COMPREHENSIVE EVIDENCE-BASED INTERVENTIONS FOR CHILDREN AND ADOLESCENTS

COMPREHENSIVE EVIDENCE-BASED INTERVENTIONS FOR CHILDREN AND ADOLESCENTS

Edited by

CANDICE A. ALFANO

DEBORAH C. BEIDEL

Library of Congress Cataloging-in-Publication Data:

Comprehensive evidence-based interventions for children and adolescents / edited by Candice A. Alfano, Deborah C. Beidel.
    1 online resource.
    Includes bibliographical references and index.
    Description based on print version record and CIP data provided by publisher; resource not viewed.
    ISBN 978-1-118-48756-3 (cloth)
    ISBN 978-1-118-86498-2 (epdf)
    ISBN 978-1-118-86482-1 (epub)
    1. Child psychopathology. 2. Adolescent psychopathology. 3. Evidence-based psychiatry. 4. Child mental health services. I. Alfano, Candice A., editor of compilation. II. Beidel, Deborah C., editor of compilation.
RJ499
618.92'8914—dc23

2013049602

Printed in the United States of America

10 9 8 7 6 5 4 3 2 1

This book is dedicated to my first love, my mother, Diane Ragusa Alfano, who passed away during its development. I have had many brilliant mentors throughout my schooling and years of training but no better teacher of how fundamentally important it is to prioritize and nurture the dreams of children.

LYD MYM,
Candice

Contents

Preface

Child mental health disorders do not discriminate. They affect boys and girls of all ages, ethnic/racial backgrounds, socioeconomic sectors, and regions of the world. In the United States alone, 13%–20% of children (up to one out of five) are diagnosed with a mental disorder in any given year (National Research Council and Institute of Medicine, 2009) and rates appear to be on the rise (Centers for Disease Control, 2013). By translation, this means that millions of young people struggle with depression, anxiety, conduct disorders, autism, eating disorders, substance use, and a host of other emotional and behavioral problems every day. In comparison to youth without a mental health disorder, these children are also more likely to suffer from health-related, interpersonal, and school-based problems such as sleep disturbances, peer rejection and victimization, and school absenteeism. Clearly, child mental disorders are a significant public health concern for individuals, families, and society.

On a more optimistic note, the range of professionals who receive training in providing mental health services to children continues to expand. This list includes psychologists, child psychiatrists, social workers, school counselors, nurse practitioners, and family therapists, among others. However, just as the training and clinical experiences of these professionals can vary, so too might the intervention approaches adopted to treat various childhood disorders. The overarching goal of this book is to provide professionals, researchers, and students in clinical psychology and allied disciplines a comprehensive resource for understanding, selecting, and delivering the most effective, evidence-based treatments for school-age children and adolescents. The term *evidence-based treatment* specifically refers to psychosocial interventions that have been subject to scientific investigation and have been empirically demonstrated to produce beneficial effects in the form of symptom reduction and/or improvements in daily functioning.

In Section I, chapters cover a range of issues and topics central to treatment delivery, including developmental and cultural considerations, ethical concerns, and efforts toward the broad dissemination of evidence-based treatments. In line with the book's focus on interventions grounded in science, we felt it important to include a chapter focused on unproven or "controversial" therapies, since awareness of treatments that are not clearly effective (and might even be harmful) should be considered equally essential for the child mental health professional. Finally, in the ever-evolving age of media and technology, we believe that readers will find Chapter 5, "New Methods of Service Delivery for Children's Mental Health Care," to be both timely and relevant.

Each chapter in Sections II and III focuses on a specific childhood disorder or problem. The decision to structure the book in this way was guided by the proliferation of evidence-based child interventions that have emerged over the past two decades. In fact, based on criteria defined by the American Psychological Association (APA), several of these treatments are now considered "well established" or "probably efficacious" interventions for children. Accordingly, rather than inviting authors to submit narrowly focused chapters describing individual treatment programs, our vision was to provide readers with in-depth coverage of a range of validated interventions and strategies for discrete types of childhood disorders/problems. We believe that this breadth of content will serve professionals and students well, both in understanding the existing research base and in developing individualized treatment plans for child patients. Chapters in Sections II and III also follow the same basic format. For example, in each chapter the same subsections appear describing core features of the disorder/problem, available evidence-based interventions, the role of parents in treatment, and circumstances where treatment modifications may be necessary to ensure effectiveness. Additional sections include review of state-of-the-art assessment tools for measuring treatment progress and clinical examples that provide valuable descriptive information and sample treatment plans.

When this book was conceptualized, *DSM-IV-TR* (American Psychiatric Association, 2000) was the standard reference for diagnostic classification. By the time of publication, *DSM-5* (American Psychiatric Association, 2013) had been introduced. In some cases, new disorders were introduced and new categories devised. We had to make decisions about how to integrate new material into the nearly completed book. For some new disorders, few data were available, suggesting that a chapter would not yet make a meaningful contribution. In the case of the newly introduced diagnostic category of Obsessive-Compulsive and Related Disorders, there was a strong empirical database and we made a decision that a separate chapter was warranted. Because the book was already in final production, we placed this chapter at the end of the volume rather than what would seem to be a more logical placement, that is, near the anxiety disorders chapter.

Even with a clear vision for the final product, we knew that the readability and utility of this book ultimately rest upon the quality of its individual chapters. We could not have wished for a more impressive list of child interventions scientists and professionals as authors. The collective expertise they brought to this shared project is immeasurable and we offer them our deepest thanks. We also wish to thank Patricia Rossi, Amanda Orenstein, and Kara Borbely from John Wiley & Sons for their guidance, support, and patience throughout the entire process. Finally, to the hundreds of child and adolescent patients we have worked with over the years, you inspire us every day!

Candice A. Alfano
Deborah C. Beidel

REFERENCES

American Psychiatric Association. (2000). *Diagnostic and statistical manual of mental disorders* (4th ed., text rev.) Washington, DC: Author.

American Psychiatric Association. (2013). *Diagnostic and statistical manual of mental disorders* (5th ed.). Alexandria, VA: American Psychiatric Publishing.

Centers for Disease Control. (2013). Mental health surveillance among children—United States, 2005–2011. *Morbidity and Mortality Weekly Report, 62*(2), 1–35.

National Research Council and Institute of Medicine. (2009). *Preventing mental, emotional, and behavioral disorders among young people: Progress and possibilities*. Washington, DC: National Academies Press.

About the Editors

Candice A. Alfano, PhD, is associate professor of psychology and director of the Sleep and Anxiety Center for Kids at the University of Houston. She received her PhD in clinical psychology in 2005 from the University of Maryland at College Park. She previously held a faculty position at the George Washington University School of Medicine and founded and directed the Child and Adolescent Anxiety Program at Children's National Medical Center in Washington, DC. Dr. Alfano serves on the Scientific Council of the Anxiety and Depression Association of America, the board of directors of the Society for Behavioral Sleep Medicine, and is associate editor for the *Journal of Anxiety Disorders*. She has authored more than 50 publications including journal articles, book chapters, books, and edited books. Her academic, research, and clinical interests focus on childhood anxiety disorders, pediatric sleep disorders, and effective interventions for these problems. Dr. Alfano is also a licensed clinical psychologist.

Deborah C. Beidel, PhD, ABPP, is professor of psychology and director of the Anxiety Disorders Clinic at the University of Central Florida. She received her PhD in clinical psychology in 1986 from the University of Pittsburgh and has held faculty positions at the University of Pittsburgh, the Medical University of South Carolina, the University of Maryland–College Park, and Penn State College of Medicine. She holds the American Board of Professional Psychology (ABPP) Diplomate in clinical psychology and behavioral psychology and is a fellow of the American Psychological Association and the Association for Psychological Science. She is the editor in chief of the *Journal of Anxiety Disorders* and has authored more than 200 publications including journal articles, book chapters, books, and edited books. Her academic, research, and clinical interests focus on child and adult anxiety disorders, including their etiology, psychopathology, and treatment. Dr. Beidel is also a licensed psychologist.

Contributors

Candice A. Alfano, PhD
Sleep and Anxiety Center for Kids,
    Department of Psychology
University of Houston
Houston, Texas

Cassidy C. Arnold, MS
Department of Psychology
Virginia Commonwealth University
Richmond, Virginia

Jessica Balderas, BA
Sleep and Anxiety Center for Kids,
    Department of Psychology
University of Houston
Houston, Texas

Deborah C. Beidel, PhD, ABPP
Anxiety Disorders Clinic
Department of Psychology
University of Central Florida
Orlando, Florida

Stephen M. Borowitz, MD
Department of Pediatrics
University of Virginia Health System
Charlottesville, Virginia

Caroline L. Boxmeyer, PhD
Department of Psychiatry and Behavioral
    Medicine
University of Alabama
Tuscaloosa, Alabama

Catherine Byrne, BA
Department of Psychiatry
University of Chicago
Chicago, Illinois

Timothy A. Cavell, PhD
Department of Psychological Science
University of Arkansas
Fayetteville, Arkansas

Priscilla T. Chan, MA
Department of Psychology
Boston University
Boston, Massachusetts

Amanda Chiapa, MA
Department of Psychology
Arizona State University
Tempe, Arizona

Winnie W. Chung, MA
Departments of Psychology and Psychiatry
Ohio State University
Columbus, Ohio

Michelle A. Clementi, BS
Sleep and Anxiety Center for Kids,
    Department of Psychology
University of Houston
Houston, Texas

Jonathan S. Comer, PhD
Mental Health Interventions
    and Technology Program,
    Department of Psychology
Florida International University
Miami, Florida

Jennifer Cowie, BA
Sleep and Anxiety Center for Kids,
Department of Psychology
University of Houston
Houston, Texas

James T. Craig, BA
Department of Psychological Science
University of Arkansas
Fayetteville, Arkansas

Megan E. Crisler, MA
Department of Psychology
University of Alabama
Tuscaloosa, Alabama

Amber L. Daigre, PhD
Department of Pediatrics
University of Miami Miller School of
    Medicine
Miami, Florida

Alan M. Delamater, PhD
Department of Pediatrics
University of Miami Miller School of
    Medicine
Miami, Florida

Peter M. Doyle, PhD
Eating and Weight Disorders Center of Seattle
Seattle, Washington

Kimberly Dunbeck, BS
Department of Psychology
Case Western Reserve University
Cleveland, Ohio

R. Meredith Elkins, MA
Department of Psychology
Boston University
Boston, Massachusetts

Brian Fisak, PhD
Department of Psychology
University of North Florida
Jacksonville, Florida

Celia B. Fisher, PhD
Center for Ethics Education
Fordham University
Bronx, New York

Adam L. Fried, PhD
Center for Ethics Education
Fordham University
Bronx, New York

Mary A. Fristad, PhD
Departments of Psychology and Psychiatry
Ohio State University
Columbus, Ohio

Samantha J. Gregus, BA
Department of Psychological Science
University of Arkansas
Fayetteville, Arkansas

Juventino Hernandez Rodriguez, BA
Department of Psychological Science
University of Arkansas
Fayatteville, Arkansas

Lindsay E. Holly, MS
Prevention Research Center, Department of
    Psychology
Arizona State University
Tempe, Arizona

Megan Jeffreys, BA
Joint Doctoral Program in Clinical
    Psychology
San Diego State University/University of
    California
San Diego, California

Luis Alberto Jimenez-Camargo, MA
Department of Psychology
University of Alabama
Tuscaloosa, Alabama

Deborah J. Jones, PhD
Department of Psychology
University of North Carolina at
    Chapel Hill
Chapel Hill, North Carolina

Heather A. Jones, PhD
Department of Psychology
Virginia Commonwealth
    University
Richmond, Virginia

Christopher A. Kearney, PhD
Department of Psychology
University of Nevada
Las Vegas, Nevada

Gerald P. Koocher, PhD
College of Science and Health
DePaul University
Chicago, Illinois

Nicole L. Kreiser, MS
Department of Psychology
Virginia Polytechnic Institute and State
    University
Blacksburg, Virginia

Daniel Le Grange, PhD
Department of Psychiatry
University of Chicago
Chicago, Illinois

Matthew D. Lerner, PhD
Department of Psychology
Stony Brook University
Stony Brook, New York

John E. Lochman, PhD
Department of Psychology
University of Alabama
Tuscaloosa, Alabama

Michael A. Mallott, PhD
Department of Psychology
University of Central Florida
Orlando, Florida

Ashley Marchante, BA
Department of Pediatrics
University of Miami Miller School of
    Medicine
Miami, Florida

Madeline McMann, BA
Department of Psychology
Simmons College
Boston, Massachusetts

Thomas H. Ollendick, PhD
Department of Psychology
Virginia Polytechnic Institute and State
    University
Blacksburg, Virginia

Freddie A. Pastrana, BA
Department of Psychological Science
University of Arkansas
Fayetteville, Arkansas

Amy T. Peters, BA
Department of Psychology
University of Illinois
Chicago, Illinois

Armando A. Piña, PhD
Prevention Research Center
Department of Psychology

Arizona State University
Tempe, Arizona

Nicole P. Powell, PhD
Department of Psychology
University of Alabama
Tuscaloosa, Alabama

Amy Przeworski, PhD
Department of Psychology
Case Western Reserve University
Cleveland, Ohio

Annie E. Rabinovitch, MA
Department of Psychology
Virginia Commonwealth University
Richmond, Virginia

Julia Revillion Cox, BA
Department of Psychology
Virginia Commonwealth University
Richmond, Virginia

Lee M. Ritterband, PhD
Department of Psychiatry and
    Neurobehavioral Sciences
University of Virginia
    Health System
Charlottesville, Virginia

Emma Ross, BA
Department of Psychology
University of Nevada
Las Vegas, Nevada

Laura D. Seligman, PhD
Department of Psychology
University of Toledo
Toledo, Ohio

Jaclyn A. Shepard, PsyD
Department of Psychiatry and
    Neurobehavioral Sciences
University of Virginia Health System
Charlottesville, Virginia

Angela Smyth, MD
Department of Psychiatry
The University of Chicago
Chicago, Illinois

Michael A. Southam-Gerow, PhD
Department of Psychology
Virginia Commonwealth University
Richmond, Virginia

Annika Stout, BA
Department of Psychology
Simmons College
Boston, Massachusetts

Sara L. Stromeyer, MA
Department of Psychology
University of Alabama
Tuscaloosa, Alabama

Erin F. Swedish, MS
Department of Psychology
University of Toledo
Toledo, Ohio

Marian Tanofsky-Kraff, PhD
Department of Medical and Clinical
    Psychology
Uniformed Services University of the
    Health Sciences
Bethesda, Maryland

Frances P. Thorndike, PhD
Department of Psychiatry and
    Neurobehavioral Sciences

University of Virginia Health System
Charlottesville, Virginia

Carrie B. Tully, MS
Department of Psychology
Virginia Commonwealth University
Richmond, Virginia

Anna Vannucci, MS
Department of Medical and Clinical Psychology
Uniformed Services University of the
    Health Sciences
Bethesda, Maryland

V. Robin Weersing, PhD
Joint Doctoral Program in Clinical Psychology
San Diego State University/University of
    California
San Diego, California

Amy E. West, PhD
Department of Psychiatry
University of Illinois
Chicago, Illinois

Susan W. White, PhD
Department of Psychology
Virginia Polytechnic Institute and State
    University
Blacksburg, Virginia

SECTION I

Treatment Considerations and Contextual Issues

CHAPTER 1

Development Considerations in Assessment and Treatment

AMY PRZEWORSKI AND KIMBERLY DUNBECK

The developmental psychopathology approach emphasizes the interplay between psychopathology and cognitive, emotional, and social development of children and adolescents (Cicchetti & Cohen, 1995; Cicchetti & Toth, 1991). This approach has long been touted as essential to the conceptualization of psychopathology and intervention for children and adolescents. Despite its utility, few inroads have been made in integrating this approach into assessment and treatment. The developmental level of child or adolescent clients is important for therapists to consider during assessment, treatment planning, and therapy implementation.

ASSESSMENT

Despite significant improvements in the empirical basis for diagnostic categorization across the years, one area where there have been few changes is the integration of developmental changes into the diagnostic criteria. The diagnostic criteria for common childhood disorders often involve the application of adult criteria to children. Although the *Diagnostic and Statistical Manual* (5th ed.; *DSM-5*) (American Psychiatric Association [APA], 2013) includes descriptions of child manifestation of symptoms for some disorders, few disorders include guidance on how symptoms may manifest differently across children and adolescents of different ages. Thus, therapists are left to use their clinical judgment to apply *DSM* criteria in a developmentally sensitive manner.

The lack of attention to developmental variations in symptoms in the *DSM* and its application is consistent with a common misconception in psychopathology, the developmental uniformity myth (Kendall, Lerner, & Craighead, 1984), which holds that disorders manifest the same no matter the age of the individual. In fact, research indicates that psychological symptoms vary quite a bit across developmental stages.

For example, there are developmental differences in the frequency of specific anxiety disorders at different ages, with separation anxiety disorder more common in young children (ages 6 to 9) and social phobia more frequent in adolescents (Weems & Costa, 2005; Weems, Hammond-Laurence, Silverman, & Ginsburg, 1998). This may be related to physical developmental changes occurring during these ages, such as that young children learn individuation and independence from parents at ages 6 to 11 and experience fears related to loss or separation from parents (Weems & Costa, 2005) and adolescents emphasize peer relationships and social interactions (Warren & Sroufe, 2004; Westenberg, van Strien, & Drewes, 2001) and therefore more often experience anxiety related to social situations.

There are also differences in the rates of depression across childhood and adolescence, with low rates in children (less than 2%) and a dramatic increase in prevalence in adolescence (4%–8%) (Hankin et al., 1998), especially in females (Silberg et al., 1999). Bipolar disorder is also rare in young children but increases in prevalence around puberty, with 15 to 19 years of age as the typical age of onset (for a review, see Kim & Miklowitz, 2002).

There are also developmental differences in depressive symptoms over the long term. For example, children who have their first depressive episode before adolescence tend to have more severe, recurrent, and treatment-resistant major depressive disorder, and as many as 40% of children who have a depressive episode will have a second episode within 5 years (Kovacs et al., 1984). Childhood-onset bipolar disorder is also typically more chronic and treatment resistant than later-onset bipolar disorder (for a review see Kim & Miklowitz, 2002). Children are less likely to see their symptoms as causing functional impairment than are their parents or other reporters (APA, 1994; Langley, Bergman, & Piacentini, 2002). As such, it is essential for assessors to be sensitive to these developmental patterns in symptoms and to rely on multiple reporters in assessing child and adolescent psychopathology.

Despite the necessity of involving multiple reporters in the assessment of child and adolescent psychopathology, there is rarely agreement on symptoms (Achenbach, McConaughy, & Howell, 1987; Comer & Kendall, 2004; Grills & Ollendick, 2002; Rapee, Barrett, Dadds, & Evans, 1994). Parent–child agreement ranges from kappas of .09 for depressive symptoms to .32 for anxiety symptoms and .29 for symptoms of attention-deficit/hyperactivity disorder (Grills & Ollendick, 2002; Rapee et al., 1994). Children often report anxiety symptoms at higher rates and intensity than their parents (Bird, Gould, & Staghezza, 1992; Edelbrock, Costello, Dulcan, Conover, & Kala, 1986; Herjanic & Reich, 1997; Hodges, Gordon, & Lennon, 1990; Kolko & Kazdin, 1993; Lagattuta, Sayfan, & Bamford, 2012); however, it is unclear which report of child anxiety is more accurate or the weight that should be given to each reporter.

Some have suggested that the age of the child should influence the degree to which assessors rely on parent versus child report. For example, it has been suggested that parental report should be relied on in assessing children below the age of 11 because such young children experience difficulties in self-report of behavior or mood problems (Achenbach et al., 1987; Ollendick & Hersen, 1993) most likely due to their limited verbal ability and insight. Further, self-report questionnaires are not commonly recommended for children under the age of 8 because children of that age typically are unable to complete such measures without assistance (Beidel & Stanley, 1993). Others have suggested that children are not always able to respond to self-report measures appropriately; for instance, they are likely to respond to questions on questionnaires based on their emotional reaction to a statement rather than based on the frequency of the event (King & Gullone, 1990; McCathie & Spence, 1991). However, the format of assessment also may influence children's ability to complete a self-report questionnaire. Questionnaires with only three anchors are the most reliable and valid way to use such measures with children (Beidel, Turner, & Morris, 1995; Ollendick, 1983). Additionally, new information indicates that children as young as 4 can report on their daily emotional states when assessed using a pictorial Likert scale and simplified wording read to them by an assessor (Lagattuta et al., 2012). Thus the most important aspect of assessment of young children's self-report may be the use of developmentally sensitive tools and techniques.

In children and adolescents 8 years of age and older, it is common to include the child's self-report; however, the degree to which the child's report is relied on may vary by the type of symptoms being assessed. Some have suggested that child report is most accurate in cases of internalizing symptoms (Jensen, Xenakis, Davis, & Degroot, 1988) versus externalizing or behavior symptoms, which are more reliably observed by parents and teachers (Kendall, 2006).

When assessing children, it can be difficult to know when and how to ask about behaviors such as sexual involvement, use of drugs or alcohol, and suicidal and homicidal ideations. The consumption of alcohol is common in late adolescents, with 4 out of 5 twelfth graders reporting that they have drunk alcohol, 50% to 62% of sixth graders reporting that they have tasted alcohol, and only 29% reporting that they have had more than a sip (Johnston, O'Malley, Bachman, & Schulenberg, 2002). This is an increase from fourth graders, where only 10% of children have had more than a sip of alcohol. Given this information and the increased rates of substance abuse in those who began drinking at age 11 and 12 (DeWit, Adlaf, Offord, & Ogborne, 2000), assessors should not assume that because a child is well below the drinking age he or she is not drinking. Therefore, while most children will not have consumed alcohol in large quantities, asking is likely recommended with children after the age of 11.

With regard to nicotine or illicit drugs, a similar pattern emerges. Sixty percent of high school seniors have smoked cigarettes; one third of them did so during the previous month. Further, 50% of high school seniors have used illicit drugs (drugs other than alcohol and nicotine) at some time in their lives (Johnston et al., 2002). Given that use of these substances is somewhat common in adolescents, assessors should be sure to ask about drug use, particularly given the association between drug use and psychological struggles (Deas & Brown, 2006; Kandel et al., 1999). Further, 7.8% of adolescents 12 to 17 years of age struggle with diagnosable substance abuse disorders; therefore, questions concerning these topics should be asked of children starting as early as late childhood (Kendall, 2006).

Other risky behaviors that should be assessed beginning in adolescence include sexual behaviors and the use of contraception. Twenty-one percent of adolescent males reported that they had sex by the age of 15 (Albert, Brown, & Flanigan, 2003; Sonenstein, Pleck, & Leighton, 1991) and 7.2% to 10% by the age of 13 (Albert et al., 2003; Kann et al., 1998). Similar rates were found in female adolescents (Albert et al., 2003). Close to 50% of high school students have had sex by the time that they graduate (Kann et al., 1998), with significantly higher rates among African American high school students (89% of males and 70% of females) (Kann et al., 1995). African American and Latino teens also report higher rates of sexual behaviors at earlier ages than Caucasians (Kann et al., 1998).

Although 57% to 74% of adolescents reported that they used contraception at their first sexual experience (Albert et al., 2003), only 10% to 20% of adolescents who are having sex use condoms consistently (DiClemente et al., 1992; Kann et al., 1995), a number that is lower in adolescents of diverse ethnicities (Airhihenbuwa, DiClemente, Wingood, & Lowe, 1992). Additionally, many adolescents have sex during monogamous relationships that are short term and therefore have multiple sexual partners over short periods of time (Overby & Kegeles, 1994). For that reason, it is important that assessment of adolescents includes assessment of sexual behaviors and the use of contraception in order to identify risky behaviors that adolescents may be engaging in as well as symptoms of psychological disorders that may be the target of treatment.

TREATMENT

Developmental sensitivity is equally important in therapy as it is in assessment. Although various types of child and adolescent therapy exist, as with adults, one of the most well-validated treatment options for children and adolescents is cognitive behavioral therapy (CBT) (Durlak, Fuhrman, & Lampman, 1991). CBT has been used with children and adolescents between the ages of 4 and 18, with the techniques included varying with the age and developmental level of the child.

Perspective Taking

One aspect of developmental level that is important to consider when choosing therapy techniques for children and adolescents is the child's level of perspective taking. Children between the ages of

2 and 3 years are often able to describe their own basic feelings, such as sadness and anger; however, they are not able to understand that other people have feelings and thoughts separate from their own (Dunn, Brown, Slomkowski, Tesla, & Youngblade, 1991). Therapy techniques that require a child to think about the impact of their behaviors on others may not be effective with young children because of their limited perspective-taking abilities (Selman, 1980). As children develop cognitively, they begin to understand that others see things differently and that others may hold opinions different from their own. However, they dismiss these opposing thoughts and feelings of others as wrong because they differ from their own. Once children have reached adolescence, they begin to understand that others' thoughts and feelings, while different from their own, are not inherently wrong but instead represent an alternative and equally valid perspective (Chandler, 1988). Due to these developmental differences in children's perspective-taking abilities, it is important to consider the child's developmental level rather than assuming that lack of ability to consider others' feelings reflects psychopathology.

A child's ability to take the perspective of others also mirrors his or her ability to consider multiple potential solutions to a problem. Before the age of 14, it is difficult for children to understand and generate numerous solutions without significant scaffolding (Sternberg, 1977; Sternberg & Nigro, 1980). A child's level of perspective taking and ability to consider numerous solutions is an important consideration when implementing cognitive restructuring. Cognitive restructuring emphasizes the notion that there are numerous ways to interpret a situation and that it is one's interpretation that influences one's emotional response to the situation. Cognitive restructuring requires that a child be able to generate and fully consider various interpretations of the same situation. Due to the limited perspective-taking abilities of children before late childhood, it may be challenging for them to identify alternative explanations for situations, let alone to consider the accuracy of each. Therefore, while cognitive restructuring is known to be an effective CBT technique, it may be somewhat challenging for children to implement.

A much more simplistic version of cognitive restructuring may be used with younger children. For example, younger children may be able to identify positive or negative aspects of a situation. One way of doing so with young children is to have them pretend to be "detective positive" or "detective negative." Each detective looks for clues in a situation that are either positive or negative. This more simplistic way of engaging in cognitive restructuring may allow a child to combat a negative attentional or interpretive bias and to identify positive cues without having to engage in the more abstract cognitive restructuring techniques of comparing the evidence for and against a thought and then revising the thought.

Abstract Reasoning

It is also important to consider the level of a child's abstract reasoning abilities when choosing among the various available therapy techniques (Weisz & Weersing, 1999). Abstract reasoning is difficult for children of all ages and is not consistently developed until approximately age 15 (Piaget, 1970; Siegler, 1986). Because of the limited abstraction ability of most children, hypothetical thinking techniques, such as role-play and brainstorming about possible outcomes, are not always helpful with children (Weisz, 1997). However, it is possible to consider multiple outcomes to an event when phrasing this concept in a developmentally sensitive manner. Children as young as 3 have hypothetical reasoning capabilities as long as they are future oriented ("What if something different happened next time?") rather than past oriented ("What if this happened instead of what actually happened?") (Robinson & Beck, 2000). Thus, therapists can introduce children to the concept that there may be various outcomes to an event by examining the possible outcomes that could occur in future situations that are similar to a current situation.

Causal Reasoning and Emotional Understanding

Another important developmental task that may influence the effectiveness of therapy techniques is causal reasoning. Causal reasoning is the understanding of complex cause-and-effect relationships—for instance, the connection among thoughts, behaviors, and emotions and understanding concepts such as rewards and punishments. Young children struggle to connect past events with current emotions or thoughts; therefore, therapeutic attempts to associate the past with the present often are unsuccessful with young children (Shirk, 1988). Young children also are likely to attribute events to conscious, concrete reasons or outside forces as opposed to psychological or internal experiences; therefore, often it is difficult for therapists to teach young children the ways in which emotions may influence one's behaviors.

Children have a limited ability to understand emotions in themselves and others (Izard, 1994), with young children (under the age of 3) able to identify only primary emotions, such as happiness, anger, sadness, and fear. Preschool-age children begin to understand emotions as they relate to themselves (emotions such as shame, pride, and guilt) but cannot describe having two feelings at the same time or blends of emotions (Harris, 1989; Harter, 1977). Preschool children also view experience and expression of emotion as synonymous, meaning they define emotional experiences by outside behavior (Nannis, 1985; Nannis & Cowan, 1987). For that reason, a child may state that a person is happy only if the individual is smiling and may not understand that emotions are internal and may be experienced but not expressed. Although this may impact a therapist's ability to teach a preschool child to inhibit emotional expression in situations, the ability of children of that age to recognize that facial expressions are linked to emotions provides an opportunity to teach them to identify their own cues for emotions, such as facial indications of fear, happiness, or sadness, and to begin to use words to describe their emotional experiences as a way of communicating their feelings. It is common for therapists to teach young children to recognize their own emotional experience by thinking about what they are expressing on their face and to convey these emotions using words rather than actions. For example, if a young child often acts out or throws temper tantrums when frustrated, a therapist may teach the child to express frustration by telling a parent that he/she is angry rather than acting out. This, when combined with the parental strategy of ignoring whining and temper tantrums that occur due to the child's attention seeking, may be an effective way of introducing adaptive emotion regulation and expression strategies with young children.

As children age (ages 6–10), they begin to see emotions as internal events that can be shared externally with others or kept a secret. Children of these ages also recognize that emotional experiences can be caused by external events (Carroll & Steward, 1984; Gnepp & Gould, 1985; Harris, Olthof, & Terwogt, 1981; Nannis, 1988). At around age 8 children also begin to understand the emotional experiences of others better and to recognize that the same situation can lead to different reactions in different people (Gnepp & Klayman, 1992). It is also around this age that children begin understanding that emotional experiences are not discrete and that an individual can experience multiple, and even opposing, emotions at the same time (Friend & Davis, 1993). By age 11 or 12, children can understand that they have control over their emotions and can choose whether to express or hide them (Nannis, 1985; Nannis & Cowan, 1987).

The emotional work that can be accomplished in therapy with children in middle childhood may involve the recognition of blends of emotions, conflicting emotions, and the link between events and subsequent emotions. Children's emotional understanding during this middle child-hood phase provides them with the abilities necessary to comprehend most cognitive behavioral techniques, such as linking antecedent events, emotions, and behaviors; using behavioral tech-niques to impact the strength of emotions, such as relaxation techniques to reduce anxiety; and the negative reinforcement that occurs when one escapes from a feared stimulus. Many of the CBT packages developed for children were developed specifically for those between the ages of 7 and 12 in mind (Barrett, Dadds, & Rapee, 1996; Kendall, 1994; Sanders, 1999; Webster-Stratton, 1992).

Language

When working with children, it is important to be aware of their language abilities. When talk-ing with a child, a therapist should always use vocabulary that the child understands (Weisz & Weersing, 1999). The type of vocabulary that a therapist uses will vary by age and across children. It is also important to understand the role that language development has on a child's emotional under-standing. It is believed that emotional competence is intertwined with the ability to use emotionally descriptive language (Beck, Kumschick, Eid, & Klann-Delius, 2012). Therefore, children who have not yet developed sophisticated emotional vocabularies will also struggle with understanding their own emotional experience and recognizing emotions in others, which will greatly impact the tech-niques that will be effective in therapy. For instance, until a child's emotional vocabulary has been fostered to a certain degree, training in emotion regulation techniques will not be effective. Further, children become better at perspective taking as they acquire more sophisticated vocabulary, par-ticularly more verbs (Astington & Filippova, 2005). Therefore, a child's language level will impact the therapist's ability to utilize role-playing and other social problem-solving techniques that rely heavily on perspective-taking ability.

Therapy Format

Children are inextricably linked to their parents because they rely on their parents for all of their basic needs as well as many of their social and emotional needs. The younger the child, the more important their parents are going to be in the therapeutic process. This is illustrated in a study by Barrett et al. (1996), which found that children ages 7 to 10 benefited from family involvement in CBT but the addition of a family component was not more beneficial than individual CBT for chil-dren ages 11 to 14. Further, adolescents showed better treatment response to individual CBT than adolescents in individual CBT plus parent training (Cobham, Dadds, & Spence, 1998). Inclusion of parents, while particularly important in younger children, also seems to be particularly important when working with children with externalizing disorders and with eating disorders. This is because parental monitoring and parental regulation of behavior are of critical importance in the treatment of both behavior problems and eating dysfunctions in children and adolescents.

When working with children and adolescents, it is also important to determine if group therapy is appropriate. Group therapy for children can be extremely beneficial, particularly when used to teach social skills and build social connections and friendships, which can be relevant for a variety of presenting problems (Harrington, Whittaker, Shoebridge, & Campbell, 1998; Larson & Lochman, 2010; Rose & Edleson, 1987). However, group settings are not ideal for addressing conduct or delinquency problems in adolescents because of the tendency for antisocial teens to encourage and reinforce antisocial tendencies, a process known as deviancy training (Dishion, McCord, & Poulin, 1999; Steinberg, 2005).

Activity in Therapy

Therapy with children is going to involve quite a bit more activity than treatment with adults. Activity is important in keeping engagement with children. Further, teaching coping skills, cognitive restructuring, and emotional awareness will need to be accomplished through concrete means. Both engagement and clarity can be achieved through the use of play. Play can make common cognitive behavioral techniques, such as modeling and role-playing, more concrete and accessible. This can be done by using puppets to demonstrate skills, to externalize the problem, or to play various roles relevant to the child's life. Active play during therapy also can allow a child to brainstorm and communicate thoughts to the therapist in an enjoyable manner. For example, the "quick decision catch" of Pincus, Chase, Chow, Weiner, and Pian (2011) asks children and the therapist to pass a ball and to give a solution to a problem quickly when they catch the ball. Once solutions have been generated, the child must choose which solution he/she would use in the situation. Because this process occurs in the context of a game, it may increase a child's engagement while also helping the child with the process of decision making and solution generation.

The use of play to act out emotions and experiences allows the child and therapist to communicate without the demands on the child's expressive language, which, as explained previously, is slower to develop. It has been hypothesized that children do not naturally communicate through dialogue; they express their inner experience through the concrete world of play and activity. Therefore, play in therapy should be viewed as a vehicle for communication, particularly with younger children (Axline, 1947; Bratton, Ray, Rhine, & Jones, 2005; Kottman, 2001; Landreth, 2002; Schaefer, 2001).

SUMMARY

Many developmental considerations need to be made when assessing and treating children. These considerations include degree of parental involvement, use of group therapy, and implementation of games or activities. Overall, in order to make clinical work applicable to children of all ages, clinicians need to be sensitive to their client's cognitive, social, and emotional developmental stage and understand what therapeutic techniques utilize only the skills the child has acquired. For instance, many traditional social problem-solving techniques, including role-play, rely on the client having developed sophisticated perspective-taking skills. Such techniques would not be appropriate to employ with a young child who has not developed these skills. By considering the various developmental concerns discussed in this chapter, the clinician can be better prepared to offer efficacious assessment and treatment for children and adolescents across ages and developmental levels.

REFERENCES

Achenbach, T. M., McConaughy, S. H., & Howell, C. T. (1987). Child/adolescent behavioral and emotional problems: Implications of cross-informant correlations for situational specificity. *Psychological Bulletin, 101*(2), 213–232. doi: 10.1037/0033-2909.101.2.213

Airhihenbuwa, C. O., DiClemente, R. J., Wingood, G. M., & Lowe, A. (1992). HIV/AIDS education and prevention among African-Americans: A focus on culture. *AIDS Education and Prevention, 4*(3), 267–276.

Albert, B., Brown, S., & Flanigan, C. (Eds.). (2003). *14 and younger: The Sexual behavior of young adolescents (summary).* Washington, DC: National Campaign to Prevent Teen Pregnancy.

American Psychiatric Association. (1994). *Diagnostic and statistical manual of mental disorders* (4th ed.). Washington, DC: Author.

American Psychiatric Association. (2013). *Diagnostic and statistical manual of mental disorders* (5th ed.). Arlington, VA: American Psychiatric Publishing.

Astington, J. W., & Filippova, E. (2005). Language as the route into other minds. In B. F. Malle & S. D. Hodges (Eds.), *Other minds: How humans bridge the divide between self and others* (pp. 209–222). New York, NY: Guilford Press.

Axline, V. M. (1947). *Play therapy: The inner dynamics of childhood.* Oxford, UK: Houghton Mifflin.

Barrett, P. M., Dadds, M. R., & Rapee, R. M. (1996). Family treatment of childhood anxiety: A controlled trial. *Journal of Consulting and Clinical Psychology, 64*(2), 333–342. doi: 10.1037/0022-006x.64.2.333

Beck, L., Kumschick, I. R., Eid, M., & Klann-Delius, G. (2012). Relationship between language competence and emotional competence in middle childhood. *Emotion, 12*(3), 503–514. doi: 10.1037/a0026320

Beidel, D. C., & Stanley, M. A. (1993). Developmental issues in the measurement of anxiety. In C. Last (Ed.), *Anxiety across the lifespan: A developmental perspective* (pp. 167–203). New York, NY: Springer.

Beidel, D. C., Turner, S. M., & Morris, T. L. (1995). A new inventory to assess childhood social anxiety and phobia: The Social Phobia and Anxiety Inventory for Children. *Psychological Assessment, 7*(1), 73–79. doi: 10.1037/1040-3590.7.1.73

Bird, H. R., Gould, M. S., & Staghezza, B. (1992). Aggregating data from multiple informants in child psychiatry epidemiological research. *Journal of the American Academy of Child & Adolescent Psychiatry, 31*(1), 78–85. doi: 10.1097/00004583-199201000-00012

Bratton, S. C., Ray, D., Rhine, T., & Jones, L. (2005). The efficacy of play therapy with children: A Meta-analytic review of treatment outcomes. *Professional Psychology: Research and Practice, 36*(4), 376–390. doi: 10.1037/0735-7028.36.4.376

Carroll, J. J., & Steward, M. S. (1984). The role of cognitive development in children's understandings of their own feelings. *Child Development, 55,* 1486–1492.

Chandler, M. J. (1988). Doubt and developing theories of mind. In J. W. Astington, P. L. Harris, & D. R. Olson (Eds.), *Developing theories of mind* (pp. 387–413). New York, NY: Cambridge University Press.

Cicchetti, D., & Cohen, D. J. (1995). *Developmental psychopathology. Vol. 1: Theory and methods.* Oxford, UK: Wiley.

Cicchetti, D., & Toth, S. (1991). A developmental perspective on internalizing and externalizing disorders. In D. Cicchetti & S. L. Toth (Eds.), *Internalizing and externalizing expressions of dysfunction* (pp. 1–19). New York, NY: Erlbaum.

Cobham, V. E., Dadds, M. R., & Spence, S. H. (1998). The role of parental anxiety in the treatment of childhood anxiety. *Journal of Consulting and Clinical Psychology, 66*(6), 893–905. doi: 10.1037/0022-006x.66.6.893

Comer, J. S., & Kendall, P. C. (2004). A symptom-level examination of parent-child agreement in the diagnosis of anxious youths. *Journal of the American Academy of Child & Adolescent Psychiatry, 43*(7), 878–886. doi: 10.1097/01 .chi.0000125092.35109.c5

Deas, D., & Brown, E. S. (2006). Adolescent substance abuse and psychiatric comorbidities. *Journal of Clinical Psychiatry, 67*(7), e02.

DeWit, D. J., Adlaf, E. M., Offord, D. R., & Ogborne, A. C. (2000). Age at first alcohol use: A risk factor for the development of alcohol disorders. *American Journal of Psychiatry, 157,* 745–750.

DiClemente, R. J., Durbin, M., Siegel, D., Krasnovsky, F., Lazarus, N., & Comacho, T. (1992). Determinants of condom use among junior high school students in a minority, inner-city school district. *Pediatrics, 89*(2), 197–202.

Dishion, T. J., McCord, J., & Poulin, F. (1999). When interventions harm: Peer groups and problem behavior. *American Psychologist, 54*(9), 755–764. doi: 10.1037/0003-066x.54.9.755

Dunn, J., Brown, J., Slomkowski, C., Tesla, C., & Youngblade, L. (1991). Young children's understanding of other people's feelings and beliefs: Individual differences and their antecedents. *Child Development, 62*(6), 1352–1366. doi: 10.1111/ j.1467-8624.1991.tb01610.x

Durlak, J. A., Fuhrman, T., & Lampman, C. (1991). Effectiveness of cognitive-behavior therapy for maladapting children: A meta-analysis. *Psychological Bulletin, 110*(2), 204–214. doi: 10.1037/0033-2909.110.2.204

Edelbrock, C., Costello, A. J., Dulcan, M. K., Conover, N. C., & Kala, R. (1986). Parent-child agreement on child psychiatry symptoms assessed via structured interview. *Journal of Child Psychology and Psychiatry, 27*(2), 181–190. doi: 10.1111/j.1469-7610.1986.tb02329.x

Friend, M., & Davis, T. L. (1993). Appearance-reality distinction: Children's understanding of the physical and affective domains. *Developmental Psychology, 29*(5), 907.

Gnepp, J., & Gould, M. E. (1985). The development of personalized inferences: Understanding other people's emotional reactions in light of their prior experiences. *Child Development, 56,* 1455–1464.

Gnepp, J., & Klayman, J. (1992). Recognition of uncertainty in emotional inferences: Reasoning about emotionally equivocal situations. *Developmental Psychology, 28*(1), 145.

Grills, A. E., & Ollendick, T. H. (2002). Issues in parent-child agreement: The case of structured diagnostic interviews. *Clinical Child and Family Psychology Review, 5*(1), 57–83. doi: 10.1023/a:1014573708569

Hankin, B. L., Abramson, L. Y., Moffitt, T. E., Silva, P. A., McGee, R., & Angell, K. E. (1998). Development of depression from preadolescence to young adulthood: Emerging gender differences in a 10-year longitudinal study. *Journal of Abnormal Psychology, 107*(1), 128–140. doi: 10.1037/0021-843x.107.1.128

Harrington, R., Whittaker, J., Shoebridge, P., & Campbell, F. (1998). Systematic review of efficacy of cognitive behaviour therapies in childhood and adolescent depressive disorder. *British Medical Journal, 316*, 1559–1563.

Harris, P. L. (1989). *Children and emotion: The development of psychological understanding*: London, UK: Basil Blackwell.

Harris, P. L., Olthof, T., & Terwogt, M. M. (1981). Children's knowledge of emotion. *Journal of Child Psychology and Psychiatry, 22*(3), 247–261.

Harter, S. (1977). A cognitive-developmental approach to children's expression of conflicting feelings and a technique to facilitate such expression in play therapy. *Journal of Consulting and Clinical Psychology, 45*(3), 417.

Herjanic, B., & Reich, W. (1997). Development of a structured psychiatric interview for children: Agreement between child and parent on individual symptoms. *Journal of Abnormal Child Psychology, 25*(1), 21–31. doi: 10.1023/a:1025703323438

Hodges, K., Gordon, Y., & Lennon, M. P. (1990). Parent-child agreement on symptoms assessed via a clinical research interview for children: The Child Assessment Schedule (CAS). *Journal of Child Psychology and Psychiatry, 31*(3), 427–436. doi: 10.1111/j.1469-7610.1990.tb01579.x

Izard, C. E. (1994). Innate and universal facial expressions: Evidence from developmental and cross-cultural research. *Psychological Bulletin, 115*(2), 288–299. doi: 10.1037/0033-2909.115.2.288

Jensen, P. S., Xenakis, S. N., Davis, H., & Degroot, J. (1988). Child psychopathology rating scales and interrater agreement: II. Child and Family Characteristics. *Journal of the American Academy of Child & Adolescent Psychiatry, 27*(4), 451–461. doi: 10.1097/00004583-198807000-00013

Johnston, L. D., O'Malley, P. M., Bachman, J. G., & Schulenberg, J. E. (2002). *Monitoring the future: National results on adolescent drug use: Overview of key findings*. NIH Pub No 02-5015. Bethesda, MD: National Institute on Drug Abuse.

Kandel, D. B., Johnson, J. G., Bird, H. R., Weissman, M. M., Goodman, S. H., Lahey, B. B., . . . Schwab-Stone, M. E. (1999). Psychiatric comorbidity among adolescents with substance use disorders: Findings from the MECA Study. *Journal of the American Academy of Child & Adolescent Psychiatry, 38*(6), 693–699. doi: 10.1097/00004583-199906000-00016

Kann, L., Kinchen, S. A., Williams, B. I., Ross, J. G., Lowry, R., Hill, C. V., . . . Kolbe, L. J. (1998). Youth risk behavior surveillance—United States, 1997. *Journal of School Health, 68*(9), 355–369. doi: 10.1111/j.1746-1561.1998.tb07202.x

Kann, L., Warren, C. W., Harris, W. A., Collins, J. L., Douglas, K. A., Collins, M. E., . . . Kolbe, L. J. (1995). Youth risk behavior surveillance—United States, 1993. *Journal of School Health, 65*(5), 163–170.

Kendall, P. C. (1994). Treating anxiety disorders in children: Results of a randomized clinical trial. *Journal of Consulting and Clinical Psychology, 62*(1), 100–110. doi: 10.1037/0022-006x.62.1.100

Kendall, P. C. (Ed.). (2006). *Child and adolescent therapy: Cognitive–behavioral procedures* (3rd ed.). New York, NY: Guilford Press.

Kendall, P. C., Lerner, R. M., & Craighead, W. E. (1984). Human development and intervention in childhood psychopathology. *Child Development, 55*(1), 71–82. doi: 10.2307/1129835

Kim, E. Y., & Miklowitz, D. J. (2002). Childhood mania, attention deficit hyperactivity disorder and conduct disorder: A critical review of diagnostic dilemmas. *Bipolar Disorders, 4*(4), 215–225. doi: 10.1034/j.1399-5618.2002.01191.x

King, N. J., & Gullone, E. (1990). Acceptability of fear reduction procedures with children. *Journal of Behavior Therapy and Experimental Psychiatry, 21*(1), 1–8. doi: 10.1016/0005-7916(90)90042-J

Kolko, D. J., & Kazdin, A. E. (1993). Emotional/behavioral problems in clinic and nonclinic children: Correspondence among child, parent, and teacher reports. *Journal of Child Psychology & Psychiatry, 34*, 991–1006.

Kottman, T. (2001). *Play therapy: Basics and beyond*. Alexandria, VA: American Counseling Association.

Kovacs, M., Feinberg, T. L., Crouse-Novak, M., Paulauskas, S. L., Pollock, M., & Finkelstein, R. (1984). Depressive disorders in childhood: II. A longitudinal study of the risk for a subsequent major depression. *Archives of General Psychiatry, 41*(7), 643–649. doi: 10.1001/archpsyc.1984.01790180013001

Lagattuta, K. H., Sayfan, L., & Bamford, C. (2012). Do you know how I feel? Parents underestimate worry and overestimate optimism compared to child self-report. *Journal of Experimental Child Psychology, 113*(2), 211–232. doi: 10.1016/j.jecp.2012.04.001

Landreth, G. L. (2002). Therapeutic limit setting in the play therapy relationship. *Professional Psychology: Research and Practice, 33*(6), 529–535. doi: 10.1037/0735-7028.33.6.529

Langley, A. K., Bergman, R. L., & Piacentini, J. C. (2002). Assessment of childhood anxiety. *International Review of Psychiatry, 14*(2), 102–113. doi: 10.1080/09540260220132626

Larson, J., & Lochman, J. (2010). *Helping schoolchildren cope with anger: A cognitive-behavioral intervention*. New York, NY: Guilford Press.

McCathie, H., & Spence, S. H. (1991). What is the Revised Fear Survey Schedule for children measuring? *Behaviour Research and Therapy, 29*(5), 495–502. doi: 10.1016/0005-7967(91)90134-O

Nannis, E. D. (1985). *Structural differences in emotional understanding and their application to clinical intervention.* Paper presented at the biennial meeting of the Society for Research in Child Development, Ontario, Canada.

Nannis, E. D. (1988). Cognitive-developmental differences in emotional understanding. *New Directions for Child and Adolescent Development, 1988*(39), 31–49. doi: 10.1002/cd.23219883904

Nannis, E. D., & Cowan, P. A. (1987). Emotional understanding: A matter of age, dimension, and point of view. *Journal of Applied Developmental Psychology, 8*(3), 289–304.

Ollendick, T. H. (1983). Reliability and validity of the Revised Fear Survey Schedule for Children (FSSC-R). *Behaviour Research and Therapy, 21*(6), 685–692.

Ollendick, T. H., & Hersen, M. (1993). *Handbook of child and adolescent assessment.* Needham Heights, MA: Allyn & Bacon.

Overby, K. J., & Kegeles, S. M. (1994). The impact of AIDS on an urban population of high-risk female minority adolescents: Implications for intervention. *Journal of Adolescent Health, 15*(3), 216–227. doi: 10.1016/1054-139X(94)90507-X

Piaget, J. (1970). Genetic epistemology (E. Duckworth, Trans.). *American Behavioral Scientist, 13,* 459–480.

Pincus, D. B., Chase, R. M., Chow, C., Weiner, C. L., & Pian, J. (2011). Integrating play into cognitive-behavioral therapy for child anxiety disorders. In S. W. Russ & L. N. Niec (Eds.), *Play in clinical practice: Evidence-based approaches.* New York, NY: Guilford Press.

Rapee, R. M., Barrett, P. M., Dadds, M. R., & Evans, L. (1994). Reliability of the DSM-III-R childhood anxiety disorders using structured interview: Interrater and parent-child agreement. *Journal of the American Academy of Child & Adolescent Psychiatry, 33*(7), 984–992. doi: 10.1097/00004583-199409000-00008

Robinson, E. J., & Beck, S. (2000). What is difficult about counterfactual reasoning? In P. Mitchell & K. J. Riggs (Eds.), *Children's reasoning and the mind* (pp. 101–119). Hove, England: Psychology Press/Taylor & Francis (UK).

Rose, S. D., & Edleson, J. L. (1987). *Working with children and adolescents in groups.* San Francisco, CA: Jossey-Bass.

Sanders, M. R. (1999). Triple P—Positive Parenting Program: Towards an empirically validated multilevel parenting and family support strategy for the prevention of behavior and emotional problems in children. *Clinical Child and Family Psychology Review, 2*(2), 71–90.

Schaefer, C. E. (2001). Prescriptive play therapy. *International Journal of Play Therapy, 10*(2), 57–73. doi: 10.1037/h0089480

Selman, R. L. (1980). *Social perception in children: Interpersonal relations in children.* New York, NY: Academic Press.

Shirk, S. R. (1988). *Cognitive development and child psychotherapy.* New York, NY: Plenum Press.

Siegler, R. S. (1986). Unities in strategy choices across domains. In M. Perlmutter (Ed.), *Minnesota symposium on child development* (Vol. 19, pp. 1–48). Hillsdale, NJ: Erlbaum.

Silberg, J., Pickles, A., Rutter, M., Hewitt, J., Simonoff, E., Maes, H., . . . Eaves, L. (1999). The influence of genetic factors and life stress on depression among adolescent girls. *Archives of General Psychiatry, 56*(3), 225–232. doi: 10.1001/archpsyc.56.3.225

Sonenstein, F. L., Pleck, J. H., & Leighton, C. K. (1991). Levels of sexual activity among adolescent males in the United States. *Family Planning Perspectives, 23*(4), 162–167. doi: 10.2307/2135739

Steinberg, L. (2005). Cognitive and affective development in adolescence. *Trends in Cognitive Sciences, 9*(2), 69–74.

Sternberg, R. J. (1977). Component processes in analogical reasoning. *Psychological Review, 84*(4), 353.

Sternberg, R. J., & Nigro, G. (1980). Developmental patterns in the solution of verbal analogies. *Child Development, 51*(1), 27–38.

Warren, S., & Sroufe, L. (2004). Developmental issues. In J. M. Ollendick (Ed.), *Phobic and anxiety disorders in children and adolescents: A clinician's guide to effective psychosocial and pharmacological interventions* (pp. 92–115). New York, NY: Oxford University Press.

Webster-Stratton, C. (1992). *The incredible years.* Retrieved from http://www.incredibleyears.com

Weems, C. F., & Costa, N. M. (2005). Developmental differences in the expression of childhood anxiety symptoms and fears. *Journal of the American Academy of Child & Adolescent Psychiatry, 44*(7), 656–663. doi: 10.1097/01.chi.0000162583.25829.4b

Weems, C. F., Hammond-Laurence, K., Silverman, W. K., & Ginsburg, G. S. (1998). Testing the utility of the anxiety sensitivity construct in children and adolescents referred for anxiety disorders. *Journal of Clinical Child Psychology, 27*(1), 69–77.

Weisz, J. R. (1997). Effects of interventions for child and adolescent psychological dysfunction: Relevance of context, developmental factors, and individual differences. In S. Luthar (Ed.), *Developmental psychopathology: Perspectives on adjustment, risk and disorder*, (pp. 3–22). New York, NY: Cambridge University Press.

Weisz, J. R., & Weersing, V. R. (1999). Developmental outcome research In W. K. Silverman & T. H. Ollendick (Eds.), *Developmental issues in the clinical treatment of children* (pp. 457–469). Needham Heights, MA: Allyn & Bacon.

Westenberg, P. M., van Strien, S. D., & Drewes, M. J. (2001). Revised description and measurement of ego development in early adolescence: An artifact of the written procedure? *Journal of Early Adolescence, 21*(4), 470–493. doi: 10.1177/0272431601021004005

CHAPTER 2

Ethical Considerations in Mental Health Treatment and Interventions With School-Age Children and Adolescents

ADAM L. FRIED AND CELIA B. FISHER

INTRODUCTION

Psychological treatments hold enormous benefit for children and adolescents and have been found to be effective across a variety of mental health conditions and disorders. Responsible professional practice with children and adolescents may differ in important ways from treatment with adults and requires an understanding of important population-specific factors that critically inform psychologists' ethical decision-making processes. Such factors include children and adolescents' evolving cognitive, social, and emotional developmental processes, differential symptom presentation and treatment response, legal status, and special ethical responsibilities when conducting treatment with minors.

Drawing on the relevant empirical and theoretical literature, laws and regulations, and principles and enforceable standards detailed in the American Psychological Association's Code of Ethics and Ethical Principles (APA Ethics Code) (American Psychological Association [APA], 2010), this chapter explores several important ethical and legal topics related to psychological treatment with school-age children and adolescents. Consistent with the goal of this volume, the chapter focuses on four areas:

1. The ethical responsibilities of mental health professionals in the selection and implementation of interventions that are based in established scientific or professional knowledge
2. The types of competence required to perform psychological treatment with children and adolescents
3. Relevant topics related to informed consent and assent
4. Navigating confidentiality and privacy procedures, which may differ considerably when working with child and adolescent populations

COMPETENCE AND THE SCIENTIFIC BASES FOR CLINICAL JUDGMENT

As professionals committed to promoting the welfare of clients, pediatric psychologists and other mental health clinicians have a special responsibility to identify, develop, and disseminate treatments for children and adolescents that reflect empirical and other types of scholarly knowledge in the field. In recent years, psychology and other mental health professions have increasingly drawn on scientific findings and established professional knowledge to empirically inform treatment and practice. Within such a model, research and practice are seen as complementary activities, each representing benefit to individual clients and society at large rather than opposing or unrelated activities (APA, 2002). Such a relationship is often bidirectional; practicing psychologists not only benefit from the fruits of scientific research, but investigators are called on to draw from real-world clinical problems and experiences often informed by practice and applied psychological activities in order to develop and empirically examine appropriate psychological questions and constructs (APA Presidential Task Force, 2006; Fisher, 2013a; Fisher, Busch-Rossnagel, Jopp, & Brown, 2012).

Treatment Selection and Empirically Based Interventions

Consistent with the APA Ethics Code General Principle A, Beneficence and Nonmaleficence, psychologists and other mental health clinicians are called on to engage in professional activities that provide benefit and do no harm. To accomplish this requires selection of treatments that have been scientifically or professionally demonstrated to show effectiveness with a particular problem and population (Standard 2.04, "Bases for Scientific and Professional Judgments") (APA, 2010). Competence is the linchpin enabling mental health professionals to fulfill these ethical obligations (Fisher, 2013a). In the field of children's mental health, professional competence requires ongoing learning and consideration of the dynamic and changing science of the field to best address the needs of their clients (Kinscherff, 1999). As evidenced throughout this volume, a growing body of research demonstrates effective treatments for children and adolescents and should form the basis of competency to treat them (Falzon, Davidson, & Bruns, 2010; Ollendick & Davis, 2004; Ollendick & King, 2004; Weisz & Hawley, 2002). Similarly, growing evidence-based ethics and best practice resources in many important areas (including competence, consent, and confidentiality) may inform practice with children and adolescents.

Clinical, Developmental, and Multicultural Competence

By definition, all professional psychological activities require some degree of competence both in terms of the focus of the activity (e.g., disorder) and the applicable population, whether it is the assessment of dementia in older adults, interventions with college-age substance users, or depression research with developmentally disabled adults. Working with child and adolescent populations requires a special competence that may well exceed one's own personal experience (either as a child/adolescent or as the parent of a child/adolescent) (Koocher, 2003) and that includes specialized training, education, experience, and/or consultation to acquire the skills necessary to provide effective professional psychological services for specific disorders or conditions (Standard 2.01, "Boundaries of Competence") (APA, 2010). Clinicians who are not appropriately trained or who cannot otherwise demonstrate necessary competencies risk providing ineffective or, in some cases, harmful services.

One important area of competence required for professional work with children and adolescents is specialized knowledge of child and adolescent development, including an understanding of the complex and evolving cognitive, social, and emotional processes, as well as related clinical knowledge to evaluate the implications of development on symptom presentation, treatment selection and implementation, and response. For example, pediatric clinicians treating mood disorders should be aware that children and adolescents may display certain depressive symptoms (such as irritability and mild antisocial behaviors) that may not be associated with depression disorders commonly diagnosed in adults (American Psychiatric Association, 2013). Interventions with child and adolescent populations also must be assessed for their developmental validity, or the extent to which the treatments have been assessed and shown to be effective across various age populations (Fisher, Hatashita-Wong, & Isman, 1999; Prout, DeMartino, & Prout, 1999). Treatment approaches that have not been adequately researched with children and adolescent populations may lack effectiveness or unintentionally worsen symptoms.

As reflected in the profession's ethical principles and standards (APA, 2010), discerning mental health professionals also understand the importance that cultural factors may play not only in symptom presentation and response to interventions but in other important facets of the child/adolescent's experience (including important values and relationships with peers and family members) that may have implications for therapeutic outcome (Arredondo & Toporek, 2004; Ponterrotto, Casas, Suzuki, & Alexander, 2001; Sue & Sue, 2003). Rather than assuming that clinicians have expertise in all types of cultural, racial, ethnic, religious, and other types of identity, the critical factor required for competent practice is a type of sensitivity to these issues, or what Fisher (2013a, 2013b) and others have described as a multicultural ethical awareness, which includes both a critical self-reflection of one's own beliefs, biases, and prejudices as well as an understanding of the ways in which cultural factors, both at the immediate and broader political levels, may affect professional work with the child/adolescent and his/her family (APA, 1993, 2003; Arredeondo & Toporek, 2004; Fowers & Davidov, 2006; Ridley, Liddle, Hill, & Li, 2001; Salter & Salter, 2012). These may include examination of broader themes, such as the basis and appropriateness of particular values, treatment goals, and determinations of deviance and psychopathology (Fisher, 2013a; Prilleltensky, 1997). A full discussion of these topics is beyond the scope of this chapter, but several authors provide excellent discussions of these topics, including Fisher (2013a, 2013b), Lemoire and Chen (2005), Ponterrotto et al. (2001), and Sue and Sue (2003).

Competence also requires an honest and critical self-evaluation and analysis of skills, knowledge training and experience, as well as any personal limitations or barriers to effective treatment; the prudent mental health professional may determine that, at times, the best way to address the clinical needs of a client adequately is to make a referral to a professional with the appropriate competencies or who may be better suited to provide the required professional services (Fisher, 2013a; Kinscherff, 1999). Referrals also may be highly appropriate for specific interventions (such as exposure therapies or behavior modification programs) that are considered highly effective but may be outside the skill repertoire of the therapist.

Finally, clinicians working with school-age children and adolescents should be aware of the specific laws, rules, and regulations governing professional interventions with minors. For example, as discussed later in the chapter, in most cases, minors are not deemed legally competent to provide informed consent to treatment; in most jurisdictions, consent must be provided by a parent or guardian. It also should be noted that rules and regulations may differ by setting or duties, and clinicians should not assume that all interventions and treatments with children and adolescents are subject to the same regulations across settings. For example, school-based interventions may be governed by additional or differing ethical standards and laws, such as the National Association of School Psychologists' *Principles for Professional Ethics* (2010) and the Family Educational Rights and Privacy Act of 1974.

INFORMED CONSENT FOR TREATMENT

Reflecting the values of respect for individual dignity and right to self-determination, informed consent procedures in professional practice provide clients and/or their appropriate decision makers with an opportunity to receive, consider, and make an informed, rational, and voluntary decision about participation in professional treatment (Standards 3.10, "Informed Consent," 10.01, "Informed Consent for Therapy") (APA, 2010). While most children and adolescents lack the legal competence to make consent decisions, their involvement in the consent process often is ethically indicated and considered essential for collaborative and productive therapeutic relationships.

Parents are assumed to be in the best position to make informed decisions for their children and are given the legal responsibility to consent to services on their behalf. In legal contexts, children and adolescents are considered incapable of providing informed consent for treatment, except in limited circumstances in which certain adolescents may be deemed competent to consent. For example, an emancipated minor is a state-determined legal status that describes an individual who has not reached the age of legal majority but who is considered (most often by law or court) competent through the assumption of adult responsibilities, such as self-support or marriage, to engage in certain types of decision making. As another example, the mature minor is a category defined by state law and refers to an individual who has not reached the age of legal competency but who has been deemed competent to make limited decisions about activities, such as engagement in treatment or assessment. Finally, court-ordered treatments may not require informed consent from parents, but ethical standards and professional guidelines recommend that both the child or adolescent client and parents/guardians be provided with pertinent consent information, such as the purpose of the treatments, limits to confidentiality, and the reporting responsibilities of the mental health professional and record keeping. Notwithstanding the aforementioned categories, when a referral of a child or adolescent is made, it is important to ensure that the referring party (often the parent/guardian) has the legal authority to do so, especially in cases in which there may be legal action (Fisher et al., 1999; Koocher, 2008). For example, a therapist who receives a referral from the local child welfare office to provide treatment for a 10-year-old child for issues related to neglect and trauma may be well advised to request a copy of court documentation confirming that the agency has the legal authority to make such a referral and consent to treatment.

Consent as an Ongoing and Developmentally Appropriate Process

It is helpful to view informed consent as an ongoing process rather than a singular event conducted at the onset of a professional relationship. Additional discussion about important consent components, including limits to confidentiality (such as mandatory disclosures) and relevant treatment information, often are necessary as treatment progresses, as the exact techniques, overall therapeutic goals, and estimated duration of therapy may change from the initial consent consultation (Fisher, 2013a; Fisher & Oransky, 2008). In addition, children and adolescents (as well as parents) may benefit especially from periodic review and discussion of these important topics.

As many point out (e.g., Fisher, 2013a; Kunin, 1997; Kuther, 2003; Melton, 1999), respect for children's and adolescents' dignity and self-determination does not necessarily imply a capacity for autonomous decision making. On the contrary, reliance on such a conclusion may lead to harm and neglects the legal and ethical responsibilities of mental health professionals. Respectful and appropriate consent procedures with child and adolescent clients take into account the developmental and other important contextual details of the decision-making process to appropriately frame the consent process and offer an opportunity to voice assent or dissent (Fisher, 2013a; Fisher, Cea, Davidson, & Fried, 2006; Masty & Fisher, 2008). For example, an advanced understanding of developmental levels and age milestones may inform methods for explaining critical consent information, such as treatment procedures, duration and frequency, and limits to confidentiality.

In most cases, it is recommended that the child/adolescent and the parents or guardians or those responsible for the care of the child/adolescent be involved in consent discussions (Fisher et al.,

1999; Molin & Palmer, 2005). Such an approach reflects respect for personhood and promotes responsibility and active participation in the therapeutic process (Byckowski, Kollar, & Britto, 2010; Kunin, 1997; Melton, 1999). In fact, recent research suggests that adolescents may expect to be involved in consent discussions. For example, Paul, Berriman, and Evans (2008) found that a majority of 14- to 16-year-olds in their study expected to be asked their opinions about participating in treatment, saw themselves (rather than parents or guardians) as primary decision maker, and believed that they had the right to terminate treatment without parental approval.

Throughout the consent process, mental health professionals also may find it helpful to solicit client attitudes toward and perceptions about mental health treatment. Rather than assume that minors or their parents/guardians accurately and adequately understand the nature and purpose of the psychotherapy (Fisher, 2013a; Fisher et al., 1999; Fisher & Oransky, 2008), providing clear explanations about the purpose, goals, and process of the therapy may help to address possible misconceptions about the purpose of treatment, offer a space to discuss feelings and values associated with mental health treatment (including possible stigma), and promote child/adolescent participation in decision-making processes in a responsible manner that reflects the principles of beneficence, nonmaleficence, integrity, and respect. Such discussions may be especially helpful in situations with families who are largely unfamiliar with the nature or purpose of psychological treatments.

Including both parents and minors in developmentally appropriate ways may hold several additional benefits, including opportunities to ensure that all parties have similar understandings about consent information and resolve any possible misconceptions regarding treatment goals, methods, and confidentiality, such as when the goals of therapy between child/adolescent and parent/guardian differ markedly. For example, research suggests that children/adolescents and parents may disagree about what types of situations therapists should report to parents (Byczkowski et al., 2010). In addition, such interactions early in the therapeutic relationship may promote a collaborative approach to treatment that may benefit the therapy process (Fisher & Oransky, 2008), and research suggests that including children and adolescents in the consent process may improve participation in and effectiveness of treatments (Redding, 1993; Sales, DeKraai, Hall, & Duvall, 2008).

Identification of the Client and Involvement of Family Members

Identification of the particular individual(s) who will be the primary client is a critical component of informed consent discussions. The identified client may be the child or adolescent, parents or guardian, or sometimes the entire family (Standard 10.02, "Therapy Involving Couples or Families") (APA, 2010). Often, therapy with children and adolescents may involve other family members in one capacity or another. Indeed, relevant collateral individuals can contribute to a more complete clinical picture, provide multiple perspectives on behaviors, and contract and enlist the assistance of family members in meeting treatment goals (Weisz & Hawley, 2002). These interactions, however, require special planning by professionals to ensure that the client is clearly identified and to delineate the nature of the participation of the collateral individuals. For example, unless clearly described during informed consent, parents may incorrectly believe that the therapist is supposed to treat not only the child/adolescent, but also address unrelated parental or family mental health concerns (Koocher & Henderson Daniel, 2012). Such situations may jeopardize the trust of the child/adolescent and lead to complex confidentiality dilemmas.

Informed Nature of Consent

Respect for the self-determination of clients requires that psychologists explain necessary components of the procedures that would be reasonably be expected to affect one's decision to participate in language that is reasonably understandable to the individual (Standard 3.10, "Informed Consent to Treatment"; Standard 10.01, "Informed Consent to Therapy") (APA, 2010). Important components include (but are not limited to) risks and benefits of the procedures, the estimated course of treatment and recommended frequency of appointments, costs and fees, and confidentiality, disclosure, and mandatory reporting procedures (see below for an extended discussion of confidentiality with children and adolescents). In addition, psychologists should also explain relevant details about suggested interventions that may affect one's decision to participate in treatment (Fisher, 2013a). For example, interventions that are new or have not yet been supported by scientific or professional data or knowledge also require the psychologist to provide information about the experimental nature of the intervention, available alternative treatments, and the client's right to end participation at any time (Standard 10.01(b), "Informed Consent to Therapy").

Distance and Internet-Based Therapies

As new and emerging technologies develop that allow practitioners to work with clients from wide geographic areas in a variety mediums, mental health professionals must consider important ethical, legal, and technological concerns to ensure that their work adheres to ethical standards and relevant laws (Baker & Bufka, 2011; Fisher, 2013a; Fisher & Fried, 2003; Maheu & Gordon, 2000). As described, consent should include relevant information about the nature of the treatment and professional interaction. Due to the relatively recent development and adoption of telehealth methods, consent may include available data on the effectiveness of such methods for mental health treatment as well as the unique risks to confidentiality and privacy associated with particular methods.

As high users of technology, children and adolescents may be especially interested in participating in electronically mediated mental health services. When therapists and clients interact solely through electronic means, however, it may be difficult to confirm the age and identity of the individual with whom the practitioner is working. For example, unless explicitly stated or confirmed, clinicians providing services exclusively through instant messages or e-mail may not be aware that they are working with children and adolescents; therefore, they may not attempt to seek or otherwise properly obtain appropriate parental or guardian permission. Experts have suggested several methods to address these concerns, such as initial in-person meetings (when feasible), video conferencing, and/or exchange of identifying documentation (Fisher, 2013a; Fisher & Fried, 2003). In general, practitioners considering using electronic and Internet-based services should also devote considerable attention to the unique privacy and confidentiality, competency, interstate practice, and other legal issues associated with these services (Barnett, 2011; Fisher, 2013a; Maheu & Gordon, 2000).

Voluntary Nature of Consent

Sometimes it is easy to overlook the fact that, for the vast majority of child and adolescent clients, the decision to enter and to remain in treatment or participate in treatment is likely made by other individuals with greater power and experience, such as parents, guardians, the legal system, or school officials (Campbell, 2003; Fisher et al., 1999; Margolin, 1982).

Due to both legal mandates and practical contextual constraints, self-determination and decision making by children and adolescents typically are limited (Fisher et al., 1999). This limitation becomes especially important when the child or adolescent is a resistant or reluctant participant in the professional relationship. In such situations, the prudent pediatric mental health professional spends time with both parent and minor client to ensure that the referral question is clear, the perspectives of all parties are discussed, the clinical goals between parent and child are (as much as possible) congruent, and participant rights are understood. Understanding consent information and rights, however, is not the same as being able to assert such rights, as these often are related to power differentials between child and parent/guardian (Fisher et al., 1999; Melton, Koocher, & Saks, 1983).

Such dynamics may make children and adolescents more vulnerable to coercion or otherwise participating in ways that may not be consistent with their personal wishes.

Rational Nature of Consent

Although the vast majority of children and adolescents are unable to legally consent to treatment, a great deal of scientific knowledge has been generated on the ability of children and adolescents to comprehend the components of consent. Grisso and Appelbaum (1998) have described four essential components to psycho-legal consent that should be demonstrated by individuals with adequate consent capacity:

1. Understanding of the key points conveyed in the consent information
2. Risk–benefit analysis about the decision to participate
3. Communicating a decision about participation
4. Demonstration of adequate reasoning about a decision

Notwithstanding the legal constraints associated with independent decision making, research suggests that, in general, minors age 14 and older often are likely to possess the cognitive skills necessary to make independent decisions about treatment (Ambuel & Rappaport, 1992; Billick, Bergert, Friberg, Downer, & Bruni-Solhkhah, 2001; Paul et al., 2008; Weithorn & Campbell, 1982; see Miller, Drotar, & Kodish [2004] for an excellent review of research and findings related to child consent and assent capabilities). As compared to adults, children and adolescents may have more difficulty identifying possible risks, may feel less vulnerable to risks, and may ascribe significantly higher value to short-term than long-term goals (Beyth-Marom, Austin, Fischoff, Palmgren, & Jacobs-Quadrel, 1993; Schachter, Kleinman, & Harvey, 2005; Scott, Reppucci, & Woolard, 1995). It is important to remember that a comprehensive developmental understanding of children and adolescents includes attention not only to evolving cognitive abilities but to other realms of their lives (including the emotional, physical, and social), all of which have the potential to impact their ability to be active and meaningful participants in decisions that affect their well-being (Parekh, 2007).

Children and Adolescents With Mental Health Conditions

Although many adolescents demonstrate the capacity to understand the information necessary to consent to treatment, research suggests that some adolescents diagnosed with a mental health condition may demonstrate key consent-related vulnerabilities. For example, research suggests that certain children and adolescents who are diagnosed with a mental health disorder have a poor understanding and difficulty appreciating their condition and subsequent treatment needs (Turrell, Peterson-Badali, & Katzman, 2011), which, in turn, may have implications for decisions about participation in treatment, such as understanding the risks and benefits of procedures and personally applying them to their situation. It should be noted, however, that individuals diagnosed with a mental disorder are an extremely heterogeneous group with tremendous variability in terms of diagnosis, type and severity of symptoms, and other comorbid conditions, all of which may impact consent capacity (Jeste, Depp, & Palmer, 2006; Jeste & Saks, 2006; Palmer & Jeste, 2006).

Informed Assent

Although children and most adolescents may be incapable of providing legal consent, often they can make personal decisions about participation. In most cases, they should be afforded the opportunity to provide their approval (known as assent) to participate in treatment (Standard 3.10(b), "Informed Consent") (APA, 2010). Providing children and adolescents with an opportunity to contribute meaningfully to the process conveys both respect for personhood and allows them to evaluate consent information and make a determination about their participation. Indeed, in a practical sense, it may be quite difficult to engage someone in the therapeutic process in a meaningful way that will lead to long-term improvements and attainment of therapeutic goals with children and adolescents who are actively opposed to participating in treatment.

Psychologists also should be aware of situations when the solicitation of child assent is contraindicated, such as when the child/adolescent is too young or otherwise lacks the cognitive or emotional capabilities to understand the basic concepts related to treatment, or when they may not have a choice in participation, such as treatment for serious disorders and conditions (Fisher, 2013a; Masty & Fisher, 2008).

Consent Context

In addition to characteristics related to the child/adolescent (such as age, developmental level, and legal status), the consent context also may be a critical factor in determining the ethical and legal responsibilities of mental health professionals (Campbell, 2003; Koocher & Keith-Spiegel, 2008). For example, methods and responsibilities related to confidentiality and record keeping may differ significantly for services offered in school-based settings compared with those offered in hospital or medical settings. As previously discussed, the nature and source of the referral (such as court-mandated psychological services) also may be critically important.

Self-Referring Clients

Although, in the vast majority of cases, children and adolescents likely are referred (sometimes reluctantly) to therapy by a parent or guardian, there are times when adolescents may seek to directly initiate services with a provider without parental or guardian knowledge. Such situations may be more common in school settings, where the school psychologist or counselor may be more accessible and already familiar to the child/adolescent (Jacob & Hartshorne, 2007). For example, an adolescent who is seeking counseling for stress related to a secret romantic relationship unknown to parents may request that the psychologist refrain from contacting them. These types of referrals raise complex questions for practitioners in terms of their responsibilities to gain informed consent from the child/adolescent's parent or guardian. As discussed, most children and adolescents are not legally deemed competent to give consent to treatment (Koocher, 2003; Melton et al., 1983), which presents a dilemma for psychologists. In many cases, initiating treatment with minors without parental consent is not ethically advisable and likely conflicts with state and local laws. (Limited exceptions may occur, depending on the state, for such conditions as substance abuse, pregnancy, or sexually transmitted diseases, states in which adolescents are considered competent to make certain decisions, or, in some cases, for emergencies.) (APA, 2010; Koocher, 2003, 2008; National Association of School Psychologists, 2010).

Best Interests

The requirement to obtain consent from a parent or guardian of a minor child recognizes both legal constraints and cognitive limitations surrounding competency and legal consent as well as the authority of parents and guardians to make decisions they feel are best for their child. When working with an individual who cannot legally provide consent, however, there may be situations in which soliciting consent from parents or guardians may potentially result in risk of harm to the child or adolescent and, therefore not in his or her "best interest" (Standard 3.10(b), "Informed Consent") (APA, 2010). In these limited cases where the psychologist determines that obtaining parental or guardian consent would not be in the child/adolescent's best interest, the practitioner may consider alternative means of ensuring comprehension of information, voluntary participation, and monitoring for any negative reactions to psychological procedures, such as appointing a consent advocate (Fisher, 2013a; Pinnock & Crosthwaite, 2005). Practitioners are advised to consult their state's laws with regard to regulations pertaining to psychological services for children and adolescents (Fisher, 2013a; Fisher et al., 1999; Koocher & Henderson Daniel, 2012).

In sum, research concerning the ability of adolescents and children to participate meaningfully in consent discussions, coupled with legal limitations on treatment-related decision making, suggest that mental health professionals should engage in a respectful and inclusive process of consent that values the self-determination and autonomy of children and adolescents that also properly protects them from decisions that may cause them harm or otherwise not be in their best interests. Children and adolescents should be afforded opportunities to be vocal and active participants in the consent process, with practitioners taking into account consent vulnerabilities to devise methods that are appropriate for the population and context, informed by evidence-based consent practices (Fisher, 2013a; Fisher et al., 2006; Fisher & Oransky, 2008; Masty & Fisher, 2008).

PRIVACY AND CONFIDENTIALITY

Trust placed in psychologists by clients to maintain promises and commitments is reflected in the ethical principle of integrity. Confidentiality, a core ethical commitment in health care settings and in mental health professions, often has been viewed as critical to the success of the therapeutic process (Collins & Knowles, 1995; Ford, Millstein, & Halpern-Felsher, 1997; Harbour, 2004; Koocher, 2008).

Privacy is often a significant concern among adolescents who are considering treatment, and there is often an expectation that clinicians will maintain privacy about information disclosed in session (Condie & Koocher, 2008; Isaacs & Stone, 2001; Kaser-Boyd, Adelman, & Taylor, 1985; McGuire, Parnell, Blau, & Abbott, 1994). Dilemmas related to privacy and confidentiality in professional settings with children and adolescents often are informed by a number of sources, including state laws, federal regulations, professional codes, and empirical research on confidentiality and privacy practices, all of which may determine (in part or totally) the degree to which psychologists may be required to divulge important clinical information related to the child or adolescents (Standard 4.01, "Maintaining Confidentiality") (APA, 2010). For example, laws in all 50 states mandate that certain professionals must report cases of suspected child abuse or neglect. Mental health professionals in particular often struggle with questions about privacy and confidentiality, especially as they relate to what information should be provided to parents/guardians about potentially risky or dangerous behaviors disclosed in therapy (Dailor & Jacob, 2011; Pope & Vetter, 1992).

Discussing Confidentiality, Limits to Confidentiality, and Mandatory Disclosures

In most cases, initial discussions about confidentiality occur at the outset of a professional relationship (Standard 10.01, "Informed Consent to Therapy"; Standard 4.02, "Discussing the Limits of Confidentiality") (APA, 2010). In psychological work with minors, psychologists must ensure that both parents and the child/adolescent are informed and understand the nature of (and limits to) confidentiality within the professional relationship. As with other elements of the informed consent process, this discussion should be revisited throughout the professional relationship as needed. For example, it may be helpful to remind children or adolescents of agreements made during the informed consent process about disclosures to parents or parents' right to request information about their care.

Adolescence often represents a time for behavioral and other types of exploration, which may lead to health-compromising or other risky behaviors, such as alcohol use, drug exploration, sexual activity, and antisocial behaviors. Unfortunately, adolescents and parents do not always view, understand, and value confidentiality in the same ways (Byczkowski et al., 2010). Parents naturally may be concerned about their child's engagement in potentially dangerous behaviors and wish to be informed immediately about potential areas of risk so that they may be addressed at home, as research suggests that increased parental monitoring may reduce adolescent risk behaviors (Beck, Boyle, & Boekeloo, 2004; DiClemente et al., 2001; Weisz & Hawley, 2002). Adolescents, however, may value confidentiality highly (Byczkowski et al., 2010) and oppose therapist disclosure of information to parents or guardians. Psychologists may be caught in the cross-fire and may be uncertain and confused about the correct course of action.

Ongoing discussions about these topics, including specific situations that may warrant disclosure at the outset of therapy (and as needed throughout treatment), often are essential for a successful therapeutic experience for a couple of reasons (Rae, Sullivan, Razo, George, & Ramirez, 2002). First, during the initial informed consent process, the therapist, child/adolescent, and parents may discuss the types of information disclosed by the adolescent/child that will and will not be communicated to parents. A key component of informed consent is disclosure of pertinent information about rules, laws, and best practices in terms of reporting dangerous behaviors to parents and other authority figures. For example, in recognition of parental responsibilities and the parents' role as acting in the best interests of their child, laws and regulations, such as the Health Information Portability and Accountability Act of 1996 (HIPAA), allow parents in most cases to request and view the contents of their child's health care records.

Second, initial and ongoing dialogue about the importance of privacy in therapy and its role in building a trusting relationship with the child/adolescent may be helpful in demystifying the psychotherapy process and reducing confusion about parent or guardian roles in the treatment process (Fisher & Oransky, 2008). As part of these discussions, it may be advisable in certain situations for therapists to recommend regular contact with parents to provide general (and specific, when warranted) feedback about the course of therapy. As Koocher (2008) points out, these discussions have the benefit of providing feedback and information that may assist in meeting treatment goals as well as to remind parents that the focus of treatment is on the issues presented by the child/adolescent, as opposed to other unrelated personal issues that parents believe are appropriate for therapy.

Secrecy Pacts and Privacy Assurances

Although privacy is considered an instrumental condition necessary to promote trust in the health care provider and initiate therapeutic work (Ford et al., 1997), therapist assurance of absolute privacy (or the promise by a practitioner not to divulge any information disclosed in session, also known as a secrecy pact), however, may be ethically irresponsible, lead to harm to the client, and place the psychologist at serious legal and professional risk (Fisher, 2013a; Isaacs & Stone, 2002; Jacob & Hartshorne, 2007). For example, therapists who feel bound to secrecy pacts and fail to report a client's active suicidal ideation may unintentionally cause harm to their client and be subject to criminal and professional disciplinary actions as well as possible malpractice litigation.

In contrast to expectations of some therapists that the maintenance of absolute privacy of all information is essential to building and maintaining the therapeutic relationship, research suggests that many adolescents may expect and prefer that health care providers disclose information about high-risk behavior or harm to parents, guardians, and responsible adults in order to obtain necessary assistance or services. For example, Ford et al. (1997) found that the majority of their adolescent sample expected providers to report concerns about physical or sexual abuse, suicide, or homicide regardless of the adolescents' attitudes or wishes. Other research with urban adolescents echo findings that suggest that adults who may be in positions of authority or responsibility may be expected or required to disclose necessary confidential information to parents or other relevant adults in order to prevent harm or otherwise act in the best interests of children/adolescents (Fisher, Higgins-D'Allesandro, Rau, Kuther, & Bélanger, 1996; O'Sullivan & Fisher, 1997).

Disclosures

Across client populations, dilemmas related to privacy and confidentiality represent one of the most challenging ethical issues for practicing mental health professionals (Dailor & Jacob, 2011; Pope & Vetter, 2002; Sullivan, Ramirez, Rae, Razo, & George, 2002). There are times when there are requirements to disclose confidential information, such as when parents request records under HIPAA or when the child is engaging in behavior that may fall under a mandated reporting rule or law, and many codes of ethics and regulations permit disclosure under specific circumstances. For example, the APA Ethics Code permits psychologists to divulge confidential information in certain situations, such as disclosure with appropriate consent (Standard 4.05, "Disclosures") (APA, 2010). There may be other times, however, when the reporting and disclosure responsibilities related to specific behaviors or topics are unclear, leaving mental health professionals uncertain about how to best proceed and possibly conflicted between ethical obligations to respect the autonomy of the clients and protecting client well-being (Isaacs & Stone, 2001).

Mandated Reporting

Clinicians should be aware of the relevant laws in their jurisdiction that require psychologists to report without consent, such as child abuse (which are enacted in all states), and, in many states, elder abuse, domestic abuse, and abuse of individuals who are disabled (Fisher, 2013a). In addition, following the rulings associated with *Tarasoff v. Regents of the University of California* (1976), many states have enacted laws that either require or permit mental health professionals to disclose information if they believe their client represents a danger. Laws may differ by jurisdiction, so clinicians should be familiar with their reporting responsibilities as well as specific definitions of abuse, dangerous, and harm (Kalichman, 1999).

Therapist Disclosure of Information

As previously described, therapists may have an ethical and legal responsibility to disclose clinical information in specific circumstances, such as situations or behaviors that represent a danger to self or others. But what are therapists' obligations to report behaviors that may represent risk but not necessarily a level that rises to the level of mandatory disclosure to parents, guardians, or other responsible adults? Discussions at the beginning and throughout therapy about what types of information disclosed during treatment are to remain private and what information merits disclosure are helpful but often insufficient, as it may be impossible to anticipate the range of possible future situations, intentions, or behaviors. Disclosure dilemmas often are complicated by behaviors that may be considered bordering between normal developmental exploration and those that may represent danger to the child/adolescent, such as sexual activities, substance use, and rule-breaking behaviors (Dailor & Jacob, 2011; Koocher, 2008; Mitchell, Disque, & Robertson, 2002; Sullivan et al., 2002). Moreover, due to evolving cognitive, emotional, and social development processes, children and adolescents may be more likely to challenge existing rules and boundaries and experiment with new and diverse behaviors. In addition, therapists may fear that reporting risky behaviors disclosed in treatment may harm the therapeutic relationship with the child/adolescent, jeopardizing future benefit of therapeutic interventions.

Unfortunately, there are few guidelines or resources to assist clinicians in determining which specific behaviors merit disclosure to parents, guardians, or responsible adults (Isaacs & Stone, 2001; Mitchell et al., 2002). Empirical investigations into confidentiality practices, such as surveys among psychologists, have led to informative but mixed results. For example, research suggests that while there appears to be some professional disagreement about which specific situations merit disclosure to parents, important determining factors in mental health professionals' decisions to disclose information include the age of the client and situational factors, including the frequency and potential magnitude of possible harm (Isaacs & Stone, 2001; Moyer & Sullivan, 2008; Rae et al., 2002, 2009). In addition, client and practitioner demographic factors also may be important in determining a therapist's decision to disclose information (Isaacs & Stone, 2001; Rae et al., 2002, 2009). For example, survey research with pediatric psychologists suggests that certain behaviors conducted by female clients (as compared to those conducted by male clients) may be viewed as more risky and/or dangerous. Finally, the decision to disclose information also may depend on the context in which the services are provided. For example, professionals working in school or insti-tutional settings may be more likely to share information with each other (Prout et al., 1999) than in other settings. Research also suggests that school psychologists (as compared with nonschool pediatric psychologists) may be more likely to view certain behaviors as being higher risk (Rae et al., 2009).

It is important to remember that the protection and promotion of the welfare of those with whom the mental health professional works is of paramount importance. This may require difficult ethical decision making that at times may be consistent with the child/adolescent's preferences and may at other times, in the interest of their welfare, be contrary to expressed wishes.

Best Practices When Making Disclosures

Decisions to disclose private information to another person, such as a parent, guardian, or other responsible adult, attempt to protect and promote the well-being and welfare of the child/adolescent while minimizing possible damage to the therapeutic relationship. As some have noted (e.g., Mitchell et al., 2002), disclosures that are conducted in a sensitive and thoughtful manner actually may serve to strengthen the therapeutic bond, enhance the parent–child relationships, enhance treatment effectiveness, and serve as a model for effective and respectful methods of communication.

In most situations, clinicians who plan to disclose confidential information should discuss such a decision with their child or adolescent client (Prout et al., 1999). Such conversations may serve important therapeutic purposes but also reflect respect for the personhood of the child/adolescent and the therapeutic agreement. Helpful recommendations have been described by several authors (Fisher, 2013a; Fisher et al., 1999; Mitchell et al., 2002; Taylor & Adelman, 1989), including these:

- *Review* confidentiality procedures, including the nature of and limits to as well as the purpose of disclosures. The clinician should attempt to engage the child/adolescent and the parents in meaningful discussions about the reasons for such disclosures and the decision to disclose in this particular situation.
- *Listen* empathically to the concerns, questions, and requests of both the child/adolescent and parents.

- When appropriate, *encourage* direct discussion between the child/adolescent and parent in communicating important information. Such exercises may serve multiple purposes, including training in effective communication skills, trust building, and child/adolescent autonomy.
- *Assess and monitor* both the reactions/implications of the disclosure and the situation regarding the information disclosed. Doing this may include observation and assessment, conversations with the child/adolescent, and follow-up meetings with parents/guardians.

CONCLUSIONS

Psychological science and practice inform each other in important ways that are increasingly being translated into effective mental health treatments for a variety of disorders and conditions affecting children and adolescents. The provision of responsible, competent, and effective mental health services to children and adolescents presents with many ethical challenges unique to these populations. Such challenges often require a specialized knowledge of the young client's developmental processes and familiarity with relevant legal requirements, regulations, enforceable professional standards, and evidence-based professional practices. Although dilemmas with child and adolescent populations may be complex, careful attention to laws, professional guidelines, and standards; sound ethical decision making; and ongoing and respectful dialogue with children, adolescents, and their families about the responsible conduct of mental health care may serve not only to further clarify professional roles and responsibilities, but to empower the child/adolescent as an active participant in the treatment process and to advance therapeutic goals. As such, these challenges may be seen as opportunities to contribute to positive treatment outcomes with children and adolescents.

REFERENCES

Ambuel, B., & Rappaport, J. (1992). Developmental trends in adolescents' psychological and legal competence to consent to abortion. *Law and Human Behavior, 16,* 129–154.

American Psychiatric Association. (2013). *Diagnostic and statistical manual of mental disorders* (5th ed.). Alexandria, VA: American Psychiatric Publishing.

American Psychological Association. (1993). Guidelines for providers of psychological services to ethnic, linguistic, and culturally diverse populations. *American Psychologist, 48,* 45–48.

American Psychological Association. (2002). *Criteria for the accreditation of psychology programs.* Washington, DC: Author.

American Psychological Association. (2003). Guidelines on multicultural education, training, research, practice and organizational change for psychologists. *American Psychologist, 58,* 377–402.

American Psychological Association. (2010). *Ethical principles of psychologists and code of conduct* (2002, amended June 1, 2010). Retrieved from www.apa.org/ethics/code/index.aspx

American Psychological Association, Presidential Task Force on Evidence-Based Practice. (2006). Evidence-based practice in psychology. *American Psychologist, 61,* 271–285.

Arredondo, P., & Toporek, R. (2004). Multicultural counseling competencies = ethical practice. *Journal of Mental Health Counseling, 26,* 44–55.

Baker, D. C., & Bufka, L. F. (2011). Preparing for the telehealth world: Navigating legal regulatory reimbursement and ethical issues in an electronic age. *Professional Psychology: Research and Practice, 42,* 405–411.

Barnett, J. E. (2011). Utilizing technological innovations to enhance psychotherapy supervision, training and outcomes. *Psychotherapy, 48,* 103–108.

Beck, K. H., Boyle, J. R., & Boekeloo, B. O. (2004). Parental monitoring and adolescent drinking: Results of a 12-month follow-up. *American Journal of Health Behavior, 28,* 272–279.

Beyth-Marom, R., Austin, L., Fischoff, B., Palmgren, C., & Jacobs-Quadrel, M. (1993). Perceived consequences of risky behaviors: Adults and adolescents. *Developmental Psychology, 29,* 549–563.

Billick, S. B., Bergert, W., Friberg, G., Downer, A. V., & Bruni-Solhkhah, S. M. (2001). A clinical study of competency to consent to treatment in pediatrics. *Journal of the American Academy of Psychiatry and Law, 29,* 298–302.

Byckowski, T. L., Kollar, L. M., & Britto, M. T. (2010). Family experiences with outpatient care: Do adolescents and parents have the same perceptions? *Journal of Adolescent Health, 47,* 92–98.

Campbell, L. F. (2003). Ethical and legal issues in working with children and adolescents. In L. VandeCreek & T. L. Jackson (Eds.), *Innovations in clinical practice: Focus on children and adolescents* (pp. 153–166). Sarasota, FL: Professional Resources Press.

Collins, N., & Knowles, A. D. (1995). Adolescents' attitudes toward confidentiality between the school counselor and the adolescent client. *Australian Psychologist, 30,* 179–182.

Condie, L. O., & Koocher, G. P. (2008). Clinical management of children's incomplete comprehension of confidentiality limits. *Journal of Child Custody, 5,* 161–191.

Dailor, A. N., & Jacob, S. 2011. Ethically challenging situations reported by school psychologists: Implications for training. *Psychology in the Schools, 48,* 619–631.

DiClemente, R. J., Wingood, G. M., Crosby, R., Sionean, C., Cobb, B. K., Harrington, K., . . . Oh, M. K. (2001). Parental monitoring: Association with adolescents' risk behaviors. *Pediatrics, 107,* 1363–1368.

Falzon, L., Davidson, K. W., & Bruns, D. (2010). Evidence searching for evidence-based psychology practice. *Professional Psychology: Research and Practice, 41,* 550–557.

Family Educational Rights and Privacy Act. (1974). 20 U.S.C. S1232g:34 C.F.R. Part 99. Retrieved from http://www.ed.gov/policy/gen/guid/fpco/ferpa/index.html

Fisher, C. B. (2013a). *Decoding the ethics code: A practical guide for psychologists* (3rd ed.). Thousand Oaks, CA: Sage.

Fisher, C. B. (2013b). Multicultural ethics in professional psychology practice, consulting and training. In F. T. L. Leong, L. Comas-Diaz, G. C. Nagayama Hall, V. C. McLoyd, & J. E. Trimble (Eds.), *APA handbook of multicultural psychology* (pp. 35–57). Washington, DC: American Psychological Association.

Fisher, C. B., Busch-Rossnagel, N. A., Jopp, D. S., & Brown, J. (2012). Applied developmental science, social justice, and socio-political well-being. *Applied Developmental Science, 16,* 54–64.

Fisher, C. B., Cea, C. D., Davidson, P. W., & Fried, A. L. (2006). Capacity of persons with mental retardation to consent to participation in randomized clinical trials. *American Journal of Psychiatry, 163,* 1813–1821.

Fisher, C. B., & Fried, A. L. (2003). Internet-mediated psychological services and the American Psychological Association ethics code. *Psychotherapy: Theory, Research, Practice, Training, 40,* 103–111.

Fisher, C. B., Hatashita-Wong, M., & Isman, L. (1999). Ethical and legal issues. In W. K. Silverman & T. H. Ollendick (Eds.), *Developmental issues in the clinical treatment of children and adolescents* (pp. 470–486). Needham Heights, MA: Allyn & Bacon.

Fisher, C. B., Higgins-D'Allesandro, A., Rau, J. M. B., Kuther, T., & Bélanger, S. (1996). Reporting and referring research participants: The view from urban adolescents. *Child Development, 67,* 2086–2099.

Fisher, C. B., & Oransky, M. (2008). Informed consent to psychotherapy: Protecting the dignity and respecting the autonomy of patients. *Journal of Clinical Psychology: In Session, 64,* 576–588.

Ford, C. A., Millstein, S. G., & Halpern-Felsher, B. L. (1997). Influence of physician confidentiality assurances on adolescents' willingness to disclose information and seek future health care. *Journal of the American Medical Association, 278,* 1029–1034.

Fowers, B. J., & Davidov, B. J. (2006). The virtue of multiculturalism: Personal transformation, character, and openness to the other. *American Psychologist, 61,* 581–594.

Grisso, T., & Appelbaum, P. S., (1998). *Assessing competence to treatment: A guide for physicians and other health professionals.* New York, NY: Oxford University Press.

Harbour, A. (2004). Understanding children and young people's right to confidentiality. *Child and Adolescent Mental Health, 9,* 187–190.

Health Information Portability and Accountability Act of 1996. Pub. L. No. 104-191, 110 Stat. 1936 (1996).

Isaacs, M. L., & Stone, C. (2001). Confidentiality with minors: Mental health counselors' attitudes toward breaching or preserving confidentiality. *Journal of Mental Health Counseling, 23,* 342–356.

Jacob, S., & Hartshorne, T. S. (2007). *Ethical and law for school psychologists* (5th ed.) Hoboken, NJ: Wiley.

Jeste, D. V., Depp, C. A., & Palmer, B. W. (2006). Magnitude of impairment in decisional capacity in people with schizophrenia compared to normal subjects: An overview. *Schizophrenia Bulletin, 32,* 121–128.

Jeste, D. V., & Saks, E. (2006). Decisional capacity in mental illness and substance use disorders: Empirical database and policy implications. *Behavioral Sciences and the Law, 24,* 607–628.

Kalichman, S. C. (1999). *Mandated reporting of suspected child abuse: Ethics, law, and policy* (2nd ed.). Washington, DC: American Psychological Association.

Kaser-Boyd, N., Adelman, H. S., & Taylor, L. (1985). Minors' ability to identify risks and benefits of therapy. *Professional Psychology: Research and Practice, 16,* 411–417.

Kinscherff, R. (1999). Empirically supported treatments: What to do until the data arrive (or now that they have)? *Clinical Child Psychology Newsletter, 14,* 4–6.

Koocher, G. P. (2003). Ethical issues in psychotherapy with adolescents. *Journal of Clinical Psychology, 59,* 1247–1256.

Koocher, G. P. (2008). Ethical challenges in mental health services to children and families. *Journal of Clinical Psychology, 64,* 601–612.

Koocher, G. P., & Henderson Daniel, J. (2012). Treating children and adolescents. In S. J. Knapp (Ed.), *American Psychological Association handbook in psychology* (Vol. 2, pp. 3–12). Washington, DC: American Psychological Association.

Koocher, G. P., & Keith-Spiegel, P. C. (2008). *Ethics in psychology and the mental health professions: Standards and cases* (3rd ed.). New York, NY: Oxford University Press.

Kunin, H. (1997). Ethical issues in pediatric life-threatening illness: Dilemmas of consent, assent and communication. *Ethics & Behavior, 7,* 43–57.

Kuther, T. L. (2003). Medical decision-making and minors: Issues of consent and assent. *Adolescence, 38,* 343–358.

Lemoire, S. J., & Chen, C. P. (2005). Applying person-centered counseling to sexual minority adolescents. *Journal of Counseling & Development, 83,* 146–154.

Maheu, M. M., & Gordon, B. L. (2000). Counseling and therapy on the Internet. *Professional Psychology: Research and Practice, 31,* 484–489.

Margolin, G. (1982). Ethical and legal considerations in marital and family therapy. *American Psychologist, 37,* 788–801.

Masty, J., & Fisher, C. B. (2008). A goodness of fit approach to parental permission and child assent in pediatric intervention research. *Ethics & Behavior, 18,* 139–160.

McGuire, J. M., Parnell, T. F., Blau, B. I., & Abbott, D. W. (1994). Demands for privacy among adolescents in multimodal alcohol and other drug abuse treatment. *Journal of Counseling & Development, 73,* 74–78.

Melton, G. B. (1999). Parents and children: Legal reform to facilitate children's participation. *American Psychologist, 54,* 935–944.

Melton, G. B., Koocher, G. P., & Saks, M. J. (1983). *Children's competence to consent.* New York, NY: Plenum Press.

Miller, V. A., Drotar, D., & Kodish, E. (2004). Children's competence for assent and consent: A review of empirical findings. *Ethics & Behavior, 14,* 255–295.

Mitchell, C. W., Disque, J. G., & Robertson, P. (2002). When parents want to know: Responding to parental demands for confidential information. *Professional School Counseling, 6,* 156–161.

Molin, E., & Palmer, S. (2005). Consent and participation: Ethical issues in the treatment of children in out-of-home care. *American Journal of Orthopsychiatry, 75,* 152–157.

Moyer, M. S., & Sullivan, J. R. (2008). Student risk-taking behaviors: When do school counselors break confidentiality? *Professional School Counseling, 11,* 236–245.

National Association of School Psychologists. (2010). *Principles for professional ethics.* Retrieved from http://www.nasponline.org/standards/2010standards/1_%20Ethical%20Principles.pdf

Ollendick, T. H., & Davis, T. E. (2004). Empirically supported treatments for children and adolescents: Where to from here? *Clinical Psychology: Science and Practice, 11,* 289–294.

Ollendick, T. H., & King, N. J. (2004). Empirically supported treatments for children and adolescence: Advances toward evidence-based practice. In P. M. Barrett & T. H. Ollendick (Eds.), *Handbook of interventions that work with children and adolescents: Prevention and treatment* (pp. 3–25). Chichester, UK: Wiley.

O'Sullivan, C., & Fisher, C. B. (1997). The effect of confidentiality and reporting procedures on parent-child agreement to participate in adolescent risk research. *Applied Developmental Science, 1,* 185–197.

Palmer, B. W., & Jeste, D. V. (2006). Relationship of individual cognitive abilities to specific components of decisional capacity among middle-aged and older patients with schizophrenia. *Schizophrenia Bulletin, 32,* 98–106.

Parekh, S. A. (2007). Child consent and the law: An insight and discussion into the law relating to consent and competence. *Child: Care, Health and Development, 33,* 78–82.

Paul, M., Berriman, J. A., & Evans, J. (2008). Would I attend child and mental health services (CAMHS)? Fourteen to sixteen year olds decide. *Child and Adolescent Mental Health, 13,* 19–25.

Pinnock, R., & Crosthwaite, J. (2005). When parents refuse consent to treatment for children and young persons. *Journal of Paediatrics and Child Health, 41,* 369–373.

Ponterotto, J. G., Casas, J. M., Suzuki, L. A., & Alexander, C. M. (2001). *Handbook of multicultural counseling* (2nd ed.). Thousand Oaks, CA: Sage.

Pope, K. S., & Vetter, V. A. (1992). Ethical dilemmas encountered by members of the American Psychological Association: A national survey. *American Psychologist, 47,* 397–411.

Prilleltensky, I. (1997). Values, assumptions, and practices: Assessing the moral implications of psychological discourse and action. *American Psychologist, 52,* 517–535.

Prout, S. M., DeMartino, R. A., & Prout, H. (1999). Ethical and legal issues in psychological interventions with children and adolescents. In H. T. Prout & D. T. Brown (Eds.), *Counseling and psychotherapy with children and adolescents* (3rd ed., pp. 26–48). New York, NY: Wiley.

Rae, W. A., Sullivan, J. R., Razo, N. P., & Garcia de Alba, R. (2009). Breaking confidentiality to report risk-taking behavior by school psychologists. *Ethics & Behavior, 19,* 449–460.

Rae, W. A., Sullivan, J. R., Razo, N. P., George, C. A., & Ramirez, E. (2002). Adolescent health risk behavior: When do pediatric psychologists break confidentiality? *Journal of Pediatric Psychology, 27,* 541–549.

Redding, R. E. (1993). Children's competence to provide informed consent for mental health treatment. *Washington and Lee Law Review, 50,* 695–753.

Ridley, C. R., Liddle, M. C., Hill, C.K.L., & Li, L. C. (2001). Ethical decision making in multicultural counseling. In J. G. Ponterotto, J. M. Casas, L. A. Suzuki, & C. M. Alexander (Eds.), *Handbook of multicultural counseling* (2nd ed., pp. 165–188). Thousand Oaks, CA: Sage.

Sales, B. D., DeKraai, M. B., Hall, S. R., & Duvall, J. C. (2008). Child therapy and the law. In R. J. Morris & T. R. Kratochwill (Eds.), *The practice of child therapy* (4th ed., pp. 519–541). Mahwah, NJ: Erlbaum.

Salter, D. S., & Salter, B. R. (2012). Competence with diverse populations. In S. Knapp, M. Gottlieb, M. Handelsman, & L. VandeCreek (Eds.), *Handbook of ethics in psychology*, Vol. 1 (pp. 217–241). Washington, DC: American Psychological Association.

Schachter, D., Kleinman, I., & Harvey, W. (2005). Informed consent and adolescents. *Canadian Journal of Psychiatry, 50,* 534–539.

Scott, E. S., Reppucci, N. D., & Wollard, J. L. (1995). Evaluating adolescent decision-making in legal contexts. *Law and Human Behavior, 19,* 221–244.

Sue, D. W., & Sue, D. (2003). *Counseling the culturally diverse.* Hoboken, NJ: Wiley.

Sullivan, J. R., Ramirez, E., Rae, W. A., Razo, N. P., & George, C. A. (2002). Factors contributing to breaking confidentiality with adolescent clients: A survey of pediatric psychologists. *Professional Psychology: Research and Practice, 33,* 396–401.

Tarasoff v. Regents of the University of California (Tarasoff II), 17 Cal. 3d 425, 51 P.2d334 (Cal. 1976).

Taylor, L., & Adelman, H. S. (1989). Reframing the confidentiality dilemma to work in children's best interests. *Professional Psychology: Research and Practice, 20,* 79–83.

Turrell, S. L., Peterson-Badali, M., & Katzman, D. K. (2011). Consent to treatment in adolescents with anorexia nervosa. *International Journal of Eating Disorders, 44,* 703–707.

Weisz, J. R., & Hawley, K. M. 2002. Developmental factors in the treatment of adolescents. *Journal of Consulting and Clinical Psychology, 70,* 21–43

Weithorn, L. A., & Campbell, S. B. (1982). The competency of children and adolescents to make informed treatment decisions. *Child Development, 53,* 1589–1598.

CHAPTER 3

Controversial Therapies for Children

GERALD P. KOOCHER, MADELINE R. MCMANN, AND ANNIKA O. STOUT

Acceptance or rejection of approaches to treating psychological problems has varied considerably over time as a function of scientific progress and the Zeitgeist of the society in question. Controversy may arise in the context of new discoveries, cultural preferences, religious values, historical trends, and other social forces. As a reaction toward improved treatment outcomes, the medical and psychological communities have increasingly supported a quest to identify and implement evidence-based practices (EBPs). In so doing, some interventions have become recognized as less effective than others, totally ineffective, or even harmful (Beyerstein, 2001; Lilienfeld, 2007). Two Delphi polls of experts have revealed a consensus about such psychological treatment and assessment techniques generally regarded as discredited for broad use (Norcross, Koocher, & Garofalo, 2006) and in the treatment of addictions (Norcross, Koocher, Fala, & Wexler, 2010). The authors of this chapter have undertaken a similar study focused on approaches used with children and adolescents.

In seeking to define controversial treatment in today's context, we have relied on criteria used as standards of evidence used for expert testimony in courts of law, such as those delineated in the *Daubert* (1993) and *Kumho Tire Company* cases (1999). For example, in *Daubert* (1993), the courts cited factors, such as testing, peer review, error rates, and acceptability in the relevant scientific community, some or all of which might prove helpful in determining the validity of a particular scientific theory or technique. The *Kumho* decision extends this reasoning to technical testimony and claims that one could prove causality by the absence of significant findings. These criteria have helped us select controversial discredited treatments, still advocated by some practitioners in narrow or remote segments of the mental health community, for discussion in this chapter.

As illustrations of discredited psychotherapeutic techniques sometimes advocated for use in treating children and adolescents, we have selected six to review in this chapter. Presented in alphabetical order, these include: aromatherapy, boot camp and disciplinary boarding schools interventions (including "Scared Straight" interventions), Drug Abuse Resistance Education (D.A.R.E.), so-called energy psychology, rebirthing, and reparative or sexual preference conversion therapies. In each instance we describe the technique, cite any available evidence for its use with children or adolescents, and provide information on any particular known harms or adverse consequences.

AROMATHERAPY

The term "aromatherapy" generally refers to a treatment that relies on plant extracts to promote physiological and psychological healing. The National Center for Complementary and Alternative Medicines (NCCAM) of the U.S. Department of Health and Human Services defines aromatherapy as a treatment "in which the scent of essential oils from flowers, herbs, and trees is inhaled to promote health and well-being" (NCCAM, 2012). However, some practitioners administer essential oil extracts topically or orally (Bradley, Brown, Chu, & Lea, 2009; Herz, 2009). Researchers have yet to agree on a standard definition of aromatherapy, thus creating one of the many problems associated with studying its efficacy.

Many societies and cultural groups have used essential oils for ritual, aromatic, and medicinal purposes for thousands of years. We have no information about how the potential healing power of aromatic plants was discovered, yet ample evidence from Egypt, India, and the Middle East indicates their use in ancient times. Hundreds of references to various oils exist in Judeo-Christian religious texts, and aromatic plants were found within royal tombs of Egypt and China. Aromatherapy is practiced globally, holding particular import in Eastern medicine and traditional native cultures. For example, in the Amazon region, some peoples use linalool, a compound found in many essential oils, to control epileptic seizures.

In the Western world, aromatherapy is regarded as a complementary and alternative medicine (CAM). However, this "nonscientific folk remedy" (Herz, 2009; Takeda, Tsujita, Kaya, Takemura, & Oku, 2008) has become increasingly popular throughout the Western world in recent years. Perry and Perry (2006), a mother and daughter research team from New Zealand who focus extensively on aromatherapy, describe it as the fastest-growing CAM today. In one study on CAM use in children with attention-deficit/hyperactivity disorder (ADHD) (Sinha & Efron, 2005), researchers reported that out of 23 CAM treatments, aromatherapy was the second most frequently used, behind diet modifications.

Review of the extant literature reveals claims that aromatherapy can successfully treat dementia, ADHD, autistic spectrum disorders, schizophrenia, anxiety, depression, and sleep disorders. Some even claim that certain essential oils can promote hippocampal neurogenesis (Perry & Perry, 2006). Thus far results have proved inconclusive. In one study, a combination of aromatherapy and massage reportedly helped to increase shared attention in four preschool-age children with comorbid autism spectrum disorders and severe learning deficits (Solomons, 2005). In another study, 5 minutes of lavender inhalation through an oxygen mask showed a significant effect on perceived pain reduction during needle insertion, lowered the need for anesthesia, and decreased stress (Kim et al., 2011). This decrease in stress may indeed be due to the pharmacological effects of the essential oil lavender. Researchers have found linalool, the sedative component of lavender, is responsible for eliciting a parasympathetic nervous system response. Sayorwan et al. (2012) found linalool to decrease blood pressure, heart rate, respiratory rate, and skin temperature. In this same study on the effects of lavender oil inhalation on emotional states, autonomic nervous system, and brain electrical activity, electroencephalograms showed significant increases in theta and alpha wave activity, both of which are associated with relaxation and inhibition.

Yet when researchers tested whether expectancy bias or the pharmacological effects of lavender were responsible for anti-anxiety effects, they found that expectations of relaxation enhance relaxation prior to a stressful cognitive task (Howard & Hughes, 2008). Additionally, aromatherapy can prove harmful. Researchers diffused bergamot for inhalation to pediatric patients undergoing stem-cell infusion and to their parents. Bergamot is an essential oil thought to reduce anxiety and nausea. The authors of this study report that patient anxiety and nausea increased significantly. Interestingly, parents of the children undergoing stem-cell infusions reported being less anxious after exposure to the essential oil (Ndao et al., 2012).

Most published research literature on aromatherapy is based on anecdotal evidence, case studies, and animal models. Many of the studies conducted on human participants have major methodological problems, such as small sample sizes, ascertainment biases, lack of control groups, and others. Most important, apart from the few studies mentioned here, very little research of any kind has focused on child and adolescent populations.

Use of aromatherapy in the clinical treatment of psychopathology in child or adolescent populations poses risks. No consensus exists on safe dosages. Little research has focused on essential oils and drug interactions. No governmental or regulatory organization ensures high quality of essential oils as the U.S. Food and Drug Administration does for prescription drugs. Another factor contributing to unreliability and invalidity in the literature on aromatherapy involves inconsistency among researchers as to what product to use or in which dose, concentration, or delivery system. In addition, by some estimates up to 70% of those using herbal and aromatic therapies do not report such use to their primary care provider (Cline et al., 2008). The current state of science in aromatherapy as a treatment for childhood ADHD or any other psychological conditions amounts to little more than traditional folkloric medicine.

BOOT CAMP INTERVENTIONS AND DISCIPLINARY BOARDING SCHOOLS

Boot camps and disciplinary boarding schools, often based in rural areas of the western United States or abroad, have become popular "treatment" alternatives for children and adolescents with conditions such as conduct disorders (CDs) and oppositional defiant disorder (ODD). So-called tough love has some broad intuitive appeal in some families and communities. Removal of the child or adolescent from their homes, peers, and communities along with imposition of rigorous physical activity demands and strict discipline form the key components of such programs, although many former participants in such programs have cited severe abuse or torture (e.g., denial of food or medical care, isolation and confinement, beatings, etc.) as integral to the experience.

The World Wide Association of Specialty Programs and Schools (WWASPS) provides an example of one controversial organization that at one time had a system of 25 such "therapeutic" schools for children ages 12 to 17 years with behavior problems. Today, fewer than 10 WWASPS schools remain open. Abuse allegations and lawsuits filed by former students and deaths of some WWASPS students have led to the majority of school closings (see, e.g., Dobner, 2011, and Janofsky, 2001). Physical and emotional abuse reports are not uncommon in such "therapeutic" boarding schools or residential boot camp facilities.

In thinking about efficacy of interventions for childhood or adolescent CDs, consider the importance of using the least restrictive and most effective treatments for children with externalizing behavior disorders. Consider, for example, the handbooks by Weisz and Kazdin (2010) and Ollendick and King (2004), which provide substantial overviews of highly effective interventions for CDs and ODD. Of course, the treatments most often recommended require considerably more effort and engagement by parents than extracting the child to a remote residential intervention. Also, consider the correlational studies showing a strong positive relationship among parenting problems, childhood abuse, and CDs (Boden, Fergusson, & Horwood, 2010; Fergusson, Boden, & Horwood, 2008; Murray & Farrington, 2010). In this context, it seems highly inappropriate to treat a childhood disorder with abusive and neglectful behaviors when the very etiology of the problem may stem in part from abuse, neglect, or inconsistent parental engagement in treatment. Indeed, Lilienfeld (2007) has particularly called out boot camps and intimidating "Scared Straight" programs as having significant potential to cause harm to child and adolescent participants.

The popularity of heavy-handed disciplinary and military-style residential programs seems particularly outrageous considering the attendant high risks and lack of scientific support. No empirical data in support of such programs has reached the peer-reviewed literature (Lilienfeld, 2007). Ethical concerns make studies on the effectiveness of coercive treatments in reducing antisocial behavior difficult. However, the research that does exist shows that boot camp programs and programs such as "Scared Straight" do more harm than good to youth with behavior problems by exacerbating painful emotions (Lilienfeld, 2007; Petrosino, Turpin-Petrosino, & Buehler, 2005). Literature on behavior disorders such as ODD and other CDs suggests that multifaceted treatments including multisystemic family therapy are far more effective (Children's Mental Health Ontario, 2011; Lilienfeld, 2007; Olendick & King, 2004; Weisz & Kazdin, 2010).

DRUG ABUSE RESISTANCE EDUCATION

While not a treatment technique in the usual sense, Drug Abuse Resistance Education, popularly known as D.A.R.E., has wide social support as a program aimed at preventing substance abuse among school-age students by using police officers to educate them on the dangers of drugs and alcohol. According to its official Web site, D.A.R.E. is currently implemented in about 75% of our nation's schools (D.A.R.E. Web site, 2012). Despite its popularity, there is no scientific evidence to support the claim that it prevents or even decreases subsequent alcohol and drug abuse.

D.A.R.E. was founded in 1983 with the mission of "teaching students good decision making skills to help them lead safe and healthy lives." This program describes itself as a "police-officer-led series of classroom lessons that teach children from kindergarten through 12th grade how to resist peer pressure and live productive drug and violence-free lives." The website includes anecdotal articles written by police officers and supporters of the program, yet no scientific empirical data support the program's ability to decrease or prevent substance use.

D.A.R.E. may not decrease substance use, but participation in the program certainly does not increase substance use either (Thombs, 2000). The high level of satisfaction community members report with the program predominantly accounts for the support it enjoys and its overall reputation in the community (Thombs, 2000). Parents, police, and school authorities all want to reduce substance abuse among children and adolescents. The program has a level of intuitive or face validity. After all, if adult authority figures all tell you that something's bad for you, you won't do it, right? Paying police officers to teach in such programs has support within the community policing movement, and what school system will say no to a free (to them) program that enhances positive collaboration with law enforcement while arguing the merits of healthy behavior?

According to Gorman and Huber (2009), the U.S. Department of Education has set very minimal standards for D.A.R.E. to meet to qualify for support, making it easy for program officials to demonstrate that they met these requirements. To qualify for use in the classroom, D.A.R.E. was required to have just one program evaluation that showed an effect on substance use or violence 1 year after the program concluded.

Several studies have shown no significant effects of D.A.R.E on participants' short-term or long-term substance use (Ennett, Tobler, Ringwalt, & Flewelling, 1994; Gorman & Huber, 2009; Rosenbaum, 1994; Thombs, 2000; Uibel, 2010). These findings should serve "as reminders to researchers and program advocates that positive outcomes are not guaranteed simply because a program is prosocial in nature and widely supported" (Rosenbaum, 1994, p. 27). These findings should also raise a red flag for donations and financial backing that goes into the program. An average of $750 million of federal funds is spent on D.A.R.E. each year (West & O'Neal, 2004). This money could be better spent on "evidence-based programs that have been shown much more promise in prevention trials" (Thombs, 2000, p. 36).

Over the past two decades, researchers have conducted a variety of different studies examining the effectiveness of the program with different methodological approaches. The results remain strikingly similar: Participation in a D.A.R.E. program produces no significant effect on later substance use. A meta-analysis of 11 previously published studies of D.A.R.E. found either no effect of the program or found that the D.A.R.E. program actually proved less effective than the control condition (West & O'Neal, 2004). A retrospective study of undergraduate college students who had earlier participated in D.A.R.E. revealed no difference in substance use when compared to their counterparts who did not participate in D.A.R.E. (Thombs, 2000). In a longitudinal evaluation of D.A.R.E., researchers determined that any initially promising results became undetectable over time (Rosenbaum, 1994). In addition, one study also provided evidence showing that D.A.R.E. participation did not alter participants' later attitudes toward these substances (Uibel, 2010). Again, the enormous amount of money poured into D.A.R.E. programs annually could be better spent developing programs with demonstrable preventive effects.

"ENERGY" PSYCHOLOGY AND THE EMOTIONAL FREEDOM TECHNIQUE

The Emotional Freedom Technique (EFT) grew out of thought field therapy. Gary Craig, an ordained minister with no training in psychotherapy, developed EFT in the mid-1990s. Practitioners of EFT believe that an imbalance in the body's energy system causes *all* negative emotions, and that tapping at particular points on the body alters brain activity to produce calming effects (Feinstein, 2008). Adherents believe that while imagining or recalling specific memories, tapping 12 "acupoints" outlined by traditional Chinese medicine practitioners and repeating encouraging phrases can cure psychiatric disorders such as insomnia, anxiety, post-traumatic stress disorder (PTSD), depression, grief, and ADHD. Some claim that the technique can also reduce symptoms of more serious disorders, such as schizophrenia. EFT is described as a brief treatment with results generally seen after between 1 and 10 sessions (Church, Yount, & Brooks, 2012; Wells, Polglase, Andrews, Carrington, & Baker, 2003).

According to Gary Craig and his wife (Craig & Craig, 2012; www.garythink.com), people of any age can use EFT, including children and even preverbal infants. What is more, Gary Craig also claims that surrogate EFT is effective in reducing symptoms of various disorders (McCaslin, 2009; www.garythink.com). Besides anecdotal evidence and a few case studies on EFT effectiveness, we could find no studies on children. However, one pilot study on the efficacy of EFT in adolescents suggests that EFT is effective in treating patients with PTSD. Church, Piña, Reategui, and Brooks (2012) conducted a randomized control trial on 16 males with PTSD from a residential treatment facility in Peru. After a single session of EFT, 14 out of the 16 participants experienced what energy psychologists call the apex effect, meaning that these patients reported reductions in the intensity of traumatic memory following the single session of treatment but credit the change to some other cause (e.g., "I felt distracted" or "It was a placebo effect."). One-month follow-up indicated that 40% of participants no longer had diagnosable PTSD. One significant methodological problem with that study involved significant reliance on the so-called subjective units of distress. Using that measure, the researcher repeatedly asks research participants to self-report their level of distress with traumatic memories using a 10-point scale, until participants report significant reductions. One can only imagine the demand characteristics inherent in applying such an outcome measure in a Peruvian juvenile detention center where significant pressures exist to show "improvement" to those in authority.

The EFT is generally supported by its adherents using case studies and anecdotal evidence. However, some currently recognize EFT as a "probably efficacious treatment" for specific phobias based on one study by Wells et al. (2003) that met the criteria set in a 1993 task force report by the Clinical Psychology Division of the American Psychological Association (Chambless & Hollon,

1998; Feinstein, 2008). Wells et al. (2003) compared the effectiveness of EFT to diaphragmatic breathing in reducing phobia to small animals and found EFT more effective. However, it is important to note that like most studies in energy psychology, the comparison treatment, diaphragmatic breathing, is not a recognized efficacious treatment either. Similarly, in the Church et al. study on the Peruvian adolescent offenders with PTSD, the treatment group was not tested against an efficacious treatment. In efficacy studies, energy treatments and tapping therapies often compared to other treatments that are not empirically supported. Thus, we can conclude little from the results of those studies. Nonetheless, the Wells et al. (2003) study did have fewer methodological problems than most other studies on EFT. Energy treatment studies tend to be riddled with methodological problems, such as biased samples, small sample sizes, and lack of adequate control groups. Whether EFT can be used effectively with clinical populations remains up for debate.

Descriptive or anecdotal research on EFT shows positive results, but how and why it works remains unclear (Benor, Ledger, Toussaint, Hett, & Zaccaro, 2009; Feinstein, 2008; Wells et al., 2003). One might conclude that so long as a treatment is effective, the method does not matter. In some respects, this conclusion is similar to supporting the merits of placebos. We often want to treat a troubling condition with whatever resources we have and with what we know to work. However, it is imperative that we understand the mechanisms behind treatment methods because such findings could alter the way we provide mental health care. For example, if we can conclude that tapping 12 "acupoints" actually lowers cortisol levels, as Church et al. (2012) claim, then psychologists might be apt to adopt tapping techniques to reduce client stress. Theoretically, clients could tap themselves to health, reduce health care costs, and potentially put psychotherapists out of business if tapping "acupoints" is solely responsible for altering brain activity. However, tapping techniques may have little or nothing to do with why EFT worked in the one reasonably well-done study by Wells and colleagues. Literature suggests that placebo effects, distraction from the issue at hand, imaginal exposure, or other cognitive processes may be responsible for the effectiveness of EFT and other energy treatments and tap therapies. Considering the other variables at play, we must wonder whether what is novel about EFT is effective or whether the effective components of any intervention using EFT are better explained using cognitive behavioral therapy principles and totally ignoring any tapping or psychic energy.

REBIRTHING THERAPY

Proponents of rebirthing therapy have claimed to treat a variety of mental disorders as well as improve the clients' daily lives with the technique. They argue that human birth constitutes a traumatic event (Lieberman & Rank, 1993) and that rebirthing breath work can cure a variety of problems that started with birth trauma. For children, the approach has been associated primarily with treating attachment disorders and related behavioral issues (Hanson & Spratt, 2001). Some therapists have advertised it to cure just about anything negative, including weight issues, anxiety, phobias, dysfunctional relationships, chronic illnesses, and concentration problems (Singer & Lalich, 1996). Although the general consensus among psychological professionals holds that this therapy technique is ineffective and potentially harmful, the alarming truth is that rebirthing is still practiced by psychotherapists (both licensed and unlicensed).

Several different rebirthing techniques appear in the literature, but the most common version applied to children involves the child being held down by several adults, rolled up in blankets, and being instructed to fight her way free (Chaffin et al., 2006). Rebirthing techniques can be traced back to Leonard Orr, who in 1974 began to submerge his friends in a hot tub with nose plugs until they "began to get in touch with certain of their own destructive behavioral patterns" (Singer & Lalich, 1996, p. 43). Since then therapists have begun "dry rebirths," where the child is wrapped up in blankets (Singer & Lalich, 1996).

Only anecdotal evidence exists to support the claims that rebirthing therapy treats children's behavioral or attachment problems. When one therapist was asked repeatedly how she knows rebirthing techniques work, she continually replied, "Because I've seen it work" (Sarner, 2001). No scientific data support the claim that rebirthing can "treat" or "cure" mental disorders in adults or children. To the contrary, a substantial body of evidence has demonstrated the potential harmfulness of this approach (Chaffin et al., 2006; Hanson & Spratt, 2001; Harvey, 2000; London, 2001; Radford, 2001; Sarner, 2001).

Although conducting a clinical trial to objectively assess the efficacy of this treatment would prove to be an ethical nightmare, more than enough evidence exists to disprove rebirthing as a safe or effective therapy technique. The case of Candace Newmaker demonstrates this well. Candace, a 10-year-old North Carolina native, was brought to Colorado rebirthing experts Connell Watkins and Julie Ponder by her adoptive mother (Josefson, 2001; London, 2001). She was diagnosed as having reactive detachment disorder, which disrupts normal bonding with the parent or caregiver (Josefson, 2001). To prepare for her rebirthing treatment, Candace was screamed at just inches away from her face, had her face licked, was forced to make eye contact, had chunks of her hair cut off, was forced to kick her legs to the point of exhaustion, and had to sit motionless for 10, 20, or 30 minutes at a time, and her head was shaken (Sarner, 2001). Finally she was wrapped tightly in a blanket and restrained by the therapists. Although past rebirthing treatments by the Colorado therapists only lasted about 6 minutes, Candace's agony was drawn out for 90 minutes (London, 2001). The therapists videotaped the entire "treatment," which later was shown to members of the jury at the trial of Watkins and Ponders (Sarner, 2001). The video shows Candace "struggling for her life" for the first 70 minutes and then falling silent for the last 20 minutes (London, 2001). When the therapists finally unwrapped the blanket, they found Candace unconscious; she died at the hospital a day later (Josefson, 2001). The jury convicted both therapists of reckless child abuse resulting in death and for practicing unlawful psychotherapy (Sarner, 2001). In April 2012 Colorado passed Candace's Law, making it illegal for licensed psychotherapists to practice rebirthing in the state (Josefson, 2001). It "prohibits the reenactment of the birthing process through therapy techniques that involve any restraint that creates a situation in which a patient may suffer physical injury or death" (Colorado House Bill 01-1238 (2001)). This terrible case led the state to formally ban the unsupported and dangerous therapeutic technique.

REPARATIVE/CONVERSION THERAPY

Reparative therapy has been a hot topic in psychology for many years, but recently it attracted sufficient attention to result in a statutory ban on its use with minors in California (Samakow, 2012). To fully understand the nature of the issue, one must focus on a bit of history. Reparative therapy is "based on the assumption that homosexuality per se is a mental disorder or based upon the a priori assumption that a patient can change his or her sexual orientation" (Samakow, 2012). As early as 1975, the American Psychological Association (APA) called on psychologists to take the lead in removing the stigma of mental illness too long associated with lesbian, gay, and bisexual orientations (http://www.apa.org/helpcenter/sexual-orientation.aspx). In addition, in 1986 homosexuality was removed entirely (after being renamed several times) from the *Diagnostic and Statistical Manual* of the American Psychiatric Association (see http://psychology.ucdavis.edu/rainbow/html/facts_mental_health.html). The World Health Organization has also taken a stance in rejecting reparative therapy: "It is a serious threat to the health and well-being—even the lives—of affected people" (O'Connor, 2012). Nonetheless, there are still therapists advertising reparative and conversion therapy as a treatment for homosexuality (Herek, 2012), often involving a religious orientation or perspective.

Reparative therapies aimed at helping people become ungay go back several centuries; however, 1992 saw the creation of the National Association for the Research and Therapy of Homosexuality (NARTH), which pushed for a treatment of homosexuality in order for homosexual individuals to "retain their membership" in society (Khan, 1998). Numerous Christian rights groups and at least one Orthodox Jewish group (http://www.jonahweb.org) also promote reparative therapy (O'Connor, 2012). Joseph Nicolosi, one of the founders of NARTH, claims a 33% success rate for reparative/conversion therapy, yet there are no scientifically validated data to support this claim (Khan, 1998). NARTH now uses the term "sexual-orientation change efforts" to describe its work and states that the goal of reparative therapy is not to necessarily "cure" the individual of all homosexual thoughts but to diminish these thoughts to the point at which they are "insignificant" (Khan, 1998).

California legislation, effective on January 1, 2013, prohibits licensed psychotherapists from practicing reparative/conversion therapy with minors (Samakow, 2012). Bill sponsor and California state senator Ted Lieu framed his support for the legislation by noting, "No one should stand idly by while children are being psychologically abused and anyone who forces a child to try and change their sexual orientation must understand this is unacceptable" (Gomstyn, 2012). In signing the bill, Governor Jerry Brown referred to conversion therapy as "quackery" (Levs, 2012).

The lack of an evidentiary basis for use of this approach to treat adults or adolescents has not silenced lay advocates or a small number of professionals. New Jersey recently provided a political backdrop for the next stage of the debate. O'Connor (2012) has studied the issue. One vocal proponent of reparative therapy, New Jersey lobbyist Greg Quinlan, reports that after engaging in the therapy, "It helped me realize that this was not biological, that is was emotional, and I did not have to accept these feelings if I didn't want to. I did not have to act on them" (O'Connor, 2012). Jeffrey Danco, a clinical psychologist in New Jersey who does not belong to the APA, advertises to his clients, "You can change homosexuality like any other sense of inadequacy or inferiority" (O'Connor, 2012). New Jersey Assemblyman Tim Eustace, who is openly gay, believes that a practitioner who "claims to be a professional, who could end up damaging a kid forever. It's a message akin to quackery" (O'Connor, 2012). He plans on introducing a bill modeled after California's that would also prohibit the practice of reparative therapy with adults. Eustace argues that it is the government's responsibility to protect children (who often do not have a choice in therapy) "much in the way it restricts other harmful activities, such as underage drinking, indoor tanning and buying cigarettes" (O'Connor, 2012). However, a potential problem with this bill and others like it arises when you look at the fine print. The bill only prohibits the practice of reparative therapy by *licensed* therapists; it does not apply to unlicensed therapists and religious figures who are promoting it and putting people, especially children, at risk.

No scientific data exist to support claims that one-third of the individuals who undergo reparative therapy are no longer influenced by their homosexual thoughts (Khan, 1998). These numbers come purely from anecdotes obtained by those who practice or advocate for reparative therapy and thus have a vested interest in documenting its success. Certainly some patients who have experienced such treatment may report a "cure"; however, such reports do not necessarily indicate a valid or good outcome. For example, some former clients may report "being cured" in an attempt to stop the noxious aspects of the treatment. Others may simply lie about continuing homosexual feelings to avoid being contacted again by reparative treatment programs.

Reparative therapy can involve a variety of cognitive, behavioral, and spiritual tactics, but the majority of them include a significant aversive conditioning component. Some former male reparative therapy participants have cited techniques that include tying their hands to blocks of ice or heated coils while simultaneously showing them pictures of men holding hands (Samakow, 2012). Another technique involved needles inserted into a participant's fingers, which delivered an electrical shock when he was shown a picture of two men (Samakow, 2012).

In a study of reparative therapy by Shidlo and Schroeder (2002), only 3% of participants reported a "successful heterosexual shift"; 88% remained homosexual. The missing 9% of participants is comprised of people who either committed suicide during the therapy or dropped out of treatment (Smith, 2012). Seventeen percent of participants reported that they had attempted suicide during the therapy process. Clearly the evidence suggests that reparative therapy is not only highly unsuccessful, but it can potentially cost people their lives.

Last, the APA's Code of Ethics forbids psychologists from making false or misleading statements about the scientific or clinical basis of their services—yet some may lead their clients to believe that homosexuality is a disease, even though it has long since been removed from consideration as pathological by both psychology and psychiatry (Smith, 2012). This raises serious ethical concerns, given that reparative therapy advocates have only questionable and unscientific evidence on which to base claims that it can cure or even decrease homosexual thoughts and behaviors. When patients present for treatment with concerns about sexual preference, they should be treated in a manner consistent with professional guidelines that do not stigmatize them for same-sex attraction per se.

SEEKING RESOLUTION

The key to ethical and effective treatment of children and adolescents involves careful assessment and intervention that flows from a sound evidentiary basis combined with individual, cultural, and family preferences that ensure the most effective outcome. We have provided six examples of supposed psychotherapeutic techniques that all lack a substantive foundation of supporting empirical data. Some such interventions, such as the D.A.R.E. program, will doubtless continue despite a lack of positive outcome data, because they feel good to many segments of society and at least seem to do no harm. Other interventions, such as intense boot camps and rebirthing techniques, actually have caused the death of some children and adolescents. Still others, such as reparative or sexual preference conversion therapies, cause harm by virtue of ineffectiveness and delaying or denying more effective interventions for children and adolescents who experience depression, stigmatization, or bullying because of same-sex attraction.

Profession ethics require us to make truthful statements about the efficacy of our work and to demonstrate competence in treating patients whom we agree to care for. When practitioners hold a license or belong to a professional association, they fall under the jurisdiction of the licensing board or an ethics committee. It is hoped that such groups will not shy away from acting in response to complaints about practicing with discredited techniques. Unfortunately, many of the practices we describe here are carried out by people whose conduct does not fall under regulation by such bodies. In such instances, speaking out to the public becomes the ethical obligation of well-trained professionals who know better.

REFERENCES

American Psychological Association, Division of Clinical Psychology. (1993). *Task force on promotion and dissemination of psychological procedures*. Retrieved from www.apa.org/divisions/div12/est/chamble2.pdf

Benor, D., Ledger, K., Toussaint, L., Hett, G., & Zaccaro, D. (2009). Pilot study of emotional freedom techniques, wholistic hybrid derived from eye movement desensitization and reprocessing and emotional freedom technique, and cognitive behavioral therapy for treatment of test anxiety in university students. *Explore, 5*(6), 338–340.

Beyerstein, B. (2001). Pseudoscience and psychotherapy—fringe psychotherapies: The public at risk. *Scientific Review of Alternative Medicine, 5*(2), 70–79.

Boden, J. M., Fergusson, D. M., & Horwood, L. (2010). Risk factors for conduct disorder and oppositional/defiant disorder: Evidence from a New Zealand birth cohort. *Journal of the American Academy of Child & Adolescent Psychiatry, 49*(11), 1125–1133.

Bradley, B. F., Brown, S. L., Chu, S., & Lea, R. W. (2009). Effects of orally administered lavender essential oil on responses to anxiety-provoking film clips. *Human Psychopharmacology: Clinical & Experimental, 24*(4), 319–330.

Chaffin, M., Hanson, R., Saunders, B., Nichols, T., Barnett, D., Zeanah, C., . . . Egeland, B. (2006). Report of the APSAC task force on attachment therapy, reactive attachment disorder, and attachment problems. *Child Maltreatment, 11*(1), 76–89. doi: 10.1177/1077559505283699

Chambless, D. L., & Hollon, S. D. (1998). Defining empirically supported therapies. *Journal of Consulting & Clinical Psychology, 66*(1), 7.

Children's Mental Health Ontario. (2011). *Evidence based practices for conduct disorder in children and adolescents*. Retrieved from http://www.kidsmentalhealth.ca/documents/EBP_conduct_disorder.pdf

Church, D., Piña, O., Reategui, C., & Brooks, A. (2012). Single-session reduction of the intensity of traumatic memories in abused adolescents after EFT: A randomized controlled pilot study. *Traumatology, 18*(3), 73–79.

Church, D., Yount, G., & Brooks, A. (2011). The effect of emotional freedom technique (EFT) on stress biochemistry: A randomized controlled trial. *Journal of Nervous and Mental Disease, 200*(10), 891–896

Cline, M., Taylor, J. E., Flores, J., Bracken, S., McCall, S., & Ceremuga, T. E. (2008). Investigation of the anxiolytic effects of linalool, a lavender extract, in the male Sprague-Dawley Rat. *AANA Journal, 76*(1), 47–52.

Colorado House Bill 01-1238 (2001).

Colorado Revised Statutes, 12-43-222 (1)(t) (2011).

Craig, G., & Craig, T. (2012). *Evening EFT for children. Emotional freedom techniques, instructions, EFT tutorials*. Retrieved from http://www.garythink.com/eft/children.html

D.A.R.E. (2012). Retrieved from http://www.dare.com

Daubert v. Merrell-Dow Pharmaceuticals, Inc. 509 U.S. 579, 113 S. Ct. 2786 (1993).

Dobner, J. (2011, September 8). *World wide association of specialty programs and schools sued by ex-students claiming abuse*. Retrieved from http://www.huffingtonpost.com/2011/09/09/world-wide-association-of_n_955459.html

Ennett, S., Tobler, N., Ringwalt, C., & Flewelling, R. (1994). How effective is drug abuse resistance education? A meta-analysis of project DARE outcome evaluations. *American Journal of Public Health, 84*(9), 1394–1401.

Feinstein, D. (2008). Energy psychology: A review of the preliminary evidence. *Psychotherapy: Theory, Research, Practice, Training, 45*(2), 199–213.

Fergusson, D. M., Boden, J. M., & Horwood, L. (2008). Exposure to childhood sexual and physical abuse and adjustment in early adulthood. *Child Abuse & Neglect, 32*(6), 607–619.

Gomstyn, A. (2012, October 1). *California bans gay conversion therapy for minors*. Retrieved from http://abcnews.go.com/blogs/health/2012/10/01/california-bans-gay-conversion-therapy-for-minors/

Gorman, D., & Huber, C. (2009). The social construction of "evidence-based" drug prevention programs: A reanalysis of data from the drug abuse resistance education (DARE) program. *Evaluation Review, 33*(4), 396–414. doi: 10.1177/0193841X09334711

Hanson, R., & Spratt, E. (2001). Reactive attachment disorder: What we know about the disorder and implications for treatment. *Child Maltreatment, 5*(137), 137–145. doi: 10.1177/1077559500005002005

Harvey, B. (2000, May 18). Girl dies in Colorado after controversial therapy. *Scientific Review of Mental Health Practice*. Retrieved from http://www.srmhp.org/archives/rebirthing-therapy.html

Herek, G. (2012, March 6). *Facts about homosexuality and mental health*. Retrieved from http://psychology.ucdavis.edu/rainbow/html/facts_mental_health.html

Herz, R. S. (2009). Aromatherapy facts and fictions: A scientific analysis of olfactory effects on mood, physiology and behavior. *International Journal of Neuroscience, 119*(2), 263–290.

Howard, S., & Hughes, B. M. (2008). Expectancies, not aroma, explain impact of lavender aromatherapy on psychophysiological indices of relaxation in young healthy women. *British Journal of Health Psychology, 13*(4), 603–617.

Janofsky, M. (2001, July 15). States pressed as 3 boys die at boot camps. *New York Times*. Retrieved from http://www.nytimes.com/2001/07/15/us/states-pressed-as-3-boys-die-at-boot-camps.html

Josefson, D. (2001). Rebirthing therapy banned after girl died in 70 minute struggle. *British Medical Journal, 322*(7293), 1014. Retrieved from http://www.ncbi.nlm.nih.gov/pmc/articles/PMC1174742/

Khan, S. (1998, July 17). *Reparative therapy: Idealized heterosexuality*. Retrieved from http://www.publiceye.org/equality/x-gay/X-Gay-04.html

Kim, S., Kim, H., Yeo, J., Hong, S., Lee, J., & Jeon, Y. (2011). The effect of lavender oil on stress, bispectral index values, and needle insertion pain in volunteers. *Journal of Alternative & Complementary Medicine, 17*(9), 823–826.

Kumho Tire Co. v. Carmichael. (97–1709), 526 U.S. 137 (1999). 131 F.3d 1433, reversed.

Levs, J. (2012, October 2). California governor oks ban on gay conversion therapy, calling it "quackery." *CNN U.S.* Retrieved from http://www.cnn.com/2012/10/01/us/california-gay-therapy-ban/index.html

Lieberman, E. J., & Rank, O. (1993). *The trauma of birth*. New York, NY: Dover.

Lilienfeld, S. O. (2007). Psychological treatments that cause harm. *Perspectives on Psychological Science, 2*, 53–70.

London, G. (2001, April 05). Jurors watch disturbing "rebirthing therapy" video. *CNN Justice*. Retrieved from http://articles.cnn.com/2001-04-05/justice/rebirthing.trial_1_jeane-newmaker-connell-watkins-rebirthing?_s=PM:LAW

McCaslin, D. L. (2009). A review of efficacy claims in energy psychology. *Psychotherapy: Theory, Research, Practice, Training, 46*(2), 249–256.

Murray, J., & Farrington, D. P. (2010). Risk factors for conduct disorder and delinquency—key findings from longitudinal studies. *Canadian Journal of Psychiatry, 55*(10), 633–642.

National Center for Complementary and Alternative Medicine. (2012). *Aromatherapy*. Retrieved from http://nccam.nih.gov/health/aromatherapy

Ndao, D. H., Ladas, E. J., Cheng, B., Sands, S. A., Snyder, K. T., Garvin, J. H., & Kelly, K. M. (2012). Inhalation aromatherapy in children and adolescents undergoing stem cell infusion: Results of a placebo-controlled double-blind trial. *Psycho-Oncology, 21*(3), 247–254.

Norcross, J. C., Koocher, G. P., Fala, N. C., & Wexler, H. K. (2010). What doesn't work? Expert consensus on discredited treatments in the addictions. *Journal of Addiction Medicine, 4*, 174–180. doi: 10.1097/ADM.0b013e3181c5f9db

Norcross, J. C., Koocher, G. P., & Garofalo, G. P. (2006). Discredited psychological treatments and tests: A Delphi poll. *Professional Psychology: Research and Practice, 37*, 515–522. doi: 10.1037/0735-7028.37.5.515

O'Connor, J. (2012, September 23). Conversion therapy for gay kids? Treatment or child abuse? *New Jersey Star-Ledger*. Retrieved from http://www.nj.com/njvoices/index.ssf/2012/09/conversion_therapy_for_gay_kid.html

Ollendick, T. H., & King, N. J. (2004). Empirically supported treatments for children and adolescents: Advances toward evidence-based practice. In P. M. Barrett & T. H. Ollendick (Eds.), *Handbook of interventions that work with children and adolescents: Prevention and treatment* (pp. 3–25). Hoboken, NJ: Wiley.

Perry, N., & Perry, E. (2006). Aromatherapy in the management of psychiatric disorders: Clinical and neuropharmacological perspectives. *CNS Drugs, 20*(4), 257.

Petrosino, A., Turpin-Petrosino, C., & Buehler, J. (2005). Scared straight and other juvenile awareness programs for preventing juvenile delinquency. *Scientific Review of Mental Health Practice, 4*(1), 48–54.

Radford, B. (2001). Rebirthing update: Therapists convicted, therapy outlawed in Colorado. *Skeptical Inquirer, 25*(4), 7.

Rosenbaum, D. (1994). Cops in the classroom: A longitudinal evaluation of drug abuse resistance education (D.A.R.E.). *Journal of Research in Crime and Delinquency, 31*(1), 3–31.

Samakow, P. (2012, October 2012). California bans "conversion" and "reparative" therapies. *Washington Times*. Retrieved from http://communities.washingtontimes.com/neighborhood/leading-edge-legal-advice-everyday-matters/2012/oct/6/change-what/

Sarner, L. (2001, June 19). *"Rebirthers" who killed child receive 16-year prison terms*. Retrieved from http://www.quackwatch.org/04ConsumerEducation/News/rebirthing.html

Sayorwan, W., Siripornpanich, V., Piriyapunyaporn, T., Hongratanaworakit, T., Kotchabhakdi, N., & Ruangrungsi, N. (2012). The effects of lavender oil inhalation on emotional states, autonomic nervous system, and brain electrical activity. *Journal of the Medical Association of Thailand [Chotmaihet Thangphaet], 95*(4), 598–606.

Shidlo, A. & Schroeder, M. (2002). Changing sexual orientation: A consumer's report. *Professional Psychology: Research and Practice, 33*, 249–259.

Singer, M., & Lalich, J. (1996). Back to the beginning: Regression, reparenting, and rebirthing. In *Crazy therapies: What are they? Do they work?* San Francisco, CA: Jossey-Bass.

Sinha, D. D., & Efron, D. D. (2005). Complementary and alternative medicine use in children with attention deficit hyperactivity disorder. *Journal of Paediatrics & Child Health, 41*(1/2), 23–26.

Smith, M. (2012, October 8). Conversion therapy hurts innocent children. *Daily Aztec*. Retrieved from http://www.thedailyaztec.com/2012/10/conversion-therapy-hurts-innocent-children/

Solomons, S. (2005). Using aromatherapy massage to increase shared attention behaviours in children with autistic spectrum disorders and severe learning difficulties. *British Journal of Special Education, 32*(3), 127–137.

Takeda, H., Tsujita, J., Kaya, M., Takemura, M., & Oku, Y. (2008). Differences between the physiologic and psychologic effects of aromatherapy body treatment. *Journal of Alternative & Complementary Medicine, 14*(6), 655–661.

Thombs, D. (2000). A retrospective study of DARE: Substantive effects not detected in undergraduates. *Journal of Alcohol and Drug Education, 46*(1), 27–40.

Uibel, B. (2010). *An evaluation of the stated student outcomes of the drug abuse resistance education (DARE) program*. (Unpublished doctoral dissertation). University of Alberta. Retrieved from https://era.library.ualberta.ca/public/view/item/uuid:28f51f60-ddac-41e1-a25a-f66926f5bfaf

Weisz, J. R., & Kazdin, A. E. (Eds.) (2010). *Evidence-based psychotherapies for children and adolescents,* (2nd ed.). New York, NY: Guilford Press.

Wells, S., Polglase, K., Andrews, H. B., Carrington, P., & Baker, A. (2003). Evaluation of a meridian-based intervention, emotional freedom techniques (EFT), for reducing specific phobias of small animals. *Journal of Clinical Psychology, 59*(9), 943–966.

West, S., & O'Neal, K. (2004). Project D.A.R.E. outcome effectiveness revisited. *American Journal of Public Health, 94*(6), 1027–1029.

CHAPTER 4

Evidence-Based Treatments for Mental, Emotional, and Behavioral Problems in Ethnic Minority Children and Adolescents

LINDSAY E. HOLLY, AMANDA CHIAPA, AND ARMANDO A. PIÑA

Over the past 20 years, the clinical child and adolescent psychology area has witnessed the rise of treatment outcome studies identifying several interventions and modalities as efficacious for targeting youth with mental, emotional, and behavioral problems (e.g., Bor, Sanders, & Markie-Dadds, 2002; Clarke, Rohde, Lewinsohn, Hops, & Seeley, 1999; Kendall, 1994; Mufson et al., 2004; Silverman et al., 1999a; Webster-Stratton, Reid, & Hammond, 2004; Wells et al., 2006). Despite these advances, relatively little is known about the use of evidence-based treatments (EBTs) with ethnic minority and culturally diverse youth (hereafter referred to as ethnic minority youth). Moreover, comprehensive information about theoretical, methodological, and practical issues in the treatment of ethnic minority youth is scant. This chapter reviews and synthetizes the little work that has been done with a focus on clinical practice.

Population estimates show that minority youth (immigrant and U.S. born) comprise a significant proportion of the nation's existing and growing population. For instance, estimates suggest there are about 18 million Hispanic/Latino, 11 million African American, 3 million Asian American, and 1 million Native American youth in the United States (U.S. Census Bureau Current Population Survey 2013, U.S. Census Bureau Population Division, 2013). Moreover, Census Bureau projections indicate that the number of ethnic minority youth in the United States will increase significantly over time (e.g., an increase of almost 6 million for Hispanic/Latino, 2 million for African Americans, and 1 million for Asian Americans is expected by 2020) (U.S. Census Bureau, 2008). With the strong emphasis on utilizing EBTs and the prominent growth of ethnic minority youth in the United States, there is urgency for determining and establishing *whether* and *how* currently available treatments developed for one cultural group can be used with another cultural group. This is an important issue as research indicates the existence of mental health disparities with ethnic minorities being at greater risk for mental health disorders but having lower levels of treatment-seeking behaviors and higher levels of attrition (U.S. Department of Health and Human Services, 2001). Furthermore, ethnic minority groups historically have been underrepresented in efficacy and effectiveness trials, so the benefit of existing treatment modalities with minority youth is largely unknown.

This chapter was supported in part by grant numbers K01MH086687 and L60MD001839 from the National Institute of Mental Health and the National Center on Minority Health and Health Disparities awarded to A. A. Pina.

DEFINING KEY TERMS

Before engaging in a discussion about culturally informed treatment protocols, it is important to delineate a few basic terms. At the core of cultural adaptations lies an understanding of the term "culture." Typically thought of as a complex and multifaceted construct, the term encompasses a group of people's shared history, values, norms, goals, and practices that are transmitted from generation to generation through social interactions. Equally important yet often overlooked in our thinking about culture are subcultures. Subcultures are generally smaller, more homogenous groups that make up the larger cultural or ethnic group. Subcultural groups, such as Mexican or Puerto Rican, often have unique cultural experiences that differentiate them from other groups within the same ethnicity. Hispanic/Latino children and families, for instance, vary across subcultures in terms of immigration circumstances (e.g., reasons for migration, generational status) and sociode-mographic characteristics (e.g., educational and income levels) (Umana-Taylor, Diversi, & Fine, 2002). Both culture and subculture can be manifested through observable factors, such as patterned behaviors, symbols, and artifacts, and through cognitive components, such as belief systems and schemas, both of which have been considered in designing and delivering treatment protocols to diverse cultural groups (Barrera, Castro, Strycker, & Toobert, 2012).

When it comes to defining parameters related to culturally informed interventions, the terminology becomes more convoluted with different theories using different terms to describe similar types of cultural modifications. Nevertheless, three distinct categories of cultural consideration in treatment modification typically emerge in the literature: cultural attunement, cultural tailoring, and cultural adaptation.

Cultural attunement, also referred to as cultural sensitivity, is the process by which culturally relevant treatment elements are added to a previously existing treatment protocol in order to enhance treatment engagement and retention of a specific ethnic minority group (Falicov, 2009). Using bilingual therapists, integrating cultural idioms into treatment, and addressing culturally specific barriers to participation are all examples of attunement strategies designed to increase the attractiveness and effectiveness of the therapy program for a specific cultural group. It is important to note, however, that the cultural attunement process focuses on adding to the standard treatment protocol without modifying core treatment components.

Cultural tailoring, or a culturally prescriptive approach, utilizes a more individualized method to modify existing treatment protocols. Kreuter and Skinner (2000) suggest that culturally tailored treatment programs incorporate culturally specific information that is intended to meet the needs of a particular client rather than an entire ethnic group. When using a tailoring approach, cultural modifications are determined by collecting information about the client's personal connection to his/her cultural background as it relates to the targeted therapeutic goal.

Cultural adaptation is a third category of treatment modification. Although this term often is used interchangeably with "cultural attunement" and/or "cultural tailoring," cultural adaptation has been defined by Bernal and colleagues as "the systematic modification of an [EBT] protocol to consider language, culture, and context in such a way that it is compatible with the client's cultural patterns, meanings, and values" (Bernal, Jimenez-Chafey, & Domenech Rodriguez, 2009, p. 362). The key feature that differentiates cultural adaptation from attunement or tailoring is the systematic nature of the modification process. As described in more detail later in this chapter, models of cultural adaptation tend to: (1) use a culture-based theoretical foundation to identify components of therapy that may need adapting in order to successfully treat a particular ethnic minority group, and (2) carefully examine the standard treatment using input from minority group members to shape the adaptation.

In our review of the literature, we found a modest body of work focusing on the treatment of mental, emotional, and behavioral problems in ethnic minority youth. In an effort to advance the knowledge base, this chapter synthesizes theory and research by discussing three key questions: Do current EBTs need to be modified for use with ethnic minority youth? What elements of EBTs should be modified for ethnic minority youth? For whom (what subgroups of ethnic minority youth or individuals) should EBTs be modified? Thus, we begin by providing an evaluative summary of the current research that supports the efficacy of standard treatment protocols with ethnic minority youth. Then we discuss theoretical and methodological approaches to developing culturally informed treatments. Challenges and recommendations to advance the treatment of disorders in ethnic minority youth are identified last with a special focus on clinical application today.

EVIDENCE FOR USING CURRENT TREATMENT PROTOCOLS WITH ETHNIC MINORITY YOUTH

There is some research evaluating the use of child and family treatment protocols with ethnic minority youth and we summarize selected studies in Table 4.1. In the table, we focus primarily on treatments for anxiety, depression, disruptive disorders, and attention-deficit/hyperactivity disorders (ADHD), but the conceptual issues discussed in the body of the chapter also are relevant to treatments for other problems and disorders (e.g., substance use, posttraumatic stress disorder). The purpose of the table is to report on treatments (e.g., cognitive and behavioral therapies [CBTs], interpersonal therapy) that have been successful in reducing symptoms and disorder rates in minority youth. In the table, we provide "exemplar" treatments for each major problem category and offer evidence for the utility of these treatments with minority youth. To this end, we provide a basic description of the research supporting each intervention, including treatment features (i.e., protocol, modality), participant characteristics (i.e., sample size, age, and ethnicity), and program effects data (primary and secondary outcomes).

Overall, our review indicates that encouraging evidence supports the use of certain procedures for targeting anxiety, depression, disruptive disorders, and ADHD among ethnic minority youth. With one exception (Arnold et al., 2003), studies have provided robust evidence that the identified treatments result in symptom reductions for Hispanic/Latino and African American youth at levels similar to what has been found for Caucasian youth. Approximately half of these studies relied on standard treatment protocols while the other half relied on treatments with at least some cultural consideration in program design and/or implementation.

In terms of cultural modifications in treatment design and implementation, there seems to be some variability in the degree of cultural consideration. Seven of the protocols use cultural attunement strategies to modify standard treatments. More specifically, six studies indicate that therapists were trained to be generally sensitive to the cultural background of the client (Garza & Bratton, 2005; Pina et al., 2003; Rossello & Bernal, 1999; Rossello et al., 2008; Szapocznik et al., 1989). The most basic and typical way therapists were sensitive to the targeted culture was by providing the treatment in the client's native language. In some cases, this was necessary for client participation in the treatment; in other cases, it served to enhance engagement by encouraging participation from parents or other family members who were less fluent in English. Often bilingual therapists were used to accommodate the possibility of differing language preferences within and across families (e.g., Garza & Bratton, 2005; Pina et al., 2012).

Culturally sensitive therapists also were charged with learning and understanding fundamental cultural values, norms, and customs associated with the client's ethnic background. Then this

TABLE 4.1   Summary of Evidence-Based Treatments for Ethnic Minority Youth

Treatment	Sample and Treatment Characteristics	Outcomes
Anxiety		
CBTs 1. Ferrell, Beidel, & Turner, 2004 2. Ginsburg & Drake, 2002 3. Pina, Silverman, Fuentes, Kurtines, & Weems, 2003 4. Pina, Zerr, Villalta, & Gonzales, 2012 5. Treadwell, Flannery-Schroeder, & Kendall, 1995	Studies utilized child-focused cognitive and behavioral protocols with varying degrees of parent involvement. Sample sizes ranged from 12 to 178 children (ages 6–17). Studies (1), (2), and (5) reported on African American children; studies (3) and (4) reported on Hispanic/Latino children.	The intervention resulted in significant reductions in child-, parent-, teacher-, and clinician-reported anxiety symptoms for African Americans. For Hispanic/Latinos, program effects were evidenced in terms of reductions in child-, parent-, and clinician-reported anxiety symptoms. Program-related reductions in child-reported depression and loneliness, parent-reported reductions in internalizing behaviors, and child-reported improvements in extraversion were found for African American youth in study (1). For Hispanic/Latinos, reductions in child-reported depression and parent-reported internalizing behaviors were evidenced in study (4).
Depression		
CBTs 1. Rossello & Bernal, 1999 2. Rossello, Bernal, & Rivera-Medina, 2008 3. Shirk, Kaplinski, & Gudmundsen, 2009	Studies utilized child-focused cognitive behavioral protocols with varying degrees of parent involvement. Studies (1) and (3) delivered the intervention in individual format. Study (2) utilized both individual and group format. Sample sizes ranged from 50 to 112 youth (ages 12–18). Studies (1) and (2) focused on a sample of Hispanic/Latino youth living in Puerto Rico; study (3) reported on Hispanic/Latino and African American youth. Studies (1) and (2) were designed to compare interpersonal therapy and CBT for depression.	The intervention resulted in significant reductions in child-reported depression symptoms for Hispanic/Latino and African American youth. For Hispanic/Latinos, improvements in child-reported self-concept and parent-reported internalizing and externalizing behaviors were evidenced in study (2). Study (2) also found that reduction of depression symptoms, internalizing and externalizing behaviors, and improvements in self-concept were greater for Hispanic/Latino youth who received CBT compared to those who received interpersonal therapy.
Interpersonal Psychotherapy 1. Rossello & Bernal, 1999 2. Rossello et al., 2008	Studies utilized interpersonal therapy protocols with varying degrees of parent involvement. Study (1) delivered the intervention in individual format. Study (2) utilized both individual and group format. Sample sizes ranged from 71 to 112 youth (ages 12–18). Studies focused on a sample of Hispanic/Latino youth living in Puerto Rico. Studies (1) and (2) were designed to compare interpersonal therapy and CBT for depression.	The intervention resulted in significant reductions in child-reported depression symptoms for Hispanic/Latino youth living in Puerto Rico. In study (1), program-related improvements in child-reported self-concept and social adaptation skills were found for Hispanic/Latino youth who received interpersonal therapy compared to wait list controls. This was not the case for youth who received CBT.
Disruptive Disorders		
Multisystemic Therapy 1. Borduin et al., 1995 2. Henggeler, Melton, & Smith, 1992	Studies utilized multisystemic therapy protocols delivered in family format. Sample sizes ranged from 84 to 176 youth (ages 12–17). Studies (1) and (2) reported on African American youth.	The intervention resulted in significant reductions in disruptive behavior problems in African American youth. Program effects were evidenced in reductions in arrests were reported for African American youth in studies (1) and (2). Program effects were also evidenced in reductions in total days incarcerated and child-reported criminal activity for African American youth in study (2).

TABLE 4.1   Summary of Evidence-Based Treatments for Ethnic Minority Youth (*continued*)

Treatment	Sample and Treatment Characteristics	Outcomes
		Program-related improvements in parent- and child-reported family cohesion and adaptability as well as observer-reported positive family interactions were also found for African American youth in study (1). Program-related improvements in child- and mother-reported family cohesion and peer aggression were found for African American youth in study (2).
CBTs 1. Hudley & Graham, 1993 2. Lochman & Wells, 2003 3. Lochman & Wells, 2004	Study (1) utilized cognitive intervention protocol delivered in group format. Studies (2) and (3) utilized a cognitive and behavioral intervention and included both child and parent components delivered in group format. Sample sizes ranged from 106 to 245 youth (fourth–sixth grade). Studies reported on African American youth.	The intervention resulted in significant reductions in disruptive behavior problems for African American youth. Program-related improvements in child-reported hostile attribution and teacher-reported aggressive behavior were evidenced for African American youth in study (1). Reductions in teacher-reported aggression were found for African American youth in study (2) and teacher-reported improvements in school behavior were evidenced for African American youth in study (3).
		Program-related decreases in child-reported substance use were found for African American youth who were older and had moderate risk in study (2). Program-related decreases in parent-reported child drug use were found for African American youth in study (3).
Brief Strategic Family Therapy 1. Santisteban et al., 2003 2. Szapocznik et al., 1989	Studies utilized brief strategic family therapy protocols delivered in family format. Sample sizes ranged from 79 to 126 youth (ages 6–18). Studies focused on samples of Hispanic/Latino youth.	The intervention resulted in significant reductions in parent- and child-reported disruptive behavior problems for Hispanic/Latino youth. Program effects were evidenced in improvements in parent-reported delinquency and aggression and reductions in child-reported drug use for Hispanic/Latino youth in study (1). In study (2), program effects were evidenced in reductions parent-reported behavior problems.
		Program-related improvements in observer-, parent-, and child-reported family functioning were also evidenced for Hispanic/Latino youth in studies (1) and (2). Child-reported improvement in self-concept was found for Hispanic/Latino youth in study (2).
Child-Centered Play Therapy Garza & Bratton, 2005	Study utilized a child-centered play therapy protocol delivered in individual format. Sample size consisted of 29 children (ages 5–11). Study focused on a sample of Hispanic/Latino children of Mexican descent.	The intervention resulted in significant reductions in parent-reported conduct problems for Hispanic/Latino youth. Program-related improvements in parent-reported internalizing and anxiety symptoms were found for Hispanic/Latino youth in the study.

Continued

TABLE 4.1   Summary of Evidence-Based Treatments for Ethnic Minority Youth (*continued*)

Treatment	Sample and Treatment Characteristics	Outcomes
Attention-Deficit/Hyperactivity Disorder		
Behavioral Treatment and Medication Management Arnold et al., 2003	Study was designed to compare behavioral intervention, medication management, and combined behavioral intervention and medication management. The medication management condition included daily parent ratings and regular doctor visits. The behavioral intervention had multiple components including parent training, full-time summer treatment program for youth, and use of a token economy. Sample size consisted of 579 children (ages 7–9). Study reported on Hispanic/Latino and African American youth.	The interventions resulted in differential program effects across ethnicity. Compared to Caucasian youth, African American youth evidenced significantly less reduction in teacher-reported attention deficit/hyperactivity and oppositional/defiant symptoms and Hispanic/Latino children evidenced significantly less reduction in parent-reported oppositional/defiant symptoms across all three treatment conditions in the study. Compared to the control condition, the behavioral intervention condition resulted in a significantly greater reduction in parent-reported oppositional/defiant symptoms for African American compared to Caucasian youth. Compared to the medication management condition, the combined behavioral intervention and medication management condition resulted in significantly greater reduction in parent-reported oppositional/defiant symptoms for Hispanic/Latino compared to Caucasian youth. Of note, all ethnic differences in outcomes were nonsignificant after controlling for an indicator of socioeconomic status.

knowledge was incorporated into the treatment protocol for delivery. For example, in their clinical trials of a CBT program for childhood anxiety, Silverman and colleagues (1999a, 1999b; also see Pina et al., 2003) trained clinicians in Hispanic and Caribbean conceptualizations of anxiety and coping styles, including on the heightened fears of the unknown and the use of folk healers (e.g., *curanderos*, *santeros*) to alleviate mental and physical health problems. Similarly, culturally attuned treatments targeting depression in Puerto Rican youth have trained clinicians to be sensitive to the cultural emphasis on the family as a source of support and also the value of absolute parental authority and respect (Rosello & Bernal, 1999; Rosello et al., 2008; Shirk et al., 2009). By acknowledging the unique role family may play in treatment of this particular cultural group, therapists can strengthen the positive aspects of these values and address associated challenges that may arise (e.g., an extended period of dependence on parents) (Rosello & Bernal, 1999). The infusion of cultural values and beliefs in this way serves to enhance the relevancy and appeal of the treatment materials and content to ethnic minority youth and their families, thereby boosting engagement and retention in the treatment program.

As described, cultural attunement can also be accomplished through the inclusion of culturally relevant add-ons to standard treatment protocols. Such add-ons typically involve incorporating culturally salient themes or elements into the treatment. Szapocznik and colleagues (1989), for example, included a Bicultural Effectiveness Training component to the standard Family Effectiveness Training protocol in their treatment of disruptive disorders in Hispanic/Latino youth.

Recognizing that varying degrees of acculturation within families may elevate intergenerational conflict, this addition incorporated bicultural skills, such as developing a shared worldview, aimed at reducing the cultural conflict that can occur as each member experiences his or her own cultural change. The addition of culturally attuned materials is also helpful in improving treatment engagement. For example, Garza and Bratton (2005) provided multicultural toys in their play therapy protocol to treat disruptive disorders in Mexico-origin youth. Culturally relevant toys such as dolls with darker skin tones and games (e.g., Loteria) were selected based on input from five Hispanic, Spanish-speaking play therapists.

Whereas culturally attuned add-ons for Hispanic youth emphasize language, customs, and values respected by one's country of origin, treatments for African American youth typically have highlighted contextual experiences that occur within the immediate ecological framework. Ginsburg and Drake (2002), for instance, incorporated specific examples of stressors often faced by low-income African American communities into their standard CBT protocol for anxiety with African American youth. Situation examples were modified to include experiences often faced by this population, such as neighborhood crime and financial hardship. Just as a culturally sensitive therapist enhances the appeal of the treatment, the use of these culturally relevant add-ons ensures that the content is engaging and directly applicable to situations likely to occur in the everyday life of certain ethnic minority youth. Despite variability in the degree and manner of culturally sensitive modifications, each of the identified culturally attuned treatments was found to be effective in improving targeted outcomes (i.e., anxiety, depression, disruptive behaviors) in ethnic minority youth.

Notably, none of the studies in the current review was consistent with current conceptualizations of a culturally adapted treatment protocol as defined herein. In fact, our review of the literature found only one study that moved beyond cultural attunement and met criteria for the culturally tailored category. Pina and colleagues (2012) used a culturally prescriptive strategy in their implementation of CBT for Hispanic/Latino children with anxiety. This approach allowed therapists to include Hispanic/Latino cultural values, traditions, and customs that are relevant to each client on an individual basis. For example, in addition to providing services in Spanish, as needed, the therapists were encouraged to share culturally relevant anecdotes and incorporated Hispanic/Latino sayings (*dichos*) into sessions for families with low acculturation. This approach was theoretically and empirically driven by the understanding that not all minority youth will be equally responsive to a one-size-fits-all approach to applying culturally sensitive psychosocial treatments (Pina, Villalta, & Zerr, 2009).

It is noteworthy that over half of the studies we highlight in Table 4.1 did not include any cultural considerations when delivering the evidence-based protocol to ethnic minority youth. Still, improvements in treatment outcomes were observed in these studies, as in the studies that included cultural considerations. As such, it is likely that not all treatments require an inclusion of culture to successfully treat ethnic minority youth. This is consistent with the idea that not all ethnic minority clients need a treatment that considers culture. However, little is known about factors that may influence whether a standard treatment will have equivalent effects for minority youth. One study we reviewed in Table 4.1 examined socioeconomic status (SES) as a factor that may elucidate ethnic differences in program outcomes. Arnold and colleagues (2003) found differences in treatment effects across Hispanic/Latino, African American, and Caucasian youth, such that the reduction in ADHD and oppositional symptoms experienced by minority youth was significantly less than that exhibited by Caucasian youth. However, ethnic group differences became nonsignificant after controlling for SES. It may be the case that the extent to which cultural considerations should be applied to current treatments varies as a function of unexamined factors that may or may not be linked to ethnic background, such as SES or acculturation level.

Overall, the studies reviewed herein suggest that aspects of EBT appear to be appropriate for use with ethnic minority youth and demonstrate that some treatment protocols that consider the unique needs and cultural values of ethnic minorities are beneficial in reducing symptoms in youth. Although this emerging research shows progress in efforts to identify effective and efficacious treatments for minority youth, a closer examination of the research does suggest that additional work is needed to fully understand the extent to which aspects of EBT are most and least appropriate for use with minority groups.

INTEGRATING CULTURE IN THE TREATMENT OF DISORDERS IN ETHNIC MINORITY YOUTH

Despite the promising effects of using current EBTs with ethnic minority youth, there is evidence to suggest that treatment efforts need to be strengthened, particularly for ethnic minority or culturally diverse child populations. For example, Cardemil, Reivich, and Seligman (2002) implemented a cognitive and behavioral treatment for depression with low-income African American and Latino children. In their study, the original structure of the program was maintained but materials were culturally attuned. Fewer depression symptoms, negative automatic thoughts, and hopeless thoughts were found immediately following the treatment program for Latino youth, including at the 6-month follow-up. In addition, at the follow-up only, Latino youth evidenced higher self-esteem compared to controls who received no treatment. For African American youth, findings were not encouraging. There were no differences between the treatment and control conditions on any of the measures or at any measurement point. At the 2-year follow-up (Cardemil, Reivich, Beevers, Seligman, & James, 2007), Latino youth showed program-related gains but African American youth did not.

In another study focusing on African American youth, Cooley, Boyd, and Grados (2004) and Cooley-Strickland, Griffin, Darney, Otte, and Ko (2011) modified the FRIENDS for Life program (a cognitive and behavioral preventive intervention program for anxious youth) to be used with African American youth living in an urban setting. Modifications focused on replacing references specific to Australian culture and including examples relevant to the contexts of inner city African American youth. In their trial, Cooley-Strickland et al. (2011) found no statistically significant program differences on any of the primary outcome variables including anxiety symptom levels (not even for those children with higher levels of pretest community violence exposure or as a function of child's sex) compared to wait-list controls.

Despite efforts made to develop culturally robust treatment programs, overall findings suggest there is still room for improvement. This appears to be true when it comes to African American children in particular (e.g., Cardemil et al., 2002; Cooley-Strickland et al., 2011). In contrast, the evidence for Latino youth seems to be more encouraging (e.g., Cardemil et al., 2002). It is important to highlight, however, that the literature is limited and predominantly exploratory in nature, with studies often lacking adequate statistical power. Moreover, these findings cannot be considered to be robust across cultures and subcultures as the research examining treatments for anxiety, depression, disruptive disorders, and ADHD has focused entirely on African American and Hispanic/Latino youth. Conclusions cannot be made about the utility of current treatments with other ethnic minority groups, such as Asian or Native American youth. Further, the use of broad ethnic categories (e.g., Hispanic/Latino versus Mexican American or Puerto Rican) to describe participants can be problematic, given variations that exist within ethnic minority groups.

TOWARD EBTS WITH ETHNIC MINORITY YOUTH: THEORY-BASED APPROACHES

Moving forward, it appears that three important questions need to be considered when it comes to culture. First, do current EBTs need to be modified for use with ethnic minority youth? Second, what elements of EBTs should be modified for ethnic minority youth? And third, for whom (what subgroups of ethnic minority youth) should EBTs be modified? An appraisal of the research literature suggests that cultural modifications are indeed warranted, as certain minority youth segments do not seem to benefit as much as their counterparts from treatment efforts considered efficacious. In terms of identifying which treatment components should be targeted in the modification process and what subgroups need to receive adapted treatments, research has yet to sufficiently examine and pinpoint the process of successful cultural modification (beyond language). Although it is clear that additional research is needed to further develop answers to these questions, theory on cultural modifications can be used to guide current practice as well as future research.

In the absence of empirical evidence to determine if and when cultural modifications are necessary, several models recently have emerged that are designed to guide a clinician or researcher through the process of culturally adapting a standard EBT (Barrera & Castro, 2006; Kumpfer, Pinyuchon, Melo, & Whiteside, 2008; McKleroy et al., 2006; Wingood & DiClemente, 2008). At the core of each of these models is an emphasis on combining both theory and data to determine whether a cultural adaptation is needed and what components should be adapted. For instance, Lau (2006) cautions against haphazardly modifying all EBTs for all ethnic minority clients and instead articulates the use of selective and directed modification strategies. The selective approach requires that there be evidence of a lack of fit between a particular treatment protocol and the targeted population. That is, a cultural modification may be warranted if there is evidence of group-specific risk and resilience processes that influence the development, maintenance, and/or amelioration of the targeted clinical problem, or characteristics that might limit engagement in the particular treatment protocol. If modifications are merited, the directed nature of Lau's approach stresses the use of data to establish and design the specific treatment modifications based on the identified group-specific qualities.

Efforts to outline the process of integrating culture into standard EBTs focus on whether and how cultural adaptations should be conducted (Barrera & Castro, 2006; Kumpfer et al., 2008; McKleroy et al., 2006; Wingood & DiClemente, 2008). A related, but often separate, body of work concentrates on which treatment parameters should be adapted and for whom. Resnicow, Baranowski, Ahluwalia, and Braithwaite (1999) and Resnicow, Soler, Braithwaite, Ahluwalia, and Butler (2000) conceptualize adaptation as happening on two levels: surface structure and deep structure. At the surface structure level, adaptations focus on adjusting the treatment materials and messages to be consistent with and relevant for the targeted minority group. This is consistent with cultural attunement defined at the beginning of this chapter. Resnicow et al. (2000) suggest that surface structure adaptations are akin to face validity of empirical measures, indicating that modifications at this level are based on observable and often superficial cultural characteristics, such as language. As such, surface-level adaptations address issues related to how a specific ethnic or cultural group will receive and engage with the treatment (Simons-Morton, Donohew, & Crump, 1997). To this end, surface structure adaptation ensures feasibility of the modified EBT. Deep structure adaptations, in contrast, determine program impact by focusing on making the treatment salient to the targeted group (Resnicow et al., 2000). This type of adaptation is complex and requires a thorough understanding of the group's cultural values, norms, and stressors (e.g., historical, environmental, social, and economic). In deep-structure adaptations, these cultural factors are considered in terms of how they influence the development and treatment of the targeted mental health issue. Currently, culturally adapted EBTs have focused on surface structure modifications; however, it is generally agreed that deep-structure adaptations may be necessary to successfully reach certain populations of minority youth.

CONCLUSIONS AND CLINICAL RECOMMENDATIONS

Theory and research relevant to the treatment of ethnic minority youth with problems related to anxiety, depression, disruptive disorders, and ADHD are growing, with empirical work suggesting that some current EBTs are successful in reducing symptoms and disorder rates in Hispanic/Latino and African American youth. However, research remains scant on the appropriateness of using EBTs with other ethnic minority groups (e.g., Asian American, Native American) and with specific subcultural groups (e.g., Dominicans, Haitians, Navajo). Moreover, there is a lack of sufficient evidence to indicate whether current treatment protocols should be modified for use with ethnic minority youth as well as which treatment elements should be modified and for whom modifications are necessary. Additional research efforts are needed to evaluate and refine treatment protocols for ethnic minority youth with a focus on identifying individual, cultural, and contextual factors that may influence efficacy. As these data accumulate, findings are likely to show the degree to which culture-related treatment modifications are warranted for specific treatments (e.g., depression) and selected populations (e.g., less acculturated Mexican immigrant adolescents undergoing discrimination stressors). As the field continues to work toward a deeper understanding of the extent to which aspects of EBTs are appropriate for use with minority youth, clinicians currently working with minority children and families should strive to provide services in a culturally competent manner. To this end, it is important that clinicians stay abreast of empirical advancements in EBTs with minority populations and utilize cultural modifications when there is evidence to do so. In the absence of research supporting culture-specific treatments and/or modifications, it is recommended that clinicians implement the standard EBTs with an awareness of and sensitivity to the cultural background of the individual client. This awareness includes knowledge of cultural characteristics relevant to the presenting problem as well as treatment engagement and participation. Clinicians should be cognizant of their own preconceived notions related to specific ethnic groups and make every effort to avoid making assumptions about the values, beliefs, and preferences of ethnic minority clients based on nondata. As clinicians increase their level of cultural competence and research moves toward the development of culturally appropriate EBTs, greater progress can be made to improve the mental health of ethnic minority children and families in the United States.

REFERENCES

Arnold, L. E., Elliot, M., Sachs, L., Bird, H., Kraemer, H. C., Wells, K. C., . . . Wigal, T. (2003). Effects of ethnicity on treatment attendance, stimulant response/dose, and 14-month outcome in ADHD. *Journal of Consulting and Clinical Psychology, 71,* 713–727.

Barrera, M., Jr., & Castro, F. G. (2006). A heuristic framework for the cultural adaptation of interventions. *Clinical Psychology: Science and Practice, 13,* 311–316.

Barrera, M., Jr., Castro, F. G., Strycker, L. A., & Toobert, D. J. (2012, January 30). Cultural adaptations of behavioral health interventions: A progress report. *Journal of Consulting and Clinical Psychology.* Advance online publication. doi: 10.1037/a0027085

Bernal, G., Jimenez-Chafey, M. I., & Domenech Rodriguez, M. M. (2009). Cultural adaptation of treatments: A resource for considering culture in evidence-based practice. *Professional Psychology: Research and Practice, 40,* 361–368.

Bor, W., Sanders, M. R., & Markie-Dadds, C. (2002). The effects of the Triple-P Positive Parenting Program on preschool children with co-occurring disruptive behavior and attentional/hyperactive difficulties. *Journal of Abnormal Child Psychology, 30,* 571–587.

Borduin, C. M., Mann, B. J., Cone, L. T., Henggeler, S. W., Fucci, B. R., Blaske, D. M., & Williams, R. A. (1995). Multisystemic treatment of serious juvenile offenders: Long-term prevention of criminality and violence. *Journal of Consulting and Clinical Psychology, 63,* 569–578.

Cardemil, E., Reivich, K. J., Beevers, C. G., Seligman, M. E. P., & James, J. (2007). The prevention of depressive symptoms in low-income, minority children: Two-year follow-up. *Behaviour Research and Therapy, 45*(2), 313–327.

Cardemil, E. V., Reivich, K. J., & Seligman, M. E. P. (2002). The prevention of depressive symptoms in low-income minority middle school students. *Prevention & Treatment, 5.* doi: 10.1037/1522-3736.5.1.58a

Clarke, G. N., Rohde, P., Lewinsohn, P. M., Hops, H., & Seeley, J. (1999). Cognitive-behavioral treatment of adolescent depression: Efficacy of acute group treatment and booster sessions. *Journal of the American Academy of Child & Adolescent Psychiatry, 38,* 272–279.

Cooley, M. R., Boyd, R. C., & Grados, J. J. (2004). Feasibility of an anxiety preventive intervention for community violence exposed African-American children. *Journal of Primary Prevention, 25*(1), 105–123.

Cooley-Strickland, M., Griffin, R. S., Darney, D., Otte, K., & Ko, J. (2011). Urban African American youth exposed to community violence: A school-based anxiety preventive intervention efficacy study. *Journal of Prevention & Intervention in the Community, 39*(2), 149–166.

Falicov, C. J. (2009). Commentary: On the wisdom and challenges of culturally attuned treatments for Latinos. *Family Process, 48,* 292–309.

Ferrell, C. B., Beidel, D. C., & Turner, S. M. (2004). Assessment and treatment of socially phobic children: A cross cultural comparison. *Journal of Clinical Child and Adolescent Psychology, 33,* 260–268.

Garza, Y., & Bratton, S. C. (2005). School-based child-centered play therapy with Hispanic children: Outcomes and cultural considerations. *International Journal of Play Therapy, 14,* 51–79.

Ginsburg, G. S., & Drake, K. L. (2002). School-based treatment for anxious African American adolescents: A controlled pilot study. *Journal of the American Academy of Child & Adolescent Psychiatry, 41,* 768–775.

Henggeler, S. W., Melton, G. B., & Smith, L. A. (1992). Family preservation using multisystemic therapy: An effective alternative to incarcerating serious juvenile offenders. *Journal of Consulting and Clinical Psychology, 60,* 953–961.

Hudley, C., & Graham, S. (1993). An attributional intervention to reduce peer-directed aggression among African-American boys. *Child Development, 64,* 124–138.

Kendall, P. C. (1994). Treating anxiety disorders in youth: Results of a randomized clinical trial. *Journal of Consulting and Clinical Psychology, 62,* 100–110.

Kreuter, M. W., & Skinner, C. S. (2000). Tailoring: What's in a name? *Health Education Research, 15,* 1–4.

Kumpfer, K. L., Pinyuchon, M., Melo, A. T., & Whiteside, H. O. (2008). Cultural adaptation process for international dissemination of the Strengthening Families Program. *Evaluation & the Health Professions, 31,* 226–239.

Lau, A. S. (2006). Making a case for selective and directed cultural adaptations of evidence-based treatments: Examples from parent training. *Clinical Psychology: Science and Practice, 13,* 295–310.

Lochman, J. E., & Wells, K. C. (2003). Effectiveness of the Coping Power program and of classroom intervention with aggressive children: Outcomes at a 1-year follow-up. *Behavior Therapy, 34,* 493–515.

Lochman, J. E., & Wells, K. C. (2004). The Coping Power program for preadolescent aggressive boys and their parents: Outcome effects at the 1-year follow-up. *Journal of Consulting and Clinical Psychology, 72,* 571–578.

McKleroy, V. S., Galbraith, J. S., Cummings, B., Jones, P., Harshbarger, C., Collins, C., . . . ADAPT Team. (2006). Adapting evidence-based behavioral interventions for new settings and target populations. *AIDS Education and Prevention, 18,* 59–73.

Mufson, L. H., Dorta, K. P., Wickramaratne, P., Nomura, Y., Olfson, M., & Weissman, M. M. (2004). A randomized effectiveness trial of interpersonal psychotherapy for depressed adolescents. *Archives of General Psychiatry, 61,* 577–584.

Pina, A. A., Silverman, W. K., Fuentes, R. M., Kurtines, W. M., & Weems, C. F. (2003). Exposure-based cognitive-behavioral treatment for phobic and anxiety disorders: Treatment effects and maintenance for Hispanic/Latino relative to European-American youths. *Journal of the American Academy of Child & Adolescent Psychiatry, 42,* 1179–1187.

Pina, A. A., Villalta, I. K., & Zerr, A. A. (2009). Exposure-based cognitive behavioral treatment of anxiety in youth: An emerging culturally-prescriptive framework. *Behavioral Psychology, 17,* 111–135.

Pina, A. A., Zerr, A. A., Villalta, I. K., & Gonzales, N. A. (2012). Indicated prevention and early intervention for childhood anxiety: A randomized trial with Caucasian and Hispanic/Latino youth. *Journal of Consulting and Clinical Psychology, 80,* 940–946.

Resnicow, K., Baranowski, T., Ahluwalia, J. S., & Braithwaite, R. L. (1999). Cultural sensitivity in public health: Defined and demystified. *Ethnicity & Disease, 9,* 10–21.

Resnicow, K., Soler, R., Braithwaite, R. L., Ahluwalia, J. S., & Butler, J. (2000). Cultural sensitivity in substance use prevention. *Journal of Community Psychology, 28*(3), 271–290.

Rosello, J., & Bernal, G. (1999). The efficacy of cognitive-behavioral and interpersonal treatments for depression in Puerto Rican adolescents. *Journal of Consulting and Clinical Psychology, 67,* 734–745.

Rosello, J., Bernal, G., & Rivera-Medina, C. (2008). Individual and group CBT and IPT for Puerto Rican adolescents with depressive symptoms. *Cultural Diversity and Ethnic Minority Psychology, 14,* 234–235.

Santisteban, D. A., Perez-Vidal, A., Coatsworth, J. D., Kurtines, W. M., Schwartz, S. J., La Perriere, A., & Szapocznik, J. (2003). Efficacy of brief strategic family therapy in modifying Hispanic adolescent behavior problems and substance use. *Journal of Family Psychology, 17,* 121–133.

Shirk, S. R., Kaplinski, H., & Gudmundsen, G. (2009). School-based cognitive-behavioral therapy for adolescent depression: A benchmarking study. *Journal of Emotional and Behavioral Disorders, 17,* 106–117.

Silverman, W. K., Kurtines, W. M., Ginsburg, G. S., Weems, C. F., Lumpkin, P. W., & Carmichael, D. H. (1999a). Treating anxiety disorders in children with group cognitive-behavioral therapy: A randomized clinical trial. *Journal of Consulting and Clinical Psychology, 67,* 995–1003.

Silverman, W. K., Kurtines, W. M., Ginsburg, G. S., Weems, C. F., Rabian, B., & Serafini, L. T. (1999b). Contingency management, self-control, and education support in the treatment of childhood phobic disorders: A randomized clinical trial. *Journal of Consulting and Clinical Psychology, 67,* 675–687.

Simons-Morton, B. G., Donohew, L., & Crump, A. D. (1997). Health communication in the prevention of alcohol, tobacco, and drug use. *Health Education & Behavior, 24,* 544–554.

Szapocznik, J., Santisteban, D. A., Rio, A., Perez-Vidal, A., Santisteban, D., & Kurtines, W. M. (1989). Family effectiveness training: An intervention to prevent drug abuse and problem behaviors in Hispanic adolescents. *Hispanic Journal of Behavioral Sciences, 11*(1), 4–27.

Treadwell, K. R. H., Flannery-Schroeder, E. C., & Kendall, P. C. (1995). Ethnicity and gender in relation to adaptive functioning, diagnostic status, and treatment outcome in children from an anxiety clinic. *Journal of Anxiety Disorders, 9,* 373–384.

Umana-Taylor, A. J., Diversi, M., & Fine, M. A. (2002). Ethnic identity and self-esteem among Latino adolescents: Distinctions among the Latino populations. *Journal of Adolescent Research, 17,* 303–327.

U.S. Census Bureau, Current Population Survey, Annual Social and Economic Supplement. (2013). *Population by sex, age, Hispanic origin, and race: 2012.* Retrieved from http://www.census.gov/population/race/data/cps.html

U.S. Census Bureau, Population Division. (2008). *2008 national population projections: Summary tables.* Retrieved from http://www.census.gov/population/projections/data/national/2008/summarytables.html

U.S. Census Bureau, Population Division. (2013). *Annual estimates of the resident population by sex, age, race, and Hispanic origin for the United States and States: April 1, 2010 to July 1, 2012.* Retrieved from http://factfinder2.census.gov/faces/tableservices/jsf/pages/productview.xhtml?src=bkmk

U.S. Department of Health and Human Services. (2001). *Mental health: Culture, race, and ethnicity—a supplement to mental health: A report of the Surgeon General.* Rockville, MD: U.S. Department of Health and Human Services, Substance Abuse and Mental Health Services Administration, Center for Mental Health Services.

Webster-Stratton, C., Reid, M., & Hammond, M. (2004). Treating children with early-onset conduct problems: Intervention outcomes for parent, child, and teacher training. *Journal of Clinical Child and Adolescent Psychology, 33,* 105–124.

Wells, K. C., Chi, T. C., Hinshaw, S. P., Epstein, J. N., Pfiffner, L. J., Nebel-Schwain, M., . . . Wigal, T. (2006). Treatment-related changes in objectively measured parenting behaviors in the multimodal treatment study of children with ADHD. *Journal of Consulting and Clinical Psychology, 74,* 649–657.

Wingood, G. M., & DiClemente, R. J. (2008). The ADAPT-ITT model: A novel method of adapting evidence-based HIV interventions. *Journal of Acquired Immune Deficiency Syndromes, 47,* S40–S46.

CHAPTER 5

New Methods of Service Delivery for Children's Mental Health Care

JONATHAN S. COMER, R. MEREDITH ELKINS, PRISCILLA T. CHAN, AND DEBORAH J. JONES

The past few decades have witnessed considerable advances in the development, evaluation, and formal identification of evidence-based psychological interventions with demonstrated success in the treatment of a considerable share of children's mental health problems (see Kendall, 2011; Silverman & Hinshaw, 2008; Weisz & Kazdin, 2010). However, despite the proliferation of these research-supported and well-tolerated treatments in laboratory settings, our current mental health service delivery models fail to reach adequate numbers of affected children and adolescents. Systematic barriers prevent large numbers of affected children from receiving timely care, and supported treatments in experimental settings are insufficiently available in the frontline service settings where the majority of youth receive mental health care (Sandler, Ostrom, Bitner, Ayers, & Wolchik, 2005; Weisz, Sandler, Durlak, & Anton, 2005).

For most affected youth, problems persist in the availability, accessibility, and acceptability of quality mental health care. Regarding care *availability*, there are inadequate numbers of trained mental health workers providing care in practice settings. Professional workforce shortages in mental health care abound, with a considerable proportion of U.S. counties lacking any psychologist, psychiatrist, or social worker (National Organization of State Offices of Rural Health, 2011). Problems in mental health care availability are particularly pronounced in remote regions, with over three quarters of federally designated Mental Health Professional Shortage Areas situated in rural areas (Bird, Dempsey, & Hartley, 2001; National Advisory Committee on Rural Health, 2002). Long wait lists at poorly funded clinics considerably slow the speed of service delivery. Given the massive discrepancy in ratio of available providers to clients in need, Kazdin and Blase (2011) have suggested that even doubling the mental health care workforce might yield only a modest reduction in the overall incidence of mental illness at a population level. Comer and Barlow (2013) have suggested that collectively these factors may help to explain, in part, recent national trends showing that psychotherapy has assumed a decreasingly prominent role in outpatient care (Olfson & Marcus, 2010).

Insufficient quality of care in many practice settings presents a further obstacle to treatment availability for many youth, as those receiving mental health care are not necessarily receiving supported services (Sandler et al., 2005). Treatments receiving the strongest support are rarely disseminated effectively on a broad level. Regrettably, limitations in the availability of quality psychological

Funding for this chapter was provided by NIMH 1K23MH090247 and NIMH 1R34MH082956 (ClinicalTrials. gov Identifier: NCT01367847).

treatment can place heavy clinical demands on the pharmacologic dimensions of children's treatment (Comer & Barlow, 2013). Geographic workforce gaps in mental health care typically are filled by primary care physicians and pediatricians, but these health workers often lack the time and training to optimally address children's mental health care needs. Not surprisingly, in recent years there has been a progressive expansion in the prescription of off-label psychotropic regimens with unfavorable side effects to treat childhood disorders for which well-tolerated, evidence-based psychological treatments are firmly established (Comer, Mojtabai, & Olfson, 2011; Comer, Olfson, & Mojtabai, 2010; Olfson, Crystal, Huang, & Gerhard, 2010).

Treatment *accessibility* is further constrained by issues of cost and transportation. Large numbers of families report having no way to get to a mental health clinic or that mental health care is either too far away or too expensive (Owens et al., 2002). These obstacles to treatment accessibility are particularly problematic for low-income families and families living in rural and otherwise remote regions. Moreover, highly prevalent rates of stigma-related beliefs constrain treatment *acceptability*. For example, roughly one quarter of families report holding negative attitudes about visiting a mental health clinic (Owens et al., 2002).

Simply put, tremendous advances in the identification and success of evidence-based psychological treatments for children have been obtained in laboratory settings; however, these scientific achievements have been seriously constrained by inadequate service delivery models and the proliferation of treatments that are not built for broad dissemination. Thus, to date, advances in evidence-based treatments (EBTs) for childhood disorders have yielded only a modest public health impact. In turn, considerable attention and large financial commitments have focused on innovative solutions to problems of treatment availability, accessibility, and acceptability. We now turn our attention to exciting and transformative new methods of service delivery for children's mental health care that have emerged in recent years that collectively hold enormous potential for meaningfully advancing the broad relevance and public health impact of EBTs for child mental disorders.

INNOVATIVE SOLUTIONS TO PROBLEMS IN CARE AVAILABILITY AND QUALITY

Leading models and solutions for redressing the problems of limited care availability and quality that dominate current theory, research, and training in children's mental health care include: (1) the strategic reformatting of EBTs, including advances in transdiagnostic protocols, modularized protocols, and intensive treatment formats; and (2) technology-based treatment delivery methods, including advances in computer-based treatments with minimal therapist involvement, smartphone applications for augmenting children's mental health care, and videoconferencing formats for remotely delivering real-time treatment.

Strategic Reformatting of Evidence-Based Treatments

Given the current crisis in the availability of children's quality mental health care, considerable scholarly attention and funding commitments have focused on broad dissemination and implementation efforts geared toward improving the quality of psychological services delivered in frontline practice settings (see McHugh & Barlow, 2010, 2012). Notably, treatment complexity influences the ongoing uptake of EBTs. Dissemination science reveals that innovations that are too complex will not get routinely incorporated, or incorporated with fidelity, into everyday practice (Rogers, 2003). The very large number of distinct manuals requiring developed expertise—each typically targeting very focused clinical problems, with significant overlap across programs (Barlow, 2004)—complicates dissemination efforts. Indeed, there has been a proliferation of single-diagnosis manuals, many with only minor and relatively negligible variations from one another. A new generation of interventions research has begun to emerge that incorporates realities about the feasibility of large-scale dissemination and implementation of EBTs in the very earliest stages of treatment development. These designs include transdiagnostic treatment formats, modular treatment designs, and intensive treatment formats.

Transdiagnostic Treatment Formats

In contrast to traditional single-diagnosis treatment protocols, transdiagnostic treatments focus on parallels and overlapping features across disorders, especially those from neighboring classes of diagnoses and those showing high levels of comorbidity. The early foundations of behavioral and cognitive therapies, as well as client-centered and psychoanalytic approaches, were intrinsically transdiagnostic (see Taylor & Clark, 2009). However, with major advances in affective neuroscience, underlying etiology, and latent structure of disorders (see Barlow, 2004; Wilamowska et al., 2010), research groups have been able to develop unifying, evidence-based protocols that can be applied flexibly across a range of diagnoses sharing common components and etiological mechanisms (Craske et al., 2009; Fairburn, Cooper, Shafran, & Wilson, 2008; Fairburn et al., 2009; Farchione et al., 2012; Norton, 2008; Norton & Hope, 2005; Sullivan et al., 2007).

A growing body of evidence supports the efficacy of transdiagnostic approaches in treating childhood disorders (Ehrenreich, Goldstein, Wright, & Barlow, 2009; Kendall, Hudson, Gosch, Flannery-Schroeder, & Suveg, 2008; Weersing, Rozenman, Maher-Bridge, & Campo, 2012). For example, instead of focusing on a single childhood disorder, the treatment protocol developed by Kendall (Kendall & Hedtke, 2006a, 2006b) applies cognitive restructuring, emotion awareness, problem-solving skills, and graduated exposure tasks to target the range of common childhood anxiety disorders. This transdiagnostic approach has undergone significant empirical examination—relative to wait lists, psychoeducation, support, pill placebo, active controls, and selective serotonin reuptake inhibitors—and has been associated with considerable clinical response across evaluations. Transdiagnostic protocols simultaneously targeting the range of anxiety *and* unipolar mood disorders in youth are also beginning to show strong promise (see Chu, 2012; Ehrenreich et al., 2009; Weersing et al., 2012).

Of course, additional research is necessary to clarify the clinical utility of transdiagnostic treatment protocols for children. However, research to date suggests that these recent advances hold the potential to meaningfully elevate the public health significance of the widespread availability of EBT practices. Specifically, by considerably reducing the number of supported protocols practitioners must learn and by introducing more parsimony into dissemination efforts, transdiagnostic protocols have the potential to increase the public health impact of our evidence-based interventions for children.

Modular Treatment Designs

Another approach to redressing the treatment manual proliferation barrier to broad dissemination in children's mental health care is the development of modular approaches to care. Whereas traditional treatment manuals apply multiple treatment components in a more linear format, it is becoming increasingly apparent that not every child will benefit comparably from each and every treatment component in an indicated treatment protocol. And, of course, practitioners encounter a broad range of sometimes unrelated, comorbid disorders across internalizing and externalizing dimensions. Thus, many children may benefit from various treatment elements found across a range of single-diagnosis treatment protocols. For the heterogeneous cases that populate practice settings, employing a linear sequence of single-diagnosis manuals may not be optimal from either a treatment delivery or dissemination standpoint.

Relative to the theoretically based transdiagnostic formats, modular treatment formats take a more empirical approach to children's mental health care and address the earlier-noted problems through strategic treatment redesign—procedures from supported protocols for specific identified problems are structured as free-standing modules, and decision flowcharts guide module selection and treatment component sequencing (Chorpita, 2007; Chorpita & Weisz, 2005; Harvey, Watkins, Mansell, & Shafran, 2004; Weisz et al., 2012). Modular approaches individualize treatment regimens to deliver supported components efficiently to each patient using evidence-based algorithms. Treatment is applied flexibly to address comorbidities by affording empirically informed sequencing of treatment elements to accommodate personalized tailoring of care for specific problems presenting in each child. Accordingly, modular approaches have the potential to address the needs of clinicians with caseloads marked by complex patterns of comorbidity and shifting clinical needs.

Modular approaches are already showing promise. For example, modular strategies and dynamic treatment regimens are distinguishing themselves from usual care for homogenous symptom classes in practice settings (Weisz et al., 2012). The MATCH (Modular Approach to Therapy for Children) program produced steeper improvement trajectories in a broad clinical child sample than usual care and standard linear manuals. At posttreatment, MATCH was also linked with significantly fewer children meeting criteria for diagnosis than usual care, whereas diagnostic outcomes of standard linear manuals did not differ from usual care outcomes (Weisz et al., 2012). Importantly, therapists trained in standard linear protocols held more negative views of manuals than did therapists trained in supported modular programs that incorporate potentially shifting treatment needs and tailor treatment sequences to individual child presentations (Borntrager, Chorpita, Higa-McMillan, & Weisz, 2009).

Intensive Treatment Formats

Whereas transdiagnostic and modular treatment formats offer opportunities to facilitate and improve broad dissemination efforts and the training of generalist mental health workers, dissemination and implementation efforts to generalists alone will not be sufficient to adequately address the incidence of children's mental illness. As noted elsewhere (Comer & Barlow, 2013), our field needs to retain a role for specialty care in the delivery of psychological treatments, given that some EBTs prove too complex for universal dissemination and the time and expenses needed for quality dissemination and implementation typically preclude large-scale training in the treatment of low base-rate disorders. Regrettably, there are considerable geographic obstacles to the broad availability of specialty mental health care, and the limited availability of specialty care is understandable from a supply and demand standpoint.

To address local workforce shortages in specialty care and problems of treatment access, many specialty programs are increasingly offering intensive treatment formats, in which patients travel for brief (e.g., 1–3 week) periods of all-day sessions in treatment not offered in their local community. Intensive treatments deliver an entire course of a treatment in a shorter period of time through longer individual sessions (Albano, 2009). This condensed modification of traditional treatment has several advantages that may make intensive treatments an attractive option for families and mental health professionals. The massed nature of the treatment sessions may reduce the negative impact of the financial, logistic, and geographic barriers to treatment attendance and completion without requiring the content of treatment to vary significantly from a traditional therapeutic approach (Ehrenreich & Santucci, 2009). Intensive treatments may be more desirable than traditional weekly treatment with respect to the necessary time commitment, travel requirements, and reduction of stigma, and as a result they may be more marketable to families (Santucci & Ehrenreich-May, 2010). Intensive treatments may be conducted during times convenient for the family, such as summer or holiday breaks, during which children have fewer academic demands. The intensive format also may allow families without easy access to settings offering intensive treatments the option to travel to such a setting and spend a week devoted to treatment (Angelosante, Pincus, Whitton, Cheron, & Pian, 2009), ensuring that patients who would not otherwise receive EBT may benefit from such approaches. Moreover, the intensive delivery of treatment may benefit children for whom previous interventions have been ineffective (e.g., Storch, Geffken, Adkins, Murphy, & Goodman, 2007).

As with traditional weekly treatment approaches, intensive treatments afford opportunities for "flexibility within fidelity" (Kendall & Beidas, 2007), relying on clinical judgment to inform the appropriate delivery of individual treatment components as well as individually tailored homework assignments and out-of-session activities that are sensitive to the individual needs of each child (Santucci, Ehrenreich, Trosper, Bennett, & Pincus, 2009). This flexibility also extends to the format and delivery of intensive treatments. For example, intensive treatments may be delivered in both individual and group formats and can be modified to incorporate varying degrees of parental involvement. The group format of some intensive treatments may be both incrementally effective and attractive to youth, as children—particularly those with low base-rate disorders—may feel less isolated by their condition in the context of peers experiencing similar symptoms, and peer interaction may provide unique opportunities for modeling and practice. Research indicates that group cohesiveness may have the added benefit of augmenting treatment effectiveness (Marziali, Monroe-Blum, & McCleary, 1997). Given that interventions flexibly delivered using creative and interactive formats may increase engagement and understanding in younger populations (e.g., Beidas, Benjamin, Puleo, Edmunds, & Kendall, 2010; Kingery et al., 2006), "camp-based" intensive group treatments represent an innovative and developmentally appropriate format for children and adolescents that have demonstrated success in treating a range of mental health concerns. As participation in camp can be a standard and attractive activity for many youth, delivering intensive psychological treatment in a camp format may attenuate the stigma associated with the receipt of traditional mental health services.

Early evaluations of intensive treatment formats across childhood disorders have yielded preliminary promise. A number of intensive protocols for individual treatment of children and adolescents have demonstrated success for a range of conditions, including specific phobia (Ollendick et al., 2009; Öst, Svensson, Hellstrom, & Lindwall, 2008), obsessive-compulsive disorder (e.g., Grabill, Storch, & Geffken, 2007; Marien, Storch, Geffken, & Murphy, 2010; Storch et al., 2008; Whiteside, Brown, & Abramowitz, 2008), school refusal (Moffitt, Chorpita, & Fernandez, 2003; Tolin et al., 2009), and panic disorder with agoraphobia (Angelosante et al., 2009; Gallo, Cooper-Vince, Hardaway, Pincus, & Comer, in press; Pincus, Ehrenreich, & Mattis, 2008). A number of innovative group and/or camp-based approaches to intensive treatments have emerged as well. These include the Summer Treatment Program, which addresses attention-deficit/hyperactivity disorder in children and adolescents (e.g., Chronis et al., 2004; Coles et al., 2005; Pelham et al., 2010; Pelham & Hoza, 1996; Sibley, Smith, Evans, Pelham, & Gnagy, 2012); Emotion Detectives, a preventive camp-based intervention that teaches emotion-focused skills for coping with anxiety and depression (Ehrenreich-May & Bilek, 2011; Laird, Santucci, & Ehrenreich, 2009); Brave Buddies, a therapeutic summer program for the treatment of selective mutism in young children (Furr et al., 2011, 2012; Kurtz, 2009); and a 1-week summer treatment program targeting separation anxiety disorder in school-age girls (Santucci & Ehrenreich-May, 2010; Santucci et al., 2009).

Despite benefits that an intensive treatment approach may provide to affected youth, the implementation of intensive treatment programs within service provision settings presents many challenges. Service provision settings require adequate training, resources, and time in order to train and deliver intensive treatments with fidelity. Although intensive approaches may be more cost effective for some payers than weekly approaches, allocating staff time for intensive treatments may decrease the feasibility of this approach in certain settings, particularly for group settings where multiple therapists provide services to the group of patients enrolled in treatment. Moreover, insurance coverage for intensive treatments may be difficult to attain, given the nontraditional format and the necessity of covering up to 24 hours of billable therapist time in one block (Angelosante et al., 2009), potentially precluding the participation of families who are unable to pay out of pocket for services.

Technology-Based Treatment Delivery Formats

Recent technological innovations offer a promising vehicle for overcoming traditional barriers to evidence-based mental health care for children. In recent years, rapidly developing computer technology, the broadening availability of the Internet and smartphones, and increasingly sophisticated capacities for live broadcasting with affordable webcams are transforming many aspects of our daily lives. For children's mental health care, a discipline that relies chiefly on verbal communication and visual observation, drawing on technological innovations can transcend traditional geographical barriers to services. Telemethods extend the availability of expert services by addressing regional workforce shortages in care, such that families living in rural or other underserved regions can participate in EBT, regardless of geographic proximity to a mental health clinic. A growing body of work supports the preliminary efficacy, feasibility, tolerability, and sustainability of telemethods for delivering evidence-based care to individuals in need (see Dimeff, Paves, Skutch, & Woodcook, 2010). To date, leading technological innovations applied to children's mental health care have concentrated in three categories: (1) computer-based treatments with minimal therapist involvement, (2) those drawing on smartphone technology, and (3) videoconferencing formats for remotely delivering real-time treatment.

Computer-Based Treatments With Minimal Therapist Involvement

Computerized treatments can improve the accessibility, fidelity, and patient engagement with treatment by delivering key elements of standardized psychological treatment in a computerized CD-ROM or web-based format. Computerized treatment programs are heterogeneous, utilizing a range of provider support depending on the preferences or needs of the patient. *Computer-based* programs are delivered entirely in a computer format, whereas *computer-assisted* programs are designed to be administered with minimal support from a clinical provider. Programs that require minimal clinician oversight are highly transportable, as these treatments can be administered with little additional support in mental health clinics, pediatrician offices, at home, or at school. Therefore, many computerized treatments are not dependent on clinician availability, operating hours of service provision settings, or the geographic limitations of patients, increasing the likelihood that children in need of mental health services will receive treatment. Importantly, minimal clinician experience, training, or supervision is necessary to implement many computerized treatments, increasing the workforce able to deliver treatments for more complex and intractable cases (Kendall, Khanna, Edson, Cummings, & Harris, 2011; Khanna & Kendall, 2010).

A potential limitation of computerized treatments is that they can have restricted adaptability and flexibility, given that care takes place within the existing constraints of a computer program. A given computerized treatment may be culturally or developmentally inappropriate for certain children or adolescents, and patient factors always should be carefully considered prior to implementing computerized treatment. Computerized treatment programs also are limited in the extent to which they can address the potential moderators of treatment response, such as parental psychopathology, family stressors, or comorbid conditions. Treatment compliance can be an issue, as evidence suggests that participants receiving computerized treatments complete fewer sessions by posttreatment than those receiving traditional in-clinic care (e.g., Cunningham et al., 2009; March, Spence, & Donovan, 2009; Spence et al., 2011).

Despite these considerations, computer-based treatments can be highly attractive and engaging for young children, combining flash animation, synchronized audio and visual information, videos, cartoons, interactive diagrams, built-in reward systems, and video games to enhance motivation and engagement (Cunningham, Rapee, & Lyneham, 2006; Khanna & Kendall, 2008, 2010). Moreover, children and adolescents are likely to be comfortable and familiar with computer formats, which can help to normalize the treatment experience and increase interest (Calam, Cox, Glasgow, Jimmieson, & Larsen, 2000; Mitchell & Gordon, 2007). Computerized treatment also affords increased patient confidentiality, as the delivery of treatment elements does not depend on the face-to-face interaction of the child and provider (Calam et al., 2000). Improvements in treatment adherence, transportability, cost effectiveness, and patient engagement further contribute to the attractiveness of computer-based formats, and a growing body of research supports the feasibility and efficacy of computerized treatments.

A number of innovative EBTs targeting child and adolescent psychopathology have been adapted to computerized formats. Computerized treatments for adolescent depression include Stressbusters (Abeles et al., 2009) and SPARX (Fleming, Dixon, Frampton, & Merry, 2012; Merry et al., 2012). Computerized treatment programs also have been adapted from manual-based cognitive behavioral treatments for anxiety disorders with minimal therapist contact. These include the BRAVE-ONLINE program (March et al., 2009; Spence et al., 2011; Spence, Holmes, March, & Lipp, 2006), Cool Teens CD-ROM (Cunningham et al., 2006, 2009; Wuthrich et al., 2012), and Camp Cope-a-Lot: the Coping Cat CD-ROM (Kendall & Khanna, 2008a, 2008b).

Randomized controlled trials have been conducted evaluating the BRAVE-ONLINE program (March et al., 2009; Spence et al., 2006, 2011), Cool Teens CD-ROM (Wuthrich et al., 2012), and Camp Cope-a-Lot (Khanna & Kendall, 2010). Overall, results indicate that treatment delivered in a computerized format produces reductions in anxiety symptoms at posttreatment that are comparable to in-clinic treatment and superior to wait-list control or education-support conditions and that treatment gains continue to accrue through follow-up assessment periods. In addition, evidence from these trials demonstrates that consumers have positive perceptions about this innovative format (e.g., Khanna & Kendall, 2010).

Leveraging Smartphone Technology in Children's Mental Health Care

The medical and pediatric community has utilized handheld mobile platforms, including smartphones, to improve patient assessment and care for quite a while; however, only recently has the field of mental health in general and children's mental health in particular considered the possibilities inherent in mobile applications (see Luxton, McCann, Bush, Mishkind, & Reger, 2011, for a related review). When one considers the multiple functionalities bundled into one portable, pocket-size, handheld device, the enthusiasm regarding the potential to leverage smartphone technology to expand the reach and efficacy of evidence-based service delivery options is perhaps not surprising. Smartphone features often include software for electronic mail (e-mail), video recording and playing, video calls, and web browsing. In addition to these default features (depending on the smartphone platform), additional software applications can be purchased or downloaded for free based on consumers' interests and needs. It is precisely the multimedia functionality of smartphones that has led to rising rates of ownership, rates that now surpass ownership of earlier-generation cellular phones (Lenhart, 2010; also see Eonta et al., 2011, for a related review).

The rise in ownership, coupled with the portability and range of potential applications, has led others to refer to smartphones as "therapeutic gold" (Aguilera & Muench, 2012, p. 70). In fact, a myriad of applications (apps) targeting a diversity of mental health issues are available to consumers, applications that target both specific diagnoses (e.g., bipolar disorder, depression, eating disorders) and more general clinical symptomatology (e.g., sleep, exercise, coping). Many of these applications appear to rely on tried and true cognitive behavioral strategies, including mood tracking, pleasant activities scheduling, and even more interactive options that target social information processing and social skills training (see Luxton et al., 2011, for a more exhaustive list of examples). However, even a preliminary review of these applications suggests that the developers may not have training in the delivery of EBTs (see Luxton et al., 2011, for a discussion of quality standards and safety). There is perhaps no better example of this than a review of the several applications relevant to behavioral parent training (BPT), the evidence-based approach for the treatment of children's disruptive behavior disorders (see Chorpita et al., 2011; Dretzke et al., 2009; Eyberg, Nelson, & Boggs, 2008, for reviews). Although several "time-out" applications exist, the primary role of these applications is to tell parents how long the child should be in time-out (i.e., based on age) and/or tracking the elapsed time-out period. Although time-out applications may be interesting gadgets for parents of typical toddlers, those who have implemented BPT with a family of a child with oppositional defiant disorder or conduct disorder know all too well that tracking time during time-out is not the biggest treatment challenge (see Jones, Forehand, McKee, Cuellar, & Kincaid, 2010). Although the potential to harness technology to drive mental health improvement has been discussed extensively within the academic literature (see Boschen & Casey, 2008; Eonta et al., 2011; Luxton et al., 2011, for examples of reviews), to date, the discussion around the potential for smartphones far exceeds the foundation of empirical inquiry or data, particularly in children's mental health (see Jones et al., 2013, for a review). Programs of research focused on the role of smartphones are rare, but we mention a few here for context. For example, SafeCare is an evidence-based child maltreatment prevention program that has examined the use of smartphones to enhance home safety (Jabaley, Lutzker, Whitaker, & Self-Brown, 2011).

Researchers in the autism community also have reported the potential utility of using smartphones to support children with autism spectrum disorders. For example, Mintz, Branch, March, and Lerman (2012) have developed a mobile cognitive support application for smartphones that includes a web-based toolkit that allows teachers to tailor interventions flexibly via prompts, social stories, daily diaries, and a "personal trainer." Qualitative results from a pilot study of four schools for children with autism spectrum disorders suggest promise for this approach to allow treatment to extend beyond the four walls of the treatment setting.

As another example, pediatric psychologists have utilized text messaging as a tool to deliver key components of intervention programs (e.g., reminders regarding medication adherence, physical activity, glycemic control) (see Militello, Kelly, & Melnyk, 2012, for a review). The bulk of this work has been conducted using cellular phones; however, the functionality of texts should operate similarly regardless of delivery vehicle, which leads to a discussion of the role of theory in guiding smartphone research.

The lag in research, particularly randomized control trials, on smartphones in particular and mobile applications more generally may be a result, at least in part, of the relative lack of theory to guide empirical work in this area (see Jones et al., 2013; Militello et al., 2012; Ritterband, Thorndike, Cox, Kovatchev, & Gonder-Frederick, 2009, for related reviews). Importantly, theory provides a framework not only for organizing the research to date; it has the potential to inform innovation in children's mental health as well. Accordingly, we provide an example of one theoretically driven evaluation of smartphone technology to engage families in one evidence-based intervention approach: BPT.

Although children with early-onset disruptive behavior disorders are overrepresented among low-income families, such families are less likely to engage in BPT than other sociodemographic groups (see Jones et al., 2013; Lundahl, Risser, & Lovejoy, 2006, for representative reviews). Data suggest that if we successfully engage low-income families in BPT services, they benefit as much as, if not more than, relatively higher income families (see Reyno & McGrath, 2006, for review). A number of approaches have been tested to improve the engagement of families in BPT, including home-based and group-focused programs as well as monetary incentives; however, these approaches have been unsuccessful in increasing rates of engagement for this population (also see Jones et al., 2013; Lundahl et al., 2006, for reviews).

Accordingly, there is a relatively untapped potential for technology to better situate BPT programs at the forefront of the daily lives of low-income families. Although originally accessible only to higher-income consumers, the proliferation in smartphone platforms, the wider availability of providers, and the increasing affordability of service plans have broadened the accessibility of smartphones to lower-income consumers as well (see Anderson & Subramanyam, 2011; Davies, 2011; Snider, 2011, for reviews). For example, smartphones are now available through subsidized programs and contract-free carriers, which do not require a credit check and offer more cost-effective smartphone models (e.g., $19.99) and service plans (e.g., $35.00/month for unlimited data). Yet it is also important to highlight that interventions delivered through smartphones can be designed to minimize data charges for those consumers who do not have unlimited plans.

The point regarding cost effectiveness brings us to the second issue. We are not aware of a review of the cost effectiveness of smartphone-delivered interventions. Relatedly, Tate, Finkelstein, Khavjou, and Gustafson (2009) highlight that while cost effectiveness is a primary rationale for developing Internet interventions, only 8 of the 420 studies on Internet interventions from 1995 to 2008 reported economic indicators. As cost-effectiveness analyses are critical to understanding the real-world sustainability of smartphone applications, future studies examining the use of smartphone technology within child mental health care would benefit from including them. Of course, technology-delivered interventions include costs to develop the intervention (e.g., programming, licensing), which would not recur for the agencies, providers, and families using them. The greater cost of delivery for end users would be the cost of the smartphone as well as the service plan. As noted, these dissemination costs conceivably will continue to decline, given the increased accessibility of smartphones and service plans that may uniquely situate smartphones and mobile applications to change the landscape of children's mental health.

Videoconferencing Methods for Remotely Delivering Real-Time Treatment

Our final section on technology-based formats for the delivery of children's mental health care focuses on the use of videoconferencing for the provision of live care traditionally delivered in person. Whereas the previously discussed technological innovations rely on technology either to complement ongoing in-person care or to provide opportunities for asynchronous communication between therapists and patients, videoconferencing methods afford real-time, remote interactions for a full treatment course. Moreover, the use of telemethods for synchronous real-time interactions between families and providers distinguishes videoconferencing methods from other forms of e-health that draw chiefly on Internet-facilitated bibliotherapy or self-management modalities. For mental health care, a discipline that relies primarily on verbal communication and visual observation, these methods may offer a transformative potential to overcome geographical barriers to live expert care by extending the availability of expert services and addressing regional workforce shortages in quality care. Families living in rural or impoverished regions—areas typically beset by insufficient availability of mental health care—can participate in real-time interactive treatment conducted by experts, regardless of geographic proximity to a mental health clinic.

Real-time, Internet-based interactive videoconferencing has shown initial success in reducing a range of diagnostic conditions in children and adults (Andersson et al., 2012; Comer, Furr, Cooper-Vince, Kerns, et al., 2013; Comer, Furr, Cooper-Vince, Madigan, et al., 2013; Herbst et al., 2012; Himle et al., 2006, 2012; Storch et al., 2011). A live, interactive, and web-based approach to treatment delivery offers the possibility to substantially expand the accessibility and availability of evidence-based care for children and families. Specifically, a videoconferencing format can offer a comparable quantity of therapist contact relative to traditional in-clinic treatment. Using videoconferencing software and webcams, treatment content can be delivered by therapists with the same speed and facility afforded in traditional in-clinic care, regardless of a family's proximity to a mental health facility, and therapists also can deliver in-the-moment feedback on child symptoms to children and families in their natural settings (e.g., homes, schools). Treating families in their homes via telehealth methods can afford live observation and feedback in many of the actual settings in which symptoms are most problematic, which may also expand on the ecological validity of EBTs.

To illustrate the potential of using videoconferencing technology to remotely deliver live, evidence-based care, let us consider the case of Parent-Child Interaction Therapy (PCIT) (Eyberg & Funderburk, 2011)—another model BPT program for several early childhood behavior problems. Although research supports the efficacy of PCIT (see Zisser & Eyberg, 2010), by some accounts it is a relatively complex treatment for broad dissemination (see Comer & Barlow, 2013). PCIT, like several other BPT programs, utilizes a highly structured coding system and provides rigorous real-time, in-session parent coaching. Although several efforts have shown some promise in the feasibility of disseminating PCIT in community settings, most care settings are not physically equipped for PCIT (i.e., they lack a one-way mirror, Bluetooth earpiece, etc.). PCIT implementation projects are forced to make substantive modifications, which some posit may be associated with more disappointing treatment outcomes (see Comer & Barlow, 2013).

Simply stated, given the complexity and specialized nature of PCIT, it may not lend itself to broad dissemination to generalist practitioners. However, a real-time, Internet-based interactive videoconferencing format may be a particularly promising vehicle for the delivery of PCIT since the therapist is not supposed to be physically present for the majority of treatment but rather unobtrusively monitoring from a separate room and providing live feedback through a Bluetooth earpiece worn by the parent. Using videoconferencing technology, PCIT therapists can provide in-the-moment feedback to parents through parent-worn earpieces during family interactions, regardless of a family's proximity to a PCIT-equipped mental health facility. Currently, we are conducting multiple randomized trials evaluating the potential of PCIT delivered via videoconferencing technology relative to traditional in-clinic PCIT and to wait list. To date, our pilot data support the preliminary feasibility, credibility, and consumer satisfaction associated with Internet-delivered PCIT (Comer, Furr, Cooper-Vince, Kerns, et al., 2013).

Several key hardware and equipment considerations warrant comment for the smooth conduct of live, remote psychological treatment via videoconferencing technology. The minimum technological requirements for such care include:

1. A computing device in the therapist's office (e.g., desktop personal computer [PC], laptop computer, smartphone, or tablet)
2. A computing device in the treated family's home
3. Broadband or Wi-Fi Internet connectivity at both sites
4. A webcam, microphone, and speaker at both sites to capture and deliver audio and visual information

For some treatments, such as in our Internet-delivered PCIT program, a family also requires a Bluetooth earpiece receiver to enable live and unobtrusive parent coaching.

Regrettably, families with insufficient mental health care accessibility (e.g., low-income and rural-dwelling families) may be those with the most limited access to PCs, webcams, and/or broadband connectivity. As such, current disparities in Internet access and technological literacy may impede Internet-based treatment accessibility for some, as 24% of households in the United States currently do not have Internet access (U.S. Census Bureau, 2012). However, demographic groups showing the poorest current access to and ease with PCs and the Internet—rural and low-income families—are, encouragingly, showing the most accelerated growth in recent years in the adoption of household Internet (Horrigan, 2009).

Importantly, only broadband Internet or Wi-Fi connections afford the quality of real-time, fluid, and discernible communication required for live treatment. Attempting to use low-bandwidth or dial-up methods for videoconferencing treatment is problematic on a number of fronts:

- Audio and visual communications will not synchronize.
- Picture resolution will be poor during movement.
- There will be a strobe effect that misses key pieces of visual information, as the frames per second of transmitted visual data will be too low.
- At times sound will be indiscernible.
- Communications will be delayed, precluding real-time interactions between the therapist and family.
- The connection between the therapist and family may be dropped frequently.

Accordingly, for families who do not have broadband or Wi-Fi connectivity, therapists or payers might consider lending them a relatively cheap temporary mobile Wi-Fi hotspot, which can be transferred forward to another family at the conclusion of treatment.

The term "videoconferencing" refers to the use of telecommunications software that allows multiple parties to communicate in real time through the simultaneous two-way transmission of video and audio signals. Most modern videoconferencing formats afford real-time and lifelike detail and motion sophisticated enough to enable quality treatment when broadband or Wi-Fi connectivity is used. Videoconferencing formats do, however, differ from one another in important ways with regard to cost, quality, encryption, and privacy. As noted elsewhere (Comer, Furr, Cooper-Vince, Madigan, et al., 2013), the lower the videoconferencing cost, typically the weaker the privacy and encryption, and the lower the communication quality. Free services, such as Skype®, typically offer relatively poorer video and audio quality compared to other available options and are associated with frequently disrupted and dropped connections. Videoconferencing services that cost money typically come with stronger encryption and improved quality of communications, with T1 and T3 line connections offering the highest quality and security. However, these connections are very expensive, limiting their role in the broad delivery of treatments to families in natural settings.

Fortunately, there are easy-to-use web conferencing applications designed to enable small to moderately size "virtual" meetings (e.g., Webex®, GoToMeeting®). These programs also afford desktop sharing, which can be useful for sharing handouts, graphs depicting weekly symptom data, and other treatment-specific documents. During treatment, graphs and handouts can be brought up on the therapist's screen, and then the desktop-sharing tool can be applied to enable the family to see the therapist's screen as the forms are explained.

Importantly, there are a number of security matters to be concerned with when selecting a videoconferencing format; these matters are detailed in greater description elsewhere (see Comer & Barlow, 2013). Specifically, providers should select a videoconferencing platform that does these things:

- Uses the Advanced Encryption Standards algorithm
- Allows meetings to be hosted in an unlisted manner, meaning that individuals not intended to attend cannot search for and find that the session is occurring
- Requires all meeting attendees to log in only after being invited by the "host" (i.e., therapist)
- Clearly identifies each attendee to all meeting attendants
- Does not store or retain any session content on a network

For additional security, it is important to select a videoconferencing format that uses at least an SSL/TLS encryption tunnel, which provides communication security over the Internet by encrypting data between the intended parties. Finally, prior to obtaining informed consent for treatment delivered via videoconferencing, it is important that all families understand that, as with all Internet-based communications, there is a potential for breaches in confidentiality. Families also should be discouraged from using last names or other identifying information, such as birth dates, during sessions.

In recent years, a number of programs have emerged that harness videoconferencing technology to overcome geographic barriers to evidence-based care (Comer, Furr, Cooper-Vince, Kerns, et al., 2013; Comer, Furr, Cooper-Vince, Madigan, et al., 2013; Himle, Olufs, Himle, Tucker, & Woods, 2010; Himle et al., 2012; Storch et al., 2011). With continued scholarly activity and empirical scrutiny in this area, videoconferencing methods may prove to be a serious and viable option for delivering real-time care to children dwelling in regions traditionally underserved by expert care.

CONCLUSIONS

Fundamental barriers interfere with the broad availability, accessibility, and acceptability of quality mental health care for the majority of affected youth. In recent years, a number of leading models and innovative solutions for remediating the problems of limited care availability and quality have dominated scholarly thought and have begun to garner preliminary empirical support. These new models and methods include the strategic reformatting of EBTs (including advances in transdiagnostic protocols, modularized protocols, and intensive treatment formats) and exciting advances in technology-based treatment delivery (including computer-based treatments with minimal therapist involvement, smartphone applications for augmenting children's mental health care, and videoconferencing formats for remotely delivering real-time treatment). Needless to say, we are just now at the very earliest stages of evaluating the potentials of each of these innovations for meaningfully improving children's mental health care, and considerable work is required before these methods are to be considered serious vehicles for the systematic delivery of mental health services. The benefits of these innovations are not self-evident and should not be accepted prima facie. Rather, due to the current scholarly excitement regarding each of these areas, it is vital that rigorous empirical evaluations of these potential advances are developed. With continued empirical support, these exciting new methods of service delivery for children's mental health care hold enormous potential for meaningfully advancing and transforming the broad relevance and public health impact of EBTs for child mental disorders.

REFERENCES

Abeles, P., Verduyn, C., Robinson, A., Smith, P., Yule, W., & Proudfoot, J. (2009). Computerized CBT for adolescent depression ("Stressbusters") and its initial evaluation through an extended case series. *Behavioural and Cognitive Psychotherapy, 37,* 151–165. doi: 10.1017/S1352465808005067

Aguilera, A., & Muench, F. (2012). There's an app for that: Information technology applications for cognitive behavioral practitioners. *Behavior Therapist, 35,* 65–73.

Albano, A. M. (2009). Special series: Intensive cognitive-behavioral treatments for child and adolescent anxiety disorders. *Cognitive and Behavioral Practice, 16,* 358–362. doi: 10.1016/j.cbpra.2009.04.002

Anderson, D., & Subramanyam, R. (2011). *The new digital American family: Understanding family dynamics, media, and purchasing behavior trends.* New York, NY: Nielson.

Andersson, E., Enander, J., Andrén, P., Hedman, E., Ljótsson, B., Hursti, T., . . . Rück, C. (2012). Internet-based cognitive behaviour therapy for obsessive-compulsive disorder: A randomized controlled trial. *Psychological Medicine, 42*(10), 2193–2203. doi: 10.1017/S0033291712000244

Angelosante, A. G., Pincus, D. B., Whitton, S. W., Cheron, D., & Pian, J. (2009). Implementation of an intensive treatment protocol for adolescents with panic disorder and agoraphobia. *Cognitive and Behavioral Practice, 16,* 345–357. doi: 10.1016/j.cbpra.2009.03.002

Barlow, D. H. (2004). Psychological treatments. *American Psychologist, 59,* 869–878. doi: 10.1037/0003–066X.59.9.869

Barlow, D. H., Farchione, T. J., Fairholme, C. P., Ellard, K. K., Boisseau, C. L., Allen, L. B., & May, J. T. E. (2010). *Unified protocol for transdiagnostic treatment of emotional disorders: Therapist guide.* New York, NY: Oxford University Press.

Beidas, R. S., Benjamin, C. L., Puleo, C. M., Edmunds, J. M., & Kendall, P. C. (2010). Flexible applications of the Coping Cat program for anxious youth. *Cognitive and Behavioral Practice, 17,* 142–153. doi: 10.1016/j.cbpra.2009.11.002

Bird, D. C., Dempsey, P., & Hartley, D. (2001). *Addressing mental health workforce needs in underserved rural areas: Accomplishments and challenges.* Portland, ME: Maine Rural Health Research Center.

Borntrager, C. F., Chorpita, B. F., Higa-McMillan, C., & Weisz, J. R. (2009). Provider attitudes toward evidence-based practices: Are the concerns with the evidence or with the manuals? *Psychiatric Services, 60*(5), 677–681. doi: 10.1176/appi.ps.60.5.677

Boschen, M. J., & Casey, L. M. (2008). The use of mobile telephones as adjuncts to cognitive behavioral psychotherapy. *Professional Psychology: Research and Practice, 39,* 546–552. doi: 10.1037/0735–7028.39.5.546

Calam, R., Cox, A., Glasgow, D., Jimmieson, P., & Larsen, S. G. (2000). Assessment and therapy with children: Can computers help? *Clinical Child Psychology and Psychiatry, 5,* 329–343. doi: 10.1177/1359104500005003004

Chorpita, B. F. (2007). *Modular cognitive-behavioral therapy for childhood anxiety disorders.* New York, NY: Guilford Press.

Chorpita, B. F., Daleiden, E. L., Ebesutani, C., Young, J., Becker, K. D., Nakamura, B. J., & Starace, N. (2011). Evidence-based treatments for children and adolescents: An updated review of indicators of efficacy and effectiveness. *Clinical Psychology: Science and Practice, 18*(2), 154–172. doi: 10.1111/j.1468–2850.2011.01247.x

Chorpita, B. F., & Weisz, J. R. (2005). *Modular approach to therapy for children with anxiety, depression, or conduct problems*. Honolulu, HI: University of Hawaii at Manoa.

Chronis, A. M., Fabiano, G. A., Gnagy, E. M., Onyango, A. N., Pelham, W. E., Lopez-Williams, A., . . . Seymour, K. E. (2004). An evaluation of the summer treatment program for children with attention-deficit/hyperactivity disorder using a treatment withdrawal design. *Behavior Therapy, 35,* 561–585. doi: 10.1016/S0005-7894(04)80032-7

Chu, B. (2012). Translating transdiagnostic approaches to children and adolescents. *Cognitive and Behavioral Practice, 19(1),* 1–4. doi: 10.1016/j.cbpra.2011.06.003

Coles, E. K., Pelham, W. E., Gnagy, E. M., Burrows-MacLean, L., Fabiano, G. A., Chacko, A., . . . Robb, J. A. (2005). A controlled evaluation of behavioral treatment with children with ADHD attending a summer treatment program. *Journal of Emotional and Behavioral Disorders, 13,* 99–112. doi: 10.1177/10634266050130020301

Comer, J. S., & Barlow, D. H. (2013). The occasional case against broad dissemination: Retaining a role for specialty care in the delivery of psychological treatments. *American Psychologist.* Advance online publication.

Comer, J. S., Furr, J. M., Cooper-Vince, C. E., Kerns, C. E., Chan, P. T., Edson, A. L., . . . Freeman, J. B. (2013). *Internet-delivered, family-based treatment for early-onset OCD: Rational, considerations, and a preliminary case series.* Manuscript under review.

Comer, J. S., Furr, J. M., Cooper-Vince, C., Madigan, R. J., Chow, C. W., Chan, P. T., . . . Eyberg, S. M. (2013). *Rationale and considerations for the Internet-based delivery of Parent-Child Interaction Therapy.* Manuscript under review.

Comer, J. S., Mojtabai, R., & Olfson, M. (2011). National trends in the antipsychotic treatment of psychiatric outpatients with anxiety disorders. *American Journal of Psychiatry, 168,* 1057–1065. doi: 10.1176/appi.ajp.2011.11010087

Comer, J. S., Olfson, M., & Mojtabai, R. (2010). National trends in child and adolescent psychotropic polypharmacy in office-based practice, 1996–2007. *Journal of the American Academy of Child & Adolescent Psychiatry, 49,* 1001–1010. doi: 10.1016/j.jaac.2010.07.007

Craske, M. G., Rose, R. D., Lang, A., Welch, S. S., Campbell-Sills, L., Sullivan, G., . . . Roy-Byrne, P. P. (2009). Computer-assisted delivery of cognitive behavioral therapy for anxiety disorders in primary-care settings. *Depression and Anxiety, 26,* 235–242. doi: 10.1002/da.20542

Cunningham, M. J., Rapee, R. M., & Lyneham, H. (2006). The Cool Teens CD-ROM: A multimedia self-help program for adolescents with anxiety. *Youth Studies Australia, 25,* 50–56.

Cunningham, M. J., Wuthrich, V. M., Rapee, R. M., Lyneham, H. J., Schniering, C. A., & Hudson, J. L. (2009). The Cool Teens CD-ROM for anxiety disorders in adolescents: A pilot case series. *European Journal of Child and Adolescent Psychiatry, 18,* 125–129. doi: 10.1007/s00787–008–0703-y

Davies, E. (2011). *Learning from the digital jugglers: New trends in smartphone adoption and usage patterns.* New York, NY: Fjord.

Dimeff, L. A., Paves, A. P., Skutch, J. M., & Woodcock, E. A. (2010). Shifting paradigms in clinical psychology: How innovative technologies are shaping treatment delivery. In D. H. Barlow (Ed.), *Handbook of clinical psychology* (pp. 618–649). New York, NY: Oxford University Press.

Dretzke, J., Davenport, C., Frew, E., Barlow, J., Stewart-Brown, S., Bayliss, S., & Hyde, C. (2009). The clinical effectiveness of different parenting programmes for children with conduct problems: A systematic review of randomized controlled trials. *Child and Adolescent Psychiatry and Mental Health, 3.* doi: 10.1186/1753–2000–3-7

Ehrenreich, J. T., Goldstein, C. R., Wright, L. R., & Barlow, D. H. (2009). Development of a unified protocol for the treatment of emotional disorders in youth. *Child and Family Behavior Therapy, 31,* 20–37. doi: 10.1080/07317100802701228

Ehrenreich, J. T., & Santucci, L. C. (2009). Special series: Intensive cognitive-behavioral treatments for child and adolescent anxiety disorders. *Cognitive and Behavioral Practice, 16,* 290–293. doi: 10.1016/j.cbpra.2009.04.001

Ehrenreich-May, J. T., & Bilek, E. L. (2011). Universal prevention of anxiety and depression in a camp setting: An initial open trial. *Child and Youth Care Forum, 40(6),* 435–455. doi: 10.1007/s10566–011–9148-4

Eonta, A. M., Christon, L. M., Hourigan, S. E., Ravindran, N., Vrana, S. R., & Southam-Gerow, M. A. (2011). Using everyday technology to enhance evidence-based treatments. *Professional Psychology: Research and Practice, 42,* 513–520. doi: 10.1037/a0025825

Eyberg, S. M., & Funderburk, B. (2011). *Parent-Child Interaction Therapy protocol.* Gainesville, FL: PCIT International.

Eyberg, S. M., Nelson, M. M., & Boggs, S. R. (2008). Evidence-based psychosocial treatments for children and adolescents with disruptive behavior. *Journal of Clinical Child and Adolescent Psychology, 37(1),* 215–237. doi: 10.1080/15374410701820117

Fairburn, C., Cooper, Z., Shafran, R., & Wilson, G. (2008). Eating disorders: A transdiagnostic protocol. In D. H. Barlow (Ed.), *Clinical handbook of psychological disorders: A step-by-step treatment manual* (pp. 578–614). New York, NY: Guilford Press.

Fairburn, C. G., Cooper, Z., Doll, H. A., O'Connor, M. E., Bohn, K., Hawker, D. M., . . . Palmer, R. L. (2009). Transdiagnostic cognitive-behavioral therapy for patients with eating disorders: A two-site trial with 60-week follow-up. *American Journal of Psychiatry, 166,* 311–319. doi: 10.1176/appi.ajp.2008.08040608

Farchione, T. J., Fairholme, C. P., Ellard, K. K., Boisseau, C. L., Thompson-Hollands, J., Carl, J. R., . . . Barlow, D. H. (2012). Unified protocol for transdiagnostic treatment of emotional disorders: A randomized controlled trial. *Behavior Therapy, 43,* 666–678. doi: 10.1016/j.beth.2012.01.001

Fleming, T., Dixon, R., Frampton, C., & Merry, S. (2012). A pragmatic randomized controlled trial of computerized CBT (SPARX) for symptoms of depression among adolescents excluded from mainstream education. *Behavioural and Cognitive Psychotherapy, 40*(5), 529–541. doi: 10.1017/S1352465811000695

Furr, J. M., Comer, J. S., Kerns, C., Feinberg, L., Wilson, L., & Kurtz, S. M. S. (2011, October). *The Boston University Brave Bunch Program: A replication of the Brave Buddies intensive, outpatient treatment program for children with selective mutism.* Poster presented at the Selected Mutism Group Annual Conference, New York, NY.

Furr, J. M., Comer, J. S., Kerns, C., Feinberg, L., Wilson, L., & Kurtz, S. M. S. (2012, November). *The Boston University Brave Buddies Program: A replication of the Brave Buddies intensive, outpatient treatment program for children with selective mutism.* Symposium presented at the 46th annual meeting of the Association for Behavioral and Cognitive Therapies, National Harbor, MD.

Gallo, K. P., Cooper-Vince, C. E., Hardaway, C., Pincus, D. B., & Comer, J. S. (in press). Trajectories of change across outcomes in intensive treatment for adolescent panic disorder and agoraphobia. *Journal of Clinical Child and Adolescent Psychology.*

Grabill, K., Storch, E. A., & Geffken, G. R. (2007). Intensive cognitive-behavioral therapy for pediatric obsessive-compulsive disorder. *Behavior Therapist, 30,* 19–21.

Harvey, A. G., Watkins, E. R., Mansell, W., & Shafran, R. (2004). *Cognitive behavioural processes across psychological disorders: A transdiagnostic approach to research and treatment.* Oxford, UK: Oxford University Press.

Herbst, N., Voderholzer, U., Stelzer, N., Knaevelsrud, C., Hertenstein, E., Schlegl, S., . . . Külz, A. (2012). The potential of telemental health applications for obsessive-compulsive disorder. *Clinical Psychology Review, 32*(6), 454–466. doi: 10.1016/j.cpr.2012.04.005

Himle, J. A., Fischer, D. J., Muroff, J. R., Van Etten, M. L., Lokers, L. M., Abelson, J. L., & Hanna, G. L. (2006). Videoconferencing-based cognitive-behavioral therapy for obsessive-compulsive disorder. *Behaviour Research and Therapy, 44*(12), 1821–1829. doi: 10.1016/j.brat.2005.12.010

Himle, M. B., Freitag, M., Walther, M., Franklin, S. A., Ely, L., & Woods, D. W. (2012). A randomized pilot trial comparing videoconference versus face-to-face delivery of behavior therapy for childhood tic disorders. *Behaviour Research and Therapy, 50*(9), 565–570. doi: 10.1016/j.brat.2012.05.009

Himle, M. B., Olufs, E., Himle, J., Tucker, B. P., & Woods, D. W. (2010). Behavior therapy for tics via videoconference delivery: An initial pilot test in children. *Cognitive and Behavioral Practice, 17,* 329–337. doi: 10.1016/j.cbpra.2010.02.006

Horrigan, J. B. (2009). *Home broadband adoption 2009.* Pew Internet & American Life Project. Retrieved from http://pewinternet.org/Reports/2009/10-Home-Broadband-Adoption-2009.aspx

Jabaley, J. J., Lutzker, J. R., Whitaker, D. J., & Self-Brown, S. (2011). Using iPhones to enhance and reduce face-to-face home safety sessions with SafeCare: An evidence-based child maltreatment prevention program. *Journal of Family Violence, 26,* 377–385.

Jones, D. J., Forehand, R., Cuellar, J., Kincaid, C., Parent, J., Fenton, N., & Goodrum, N. (2013). Harnessing innovative technologies to advance children's mental health: Behavioral parent training as an example. *Clinical Psychology Review.* doi: 10.1016/j.cpr.2012.11.003

Jones, D. J., Forehand, R., Cuellar, J., Parent, J., Honeycutt, A., Khavjou, O., . . . Newey, G. (2013). *Technology-enhanced program for child disruptive behavior disorders: Development and pilot randomized control trial.* Manuscript under review.

Jones, D. J., Forehand, R., McKee, L., Cuellar, J., & Kincaid, C. (2010). Behavioral parent training: Is there an "app" for that? *Behavior Therapist, 33,* 72–77.

Kazdin, A. E., & Blase, S. L. (2011). Rebooting psychotherapy research and practice to reduce the burden of mental illness. *Perspectives on Psychological Science, 6,* 21–37.

Kendall, P. C. (2011). *Child and adolescent therapy: Cognitive-behavioral procedures* (4th ed.). New York, NY: Guilford Press.

Kendall, P. C., & Beidas, R. S. (2007). Smoothing the trail for dissemination of evidence-based practices for youth: Flexibility within fidelity. *Professional Psychology: Research and Practice, 38,* 13–20. doi: 10.1037/0735–7028.38.1.13

Kendall, P. C., & Hedtke, K. (2006a). *Cognitive-behavioral therapy for anxious children: Therapist manual* (3rd ed.). Ardmore, PA: Workbook Publishing.

Kendall, P. C., & Hedtke, K. (2006b). *The Coping Cat workbook* (2nd ed.). Ardmore, PA: Workbook Publishing.

Kendall, P. C., Hudson, J. L., Gosch, E., Flannery-Schroeder, E., & Suveg, C. (2008). Cognitive-behavioral therapy for anxiety disordered youth: A randomized clinical trial evaluating child and family modalities. *Journal of Consulting and Clinical Psychology, 76,* 282–297. doi: 10.1037/0022–006X.76.2.282

Kendall, P. C., & Khanna, M. S. (2008a). *Camp Cope-a-Lot: The Coping Cat CD ROM* [Software]. Ardmore, PA: Workbook Publishing.

Kendall, P. C., & Khanna, M. S. (2008b). *Coach's manual for Camp Cope-a-Lot: The Coping Cat CD ROM.* Ardmore, PA: Workbook Publishing.

Kendall, P. C., Khanna, M. S., Edson, A., Cummings, C., & Harris, M. S. (2011). Computers and psychological treatment for child anxiety: Recent advances and ongoing efforts. *Depression and Anxiety, 28*(1), 58–66.

Khanna, M. S., & Kendall, P. C. (2008). Computer-assisted CBT for child anxiety: The Coping Cat CD-ROM. *Cognitive and Behavioral Practice, 15,* 159–165. doi: 10.1016/j.cbpra.2008.02.002

Khanna, M. S., & Kendall, P. C. (2010). Computer-assisted cognitive behavioral therapy for child anxiety: Results of a randomized clinical trial. *Journal of Consulting and Clinical Psychology, 78,* 737–745. doi: 10.1037/a0019055

Kingery, J. N., Roblek, T. L., Suveg, C., Grover, R. L., Sherrill, J. T., & Bergman, R. L. (2006). They're not just "little adults": Developmental considerations for implementing cognitive-behavioral therapy with anxious youth. *Journal of Cognitive Psychotherapy: An International Quarterly, 20,* 263–273. doi: 10.1891/jcop.20.3.263

Kurtz, S. (2009). *Camp Brave Buddies, 2009: Summer day camp for children with selective mutism.* Retrieved from http://www.selectivemutism.org/events/CampBraveBuddies_2009_brochure.pdf

Laird, E. A., Santucci, L. C., & Ehrenreich, J. T. (2009, November). *Emotion detectives: Preliminary results from an investigation of a novel universal prevention program targeting the development of anxiety and depression in youth.* Poster session presented at the Association for Behavioral and Cognitive Therapies annual conference, New York, NY.

Lenhart, A. (2010). *Cell phones and American adults.* Retrieved from http://pewinternet.org/Reports/2010/Cell-Phones-and-American-Adults.aspx

Lundahl, B., Risser, H. J., & Lovejoy, M. C. (2006). A meta-analysis of parent training: Moderators and follow-up effects. *Clinical Psychology Review, 26,* 86–104. doi: 10.1016/j.cpr.2005.07.004

Luxton, D. D., McCann, R. A., Bush, N. E., Mishkind, M. C., & Reger, G. M. (2011). mHealth for mental health: Integrating smartphone technology in behavioral healthcare. *Professional Psychology: Research and Practice, 42,* 505–512. doi: 10.1037/a0024485

March, S., Spence, S. H., & Donovan, C. L. (2009). The efficacy of an Internet-based cognitive-behavioral therapy intervention for child anxiety disorders. *Journal of Pediatric Psychology, 34,* 474–487. doi: 10.1093/jpepsy/jsn099

Marien, W. E., Storch, E. A., Geffken, G. R., & Murphy, T. K. (2009). Intensive family-based cognitive-behavioral therapy for pediatric obsessive-compulsive disorder: Applications for treatment of medication partial- or nonresponders. *Cognitive and Behavioral Practice, 16,* 304–316. doi: 10.1016/j.cbpra.2008.12.006

Marziali, E., Monroe-Blum, H., & McCleary, L. (1997). The contribution of group cohesion and group alliance to the outcome of group psychotherapy. *International Journal of Group Psychotherapy, 47,* 475–497.

McHugh, R. K., & Barlow, D. H. (2010). The dissemination and implementation of evidence-based psychological treatments: A review of current efforts. *American Psychologist, 65,* 73–84. doi: 10.1037/a0018121McHugh, R. K., & Barlow, D. H. (2012). *Dissemination and implementation of evidence-based psychological interventions.* New York, NY: Oxford University Press.

McMahon, R. J., & Forehand, R. L. (2003). *Helping the noncompliant child: Family-based treatment for oppositional behavior* (2nd ed.). New York, NY: Guilford Press.

Merry, S. N., Stasiak, K., Shepherd, M., Frampton, C., Fleming, T., & Lucassen, M. F. G. (2012). The effectiveness of SPARX, a computerized self-health intervention for adolescents seeking help for depression: Randomized controlled non-inferiority trial. *British Medical Journal, 344*(7857), 1–16.

Militello, L. K., Kelly, S. A., & Melnyk, B. M. (2012). Systematic review of text-messaging interventions to promote healthy behaviors in pediatric and adolescent populations: Implications for clinical practice and research. *Worldviews of Evidence-Based Nursing, 9*(2), 66–77.

Mintz, J., Branch, C., March, C., & Lerman, S. (2012). Key factors mediating the use of mobile technology tool designed to develop social and life skills in children with autistic spectrum disorders. *Computers & Education, 58,* 53–62. doi: 10.1016/j.compedu.2011.07.013

Mitchell, N., & Gordon, P. K. (2007). Attitudes towards computerized CBT for depression amongst a student population. *Behavioural and Cognitive Psychotherapy, 35,* 421–430. doi: 10.1017/S1352465807003700

Moffitt, C. E., Chorpita, B. R., & Fernandez, S. N. (2003). Intensive cognitive-behavioral treatment of school refusal behavior. *Cognitive and Behavioral Practice, 10,* 51–60. doi: 10.1016/S1077–7229(03)80008–1

National Advisory Committee on Rural Health. (2002). *A targeted look at the rural health care safety net: A report to the secretary, U.S. Department of Health and Human Services.* Washington, DC: National Advisory Committee on Rural Health.

National Organization of State Offices of Rural Health. (2011). *Statement on reducing behavioral health disparities in rural communities.* Sterling Heights, MI: Author.

Norton, P. J. (2008). An open trial of a transdiagnostic cognitive-behavioral group therapy for anxiety disorder. *Behavior Therapy, 39,* 242–250. doi: 10.1016/j.beth.2007.08.002

Norton, P. J., & Hope, D. A. (2005). Preliminary evaluation of broad spectrum cognitive behavioral group therapy for anxiety. *Journal of Behavior Therapy and Experimental Psychiatry, 36*(2), 79–97. doi: 10.1016/j.jbtep.2004.07.002

Olfson, M., Crystal, S., Huang, C., & Gerhard, T. (2010). Trends in antipsychotic drug use by very young, privately insured children. *Journal of the American Academy of Child & Adolescent Psychiatry, 49,* 13–23. doi: 10.1097/00004583–201001000–00005

Olfson, M., & Marcus, S. C. (2010). National trends in outpatient psychotherapy. *American Journal of Psychiatry, 167,* 1456–1463. doi: 10.1176/appi.ajp.2010.10040570

Ollendick, T. H., Öst, L. G., Rueterskiöld, L., Costa, N., Cederlund, R., Sirbu, C., . . . Jarrett, M. A. (2009). One-session treatment of specific phobia in youth: A randomized clinical trial in the United States and Sweden. *Journal of Consulting and Clinical Psychology, 77,* 54–57. doi: 10.1037/a0015158

Öst, L. G., Svensson, L., Hellstrom, K., & Lindwall, R. (2001). One-session treatment of specific phobias in youth: A randomized clinical trial. *Journal of Consulting and Clinical Psychology, 69,* 814–824. doi: 10.1037/0022–006X.69.5.814

Owens, P. L., Hoagwood, K., Horowitz, S. M., Leaf, P. J., Poduska, J. M., Kellam, S. G., & Ialongo, N. S. (2002). Barriers to children's mental health services. *Journal of the American Academy of Child & Adolescent Psychiatry, 41,* 731–738. doi: 10.1097/00004583–200206000–00013

Pelham, W. E., Gnagy, E. M., Greiner, A. R., Waschbusch, D. A., Fabiano, G. A., & Burrows-Maclean, L. (2010). Summer treatment programs for attention-deficit/hyperactivity disorder. In J. R. Weisz & A. E. Kazdin (Eds.), *Evidence-based psychotherapies for children and adolescents* (2nd ed., pp. 277–292). New York, NY: Guilford Press.

Pelham, W. E., & Hoza, B. (1996). Intensive treatment: A summer program for children with ADHD. In E. D. Hibbs & P. S. Jensen (Eds.), *Psychosocial treatments for child and adolescent disorders: Empirically based strategies for clinical practice* (pp. 311–340). Washington, DC: American Psychological Association.

Pincus, D. B., Ehrenreich, J. T., & Mattis, S. G. (2008). *Mastery of your anxiety and panic for adolescents: Riding the wave, therapist guide.* New York, NY: Oxford University Press.

Reyno, S. M., & McGrath, P. J. (2006). Predictors of parent training efficacy for child externalizing behavior problem—a meta-analytic review. *Journal of Child Psychology and Psychiatry, 47,* 99–111. doi: 10.1111/j.1469–7610.2005.01544.x

Ritterband, L. M., Thorndike, F. P., Cox, D. J., Kovatchev, B. P., & Gonder-Frederick, L. A. (2009). A behavior change model for Internet interventions. *Annals of Behavior Medicine, 38*(1), 18–27. doi: 10.1007/s12160-009-9133-4

Rogers, E. M. (2003). *Diffusion of innovations* (5th ed.). New York, NY: Free Press.

Sandler, I. N., Ostrom, A., Bitner, M. J., Ayers, T. S., & Wolchik, S. (2005). Developing effective prevention services for the real world: A prevention service development model. *American Journal of Community Psychology, 35,* 127–142.

Santucci, L., Ehrenreich, J. T., Trosper, S. E., Bennett, S. M., & Pincus, D. B. (2009). Development and preliminary evaluation of a one-week summer treatment program for separation anxiety disorder. *Cognitive and Behavioral Practice, 16,* 317–331. doi: 10.1016/j.cbpra.2008.12.005

Santucci, L. C., & Ehrenreich-May, J. (2010, November). A one-week summer treatment program for children with separation anxiety disorder: Results of a randomized controlled trial. In K. P. Gallo & D. B. Pincus (Chairs), *Innovative formats of CBT for child anxiety: Efficacy, feasibility, and acceptability.* Symposium conducted at the 44th annual convention of the Association for Behavioral and Cognitive Therapies, San Francisco, CA.

Sibley, M. H., Smith, B. H., Evans, S. W., Pelham, W. E., & Gnagy, E. M. (2012). Treatment response to an intensive summer treatment program for adolescents with ADHD. *Journal of Attention Disorders, 16*(6), 443–448. doi: 10.1177/1087054711433424

Silverman, W. K., & Hinshaw, S. P. (2008). The second special issue of evidence-based psychosocial treatments for children and adolescents: A 10-year update. *Journal of Clinical Child and Adolescent Psychology, 37*(1), 1–7. doi: 10.1080/15374410701817725

Snider, M. (2011). *A quarter of American homes have hung up on landlines.* Retrieved from http://www.usatoday.com/tech/news/2011–04–20-cellphone-study.htm

Spence, S. H., Donovan, C. L., March, S., Gamble, A., Anderson, R. E., Prosser, S., & Kenardy, J. (2011). A randomized controlled trial of online versus clinic-based CBT for adolescent anxiety. *Journal of Consulting and Clinical Psychology, 79*(5), 629–642. doi: 10.1037/a0024512

Spence, S. H., Holmes, J. M., March, S., & Lipp, O. V. (2006). The feasibility and outcome of clinic plus internet delivery of cognitive-behavior therapy for childhood anxiety. *Journal of Consulting and Clinical Psychology, 74,* 614–621. doi: 10.1037/0022–006X.74.3.614

Storch, E. A., Caporino, N. E., Morgan, J. R., Lewin, A. B., Rojas, A., Brauer, L., . . . Murphy, T. K. (2011). Preliminary investigation of web-camera delivered cognitive-behavioral therapy for youth with obsessive-compulsive disorder. *Psychiatry Research, 189*(3), 407–412. doi: 10.1016/j.psychres.2011.05.047

Storch, E. A., Geffken, G. R., Adkins, J. W., Murphy, T. K., & Goodman, W. K. (2007). Sequential cognitive-behavioral psychotherapy for children with obsessive-compulsive disorder with an inadequate medication response: A case series of five patients. *Depression and Anxiety, 24,* 375–381. doi: 10.1002/da.20260

Storch, E. A., Geffken, G. R., Merlo, L. J., Mann, G., Duke, D., Munson, M., . . . Goodman, W. K. (2007). Family-based cognitive-behavioral therapy for pediatric obsessive-compulsive disorder: Comparison of intensive and weekly approaches. *Journal of the American Academy of Child & Adolescent Psychiatry, 26,* 469–478. doi: 10.1097/chi.0b013e31803062e7

Storch, E. A., Merlo, L. J., Lehmkuhl, H., Geffken, G. R., Jacob, M., Ricketts, E., . . . Goodman, W. K. (2008). Cognitive-behavioral therapy for obsessive-compulsive disorder: A non-randomized comparison of intensive and weekly approaches. *Journal of Anxiety Disorders, 22,* 1146–1158. doi: 10.1016/j.janxdis.2007.12.001

Sullivan, G., Craske, M. G., Sherbourne, C., Edlund, M. J., Rose, R. D., Golinelli, D., . . . Roy-Byrne, P. P. (2007). Design of the coordinated anxiety learning and management (CALM) study: Innovations in collaborative care for anxiety disorders. *General Hospital Psychiatry, 29,* 379–387. doi: 10.1016/j.genhosppsych.2007.04.005

Tate, D. F., Finkelstein, E. A., Khavjou, O., & Gustafson, A. (2009). Cost effectiveness of internet interventions: Review and recommendations. *Annals of Behavioral Medicine, 38,* 40–45. doi: 10.1007/s12160–009–9131–6

Taylor, S., & Clark, D. A. (2009). Transdiagnostic cognitive-behavioral treatments for mood and anxiety disorders: Introduction to the special issue. *Journal of Cognitive Psychotherapy, 23,* 3–5. doi: 10.1891/0889–8391.23.1.3

Tolin, D. F., Whiting, S., Maltby, N., Diefenbach, G. J., Lothstein, M. A., Hardcastle, S., . . . Gray, C. (2009). Intensive (daily) behavior therapy for school refusal: A multiple baseline case series. *Cognitive and Behavioral Practice, 16*(3), 332–344. doi: 10.1016/j.cbpra.2009.02.003

U.S. Census Bureau. (2012). *Computer and Internet use in the United States: 2010.* Retrieved from http://www.census.gov/hhes/computer/publications/2010.html

Weersing, V., Rozenman, M. S., Maher-Bridge, M., & Campo, J. V. (2012). Anxiety, depression, and somatic distress: Developing a transdiagnostic internalizing toolbox for pediatric practice. *Cognitive and Behavioral Practice, 19,* 68–82. doi: 10.1016/j.cbpra.2011.06.002

Weisz, J. R., Chorpita, B. F., Palinkas, L. A., Schoenwald, S. K., Miranda, J., Bearman, S. K., . . . Gibbons, R. D. (2012). Testing standard and modular designs for psychotherapy with youth depression, anxiety, and conduct problems: A randomized effectiveness trial. *Archives of General Psychiatry, 69,* 274–282. doi: 10.1001/archgenpsychiatry.2011.147

Weisz, J. R., & Kazdin, A. E. (2010). *Evidence-based psychotherapies for children and adolescents* (2nd ed.). New York, NY: Guilford Press.

Weisz, J. R., Sandler, I. N., Durlak, J. A., & Anton, B. S (2005). Promoting and protecting youth mental health through evidence-based prevention and treatment. *American Psychologist, 60,* 628–648. doi: 10.1037/0003–066X.60.6.628

Whiteside, S. P., Brown, A. M., & Abramowitz, J. S. (2008). Five-day intensive treatment for adolescents OCD: A case series. *Journal of Anxiety Disorders, 22,* 495–504. doi: 10.1016/j.janxdis.2007.05.001

Wilamowska, Z. A., Thompson-Hollands, J., Fairholme, C. P., Ellard, K. K., Farchione, T. J., & Barlow, D. H. (2010). Conceptual background, development, and preliminary data from the unified protocol for transdiagnostic treatment of emotional disorders. *Depression and Anxiety, 27,* 882–890. doi: 10.1002/da.20735

Wuthrich, V. M., Rapee, R. M., Cunningham, M. J., Lyneham, H. J., Hudson, J. L., & Schniering, C. A. (2012). A randomized controlled trial of the Cool Teens CD-ROM computerized program for adolescent anxiety. *Journal of the American Academy of Child & Adolescent Psychiatry, 51*(3), 261–270. doi: 10.1016/j.jaac.2011.12.002

CHAPTER 6

Dissemination and Implementation of Evidence-Based Treatments for Children and Adolescents

MICHAEL A. SOUTHAM-GEROW, CASSIDY C. ARNOLD, CARRIE B. TULLY, AND JULIA REVILLION COX

The field of psychological science has made enormous progress developing and testing psychological and combined medication/psychological treatments to address the increasing prevalence of psychopathology in children (e.g., Hoagwood & Olin, 2002). Indeed, a recent review found more than 350 randomized controlled trials testing treatments for childhood mental health problems (Chorpita, Bernstein, & Daleiden, 2011). However, there remains a significant number of children not receiving adequate treatments (e.g., Fulda, Lykens, Bae, & Singh, 2009; Tang et al., 2008), a reminder of the oft-lamented science–practice gap (e.g., U.S. Department of Health and Human Services, 2002). Researchers and other children's mental health stakeholders have identified dissemination and implementation (D&I) of psychological treatments as a key goal for the field (e.g., Aarons, Hurlburt, & Horwitz, 2011; Proctor et al., 2009; Schoenwald & Hoagwood, 2001; Southam-Gerow, Rodriguez, Chorpita, & Daleiden, 2012). This chapter provides an overview of the D&I field related to child and adolescent mental health treatment and services research. Specifically, we provide a brief conceptual primer related to D&I science; provide a succinct rationale for why D&I has emerged as a focus; outline several prominent D&I models; and describe some recent empirical D&I studies.

CONCEPTUAL PRIMER ON DISSEMINATION AND IMPLEMENTATION

Given the relative novelty of D&I science, there is not yet absolute convergence on the definition of key terms. Our definitions are based on a careful reading of the literature, with particular emphasis on the work of Chambers, Ringeisen, and Hickman (2005); Fixsen, Naoom, Blasé, Friedman, and Wallace (2005); Proctor et al. (2009); and Rabin and Brownson (2012).

First, we provide some clarification of three terms that are similar but distinct: diffusion, dissemination, and implementation. The term "diffusion" means the planned or unplanned/spontaneous spread of an innovation. In other words, "diffusion" refers to both the *natural* distribution of a new idea and the more intentional spread of that idea (Chambers et al., 2005; Rogers, 2003). The term "dissemination" refers to the *directed* and *planned* spread of an innovation or, as Chambers et al. (2005) wrote, the "targeted distribution of a well designed set of information" (p. 323). Because dissemination involves the consistent spread or distribution of information, such as a treatment approach, the process of dissemination involves identifying ways to communicate the innovation to maximize its consistent and accurate receipt by the desired end users.

Finally, the term "implementation" refers to the processes and strategies needed to adapt the innovation (e.g., a treatment program) to fit within a specific context. This definition of implementation is similar to that provided by Fixsen et al. (2005) in their treatise on implementation research: "a specified set of activities designed to put into practice an activity or program of known dimensions" (p. 5). Fixsen et al. also distinguished among different degrees of implementation, ranging from paper (i.e., enacting policies consistent with the innovation), to process (i.e., creating procedures that enable training and supervision in the use of a new innovation), to performance implementation (i.e., creating procedures that identify ways to ensure that the innovation is being used properly *and* that its use is having the expected consequence—that is, benefit for the consumer). It bears mention that others have used the term in a more proximal sense to mean the enactment of a specific treatment approach or treatment strategy, thereby creating some confusion about this term. In general, in the context of D&I science, the term "implementation" has a broader sense and refers to the processes used to bring a program (or other innovation) into a new context. Thus, dissemination involves spreading the word about an innovation, whereas implementation involves specific processes and procedures designed to improve the adoption, correct use, and sustainment of the innovation in a specific place. In short, implementation is the *how* of dissemination.

A few other terms often used in relation to D&I research warrant brief mention. The term "technology transfer" has long been applied to the process of taking scientific findings and adapting them to have broader applications for public use and/or for sale in the commercial sector. Along these lines, then, D&I research can represent a specific example of technology transfer. Additionally, the term "translational research" is used to refer to work that translates "bench science" for the bedside (and vice versa), a process that fits with the aims of D&I science.

WHY IS DISSEMINATION AND IMPLEMENTATION SCIENCE NEEDED?

It is noteworthy that a dictionary of terms is needed for dissemination and implementation. Obviously, the field of treatment of child/adolescent mental health problems is not a build-it-and-they-will-come context. Simple dissemination efforts like publishing papers and generating lists of evidence-based treatments (EBTs) have not been sufficient methods for widespread adoption of EBTs. D&I science has emerged because of the need to identify ways to implement treatments in a variety of settings. But why have simple dissemination strategies failed? That is, why has strong evidence about potent treatments for child/adolescent mental health problems not generated a mass effort on the part of therapists and agencies to adopt these treatments? In this section, we grapple with this question.

Most treatment programs are developed for a single, specific child disorder (e.g., obsessive-compulsive disorder) or problem type (e.g., disruptive behavior). The focus on a single child problem is consistent with decades of medical research and has led to incredible and important developments in the science of mental health treatment for children and adolescents. However, as the field has moved toward widespread dissemination of treatments developed in this manner, some limitations of the approach have become apparent. Specifically, multiple factors beyond the child's disorder appear to influence how potent a treatment will be, as has been described by several scientists (e.g., Damschroder & Hagedorn, 2011; Fixsen et al., 2005; Proctor et al., 2009; Schoenwald & Hoagwood, 2001; Southam-Gerow et al., 2012). For example, Southam-Gerow et al. (2012) describe an array of factors that may have an impact on how well a treatment works in a particular setting; these include child and family factors, therapist factors, organization factors, and service system factors. We review each of these briefly and discuss how they might function as barriers to simple dissemination strategies.

Child and Family Factors

A number of child- and family-specific variables can influence how well psychological treatments for youth work. Many of these variables are largely neglected as targets of treatment and/or remain underrepresented within efficacy study samples. Past research efforts across different primary diagnoses have demonstrated that children served by community clinics often present with comorbidities, impaired academic and social functioning, and other stressors (Ehrenreich-May et al., 2011; Southam-Gerow, Chorpita, Miller, & Gleacher, 2008; Weersing & Weisz, 2002), factors that are often unaddressed by manualized treatments (Hammen, Rudolph, Weisz, Rao, & Burge, 1999). When compared to those referred to university-based research clinics, children receiving services in the community are more likely to have parents with less education (Southam-Gerow et al., 2008) and lower incomes (Ehrenreich-May et al., 2011). Single-parent families are also more frequent among this population (Southam-Gerow, Weisz, & Kendall, 2003), and, even when controlling for geographic differences, ethnic minority families are overrepresented (Ehrenreich-May et al., 2011). Echoing these findings, one study of youth receiving school-based services found higher rates of trauma and past suicide attempts when compared to efficacy studies (Shirk, Kaplinski, & Gudmundsen, 2009), highlighting the many ways that clinical complications can impede successful child outcomes. These client and family variable differences have contributed to the rise of D&I science.

Therapist Factors

Efficacy studies attempt to ensure the integrity and maximize the dose of a given treatment by employing therapists who are specially trained and receive ongoing supervision and consultation (usually doctoral-level students/professionals). In contrast, master's-level therapists with varied training backgrounds comprise the majority of the workforce in community mental health settings (Garland, Kruse, & Aarons, 2003; Weisz, Chu, & Polo, 2004). This difference may influence how an EBT will fare when transported to community settings for a variety of reasons. Community providers' motivation to learn and use EBTs is variable: Several studies have documented clinicians' concerns that manualized treatments are inflexible and inhibit individualized case conceptualization and treatment planning (Addis & Krasnow, 2000; Becker, Zayfert, & Anderson, 2004; Walrath, Sheehan, Holden, Hernandez, & Blau, 2006). While openness to and knowledge about EBTs may facilitate the implementation at the therapist level (Aarons, McDonald, Sheehan, & Walrath-Greene, 2007), recent surveys of the attitudes of community-based clinicians toward evidence-based practice have not revealed consistent correlates by theoretical orientation, training, or years of experience (Nakamura, Higa-McMillan, Okamura, & Shimabukuro, 2011).

Yet another element to consider is the limited effectiveness of specialized training in EBTs. Self-directed learning and workshops, both in person and online, are by far the most popular training vehicles: Several studies have documented significant gains in clinician knowledge and self-reported efficacy (see Beidas & Kendall, 2010, for a review). There is, however, very little evidence that these methods result in substantive behavioral change (Beidas & Kendall, 2010; Herschell, Kolko, Baumann, & Davis, 2010). However, the use of behavioral strategies, including observation, feedback, ongoing consultation, and coaching, has been shown to increase EBT adoption and impact client outcomes (Becker & Stirman, 2011; Herschell et al., 2010).

Organizational Factors

Therapists within the community are often part of an agency or organization, each with its own unique characteristics and culture that can influence the successful implementation of EBTs.

As Glisson et al. (2012) discuss, *organizational climate* (e.g., norms, expectations) and policies drive clinician behavior (e.g., willingness and ability to pursue training opportunities, or resistance) and attitudes (e.g., job satisfaction, morale). Beyond the diffuse impact on therapist attitudes and behavior, organizations are integral to successful implementation of EBTs in these ways:

- Leading the implementation process through goal setting, planning, and task operationalization
- Involving other stakeholders in EBT selection
- Creating an implementation task force or committee to oversee the process
- Involving consultants and reinforcing organizational change
- Allocating resources for implementation tasks
- Integrating implementation goals into human resource sectors
- Facilitating the training and development of management and support staff
- Committing resources to support ongoing implementation activities (Fixsen et al., 2005)

This organizational infrastructure supports ongoing training, fidelity monitoring, and supervision/coaching in an effort to sustain meaningful change (Fixsen et al., 2005).

System Factors

Just as therapists work within the parameters of an organization, all community mental health organizations are subject to influences at the system level, what Aarons et al. (2011) refer to as the *outer context*. These influences include relevant local, state, and federal policies; the availability and priorities of funding sources (e.g., public and private insurance, community resources); referral mechanisms; legal obligations or mandates; relationships with other agencies and organizations; and the needs of local mental health consumers (Fixsen et al., 2005; Schoenwald & Hoagwood, 2001). These distal variables can have profound influence on implementation efforts (e.g., Aarons & Sommerfeld, 2012; Metz & Bartley, 2012).

Thus, the short answer to why the field has strongly emphasized D&I science in recent years is that myriad complex factors can influence whether and how EBTs (or any new treatment or other innovation) are used in community settings. Developing methods to implement EBTs in community settings, thereby maximizing the public health benefits of our considerable science on treatments, represents the focus of D&I science. Given the complex nature of this work, there has been effort to identify models and frameworks to guide work. In the next section, we consider the most influential current models.

MODELS OF DISSEMINATION

As reflected in the previous section, the challenges facing the dissemination and implementation of psychological interventions in community practices are numerous. As a result, the availability of EBTs, directives to use EBTs, and other "push" forces (i.e., forces on the research side of the science–practice gap) seem to be insufficient on their own (e.g., Proctor et al., 2009; Southam-Gerow et al., 2012). At the same time, "pull" forces (i.e., forces on the community side of the gap), such as patients requesting a particular EBT or practitioners requesting training in, organizational support for, and reimbursement of EBT, do not seem to occur organically at a sufficient strength to promote a high rate of dissemination and implementation of EBTs.

The sophistication of D&I research and the models that describe them is at an interesting stage. On one hand, the development of D&I models and their use in D&I projects, along with measures of the key variables within models, increases the interpretability of findings from these efforts (Tabak, Khoong, Chambers, & Brownson, 2012). However, the abundance of models and their relative lack of empirical evaluation mean that it is currently impossible to definitively support the use of one model over another (Proctor et al., 2009). To move beyond this stage, for the empirical support to grow and support the use of the best models, more D&I projects that use and compare models with strong research designs are needed.

The remainder of this section describes six D&I models, selected because they demonstrate the breadth of characteristics within the D&I models:

1. Rogers' diffusion of innovations theory (2003)
2. Fixsen et al.'s conceptual framework of implementation (2005)
3. The mental health systems ecological model (e.g., Schoenwald & Hoagwood, 2001; Southam-Gerow et al., 2012)
4. Proctor et al.'s implementation research model (2009)
5. Aarons et al.'s multilevel, multiphase implementation model (2011)
6. Meyers, Durlak, and Wandersman's quality implementation framework (2012)

Rogers' Diffusion of Innovations Model

Rogers' (2003) diffusion of innovations model is the broadest one presented here and was not originally developed to explain or understand the dissemination of mental health treatments. The model describes the spreading of an idea, practice, or object that is new or perceived to be new to the unit of adoption (e.g., individuals, therapists, hospitals, etc.) through a social system. Within this model, the term "diffusion" refers to the ways an idea moves through a social system via communication between parts or individuals within the system (Rogers, 2003). Unlike the other models discussed in this section, the four factors in Rogers' model do not explicitly include (or prohibit) effortful processes or require individuals who actively drive the innovation into new areas. That is, the model emphasizes both intentional implementation efforts as well as less (or even un-) intentional dissemination of innovations. The four primary factors emphasized in Rogers' model are:

1. The innovation and its characteristics
   Important aspects of the innovation include: (a) the innovation's perceived *relative advantages* over the idea, practice, or object that is being replaced; (b) the *compatibility* of the innovation with established values and needs of the adopters; (c) the *complexity* or perceived difficulty of using the innovation; (d) the *trialability* of the innovation (i.e., the degree to which the innovation can be used on a trial basis) versus the degree to which adopters must fully commit to adoption; and (e) the *observability* or visibility of beneficial outcomes (Rogers, 2003). All of these characteristics have clear application to EBTs.
2. Channels of communication within the social system
3. Time
4. The social system

The communication channels through which information can spread also influence the dissemination of an innovation. Different communication channels (e.g., mass media and interpersonal channels) spread information at different rates, reach different potential adopters, and influence the adopter differently. Time, in Rogers' model, refers to the lapse between when adopters first learn of an innovation and when they decide to adopt or reject the innovation, the earliness or lateness of adoption versus other members of the system, and the rate at which adoption takes place across the system.

The fourth and final major factor is the social system: the complete collection of potential adopters of a given innovation (Rogers, 2003). Within the mental health field, this may be therapists within a community or practice, community mental health centers, localities and states establishing policy relevant to mental health treatment, and/or insurance companies that pay for mental health services. According to Rogers, key aspects of social systems, such as local norms and key opinion leaders, significantly influence the rate of diffusion within them.

Although not originally developed with mental health services in mind, Rogers' model has important implications for D&I efforts. For example, consider the fact that the design of an EBT (i.e., more versus less flexible) appears to influence potential adopters' perception of that EBT as well as the outcomes achieved by those adopters (Borntrager, Chorpita, Higa-McMillan, & Weisz, 2009; Weisz et al., 2012). The therapist training literature described earlier (e.g., Beidas & Kendall, 2010; Herschell et al., 2010) supports the importance of Rogers' notion of communication channels. Finally, key opinion leaders (i.e., influential individuals within their social network and whose behavior serves as a model for others) have been found to be instrumental in the implementation of teacher-delivered mental health interventions in schools serving low-income minority children with behavioral problems (Atkins et al., 2008).

Fixsen et al.'s Implementation Framework

In their 2005 monograph, Fixsen and colleagues synthesized the dissemination and implementation literature from diverse fields in an effort to provide both an overarching theoretical framework and a concrete step-by-step description of the implementation process, with an eye toward applying their findings to mental health services. While the authors pull broadly from the human services and technology fields, their model for implementation occurs within the context of a specific community (e.g., agency, city) that has unique needs, assets, and challenges.

The broad "conceptual framework" for implementation of programs or practices includes five essential components:

1. A *source*, the innovation to be implemented as originally conceived by the developers
2. A *destination*, both the individual professional and the community that implements the programs and practices
3. A *communication link*, those individuals (or "purveyors") who actively work to efficiently implement a defined innovation with fidelity
4. A *feedback mechanism*, an ongoing mechanism that provides each level of the organization with feedback
5. The combined *influences* of the *myriad proximal and distal* factors that affect any one involved person or system (e.g., insurance policies, national funding priorities)

Building on the work of Rogers and others, Fixsen et al. (2005) also delineate more concrete stages of the implementation model that describes six categories:

1. *Exploration and adoption*, in which an organization assesses its needs and resources and identifies an intervention program to meet those needs
2. *Program installation*, in which an organization makes structural changes in preparation for implementation of the chosen intervention program (e.g., training and/or hiring staff, creating referral mechanisms, planning evaluation strategies)

3. *Initial implementation*, in which organizational change struggles to build momentum, stymied by the "compelling forces of fear of change, inertia, and investment in the status quo" (p. 16)
4. *Full operation*, in which the intervention program becomes embedded within the organization, from individual practitioners to organization policy
5. *Innovation*, in which an organization uses its collective expertise to refine the intervention, while being careful to monitor program fidelity
6. *Sustainability*, in which an organization is able to shift with inevitable changes (e.g., staff turnover, funding priorities) while continuing to provide the intervention program with fidelity

Along with a thorough review of implementation research efforts, Fixsen et al. (2005) also identify core intervention and implementation components. Core intervention components include the "active ingredients," the essential techniques and principles of the treatment program being implemented. Similarly, core implementation components are the elements that contribute to the successful implementation of a program with fidelity. These components include training and consultation, selection of staff to directly implement the treatment model, monitoring treatment fidelity, and evaluating program outcomes.

Mental Health Systems Ecological Model

The mental health systems ecological (MHSE) model was developed explicitly with children's mental health services in mind. As discussed earlier, multiple factors influence how potent a treatment will be in treating a child's mental health problems. The MHSE model (e.g., Schoenwald & Hoagwood, 2001; Southam-Gerow et al., 2012; Southam-Gerow, Ringeisen, & Sherrill, 2006) specifically outlines the importance of four different levels of the ecology to consider when planning D&I science: (1) child and family factors, (2) therapist factors, (3) organization factors, and (4) service system factors. As will be clearer shortly, this broad ecological approach is consistent with other models (e.g., Aarons et al., 2011; Damschroder & Hagedorn, 2011; Fixsen et al., 2005; Proctor et al., 2009).

The MHSE model posits that implementation efforts should be designed with the key variables at one or more of these levels in mind. For example, given the possibility of therapist opposition to a particular EBT (e.g., Aarons, Wells, Zagursky, Fettes, & Palinkas, 2009), some D&I researchers have emphasized the use of partnership approaches to build collaboration from the outset of an implementation effort (e.g., Baptiste et al., 2007; Fox, Mattek, & Gresl, 2013; Southam-Gerow, Hourigan, & Allin, 2009). Others have used organization-level interventions to influence EBT uptake (e.g., Glisson et al., 2010) or have been able to synergize EBT implementation efforts with system-wide financing changes (e.g., Southam-Gerow et al., in press).

Proctor et al.'s Implementation Research Model

Proctor and colleagues (2009) aimed to use a review of earlier models to develop a broader D&I model. In contrast to the assumption that the progression from intervention development through evaluation to dissemination and implementation was unidirectional, the model that they proposed accounted for nonlinear movement through these stages. Next, similar to the MHSE model, their model addressed the multilevel nature of the forces on dissemination and implementation by accounting for the influence of variables at four levels: (1) large system/environment, (2) organization, (3) group/team, and (4) individual. Finally, their model included multiple outcome domains. Whereas client outcomes (e.g., symptom reduction and improved well-being) are the most important for any mental health or social service innovation, measuring other forms of outcomes, such as implementation outcomes (e.g., treatment integrity and feasibility) and service outcomes (e.g., safety and efficiency) allows for analysis of the innovation's success within the larger system and potential mediators and moderators of success.

Aarons et al.'s Multilevel, Multiphase Implementation Model

Aarons and colleagues (2011) carefully reviewed research in the fields of mental health, health care, public health, organizational development, and business that addresses moving practices from research settings to practice to develop their multiphase, multilevel model. They identified four phases to guide D&I science: (1) exploration, (2) adoption decision/preparation, (3) implementation, and (4) sustainment. Within each phase, they emphasize the importance of specific factors across an ecological model (cf. Fixsen et al., 2005; Proctor et al., 2009; Southam-Gerow et al., 2012): an *outer context*, an *inner context*, and *interconnections* between the outer and inner contexts. Similar factors are posited to influence the implementation of innovations at each of the four phases, although each phase also has unique factors. For example, sociopolitical context and funding sources are identified as important outer context variables within each phase, while organizational characteristics are included as inner context factors in each phase. Aarons et al. provide a description of the many outer and inner context factors at each phase; interested readers are encouraged to review their work, as a detailed description of the many variables within this model is beyond the scope of this chapter.

D&I research, including models and conceptual frameworks, can serve as the *technology* to guide the practice of spanning the research–practice gap. The models discussed here represent part of a rapidly growing literature on this science but also indicate how far this work needs to go. For example, each of the models includes variables that influence one or more stages in the process of moving a treatment from development to implementation but does not explicitly specify how to measure and modify each variable. Indeed, the breadth of these models reflects a key challenge for D&I science. As we discuss shortly, the field is in dire need of measurement tools to help assess the many levels of influence across the ecology.

Meyers et al.'s Quality Implementation Framework

Finally, we consider the recent model delineated by Meyers and colleagues (2012) as an effort to synthesize past implementation framework efforts. After a careful review of more than 150 papers, Meyers et al. identified a synthetic model containing 14 critical steps across four phases. Their first phase, called "initial considerations regarding the host setting," contains 8 of the 14 steps of the entire model, underscoring its importance. Essentially, in phase 1, three tasks are completed.

1. An assessment is conducted of the potential setting for implementation: needs and resources are gauged, the fit of the proposed intervention and the setting are considered, and the readiness of the setting is examined carefully.
2. Assuming the assessment yields a "move forward" decision, the implementation team explicitly deliberates the boundaries of adaptation allowable for the innovation.
3. The final steps in the first phase involve more intensive collaboration with relevant stakeholders to build capacity for implementation.

Phase 1 is a preparation phase, and its extensiveness underscores a theme of this chapter—that implementation is, to riff on the adage, largely about preparation (and perspiration). In phase 2, the implementation of the innovation begins. Specifically, structures are created to support the implementation: Teams that will do the work are identified, and a plan that will guide that work is crafted. The green flag is then raised, and implementation begins.

With teams and a plan in place, the process moves to phase 3, a set of steps to build lasting organizational structures with the goal of sustaining implementation. Here, technical assistance/consultation is used to help maintain innovation fidelity as well as troubleshoot obstacles. Further, a process is identified for collecting and feeding back data about the results of the work. This phase may remind the reader of findings from the training literature reviewed earlier: Ongoing consultation after an initial training may improve provider use of and fidelity with new programs (e.g., Beidas & Kendall, 2010).

Phase 4 of the Meyers et al. (2012) model asserts that, beyond sustainability of the program, implementation efforts also must include mechanisms that can help the implementation team improve. In other words, phase 4 requires that the implementation team reflect on the results of the first three phases with an eye toward questions like "What have we learned?" and "How can we keep getting better at meeting our goals/serving our mission?"

Closing with the Meyers et al. (2012) model is fitting, given their efforts to synthesize a broad literature. Readers likely noted similarities across all six models reviewed here. Indeed, although models may not converge 100% in terms of the number of phases or stages or steps needed for implementation, there is wide agreement on a few key concepts. First, there are multiple levels of influence that must be considered. Second, implementation efforts must proceed through phases. Finally, the models also converge on the notion that implementation is not a linear process: There is need for feedback and feed-forward processes to help inform stakeholders involved in and/or affected by the implementation effort. As the field continues to mature, it is possible that a single or a small number of conceptual models will become prominent. The current status of many models, all relatively new, is consistent with the relative novelty of the research field. We turn next to an illustrative review of three recent D&I studies.

RECENT EXEMPLARS OF EBT IMPLEMENTATION RESEARCH

A thorough review of all D&I efforts would require an entire volume—and indeed, the topic of D&I has been the focus of recent books (e.g., Brownson, Colditz, & Proctor, 2012). Instead, we highlight three different implementation efforts, each focused on a different aspect of the D&I process. Specifically, the studies chosen highlight adaptation of the treatment, therapist training and supervision methods, and organizational readiness.

Our first example is drawn from the programmatic work of the Research Network on Youth Mental Health Care, an effort supported by the John D. and Catherine T. MacArthur Foundation from 2001 through 2011. The work of the network was diverse and broad, although one major focus was the Child System and Treatment Enhancement Projects (Child STEPs), an initiative with the goal of bridging the science–practice gap in children's mental health in part by developing and testing dissemination strategies (e.g., Schoenwald, Kelleher, & Weisz, 2008). Child STEPs used a broad conceptual framework for dissemination that examined elements that interact with the mental health system, including governance structures, financing structures and reimbursement, provider organizations, clinical supervisors and clinicians, and treatment and service content (Schoenwald et al., 2008). For the purposes of this chapter, however, we focus solely on the Clinic Treatment Project (CTP), a randomized controlled trial designed to ascertain whether modularized EBT would produce superior outcomes in a community setting compared to standard manual treatment and usual care. The focus of the CTP was EBTs for children and adolescents with anxiety, depression, and disruptive behavior problems. Three different treatments for each of three different problem areas (i.e., nine study arms) were included. The three broad treatment groups were (1) modular manualized treatment (MMT), (2) standard manualized treatment (SMT), and (3) usual care. For MMT, there was a single manual regardless of problem type: the Modular Approach to Therapy for Children with Anxiety, Depression, or Conduct Problems (MATCH) (Chorpita, Daleiden, & Weisz, 2005). For SMT, there was a different program for each of the three problem types: (1) anxiety—Coping Cat (Kendall, 1994); (2) depression—Primary and Secondary Enhancement Training (Weisz, Thurber, Sweeney, Proffitt, & LeGagnoux, 1997), and (3) disruptive behavior—Defiant Child (Barkley, 1997). The final treatment group was usual care.

A key element of the design of the trial was the difference between MMT and SMT. Both represented manualized treatments based on years of scientific evidence. SMT involved three different treatment manuals, each with a set order of contents. MMT, however, involved a more flexible approach. Comprised of a single manual, MMT provided the therapist with a default decision flowchart to guide treatment, with optional modules to address common treatment interference issues. As one example, a client with primary anxiety would receive specific anxiety interventions (psychoeducation, fear ladder, exposure). However, if client disruptive behavior interfered with treatment, the therapist, in consultation with his/her supervisor, could consider adding one or more modules from those targeting disruptive behaviors (e.g., parent praise, time out).

In the study, MMT, SMT, and usual care were compared. First, clinicians from across multiple agencies and two states were randomly assigned to one of the three treatment conditions; those assigned to SMT or MMT received extensive training and supervision in the models. Youth with primary problems related to anxiety, depression, or disruptive behavior were randomly assigned to one of the three conditions. Trajectories of change were measured through weekly collection of brief measures of youth psychopathology and measures of progress on specific areas identified as problematic (see Weisz et al., 2012). In the end, youth receiving MMT improved faster at clinically and statistically significant rates as compared to youth receiving SMT. Advantages of MMT over usual care were even more pronounced and included fewer diagnoses at posttreatment (Weisz et al., 2012). A 2-year follow-up study reported continued superiority of MMT over usual care (Chorpita et al., 2013). As noted earlier, these findings support the notion that design of the treatment (i.e., allowing for flexibility) may influence not only therapist perception of the intervention but the outcomes achieved (see also Stewart, Stirman, & Chambless, 2012). Overall, the work of the Child STEPs team is exemplary of adapting EBTs in community settings.

A second example involves a study focused on training and supervision of therapists. Chamberlain, Price, Reid, and Landsverk (2008) presented a study focusing on the supervisor's role using a cascaded training model to implement a multidimensional training for foster care parents. This study involved testing the transferability of multidimensional treatment foster care from a research-based setting to foster parents in San Diego County. The effects of treatment on child outcomes were examined during two phases of implementation: (1) comparing training with and without the treatment development team present, and (2) a cascaded training (i.e., training the trainer) model.

There were three phases of intervention developer involvement in this project. In phase 1, treatment developers supervised experienced foster parents who delivered treatment to foster family participants. In phase 2, paraprofessionals provided the training, with weekly in-person supervision from an on-site supervisor and phone supervision from a clinical consultant treatment developer. In phase 3, the paraprofessional staff from phase 2 trained a new cohort of paraprofessionals, with no direct contact between the treatment developers and the second cohort of interventionists. Developers provided regular supervision of the first cohort of paraprofessionals' training for the second cohort. Results showed no significant differences in child behavior problems between phases 2 and 3 of the study, supporting the use of the cascade approach. The study suggests that third-generation interventionists with no direct contact with treatment developers are able, with training and continued supervision, to deliver treatment.

Our final example concerns a study focused at the level of the organization. Through years of foundational work, Glisson and colleagues have demonstrated the influence of organizational characteristics such as organizational climate and organizational culture on D&I efforts (e.g., Hemmelgarn, Glisson, & James, 2006; Glisson & James, 2002). In a randomized controlled trial, Glisson et al. (2010) tested the benefits of an organizational intervention in implementing an EBT in community-based mental health services in rural Tennessee. In the study, there were two levels of randomization: (1) children assigned to either multisystemic therapy (MST) or usual services; and (2) counties assigned to receive a dissemination intervention or usual services.

At the individual level, the study compared MST to usual services for 615 youth referred to juvenile court for status offenses or delinquent behavior. MST is an empirically supported treatment for youth delinquency that targets each level of a child's ecological system: family, peers, school, neighborhood, and community (Henggeler, Schoenwald, Borduin, Rowland, & Cunningham, 2009). The system randomization involved the 14 rural counties assigned either to an organizational intervention called availability, responsiveness, and continuity (ARC; $n = 6$ counties) or to a "usual services" comparison ($n = 8$ counties). The ARC intervention is guided by three assumptions making up the social context of mental health services: (1) Implementation of any new technology, including evidence-based treatment, includes social and technical processes; (2) mental health services exist within a social context; and (3) treatment effectiveness is determined by how well the social context supports the goals of the new technology (Glisson & Schoenwald, 2005). In this way, ARC is designed to address barriers between a specific community and specific mental health service technology, by focusing the community on the problem area, building community support for change, creating alliances between providers and stakeholders, and developing a social context for effective services (Glisson & Schoenwald, 2005).

ARC is a complex intervention, comprised of 12 components across three stages, made explicit and replicable via a manual (Glisson, 2009; Glisson, Dukes, & Green, 2006). Stage 1 is collaboration, wherein ARC specialists support the organizational leadership's use of the ARC model and set high performance standards, cultivate personal relationships with key stakeholders, and access and develop networks for collaboration (Glisson et al., 2006). Stage 2, participation, consists of:

- Building teamwork
- Training about the intervention model
- Creation of a feedback system to monitor implementation and outcome variables
- Establishment of a participatory decision-making process
- Focus on resolving conflicts across organizational levels

The last stage, innovation, includes:

- Developing goal-setting procedures
- Using short- and long-term goals
- Using feedback systems
- Implementation of continued quality improvement techniques
- Revision of job characteristics
- Provision of training and information to contribute to continuous self-regulation and improvement

In short, the study used a 2×2 factorial design allowing for comparisons of youth receiving MST within ARC implementation systems and youth receiving MST in counties without ARC implementation. MST fidelity, efficiency of therapeutic effort, and MST treatment outcomes (e.g., psychosocial and systems level) were monitored. Results revealed that youth who received MST in the ARC counties improved at a faster rate during treatment, resulting in significant differences at 6-month treatment outcomes. While scores on behavioral checklists showed no difference at 18 months, individuals in the MST condition in ARC counties were less likely to enter out-of-home placement. The interaction of MST plus ARC implementation suggests that changes in the organizational and community social contexts for individuals led to change, rather than changes in therapist fidelity to MST treatment. Overall, the study provides an excellent example of a D&I focus on the level of organizational change as a facilitator of EBT adoption and use.

Each of the three different D&I studies emphasizes a focus at a different level of the ecology in which children's mental health services is situated. Each study demonstrated the great promise of D&I science, and there is hope that the gap between science and practice will lessen.

CONCLUSION

The public health importance of addressing children's mental health needs cannot be overstated. The future of our society has always depended on children. Research on treatment in the latter part of the 20th century was pivotal in moving our field forward. We now have a wealth of data on hundreds of different treatment programs addressing a variety of clinical problems (e.g., Chorpita et al., 2011). As this chapter has made clear, one of the critical challenges facing the field in the early part of the 21st century concerns how best to leverage the evidence base we have accumulated to meet the diverse and changing needs of children and families across a variety of contexts. D&I research represents an excellent path forward in this direction. Given the multifarious ways that D&I research can be conducted, we are hopeful that despite the challenges, our science will continue to generate innovations that improve the lives of children and families. We conclude the chapter by briefly describing several future directions for current and future D&I research.

All of the D&I models reviewed earlier explicitly or implicitly involved measurement of various processes relevant to implementation. For example, the Meyers et al. (2012) model involves measurement throughout all four of their implementation phases. The good news is that there is reasonable measurement for some of the key variables for implementation. Specifically, there are a bevy of measures of child symptoms and functioning (see Klein, Dougherty, & Olino, 2005; McKinney & Morse, 2012; Southam-Gerow & Chorpita, 2007) as well as measures of parent and family characteristics (see Alderfer et al., 2008; Smith, 2011). Although there are a growing number of measures of therapist variables, such as attitudes, there is much less research in this area (see Aarons, 2004; Nakamura et al., 2011). For example, McLeod, Southam-Gerow, Bair Tully, Rodriguez, and Smith (2013) and Sburlati, Schniering, Lyneham, and Rapee (2011) have recently highlighted the relevance of measuring aspects of treatment integrity (e.g., adherence, competence) for D&I efforts. When measuring constructs beyond client and therapist, the evidence base also is growing but still relatively sparse. For example, there have been strong efforts to develop measures for gauging an organization's readiness for implementation (Glisson, 2007; Hemmelgarn et al., 2006). However, measurement remains a key gap in the D&I literature and represents a significant growth industry in the coming years (e.g., Aarons et al., 2011; Newhouse, Bobay, Dykes, Stevens, & Titler, 2013; Proctor & Brownson, 2012).

Another common theme across the D&I models reviewed in this chapter is the paramount importance to implementation efforts of collaboration with stakeholders. Partnership and collaborative research has been promoted across diverse public health concerns for decades (e.g., Adelman & Taylor, 2004; Harper, Bangi, Contreras, Pedraza, Tolliver, & Vess, 2004; Radda, Schensul, Disch, Levy, & Reyes, 2003; Stein et al., 2002). Such partnership approaches have now become much more common in children's mental health research (e.g., Becker, Stice, Shaw, & Woda, 2009), focusing on child welfare (e.g., Aarons, Sommerfeld, Hecht, Silovsky, & Chaffin, 2009), mental health (e.g., Southam-Gerow et al., 2009), or other community (e.g., Stahmer, Brookman-Frazee, Lee, Searcy, & Reed, 2011) contexts. Given the potential for stakeholders at different levels of the system to influence implementation efforts, partnership research is another key growth industry for D&I scientists.

Taking a systems-level view of the challenges facing D&I science, assume for a minute you are the director of a large organization providing children's mental health services that serves thousands of children and families annually. Like many state governments, yours has strongly urged mental health organizations to deliver EBTs, and there is talk of tying funding to use of EBTs. You decide to align your organization with EBTs. How do you accomplish that goal? There are more than 100 prevention and intervention EBTs in existence (Chorpita et al., 2011), and your organization can feasibly implement only a fraction of those, given current staffing levels (i.e., you have a fixed number of therapists). To guide your choice, there are various lists and catalogs of EBTs that summarize the available options (e.g., the National Registry of Effective Practices and Programs) (Substance Abuse and Mental Health Services Administration, 2013), but little formal guidance is available for how to make the optimal selection for a particular local population. Moreover, even for highly resourced service systems, the number of EBTs that can be integrated and managed successfully is likely to be small (i.e., burden of training and maintaining a staff skilled in multiple EBTs).

Chorpita and colleagues (2011) introduced a novel method for solving that problem while leveraging the evidence base, an approach they called relevance mapping. Relevance mapping gauges the generalizability of any treatment or set of treatments to a given population. Specifically, the demographic and diagnostic data from a particular agency or organization can be mapped onto a database of the entire evidence base of randomized controlled trials. The process seeks to match each client in the system to a treatment, with the end result a solution identifying the smallest set of treatments covering the largest proportion of the children. In their paper, Chorpita et al. identified the eight additional treatments (MST was already in place in the system) that covered the maximum number of youth for the large mental health system, in this case 71%. They found further that with those nine total treatments, as many youth would be covered as would be if the therapists could be trained in every treatment available.

The relevance-mapping approach solves a significant problem for mental health agencies and larger systems—how to cover as many children in their system efficiently. Training therapists in EBTs is costly, and selecting which EBTs to use can be confusing. The relevance-mapping approach represents one possible way to solve the problem. Innovative ways to solve large system problems like this represent a third growth industry in D&I science.

One final point to make that stems from the results of Chorpita et al.'s (2011) study. Even with nine (or *every*) EBT, almost 30% of children were *not* covered. That is, after decades of scientific inquiry, we still have no EBT for 3 of 10 children who came in for treatment at a large mental health services agency. Although the chapter has focused on disseminating and implementing EBTs that are already developed, there is clearly room for the development of innovative treatment approaches to help improve the functioning of these children. Indeed, invention is needed across the entire field, from basic science to treatment development through to D&I.

As this chapter makes clear, advances in D&I science are likely to be considerable in the coming years. The rising importance of D&I work is evident by the proliferation of publications in the area, including a dedicated journal, *Implementation Science* (http://www.implementationscience.com/), and the funding priorities of funding agencies in the United States (e.g., National Institutes of Health [NIH]). For example, there are dedicated program announcements for D&I research via the NIH (e.g., http://grants.nih.gov/grants/guide/pa-files/PAR-10-038.html), and the NIH has hosted a D&I conference since 2007. We are heartened by these developments, as D&I science represents an important avenue for improving the lives of the large numbers children and families struggling with mental health concerns. We hope that this chapter has informed and inspired some readers to consider a career focused on D&I science.

REFERENCES

Aarons, G. A. (2004). Mental health provider attitudes toward adoption of evidence-based practice: The Evidence-Based Practice Attitude Scale (EBPAS). *Mental Health Services Research, 6*(2), 61–74. doi: 10.1023/B:M HSR.0000024351.12294.65

Aarons, G. A., Hurlburt, M., & Horwitz, S. M. (2011). Advancing a conceptual model of evidence-based practice implementation in public service sectors. *Administration and Policy in Mental Health, 38*(1), 4–23. doi: 10.1007/s10488-010-0327-7

Aarons, G. A., McDonald, E. J., Sheehan, A. K., & Walrath-Greene, C. M. (2007). Confirmatory factor analysis of the Evidence-Based Practice Attitude Scale (EBPAS) in a geographically diverse sample of community mental health providers. *Administration and Policy in Mental Health Services Research, 34*(5), 465–469. doi: 10.1007/s10488-007-0127-x

Aarons, G. A., & Sommerfeld, D. H. (2012). Leadership, innovation climate, and attitudes toward evidence-based practice during a statewide implementation. *Journal of the American Academy of Child & Adolescent Psychiatry, 51*(4), 423–431. doi: 10.1016/j.jaac.2012.01.018

Aarons, G. A., Sommerfeld, D. H., Hecht, D. B., Silovsky, J. F., & Chaffin, M. J. (2009). The impact of evidence-based practice implementation and fidelity monitoring on staff turnover: Evidence for a protective effect. *Journal of Consulting and Clinical Psychology, 77,* 270–280.

Aarons, G. A., Wells, R., Zagursky, K., Fettes, F., & Palinkas, L. A. (2009). Implementing evidence-based practice in community mental health agencies: Multiple stakeholder perspectives. *American Journal of Public Health, 99*(11): 2087–2095.

Adelman, H. S., & Taylor, L. (2004). Mental health in schools: A shared agenda. *Emotional & Behavioral Disorder in Youth, 4*(3), 59–78.

Addis, M. E., & Krasnow, A. D. (2000). A national survey of practicing psychologists' attitudes toward psychotherapy treatment manuals. *Journal of Consulting and Clinical Psychology, 68*(2), 331–339. doi: 10.1037/0022-006X.68.2.331

Alderfer, M. A., Fiese, B. H., Gold, J., Cutuli, J. J., Holmbeck, G. N., Chambers, C. T., . . . Patterson, J. (2008). Evidence-based assessment in pediatric psychology: Family measures. *Journal of Pediatric Psychology, 33*(9), 1046–1061.

Atkins, M. S., Frazier, S. L., Leathers, S. J., Graczyk, P. A., Talbott, E., Jakobsons, L., . . . Bell, C. C. (2008). Teacher key opinion leaders and mental health consultation in low-income urban schools. *Journal of Consulting and Clinical Psychology, 76*(5), 905.

Baptiste, D., Bhana, A., Peterson, I., Voisin, D., Mckay, M., Bell, C., et al. (2007). A community participatory framework for international youth-focused HIV/AIDS prevention in South Africa and Trinidad. *Journal of Pediatric Psychology, 31*(9), 905–916.

Barkley, R. A. (1997). *Defiant children: A clinician's manual for assessment and parent training*. New York, NY: Guilford Press.

Becker, C. B., Stice, E., Shaw, H., & Woda, S. (2009). Use of empirically supported interventions for psychopathology: Can the participatory approach move us beyond the research-to-practice gap? *Behaviour Research and Therapy, 47*(4), 265–274. doi: 10.1016/j.brat.2009.02.007

Becker, C. B., Zayfert, C., & Anderson, E. (2004). A survey of psychologists' attitudes towards and utilization of exposure therapy for PTSD. *Behaviour Research and Therapy, 42,* 277–292. doi: 10.1016/S0005-7967(03)00138-4

Becker, K. D., & Stirman, S. W. (2011). The science of training in evidence-based treatments in the context of implementation programs: Current status and prospects for the future. *Administration and Policy in Mental Health, 38*(4), 217–222. doi: 10.1007/s10488-011-0361-0

Beidas, R. S., & Kendall, P. C. (2010). Training therapists in evidence-based practice: A critical review of studies from a systems-contextual perspective. *Clinical Psychology: Science and Practice, 17*(1), 1–30. doi: 10.1111/j.1468–2850 .2009.01187.x

Borntrager, C. F., Chorpita, B. F., Higa-McMillan, C., & Weisz, J. R. (2009). Provider attitudes toward evidence-based practices: Are the concerns with the evidence or with the manuals? *Psychiatric Services, 60*(5), 677–681. doi: 10.1176/appi. ps.60.5.677

Brownson, R. C., Colditz, G. A., & Proctor, E. K. (2012). *Dissemination and implementation research in health: Translating science to practice.* New York, NY: Oxford University Press.

Chamberlain, P., Price, J., Reid, J., & Landsverk, J. (2008). Cascading implementation of a foster and kinship parent intervention. *Child Welfare, 87*(5), 27–48.

Chambers, D. A., Ringeisen, H., & Hickman, E. E. (2005). Federal, state, and foundation initiatives around evidence-based practices child and adolescent mental health. *Child and Adolescent Psychiatric Clinics of North America, 14*(2), 307–327. doi: 10.1016/j.chc.2004.04.006

Chorpita, B. F., Bernstein, A., & Daleiden, E. L. (2011). Empirically guided coordination of multiple evidence-based treatments: An illustration of relevance mapping in children's mental health services. *Journal of Consulting and Clinical Psychology, 79*(4), 470–480. doi: 10.1037/a0023982

Chorpita, B. F., Daleiden, E. L. Ebesutani, C., Young, J., Becker, K. D., Nakamura, B. J., . . . Starace, J. (2011). Evidence-based treatments for children and adolescents: An updated review of indicators of efficacy and effectiveness. *Clinical Psychology: Science and Practice, 18*(2), 154–172. doi: 10.1111/j.1468–2850.2011.01247.x

Chorpita, B. F., Daleiden, E. L., & Weisz, J. R. (2005). Modularity in the design and application of therapeutic interventions. *Applied and Preventive Psychology, 11,* 141–156. doi: 10.1016/j.appsy.2005.05.002

Chorpita, B. F., Weisz, J. R., Daleiden, E. L., Schoenwald, S. K., Palinkas, L. A., Miranda, J., . . . the Research Network on Youth Mental Health. (in press). Long term outcomes for the Child STEPs randomized effectiveness trial: A comparison of modular and standard treatment designs with usual care. *Journal of Consulting and Clinical Psychology, 81,* 999–1009.

Damschroder, L. J., & Hagedorn, H. J. (2011). A guiding framework and approach for implementation research in substance use disorders treatment. *Psychology of Addictive Behaviors, 25*(2), 194–205. doi: 10.1037/a0022284

Ehrenreich-May, J., Southam-Gerow, M. A., Hourigan, S. E., Wright, L. R., Pincus, D. B., & Weisz, J. R. (2011). Characteristics of anxious and depressed youth seen in two different clinical contexts. *Administration and Policy in Mental Health and Mental Health Services Research, 38*(5), 398–411. doi: 10.1007/s10488–010–0328–6

Fixsen, D. L., Naoom, S. F., Blasé, K. A., Friedman, R. M., & Wallace, F. (2005). *Implementation research: A synthesis of the literature.* Tampa, FL: University of South Florida, Louis de la Parte Florida Mental Health Institute, National Implementation Research Network (FMHI Publication #231).

Fox, R. A., Mattek, R. J., & Gresl, B. L. (2013). Evaluation of a university-community partnership to provide home-based, mental health services for children from families living in poverty. *Community Mental Health Journal, 49,* 599–610.

Fulda, K. G., Lykens, K. K., Bae, S., & Singh, K. P. (2009). Unmet mental health care needs for children with special health care needs stratified by socioeconomic status. *Child and Adolescent Mental Health, 14*(4), 190–199. doi: 10.1111/j.1475–3588.2008.00521.x

Garland, A. F., Kruse, M., & Aarons, G. A. (2003). Clinicians and outcome measurement: What's the use? *Journal of Behavioral Health Services & Research, 30*(4), 393–405. doi: 10.1007/BF02287427

Glisson, C. (2007). Assessing and changing organizational culture and climate for effective services. *Research on Social Work Practice, 17*(6), 736–747. doi: 10.1177/1049731507301659

Glisson, C. (2009). Organizational climate and service outcomes in child welfare agencies. In M. B. Webb, K. Dowd, B. J. Harden, J. Landsverk, & M. F. Testa (Eds.), *Child welfare and child protection: New perspectives from the National Survey of Child and Adolescent Well-Being* (pp. 380–408). New York, NY: Oxford University Press.

Glisson, C., Dukes, D., & Green, P. (2006). The effects of the ARC organizational intervention on caseworker turnover, climate, and culture in children's service systems. *Child Abuse and Neglect, 30,* 855–880.

Glisson, C., Hemmelgarn, A., Green, P., Dukes, D., Atkinson, S., & Williams, N. J. (2012). Randomized trial of the Availability, Responsiveness, and Continuity (ARC) organizational intervention with community-based mental health programs and clinicians serving youth. *Journal of the American Academy of Child & Adolescent Psychiatry, 51*(8), 780–787. doi: 10.1016/j.jaac.2012.05.010

Glisson, C., & James, L.R. (2002). The cross-level effects of culture and climate in human service teams. *Journal of Organizational Behavior, 23,* 767–794. doi: 10.1002/job.162

Glisson, C., & Schoenwald, S. K. (2005). The ARC organizational and community intervention strategy for implementing evidence-based children's mental health treatments. *Mental Health Services Research, 7*(4), 243–259. doi: 10.1007/ s11020–005–7456–1

Glisson, C., Schoenwald, S. K., Hemmelgarn, A., Green, P., Dukes, D., Armstrong, K. S., & Chapman, J. E. (2010). Randomized trial of MST and ARC in a two-level evidence-based treatment implementation strategy. *Journal of Consulting and Clinical Psychology, 78*(4), 537–550. doi: 10.1037/a0019160

Hammen, C., Rudolph, K., Weisz, J., Rao, U., & Burge, D. (1999). The context of depression in clinic-referred youth: Neglected areas in treatment. *Journal of the American Academy of Child & Adolescent Psychiatry, 38*(1), 64–71. doi: 10.1097/00004583–199901000–00021

Harper, G. W., Bangi, A. K., Contreras, R., Pedraza, A., Tolliver, M., & Vess, L. (2004). Diverse phases of collaboration: Working together to improve community-based HIV interventions for adolescents. *American Journal of Community Psychology, 33,* 193–204.

Hemmelgarn, A. L., Glisson, C., & James, L. R. (2006). Organizational culture and climate: Implications for services and interventions research. *Clinical Psychology: Science and Practice, 13,* 73–89, doi: 10.1111/j.1468–2850.2006.00008.x

Henggeler, S. W., Schoenwald, S. K., Borduin, C. M., Rowland, M. D., & Cunningham, P. B. (2009). *Multisystemic therapy for antisocial behavior in children and adolescents* (2nd ed.). New York, NY: Guilford Press.

Herschell, A. D., Kolko, D. J. Baumann, B. L., & Davis, A. C. (2010) The role of therapist training in the implementation of psychosocial treatments: A review and critique with recommendations. *Clinical Psychology Review, 30*(4), 448–466. doi: 10.1016/j.cpr.2010.02.005

Hoagwood, K., & Olin, S. (2002). The NIMH blueprint for change report: Research priorities in child and adolescent mental health. *Journal of the American Academy of Child & Adolescent Psychiatry, 41*(7), 760–767. doi: 10.1097/00004583–200207000–00006

Kendall, P. C. (1994). Treating anxiety disorders in children: Results of a randomized clinical trial. *Journal of Consulting and Clinical Psychology, 62,* 100–110.

Klein, D. N., Dougherty, L. R., & Olino, T. M. (2005). Toward guidelines for evidence-based assessment of depression in children and adolescents. *Journal of Clinical Child and Adolescent Psychology, 34*(3), 412–432. doi: 10.1207/s15374424jccp3403_3

McKinney, C., & Morse, M. (2012). Assessment of disruptive behavior disorders: Tools and recommendations. *Professional Psychology: Research and Practice, 43,* 641–649. doi: 10.1037/a0027324

McLeod, B. D., Southam-Gerow, M. A., Tully, C. B., Rodriguez, A., & Smith, M. M. (2013). Making a case for treatment integrity as a psychosocial treatment quality indicator for youth mental health care. *Clinical Psychology: Science and Practice, 20,* 14–32.

Metz, A., & Bartley, L. (2012). Active implementation frameworks for program success. *Zero to Three, 32*(4), 11–18.

Meyers, D. C., Durlak, J. A., & Wandersman, A. (2012). The quality implementation framework: A synthesis of critical steps in the implementation process. *American Journal of Community Psychology, 50*(3–4), 462–480. doi: 10.1007/s10464–012–9522-x

Nakamura, B. J., Chorpita, B. F., Hirsch, M., Daleiden, E., Slavin, L., Amundson, M. J., . . . Vorsino, W. M. (2011). Large-scale implementation of evidence-based treatments for children 10 years later: Hawaii's evidence-based services initiative in children's mental health. *Clinical Psychology: Science and Practice, 18*(1), 24–35. doi: 10.1111/j.1468–2850.2010.01231.x

Nakamura, B. J., Higa-McMillan, C. K., Okamura, K. H., & Shimabukuro, S. (2011). Knowledge of and attitudes towards evidence-based practices in community child mental health practitioners. *Administration and Policy in Mental Health and Mental Health Services Research, 38*(4), 287–300. doi: 10.1007/s10488–011–0351–2

Newhouse, R., Bobay, K., Dykes, P. C., Stevens, K. R., & Titler, M. (2013). Methodology issues in implementation science. *Medical Care, 51*(4), S32–S40. doi: 10.1097/MLR.0b013e31827feeca

Proctor, E. K., & Brownson, R. C. (2012). Measurement issues in dissemination and implementation research. In R. C. Brownson, G. A. Colditz, & E. K. Proctor (Eds.), *Dissemination and implementation research in health: Translating science to practice* (pp. 261–280). New York, NY: Oxford University Press.

Proctor, E. K., Landsverk, J., Aarons, G., Chambers, D., Glisson, C., & Mittman, B. (2009). Implementation research in mental health services: An emerging science with conceptual, methodological, and training challenges. *Administration and Policy in Mental Health and Mental Health Services Research, 36,* 24–34. doi: 10.1007/s10488–008–0197–4

Rabin, B. A., & Brownson, R. C. (2012). Measurement issues in dissemination and implementation research. In R. C. Brownson, G. A. Colditz, & E. K. Proctor (Eds.), *Dissemination and implementation research in health: Translating science to practice* (pp. 23–51). New York, NY: Oxford University Press.

Radda, K. E., Schensul, J. J., Disch, W. B., Levy, J. A., & Reyes, C. Y. (2003). Assessing human immunodeficiency virus (HIV) risk among older urban adults. *Family & Community Health, 26*(3), 203–213.

Rogers, E. M. (2003). *Diffusion of innovations* (5th ed.). New York, NY: Free Press.

Sburlati, E. S., Schniering, C. A., Lyneham, H. J., & Rapee, R. M. (2011). A model of therapist competencies for the empirically supported cognitive behavioral treatment of child and adolescent anxiety and depressive disorders. *Clinical Child and Family Psychology Review, 14*(1), 89–109. doi: 10.1007/s10567–011–0083–6

Schoenwald, S. K., & Hoagwood, K. (2001). Effectiveness, transportability, and dissemination of interventions: What matters when? *Psychiatric Services, 52*(9), 1190–1197. doi: 10.1176/appi.ps.52.9.1190

Schoenwald, S. K., Kelleher, K., & Weisz, J. R. (2008). Building bridges to evidence-based practice: The MacArthur Foundation Child System and Treatment Enhancement Projects (Child STEPs). *Administration and Policy in Mental Health and Mental Health Services Research, 35*(1–2), 66–72. doi: 10.1007/s10488–007–0160–9

Shirk, S. R., Kaplinski, H., & Gudmundsen, G. (2009). School-based cognitive-behavioral therapy for adolescent depression: A benchmarking study. *Journal of Emotional and Behavioral Disorders, 17*(2), 106–117. doi: 10.1177/1063426608326202

Smith, M. (2011). Measures for assessing parenting in research and practice. *Child and Adolescent Mental Health, 16,* 158–166. doi: 10.1111/j.1475–3588.2010.00585.x

Southam-Gerow, M. A., & Chorpita, B. F. (2007). Anxiety in children and adolescents. In E. J. Mash & R. A. Barkley (Eds.), *Assessment of childhood disorders* (4th ed., pp. 347–397). New York, NY: Guilford Press.

Southam-Gerow, M. A., Chorpita, B. F., Miller, L. M., & Gleacher, A. A. (2008). Are children with anxiety disorders privately referred to a university clinic like those referred from the public mental health system? *Administration and Policy in Mental Health and Mental Health Services Research, 35*(3), 168–180. doi: 10.1007/s10488–007–0154–7

Southam-Gerow, M. A., Daleiden, E. L., Chorpita, B. F., Bae, C., Mitchell, C., Faye, M., & Alba, M. (in press). MAPping Los Angeles County: Taking an evidence-informed model of mental health care to scale. *Journal of Clinical Child & Adolescent Psychology.*

Southam-Gerow, M. A., Hourigan, S. E., & Allin, R. B. (2009). Adapting evidence-based mental health treatments in community settings: Preliminary results from a partnership approach. *Behavior Modification, 33*(1), 82–103. doi: 10.1177/0145445508322624

Southam-Gerow, M. A., Ringeisen, H. L., & Sherrill, J. T. (2006). Integrating interventions and services research: Progress and prospects. *Clinical Psychology: Science and Practice, 13*(1), 1–8. doi: 10.1111/j.1468–2850.2006.00001.x

Southam-Gerow, M. A., Rodríguez, A., Chorpita, B. F., & Daleiden, E. L. (2012). Dissemination and implementation of evidence based treatments for youth: Challenges and recommendations. *Professional Psychology: Research and Practice, 43*(5), 527–534. doi: 10.1037/a0029101

Southam-Gerow, M. A., Weisz, J. R., & Kendall, P. C. (2003). Youth with anxiety disorders in research and service clinics: Examining client differences and similarities. *Journal of Clinical Child and Adolescent Psychology, 32*(3), 375–385. doi: 10.1207/S15374424JCCP3203_06

Stahmer, A. C., Brookman-Frazee, L., Lee, E., Searcy, K., & Reed, S. (2011). Parent and multidisciplinary provider perspectives on earliest intervention for children at risk for autism spectrum disorders. *Infants & Young Children, 24,* 344–363. doi: 10.1097/IYC.0b013e31822cf700

Stein, B. D., Kataoka, S., Jaycox, L. H., Wong, M., Fink, A., & Escudero, P. (2002). Theoretical basis and program design of a school-based mental health intervention for traumatized immigrant children: A collaborative research partnership. *Journal of Behavioral Health Services & Research, 29*(3), 318–326.

Stewart, R. E., Stirman, S. W., & Chambless, D. L. (2012). A qualitative investigation of practicing psychologists' attitudes toward research-informed practice: Implications for dissemination strategies. *Professional Psychology, Research and Practice, 43*(2), 100–109. doi: 10.1037/a0025694

Substance Abuse and Mental Health Services Administration. (2013). *National Registry of Effective Programs and Practices.* Retrieved from http://nrepp.samhsa.gov

Tabak, R. G., Khoong, E. C., Chambers, D. A., & Brownson, R. C. (2012). Bridging research and practice: Models for dissemination and implementation research. *American Journal of Preventive Medicine, 43*(3), 337–350.

Tang, M. H., Hill, K. S., Boudreau, A. A., Yucel, R. M., Perrin, J. M., & Kuhlthau, K. A. (2008). Medicaid managed care and the unmet need for mental health care among children with special health care needs. *Health Services Research, 43*(3), 882–900. doi: 10.1111/j.1475–6773.2007.00811.x

U.S. Department of Health and Human Services. (2002). *Closing the gap: A national blueprint to improve the health of persons with mental retardation.* Report of the Surgeon General's Conference on Health Disparities and Mental Retardation. Washington, DC: Office of the Surgeon General.

Walrath, C. M., Sheehan, A. K., Holden, E. W., Hernandez, M., & Blau, G. M. (2006). Evidence-based treatments in the field: A brief report on provider knowledge, implementation, and practice. *Journal of Behavioral Health Services & Research, 33*(2), 244–253. doi: 10.1007/s11414–005–9008–9

Weersing, V. R., & Weisz, J. R. (2002). Community clinic treatment of depressed youth: Benchmarking usual care against CBT clinical trials. *Journal of Consulting and Clinical Psychology, 70*(2), 299–310. doi: 10.1037//0022–006X.70.2.299

Weisz, J. R., Chorpita, B. F., Palinkas, L. A., Schoenwald, S. K., Miranda, J., Bearman, S. K., . . . the Research Network on Youth Mental Health. (2012). Testing standard and modular designs for psychotherapy treating depression, anxiety, and conduct problems in youth: A randomized effectiveness trial. *Archives of General Psychiatry, 69*(3), 274–282. doi: 10.1001/archgenpsychiatry.2011.147

Weisz, J. R., Chu, B. C., & Polo, A. J. (2004). Treatment dissemination and evidence-based practice: Strengthening intervention through clinician-researcher collaboration. *Clinical Psychology: Science and Practice, 11*(3), 300–307. doi: 10.1093/clipsy.bph085

Weisz, J. R., Thurber, C. A., Sweeney, L., Proffitt, V. D., & LeGagnoux, G. L. (1997). Brief treatment of mild-to-moderate child depression using Primary and Secondary Control Enhancement Training. *Journal of Consulting and Clinical Psychology, 65*(4), 703–707.

SECTION II

Disorder-Focused Interventions

CHAPTER 7

Anxiety Disorders in Children

LAURA D. SELIGMAN, ERIN F. SWEDISH, AND THOMAS H. OLLENDICK

BRIEF OVERVIEW OF DISORDERS

Anxiety disorders in children describe a broad spectrum of syndromes (Grills-Taquechel & Ollendick, 2013). According to the *Diagnostic and Statistical Manual*, 4th ed. (*DSM-IV*) (American Psychiatric Association [APA], 1994), children with significant and interfering anxiety can be diagnosed with one or more of eight anxiety disorders (APA, 1994; World Health Organization, 1992):

1. Panic disorder with agoraphobia
2. Panic disorder without agoraphobia
3. Agoraphobia without history of panic
4. Specific phobia
5. Social phobia
6. Obsessive-compulsive disorder
7. Posttraumatic stress disorder
8. Generalized anxiety disorder

   Additionally, the *DSM-IV* and the *International Classification of Diseases*, 10th revised ed. (ICD-10) specify one anxiety diagnosis specific to childhood: separation anxiety disorder (SAD). However, in the most recent version of the *DSM*, the *DSM-5* (APA, 2013), the age-of-onset requirement for SAD has been dropped; thus, SAD is listed among the anxiety disorders. In addition, *DSM-5* moves obsessive-compulsive disorder to a new chapter for obsessive-compulsive and related disorders and removes posttraumatic stress disorder (PTSD) from anxiety disorders and places it in a section titled "Trauma and Stressor-Related Disorders."

   As is evident from this discussion, what is and what is not considered an anxiety disorder by diagnostic classification systems is especially fluid right now. Generally speaking, a broad range of topics can be subsumed under the heading of anxiety disorders in childhood. Due to space constraints, however, we have chosen to limit the more specific aspects of our discussion to the examination of SAD, generalized anxiety disorder (GAD), social anxiety disorder (SOC), and specific phobias (SPs); several papers provide excellent resources for the reader interested in review of the literature on other anxiety disorders in youth (Cary & McMillen, 2012; Franklin, Harrison, & Benavides, 2012; Leenarts, Diehle, Doreleijers, Jansma, & Lindauer, 2012; Ollendick, Mattis, & King, 1994).

This review was funded in part by the National Institute of Mental Health Grant R01 074777 to Thomas H. Ollendick (PI).

Separation Anxiety Disorder

Developmentally inappropriate or excessive anxiety or fear upon separation from attachment figures (usually a parent or primary caregiver) or from home for a duration of at least 4 weeks is the core feature of SAD as defined by both the *DSM-5* and the *ICD-10* diagnostic criteria (APA, 2013; WHO, 1992). Children with SAD may experience a variety of behavioral (e.g., clinging to attachment figure, crying) and somatic symptoms (e.g., muscle aches, headaches) upon separation from or in anticipation of separation from the attachment figure. Children with SAD experience intrusive worries that something might happen to the attachment figure or to the child him-/herself. Furthermore, a child with SAD may be reluctant to sleep alone or to sleep away from home. School refusal is associated frequently with SAD and can be one of the most debilitating symptoms for both the child and the family. Moreover, comorbidity of SAD with other anxiety disorders and with depression is common (Black, 1995; Last, Hersen, & Kazdin, 1987).

Of note, there is a good deal of variation across cultures regarding expectations for separation; thus, the severity of clinical symptoms that warrant a diagnosis of SAD may vary widely depending on the child's contextual environment. Thus, it is important to assess for and take into account cultural norms regarding separation when considering a diagnosis of SAD.

Generalized Anxiety Disorder

The core feature of GAD is excessive worrying related to a number of events or activities (e.g., world events) that lasts for a period of six months or more (APA, 2013; WHO, 1992). This worry is difficult to control or stop; children with GAD may experience difficulty concentrating on schoolwork or social interactions because of their focus on their worries. Additionally, the worry is accompanied by somatic complaints and distress. As with SAD, children with GAD have a high rate of concurrent mental health disorders (Costello, Egger, & Angold, 2005).

Social Anxiety Disorder (Social Phobia)

Social anxiety disorder or social phobia is characterized by an excessive fear of negative evaluation by others. Often this extreme fear of judgment and evaluation is in situations with unfamiliar people or situations that could possibly result in scrutiny. The anxiety must be present in a variety of interactions (e.g., with peers, not just in interactions with adults) for a diagnosis of SOC to be made. Typically, children with social anxiety avoid social interactions to the extent that normal daily functioning can be greatly impaired (Stein & Gorman, 2001). The onset of SOC generally occurs during adolescence (approximately 13 years of age, on average); however, SOC can become evident during early childhood (Beidel, Turner, & Morris, 1999). As with other anxiety disorders, children with SOC often present with comorbid disorders; moreover, SOC in youth is associated with increased risk of substance abuse disorders later in life (Buckner et al., 2008).

Specific/Simple Phobia

Specific (simple) phobia is defined by excessive and marked fear in response to encountering or anticipating an object or situation (e.g., heights, small places, animals) (APA, 1994). The fear causes distress and interference in the child's routine, and the feared stimulus is generally avoided. Although adults often realize that their fears are excessive and unreasonable, this may not always be the case for children. It is estimated that SPs occur in about 8% of children (Kim et al., 2010). Again, children with SPs often present with comorbid disorders (Kim et al., 2010).

EVIDENCE-BASED APPROACHES

Over the past few decades, research has identified various evidence-based approaches for children with anxiety disorders. More specifically, research suggests that some treatments work better than others for children who experience anxiety and that cognitive behavioral therapy (CBT) has a relatively strong evidence base (Seligman & Ollendick, 2011). Although there are variations in the specific approaches for different anxiety disorders, in general CBT for child anxiety focuses on the cognitive and behavioral processes hypothesized to lead to and maintain anxiety. More specifically, the core components of CBT for anxious youth include psychoeducation, emotion education, problem solving, cognitive restructuring, exposure, and relapse prevention. Treatment programs typically last from 12 to 18 sessions, although some treatments have been shown to be efficacious with as few as 8 to 10 sessions (Rapee, 2000).

COMMON COMPONENTS OF EVIDENCE-BASED TREATMENTS FOR CHILDREN WITH ANXIETY DISORDERS

Although many evidence-based treatment programs and packages have been identified, these treatments are based on common core components. These components are discussed next.

Psychoeducation and Emotion Education

Psychoeducation efforts are aimed at helping the child and his/her family understand the treatment rationale and lay the foundation for the skills that are the focus of later sessions. Children and their families are given basic information regarding anxiety and are introduced to the CBT model and specifically the interaction among thoughts, feelings, and behavior. Maintaining factors of anxiety are discussed, with a particular focus on avoidance and accommodation. This may be the first time that the family begins to consider that accommodation of anxious behavior and/or avoidance of anxiety-provoking stimuli are not necessary reactions to anxiety. Therapists focus on helping families understand that the experience of anxiety is not, in and of itself, dangerous and that anxiety does not spiral out of control and continue indefinitely, as many people believe.

Psychoeducation also typically involves helping children to recognize and distinguish feelings and increase their awareness of their emotions. Emotion education can help children to identify the specific situations that lead to anxiety. This process can set the stage for later efforts at using coping strategies and monitoring anxious cognitions.

Problem Solving

Problem-solving methods are taught and practiced in order to help children identify new methods for addressing anxiety-provoking situations. Children are taught to use a step-by-step process that includes finding multiple solutions to a problem, examining the costs and benefits of each, and implementing the preferred solution. Given that research suggests that children with anxiety disorders prefer avoidant ways to cope with anxiety and that this behavior may be encouraged by parents

(Dadds, Marrett, & Rapee, 1996), problem solving can serve the important function of allowing children to recognize that other approach-oriented options are available and to examine the pros and cons of avoidant versus approach behaviors.

Cognitive Restructuring

Cognitive restructuring helps children identify and replace maladaptive thoughts and beliefs with more adaptive thoughts and beliefs. Learning to think more realistically is an important strategy for helping children overcome anxiety. In order for children to change their thoughts, it is important for them to first understand the relationship among thoughts, feelings, and behaviors. That is, it is important for children to understand that their feelings and emotions are not directly caused by the events and situations that occur but instead by the way events are thought about and interpreted. Such an approach may also allow anxious children to begin to feel more control over their emotions.

Cognitive restructuring efforts often focus on two common errors made by children with anxiety disorders: overestimation of the probability of threat or negative outcomes and overestimation of the negative consequences of an event, should it occur. For example, a little boy who experiences social anxiety when starting a conversation with peers may be taught to examine and modify his automatic thought that other children will laugh at him if he says something wrong when joining a group, or he may be encouraged to modify his beliefs about how bad it would be if the other children did indeed laugh at him.

Given that most anxious children think in these unrealistic ways, it is important for children to recognize their thought patterns and identify their dysfunctional beliefs so they might begin to develop more adaptive ways of thinking. However, the concept of cognitive restructuring and the process of actually changing thoughts is difficult, even for adults. Therefore, when working with children, cognitive restructuring often is introduced as a game in which children are encouraged to become detectives to first find anxiety-provoking thoughts and then to find various clues to determine whether their anxious thought is accurate.

Exposure

Most anxious children have developed ways to avoid the situations that are frightening for them. Therefore, they never allow themselves the opportunity to learn that neither the feared situation nor the experience of anxiety is dangerous. As such, a central component of almost all evidence-based approaches to the treatment of anxiety disorders in children is some form of exposure and response prevention. Often children are exposed to feared stimuli in a graduated process, using a fear hierarchy. Children often are encouraged to conceptualize the hierarchy as a stepladder or hill that they are climbing, taking small steps in order to climb the entire way. Exposure can be in vivo or imaginal, but often a combination of the two is used.

Relapse Prevention

Treatment usually terminates as children become more adept at using the skills taught and generalizing these skills to other settings. As such, concluding sessions often focus on consolidation and assessment of skills. Many times relapse prevention is the focus of the final sessions. Reoccurrence of anxiety symptoms can occur for several reasons (see Bouton, Woods, Moody, Sunsay, & Garcia-Gutierrez, 2006); when anxiety does reoccur, it is important for children and the parent to know that they have acquired the necessary skills to prevent the anxiety from becoming impairing and out of control. Relapse prevention focuses on combining the skills learned during treatment and applying them with decreased reliance on the therapist. During relapse prevention, situations are identified that potentially could be problematic in the future, and children and their family are asked to identify skills that could help them in managing these situations. The therapist must assess whether each child and family has the ability to use the skills independently and to generalize the skills to novel problems. Treatment ends when these conditions are met, not when anxiety is absent or when stressful situations cease, as anxiety and potential stressors are considered normal experiences that are not inherently dangerous.

EVIDENCE FOR THE EFFICACY OF CBT FOR THE TREATMENT OF ANXIETY DISORDERS IN CHILDHOOD

There is growing evidence for the use of CBT as a first-line treatment for anxiety disorders in childhood. This evidence is reviewed below.

Generalized Anxiety Disorder, Separation Anxiety Disorder, and Social Anxiety Disorder

Randomized controlled trials (RCTs) provide strong evidence for the use of CBT for the treatment of GAD, SAD, and SOC for youth as young as 3 years of age (e.g., Kendall, 1994; Minde, Roy, Bezonsky, & Hashemi, 2010; Silverman, Kurtines, Ginsburg, Weems, Lumpkin, et al., 1999). More specifically, individual cognitive behavioral therapy (ICBT), group cognitive therapy (GCBT) with parents, and group cognitive therapy (GCBT) without parents all have been shown to be efficacious. Overall, studies indicate that ICBT and GCBT are comparable (e.g., Flannery-Schroeder & Kendall, 2000), as is CBT with or without parent involvement (see the Parent Involvement section further on). Remission rates, defined as youth diagnosis free at posttreatment, are as high as 65% to 70% (Barrett, Dadds, & Rapee, 1996; Flannery-Schroeder & Kendall, 2000). Specific manualized evidence-based treatments have been developed for GAD, SAD, and SOC in youth. One of the most widely researched, the Coping Cat program (Kendall, 1994), a manual for use with children 6 to 13 years of age, addresses impairing and distressing symptoms related to anxiety using CBT as described earlier. Included in the program is a therapist manual and child workbook. Early trials have shown the Coping Cat program to be effective compared to a wait list, with approximately 53% of children free of their primary diagnosis at the end of treatment (Kendall et al., 1997). Additionally, children treated with the Coping Cat program show significant improvement in symptomatology based on parent and child reports, and multiple long-term follow-up studies provide evidence that positive outcomes are maintained across time. For example, at an average of 3.35 years after the conclusion of treatment, anxious youth maintained treatment gains such as positive changes in coping and decreased levels of distress (Kendall & Southam-Gerow, 1996). Similarly, adolescents who had completed the Coping Cat program on average 7.4 years earlier also maintained positive treatment gains, with 81% of the adolescents no longer carrying their initial anxiety diagnosis, based on parents' interview (Kendall, Safford, Flannery-Schroeder, & Webb, 2004). Importantly, this suggests that the benefits of CBT treatment are maintained across developmental periods. In addition, the Coping Cat program has been adapted and extended in other countries. For example, in Australia, studies suggest that treatment programs stemming from the program provide similar positive outcomes (e.g., Barrett, 1998).

Specific Phobia

Research also supports CBT for the treatment of SPs in youth (Davis, Ollendick, & Öst, 2009, 2012; Ollendick et al., 2009). More specifically, evidence suggests that exposure to the feared stimulus is crucial in the treatment of SP in children (Cornwall, Spence, & Schotte, 1996). For example, Cornwall and colleagues found emotive imagery to be superior to a wait-list control for the treatment of SPs. More specifically, results revealed that children who received emotive imagery tolerated a dark room longer compared to children in the wait-list group, and parents of children in the emotive imagery group reported their child experienced an overall reduction of the fear of darkness, with outcomes maintained at 3-month follow-up (Cornwall et al., 1996).

In another study, children age 6 to 16 with a phobic disorder were assigned to exposure with self-control, exposure plus contingency management, or education support. Eighty-eight percent of children who received exposure therapy with self-control were diagnosis free at posttreatment as compared to 56% of the youth who received education support (Silverman, Kurtines, Ginsburg, Weems, Rabian, et al., 1999). Further, positive treatment gains were maintained at 3-, 6-, and 12-month follow-up assessments (Silverman, Kurtines, Ginsburg, Weems, Rabian, et al., 1999). Interestingly, more recent research suggests that treatment for SPs can be delivered effectively in a single, intensive session (see adaptions and modifications as well as Ollendick et al., 2009).

In sum, CBT has been shown to be effective for children with a variety of anxiety disorders. Although CBT can be delivered in a variety of formats depending on the specific anxiety disorder, numerous randomized controlled studies suggest that CBT can be efficacious in both the short and the long term.

PARENTAL INVOLVEMENT

Numerous studies have demonstrated a link between anxiety disorders in youth and parental psychopathology, particularly anxiety and affective disorders (e.g., Beidel & Turner, 1997; Lieb et al., 2000). Additionally, research has shown that parenting behavior may lead to, or at least help maintain, anxious symptomatology in children. For example, parental overcontrol and overinvolvement have been associated with anxiety symptoms in children (Hudson & Rapee, 2001, 2002; Muris & Merckelbach, 1998). Furthermore, several studies have suggested that parents may transmit information about threat and harm, either verbally or through modeling, that may lead to increased anxiety in their offspring (Ehlers, 1993; Lester, Seal, Nightingale, & Field, 2010; Muris, Mayer, Borth, & Vos, 2012). Similarly, some studies have suggested that parenting behavior can interfere with nonanxious learning once anxiety symptoms become evident, either by encouraging avoidant responses on the part of the child or by making modifications in family behavior that allow for avoidance (e.g., Dadds et al., 1996; Futh, Simonds, & Micali, 2012). Because of these findings linking parent psychopathology and parenting behavior to anxiety disorders in youth, it often has been hypothesized that parental involvement in the treatment of children with anxiety disorders is necessary or, at a minimum, parental involvement should result in better outcomes than treatments that focus exclusively on the child. Research testing these hypotheses, however, has yielded less than strong support.

Dadds and colleagues were the first to examine parental involvement in the treatment of anxious youth, conducting a small open trial of a CBT treatment with a parent component over 20 years ago

(Dadds, Heard, & Rapee, 1992). Five of the seven children receiving treatment for SAD, avoidant disorder, or overanxious disorder[1] were diagnosis free after the 12-week treatment, offering promise for involving parents in the treatment of anxious youth. Since that time several other studies have supported the efficacy of parent involvement in the treatment of children with anxiety disorders, either in individual or group format, for problems ranging from anxiety symptoms, to phobias, to severe obsessive compulsive disorder (Barrett, Healy-Farrell, & March, 2004; Dadds, Spence, Holland, Barrett, & Laurens, 1997; Manassis et al., 2002; Shortt, Barrett, & Fox, 2001; Silverman, Kurtines, Ginsburg, Weems, Lumpkin, et al., 1999; Silverman, Kurtines, Ginsburg, Weems, Rabian, et al., 1999; Storch et al., 2007). Across these studies, results suggest that children get better with CBT aimed at the child and the parent and that their outcomes are superior to untreated youth followed on a wait list. However, results are more equivocal when studies examine whether treatment for the child and the parent is superior to treatment for the child alone.

Promising findings in the Dadds et al. (1997) trial led to a more methodologically rigorous test of the effects of parent treatment—a controlled trial in which CBT with parent involvement was compared to child-focused CBT and a wait-list control (Barrett et al., 1996). The parent component of treatment taught skills such as planned ignoring and the use of social and tangible rewards to increase nonanxious, approach-oriented behavior. Additionally, parents were trained in communication and problem-solving techniques aimed at increasing their ability to work together and decreasing parental conflict concerning child rearing. In general, findings favored the CBT with parental involvement treatment. For example, at posttreatment assessment, significantly more children in the CBT plus parent treatment group were diagnosis free: 84% in the CBT plus parent treatment group compared to 57% in the group in which only the child was treated. Parent report of child symptoms also suggested that the addition of the parent treatment component was beneficial. Child reports of symptoms did not differentiate among any of the treatments—including the wait-list control; however, this seems to be a common finding in treatment trials for pediatric anxiety disorders, suggesting that child self-reports may not be the best method for measuring treatment effects (see the section titled "Measuring Treatment Effects"). Interestingly, the benefit of parent treatment was not universal. Results suggested that younger children (7–10 years) and girls had better results with the CBT plus parent treatment; for boys and older children (11–14 years), the CBT with parent treatment was comparable to the CBT treatment for the child alone.

The findings from this trial regarding the long-term effects of adding parent treatment to child CBT were more mixed. At 6-month follow-up, the differences in recovery (i.e., absence of anxiety disorder diagnosis) between the two active treatments disappeared (71.4% for the CBT for the child-only group; 84.0% for the CBT plus parent treatment group). However, at 12-month follow-up, the recovery rate in the child-only group was relatively stable, with 70.3% judged to be diagnosis free. The children whose parents also received treatment seemed to show continued improvement over time, with 95.6% diagnosis free at the 1-year mark. Again, parent reports also provided evidence of superiority for parental involvement in treatment, but child reports generally did not.

More recent studies, however, show somewhat weaker effects for the addition of parent involvement. For example, one study (Nauta, Scholing, Emmelkamp, & Minderaa, 2003) compared a wait-list control group to CBT for the child only and CBT for the child plus cognitive parent training in a trial for children and adolescents with a *DSM-IV* diagnosis of anxiety disorders. Results suggested that both active treatments were better than the wait list but that the two treatments did not differ.

---

[1] Avoidant disorder and overanxious disorder were subsumed under the diagnoses of social anxiety disorder and generalized anxiety disorder, respectively, in the *DSM-IV*.

Similar results were found in a treatment study to address PTSD and PTSD symptoms in youth with histories of sexual trauma (King et al., 2000). In this trial, CBT was compared to family CBT and a wait-list control. Although active treatment was superior to wait list, again there was little evidence to suggest that the addition of the family component was beneficial. Spence and colleagues also found that parent involvement did offer significant improvement over child-only CBT for youth with SOC (Spence, Donovan, & Brechman-Toussaint, 2000). Although a similar study (Mendlowitz et al., 1999) tested the hypothesis that parental involvement would be better than CBT for the child alone for a more varied group (i.e., children with any *DSM-IV* anxiety disorder), they also found little evidence for the superiority of additional treatment with the parents. Moreover, it should be noted that across these trials, the addition of parent involvement typically was confounded with more treatment time; that is, not only did families in the CBT with parent involvement treatment groups receive additional treatment components (e.g., contingency management training), they also received more treatment—up to twice as many sessions or treatment time—yet little additional benefit was observed. Moreover, some trials actually have found that behavioral indicators suggest child treatment alone or parent/teacher treatment alone may outperform combined parent and child treatment (Öst, Svensson, Hellstrom, & Lindwall, 2001).

Thus, while these studies suggest limited cause for enthusiasm, conclusive statements about added benefit of parental involvement may require more targeted investigations. For example, although the earliest study to examine parental involvement suggested that benefits may be limited to younger children and girls, many subsequent trials that have found no added effect have included adolescents up to 17 or 18 years of age (King et al., 2000; Nauta et al., 2003) and almost all of the studies to examine the additional benefit of parent treatment involved both boys and girls. Additionally, sometimes parent involvement has been minimal. For example, in Öst's trial examining the effects of single-session treatment for SPs with or without parental involvement, the parent involvement could range from active modeling of nonanxious behavior in session to simply being present while the therapist delivered the treatment (Öst et al., 2001). Concerns about the strength of the parent treatment in the combined treatment groups are compounded by the fact that CBT treatments for the child only often necessarily include some parent involvement (see, e.g., Kendall, 1994).

Also, parent treatments sometimes have been limited in the degree to which empirical data and theory have guided treatments. For example, despite studies that have shown problematic communication patterns in the families of anxious children, few parent treatments have focused on changing these patterns in much depth. Additionally, although parent treatment is hypothesized to be beneficial in part because of the association between parental psychopathology and child anxiety disorder and, in fact, studies have found parent psychopathology to be a negative prognostic indicator in the treatment of child anxiety (Berman, Weems, Silverman, & Kurtines, 2000; Southam-Gerow, Kendall, & Weersing, 2001), the aforementioned studies have examined the effects of the addition of parent treatment without regard to whether parental psychopathology was present.

Two studies that have taken a more targeted approach to the question of whether parental involvement confers benefits over child treatment alone have shown some promise. In one, Wood and colleagues (Wood, Piacentini, Southam-Gerow, Chu, & Sigman, 2006) examined the effects of a parent treatment component focused specifically on modifying some of the problematic communication patterns found in the families of youth with anxiety disorders. More specifically, they compared CBT for the child only to CBT with parent treatment focused on increasing autonomy granting and decreasing parental intrusiveness. Moreover, consistent with past findings, the trial included relatively young children (i.e., 8 to 13 years). At post, parent reports of child anxiety were significantly better in the CBT with parent involvement group, as were clinician ratings of severity and improvement; differences in diagnostic recovery did not reach statistical significance, although there was a trend favoring the CBT with parental involvement group. Of note, these effects could not be attributed to the CBT with parental involvement group receiving more treatment because, unlike earlier trials, treatment time was equated in both groups. That is, the parent group differed only in the focus of the treatment, not in the amount of the treatment. Interestingly, parental anxiety did not predict treatment outcome. Unfortunately, no analysis of whether parent disorder interacted with treatment condition (i.e., whether parents with anxiety disorders were the ones who needed the additional parent treatment) was reported. However, this matching hypothesis was tested in a trial conducted by Cobham and colleagues (Cobham, Dadds, & Spence, 1998). In this study, children and early adolescents (7–14 years) with anxiety disorders were assigned to CBT or CBT plus parent anxiety management (PAM). In some families, only the child was anxious; in other families, the parent(s) also had significant problems with anxiety. As with Wood and colleagues (Wood et al., 2006), the amount of treatment time was equated across groups. When comparing the two treatments without regard to parent anxiety status, results were similar to other trials. Although there was a trend toward greater recovery in the CBT + PAM group, the difference was not statistically significant; however, an interaction between treatment condition and parental anxiety status was found. If parental anxiety was absent, there was no difference between treatments; however, if the parents were anxious, CBT + PAM was superior. Although these results seem promising and could offer specific suggestions to clinicians about when it may be worthwhile to add parent treatment, the benefit of matching seemed to disappear by 12 months. In this case, however, the parent treatment was only four sessions; it may be that more treatment is needed.

In sum, despite research and theory that suggests that the addition of parent treatment to child-focused CBT for child anxiety should be beneficial, tests of this hypothesis have yielded mixed results and do not provide strong evidence of the long-term benefits. This may be because treatment focused on the child changes the child's behavior, which in turn changes the family dynamic, or it may be that parental involvement could be beneficial in specific cases (e.g., for young girls whose parents are anxious), but these fine-grained relationships have yet to be examined. Extant studies, both successful and unsuccessful, have clearly provided multiple hypotheses for further study, and we must await these studies to make a more definitive statement on the role of parental involvement in child treatment (also see Breinholst, Esbjørn, Reinholdt-Dunne, & Stallard, 2012). This caveat notwithstanding, however, the current options for parent treatment seem to have significant costs, with many requiring additional treatment time and training on the part of therapists, without the expected benefits.

ADAPTATIONS AND MODIFICATIONS

Current evidence-based treatments for child anxiety, although manualized, are inherently flexible in that proper implementation requires adapting the treatment procedures for the specific child and the context in which the child's symptoms are present (Kendall, Gosch, Furr, & Sood, 2008). Several specific adaptations of current treatments have been examined in the literature. Here we briefly review efforts addressing single-session treatments, nontraditional treatment delivery methods, and evidence-based approaches to prevention and early intervention.

Single-Session Treatment

Ollendick and colleagues have found support for an intensive version of CBT for youth with SPs (Davis et al., 2009; Ollendick et al., 2009). More specifically, results from an RCT conducted in the United States and Sweden show that a single session, lasting up to 3 hours and focusing on graduated exposure with the aim of modifying catastrophic conditions, can be effective for a sizable proportion of youth with clinically significant SPs (Ollendick et al., 2009). Although there was some evidence from this trial that girls' long-term outcome was superior to boys', in general the treatment seemed to be effective across a range of sociodemographic variables as well as comorbid conditions (Ollendick, Öst, Reuterskiöld, & Costa, 2010). Moreover, dropout was nonexistent (since there was only one prolonged session), so this may be an especially attractive option for families that may not have the resources to attend sessions regularly over 4 to 6 months. Whether intensive treatment programs such as this can be used with children with other anxiety disorders awaits further research.

Alternative Methods of Treatment Delivery

Parent-directed bibliotherapy, in which parents are taught to implement a CBT treatment with their child, has been shown to be effective (Rapee, Abbott, & Lyneham, 2006); however, studies suggest that many families need support in the form of therapist contact in order to stay engaged with and benefit from such treatments (Lyneham & Rapee, 2006). Of note, this is not to say that all forms of self-help books that address anxiety in youth would be expected to be efficacious; the book used in these trials was based on a treatment approach with empirical support.

Similarly, Kendall and colleagues have examined computer-assisted treatment delivery as a method for disseminating the empirically supported Coping Cat treatment. In this program, children first work through six computerized sessions to learn CBT skills such as problem solving and relaxation, then they continue to use the computerized treatment package with assistance from a therapist to complete tailored exposure sessions. Research suggests that this method of delivery is better than an education support condition and produces outcomes similar to standard CBT with about half of the investment of therapist time (Khanna & Kendall, 2010).

Community Intervention and Prevention Efforts

Several studies have shown some support for the use of CBT strategies either as a universal prevention program or for use with children who evidence high levels of anxiety symptoms but not necessarily a full-blown anxiety disorder (Aune & Stiles, 2009; Essau, Conradt, Sasagawa, & Ollendick, 2012; Neil & Christensen, 2009; Simon, Dirksen, Bögels, & Bodden, 2012; Stopa, Barrett, & Golingi, 2010). These interventions often use strategies similar to those found effective in trials of diagnosed youth but often with fewer sessions. Typically these programs are delivered in a group format and by classroom teachers. Studies generally have shown a reduction in anxiety over time with such interventions, although some have found this reduction to be similar to that found in control conditions; additionally, further research is needed to determine whether such interventions for high-risk youth prevent the development of later anxiety disorders.

MEASURING TREATMENT EFFECTS

The effects of treatment for children with anxiety disorders generally have been measured using three primary methods: structured or semistructured diagnostic interviews, child self-report questionnaires, and parent questionnaires. Other methods, including teacher reports, behavioral observations, physiological assessment, and parent or self-monitoring, sometimes are used. A thorough review of each of these methods and their empirical support for measuring reactions to treatment is beyond the scope of this chapter; therefore, our discussion focuses on the most commonly used methods. We refer the reader to Silverman and Ollendick (2005) for a more extensive review of the current state of empirically based assessment for child anxiety disorders. Additionally, although projective techniques sometimes are used in clinical practice for the assessment and monitoring of anxiety in children, data on the validity and cost effectiveness of these measures do not support their continued use (Lilienfeld, Wood, & Garb, 2000); therefore, such measures are not included in our discussion.

Evaluation of treatment effects in children with anxiety and anxiety disorders is a complex undertaking for several reasons. For one, given the high rates of comorbidity within the anxiety disorders and between the anxiety disorders and depression (Seligman & Ollendick, 1998), a thorough assessment of treatment outcome in children with anxiety disorders must include evaluation of co-occurring disorders and symptoms. Additionally, unlike externalizing disorders, in which symptoms often are readily observable by significant others, such as parent and teachers, many of the most significant symptoms of anxiety disorders in youth (e.g., worry, physiological symptoms) are internal and may not be detected by even close family members. Theoretically, then one would expect children with an anxiety disorder to be in the best position to report on their symptoms and changes in their symptoms; however, this may not be true. Children with anxiety disorders may be embarrassed to admit to their symptoms; in fact, such fear of negative evaluation by others may be a central problem for some of these children. Social desirability in the reporting of anxiety symptoms may be especially problematic for young children, and this may be compounded by cultural differences in that African American and Latino/a youth may respond in a more socially desirable manner on self-reports of anxiety in comparison with European American/Caucasian youth (Dadds, Perrin, & Yule, 1998; Pina, Silverman, Saavedra, & Weems, 2001). Developmental considerations also add to the complexity of the assessment of treatment outcome in youth in that the nature of severity of normative fears and anxiety covary with development (Gullone & King, 1993; Westenberg, Gullone, Bokhorst, Heyne, & King, 2007); therefore, ideal measures of treatment effects would be sensitive to change in symptoms while at the same time accounting for predicted change due to development. Unfortunately, the technology of the assessment of anxiety symptoms in youth has not advanced to this stage just yet. Given these complexities and the limitations of any one measure or class of measures, the assessment of treatment outcome in clinical trials has used a multi-method, multi-informant method. While this is probably a wise decision, research has shown that such measures rarely converge into one cohesive picture (Grills & Ollendick, 2002; Ollendick, Allen, Benoit, & Cowart, 2011; Safford, Kendall, Flannery-Schroeder, Webb, & Sommer, 2005). Therefore, it is important to consider how to integrate discrepant information and which data to weigh most heavily.

In this regard, structured and semistructured diagnostic interviews and rates of recovery (i.e., diagnosis free at posttreatment) largely have been considered the gold standard for measuring treatment effects in most trials of treatment for anxiety disorders in youth. These interviews, particularly the Anxiety Disorders Interview Schedule for Children for *DSM-IV*: Child and Parent Versions (ADIS-IV: C/P) (Silverman & Albano, 1996; Silverman, Saavedra, & Pina, 2001), have good reliability (see Table 7.1), and evaluation of comorbidity is easily accomplished because these interviews generally include a thorough assessment of all of the anxiety disorders as well as the most frequently co-occurring disorders. Screening questions for less commonly occurring disorders are included in the parent version (i.e., the ADIS-IV: C/P). Moreover, in the hands of a well-trained clinician, these instruments have the potential to be sensitive to developmental considerations. Treatment studies have shown that diagnostic status, as measured by the structured and semistructured diagnostic

TABLE 7.1   Reliability of Common Childhood Anxiety Diagnoses With the Use of Structured or Semistructured Interviews

Interview Name	Age (Years)	Diagnostic Reliability (k coefficients)
Anxiety Disorders Interview Schedule for C/P *DSM-IV:* Child and Parent Versions (Silverman & Albano, 1996; Silverman et al., 2001)	6 to 18	Child: SAD = .78; SOC = .71; SP = .80; GAD = .63 Parent: SAD = .88; SOC = .86 Combined: SAD = .84; SOC = .92; SP = .81; GAD = .80
Child and Adolescent Psychiatric Assessment (Angold & Costello, 2000)	9 to 13	Child: GAD = .79
Diagnostic Interview for Children and Adolescents (Herjanic & Reich, 1982; Reich, 2000; Reich, Herjanic, Welner, & Gandhy, 1982)	6 to 17	Child: SAD = .60; SP = .65
NIMH Diagnostic Interview Schedule for Children Version IV (Shaffer, Fisher, Lucas, Dulcan, & Schwab-Stone, 2000)	9 to 17	Child: SP = .68; SOC = .25; SAD = .46 Parent: SP = .96; SOC = .54; SAD = .58; GAD = .65 Combined: SP = .86; SOC = .48; SAD = .51; GAD = .58
Schedule for Affective Disorders and Schizophrenia for School-Age Children (Ambrosini, 2000)	6 to 18	Combined: SP = .80

Note: *DSM-IV = Diagnostic and Statistical Manual of Mental Disorders*, 4th ed. (APA, 1994); SAD = separation anxiety disorder; SOC = social anxiety disorder; SP = specific phobia: GAD = generalized anxiety disorder; NIMH = National Institute of Mental Health.

interviews reviewed in Table 7.1, is sensitive to treatment effects in that they distinguish between treated and untreated children and, in some cases, between children treated with different types of treatment (e.g., Barrett et al., 1996).

Self-reports, including those that map to *DSM* symptoms of anxiety disorders as well as more general measures of anxiety, have been used frequently to measure treatment effects in outcome trials; however, their utility in this regard seems suspect. Although we have found that self-reports are sensitive to change over time (Seligman, Ollendick, Langley, & Bechtoldt Baldacci, 2004), it might be that these measures are *too* sensitive, picking up on demand characteristics, regression to the mean, and possibly expectations and normal developmental changes to the degree that they do not distinguish between treated children and nontreated children. For example, our analysis of 31 studies that used various self-reports of anxiety symptoms as outcome measures suggests a pre–post effect size of 0.44 for the *wait-list* group, between a small and medium effect according to Cohen's guidelines. Of note, these youth received no treatment, nor were they purposefully given expectations of improvement as with a placebo control group. While it could be that self-reports are doing their job and treatments do not offer any benefit above and beyond the passage of time, it should be noted that self-reports across several trials have diverged from other indicators of outcome; that is, while clinician measures, diagnosis, parent reports, and sometimes behavioral indicators have distinguished between treated and nontreated children, self-reports often fail to do so.

Parent and teacher reports, most notably the Child Behavior Checklist and the Teacher Report Form (Achenbach & Rescorla, 2001), commonly are used to measure treatment effects for youth with anxiety disorders. Parent reports, in particular, appear to be sensitive to changes that result from treatment while also distinguishing between children who are treated and those who are not.

Last, few studies have examined behavioral indices of treatment outcome, such as behavioral approach tests for children with fears and phobias or absenteeism for children with school refusal behavior secondary to SAD or SOC; however, the studies that have used such measures suggest they may be useful for measuring change in response to treatment (Ollendick et al., 2011). One would guess that these might be the best indicators of real-world functioning as they provide a direct assessment of the types of problems that bring many children with anxiety disorders in for treatment; however, the psychometric properties of such measures have received little attention. More conclusive statements regarding the utility of these measures as indicators of treatment effects await such studies.

CLINICAL CASE EXAMPLE: SEPARATION ANXIETY DISORDER

Ashley is a 7-year-old girl who has been diagnosed SAD. Ashley is an only child who lives with her divorced mother. Ashley often worries about her mother and is terrified something bad will happen to her mother while they are separated. As a young child Ashley typically had trouble being away from her mother; however, after starting kindergarten Ashley's separation anxiety became increasingly problematic. Ashley's mother reported that the girl has difficulty going to school and staying in school, and Mom indicates that it has been a struggle every morning to get Ashley onto the school bus. When Ashley did go to school, she often refused to do schoolwork and instead spent her time crying and requesting to be with her mom. As a result, Ashley had missed several days of school and had fallen behind academically. When Ashley's separation problems evidenced themselves in kindergarten, her anxiety was more severe than that of her classmates but not so markedly atypical or developmentally inappropriate that it caused problems with peers. Over time, as the other children in Ashley's cohort began having fewer problems with separation and started to develop stronger peer relationships, Ashley was left out of this process because her peers viewed her as odd and because she was unable to focus on peer activities because of her anxiety.

Ashley's SAD also interfered with Mom's daily routines in that Mom had taken days off work when she was not able to get Ashley to go to school. Mom was unable to socialize because Ashley refused to be left alone with a babysitter or even to be left at other family members' homes. As a result, Ashley's mother rarely went out on her own. Ashley also slept with her mom every night because she was afraid something might happen. Ashley's mother had tried to have her sleep in her own room, but Ashley threw tantrums and Mom indicated that it was easier just to have her sleep in the same bedroom.

Treatment

Ashley's treatment first focused on helping her and her mom to understand the rationale behind CBT and to understand the nature of anxiety. Ashley and her therapist then worked to identify the thoughts that made Ashley anxious (e.g., Mom might be in a car accident and I will never see her again) and to replace these thoughts with more realistic and adaptive thoughts (e.g., Mom is a good driver, she always wears her seat belt, and drives a safe car so even if she is in an accident she will probably be okay). Ashley and her therapist then worked to develop a coping plan for when she got anxious and upset at school—Ashley would review coping cards that had her adaptive thoughts on them. Next, the therapist helped Ashley to generate a list of challenging anxiety-provoking situations (e.g., staying over at Grandma's house without Mom, going to school and staying at school) and to order the situations from least challenging to most challenging. The therapist and Ashley, sometimes with Mom's help, worked to develop exposures to each of these situations that would allow Ashley the opportunity to learn that she could cope with her anxiety, her anxiety would get better, and that her mom would be safe. Ashley was encouraged to engage in the exposures with reminders from Mom and the therapist that each step was just slightly more difficult than the one she had just mastered. As Ashley progressed through her hierarchy, she become more and more confident and more willing to engage in the exposure sessions. Moreover, she started to gain access to naturally occurring reinforcers in her everyday environment that encouraged her progress. For example, once Ashley was able to attend school regularly and to engage in group activities with her classmates, she starting to make friends. Her decrease in separation anxiety allowed her to engage in play dates outside of school for the first time, and a glimpse of what she had been missing motivated Ashley to keep working on her exposures both in session and outside of session. The therapist and Mom monitored Ashley's school attendance and social activities. Once these started to increase, they began to discuss plans for termination. As Ashley and Mom started to develop new coping statements and exposures in response to problems Ashley encountered, the therapist realized that the family was ready to work independently and after a few spaced-out booster sessions focused on skills review, treatment was terminated.

REFERENCES

Achenbach, T. M., & Rescorla, L. A. (2001). *Manual for the ASEBA School-Age Forms & Profiles*. Burlington, VT: University of Vermont, Research Center for Children, Youth, & Families.

American Psychiatric Association. (1994). *Diagnostic and statistical manual of mental disorders* (4th ed.). Washington, DC: Author.

American Psychiatric Association. (2013). *Diagnostic and statistical manual of mental disorders* (5th ed.). Arlington, VA: American Psychiatric Publishing.

Aune, T., & Stiles, T. C. (2009). Universal-based prevention of syndromal and subsyndromal social anxiety: A randomized controlled study. *Journal of Consulting and Clinical Psychology, 77*(5), 867–879. doi: 10.1037/a0015813

Barrett, P. M. (1998). Evaluation of cognitive-behavioral group treatments for childhood anxiety disorders. *Journal of Clinical Child Psychology, 27*(4), 459–468.

Barrett, P. M., Dadds, M. R., & Rapee, R. M. (1996). Family treatment of childhood anxiety: A controlled trial. *Journal of Consulting & Clinical Psychology, 64*(2), 333–342.

Barrett, P. M., Healy-Farrell, L., & March, J. S. (2004). Cognitive-behavioral family treatment of childhood obsessive-compulsive disorder: A controlled trial. *Journal of the American Academy of Child & Adolescent Psychiatry, 43*(1), 46–62. doi: 10.1097/01.chi.000096367.43887.13

Beidel, D. C., & Turner, S. M. (1997). At risk for anxiety: I. Psychopathology in the offspring of anxious parents. *Journal of the American Academy of Child & Adolescent Psychiatry, 36*(7), 918–924. doi: 10.1097/00004583-199707000-00013

Beidel, D. C., Turner, S. M., & Morris, T. L. (1999). Psychopathology of childhood social phobia. *Journal of the American Academy of Child & Adolescent Psychiatry, 38*(6), 643–650. doi: 10.1097/00004583-199906000-00010

Berman, S. L., Weems, C. F., Silverman, W. K., & Kurtines, W. M. (2000). Predictors of outcome in exposure-based cognitive and behavioral treatments for phobic anxiety disorders in children. *Behavior Therapy, 31*(4), 19.

Black, B. (1995). Separation anxiety disorder and panic disorder. In J. S. March (Ed.), *Anxiety disorders in children and adolescents* (pp. 212–234). Philadelphia, PA: Guilford Press.

Bouton, M. E., Woods, A. M., Moody, E. W., Sunsay, C., & Garcia-Gutierrez, A. (2006). Counteracting the context-dependence of extinction: Relapse and tests of some relapse prevention methods. In M. G. Craske, D. Hermans, & D. Vansteenwegen (Eds.), *Fear and learning: From basic processes to clinical implications* (pp. 175–196). Washington, DC: American Psychological Association.

Breinholst, S., Esbjørn, B. H., Reinholdt-Dunne, M. L., & Stallard, P. (2012). CBT for the treatment of child anxiety disorders: A review of why parental involvement has not enhanced outcomes. *Journal of Anxiety Disorders, 26*(3), 416–424. doi: 10.1016/j.janxdis.2011.12.014

Buckner, J. D., Schmidt, N. B., Lang, A. R., Small, J. W., Schlauch, R. C., & Lewinsohn, P. M. (2008). Specificity of social anxiety disorder as a risk factor for alcohol and cannabis dependence. *Journal of Psychiatric Research, 42*(3), 230–239. doi: 10.1016/j.jpsychires.2007.01.002

Cary, C. E., & McMillen, J. C. (2012). The data behind the dissemination: A systematic review of trauma-focused cognitive behavioral therapy for use with children and youth. *Children and Youth Services Review, 34*(4), 748–757. doi: 10.1016/j.childyouth.2012.01.003

Cobham, V. E., Dadds, M. R., & Spence, S. H. (1998). The role of parental anxiety in the treatment of childhood anxiety. *Journal of Consulting and Clinical Psychology, 66*(6), 893–905.

Cornwall, E., Spence, S. H., & Schotte, D. (1996). The effectiveness of emotive imagery in the treatment of darkness phobia in children. *Behaviour Change, 13*(4), 223–229.

Costello, E. J., Egger, H. L., & Angold, A. (2005). The developmental epidemiology of anxiety disorders: Phenomenology, prevalence, and comorbidity. *Child and Adolescent Psychiatric Clinics of North America, 14*(4), 631–648. doi: 10.1016/j.chc.2005.06.003

Dadds, M. R., Heard, P. M., & Rapee, R. M. (1992). The role of family intervention in the treatment of child anxiety disorders: Some preliminary findings. *Behaviour Change, 9*(3), 171–177.

Dadds, M. R., Marrett, P. M., & Rapee, R. M. (1996). Family process and child anxiety and aggression: An observational analysis. *Journal of Abnormal Child Psychology, 24*(6), 715–734. doi: 10.1007/BF01664736

Dadds, M. R., Perrin, S., & Yule, W. (1998). Social desirability and self-reported anxiety in children: An analysis of the RCMAS Lie Scale. *Journal of Abnormal Child Psychology, 26*(4), 311–317.

Dadds, M. R., Spence, S. H., Holland, D. E., Barrett, P. M., & Laurens, K. R. (1997). Prevention and early intervention for anxiety disorders: A controlled trial. *Journal of Consulting and Clinical Psychology, 65*(4), 627–635.

Davis, T. E., Ollendick, T. H., & Öst, L. G. (2009). Intensive treatment of specific phobias in children and adolescents. *Cognitive and Behavioral Practice, 16,* 294–303.

Davis, T. E., Ollendick, T. H., & Öst, L.-G. (2012). *Intensive one-session treatment of specific phobias.* New York, NY: Springer.

Ehlers, A. (1993). Somatic symptoms and panic attacks: A retrospective study of learning experiences. *Behaviour Research and Therapy, 31*(3), 269–278. doi: 10.1016/0005-7967(93)90025-P

Essau, C. A., Conradt, J., Sasagawa, S., & Ollendick, T. H. (2012). Prevention of anxiety symptoms in children: Results from a universal school-based trial. *Behavior Therapy, 43*(2), 450–464. doi: 10.1016/j.beth.2011.08.003

Flannery-Schroeder, E. C., & Kendall, P. C. (2000). Group and individual cognitive-behavioral treatments for youth with anxiety disorders: A randomized clinical trial. *Cognitive Therapy and Research, 24*(3), 251–278.

Franklin, M. E., Harrison, J. P., & Benavides, K. L. (2012). Obsessive-compulsive and tic-related disorders. *Child and Adolescent Psychiatric Clinics of North America, 21*(3), 555–571. doi: 10.1016/j.chc.2012.05.008

Futh, A., Simonds, L. M., & Micali, N. (2012). Obsessive-compulsive disorder in children and adolescents: Parental understanding, accommodation, coping and distress. *Journal of Anxiety Disorders, 26*(5), 624–632. doi: 10.1016/j.janxdis.2012.02.012

Grills, A. E., & Ollendick, T. H. (2002). Issues in parent-child agreement: The case of structured diagnostic interviews. *Clinical Child and Family Psychology Review, 5*(1), 57–83. doi: 10.1023/A:1014573708569

Grills-Taquechel, A. E., & Ollendick, T. H. (2013). *Phobic and anxiety disorders in children and adolescents.* Cambridge, MA: Hogrefe.

Gullone, E., & King, N. J. (1993). The fears of youth in the 1990s: Contemporary normative data. *The Journal of Genetic Psychology: Research and Theory on Human Development, 154*(2), 137–153. doi: 10.1080/00221325.1993.9914728

Hudson, J. L., & Rapee, R. M. (2001). Parent-child interactions and anxiety disorders: An observational study. *Behaviour Research & Therapy, 39*(12), 1411–1427.

Hudson, J. L., & Rapee, R. M. (2002). Parent-child interactions in clinically anxious children and their siblings. *Journal of Clinical Child and Adolescent Psychology, 31*(4), 548–555.

Kendall, P. C. (1994). Treating anxiety disorders in children: Results of a randomized clinical trial. *Journal of Consulting & Clinical Psychology, 62*(1), 100–110.

Kendall, P. C., Flannery-Schroeder, E., Panichelli-Mindel, S. M., Southam-Gerow, M., Henin, A., & Warman, M. (1997). Therapy for youths with anxiety disorders: A second randomized clincal trial. *Journal of Consulting and Clinical Psychology, 65*(3), 366–380. doi: 10.1037/0022-006X.65.3.366

Kendall, P. C., Gosch, E., Furr, J. M., & Sood, E. (2008). Flexibility within fidelity. *Journal of the American Academy of Child & Adolescent Psychiatry, 47*(9), 987–993. doi: 10.1097/CHI.0b013e31817eed2f

Kendall, P. C., Safford, S., Flannery-Schroeder, E., & Webb, A. (2004). Child anxiety treatment: Outcomes in adolescence and impact on substance use and depression at 7.4-year follow-up. *Journal of Consulting and Clinical Psychology, 72*(2), 276–287. doi: 10.1037/0022-006x.72.2.276

Kendall, P. C., & Southam-Gerow, M. A. (1996). Long-term follow-up of a cognitive-behavioral therapy for anxiety-disordered youth. *Journal of Consulting & Clinical Psychology, 64*(4), 724–730.

Khanna, M. S., & Kendall, P. C. (2010). Computer-assisted cognitive behavioral therapy for child anxiety: Results of a randomized clinical trial. *Journal of Consulting and Clinical Psychology, 78*(5), 737–745. doi: 10.1037/a0019739

Kim, S.-J., Kim, B.-N., Cho, S.-C., Kim, J.-W., Shin, M.-S., Yoo, H.-J., & Kim, H. W. (2010). The prevalence of specific phobia and associated co-morbid features in children and adolescents. *Journal of Anxiety Disorders, 24*(6), 629–634. doi: 10.1016/j.janxdis.2010.04.004

King, N. J., Tonge, B. J., Mullen, P., Myerson, N., Heyne, D., Rollings, S., . . . Ollendick, T. H. (2000). Treating sexually abused children with posttraumatic stress symptoms: A randomized clinical trial. *Journal of the American Academy of Child & Adolescent Psychiatry, 39*(11), 1347–1355.

Last, C., Hersen, M., & Kazdin, A. (1987). Comparison of DSM-III separation anxiety and overanxious disorders: Demographic characteristics and patterns of comorbidity. *Journal of the American Academy of Child & Adolescent Psychiatry, 26,* 527–531.

Leenarts, L. E. W., Diehle, J., Doreleijers, T. A. H., Jansma, E. P., & Lindauer, R. J. L. (2012). Evidence-based treatments for children with trauma-related psychopathology as a result of childhood maltreatment: A systematic review. *European Child & Adolescent Psychiatry.* doi: 10.1007/s00787-012-0367-5

Lester, K. J., Seal, K., Nightingale, Z. C., & Field, A. P. (2010). Are children's own interpretations of ambiguous situations based on how they perceive their mothers have interpreted ambiguous situations for them in the past? *Journal of Anxiety Disorders, 24*(1), 102–108. doi: 10.1016/j.janxdis.2009.09.004

Lieb, R., Wittchen, H.-U., Hoefler, M., Fuetsch, M., Stein, M. B., & Merikangas, K. R. (2000). Parental psychopathology, parenting styles, and the risk of social phobia in offspring: A prospective-longitudinal community study. *Archives of General Psychiatry, 57*(9), 859–866.

Lilienfeld, S. O., Wood, J. M., & Garb, H. N. (2000). The scientific status of projective techniques. *Psychological Science in the Public Interest, 1*(2), 27–66. doi: 10.1111/1529-1006.002

Lyneham, H. J., & Rapee, R. M. (2006). Evaluation of therapist-supported parent-implemented CBT for anxiety disorders in rural children. *Behaviour Research and Therapy, 44*(9), 1287–1300. doi: 10.1016/j.brat.2005.09.009

Manassis, K., Mendlowitz, S. L., Scapillato, D., Avery, D., Fiksenbaum, L., Freire, M., . . . Owens, M. (2002). Group and individual cognitive-behavioral therapy for childhood anxiety disorders: A randomized trial. *Journal of the American Academy of Child & Adolescent Psychiatry, 41*(12), 1423–1430. doi: 10.1097/01.Chi.0000024879.60748.5e

Mendlowitz, S. L., Manassis, K., Bradley, S., Scapillato, D., Miezitis, S., & Shaw, B. F. (1999). Cognitive-behavioral group treatments in childhood anxiety disorders: The role of parental involvement. *Journal of the American Academy of Child & Adolescent Psychiatry, 38*(10), 1223–1229.

Minde, K., Roy, J., Bezonsky, R., & Hashemi, A. (2010). The effectiveness of CBT in 3–7 year old anxious children: Preliminary data. *Journal of the Canadian Academy of Child & Adolescent Psychiatry, 19*(2), 19–115.

Muris, P., Mayer, B., Borth, M., & Vos, M. (2012). Nonverbal and verbal transmission of disgust from mothers to offspring: Effects on children's evaluation of a novel animal. *Behavior Therapy.* doi: 10.1016/j.beth.2012.10.002

Muris, P., & Merckelbach, H. (1998). Perceived parental rearing behaviour and anxiety disorders symptoms in normal children. *Personality & Individual Differences, 25*(6), 1199–1206.

Nauta, M. H., Scholing, A., Emmelkamp, P. M. G., & Minderaa, R. B. (2003). Cognitive-behavioral therapy for children with anxiety disorders in a clinical setting: No additional effect of a cognitive parent training. *Journal of the American Academy of Child & Adolescent Psychiatry, 42*(11), 1270–1278. doi: 10.1097/01.chi.0000085752.71002.93

Neil, A. L., & Christensen, H. (2009). Efficacy and effectiveness of school-based prevention and early intervention programs for anxiety. *Clinical Psychology Review, 29*(3), 208–215. doi: 10.1016/j.cpr.2009.01.002

Ollendick, T. H., Allen, B., Benoit, K., & Cowart, M. (2011). The tripartite model of fear in children with specific phobias: Assessing concordance and discordance using the behavioral approach test. *Behaviour Research and Therapy, 49*(8), 459–465. doi: 10.1016/j.brat.2011.04.003

Ollendick, T. H., Mattis, S. G., & King, N. J. (1994). Panic in children and adolescents: A review. *Journal of Child Psychology & Psychiatry, 35*(1), 113–134.

Ollendick, T. H., Öst, L.-G., Reuterskiöld, L., & Costa, N. (2010). Comorbidity in youth with specific phobias: Impact of comorbidity on treatment outcome and the impact of treatment on comorbid disorders. *Behaviour Research and Therapy, 48*(9), 827–831. doi: 10.1016/j.brat.2010.05.024

Ollendick, T. H., Öst, L.-G., Reuterskiöld, L., Costa, N., Cederlund, R., Sirbu, C., . . . Jarrett, M. A. (2009). One-session treatment of specific phobias in youth: A randomized clinical trial in the United States and Sweden. *Journal of Consulting and Clinical Psychology, 77*(3), 504–516. doi: 10.1037/a0015158

Öst, L. G., Svensson, L., Hellstrom, K., & Lindwall, R. (2001). One-session treatment of specific phobias in youths: A randomized clinical trial. *Journal of Consulting and Clinical Psychology, 69*(5), 814–824.

Pina, A. A., Silverman, W. K., Saavedra, L. M., & Weems, C. F. (2001). An analysis of the RCMAS lie scale in a clinic sample of anxious children. *Journal of Anxiety Disorders, 15*(5), 443–457.

Rapee, R. M. (2000). Group treatment of children with anxiety disorders: Outcome and predictors of treatment response. *Australian Journal of Psychology, 52*(3), 125–130. doi: 10.1080/00049530008255379

Rapee, R. M., Abbott, M. J., & Lyneham, H. J. (2006). Bibliotherapy for children with anxiety disorders using written materials for parents: A randomized controlled trial. *Journal of Consulting and Clinical Psychology, 74*(3), 436–444. doi: 10.1037/0022-006x.74.3.436

Safford, S. M., Kendall, P. C., Flannery-Schroeder, E., Webb, A., & Sommer, H. (2005). A longitudinal look at parent-child diagnostic agreement in youth treated for anxiety disorders. *Journal of Clinical Child and Adolescent Psychology, 34*(4), 747–757. doi: 10.1207/s15374424jccp3404_16

Seligman, L. D., & Ollendick, T. H. (1998). Comorbidity of anxiety and depression in children and adolescents: An integrative review. *Clinical Child and Family Psychology Review, 1*(2), 125–144.

Seligman, L. D., & Ollendick, T. H. (2011). Cognitive-behavioral therapy for anxiety disorders in youth. *Child and Adolescent Psychiatric Clinics of North America, 20*(2), 217–238. doi: 10.1016/j.chc.2011.01.003

Seligman, L. D., Ollendick, T. H., Langley, A. K., & Bechtoldt Baldacci, H. (2004). The utility of measures of child and adolescent anxiety: A meta-analytic review of the Revised Children's Anxiety Scale, the State-Trait Anxiety Inventory for Children, and the Child Behavior Checklist. *Journal of Clinical Child and Adolescent Psychology, 33*(3), 557–565.

Shortt, A. L., Barrett, P. M., & Fox, T. L. (2001). Evaluating the FRIENDS program: A cognitive-behavioral group treatment for anxious children and their parents. *Journal of Clinical Child Psychology, 30*(4), 525–535.

Silverman, W. K., & Albano, A. M. (1996). *Anxiety Disorders Interview Schedule for DSM-IV, Child Version.* San Antonio, TX: The Psychological Corporation.

Silverman, W. K., Kurtines, W. M., Ginsburg, G. S., Weems, C. F., Lumpkin, P. W., & Carmichael, D. H. (1999). Treating anxiety disorders in children with group cognitive-behaviorial therapy: A randomized clinical trial. *Journal of Consulting and Clinical Psychology, 67*(6), 995–1003.

Silverman, W. K., Kurtines, W. M., Ginsburg, G. S., Weems, C. F., Rabian, B., & Serafini, L. T. (1999). Contingency management, self-control, and education support in the treatment of childhood phobic disorders: A randomized clinical trial. *Journal of Consulting and Clinical Psychology, 67*(5), 675–687.

Silverman, W. K., & Ollendick, T. H. (2005). Evidence-based assessment of anxiety and its disorders in children and adolescents. *Journal of Clinical Child and Adolescent Psychology, 34*(3), 380–411.

Silverman, W. K., Saavedra, L. M., & Pina, A. A. (2001). Test-retest reliability of anxiety symptoms and diagnoses with anxiety disorders interview schedule for DSM-IV: Child and parent versions. *Journal of the American Academy of Child & Adolescent Psychiatry, 40*(8), 937–944. doi: 10.1097/00004583-200108000-00016

Simon, E., Dirksen, C., Bögels, S., & Bodden, D. (2012). Cost-effectiveness of child-focused and parent-focused interventions in a child anxiety prevention program. *Journal of Anxiety Disorders, 26*(2), 287–296. doi: 10.1016/j.janxdis.2011.12.008

Southam-Gerow, M. A., Kendall, P. C., & Weersing, V. R. (2001). Examining outcome variability: Correlates of treatment response in a child and adolescent anxiety clinic. *Journal of Clinical Child Psychology, 30*(3), 422–436.

Spence, S. H., Donovan, C., & Brechman-Toussaint, M. (2000). The treatment of childhood social phobia: The effectiveness of a social skills training-based, cognitive-behavioural intervention, with and without parental involvement. *Journal of Child Psychology and Psychiatry and Allied Disciplines, 41*(6), 713–726.

Stein, M. B., & Gorman, J. M. (2001). Unmasking social anxiety disorder. *Journal of Psychiatry and Neuroscience, 26*(3), 185.

Stopa, J. E., Barrett, P. M., & Golingi, F. (2010). The prevention of childhood anxiety in socioeconomically disadvantaged communities: A universal school-based trial. *Advances in School Mental Health Promotion, 3*(4), 5–24. doi: 10.1080/1754730X.2010.9715688

Storch, E. A., Geffken, G. R., Merlo, L. J., Mann, G., Duke, D., Munson, M., . . . Goodman, W. K. (2007). Family-based cognitive-behavioral therapy for pediatric obsessive-compulsive disorder: Comparison of intensive and weekly approaches. *Journal of the American Academy of Child & Adolescent Psychiatry, 46*(4), 469–478. doi: 10.1097/chi.0b013e31803062e7

Westenberg, P. M., Gullone, E., Bokhorst, C. L., Heyne, D. A., & King, N. J. (2007). Social evaluation fear in childhood and adolescence: Normative developmental course and continuity of individual differences. *British Journal of Developmental Psychology, 25*(3), 471–483. doi: 10.1348/026151006X173099

Wood, J. J., Piacentini, J. C., Southam-Gerow, M., Chu, B. C., & Sigman, M. (2006). Family cognitive behavioral therapy for child anxiety disorders. *Journal of the American Academy of Child & Adolescent Psychiatry, 45*(3), 314–321. doi: 10.1097/01.chi.0000196425.88341.b0

World Health Organization. (1992). *International classification of diseases* (10th rev. ed.). Geneva, Switzerland: Author.

CHAPTER 8

Anxiety Disorders in Adolescents

MICHAEL A. MALLOTT AND DEBORAH C. BEIDEL

BRIEF OVERVIEW OF ADOLESCENT ANXIETY DISORDERS

The development period of adolescence is marked by physical, social, and psychological changes. Early adolescence marks the development of metacognition and thus the ability to worry about the future. Socially, early adolescence is associated with the importance of peer groups and social status within those groups, requiring the ability to interact effectively and comfortably with others. Given these developmental milestones as well as others, it is not surprising that anxiety disorders are among the most common psychiatric disorders in adolescence (e.g., Costello, Egger, & Angold, 2005). Highlighting the importance of this developmental stage, the collective median age of onset for anxiety disorders appears to fall in early adolescence (Kessler, Berglund, Demler, Merikangas, & Walters, 2005). Although acknowledging the considerable heterogeneity in the age of onset for any specific anxiety disorders, it is clear that for many individuals, their anxiety symptoms will have developed by or will develop during adolescence.

Among adolescents, prevalence is highest for specific phobia (19.3%), followed by social phobia (9.1%), separation anxiety disorder (7.6%), posttraumatic stress disorder (5.0%), agoraphobia (2.4%), panic disorder (PD) (2.3%), and generalized anxiety disorder (GAD) (2.2%) (Merikangas et al., 2010), illustrating the number of adolescents who are seriously impacted by these disorders. Even though highly prevalent, the impact of these disorders may be underestimated. Parents may not seek treatment for an anxious adolescent because they incorrectly assume that the adolescent will simply grow out of the problem. However, the importance of early treatment for adolescents with anxiety disorders is highlighted by a number of studies that reflect the chronicity and severity of these issues. Anxiety disorders are characterized by a chronic unremitting course (Woodward & Fergusson, 2001), and the trajectory of anxiety disorders is generally in the direction of increased rather than decreased prevalence over the period of adolescence (Essau, Conradt, & Petermann, 2000; Newman et al., 1996). These disorders also are associated with significant impairment in a number of domains that affect development (Langley, Bergman, McCracken, & Piacentini, 2004). Consequently, delays in treatment may exacerbate the already negative impact associated with anxiety disorders.

Although some adolescents may suffer from only one anxiety disorder, comorbidity is a significant problem; 42% of one sample who met criteria for one disorder also met criteria for at least one other disorder (Merikangas et al., 2010). The most common co-occurring disorders are other anxiety disorders, depression, conduct disorder, and alcohol abuse (Clark, Smith, Neighbors, Skerlec, & Randal, 1994; Ollendick, Jarrett, Grills-Taquechel, Howey, & Wolff, 2008). Some studies suggest that comorbidity is a bigger problem in adolescent anxiety disorders than in adult disorders (Lewinsohn, Hops, Roberts, Seeley, & Andrews, 1993; Rohde, Lewinsohn, & Seeley, 1996). Although comorbidity does not necessarily affect the overall rate of symptom reduction (Kendall,

Brady, & Verduin, 2001; Rapee, 2003), it may affect the end point of treatment as comorbidity may serve as a marker for symptom severity (Rapee et al., 2013).

EVIDENCE-BASED APPROACHES

Most studies and meta-analyses examining treatment outcome reveal consistent support for exposure-based cognitive behavioral therapies (CBTs). In fact, the outcome data are so consistently positive that CBT is recognized as the treatment of choice for adolescents with anxiety disorders (e.g., Kendall, 1994; Ollendick & King, 1998; Silverman, Pina, & Viswesvaran, 2008). Often, treatment samples have been transdiagnostic in nature and the CBT interventions are likewise transdiagnostic, allowing their implementation across the broad spectrum of anxiety disorders. Thus, the core elements of CBT are seen as equally applicable to separation anxiety disorder, social phobia, and GAD as these disorders share many features and appear to be distinct from other anxiety disorders (cf. Velting, Setzer, & Albano, 2004). These interventions attempt to address underlying commonalities across forms of problematic anxiety (physiological arousal, subjective distress, behavioral avoidance). Many CBT protocols follow a similar format and include identical elements: psychoeducation, skills training (somatic management and problem solving), cognitive restructuring, exposure, and relapse prevention (Velting et al., 2004). Next, we describe each of these elements as they pertain to the treatment of anxiety disorders in adolescents.

Common Features of CBT

There are many different interventions that are included under the umbrella term of cognitive behavioral treatment (CBT). Psychosocial intervention typically proceeds the implementation of any active intervention.

Psychoeducation

Usually didactic in nature, information is provided about the nature of anxiety and emotions in general, features of the specific anxiety disorder being targeted in treatment, and the critical function of exposure therapy as part of the treatment program. This initial phase of treatment is not intended to be an active intervention but provides the rationale for CBT and may include attention to the role of behavioral avoidance and the recognition of anxious emotional states, including somatic cues of distress. For some forms of CBT, understanding when to implement anxiety management skills requires recognition of an anxious emotional state. Thus, the psychoeducation portion of treatment serves as the foundation for other components introduced later in treatment.

Coping Skill Training

After providing psychoeducation, many CBT protocols address coping skill development. Across many protocols, skill development includes a focus on managing the somatic symptoms through the use of relaxation training and/or problem-solving skills. For example, the C.A.T. program, an adolescent version of the Coping Cat protocol (Kendall, Choudhury, Hudson, & Webb, 2002), teaches adolescents how to engage in relaxation techniques (deep breathing, progressive muscle relaxation, use of relaxation aids) and identify the presence of somatic cues that indicate the need to implement coping responses (O'Neil, Brodman, Cohen, Edmunds, & Kendall, 2012). After acquiring relaxation skills, the C.A.T. protocol moves to training problem-solving skills. First, these problem-solving skills are practiced with nonstressful situations. Later, the skills are applied to more stressful situations. Problem-solving skills teach a method to deal with anxiety-provoking situations rather than feeling helpless about them. An adolescent dealing with test anxiety, for example, can learn to engage in positive study habits to prepare for tests rather than allowing worry about tests to result in avoidance of thoughts about and lack of preparation for tests. The development of problem-solving skills therefore can lead adolescents from behavioral avoidance to active engagement in problematic situations.

Cognitive Restructuring

Another common component of CBT for adolescents with anxiety disorders is the use of cognitive restructuring. Although the central importance of cognition and cognitive restructuring in the etiology and treatment of anxiety disorders in children and adolescents remains an open question (Beidel & Turner, 2007), research has been relatively consistent concerning the association between maladaptive cognitive processes and anxiety in children and adolescents. One study suggests that certain types of cognitive processes may play a casual role in the development and maintenance of posttraumatic stress disorder (Meiser-Stedman, Dalgleish, Glucksman, Yule, & Smith, 2009). Other data suggest that specific cognitive coping skills may be associated with problematic anxiety (Garnefski, Legerstee, Kraaij, Van den Kommer, & Teerds, 2002), and these coping skills may differentiate anxiety-disordered and nonanxious adolescents (Legerstee, Garnefski, Verhulst, & Utens, 2011), suggesting a role for cognitive processes in the maintenance of the disorder but not necessarily its onset. For a review of the role of cognitions in the development and maintenance of anxiety in children and adolescence, see Muris and Field (2008). Regardless of its hypothesized role in etiology, cognitive restructuring is a significant component of many CBT protocols, and its general principles are discussed here.

The general goals of cognitive restructuring are the identification of thoughts that may serve to produce or perpetuate anxiety and the use of techniques to challenge these thoughts. Therapists help identify inaccurate and negative thought patterns. For example, an adolescent with social anxiety disorder may identify a number of cognitive distortions, such as: overestimating the amount of attention directed at him/her, misinterpreting the outcome of social encounters as more negative than they actually are, and foreclosing on the belief that he/she will ever be socially competent. After identifying these thoughts, techniques are used to develop more realistic and accurate assessments of situations and alter self-talk to be more positive and proactive. These techniques include but are not limited to Socratic questioning, behavioral experiments, evidence examination, and cognitive rehearsal (Basco, Glickman, Weatherford, & Ryser, 2000; Kendall, Chu, Pimentel, & Choudhury, 2000). To continue the example, the adolescent might be asked to engage in social situations to observe how much attention is really focused on him/her and provide examples of positive and negative outcomes. The adolescent may be asked to reflect on what went right in the situations or recall times when he/she displayed adequate social skills, such as situations with family members when anxiety may have been minimal. Although many cognitive restructuring techniques exist, the results of their use should be more flexible, positive, and objective beliefs about anxiety-provoking situations.

Exposure

Although there are variations among CBT protocols, one common and essential feature is the inclusion of exposure to effect reduction of anxiety and associated symptoms (Kazdin & Weisz, 1998; Kendall et al., 2005). Exposure involves having adolescents face their fear directly. Exposure typically is done in a graduated fashion in which less feared situations are attempted before more challenging ones. Although the specific exposure instructions vary by protocol, typically the individual is asked to remain in contact with the feared situation or object until a specific length of time has passed or until habituation occurs (i.e., a reduction or elimination of anxiety in the situation). When situations cannot be reproduced in the clinic environment, imaginal exposure can be used. In imaginal exposure, the adolescent is asked to imagine feared stimuli using mental sensory cues to produce an accurate and realistic depiction of the feared stimuli. Depending on the availability, reproducibility, and actual threat value of the feared stimuli, treatment can make use of either or both types of exposure, imaginal and/or in vivo (actual live exposure to stimuli), although in-vivo exposure may produce more favorable results (Ultee, Griffioen, & Schellekens, 1982).

Regardless of the type of exposure, the procedure for carrying out exposure exercises is generally the same and consists of developing a list of anxiety-provoking situations, rating identified situations according to amount of anxiety elicited, and exposing the adolescent to these situations according to a graded hierarchy (Kendall et al., 2005). First, the adolescent, parent(s), teacher, or other parties knowledgeable about the adolescent are consulted about situations that typically provoke anxiety. Identification of these situations can be obtained through self-report scales, interviews, diaries, and/or behavioral observations. It may be particularly useful to gain information about situations that pose the most impairment, so these situations can be addressed specifically in treatment. It is useful to construct a list of situations with varying levels of distress to facilitate treatment and provide a graduated experience of exposure to increasing levels of distress in treatment sessions. Once a working list of situations is developed, the adolescent provides ratings using a Subjective Units of Distress Scale (SUDS) (Wolpe, 1969). Although the exact numerical anchors used for the SUDS ratings are somewhat arbitrary, some recommend making use of smaller numbers (e.g., 0–8 scale) and additional visual aids (e.g., fear thermometer) to help keep ratings simple and clear for children and adolescents (Kendall et al., 2005). Once situations have been assigned an associated SUDS level, the SUDS ratings are used to determine which situations will be addressed first in treatment. In some protocols, adolescents are encouraged to use their coping skills while engaged in the exposure task. In other cases, distraction is considered counterproductive. To date, there are no data regarding which of these strategies is more effective.

Relapse Prevention

The last element of many CBT protocols is consolidation of skills and experiences introduced in treatment and increasing the independent implementation of these strategies by the adolescent. Sessions become less frequent (e.g., move from weekly to biweekly sessions) in this phase of treatment. Before complete termination, booster sessions may occur at longer intervals (e.g., monthly sessions). Empirical studies are needed to determine whether these extra sessions increase effectiveness of treatment (Compton et al., 2004), but, nonetheless, many protocols formally outline their inclusion.

In addition to transdiagnostic CBT protocols, other empirically supported treatments are designed to address specific anxiety disorders. These specific interventions often include some of the same elements contained in more generic CBT interventions, but these elements are tailored to the unique symptom characteristics of specific anxiety disorders. To reduce redundancy, only the unique aspects of these interventions are described next.

Features of CBT for Specific Anxiety Disorders

With that general framework in mind, we now turn attention to interventions used for some of the individual anxiety disorders.

Social Anxiety Disorder

Even though developers of many transdiagnostic CBT protocols have indicated that these general treatments are appropriate for adolescents with social anxiety disorders, there is evidence that socially phobic children do not respond as well to these treatments as children with other anxiety disorders (Crawley, Beidas, Benjamin, Martin, & Kendall, 2008). Fortunately, specific treatments for child and adolescent social anxiety disorder have been relatively well researched. A number of studies have provided evidence for the effectiveness of these social phobia–specific treatments in the short and long term (Albano, Marten, Holt, Heimberg, & Barlow, 1995; Beidel et al., 2007; Beidel, Turner, & Morris, 2000; García-López et al., 2006; Spence, Donovan, & Brechman-Toussant, 2000).

Although most of the elements common to CBT for other anxiety disorders are part of the interventions developed for social anxiety disorder, several protocols include additional treatment elements. For instance, most of these specific protocols focus on the development of social skills, sometimes substituting this element for skills to manage somatic symptoms of anxiety. For example, Social Effectiveness Therapy for Children and Adolescents (SET-C) (Beidel et al., 2003) devotes 12 sessions to teaching and practicing social skills (e.g., conversational skills, establishing and maintaining friendships, appropriate assertiveness). Many of these treatments also are delivered in a group format (e.g., Group Cognitive Behavioral Treatment for Adolescents [GCBT-A]) (Albano, Marten, & Holt, 1991), and some incorporate nonanxious peers to practice social skill development (Beidel et al., 2000; Olivares & García-López, 1998). The group format may provide additional exposure opportunities, given the interpersonal nature of social phobia. The setting of treatment also has been adapted in some treatments to include implementation in schools (e.g., Skills for Academic and Social Success [SASS]) (Masia, Klein, Storch, & Corda, 2001). One of the advantages of implementing treatment in school is the environment may be the primary setting in which adolescents experience social distress. Even when social skills training is included as an element of the treatment package, the emphasis of these protocols remains on exposure, and some treatments omit explicit focus on cognitive elements entirely in favor of behavioral techniques (e.g., SET-C).

Panic Disorder and Agoraphobia

Treatments specifically designed for adolescents with PD have received little attention until relatively recently. Work by Mattis and colleagues (Mattis et al., 2001; Mattis & Pincus, 2004; Pincus, Ehrenreich, Whitton, Mattis, & Barlow, 2010) has provided evidence for the efficacy of panic control treatment (PCT) adapted for use with adolescents. Similar to other forms of CBT, PCT includes psychoeducation, skills training, cognitive restructuring, exposure, and relapse prevention; however, the focus of the elements is specific to symptoms of PD and agoraphobic avoidance (see Hoffman & Mattis, 2000, for an overview of PCT session by session). One unique aspect of PCT compared with generic CBT for adolescents with anxiety disorders is the inclusion of breathing retraining to counteract the hyperventilatory response associated with PD. Adolescents are taught to breathe deeply from the diaphragm to counteract escalating physical symptoms associated with hyperventilation during a panic attack. Another unique aspect of PCT is the focus on interoceptive cues in exposure. Physiological sensations are induced during exposure to help adolescents habituate to these feared sensations. For example, an adolescent who fears feeling dizzy may be asked to spin in a chair during a session to induce feelings of dizziness and repeat this activity to habituate to the sensation of dizziness. When present, agoraphobic avoidance is also addressed with exposure. The cognitive restructuring component of PCT focuses on the probability overestimation of feared events and the belief in the catastrophic consequences of the feared event (e.g., I'm going to faint in the mall, and I'll hit my head and die).

Generalized Anxiety Disorder

Although most transdiagnostic treatments for adolescent anxiety were developed to treat a cluster of anxiety disorders including GAD, some have begun to develop treatments specifically tailored for GAD (e.g., Léger, Ladouceur, Dugas, & Freeston, 2003; Payne, Bolton, & Perrin, 2001). Adaptations to CBT for GAD generally have not deviated from transdiagnostic CBT but rather focus on individual elements of CBT most related to the GAD clinical syndrome. For instance, these treatments tend to emphasize remediating problematic worry and develop better tolerance to uncertainty in cognitive restructuring and exposure. Specifically, cognitive restructuring focuses on evaluating beliefs about worry, including the usefulness of worry. Treatment also may focus on the development of tolerance to uncertainty by engaging in situations with uncertain outcomes and exposing adolescents to threatening mental images, especially images related to worry content. Problem-solving skills typically are part of GAD-specific treatment and include understanding the difference between solvable and unsolvable problems. Adolescents also are taught to redirect their focus on elements of threat in problematic situations and to identify benefits that can be obtained from problematic situations, such as preparing them for similar situations in the future.

The length of treatment and resources involved in implementing treatment protocols vary considerably. Reviews of CBT protocols for anxiety disorders list ranges of 6 to 24 sessions, with most treatments outlining 10 to 15 sessions (Ishikawa, Okajima, Matsuoka, & Sakano, 2007; Silverman et al., 2008). These reviews also point out that treatment sessions may be delivered in a group format or individually and may or may not incorporate parents and/or other family members.

PARENTAL INVOLVEMENT IN TREATMENT

Research on the role of incorporating parents and family into treatment of adolescents with anxiety disorders has yielded mixed findings. Some studies report that parental involvement in treatment may lead to better outcomes (Barrett, Dadds, & Rapee, 1996, Mendlowitz et al., 1999), but these better outcomes may be limited to younger children (Barrett et al., 1996). Other studies have suggested that parental involvement may enhance treatment when the parents themselves also have anxiety (Cobham, Dadds, & Spence, 1998). Also, studies suggest that parenting characteristics can affect adolescent anxiety symptomology (Hale, Engels, & Meeus, 2006). A few issues related to implementing parental involvement in treatment have been provided.

A number of studies have established a link between parental and child anxiety (Ginsburg & Schlossberg, 2002; Rapee, 2001), so it seems reasonable that the focus of parental involvement in treatment may address how anxiety in parents might impact the maintenance of anxiety in the children. Four characteristics of parental anxiety that may be particularly relevant to parental involvement in the treatment of adolescents with anxiety disorders include: parental overinvolvement/overcontrol, parental assumptions/beliefs, modeling/reinforcement of anxious behavior, and family conflict/dysfunction (Breinholst, Esbjørn, Reinholdt-Dunne, & Stallard, 2012). In an effort to manage their anxiety, anxious parents may develop an overcontrolling style that may hinder efforts of adolescents to develop confidence in their own ability to navigate new situations (Breinholst et al., 2012). To counteract these issues, they recommend that treatment include components that address the parents' own difficulty with allowing their adolescent to face fears adaptively. Parents need to understand how excessive control may inadvertently foster increased anxiety in their adolescent. Along these lines, parents may need to face and challenge underlying assumptions and beliefs about their adolescent and/or their own ability to protect him/her. Doing this may allow parents to relinquish control and allow the adolescent to engage in exposure necessary to treatment progress.

In addition, contingency management strategies (e.g., Cartwright-Hatton, Laskey, Rusk, & McNally, 2010) can be used in treatment to help parents model and reinforce appropriate, adaptive behavior in anxiety-provoking situations. Parents can learn to identify and reward these behaviors and provide consistent encouragement of approach-related behavior in these situations. Finally, treatment may include parental skill development in the areas of positive communication and problem solving (Breinholst et al., 2012). Parents may need to develop more positive and proactive behavior rather than rely on rejection and criticism as parenting tools. Parents are taught about the importance of consistency, develop conflict-resolution skills, and model these skills for their adolescent.

ADAPTATIONS AND MODIFICATIONS

Although many interventions for adolescents with anxiety disorders were developed concurrently with treatments for younger children, treatment with adolescents poses unique challenges. First, attention to developmental issues may be a particularly important part of treatment planning, given the wide range of physical, cognitive, and emotional maturation found even among same-age adolescents (Oetzel & Scherer, 2003). For example, it may be more important in group treatment to consider developmental age rather than chronological age when making group composition decisions. Group dynamics may be affected by the social and cognitive development of its constituents, and individuals in the group may benefit more from a group composed of developmentally similar adolescents to maximize relevance, interpersonal interactions, and comprehension. In individual treatment, emphasis on cognitive components of treatments likewise should consider development rather than age to determine how much time and complexity should be devoted to cognitive therapeutic techniques. Further, engagement in treatment can be complicated in adolescents because of normal developmental processes that favor the development of autonomy and resistance to authority (Sauter, Heyne, & Westenberg, 2009). Compounding this problem, adolescents typically do not seek therapy (Piacentini & Bergman, 2001), so they may enter treatment already resistant to the process. As a consequence, motivational issues need to be addressed early in treatment. Promoting an open, active, and cooperative treatment environment may help mitigate some of these issues (Friedberg & McClure, 2002).

In addition to developmental issues that may drive treatment decisions, other adaptations and modifications related to treatment delivery may be considered. One adaptation that may reduce the cost and burden of treatment is the use of group format as opposed to treatment with individual adolescents. Research generally supports group CBT as an effective alternative to individual treatment of adolescent anxiety disorders (Liber et al., 2008), although in some cases individual treatment may be somewhat more potent than group treatment (Flannery-Schroeder & Kendall, 2000). Further, many of the treatments for social phobia, such as SET-C, are specifically designed as group interventions since the focus of treatment is social fears. An additional benefit of utilizing a group format in the treatment of socially phobic adolescents is that exposure is built into the format given the interpersonal nature of group treatment, although in at least one study children with very high levels of social anxiety benefited more from individual rather than group treatment (Manassis et al., 2002).

Because of rapid advances in computer and telecommunications technologies, many researchers are investigating how these technologies can be incorporated into treatment. Some have suggested that CBT is a good candidate for computer-based delivery (Anderson, Jacobs, & Rothbaum, 2004), given its structure and focus. Although research on computer-based treatments is in a relatively early stage, several studies show promise in altering existing protocols for computer-based delivery. A series of studies provided preliminary evidence for effective delivery of the BRAVE transdiagnostic anxiety treatment over the Internet (March, Spence, & Donovan, 2009; Spence, Holmes, March, & Lipp, 2006; Spence et al., 2008). Cool Teens, a computerized version of the C.A.T. project, is currently in development as well (Cunningham et al., 2009). Virtual environments also are being developed to assist in social skill generalization for children and adolescents with social anxiety disorder (Wong Sarver, Beidel, & Spitalnick, 2014). Many technologies offer the potential to augment or replace traditional delivery of CBT, including: laptops, smartphones, other palm-held devices, tablet computers, and virtual reality/ virtual enhancement. More research is needed to determine which computer-based interventions are effective treatments for adolescent anxiety. The progress of this research should be monitored as cost and access issues may make computer-based delivery of CBT an attractive therapeutic option.

MEASURING TREATMENT EFFECTS

A number of well-validated measures exist to provide objective data about treatment outcome with general and specific anxiety symptoms. In most cases, use of multiple informants will provide the most robust outcome data (De Los Reyes, Alfano, & Beidel, 2011; March & Albano, 1996). Relying solely on data from adolescents may result in the underreporting of symptoms (Silverman & Eisen, 1992), and parents may provide more reliable data for some sets of symptoms than adolescents (Schniering, Hudson, & Rapee, 2000). Although not inclusive, the measures listed next provide a good overview of some of the better-supported instruments for measuring treatment change in adolescent anxiety disorders.

Assessment of Anxiety Disorders

Next we review the most commonly used strategies for the assessment of anxiety disorders.

Anxiety Disorders Interview Schedule for DSM-IV, Child and Parent Versions

One commonly used semistructured interview to assess the presence of anxiety disorders in adolescents (and children) is the Anxiety Disorders Interview Schedule for *DSM-IV*, child and parent versions (ADIS-IV-C/P) (Silverman & Albano, 1996). Both the child and parent versions assess the presence of anxiety, mood, and externalizing disorders and also allow the clinician to record distress ratings for individual situations/stimuli related to most anxiety disorders, interference ratings for all disorders, and overall clinician severity ratings for each diagnosis. The ADIS-IV-C/P is a well-validated interview that is useful as a measure of diagnostic and severity change over the course of treatment (Piacentini & Bergman, 2000; Silverman & Berman, 2001; Silverman et al., 1999).

Multidimensional Anxiety Scale for Children

The Multidimensional Anxiety Scale for Children (MASC) (March, 1997) is a 39-item self-report measure that assesses overall anxiety and provides anxiety disorder index scores along with scale scores for physical symptoms of anxiety, social anxiety, harm avoidance, and separation/panic. The MASC is appropriate through adolescence and has been established as a measure of treatment outcome for anxious youth (Barrett, Healy-Farrell, & March, 2004; White, Ollendick, Scahill, Oswald, & Albano, 2009).

Child Behavior Checklist

The Child Behavior Checklist (CBCL) (Achenbach & Rescorla, 2001) is one of the most widely used parental measures of child and adolescent psychopathology (Bérubé & Achenbach, 2002).

In addition to the CBCL, there is also a teacher's report form (TRF) for ages 6 to 18 and a youth self-report (YSR) for ages 11 to 18. All versions yield normative scores for symptom scales on eight factors:

1. Anxious/depressed
2. Withdrawn/depressed
3. Somatic complaints
4. Social problems
5. Thought problems
6. Attention problems
7. Rule-breaking behavior
8. Aggressive behavior

The YSR and CBCL also provide scores for activity, social, and academic competency. The TRF provides academic performance and adaptive functioning scores. The CBCL and related measures can be helpful to assess treatment improvement in anxiety and other comorbid conditions as they tap a broad spectrum of symptoms in addition to anxiety problems.

Disorder-Specific Measures

In addition to multidimensional measures, other measures are geared specifically toward the assessment of one specific anxiety disorder

Social Anxiety Disorder

The Social Phobia and Anxiety Inventory for Children (SPAI-C) (Beidel, Turner, & Morris, 1995) is a 26-item self-report used to measure somatic, cognitive, and behavioral symptoms associated with social phobia. Although originally recommended to be used with children ages 8 to 13, further research supported its use with older children (Storch, Masia-Werner, Dent, Roberti, & Fisher, 2004). Alternatively, the version designed for adults, SPAI (Turner, Beidel, Dancu, & Stanley, 1989), also has been validated for use with adolescents (Clark et al., 1994). When deciding which version to administer to an individual adolescent, it may be important to evaluate the item content from both measures to determine which measure best reflects the individual adolescent's experience since some items on the adult version may not relate to everyday experiences of youth. The SPAI-C and SPAI have been shown to be sensitive to the effects of treatment (Beidel et al., 2007; Hayward et al., 2000).

Another widely used measure of social phobia in adolescence is the Social Anxiety Scale for Adolescents (SAS-A) (La Greca & Lopez, 1998). The SAS-A is a self-report measure containing 18 anxiety-related items and four "filler" items and provides a total score of social anxiety as well as scores on three factors: fear of negative evaluation, social avoidance and distress specific to new situations, and generalized social avoidance and distress. The SAS-A has demonstrated good discriminate validity in differentiating adolescents with and without social phobia (Storch et al., 2004) and has shown good treatment sensitivity (March, Entusah, Rynn, Albano, & Tourian, 2007; Wagner et al., 2004).

Behavioral assessment of social skills is a method by which to assess the ability of adolescents to engage in social interactions with peers. Adolescents are presented with role-play scenarios or a "typical peer situation" (e.g., play a game on Wii with a peer) and their behaviors are digitally recorded and later scored for elements of social behavior (conversation initiation, eye contact, length of speech, etc.). The use of behavioral assessment to assess social skills in children and adolescents with social anxiety disorder has been repeatedly validated both to document their presence in youth with social anxiety disorder (e.g., Scharfstein, Beidel, Sims, & Finnell, 2011) and as a sensitive measure of treatment outcome (Scharfstein, Beidel, Finnell, Distler, & Carter, 2011).

Panic Disorder

Anxiety sensitivity is a construct that, like the work in adult PD, has been shown to be associated with PD in children and adolescents (Kearney, Albano, Eisen, Allan, & Barlow, 1997) and a risk factor for PD (Hale & Calamari, 2006). Therefore, it may be useful to obtain information about anxiety sensitivity levels when assessing treatment progress in adolescents with PD. Anxiety sensitivity is a fear of and sensitivity to anxiety-related physiological symptoms (Taylor, 1995). The Child Anxiety Sensitivity Index (CASI) (Silverman, Fleisig, Rabian, & Peterson, 1991) is an 18-item self-report measure of anxiety sensitivity. In addition to an overall anxiety sensitivity score, the CASI also provides scores on three lower-order factors: physical, social, and cognitive concerns. There is some evidence that these lower-order factors may be incrementally predictive of clusters of anxiety symptoms after controlling for trait anxiety (McLaughlin, Stewart, & Taylor, 2007); therefore, there may be utility in employing the CASI as a general measure of anxiety in addition to its use in adolescents with PD.

Generalized Anxiety Disorder

Given the importance of the construct of worry to GAD, the inclusion of a worry-specific measure in a treatment outcome assessment battery for GAD may be informative. The Penn State Worry Questionnaire for Children (PSWQ-C) (Chorpita, Tracey, Brown, Collica, & Barlow, 1997) is a 14-item self-report measure of worry in children and adolescents ages 7 to 17. At least one study found that the PSWQ-C was able to differentiate children with GAD from children with other anxiety disorders (Pestle, Chorpita, & Shiffman, 2008). One note of caution has been provided by several studies about three reverse-scored items on the PSWQ-C (Chorpita et al., 1997; Muris, Meesters, & Goble, 2001; Pestle et al., 2008); however, it is recommended that these three items be retained because they may increase the validity of the PSWQ-C (Pestle et al., 2008). Several studies have used the PSWQ-C successfully as a measure of treatment outcome (Léger et al., 2003; Muris et al., 2002; Payne et al., 2011).

CLINICAL CASE EXAMPLE

Tyler is a 14-year-old male with social anxiety disorder. His parents referred him for treatment because his fear of negative evaluation was disrupting his and his family's life. To understand the full extent of Tyler's symptoms and severity of impairment, the SPAI-C was administered. Although all types of evaluation elicited anxiety in Tyler, he was particularly bothered by speaking to boys his own age. He loved sports but would not join any teams because he might "make a mistake" and the "other guys will laugh at me." He would pretend that he did not know the answer if called on in class because he was afraid of making a mistake. He refused to go to restaurants with his family because one time, when he was 8 years old, he spilled a glass of water in a restaurant and other people looked at him when the waitstaff came to clean up. He was also uncomfortable around girls his age and adults. At family gatherings, he would hide in his room, unable to even interact with his

Note: Identifying information has been altered.

grandparents. As a consequence of these behaviors, other adolescents viewed him as odd and aloof, and his parents noted that he had few, if any, friends. His parents also noted that Tyler had been shy since he was a toddler, and had never engaged in interactions with other children. Tyler was able to acknowledge a desire to engage in peer activities, but fear of negative evaluation took precedence over cultivation of peer relationships. He stated that he "did not know how" to talk to other adolescents and he "could not think of anything to say" when thrust into a social interaction with another person. At times, Tyler was verbally abusive toward his sister if she would not order for him in a restaurant or answer the telephone if their parents were not home. His fears were becoming more severe, and he was beginning to skip school so he would not have to interact with other people. The ADIS-IV-C and ADIS-IV-P were also administered as part of the diagnostic process. Both child and parent interviews confirmed the diagnosis of social anxiety disorder, but no other comorbid disorder was appropriate. A behavioral assessment of social skill indicated that Tyler indeed did not have the social skills necessary to engage with peers in typical social situations.

Given Tyler's presentation, Social Effectiveness Therapy for Children (SET-C), which consists of both exposure and social skills training, was the most appropriate intervention. The initial treatment session was spent helping Tyler and his parents understand the nature of social anxiety disorder, and the function of exposure and social skills training in treatment. It was also explained that an important part of the exposure was the need to stay in the situation until his anxiety dissipated. They also learned that exposure alone would not be effective for eliminating his anxiety in social encounters, if he did not also possess the knowledge and skills necessary to engage in effective social interactions. Therefore, in addition to exposure, Tyler would learn the skills necessary to interact in social settings.

Tyler's treatment plan consisted of two sessions per week. One session was devoted to social skills training and the second to exposure therapy. Social skills training was conducted using the SET-C manual (Beidel, Turner & Morris, 1998) and included the following topics:

- Social Environment Awareness
  - Recognition of social cues
  - Greeting others
- Conversational Skills
  - Initiating conversations
  - Appropriate conversational topics
  - Maintaining and ending conversations
- Interpersonal Skills Enhancement
  - Skills for joining groups
  - Establishing and maintaining friendships
  - Giving and receiving compliments
  - Assertiveness
  - Telephone skills

Social skills training sessions included a review of the prior skills session, the acquisition of the new skills (using instruction, modeling, behavior rehearsal, positive reinforcement, and feedback), and homework assignments designed to promote skill generalization. Social skills training is typically conducted using a group format, as it allows practice with different interpersonal partners. Groups are formed based on similar ages to address developmental issues. At the time Tyler was seeking treatment, there were no other adolescents of similar age requesting treatment. Therefore, social skills training was conducted individually with the use of the *Pegasys-VR*™ system (Spitalnick &

Beidel, in preparation), which allows clinicians in nonresearch settings to provide social skills training and peer generalization experiences without the need for same-age peers. Using virtual humans (male teacher, female teacher, principal, gym teacher, school bully, smart peer, friendly boy peer, friendly girl peer), the clinician is able to provide practice partners and skill generalization opportunities using a virtual environment. Furthermore, the clinician has a total of 744 unique verbal responses across these eight characters, allowing for a rich dialogue between the adolescent and the various avatars. Therefore, the therapist can arrange for a dose-controlled strategy to control the speed of skill acquisition, assuring acquisition of basic skills before moving to more advanced interactions (Wong Sarver et al., 2014).

In vivo exposure sessions also were conducted once per week based on a hierarchy established by Tyler and his therapist. The hierarchy was constructed as follows:

1. Greet and say hello to unknown persons.
2. Conduct a survey of people on campus (requires asking questions).
3. Go to a mall and ask salespeople questions about products for sale.
4. Go to a local ice cream shop with a same-age, unfamiliar peer. Purchase ice cream and talk with peer.
5. Repeat task above with two peers.

Initially, Tyler was required to walk around the college campus where the sessions were conducted, making eye contact and saying hello to strangers who walked by. During the sessions, Tyler's anxiety was monitored using an 8-point SUDS. Items higher on the hierarchy were introduced once Tyler no longer exhibited or reported anxiety on the lower items.

After the completion of the 24 SET-C sessions, the ADIS-IV-C, ADIS-IV-P, and SPAI-C were readministered. Tyler exhibited marked changes on these measures. Both he and his parents noticed significant changes in his social life. He had developed significant friendships with three other boys his age and was invited and attended a sleepover, which he reported would have been impossible to do at the beginning of treatment. He was attending school regularly, was raising his hand in class, joined the chess club, and was going to restaurants with his family.

REFERENCES

Achenbach, T. M., & Rescorla, L. A. (2001). *Manual for the ASEBA School-Age Forms & Profiles*. Burlington, VT: University of Vermont, Research Center for Children, Youth, & Families.

Albano, A. M., Marten, P. A., & Holt, C. S. (1991). *Cognitive-behavioral treatment for adolescent social phobia: A treatment manual*. Unpublished manuscript, State University of New York at Albany.

Albano, A. M., Marten, P. A., Holt, C. S., Heimberg, R. G., & Barlow, D. H. (1995). Cognitive-behavioral group treatment for social phobia in adolescents: A preliminary study. *Journal of Nervous and Mental Disease, 183,* 649–656.

Anderson, P., Jacobs, C., & Rothbaum, B. O. (2004). Computer-supported cognitive behavioral treatment of anxiety disorders. *Journal of Clinical Psychology, 60,* 253–267.

Barrett, P., Healy-Farrell, L., & March, J. (2004). Treatment of OCD in children and adolescents. In P. Barrett & T. Ollendick (Eds.), *Handbook of interventions that work with children and adolescents: Prevention and treatment* (pp. 187–216). West Sussex, UK: Wiley.

Barrett, P. M., Dadds, M. R., & Rapee, R. M. (1996). Family treatment of childhood anxiety: A controlled trial. *Journal of Consulting and Clinical Psychology, 64,* 333–342.

Basco, M. R., Glickman, M., Weatherford, P., & Ryser, N. (2000). Cognitive-behavioral therapy for anxiety disorders: Why and how it works. *Bulletin of the Menninger Clinic, 64,* A52–70.

Beidel, D. C., & Turner, S. M. (2007). *Painfully shy, socially phobic: An inquiry into the world of social anxiety.* Washington, DC: American Psychological Association.

Beidel, D. C., Turner, S. M., & Morris, T. L. (1995). A new inventory to assess childhood social anxiety and phobia: The Social Phobia and Anxiety Inventory for Children. *Psychological Assessment, 7,* 73–79.

Beidel, D. C., Turner, S. M., & Morris, T. L. (1998). *The Social Phobia and Anxiety Inventory for Children.* Toronto, Ontario, Canada: Multi-Health Systems.

Beidel, D. C., Turner, S. M., & Morris, T. L. (2000). Behavioral treatment of childhood social phobia. *Journal of Consulting and Clinical Psychology, 68,* 1072–1080.

Beidel, D. C., Turner, S. M., Sallee, F. R., Ammerman, R. T., Crosby, L. A., &, Pathak, S. (2007). SET-C vs. fluoxetine in the treatment of childhood social phobia. *Journal of the American Academy of Child and Adolescent Psychiatry, 46,* 1622–1632.

Bérubé, R. L., & Achenbach, T. M. (2002). *Bibliography of published studies using the Achenbach System of Empirically Based Assessment (ASEBA): 2002 edition.* Burlington, VT: University of Vermont, Research Center for Children, Youth, & Families.

Breinholst, S., Esbjørn, B. H., Reinholdt-Dunne, M. L., & Stallard, P. (2012). CBT for treatment of child anxiety disorders: A review of why parental involvement has not enhanced outcomes. *Journal of Anxiety Disorders, 26,* 416–424.

Cartwright-Hatton, S., Laskey, B., Rust, S., & McNally, D. (2010). *From timid to tiger: A treatment manual for parenting the anxious child.* West Sussex, UK: Wiley-Blackwell.

Chorpita, B. F., Tracey, S. A., Brown, T. A., Collica, T. J., & Barlow, D. H. (1997). Assessment of worry in children and adolescents: An adaptation of the Penn State worry questionnaire. *Behavior Research and Therapy, 35,* 569–581.

Clark, D. B., Smith, M. G., Neighbors, B. D., Skerlec, L. M., & Randal, J. (1994). Anxiety disorders in adolescence: Characteristics, prevalence, and comorbidities. *Clinical Psychology Review, 14,* 113–137.

Clark, D. B., Turner, S. M., Beidel, D. C., Donovan, J. E., Kirisci, L., & Jacob, R. G. (1994). Reliability and validity of the Social Phobia and Anxiety Inventory for adolescents. *Psychological Assessment, 6,* 135–140.

Cobham, V. E., Dadds, M. R., & Spence, S. H. (1998). The role of parental anxiety in the treatment of childhood anxiety. *Journal of Consulting and Clinical Psychology, 66,* 893–905.

Cohen, P., Cohen, J., Kasen, S., Velez, C. N., Hartmark, C., Johnson, J., . . . Streuning, E. L. (1993). An epidemiologic study of disorders in late childhood and adolescence: I. Age- and gender-specific prevalence. *Journal of Child Psychology and Psychiatry, 34,* 851–867.

Compton, S. N., March, J. S., Brent, D., Albano, A. M., Weersing, V. R., & Curry, J. (2004). Cognitive-behavioral psychotherapy for anxiety and depressive disorders in children and adolescents: An evidence-based medicine review. *Journal of the American Academy of Child & Adolescent Psychiatry, 43,* 930–959.

Costello, J., Egger, H., & Angold, A. (2005). 10-year research update review: The epidemiology of child and adolescent psychiatric disorders: I. Methods and public health burden. *Journal of the American Academy of Child and Adolescent Psychiatry, 44,* 972–986.

Crawley, S. A., Beidas, R. S., Benjamin, C. L., Martin, E., & Kendall, P. C. (2008). Treating socially phobic youth with CBT: Differential outcomes and treatment considerations. *Behavioural and Cognitive Psychotherapy, 36,* 379–389.

Cunningham, M. J., Wuthrich, V. M., Rapee, R. M., Lyneham, H. J., Schniering, C. A., & Hudson, J. L. (2009). The Cool Teens CD-ROM for anxiety disorders in adolescents: A pilot case series. *European Journal of Child and Adolescent Psychiatry, 18,* 125–129.

De Los Reyes, A., Alfano, C. A., & Beidel, D. C. (2011). Are clinicians' assessments of improvements in children's functioning "global"? *Journal of Clinical Child and Adolescent Psychology, 40,* 281–294.

Essau, C. A., Conradt, J., & Petermann, F. (2000). Frequency, comorbidity and psychosocial impairment of anxiety disorders in German adolescents. *Journal of Anxiety Disorders, 14,* 263–279.

Flannery-Schroeder, E. C., & Kendall, P. C. (2000). Group and individual cognitive-behavioral treatments for youth with anxiety disorders: A randomized clinical trial. *Cognitive Therapy and Research, 24,* 251–278.

Friedberg, R. D., & McClure, J. M. (2002). *Clinical practice of cognitive therapy with children and adolescents: The nuts and bolts.* New York, NY: Guilford Press.

García-López, L. J., Olivares, J., Beidel, D. C., Albano, A. M., Turner, S. M., and Rosa, A. I. (2006). Efficacy of three treatment protocols for adolescents with social anxiety disorder: A 5-year follow-up assessment. *Journal of Anxiety Disorders, 20,* 175–191.

Garnefski, N., Legerstee, J., Kraaij, V., Van den Kommer, T., & Teerds, J. (2002). Cognitive coping strategies and symptoms of depression and anxiety: A comparison between adolescents and adults. *Journal of Adolescence, 25,* 603–611.

Ginsburg, G. S., & Schlossberg, M. C. (2002). Family-based treatment of childhood anxiety disorders. *International Review of Psychiatry, 14,* 143–154.

Hale, L. R., & Calamari, J. E. (2006). Panic symptoms and disorder in youth: What role does anxiety sensitivity play? In C. Velotis (Ed.), *New developments in anxiety disorder research* (pp. 131–162). Hauppauge, NY: Nova Science.

Hale, W. W., III, Engels, R., & Meeus, W. (2006). Adolescent's perceptions of parenting behaviors and its relationship to adolescent generalized anxiety disorder symptoms. *Journal of Adolescence, 29,* 407–417.

Hayward, C., Varady, S., Albano, A. M., Thienemann, M., Henderson, L., & Schatzberg, A. F. (2000). Cognitive-behavioral group therapy for social phobia in female adolescents: Results of a pilot trial. *Journal of the American Academy of Child & Adolescent Psychiatry, 39,* 721–726.

Hoffman, E. C., & Mattis, S. G. (2000). A developmental adaptation of panic control treatment for panic disorder in adolescence. *Cognitive and Behavioral Practice, 7,* 253–261.

Ishikawa, S., Okajima, I., Matsuoka, H., & Sakano Y. (2007). Cognitive behavioural therapy for anxiety disorders in children and adolescents: A meta-analysis. *Child and Adolescent Mental Health, 12,* 164–172.

Kazdin, A. E., & Weisz, J. R. (1998). Identifying and developing empirically supported child and adolescent treatments. *Journal of Consulting and Clinical Psychology, 66,* 19–36.

Kearney, C. A., Albano, A. M., Eisen, A. R., Allan, W. D., & Barlow, D. H. (1997). The phenomenology of panic disorder in youngsters: An empirical study of a clinical sample. *Journal of Anxiety Disorders, 11,* 49–62.

Kendall, P., Choudhury, M., Hudson, J., & Webb, A. (2002). *The CAT project manual.* Ardmore, PA: Workbook.

Kendall, P., Chu, B. C., Pimentel, S. S., & Choudhury, M. (2000). Treating anxiety disorders in youth. In P. C. Kendall (Ed.), *Child and adolescent therapy: Cognitive-behavioral procedures* (pp. 235–287). New York, NY: Guilford Press.

Kendall, P. C. (1994). Treating anxiety disorders in children: Results of a randomized clinical trial. *Journal of Consulting and Clinical Psychology, 62,* 100–110.

Kendall, P. C., Brady, E. U., & Verduin, T. L. (2001). Comorbidity in childhood anxiety disorders and treatment outcome. *Journal of the American Academy of Child & Adolescent Psychiatry, 40,* 787–794.

Kendall, P. C., Robin, J. A., Hedtke, K., Suveg, C., Flannery-Schroeder, E., & Gosch, E. (2005). Considering GBT with anxious youth? Think exposures. *Journal of Cognitive and Behavioral Practice, 12,* 136–150.

Kessler, R. C., Berglund, P., Demler, O., Jin, R., Merikangas, K. R., & Walters, E. E. (2005). Lifetime prevalence and age-of-onset distributions of DSM-IV disorders in the National Comorbidity Survey Replication. *Archives of General Psychiatry, 62,* 593–602.

La Greca, A. M., & Lopez, N. (1998). Social anxiety among adolescents: Linkages with peer relations and friendships. *Journal of Abnormal Child Psychology, 26,* 83–94.

Langley, A. K., Bergman, R. L., McCracken, J., & Piacentini, J. C. (2004). Impairment in childhood anxiety disorders: Preliminary examination of the Child Anxiety Impact Scale–Parent Version. *Journal of Child and Adolescent Psychopharmacology, 14,* 105–114.

Léger, E., Ladouceur, R., Dugas, M. J., & Freeston, M. H. (2003). Cognitive-behavioral treatment of generalized anxiety disorder among adolescents: A case series. *Journal of the American Academy of Child and Adolescent Psychiatry, 42,* 327–330.

Legerstee, J. S., Garnefski, N., Verhulst, F. C., & Utens, E. M. (2011). Cognitive coping in anxiety-disordered adolescents. *Journal of Adolescence, 34,* 319–326.

Lewinsohn, P. M., Hops, H., Roberts, R. E., Seeley, J. R., & Andrews, J. A. (1993) Adolescent psychopathology: I. Prevalence and incidence of depression and other DSM-III-R disorders in high school students. *Journal of Abnormal Psychology, 102,* 133–144.

Liber, J. M., van Widenfelt, B. M., Goedhart, A. W., Utens, E. M., van der Leeden, A. J., Markus, M. T., & Treffers, P. D. (2008). Parenting and parental anxiety and depression as predictors of treatment outcome for childhood anxiety disorders: Has the role of fathers been underestimated? *Journal of Clinical Child and Adolescent Psychology, 37,* 747–758.

Manassis, K., Mendlowitz, S. L., Scapillato, D., Avery, D., Fiksenbaum, L. Freire, M., . . . Owens, M. (2002). Group and individual cognitive-behavioral therapy for childhood anxiety disorders: A randomized trial. *Journal of the American Academy of Child & Adolescent Psychiatry, 41,* 1423–1430.

March, J., & Albano, A. (1996). Assessment of anxiety in children and adolescents. In L. Dickstein, M. Riba, & M. Oldham (Eds.), *Review of psychiatry,* Vol. 15 (pp. 405–427). Washington, DC: American Psychiatric Press.

March, J. S. (1997). *Manual for the Multidimensional Anxiety Scale for Children (MASC).* Toronto, Canada: Multi-Health Systems.

March, J. S., Entusah, A. R., Rynn, M., Albano, A. M., & Tourian, K. A. (2007). A randomized controlled trial of venlafaxine versus placebo in pediatric social anxiety disorder. *Biological Psychiatry, 62,* 1149–1154.

March, S., Spence, S. H., & Donovan, C. L. (2009). The efficacy of an Internet-based cognitive-behavioral therapy intervention for child anxiety disorders. *Journal of Pediatric Psychology, 34,* 474–487.

Masia, C. L., Klein, R. G., Storch, E. A., & Corda, B. (2001). School-based behavioral treatment for social anxiety disorder in adolescents: Results of a pilot study. *Journal of the American Academy of Child & Adolescent Psychiatry, 40,* 780–786.

Mattis, S. G., Cohen, E. M., Hoffman, E. C., Pincus, D. P., Choate, M. L., & Micco, J. A. (2001, March). *Cognitive-behavioral treatment of panic disorder in adolescents.* Symposium conducted at the 21st annual meeting of the Anxiety Disorders Association of America, Atlanta, GA.

Mattis, S. G., & Pincus, D. B. (2004). Treatment of SAD and panic disorder in children and adolescents. In P. M. Barrett & T. H. Ollendick (Eds.), *Handbook of interventions that work with children and adolescents: Prevention and treatment* (pp. 145–168). Hoboken, NJ: Wiley.

McLaughlin, E. N., Stewart, S. H., & Taylor, S. (2007). Childhood anxiety sensitivity index factors predict unique variance in DSM-IV anxiety disorder symptoms. *Cognitive Behaviour Therapy, 36,* 210–219.

Meiser-Stedman, R., Dalgleish, T., Glucksman, E., Yule, W., & Smith, P. (2009). Maladaptive cognitive appraisals mediate the evolution of posttraumatic stress reactions: A 6-month follow up of child and adolescent assault and motor vehicle accident survivors. *Journal of Abnormal Psychology, 118,* 778–787.

Mendlowitz, S. L., Manassis, K., Bradley, S., Scapillato, D., Miezitis, S., & Shaw, B. F. (1999). Cognitive-behavioral group treatments in childhood anxiety disorders: The role of parental involvement. *Journal of the American Academy of Child & Adolescent Psychiatry, 38,* 1223–1229.

Merikangas, K. R., Jian-ping, H., Burstein, M., Swanson, S. A., Avenevoli, S., Cui, L., . . . Swendsen, J. (2010). Lifetime prevalence of mental disorders in U.S. adolescents: Results from the National Comorbidity Survey Replication—Adolescent supplement (NCS-A). *Journal of the American Academy of Child & Adolescent Psychiatry, 49,* 980–989.

Muris, P., & Field, A. P. (2008). Distorted cognition and pathological anxiety in children and adolescents. *Cognition and Emotion, 22,* 395–421.

Muris, P., Meesters, C., & Goble, M. (2001). Reliability, validity, and normative data of the Penn State Worry Questionnaire in 8–12-yr-old children. *Journal of Behavior Therapy and Experimental Psychiatry, 32,* 63–72.

Newman, D. L., Moffit, T. E., Caspi, A., Mogdol, L., Silva, P. A., & Stanton, W. R. (1996). Psychiatric disorder in a birth cohort of young adults: Prevalence, comorbidity, clinical significance, and new case incidence from ages 11–21. *Journal of Consulting and Clinical Psychology, 64,* 552–562.

Oetzel, K. B., & Scherer, D. G. (2003). Therapeutic alliance with adolescents in psychotherapy. *Psychotherapy: Theory, Research, Practice, Training, 40,* 215–225.

Olivares, J., & García-López, L. J. (1998). *Intervención en adolescentes con fobia social generalizada (IAFS).* Unpublished manuscript.

Ollendick, T. H., Jarrett, M. A., Grills-Taquechel, A. E., Hovey, L. D., & Wolff, J. C. (2008). Comorbidity as a predictor and moderator of treatment outcome in youth with anxiety, affective, attention deficit/hyperactivity disorder, and oppositional/conduct disorders. *Clinical Psychology Review, 28,* 1447–1471.

Ollendick, T. H., & King, N. J. (1998). Empirically supported treatments for children with phobic and anxiety disorders: current status. *Journal of Clinical Child Psychology, 27,* 156–167.

O'Neil, K. A., Brodman, D. M., Cohen, J. S., Edmunds, J. M., & Kendall, P. C. (2012). Cognitive-behavioral therapy for childhood anxiety disorders: The Coping Cat program. In E. Szigethy, J. Weisz, & R. L. Findling (Eds.), *Cognitive behavioral therapy for children and adolescents* (pp. 227–261). Arlington, VA: American Psychiatric Publishing.

Payne, S., Bolton, D., & Perrin, S. (2011). A pilot investigation of cognitive therapy for generalized anxiety disorder in children aged 7–17 years. *Cognitive Therapy and Research, 35,* 171–178.

Pestle, S. L., Chorpita, B. F., & Shiffman, J. (2008). Psychometric properties of the Penn State Worry Questionnaire for children in a large clinical sample. *Journal of Clinical Child & Adolescent Psychiatry, 37,* 465–471.

Piacentini, J., & Bergman, R. L. (2000). Obsessive-compulsive disorder in children. *Psychiatric Clinics of North America, 23,* 519–533.

Piacentini, J., & Bergman, R. L. (2001). Developmental issues in the cognitive treatment of childhood anxiety disorders. *Journal of Cognitive Psychotherapy, 15,* 165–182.

Pincus, D. B., Ehrenreich, J. T., Whitton, S. A., Mattis, S. M., & Barlow, D. H. (2010). Cognitive behavioral treatment of panic disorder in adolescence. *Journal of Clinical Child and Adolescent Psychology, 39,* 1–12.

Rapee, R. M. (2001). The development of generalized anxiety. In M. W. Vasey & M. R. Dadds (Eds.), *The developmental psychopathology of anxiety* (pp. 481–503). New York, NY: Oxford University Press.

Rapee, R. M. (2003). The influence of comorbidity on treatment outcome for children and adolescents with anxiety disorders. *Behavior Research and Therapy, 41,* 105–112.

Rapee, R. M., Lyneham, H. J., Hudson, J. L., Kangas, M., Wuthrich, V. M., & Schniering, C. A. (2013). Effect of comorbidity on treatment of anxious children and adolescents: Results from a large, combined sample. *Journal of the American Academy of Child & Adolescent Psychiatry, 52,* 47–56.

Rohde, P., Lewinsohn, P. M., & Seeley, J. R. (1996). Psychiatric comorbidity with problematic alcohol use in high school adolescents. *Journal of the American Academy of Child & Adolescent Psychiatry, 35,* 101–109.

Sauter, F. M., Heyne, D., & Westenberg, P. M. (2009). Cognitive behavior therapy for anxious adolescents: Developmental influences on treatment design and delivery. *Clinical Child and Family Psychology Review, 12,* 310–335.

Scharfstein, L. A., Beidel, D. C., Finnell, L. R., Distler, A., & Carter, N. T. (2011). Do pharmacological and behavioral interventions differentially affect treatment outcome for children with social phobia? *Behavior Modification, 35,* 451–467.

Scharfstein, L. A., Beidel, D. C., Sims, V. K., & Finnell, L. R. (2011). Social skills deficits and vocal characteristics of children with social phobia or Asperger's disorder: A comparative study. *Journal of Abnormal Child Psychology, 39,* 865–875.

Schniering, C. A., Hudson, J. L., & Rapee, R. M. (2000). Issues in the diagnosis and assessment of anxiety disorders in children and adolescents. *Clinical Psychology Review, 20,* 453–478.

Silverman, W. K., & Albano, A. M. (1996). *The Anxiety Disorders Interview Schedule for DSM-IV—Child and Parent versions.* London, UK: Oxford University Press.

Silverman, W. K., & Berman, S. L. (2001). Psychosocial interventions for anxiety disorders in children: Status and future directions. In W. K. Silverman and P. D. A. Treffers (Eds.), *Anxiety disorders in children and adolescents: Research, assessment and intervention* (pp. 313–334). Cambridge, UK: Cambridge University Press.

Silverman, W. K., & Eisen, A. R. (1992). Age differences in the reliability of parent and child reports of child anxious symptomatology using a structured interview. *Journal of the American Academy of Child & Adolescent Psychiatry, 31,* 117–124.

Silverman, W. K., Fleisig, W., Rabian, B., & Peterson, R. A. (1991). Child Anxiety Sensitivity Index. *Journal of Clinical Child Psychology, 20,* 162–168.

Silverman, W. K., Kurtines, W. M., Ginsburg, G. S., Weems, C. F., Lumpkin, P. W., & Carmichael, D. H. (1999). Treating anxiety disorders in children with group cognitive-behaviorial therapy: A randomized clinical trial. *Journal of Consulting and Clinical Psychology, 67,* 995–1003.

Silverman, W. K., Pina, A. A., & Viswesvaran, C. (2008). Evidence-based psychosocial treatments for phobic and anxiety disorders in children and adolescents. *Journal of Clinical Child and Adolescent Psychology, 37,* 105–130.

Spence, S. H., Donovan, C., & Brechman-Toussant, M. (2000). The treatment of childhood social phobia: The effectiveness of a social skills training based, cognitive-behavioural intervention, with and without parental involvement. *Journal of Child Psychology and Psychiatry, 41,* 713–726.

Spence, S. H., Donovan, C. L., March, S., Gamble, A., Anderson, R., Prosser, S., & Kenardy, J. (2008). Online CBT in the treatment of child and adolescent anxiety disorders: Issues in the development of BRAVE-ONLINE and two case illustrations. *Behavioural & Cognitive Psychotherapy, 36,* 411–430.

Spence, S. H., Holmes, J. M., March, S., & Lipp, C. V. (2006). The feasibility and outcome of clinic plus Internet delivery of cognitive-behavior therapy for childhood anxiety. *Journal of Consulting and Clinical Psychology, 74,* 614–621.

Spitalnick, J., & Beidel, D. C. (in preparation). *Pegasys-VR™: Integrating virtual humans in the treatment of child social anxiety.* Unpublished manuscript, Virtually Better.

Storch, E. A, Masia-Warner, C., Dent, H. C., Roberti, J. W., & Fisher, P. H. (2004). Psychometric evaluation of the Social Anxiety Scale for Adolescents and the Social Phobia and Anxiety Inventory for Children: Construct validity and normative data. *Anxiety Disorders, 18,* 665–679.

Taylor, S. (1995). Anxiety sensitivity: Theoretical perspectives and recent findings. *Behaviour Research and Therapy, 33,* 243–258.

Turner, S. M., Beidel, D. C., Dancu, C. V., & Stanley, M. A. (1989). An empirically derived inventory to measure social fears and anxiety: The social phobia and anxiety inventory. *Psychological Assessment: A Journal of Consulting and Clinical Psychology, 1,* 35–40.

Ultee, C. A., Griffioen, D., & Schellekens, J. (1982). The reduction of anxiety in children: A comparison of the effects of "systematic desensitization in vitro" and "systematic desensitization in vivo." *Behaviour Research and Therapy, 20,* 61–67.

Velting, O. N., Setzer, N., & Albano, A. M. (2004). Update on and advances in assessment and cognitive-behavioral treatment of anxiety disorders in children and adolescents. *Professional Psychology: Research and Practice, 35,* 42–54.

Wagner, K. D., Berard, R., Stein, M. B., Wetherhold, E., Carpenter, D. J., Perera, P., et al. (2004). A multicenter, randomized, double-blind, placebo-controlled trial of paroxetine in children and adolescents with social anxiety disorder. *Archives of General Psychiatry, 61,* 1153–1162.

White, S. W., Ollendick, T., Scahill, L., Oswald, D., & Albano, A. (2009). Preliminary efficacy of a cognitive-behavioral treatment program for anxious youth with autism spectrum disorders. *Journal of Autism and Developmental Disorders, 39,* 1652–1662.

Wolpe, J. (1969). *The practice of behavior therapy.* New York, NY: Pergamon Press.

Wong Sarver, N., Beidel, D. C., & Spitalnick, J. (2014). The feasibility and acceptability of virtual environments in the treatment of childhood social anxiety disorder. *Journal of Clinical Child and Adolescent Psychology, 43,* 63–73.

Woodward, L. J., & Fergusson, D. M. (2001). Life course outcomes of young people with anxiety disorders in adolescence. *Journal of the American Academy of Child & Adolescent Psychiatry, 40,* 1086–1093.

CHAPTER 9

Depressive Disorders in Children

WINNIE W. CHUNG AND MARY A. FRISTAD

OVERVIEW OF THE DISORDER

Childhood depression is an impairing condition and can lead to lifelong physical and mental health concerns. Major depressive disorder (MDD) is estimated to affect 2.8% of children under age 13, with 12-month prevalence rates ranging from approximately 1% to 3% in school-age children (Costello, Erkanli, & Angold, 2006) and 1% to 2% in preschoolers (Egger et al., 2006). An additional 5% to 10% of youth experience significant depressive symptoms that do not meet diagnostic criteria for MDD (Birmaher, Brent, & the American Academy of Child and Adolescent Psychiatry [AACAP] Work Group on Quality Issues, 2007). The review of adolescent depression appears elsewhere in this book; this chapter primarily focuses on the assessment and treatment of depressive disorders and symptoms in children age 12 years and under.

In the treatment outcome studies presented later in this chapter that focus on children with depressive spectrum disorders (DSDs), diagnoses are based on criteria described in the *Diagnostic and Statistical Manual of Mental Disorders*, 4th ed. (*DSM-IV*) (American Psychiatric Association [APA], 1994). DSD diagnostic categories in the *DSM-IV* include MDD, dysthymic disorder (DD), and depressive disorder not otherwise specified (D-NOS). MDD requires the presence of depressed or irritable mood, or loss of interest in activities for most of the time during a 2-week period, along with symptoms including appetite changes, sleep disturbances, fatigue, feelings of worthlessness, concentration difficulties, and suicidal thoughts and behaviors. DD has a more chronic and pervasive presentation, with depressed or irritable mood and associated symptoms lasting most days for at least 1 year. Finally, a D-NOS diagnosis is reserved for depressive symptoms and features that do not meet criteria for MDD, DD, or an adjustment disorder. In the fifth edition of the *DSM* (*DSM-5*), bereavement is no longer an exclusion criterion for MDD (APA, 2013). A new diagnostic category, persistent depressive disorder, replaces the former DD diagnosis, and allows for the continuous presence of MDD in the first year of depressive symptoms, thereby consolidating the *DSM-IV* chronic MDD and DD diagnoses. Further, the multiaxial system used in the *DSM-IV* is replaced by a nonaxial approach in the *DSM-5* to document diagnoses.

Children experiencing depressive symptoms or disorders are at greater risk for attention and behavioral problems; disruptions in family, academic, and social functioning; and suicide and drug or alcohol abuse (Birmaher, Arbelaez, & Brent, 2002; Birmaher et al., 2007). While most recover from an index episode, 30% to 70% will experience a relapse or recurrence (Birmaher et al., 2002). Early age of onset, greater depression severity, conflict with parents, and various comorbid conditions predict longer episode duration and relapse or recurrence (Birmaher et al., 2002). Other influences include low socioeconomic status, family history of mood disorders, and negative patterns of cognition. Most (80%–95%) children diagnosed with MDD experience a comorbid condition, often an anxiety or behavior disorder, which are also of significant concern (Kovacs, 1996).

Children with MDD who also exhibit psychotic symptoms, psychomotor retardation, have a family history of bipolar disorder (BD), or exhibit pharmacologically induced mania symptoms are at risk for subsequent development of BD (e.g., Akiskal et al., 1983; Birmaher et al., 2002, 2007; Geller, Fox, & Clark, 1994). Careful monitoring of symptom development and responses to pharmacological interventions (e.g., antidepressant medications) is of particular importance with these children. Additionally, sex and age differences are notable. In childhood, girls and boys are equally likely to have MDD (Birmaher et al., 1996); by adolescence, girls are twice as likely to have MDD.

EVIDENCE-BASED APPROACHES

Psychotherapeutic approaches, for both prevention and intervention, have received increasing attention. More research has focused on adolescents than children (Weisz, McCarty, & Valeri, 2006). Two reviews using the Task Force on the Promotion and Dissemination of Psychological Procedures criteria (Chambless et al., 1996; Chambless et al., 1998; Chambless & Hollon, 1998) have evaluated the evidence base for youth depression treatments (David-Ferdon & Kaslow, 2008; Kaslow & Thompson, 1998). In the first review (Kaslow & Thompson, 1998), seven studies involved 13- to 18-year-old adolescents only while seven studies focused exclusively on children in grades 3 to 8. The latter included children with "elevated symptoms of depression" determined by children's self-reported symptoms on measures such as the Children's Depression Inventory (CDI) (Kovacs, 1985). No studies reported on children with a DSD diagnosis. These child studies all used treatments that were downward extensions of adult approaches, primarily based on cognitive behavioral principles, and typically administered in group formats. Only Stark and colleagues' school-based Self-Control Therapy (SCT) (Stark, Reynolds, & Kaslow, 1987; Stark, Rouse, & Livingston, 1991) emerged as a *probably efficacious* treatment; no treatments met criteria and standards for a *well-established* intervention.

Ten years after Kaslow and Thompson's review (1998), David-Ferdon and Kaslow (2008) examined randomized controlled trials (RCTs) conducted subsequent to the previous review. Eighteen adolescent-only, five child-only, and five mixed-aged studies were identified. Of the 10 new studies that included child participants, 3 included those diagnosed with a DSD; the remainder focused on children with elevated depressive symptoms. Treatments examined in the child studies were more developmentally informed than those in the prior review. Most included cognitive behavioral principles, although treatments utilizing psychodynamic, family systems, and a combination of psychoeducational and supportive approaches were also represented. In addition to Stark and colleagues' SCT, the Penn Prevention Program (including the modified Penn Optimism Program) (e.g., Jaycox, Reivich, Gillham, & Seligman, 1994; Yu & Seligman, 2002) was deemed a *probably efficacious* intervention. As a group, cognitive behavioral therapy (CBT) is considered a *well-established* treatment approach, and specifically, child-only group CBT and child-group CBT with a parent component are *well-established* treatment modalities. Behavior therapy as a theoretical approach is considered *probably efficacious*; nondirected support, psychoeducational, and family systems approaches are deemed *experimental*. Parent–child and individual video self-monitoring modalities are also considered *experimental*, reflecting the limited research on these modalities.

Since the 2008 review, two additional RCTs have been published (Fristad, Verducci, Walters, & Young, 2009; Luby, Lenze, & Tillman, 2012). Fristad and colleagues (2009) evaluated the efficacy of Multi-Family Psychoeducational Psychotherapy (MF-PEP), which incorporates CBT and family systems therapy techniques, in children diagnosed with either a DSD or bipolar spectrum disorder. Luby and colleagues (2012) examined the efficacy of a modified version of Parent-Child

Interaction Therapy (PCIT) among preschool-age children diagnosed with MDD. While both RCTs demonstrated favorable results, they remain in the experimental stage, given their initial evaluation status.

A recent meta-analysis examining the effects of psychotherapy in treating youth depression revealed positive though modest effects (Weisz et al., 2006). Weisz et al. (2006) also found that both cognitive and noncognitive (e.g., behavioral activation techniques) approaches demonstrated similar effects, and self-report outcome data from youth were more favorable than that provided by parents. Weisz and colleagues (2012) conducted an RCT to examine the Modular Approach to Therapy for Children with Anxiety, Depression, or Conduct Problems in children and adolescents. This approach includes techniques from various evidence-based approaches, with flowcharts directing the sequence of modules to guide clinicians as they target specific symptoms of concern. Results suggest that youth who received modular treatment demonstrated steeper improvement trajectories compared to those who received usual care or standard evidence-based treatment and had fewer diagnoses posttreatment than those in usual care. Future studies to further elucidate the unique contributions of these elements to treatment outcomes, specifically with children, would be highly informative.

SPECIFIC TREATMENT APPROACHES

Reviews suggest that psychotherapy has some efficacy in ameliorating children's depressive symptoms; brief descriptions of such interventions, including child-only group CBT, group CBT with parental involvement, parent–child CBT, individual therapy with parent component, family-based therapy, parenting-based treatment, and psychodynamic therapy, are discussed next.

Child-Only Group CBT

The following describes child-only interventions employing CBT techniques delivered in a group format.

Penn Prevention Program

The Penn Prevention Program (PPP) was developed to prevent depressive symptoms and related impairment in at-risk children with elevated depressive symptoms and perception of parental conflict (Gillham, Reivich, Jaycox, & Seligman, 1995; Jaycox et al., 1994). This 12-week group treatment conducted in schools includes a cognitive component (e.g., identifying and accurately evaluating negative beliefs, engaging in flexible thinking, and adopting a more optimistic explanatory style) and a social problem-solving component (e.g., learning perspective-taking and problem-solving skills). Other techniques to cope with family conflict and stressful events are also introduced. PPP has been evaluated in 143 at-risk 10- to 13-year-old youth, randomized to treatment and control conditions by school (Jaycox et al., 1994). Those who received PPP self-reported significantly greater decreases in depressive symptoms postintervention compared to those in the control group; results were maintained at 6-month follow-up. Although children who participated in PPP did not demonstrate significant changes in overall explanatory style, they were less likely than those in the control condition to make stable and enduring attributions to negative events postintervention. Effects were maintained 2 years postintervention (Gillham et al., 1995). By 3 years posttreatment, effects on depressive symptoms had diminished, although effects on explanatory style were maintained (Gillham & Reivich, 1999). PPP has also been evaluated in an RCT of 189 seventh-grade students with elevated symptoms of depression in rural Australia (Roberts, Kane, Thomson, Bishop, & Hart, 2003). While there were no intervention effects on depressive symptoms at posttreatment and 6-month follow-up, children who participated in PPP showed lower levels of anxiety symptoms at both time points.

Gillham, Reivich, and colleagues (2006) incorporated a six-session group parent component to PPP to equip parents with the same resiliency skills taught to the children. This revised Penn Resilience Program (PRP) reduced symptoms of depression and anxiety at 6- and 12-month follow-ups in 44 at-risk sixth and seventh graders, compared to those in a control condition. PRP has also been evaluated in primary care with 271 children 11 and 12 years of age exhibiting elevated depressive symptoms (Gillham, Hamilton, Freres, Patton, & Gallop, 2006). While there were no overall intervention effects on depressive symptoms or disorders, girls (not boys) in PRP reported lower levels of depressive symptoms, and all who participated in PRP demonstrated improvements in explanatory style for positive events over the subsequent 2 years. A PRP effectiveness study that used an active control condition (the Penn Enhancement Program) demonstrated mixed results (Gillham et al., 2007). Specifically, while PRP was effective in reducing depressive symptoms through the 30-month follow-up among 697 sixth to eighth graders with elevated symptoms of depression in two schools, no effects of PRP were found for a third school.

Primary and Secondary Control Enhancement Training

The Primary and Secondary Control Enhancement Training program (PASCET) was originally developed as an eight-session small-group treatment to reduce elevated depressive symptoms among elementary school–age children by increasing their primary and secondary control coping strategies (Weisz, Thurber, Sweeney, Proffitt, & LeGagnoux, 1997). Primary control strategies involve modifying one's objective environment when possible to fit one's needs and desires; secondary control strategies involve changing one's interpretations of objective situations that are not modifiable. PASCET is also available as an 18-session individual treatment for 8- to 15-year-olds, with options for parental and school involvement (Bearman, Ugueto, Alleyne & Weisz, 2010). Practice homework is assigned between sessions, and a final project is completed to summarize and integrate skills learned throughout treatment.

An RCT of PASCET in 48 third to sixth graders with elevated depressive symptoms revealed that participation in PASCET in the school setting resulted in lowered depressive symptoms, including scores that normalized, compared to peers in a control condition (Weisz et al., 1997). Effects were maintained at 9-month follow-up. A version of PASCET plus parenting training has been developed (PASCET plus caregiver–child relationship enhancement training; PASCET-C-CRET). Children with mild to moderate depressive symptoms showed improvement in depressive symptoms, psychosocial functioning, coping, and the caregiver–child relationship after participation in PASCET-C-CRET (Eckshtain & Gaynor, 2009). PASCET appears to be promising in treating depressive symptoms in children; further evaluations are warranted.

Coping with Depression

The Coping with Depression (CWD) course, developed to address depression in adolescents (Clarke & Lewinsohn, 1984; Lewinsohn & Clarke, 1984), has been adapted to treat moderate to severe depressive symptoms among sixth- to eighth-grade students (Kahn, Kehle, Jenson, & Clark, 1990). Consisting of 12 sessions delivered in a small-group format, CWD teaches children self-change skills, pleasant-activities scheduling, cognitive techniques, communication, problem solving, social skills, and strategies to maintain and generalize treatment gains. A school-based RCT with 68 sixth to eight graders experiencing elevated depressive symptoms compared CWD, a relaxation protocol, an individual self-modeling intervention, and a wait-list control (WLC) group. Participants in all three treatment conditions had significantly lower depression scores at posttreatment and 1-month follow-up; youth who participated in CWD showed improved self-concept compared to those in the WLC group. Further, CWD participants were almost twice as likely to function in the nondepressed range compared with those in the self-modeling condition; effects were more strongly maintained at follow-up for the CWD group than for the self-modeling group, suggesting CWD helps to improve depressive symptoms.

Group CBT With Parental Involvement

The following describes group interventions for children employing CBT techniques that incorporate parental involvement.

Self-Control Therapy

Stark and colleagues' SCT is a school-based group treatment (Stark, Brookman, & Frazier, 1990; Stark et al., 1987, 1991) that incorporates cognitive training, teaches self-control and behavioral skills, and includes ongoing consultation with children's teachers to support their functioning at school and with peers. Parent training and education are provided in monthly family meetings. Sessions begin and end discussing homework previously assigned or to be assigned; the remaining time is spent discussing children's personal concerns and skills training. The cognitive component involves cognitive restructuring and attribution retraining. Self-control training consists of teaching accurate self-monitoring skills, training in self-reinforcement, and accurate self-evaluations. The behavioral training component includes planning pleasant activities, and training in assertiveness, social skills, and relaxation.

Stark and colleagues (1987) compared a 12-session version of SCT with behavioral problem-solving therapy and a WLC group among 29 fourth to sixth graders with elevated depression symptoms. Children in both active treatments reported decreases in depression and anxiety posttreatment; those in SCT reported lower levels of depressive symptoms than those in the WLC condition. Improvements in depressive symptoms were maintained at 8-week follow-up, and children in the SCT group showed reduced depression scores and greater self-concept scores than those in the behavioral problem-solving condition. In a second study, Stark and colleagues (1991) examined an expanded, 24- to 26-session version of SCT. Twenty-six fourth to seventh graders with elevated depressive symptoms were randomly assigned to this expanded SCT or a counseling control condition. While children in both conditions showed reduced depressive symptoms at posttreatment and 7-month follow-up, those in SCT reported lower levels of depression and depressive cognitions than those in the control group postintervention.

Stress-Busters Intervention

The Stress-Busters program is a 10-session after-school group intervention that includes general skill building, depression-specific CBT, the creation of a videotape summarizing therapeutic skills, and a family education session to facilitate skills generalization and to foster positive parent–child interactions (Asarnow, Scott, & Mintz, 2002). Skills taught include problem solving, relaxation, social skills, scheduling pleasant activities, cognitive restructuring, and developing a personal coping plan. Therapists also discuss the notion of emotional spirals and how one's thoughts and actions can influence the direction of spirals. Twenty-three fourth to sixth graders with tentative depression diagnoses (based on symptoms endorsed on the CDI [Kovacs, 1985]) who were randomly assigned to Stress-Busters demonstrated greater reductions in depressive symptoms, negative automatic thoughts, and internalized coping than those in the WLC group. Participants expressed high satisfaction with the treatment, also supporting the promise of this intervention in reducing children's depressive symptoms.

Parent–Child CBT

The following describes an intervention employing CBT techniques that incorporates individual child and family sessions delivered in a videoconferencing format.

CBT via Videoconferencing

Nelson, Barnard, and Cain (2003, 2006) implemented an 8-week CBT protocol using video-conferencing. During each session, the therapist meets with the target child and his/her parent separately. Content covered in child sessions includes scheduling positive activities, monitoring feelings, cognitive-behavioral techniques, as well as training in social, problem-solving, anger management, and relaxation skills. Similar content is presented in parent sessions, with additional material relating to positive parenting, discipline strategies, and family activities. Comparing CBT via Videoconferencing (CBT-VC) with CBT delivered in the traditional face-to-face format in the clinic setting, Nelson and colleagues (2003, 2006) found that 8- to 14-year-old children diagnosed with depression who were randomized to either version of CBT demonstrated decreased depression scores posttreatment; 82% of participants no longer met criteria for a depression diagnosis. Those in CBT-VC showed a significantly greater rate of decline in symptoms than children in traditional CBT, suggesting that CBT-VC is a promising mode of treatment delivery.

Individual Therapy With Parent Component

The following describes an individual child intervention incorporating parental involvement.

Contextual Emotion-Regulation Therapy

Kovacs and colleagues' (2006) contextual emotion-regulation therapy (CERT) is a 30-session problem-focused and developmentally sensitive treatment targeting children's self-regulation of distress and dysphoria. Presented individually in a clinic, the core goals of CERT include reducing depressive symptoms, increasing effective regulation of negative emotions, and enabling children to adaptively respond to upsetting events. Didactic training in and practice of emotion-regulation responses are key treatment components. Other strategies presented include tracking symptoms, improving sleep hygiene, and scheduling social activities. As mentioned, parents are asked to play a significant role in CERT, by serving as "assistant coaches" and improving their relationship with their child. An open-label evaluation of CERT was conducted among 20 7- to 12-year-old children with a diagnosis of DD (Kovacs et al., 2006). Children's depressive and anxiety symptoms decreased significantly posttreatment; effects were maintained 6 and 12 months later. For children with superimposed MDD, 80% of MDD diagnoses remitted posttreatment. Over half (53%) of the DD diagnoses remitted posttreatment; by the end of the 12-month follow-up, an additional 40% of DD cases remitted. CERT is currently being investigated in an RCT, which will provide further data regarding its efficacy.

Family-Based Therapy

The following describes family-based interventions for children with diagnosed depressive disorders.

Family-Focused Treatment for Childhood Depression

Family-Focused Treatment for Childhood Depression (FFT-CD) was developed to treat school-age children with depressive disorders in the clinic setting. It incorporates family systems and cognitive behavioral approaches to interrupt and reverse negative emotional spirals through psychoeducation and skills building with the family (Tompson et al., 2007; Tompson, Boger, & Asarnow, 2012). Consisting of five modules, FFT-CD focuses on psychoeducation, communication skills, scheduling fun activities, problem solving, and promoting skills generalization. An open trial of FFT-CD with nine 9- to 14-year-old children diagnosed with a depressive disorder revealed that children's depression severity was significantly reduced and global functioning significantly improved posttreatment (Tompson et al., 2007). Two-thirds (six of nine) no longer met diagnostic criteria for a depressive disorder posttreatment, and by 9 months, 77% no longer met diagnostic criteria. Children also reported significant improvement in family cohesion at posttreatment and 9-month follow-up. An RCT is currently examining the impact of FFT-CD on children with depressive disorders and will identify potential mediators and moderators of treatment (Tompson et al., 2012).

Multi-Family Psychoeducational Psychotherapy

Multi-family psychoeducational psychotherapy (MF-PEP) is an eight-session manualized intervention developed as an adjunctive treatment for children with unipolar depressive or bipolar disorders (Fristad, Goldberg-Arnold, & Leffler, 2011). MF-PEP incorporates psychoeducation, family systems, and CBT techniques delivered in separate parent and child groups in the clinic. Sessions begin and end with parents and children together to review between-session projects. Key goals include teaching children and parents about symptoms and evidence-based treatments, providing social support, improving emotion regulation, developing mental health and school teams, recognizing and altering maladaptive family interaction patterns, managing difficult mood symptoms (e.g., suicidal behavior), learning cognitive behavioral techniques, and improving problem-solving and communication skills within the family. Family projects completed between sessions help facilitate skill acquisition and generalization; children play a review game at the final session to enhance knowledge retention.

In an RCT of MF-PEP with 165 8- to 12-year-old children diagnosed with MDD, DD, or a bipolar spectrum disorder, those assigned to MF-PEP plus treatment as usual (TAU) exhibited lower levels of mood severity over a year-long follow-up period compared to those in the WLC plus TAU group (Fristad et al., 2009). Participation in MF-PEP improved the quality of services children received, mediated by parents' treatment beliefs (Mendenhall, Fristad, & Early, 2009), and the quality of services children received mediated improvement in mood symptoms. Comorbid behavior and anxiety disorders did not impede improvement in mood (Boylan, MacPherson, & Fristad, 2013; Cummings & Fristad, 2012), and behavioral symptoms improved with treatment (Boylan et al., 2013). Children who benefited the most from MF-PEP were those with greater impairment, had significant stress and trauma histories, and whose parents exhibited fewer dramatic, emotional, and erratic personality features (MacPherson, Algorta, Mendenhall, Fields, & Fristad, 2013). Although not developed specifically for children with a DSD, MF-PEP appears promising in improving mood symptoms in children with unipolar depressive and bipolar disorders. A 24-session individual-family version is available (IF-PEP) (Fristad et al, 2011); its efficacy among children with depressive disorders is currently being evaluated in an RCT.

Parenting-Based Treatment

The following describes interventions focused on parenting techniques to improve children's depressive symptoms.

Parent–Child Interaction Therapy Emotion Development

Based on the original version of PCIT developed for children exhibiting oppositional behavior (Brinkmeyer & Eyberg, 2003), Luby and colleagues (2012) adapted PCIT to treat depression in 3- to 7-year-old children. PCIT is presented in a dyadic format in the clinic setting; both parents and children attend sessions. Child-Directed Interaction and Parent-Directed Interaction modules aim to improve and strengthen the parent–child relationship through in vivo coaching of positive play strategies, giving clear commands, and effectively managing noncompliant and disruptive behavior. In this 14-session version, parents and children participating in Parent–Child Interaction Therapy Emotion Development (PCIT-ED) also engage in a 6-session module focused on increasing emotional competence. Skills taught include accurate identification of emotions and the implementation of various coping techniques.

Comparing PCIT-ED to a psychoeducational, didactic control condition among 54 young children with MDD and their parents (Luby et al., 2012), children in both conditions showed decreased internalizing symptoms, depressive symptoms, and functional impairment posttreatment. However, those participating in PCIT-ED also demonstrated significant decreases in overanxious symptoms, externalizing/ADHD symptoms, conduct problems, overt hostility, inattention, family-related impairment, and parental stress along with significantly improved executive functioning and emotion recognition abilities. This preliminary examination suggests that PCIT-ED produces favorable results among preschoolers with depression and their parents.

Emotionally Attuned Parenting

Flory (2004) developed Emotionally Attuned Parenting (EAP) to improve parents' empathy toward children with severe depressive and anxiety disorders and comorbid conditions. EAP is a parent-only, individually based intervention based on the theory that parental cognition can both support and hinder parents' displays of empathy toward their child. Parents are first provided with psychoeducation regarding their child's disorder and the importance of understanding their child's emotions and improving the parent–child relationship. In subsequent sessions (the number of sessions varies from family to family), parents discuss with therapists problematic times they have had with their child since the last session, highlighting any negative cognitions parents had toward their situation or their child. Parents are taught to evaluate and challenge their negative thoughts. Throughout treatment, there is a strong focus on recognizing and understanding the influence of children's feelings and emotions on their behaviors. In an open-label evaluation of EAP among 11 clinic-referred 6- to 13-year-old children, EAP significantly reduced the number of DD diagnoses, and there were significant reductions in child-reported depressive and anxiety symptoms and mother-reported parenting stress posttreatment. Treatment gains were maintained at 6 months for the five children with available data. While further examinations of the EAP are necessary, preliminary evidence suggests EAP may be efficacious in reducing depressive symptomatology and parenting stress among children with depressive disorders.

Psychodynamic Approaches

Trowell and colleagues (2007) compared systems integrative family therapy (SIFT) (focuses on family dysfunction) with focused individual psychodynamic psychotherapy (FIPP) among 72 youth 9 to 15 years old with diagnoses of MDD and/or DD. FIPP emphasizes interpersonal relationships, stressful life events, and problematic attachments using psychodynamic principles. Youth randomized to SIFT and FIPP showed reduced rates of depressive disorder diagnoses at posttreatment and

6-month follow-up. Participants in both conditions showed improvements in depressive symptoms and global functioning at both assessment time points.

Muratori, Picchi, Bruni, Patarnello, and Romagnoli (2003) evaluated an 11-week course of psychodynamic psychotherapy (PP) in children diagnosed with a depressive or anxiety disorder. The overall goal of PP is to identify core conflictual themes and point out their relationship to target children's symptoms as well as to their parents' representational world. Treatment proceeds in three phases, beginning with five parent–child sessions, then five child-only sessions, and concludes with a final parent–child session. Fifty-eight 6- to 11-year-old children and a parent were randomly assigned to participate in PP or to a usual-care control condition. While both groups exhibited significant improvement in overall functioning within the first 6 months of initiating treatment, the PP group showed greater overall functioning compared to the control condition at the 6-month post-baseline and 2-year follow-up assessments. There were no significant group differences in total, internalizing, and externalizing problems 6 months post-baseline; however, only children in the PP condition showed improvement in each of these three domains. Further, at the 2-year follow-up, children in the PP condition had significantly fewer total, internalizing, and externalizing problems compared to those in the control group, although children in the control condition also demonstrated improvement in total problems compared to baseline.

Summary of Specific Treatment Protocols

Table 9.1 provides a summary of the commonly or more frequently implemented techniques across the range of intervention protocols developed and tested, as described earlier.

PARENTAL INVOLVEMENT IN TREATMENT

Practice parameters published by AACAP (Birmaher et al., 2007) recommend that families, particularly parents, be centrally involved in the treatment of their child with depression. Not only can parents provide insight into their child's functioning, they also serve as gatekeepers for the types and levels of care their child receives. In addition, they play a vital role in monitoring their child's progress and acting as a safety net (p. 1510). Research supports this position. Parent and child depressive symptoms are mutually linked, such that symptom improvement exhibited by one often corresponds to symptom improvement in the other (Stark, Banneyer, Wang, & Arora, 2012; Weissman et al., 2006). Parental characteristics and behaviors postulated to contribute to children's depressive symptoms include inconsistent and hostile parenting, insecure attachment, inattentiveness to the child's needs, high maternal criticism, poor interpersonal skills, and ineffective coping styles. These behaviors are magnified in parents who themselves suffer from depression; consequently, their adverse impact on children's depression is also magnified (Stark et al., 2012). Particularly since children are highly embedded within their family contexts (Tompson et al., 2012), involving parents in treatment is critical. As will be shown, many treatment approaches include a primary or adjunctive parent component.

ADAPTATIONS AND MODIFICATIONS

Researchers have adapted and modified depression treatments to tailor interventions to specific child populations, including those of different cultural backgrounds. This section presents adaptations and modifications to the interventions discussed earlier.

TABLE 9.1   Summary of Common Intervention Strategies Implemented in Childhood Depression Treatments

Broad Intervention Strategy	Examples of Specific Techniques
Behavioral activation	Schedule pleasant activities
Cognitive reframing	Identify, challenge, and replace maladaptive thoughts
	Promote optimistic explanatory style and attribution retraining
Emotion regulation	Develop and practice relaxation skills
	Develop personal coping strategies and plan
	Improve appropriate use of primary (e.g., modifying objective environment, implementing behavioral activation techniques) and secondary coping (e.g., implementing cognitive techniques)
Family involvement	Involve parents as models and coaches
	Improve family dynamics
	Improve parent–child relationship
Maintenance and generalization of gains	Assign between-session homework projects
	Create final project or play review game summarizing skills covered in treatment
Parenting	Teach positive parenting skills
	Teach effective discipline skills
	Increase parental empathy
Psychoeducation	Increase knowledge of childhood depression and its treatment
	Increase knowledge of importance of family's role in depression
	Discuss concept of emotional spirals
Self-monitoring	Track symptoms
	Track activity
Social skills training	Improve perspective-taking skills
	Improve communication skills
	Improve problem-solving skills
	Teach assertive communication

ACTION Treatment Program for Girls

The ACTION Treatment Program for Girls has its basis in SCT (Stark et al., 1987, 1991), and is a developmentally appropriate, group CBT protocol designed for 9- to 13-year-old girls diagnosed with a depressive disorder and their parents (Stark et al., 2006, 2008, 2010). Consisting of 20 group and 2 individual meetings delivered in the school setting, ACTION emphasizes cognitive restructuring and self-monitoring of pleasant activities, as in SCT. While a substantial portion of SCT is devoted to training in social skills, ACTION focuses on providing affective education, teaching effective coping, and helping girls develop a positive sense of self. Parents also attend 10 weekly group meetings to receive training in modeling and reinforcing their daughter's use of skills and in improving family communication patterns and fostering a supportive family environment.

ACTION has been evaluated in an RCT of 159 9- to 13-year-old girls diagnosed with MDD, DD, or D-NOS. Participants were randomly assigned to ACTION at their school with or without parent training, or to a minimal contact control group (Stark, Streusand, Krumholz, & Patel, 2010). The sample was ethnically diverse, and approximately half had at least one comorbid condition. Posttreatment, children in both ACTION conditions reported lower levels of depressive symptoms than those in the control condition, with no significant differences between the ACTION groups. Over 80% of those who participated in ACTION no longer met diagnostic criteria for a depressive disorder, compared to 47% of those in the control condition. Gains were largely maintained at the 1-year follow-up. In addition, only girls in the ACTION program without parent training reported improved sense of self and of the future, and only those in the ACTION program with parent training condition reported improved family cohesion and communication posttreatment.

Adaptations of the Penn Resiliency Program

Cardemil, Reivich, and Seligman (2002) and Cardemil, Reivich, and Seligman (2002) adapted the 12-session PRP for 168 low-income Latino and African American fifth- to eighth-grade children. Content was adjusted so that the role-plays, exercises, and other therapeutic activities presented would be relevant for children in low-income communities and urban settings. At posttreatment and over a 2-year follow-up period, Latino children randomly assigned to participate in PRP showed significant improvement in depressive symptoms compared to Latino children in the control condition; these effects were not found among African American children. Across the 6-month but not 2-year follow-up, Latino children in PRP showed significant reductions in negative cognitions and increased self-esteem compared to Latino children in the control group; again, these effects were not detected among the African American children. In sum, this culturally adapted version of PRP may be efficacious in improving depressive symptoms among Latino, but not African American, children.

PRP has also been adapted to treat at-risk Chinese children with elevated symptoms of depression and perceptions of family conflict (Yu & Seligman, 2002). Modifications included: shortening the 12-week program in 10 sessions to facilitate attendance and improve efficiency; altering assertiveness training components to be sensitive to values of social harmony and conformity promoted by the Chinese culture; and to increase feasibility, teachers rather than graduate students or mental health professionals were recruited to deliver the treatment. In China, 220 fourth- to sixth-grade children were randomly assigned to participate in the Penn Optimism Program (POP) or to a control group (Yu & Seligman, 2002). Children in POP showed significant reductions in depressive symptoms and more optimistic explanatory styles compared to those in the control group at posttreatment as well as 3- and 6-month follow-up assessments. Changes in explanatory styles mediated improvements in depressive symptoms. As such, it seems this cultural adaptation is successful in improving at-risk Chinese children's depressive symptoms.

MEASURING TREATMENT EFFECTS

Effects of treatments just discussed have been assessed using various self- and informant-report measures and clinician ratings. The next discussion is by no means an exhaustive list of all measures implemented in childhood depression intervention studies. Rather, those frequently used to determine diagnoses, assess depressive symptoms and global functioning, and evaluate more specific outcomes, such as attributional styles and automatic thoughts, are mentioned.

Determining Depression Diagnosis

The Kiddie-Schedule for Affective Disorders and Schizophrenia for school-age children (K-SADS) (Chambers et al., 1985) is a semistructured interview that incorporates information from parents, children, and clinical judgment to determine pre- and posttreatment diagnoses based on *DSM-IV* (APA, 1994). The Preschool Age Psychiatric Assessment (PAPA) (Egger, Ascher, & Angold, 1999) is a structured, interviewer-based parent interview used to determine psychiatric diagnoses in preschool-age children ages 2 to 5. The PAPA also assesses family functioning, parental variables, and school and peer functioning. The Children's Interview for Psychiatric Syndromes (ChIPS) is a structured interview with child and parent (P-ChIPS) forms that assesses 20 behavioral, anxiety, mood, and other syndromes according to *DSM-IV* criteria as well as psychosocial stressors in youth ages 6 to 18 (Weller, Weller, Rooney, & Fristad, 1999).

Assessing Symptoms and Global Functioning

The Children's Depression Inventory (CDI) (Kovacs, 1985) is a commonly used 27-item self-report measure of children's depressive symptoms in the previous 2 weeks. Scores range from 0 to 54, with higher scores indicating greater levels of depression. The Mood and Feelings Questionnaire (MFQ) (Angold, Costello, Messer, Pickles, Winder, & Silver, 1995) has also been used as an outcome measure; it is a 32-item parent- and child-report rating scale that assesses symptoms of depression. Items are rated on a 3-point Likert scale, with higher total scores indicating higher levels of depressive symptoms. A parent-report omnibus measure, the Child Behavior Checklist (CBCL) (Achenbach, 1991), is another measure frequently used to assess externalizing and internalizing problems, including depressive and somatic symptoms. *T*-scores are provided in several domains of functioning (e.g., social competence, total problems, and specific syndromes such as anxious/depressed, withdrawn/depressed, and somatic complaints), and scores are described to be in the normal, subclinical, or clinical range.

The Children's Depression Rating Scale–Revised (CDRS-R) (Poznanski et al., 1984) is a semistructured interview that combines parent and child input. Scores range from 17 to 113, with higher scores indicating greater severity of depressive symptoms. A clinician-rated measure, the Children's Global Assessment Scale (CGAS) (Shaffer, Gould, & Brasic, 1993), provides an overall summary score that ranges from 0 to 100. Clinicians rate children's functioning based on their home, school, and peer functioning, with higher scores indicating better functioning.

Assessing Targeted Treatment Outcomes

Two commonly used measures assess cognitive patterns. The Children's Attributional Style Questionnaire (CASQ) (Seligman et al., 1984), a 24-item child-report measure, assesses children's explanatory styles. Children are presented with both positive and negative events and are asked to select one of two responses that correspond to three dimensions of causality (i.e., stable-unstable, internal-external, global-specific). Explanatory style scores for positive events, negative events, and an overall score are obtained. The Automatic Thoughts Questionnaire (ATQ) (Hollon & Kendall, 1980), a 30-item self-report measure, assesses the frequency at which children make negative self-statements and have negative automatic thoughts. Each item is rated on a 5-point scale; scores range from 30 to 150, with higher scores indicating more negative cognitions.

To assess family functioning, the Family Environment Scale (FES) (Moos & Moos, 1994) is frequently used. Consisting of 90 self-reported items, the FES examines the characteristics of families on three dimensions: interpersonal relationship, personal growth, and system maintenance. Using a true-or-false response format, higher scores on the FES suggest more positive functioning in the particular domain assessed.

CLINICAL CASE EXAMPLE

As discussed, CBT as a broad theoretical approach is considered a well-established treatment approach. This case illustrates the use of CBT techniques (using strategies outlined in the IF-PEP treatment manual [Fristad et al., 2011]) in the treatment of a 9-year-old girl, Janelle (identifying information has been altered to protect confidentiality), for whom her single mother, Ms. Smith, sought treatment at a community mental health outpatient clinic. At intake, Janelle presented with symptoms of dysphoric mood, irritable mood, withdrawn behavior, fatigue, and feelings of worthlessness. Ms. Smith described Janelle to have been grumpy and cranky approximately 50% of the time, exhibiting anger outbursts (triggered by minor events) that lasted up to 1 hour several times a week. Janelle expressed frequently feeling sad and mad and reported crying often and experiencing fatigue daily. Janelle would state that she is "dumb," "no good," and "has no friends" every other day and would express feeling lonely because no one liked her at school. After a thorough assessment of Janelle's presenting concerns, relevant history, and family functioning through parent and child interviews and consultation with Janelle's teacher at school, a diagnosis of D-NOS was assigned. No comorbid diagnoses were given. Ms. Smith noted that Janelle did exhibit occasional oppositional behaviors that seemed age appropriate and were not concerning to her at the time.

Rapport was easily established with both Janelle and Ms. Smith. The therapist collaborated with them to develop a treatment plan with four broad goals: (1) reduce the frequency and intensity of Janelle's depressed and irritable moods; (2) improve Janelle's self-esteem; (3) equip Janelle with coping skills to manage her moods; and (4) improve Janelle's social relationships. The therapist met with Janelle and Ms. Smith together at the beginning of each session to assess Janelle's functioning and address any new concerns. The three met together again at the end of each session to provide Janelle the opportunity to share with Ms. Smith the content of that day's session and to aid Ms. Smith in facilitating Janelle's skills generalization.

To accomplish the first therapy goal, treatment began by providing psychoeducation regarding depressive symptoms to the family. Next, the therapist worked with Janelle on identifying and labeling her feelings and rating the intensity of those feelings. This exercise was completed at the start of each subsequent session. Using age-appropriate and engaging worksheets and games, Janelle was also taught the physiological responses of emotions and environmental triggers for different emotions. Janelle was encouraged to chart her mood and identifiable triggers using a feelings log; this was also completed as a between-session project with help from her mother. Further, in collaboration with Janelle's mother, a list of pleasant and fun activities was generated, and Janelle was asked to document the times when she engaged in those activities and her moods associated with participation. To improve Janelle's self-esteem, she completed an activity in which she was asked to differentiate her depressive symptoms from herself.

Developing behavioral coping strategies to manage "hurtful feelings" was the next focus. With input from Ms. Smith, Janelle brainstormed tools to use when feeling upset. Strategies identified include engaging in physical and social activities, practicing relaxation techniques, and participating in creative activities such as drawing and dancing. Janelle decorated a shoebox to create a toolkit that she filled with reminders of strategies she could use when experiencing hurtful feelings. She was asked to track the times when she used those coping strategies and their effectiveness in improving her mood.

The relationship among thoughts, feelings, and behaviors was then presented to Janelle in an age-appropriate manner, followed by examples of cognitive restructuring. These concepts were reviewed with Ms. Smith. The skills of identifying negative automatic thoughts, evaluating their accuracy, and developing more balanced thinking were introduced and practiced in session and at home with Janelle and Ms. Smith. Next, problem-solving and communication skills were taught. Concrete steps to solve interpersonal problems were introduced, and Janelle practiced implementing those steps in daily social conflicts. Ways to improve both nonverbal and verbal communication were presented. Janelle first practiced those skills in session, then at home with Ms. Smith, and finally applied them in her interactions with peers and teachers at school.

Janelle and Ms. Smith attended a combined total of 18 sessions over 4 months. Both reported steady improvements in Janelle's moods and behaviors. By session 15, Ms. Smith expressed satisfaction with Janelle's progress in treatment, and both Janelle and Ms. Smith expressed being ready to terminate treatment within the next few weeks. The final two sessions were spent reviewing newly learned skills. Strategies to maintain treatment gains and prevent relapse were discussed (e.g., continued practice and implementation of skills, seek treatment if symptoms return or worsen). Throughout treatment, Janelle was friendly and engaged, and consistently completed between-session projects. Ms. Smith was also eager and pleasant, and was reliable in facilitating Janelle's skills generalization between sessions. At the conclusion of treatment, Janelle no longer exhibited frequent periods of dysphoric and irritable moods and seldom made negative self-statements but rather began describing positive characteristics of herself to Ms. Smith. She also began participating in extracurricular activities at school and developed several satisfying friendships with girls in her class. In addition, Ms. Smith continued to encourage and support Janelle in implementing therapeutic skills. At termination of treatment, Janelle had successfully met her treatment goals and no longer met diagnostic criteria for a depressive disorder.

CONCLUSION

Whether children suffer from depressive symptoms or disorder, their lives are adversely impacted in a plethora of ways. Their academic performance, friendships with peers, and relationships with family members can all be affected directly and/or indirectly by depression. In this chapter, we have presented a summary of currently available interventions for children with depressive symptoms or disorders. We have highlighted the evidence for various treatments, described adaptations made to interventions, and illustrated the implementation of strategies that fall under the rubric of CBT, a well-established theoretical approach. Despite the distance the field has come in developing and evaluating interventions for childhood depression, critical work remains to further inform evidence-based clinical practice. With persistent efforts to evaluate and refine promising approaches in well-designed outcome studies, there can be confidence that the field is moving forward to improve the lives of children with depression and their families.

REFERENCES

Achenbach, T. M. (1991). *Manual for the Child Behavior Checklist/4–18 and 1991 profile*. Burlington, VT: University Associates in Psychiatry.

Akiskal, H. S., Walker, P., Puzantian, V. R., King, D., Rosenthal, T. L., & Dranon, M. (1983). Bipolar outcome in the course of depressive illness. *Journal of Affective Disorders, 5,* 115–128.

American Psychiatric Association. (1994). *Diagnostic and statistical manual of mental disorders* (4th ed.). Washington, DC: Author.

American Psychiatric Association. (2013). *Diagnostic and statistical manual of mental disorders* (5th ed.). Arlington, VA: American Psychiatric Publishing.

Angold, A., Costello, E. J., Messer, S. C., Pickles, A., Winder, F., & Silver, D. (1995). The development of a short question-naire for use in epidemiological studies of depression in children and adolescents. *International Journal of Methods in Psychiatric Research, 5,* 237–249.

Asarnow, J. R., Scott, C. V., & Mintz, J. (2002). A combined cognitive-behavioral family education intervention for depression in children: A treatment development study. *Cognitive Therapy and Research, 26*(2), 221–229.

Bearman, S. K., Ugueto, A., Alleyne, A., & Weisz, J. R. (2010). Adapting cognitive-behavioral therapy for depression to fit diverse youths and contexts. In J. R. Weisz & A. E. Kazdin (Eds.), *Evidence-based psychotherapies for children and adolescents* (2nd ed., pp. 466–481). New York, NY: Guilford Press.

Birmaher, B., Arbelaez, C., & Brent, D. (2002). Course and outcome of child and adolescent major depressive disorder. *Child and Adolescent Psychiatric Clinics of North America, 11,* 619–637.

Birmaher, B., Brent, D., & the American Academy of Child and Adolescent Psychiatry Work Group on Quality Issues. (2007). Practice parameter for the assessment and treatment of children and adolescents with depressive disorders. *Journal of the American Academy of Child & Adolescent Psychiatry, 46*(11), 1503–1526.

Birmaher, B., Ryan, N., Williamson, D. E., Brent, D. A., Kaufman, J., Dahl, R. E., . . . Nelson, B. (1996). Childhood and adolescent depression: A review of the past 10 years. Part 1. *Journal of the American Academy of Child & Adolescent Psychiatry, 35*(11), 1427–1439.

Boylan, K., MacPherson, H. A., & Fristad, M. A. (2013). Impact of disruptive behavior on outcomes in a randomized psychotherapy trial for mood disorders. *Journal of the American Academy of Child & Adolescent Psychiatry, 52*(7), 699–708.

Brinkmeyer, M., & Eyberg, S. (2003). Parent–child interaction therapy for oppositional children. In A. E. Kazdin & J. Weisz (Eds.), *Evidence-based psychotherapies for children and adolescents* (pp. 204–223). New York, NY: Guilford Press.

Cardemil, E. V., Reivich, K. J., Beevers, C. G., Seligman, M. E. P., & James, J. (2007). The prevention of depressive symptoms in low-income, minority children: Two-year follow-up. *Behaviour Research and Therapy, 45*(2), 313–327.

Cardemil, E. V., Reivich, K. J., & Seligman, M. E. P. (2002). The prevention of depressive symptoms in low-income minority middle school students. *Prevention and Treatment, 5*(1).

Chambers, W. J., Puig-Antich, J., Hirsch, M., Paez, P., Ambrosini, P. J., Tabrizi, M. A., & Davies, M. (1985). The assessment of affective disorders in children and adolescents by semistructured interview: Test-retest reliability of the Schedule for Affective Disorders and Schizophrenia for school-age children, present episode version. *Archives of General Psychiatry, 42*(7), 696–702.

Chambless, D. L., Baker, M. J., Baucom, D. H., Beutler, L. E., Calhoun, K. S., Crits-Christoph, P., . . . Woody, S. R. (1998). Update on empirically validated therapies II. *Clinical Psychologist, 51*(1), 3–16.

Chambless, D. L., & Hollon, S. D. (1998). Defining empirically supported therapies. *Journal of Consulting and Clinical Psychology, 66*(1), 7–18.

Chambless, D. L., Sanderson, W. C., Shoham, V., Bennett, J. S., Pope, K. S., Crits-Christoph, P., . . . McCurry, S. (1996). An update on empirically validated therapies. *Clinical Psychologist, 49*(2), 5–18.

Clarke, G. N., & Lewinsohn, P. M. (1984). *The Coping with Depression Course Adolescent Version: A psychoeducational intervention for unipolar depression in high school students.* Eugene, OR: Castalia Press.

Costello, E. J., Erkanli, A., & Angold, A. (2006). Is there an epidemic of child or adolescent depression? *Journal of Child Psychology and Psychiatry, 47*(12), 1263–1271.

Cummings, C. M., & Fristad, M. A. (2012). Anxiety in children with mood disorders: A treatment help or hindrance? *Journal of Abnormal Child Psychology, 40*(3), 339–351.

David-Ferdon, C., & Kaslow, N. J. (2008). Evidence-based psychosocial treatments for child and adolescent depression. *Journal of Clinical Child and Adolescent Psychology, 37*(1), 62–104.

Eckshtain, D., & Gaynor, S. T. (2009). Assessing outcome in cognitive behavior therapy for child depression: An illustrative case series. *Child and Family Therapy, 31*(2), 94–116.

Egger, H., Ascher, B., & Angold, A. (1999). *Preschool Age Psychiatric Assessment (PAPA): Version 1.1.* Durham, NC: Department of Psychiatry and Behavioral Sciences, Center for Developmental Epidemiology, Duke University Medical Center.

Egger, H. L., Erkanli, A., Keeler, G., Potts, E., Walter, B. K., & Angold, A. (2006). Test-retest reliability of the Preschool Age Psychiatric Assessment (PAPA). *Journal of the American Academy of Child & Adolescent Psychiatry, 45*(5), 538–549.

Flory, V. (2004). A novel clinical intervention for severe childhood depression and anxiety. *Clinical Child Psychology and Psychiatry, 9*(1), 9–23.

Fristad, M. A., Goldberg-Arnold, J. S., & Leffler, J. M. (2011). *Psychotherapy for children with bipolar and depressive disorders.* New York, NY: Guilford Press.

Fristad, M. A., Verducci, J. S., Walters, K., & Young, M. E. (2009). Impact of multifamily psychoeducational psychotherapy in treating children aged 8 to 12 years with mood disorders. *Archives of General Psychiatry, 66*(9), 1013–1020.

Geller, B., Fox, L. W., & Clark, K. A. (1994). Rate and predictors of prepubertal bipolarity during follow-up of 6- to 12-year-old depressed children. *Journal of the American Academy of Child & Adolescent Psychiatry, 33*(4), 461–468.

Gillham, J. E., Hamilton, J., Freres, D., Patton, K., & Gallop, R. (2006). Preventing depression among early adolescents in the primary care setting: A randomized controlled study of the Penn Resiliency Program. *Journal of Abnormal Child Psychology, 34*(2), 203–219.

Gillham, J. E., & Reivich, K. J. (1999). Prevention of depressive symptoms in schoolchildren: A research update. *Psychological Science, 10*(5), 461–462.

Gillham, J. E., Reivich, K. J., Freres, D. R., Chaplin, T. M., Shatte, A. J., Samuels, B., . . . Seligman, M. E. P. (2007). School-based prevention of depressive symptoms: A randomized controlled study of the effectiveness and specificity of the Penn Resiliency Program. *Journal of Consulting and Clinical Psychology, 75*(1), 9–19.

Gillham, J. E., Reivich, K. J., Freres, D. R., Lascher, M., Litinger, S., Shatte, A., & Seligman, M. E. P. (2006). School-based prevention of depression and anxiety symptoms in early adolescence: A pilot of a parent intervention component. *School Psychology Quarterly, 21*(3), 323–348.

Gillham, J. E., Reivich, K. J., Jaycox, L. H., & Seligman, M. E. P. (1995). Prevention of depressive symptoms in school children: Two-year follow-up. *Psychological Science, 6*(6), 343–351.

Hollon, S. D., & Kendall, P. C. (1980). Cognitive self-statements in depression: Development of an Automatic Thoughts Questionnaire. *Cognitive Therapy and Research, 4*, 383–397.

Jaycox, L. H., Reivich, K. J., Gillham, J., & Seligman, M. E. P. (1994). Prevention of depressive symptoms in school children. *Behaviour Research and Therapy, 32*(8), 801–816.

Kahn, J. S., Kehle, T. J., Jenson, W. R., & Clark, E. (1990). Comparison of cognitive-behavioral, relaxation, and self-modeling interventions for depression among middle-school students. *School Psychology Review, 19*(2), 196–211.

Kaslow, N. J., & Thompson, M. P. (1998). Applying the criteria for empirically supported treatments to studies of psychosocial interventions for child and adolescent depression. *Journal of Clinical Child Psychology, 27*(2), 146–155.

Kovacs, M. (1985). The Children's Depression Inventory (CDI). *Psychopharmacology Bulletin, 21*, 995–1124.

Kovacs, M. (1996). The course of childhood-onset depressive disorders. *Psychiatric Annals, 26*(6), 326–330.

Kovacs, M., Sherrill, J., George, C. J., Pollock, M., Tumuluru, R. V., & Ho, V. (2006). Contextual emotion regulation therapy for childhood depression: Description and pilot testing of a new intervention. *Journal of the American Academy of Child & Adolescent Psychiatry, 45*(8), 892–903.

Lewinsohn, P. M., & Clarke, G. N. (1984). *The Coping with Depression Course Adolescent Version: Instructor's manual for parent course.* Eugene, OR: Castalia Press.

Luby, J., Lenze, S., & Tillman, R. (2012). A novel early intervention for preschool depression: Findings from a pilot randomized controlled trial. *Journal of Child Psychology and Psychiatry, 53*(3), 313–322.

MacPherson, H. A., Algorta, G. P., Mendenhall, A. N., Fields, B. W., & Fristad, M. A. (2013). Predictors and moderators in the randomized trial of multi-family psychoeducational psychotherapy for childhood mood disorders. *Journal of Clinical Child and Adolescent Psychology.* Advance online publication. doi: 10.1080/15374416.2013.807735

Mendenhall, A. N., Fristad, M. A., & Early, T. J. (2009). Factors influencing service utilization and mood symptom severity in children with mood disorders: Effects of multifamily psychoeducation groups (MFPGs). *Journal of Consulting and Clinical Psychology, 77*(3), 463–473.

Moos, R., & Moos, B. (1994). *Family Environment Scale manual: Development, applications, research* (3rd ed.). Palo Alto, CA: Consulting Psychologist Press.

Muratori, F., Picchi, L., Bruni, G., Patarnello, M., & Romagnoli, G. (2003). A two-year follow-up of psychodynamic psychotherapy for internalizing disorders in children. *Journal of the American Academy of Child & Adolescent Psychiatry, 42*(3), 331–339.

Nelson, E., Barnard, M., & Cain, S. (2003). Treating childhood depression over videoconferencing. *Telemedicine Journal and e-Health, 9*(1), 49–55.

Nelson, E., Barnard, M., & Cain, S. (2006). Feasibility of telemedicine intervention for childhood depression. *Counselling and Psychotherapy Research, 6*(3), 191–195.

Poznanski, E. O., Grossman, J. A., Buchsbaum, Y., Banegas, M., Freeman, L., & Gibbons, R. (1984). Preliminary studies of the reliability and validity of the Children's Depression Rating Scale. *Journal of the American Academy of Child & Adolescent Psychiatry, 23*(2), 191–197.

Roberts, C., Kane, R., Thomson, H., Bishop, B., & Hart, B. (2003). The prevention of depressive symptoms in rural school children: A randomized controlled trial. *Journal of Consulting and Clinical Psychology, 71*(3), 622–628.

Seligman, M. E. P., Peterson, C., Kaslow, N. J., Tanenbaum, R. L., Alloy, L. B., & Abramson, L. Y. (1984). Attributional style and depressive symptoms among children. *Journal of Abnormal Psychology, 93*, 235–238.

Shaffer, D., Gould, M. S., & Brasic, J. (1983). A children's global assessment scale (CGAS). *Archives of General Psychiatry, 40,*1228–1231.

Stark, K. D., Banneyer, K. N., Wang, L. A., & Arora, P. (2012). Child and adolescent depression in the family. *Couple and Family Psychology, 3,* 161–184.

Stark, K. D., Brookman, C. S., & Frazier, R. (1990). A comprehensive school-based treatment program for depressed children. *School Psychology Quarterly, 5*(2), 111–140.

Stark, K. D., Hargrave, J., Hersh, B., Greenberg, M., Herren, J., & Fisher, M. (2008). Treatment of childhood depression: The ACTION Treatment Program. In J. R. Z. Abela & B. L. Hankin (Eds.), *Handbook of depression in children and adolescents* (pp. 224–249). New York, NY: Guilford Press.

Stark, K. D., Reynolds, W. M., & Kaslow, N. J. (1987). A comparison of the relative efficacy of self-control therapy and a behavioral problem-solving therapy for depression in children. *Journal of Abnormal Child Psychology, 15*(1), 91–113.

Stark, K. D., Rouse, L., & Livingston, R. (1991). Treatment of depression during childhood and adolescence: Cognitive behavioral procedures for the individual and family. In P. Kendall (Ed.), *Child and adolescent therapy* (pp. 165–206). New York, NY: Guilford Press.

Stark, K. D., Simpson, J., Schnoebelen, S., Hargrave, J., Glenn, R, & Molnar, J. (2006). *Therapist's manual for ACTION.* Broadmore, PA: Workbook.

Stark, K. D., Streusand, W., Krumholz, L. S., & Patel, P. (2010). Cognitive-behavioral therapy for depression: The ACTION treatment program for girls. In J. R. Weisz & A. E. Kazdin (Eds.), *Evidence-based psychotherapies for children and adolescents* (pp. 93–109). New York, NY: Guilford Press.

Tompson, M. C., Boger, K. D., & Asarnow, J. R. (2012). Enhancing the developmental appropriateness of treatment for depression in youth: Integrating the family in treatment. *Child and Adolescent Psychiatric Clinics of North America, 21*(3), 345–384.

Tompson, M. C., Pierre, C. B., Haber, F. M., Fogler, J. M., Groff, A. R., & Asarnow, J. R. (2007). Family-focused treatment for childhood-onset depressive disorders: Results of an open trial. *Clinical Child Psychology and Psychiatry, 12*(3), 403–420.

Trowell, J., Joffe, I., Campbell, J., Clemente, C., Almqvist, F., Soininen, M., . . . Tsiantis, J. (2007). Childhood depression: A place or psychotherapy: An outcome study comparing individual psychodynamic psychotherapy and family therapy. *European Child and Adolescent Psychiatry, 16*(3), 157–167.

Weissman, M. M., Pilowsky, D. J., Wickramaratne, P. J., Talati, A., Wisniewski, S. R., Fava, M., . . . Rush, A. J. (2006). Remissions in maternal depression and child psychopathology. *Journal of the American Medical Association, 295*(12), 1389–1398.

Weisz, J. R., Chorpita, B. F., Plinkas, L. A., Schoenwald, S. K., Miranda, J., Bearman, S. K., . . . the Research Network on Youth Mental Health. (2012). Testing standard and modular designs for psychotherapy treating depression, anxiety, and conduct problems in youth. *Archives of General Psychiatry, 69*(3), 274–282.

Weisz, J. R., McCarty, C. A., & Valeri, S. M. (2006). Effects of psychotherapy for depression in children and adolescents: A meta-analysis. *Psychological Bulletin, 132*(1), 132–149.

Weisz, J. R., Thurber, C. A., Sweeney, L., Proffitt, V. D., & LeGagnoux, G. L. (1997). Brief treatment of mild-to-moderate child depression using primary and secondary control enhancement training. *Journal of Consulting and Clinical Psychology, 65*(4), 703–707.

Weller, E. B., Weller, R. A., Rooney, M. T., & Fristad, M. A. (1999). *Children's Interview for Psychiatric Syndromes (ChIPS).* Washington, DC: American Psychiatric Press.

Yu, D. L., & Seligman, M. E. P. (2002). Preventing depressive symptoms in Chinese children. *Prevention and Treatment, 5*(1).

CHAPTER 10

Depressive Disorders in Adolescents

MEGAN JEFFREYS AND V. ROBIN WEERSING

OVERVIEW OF THE DISORDERS

Depression is widely prevalent in adolescence, with 1 in 5 youth experiencing a depressive episode before reaching the age of 18 (Lewinsohn, Hops, Roberts, Seeley, & Andrews, 1993). Depressive episodes are impairing at any age, with depression being a leading cause of disability worldwide (World Health Organization, 2012); however, this disorder may be particularly consequential with adolescent onset. Youth who first experience a depressive episode in adolescence are at substantially greater risk of experiencing recurrent depressive episodes in adulthood (Weissman et al., 1999). Adolescent depression also predicts impaired educational attainment, deficits in social support, and increased risk of suicide attempt (Gould et al., 1998; Weissman et al., 1999). Even once recovered from a depressive episode, youth continue to experience impaired functioning. Compared to healthy controls, youth with a prior depressive episode experience higher levels of anxiety, elevated depressive symptoms, impaired social functioning, and higher levels of substance abuse (Rohde, Lewinsohn, & Seeley, 1994).

By far, cognitive behavioral therapy (CBT) is the most well researched intervention for adolescent depression, with the vast majority of published clinical trials investigating CBT effects. In this chapter, we attempt to bring clarity to the pattern of results in CBT studies for adolescent depression while reviewing the burgeoning evidence base for interpersonal psychotherapy for adolescents (IPT), an alternate evidence-based treatment (EBT) for this population. In addition, we discuss expectations for parental involvement in treatment and evidence supporting need for parent inclusion across these interventions, and we further emphasize findings, as available, on effects of treatment for adolescent depression in diverse samples and outside of traditional, lab-based settings. Finally, we conclude with a clinically relevant discussion of the use of standardized assessment in the provision of evidence-based care for adolescent depression and provide a case example of how evidence-based approaches could be used to treat depression in adolescence.

EVIDENCE-BASED APPROACHES

Depression is thought to arise from the interplay of heightened intrapersonal sensitivity to stress, experience of stressful life events, and maladaptive responses to these stressors (Caspi et al., 2003; Gazelle & Rudolph, 2004; Kendler, Thorton, & Gardner, 2001). Evidence-based psychosocial treatments for adolescent depression aim at disrupting these processes. In CBT, therapists collaborate with the adolescent to identify depressogenic patterns of thinking and behavior and explicitly teach the adolescent new skills for managing thoughts and mood. In contrast, IPT focuses on current interpersonal stressful life events that appear to play a role in the development or maintenance of the depressive episode. The role of the therapist in IPT is to help the adolescent identify a core problem area in interpersonal functioning and develop interpersonal stress management skills.

Both CBT and IPT have been tested using several similar, but distinct, treatment manuals. Here we examine the literature testing each treatment manual specifically and provide a cumulative review of the evidence for each broad type of treatment. For the purposes of the current review, only intervention trials targeting youth with diagnosable levels of depression are included. Trials including youth with elevated symptoms alone and trials focusing on prevention of depressive illness are excluded.

Cognitive Behavioral Therapy

The term "cognitive behavioral therapy" does not refer to one specific manual, structure, or format for delivering treatment. Rather, CBT refers to the use of a number of techniques the core of which is in the very name, *cognitive* restructuring and *behavioral* activation. Depending on the treatment manual used, CBT for depression may also consist of a number of other treatment techniques, including problem solving, parent management training, relaxation, social skills training, and motivational interviewing (Weersing, Rozenman, & Gonzalez, 2008). The format in which these techniques are used also differs among manuals, ranging from highly didactic group formats to principle-driven, more flexibly applied individual sessions (Weersing & Brent, 2006). This cluster of techniques is united by a focus on *current* problems and symptoms that can be corrected through cognitive and behavioral modification. Under this broad umbrella, four core CBT manuals have been tested in clinical trials with depressed adolescents. We briefly describe and review the evidence for each treatment manual.

Coping with Depression

The Adolescent Coping with Depression Course (CWD-A) is the most extensively tested treatment manual for depression in adolescence. CWD-A was adapted from an adult treatment manual (Lewinsohn, Antonuccio, Steinmetz-Brekenridge, & Teri, 1984) and aims at building skills in a didactic, highly structured format delivered within a group setting. Skills taught in treatment include relaxation, behavioral activation, social skills training, problem solving/conflict resolution, and recognizing and challenging distorted thoughts.

In the initial test of this manual in adolescents, 59 youth with moderate depression were recruited through health professionals, school counselors, and the media (Lewinsohn, Clarke, Hops, & Andrews, 1990). Enrolled youth were randomized to CWD-A, CWD-A with additional parent sessions, or a wait-list control group. CWD-A was delivered in 14 2-hour sessions over the course of 7 weeks. Upon termination from treatment, youth randomized to CWD-A and CWD-A with additional parental support had significantly lower rates of depressive diagnoses (57.1% and 52.4%, respectively) relative to youth randomized to the wait-list control group (94.7%). Six- and 24-month data suggested gains made by youth in active treatment were maintained after termination from treatment (Lewinsohn et al., 1990). A second test of the manual was conducted with 124 adolescents with moderate depression (Clarke, Rohde, Lewinsohn, Hops, & Seeley, 1999). Youth were randomized to CWD-A, CWD-A with parent group, or wait-list control. Youth in both active treatment arms were randomized to receipt of booster sessions following the acute phase of treatment. As in the prior trial, youth randomized to either CWD-A group had higher rates of recovery from depressive disorder diagnosis (66.7% for both groups combined) relative to rates of recovery among youth in the wait-list control (48.1%). Two years following treatment, youth in the active treatment arms experienced low rates of depression recurrence with no statistically significant difference associated with the receipt of booster sessions (25%).

The CWD-A manual has since been tested in more clinically complicated samples. Rohde, Clarke, Mace, Jorgensen, and Seeley (2004) recruited a sample of 93 youth from juvenile justice with comorbid major depressive disorder (MDD) and conduct disorder. Youth were randomized to either a modified version of CWD-A or an alternative intervention targeting potential skill deficits associated with their conduct disorder diagnoses, life skills (LS) training. Rohde and colleagues found youth assigned to CWD-A experienced significantly greater rates of recovery from MDD (39%) relative to youth randomized to the LS training (19%) at the posttreatment assessment; however, the groups did not differ significantly at 6-month (46.3% and 40.05% for CWD-A and LS training, respectively) and 12-month follow-up assessments (36.6% and 37.0%) (Rohde et al., 2004). Rates of recovery from conduct disorder diagnoses did not differ significantly between the CWD-A (9%) and LS training (17%) groups. Notably, in this comorbid sample the rate of recovery from MDD (39%) was lower than rates of recovery in the Clarke et al. (1999) trial (67%). Despite the superiority of CBT to control, overall lower rates of recovery in this comorbid sample may suggest the CWD-A manual is more efficacious when treating moderate depression without co-occurring disruptive behavior problems.

In a further test of the robustness of CWD-A, efficacy of the manual has been examined in treatment for the depressed adolescent offspring of depressed parents. Clarke and colleagues (2002) enrolled 88 depressed youth through large health maintenance organizations (HMOs) whose parents had a current or a recent (within the past 12 months) depressive episode. Adolescents were randomized to either 16 sessions of CWD-A delivered in a group format or treatment as usual (TAU) through their HMO. Rates of recovery from depressive illness did not differ significantly between youth randomized to CWD-A (31.6%) and TAU (29.8%) upon termination from treatment, nor were significant group differences found at 12- or 24-month follow-up assessments. Notably, the posttreatment response rate for CWD-A is lower in this trial than in any previous trials of this manual. This result is consistent with the broader negative impact of parental depression on youth mental health and response to treatment seen in other investigations (Garber et al., 2009; Rishel et al., 2006).

Overall, research on the CWD-A manual suggests that this intervention has acute benefits in reducing depressive symptoms in four randomized clinical trials. Youth receiving this intervention maintain gains as far as 2 years posttreatment. However, the efficacy of this intervention in samples with more clinically complicated presentations has been less well supported.

Pittsburgh Cognitive Therapy Study

In contrast with the highly structured, group-based CWD-A manual, the cognitive therapy manual developed in Pittsburgh by Brent and colleagues was developed to be delivered in an individual setting over 12 to 16 sessions (Weersing & Brent, 2003, 2006). The manual is principle based, allowing greater flexibility in the implementation of three core techniques: cognitive restructuring, behavioral activation, and problem solving. Application of these techniques is tailored to the individual patient and guided by cognitive case conceptualization. One randomized clinical trial of this treatment manual has been conducted to date (Brent et al., 1997). Adolescents ($N = 107$) with moderate to severe levels of depression were recruited through psychiatric referral and advertisement and randomized to one of three conditions: CBT, systemic behavior family therapy (SBFT), or nondirective supportive therapy (NST). Notably, youth in all three treatment arms received extensive psychoeducation. Youth in the study were clinically complicated, with over half the sample meeting criteria for a comorbid diagnosis and approximately one quarter with a history of suicide attempt. Rates of recovery were significantly higher for youth randomized to CBT (60%) relative to SBFT (37.9%) and NST (39.4%). At 2 years posttreatment, 80% of youth across groups had recovered, with no significant difference between groups (Birmaher et al., 2000), although high rates of service utilization among youth over follow-up make interpretation of this finding difficult.

Brief CBT

A briefer manual for CBT has been developed and tested among youth with a depressive disorder diagnosis within two randomized clinical trials in the United Kingdom. Vostanis, Feehan, Grattan, and Bickerton (1996b) randomized 57 moderately depressed youth to either brief CBT or a control intervention involving nondirective supportive treatment. Brief CBT included emotion recognition and labeling, social skill building, and challenging distorted cognitions. Treatment consisted of nine individual sessions delivered every other week over a maximum of 6 months; this is notably a lower dose of treatment spread over a longer length of time than in previous trials. As in the coping with depression course, sessions were highly structured and didactic. Youth treated with brief CBT did not demonstrate significantly lower rates of depression than youth treated with supportive therapy upon termination from treatment (Vostanis et al., 1996b). Rates of depressive disorders were low both among youth randomized to CBT (13%) and for youth randomized to supportive therapy (25%). This lack of a significant difference between treatment arms was also evident at 9-month and 2-year follow-up periods (Vostanis, Feehan, & Grattan, 1998; Vostanis, Feehan, Grattan, & Bickerton, 1996a). This lack of an effect may be compounded by natural remission rates of depression over time and relativity low doses of CBT.

In a second trial of a similar manual, Wood, Harrington, and Moore (1996) randomized 53 moderately depressed youth to brief CBT or a relaxation training (mean number of sessions = 6.4). In contrast to the results of Vostanis and colleagues, youth randomized to CBT had lower levels of depressive symptoms than youth in relaxation training immediately after treatment (Wood et al., 1996). Clinical remission was defined as a score ≤ 3 on the Clinical Global Impressions Scale (CGI). Youth randomized to CBT experienced greater levels of improvement at posttreatment assessment (54%) relative to youth in relaxation training (21%), but these differences were not significant at 3-month (45% and 25% for CBT and relaxation training, respectively) and 6-month (54% and 38%) follow-up.

Modular CBT

A final, critical manual in the treatment for depression in adolescents is modular CBT. This manual was developed through combining elements of the CWD-A and Pittsburgh cognitive manuals. This treatment takes a modular approach in which all youth receive six sessions building core skills in CBT. These core sessions include psychoeducation, goal-setting, mood monitoring, behavioral activation, social problem solving, and cognitive restructuring. In addition to these core sessions, modular CBT includes a number of additional sessions that can be used as needed for the individual teen in sessions 7 through 12. Additional sessions include a variety of potential skills to learn, including increasing social engagement, improving skills in communication, assertiveness training, and additional work with parents (Treatment for Adolescents with Depression Study [TADS] Team, 2004).

This manual was used in the largest treatment trial for depressed adolescents to date, the TADS. The sample of the TADS study was comprised of youth with moderate to severe depression. Youth enrolled in the TADS study were randomized to CBT, fluoxetine, combination treatment with fluoxetine and CBT, or pill placebo. After acute treatment, youth receiving combination treatment had the highest rates of response (71%) followed by the rates of response in youth receiving fluoxetine alone (61%). Youth receiving CBT experienced lower rates of response (43%), with no significant difference found between this condition and pill placebo (35%). Youth in the CBT condition continued to make gains over follow-up at weeks 18 and 36. Rates of response at week 18 were highest for combination treatment (85%), with rates of response to CBT alone (65%) comparable to rates of response in youth treated with fluoxetine (69%). By week 36, rates of response to CBT were comparable to both combination treatment and fluoxetine alone (TADS Team, 2007).

This finding lies in stark contrast with the above literature showing notably lower acute response rates than found in prior CBT trials. This outcome is particularly surprising given the support for both manuals used to develop the modular CBT manual; each of the contributing manuals had response rates approximately 20 percentage points higher (Brent et al., 1997; Clarke et al., 1999). Moreover, this finding lies in contrast to later tests of the same manual. Brent and colleagues (2008) recruited adolescents with clinically significant depression despite currently taking a selective serotonin reuptake inhibitor (SSRI). Youth were randomized to a change in medication alone or change in medication along with modular CBT. Youth in all treatment arms improved; however, youth receiving CBT in addition to either change in medication improved more than youth receiving medication alone (14% difference in response rate). Though data on use of the various modules in the TADS trial have not been published, one possible explanation for the difference in these two trials may lie in dosage of core components of CBT. Indeed, within the TORDIA sample, superior response was associated with receiving a higher dose of problem-solving skills and social skills training, relative to other components of the modular intervention (Kennard et al., 2009).

Cumulative Evidence for CBT

Across manuals, when core CBT skills (e.g., cognitive restructuring and behavioral activation) are delivered at an optimal dose and intensity (weekly for at least 12 weeks), CBT appears to be efficacious in treating depression in adolescence. The evidence to date supports the acute efficacy of CBT either when implemented in a highly structured group setting or more flexibly implemented in individual treatment. Despite consistent positive effects at posttreatment, the superiority of CBT as compared to other treatments diminishes over follow-up. This pattern of results appears to be driven in large part by catch-up effects in control conditions, as might be expected given the cyclical nature of depressive disorder (e.g., untreated episodes resolve in 9 months, on average [see Weersing & Weisz, 2002, for discussion; Kovacs, Obrosky, Gatsonis, & Richards, 1997]). The efficacy of CBT for clinically complicated youth and the effectiveness of CBT when delivered in real-world service settings are less clear. These issues are covered in greater detail in sections that follow.

Interpersonal Psychotherapy

The second major evidence-based psychosocial treatment for depression in adolescence is IPT. Similar to CBT, IPT is a treatment that targets practicing and building skills to reduce *current* symptoms and impairment associated with depression. In contrast to CBT, IPT focuses primarily on the social context in which symptoms develop and are maintained. IPT treats depressive symptoms and problematic social functioning using three primary treatment strategies: identification of a social problem area tied with onset of the depressive episode; development of effective communication and problem-solving skills for this problem area; and building and practicing skills taught in treatment (Mufson & Sills, 2006). To date, two IPT manuals have been tested in randomized controlled trials for treatment of depression in adolescence. Evidence for each treatment manual as well as the cumulative evidence for IPT are discussed.

Interpersonal Psychotherapy for Depressed Adolescents

The IPT-A manual is based on an efficacious interpersonal therapy manual for depressed adults (Klerman, Weissman, Rounsaville, & Chevron, 1984). IPT-A is a structured treatment that works through active skill building in and out of session. In an initial randomized controlled trial of IPT-A, Mufson, Weissman, Moreau, and Garfinkel (1999) enrolled 48 moderately depressed adolescents who were then randomized to either IPT-A or clinical monitoring. Patients received weekly individual treatment for 12 weeks and additional weekly phone contact for the first 4 weeks of treatment. Results indicated that youth randomized to IPT-A improved significantly relative to youth randomized to clinical monitoring. Rates of recovery were defined by scores equal to or lower than 6 on the Hamilton Rating Scale for Depression (HRSD) and 9 on the Beck Depression Inventory (BDI), respectively. Youth receiving IPT-A had higher rates of recovery (75%) upon treatment termination as compared to youth receiving clinical monitoring (46%).

The effects of IPT-A were further tested in a second randomized controlled trial. Mufson and colleagues (2004) worked with clinicians (primarily social workers and two psychologists) at five schools. Half of the clinicians at each school received training in IPT-A; training included: reading the manual, didactic training for two half days, and weekly supervision. IPT-A consisted of eight 35-minute weekly sessions followed by an additional four sessions that could be administered weekly or biweekly. Enrolled youth ($N = 63$) were randomized to either IPT-A provided by a school clinician or TAU (e.g., supportive counseling with a school counselor not trained in the IPT-A protocol). Youth randomized to IPT-A improved significantly relative to youth receiving routine care through the school. Upon termination of treatment, 50% of youth receiving IPT-A and 34% of youth receiving TAU met criteria for recovery on the Hamilton Rating Scale for Depression (HAM-D); on the Beck Depression Inventory (BDI), 74% and 52% of youth in IPT-A and TAU conditions, respectively, met criteria for recovery. Across these two trials, the evidence base supports the acute efficacy of IPT-A with preliminary support of the effectiveness of this treatment when implemented in a real-world service setting.

Cumulative Evidence for IPT-A

There is evidence to suggest the efficacy of IPT-A in treating depression in adolescence. Rates of recovery from depression in youth receiving IPT-A treatments (82%–75%) were considerably higher than rates of recovery among youth in no-treatment or TAU conditions (52%–34%). Preliminary evidence exists to support the effectiveness of IPT-A when implemented in school settings by school practitioners with no IPT-A experience prior to the study (Mufson et al., 2004). Long-term maintenance of gains made after treatment in IPT-A requires further examination. Additional evidence for the efficacy of IPT comes from two trials comparing IPT adapted for Puerto Rican adolescents with depression to both wait-list control and CBT. These two trials are further discussed in the Adaptations and Modifications Section.

PARENTAL INVOLVEMENT IN TREATMENT

In treating youth psychopathology broadly, and adolescent depression specifically, one question that may arise is what role parents should play in treatment. Certainly there is strong empirical ground to suggest that parental psychopathology is involved in the development and maintenance of adolescent depression. Offspring of parents with a history of depression experience two- to three-fold increases in depressive illness (Weissman et al., 2006) due to both shared genetic vulnerability to the effects of stress and the direct stressful effects of living with an impaired parent (Hammen, 2002; Lewis, Rice, Harold, Collishaw, & Thapar, 2011). Further, there is evidence to suggest that current parental depression at the time of intervention delivery predicts poor response for depressed teens and may moderate treatment effects, erasing the positive impact of CBT (Brent et al., 1998; Clarke et al., 2002; Jayson, Wood, Kroll, Fraser, & Harrington, 1998).

CBT manuals for adolescent depression have involved parents to differing degrees. The role of parental involvement in treatment has been most extensively examined in the CWD-A manual. In two trials of this protocol, an adolescent-only treatment was compared to treatment augmented with a parallel parent group (Clarke et al., 1999; Lewinsohn et al., 1990). The parent group was designed to review skills taught to adolescents while also targeting family conflict reduction. Lewinsohn and colleagues (1990; $N = 59$) found that both groups improved significantly compared with wait-list control. Although the adolescent-alone and parent groups did not differ significantly on most measures, youth randomized to treatment with the parallel parent group had lower rates of depressive illness at posttreatment (52.4% compared with 57.1%). In a larger trial of the same manual ($N = 123$), Clarke and colleagues (1999) found that the adolescent-only and adolescent plus parent groups improved, but the groups did not differ significantly. In this trial, a trend was found as well for adolescents randomized to the treatment plus parent group to have higher rates of being diagnosis free (68.8%) compared with adolescents not receiving the parent component (64.9%). Failure to detect a significant difference across treatments may be due to low power or moderate to poor attendance, especially for fathers ($M = 5.8$ of 9 sessions).

As IPT-A is a treatment designed to address interpersonal problems, there is reason to believe the relationship with the parent is critical to program success. Indeed, modifications made in the development of the IPT-A protocol from the original adult manual include discussion of parental relationship issues (e.g., separation, negotiating autonomy) and addition of a fifth problem related to single-parent households (Mufson et al., 1999). Although IPT-A is designed to target interpersonal problems, the treatment itself is largely implemented through building skills in session with the therapist that can later be applied in real-life interpersonal contexts. Examination of the impact of explicitly including the parent in session in IPT-A with adolescents diagnosed with a depressive disorder is needed.

Notably, there has been limited empirical exploration of the efficacy of family-based treatment for adolescent depression; family therapies for adolescent depression are not currently considered an evidence-based approach (David-Ferdon & Kaslow, 2008). In the Pittsburgh cognitive therapy trial, Brent and colleagues (1997) compared CBT to systemic behavior family therapy (SBFT) in addition to a supportive, nondirective therapy control condition. The authors found that youth receiving CBT had substantially higher rates of remission (64.7%) than youth receiving SBFT (37.9%). Despite this negative result, work on family-focused treatments continues, including Attachment-Based Family Therapy (ABFT) (Diamond, Reis, Diamond, Siqueland, & Isaacs, 2002; Diamond et al., 2010), as well as on models that utilize parents as cotherapists, such as Contextual Emotion-Regulation Therapy (CERT) (Kovacs et al., 2006).

ADAPTATIONS AND MODIFICATIONS

Throughout our review, we have sought to highlight studies in which investigators have stepped beyond the confines of traditional lab-based clinical trials and tested the effectiveness of interventions in real-world delivery settings with populations diverse in demographic and clinical characteristics. This section reviews the evidence for the effectiveness of CBT when used in real-world settings and adaptations made to enhance cultural sensitivity of these evidence-based interventions.

Adaptations for and Effectiveness in Practice

Results have been mixed on the effectiveness of CBT compared to TAU conditions. Effectiveness of brief CBT was examined by Kerfoot and colleagues (2004) in adolescents with elevated depressive symptoms. Practicing social workers were randomized to be trained using several days of didactic instruction and biweekly supervision in CBT. In the comparison arm, youth received routine care through their social worker without the CBT training augmentation. Although youth receiving CBT did not experience greater levels of remission in depressive symptoms than did youth in usual services, this may in part be due to low attendance to supervision by the providers. With median attendance of three supervision sessions, it is difficult to know how well the principles of CBT were implemented in this trial. Indeed, in a later effectiveness trial of CBT in children and adolescents that relied on extensive supervision, Weisz and colleagues (2009) found that youth receiving CBT had earlier treatment termination (24 weeks instead of 39), stronger therapeutic alliance, decreased service utilization, and fewer health care costs.

Several trials testing the combination of medication and CBT have also occurred in primary care and outpatient mental health settings. Clarke and colleagues (2005) tested the effectiveness of using brief CBT to supplement SSRI medication treatment in pediatric primary care. In the CBT arm, youth were presented with psychoeducation and the treatment rationale. Youth then completed either four sessions of behavioral activation or four sessions of cognitive restructuring, according to their preference. If the youth did not recover after these four sessions, four additional sessions were allocated to cover the alternate skill. Although no difference was found on presence of a depression diagnosis, youth receiving CBT reported a decrease in outpatient visits and use of SSRI medication compared to youth in the usual care medication-only condition. In a similar study, Goodyer and colleagues (2007) examined the effectiveness of CBT in combination with receipt of an SSRI. The study was conducted in a sample of youth seen through the National Health Service (NHS) who had failed to respond to brief intervention. Again, no difference was found between youth receiving combination treatment and those receiving medication and routine care alone. However, the sample was comprised of a particularly difficult-to-treat sample of youth with high levels of suicidality representative of youth seen in this outpatient setting. Finally, Asarnow and colleagues (2005) tested the impact of a quality improvement intervention in pediatric primary care, a package of training and services that included access to CBT. Adolescents with probable depression were randomized to either TAU through primary care or to this quality improvement condition ($N = 418$; ages 13–21). Youth randomized to the quality improvement treatment arm had significantly lower depressive symptoms and better quality of life, in addition to higher rates of mental health care, psychosocial treatment (CBT), and greater satisfaction with care.

Data on the effectiveness of IPT-A are less ambiguous. As discussed previously, Mufson and colleagues (2004) have demonstrated effectiveness of IPT-A when delivered in school settings by school counselors naive to evidence-based intervention prior to study involvement. Clinicians in the intervention arm received training that included reading the manual, didactic training for two half days, and weekly supervision. Treatment consisted of twelve 35-minute sessions that were held weekly for the initial eight sessions; after session 8, clinicians were free to continue weekly sessions or taper to biweekly sessions. As noted above, IPT-A significantly outperformed usual school counseling services in this study; furthermore, absolute recovery rates for youth receiving IPT-A in this effectiveness design were similar to those reported in prior efficacy trials (74%–50%).

Cultural Adaptations

To date, randomized clinical trials for adolescent depression have largely included Caucasian-majority samples or failed to provide information on the culture, race, and ethnicity of enrolled adolescents (see, e.g., Lewinshohn et al., 1990). The work of Rosselló, Bernal, and colleagues is a notable exception, focusing on testing culturally adapted treatments for adolescent depression in adolescents in Puerto Rico. In two randomized trials (Rosselló & Bernal, 1999; Rosselló, Bernal, & Rivera-Medina, 2008), culturally adapted versions of CBT and IPT (in individual and group formats) were compared to each other and, in one trial, to a wait-list control condition. The CBT program was based on a manual used successfully with depressed Latino adults, primarily of South American descent, in the mainland United States (Muñoz et al., 1995). Adaptations to this program include tying discussion of pleasant activity scheduling to an analysis of the adolescent's broad social networks and the role of family obligation (including the option of bringing family members to sessions). As a result, this CBT protocol is more interpersonal than many other nonadapted manuals, with one third of sessions containing explicit interpersonal content (Rosselló & Bernal, 1999). To adapt IPT for Puerto Rican youth, the research team also began with an adult manual, the original IPT work of Klerman and colleagues (1984). As this adult manual had not been previously adapted for use in a Latino population, the level of modification was more extensive than with the CBT protocol, including translation of materials into Puerto Rican idiomatic Spanish, development and use of culturally relevant metaphors, greater involvement of family members in treatment sessions, and adjustment of therapy goals and definition of interpersonal "problem" areas to respect the structure and values of Puerto Rican families (Rosselló & Bernal, 1999). For example, *familism* was identified as a core cultural value, with family obligation and family support central to definitions of self and feelings of self-esteem. Therapists were trained to treat parents with formality and respect and to vary their practice to include separate parent meetings, as necessary, to discuss the youth's treatment and role of the family. Both trials found positive outcomes of culturally adapted CBT and IPT. In the initial trial, Rosselló and Bernal (1999) randomized 71 Puerto Rican adolescents with a depressive disorder to CBT, IPT, or a wait-list control. Both active treatments resulted in greater reductions in depressive symptoms compared with wait-list control, with no significant difference between the two active treatments. An additional randomized clinical trial has been conducted in a mixed sample of adolescents with a depressive disorder diagnosis and elevated symptoms alone (Rosselló, Bernal, & Rivera-Medina, 2008). Youth were randomized to either group or individual IPT or CBT. No significant difference emerged between group and individual delivery formats. Though CBT outperformed IPT, across theoretical orientations recovery rates were comparable to previously established outcomes for CBT and IPT.

MEASURING TREATMENT EFFECTS

Why invest in evidence-based assessment when treating depressed teens? At intake, use of standardized assessments is a way to conduct a thorough assessment of a youth's symptoms and functioning and to assess the match between an adolescent's presenting symptoms and any EBTs being considered. Use of standardized assessment can also help in assessing adequacy of change in symptoms over the course of treatment. Throughout our review of the CBT and IPT evidence base, we have included reference to specific definitions of treatment response. The response rates of these studies serve as a useful benchmark for clinical practice. Moreover, use of frequent assessment can aid in a clinician's understanding of when change occurred for the patient and perhaps what occurred in treatment to facilitate change—a critical task in the use of modular EBTs for depressed teens, in which therapists have considerable flexibility in optimizing the dose of especially helpful treatment components.

Clinician-Rated Assessments

The Schedule for Affective Disorders and Schizophrenia for School Aged Children (K-SADS) (Kaufman, Birmaher, Brent, & Rao, 1997) is the research gold standard for psychodiagnostic assessment of depression. The K-SADS is a semistructured assessment that probes for current and past episodes of psychiatric illness. The K-SADS includes assessment of internalizing, external-izing, eating, psychotic, and substance abuse disorders as well as disorders diagnosed in childhood. Excellent psychometric properties have been established for the K-SADS with high interrater and test-retest reliability as well as convergent and discriminant validity (Kaufman et al., 1997). In clini-cal practice, the K-SADS may be useful for establishing primary mood and comorbid diagnoses at intake and in providing a strong assessment of treatment response (i.e., diagnostic remission). However, as with all comprehensive diagnostic evaluations, the K-SADS is lengthy to complete and requires advanced training to achieve adequate reliability.

In addition to diagnostic assessment, clinician-rated severity scales can be used to assess depressive symptoms. The Children's Depression Rating Scale–Revised (CDRS-R) (Poznanski, Freeman, & Mokros, 1984) is a rating scale in which the clinician uses both youth and parent report as well as clinical observation to make summary ratings for each specific symptom of youth depression. The CDRS-R has exceptional psychometric properties with good interrater reliability, internal consistency, and convergent validity (Mayes, Bernstein, Hayley, Kennard, & Emslie, 2010). Additionally, the CDRS-R is a sensitive measure that has been used to assess outcomes in sev-eral clinical trials (Brent et al., 2008; TADS Team, 2004). The CDRS-R provides a state-of-the-art assessment of depression symptoms at a significant time savings over a full diagnostic assessment, albeit with a much more limited scope (i.e., no information on comorbid diagnoses).

Youth- and Parent-Report Assessments

Youth- and parent-report assessments are useful primarily for assessing change in depressive symptoms over the course of treatment, rather than establishing depressive diagnoses at intake. Common youth- and parent-report assessments include the Center for Epidemiological Studies Depression Scale for Children (CES-DC) (Radloff, 1977), the Children's Depression Inventory (CDI) (Kovacs, 1983), Depression Self Rating Scale (DSRS) (Birleson, 1981), as well as the short and long forms of the Mood and Feelings Questionnaire (MFQ) (Costello & Angold, 1988). In a systematic review of the content validity of the CES-DC, CDI, DSRS, CDS, and MFQ, Costello and Angold (1988) found that despite coverage of 80 symptoms total among the scales, only six items were covered in each measure (depressed mood, anhedonia, insomnia, fatigue, crying, loneliness). Criterion validity of each of these measures varies according to the cut point used, with specificity increasing and sensitivity decreasing with higher cut points. Of these options, the most widely used measure for assessing youth depression is the CDI. Using a cut point of 19, 88% of depressed youth were correctly identified and 90% of nonreferred youth scored below this point (Friedman & Butler, 1979), demonstrating excellent sensitivity and specificity. Although less widely used, the MFQ is a free-of-cost alternative with similar psychometric properties to the

CDI and may be a useful alternate in budget-conscious clinical applications. In an examination of the psychometric properties of the MFQ, Wood, Kroll, Moore, and Harrington (1995) found superior criterion validity on the youth report MFQ (MFQ-C) as compared to parent-report MFQ. The MFQ-C had high specificity (78%) and sensitivity (78%).

CLINICAL CASE EXAMPLE

Cecilia is a 14-year-old female who is experiencing a first episode of MDD. Prior to the onset of the disorder, Cecilia was functioning well academically and socially. Cecilia was on the honor roll and actively involved with the soccer team. Although Cecilia was somewhat shy, this did not get in the way of her ability to make or maintain her friendships. Family life had been difficult after Cecilia's parents separated 2 years prior to the onset of her depressive episode. Cecilia's mother, her primary guardian, with whom she was close, began working more hours after the divorce, which meant Cecilia was spending more time home alone and less time with this source of support. Cecilia's symptoms started during her transition to high school; she was going to a different high school from many of her middle school friends. After initially struggling to make friends, Cecilia became socially withdrawn and quit the soccer team she had tried out for over the summer. Cecilia started spending increasingly more time in her room watching television. At the intake appointment, Cecilia's mother noted a sharp change in the way her daughter talked about herself in which Cecilia began to see herself in a more negative light. Over time, Cecilia began to feel hopeless and had passing thoughts wishing she were not alive. Based on information collected during the intake appointment, Cecilia met criteria for MDD with comorbid social phobia. Cecilia was above the clinical cutoff on both a clinician-rated measure of depressive symptoms (CDRS-R = 49) and self-report measure (MFQ-C = 52).

Cecilia's therapist began treatment by providing psychoeducation regarding depression, including the relationship between stress and depression, prevalence rates of depressive disorders in youth, and a discussion of when normal sadness can spiral into depression. Cecilia's therapist introduced a model of depression comprised of thoughts, behaviors, and physical symptoms and how Cecilia's current symptoms fit within this model. Specifically, Cecilia's therapist discussed the distorted thoughts the family noted during the initial appointment. Cecilia identified the thought "no one cares about me" and belief that "I am a burden." Her therapist discussed how these thoughts impacted her behavior and served to maintain her symptoms over time. Cecilia and her therapist discussed how these thoughts led to avoidance and withdrawal. Cecilia endorsed believing that these thoughts prevented her from attempting to make new friends and initiate social contact. Her therapist discussed how these thoughts and behaviors became automatic with the initial goal of treatment as identifying what the thoughts and behaviors were for her. Cecilia agreed to monitoring her mood, including monitoring the thoughts and behaviors she had when feeling down.

Cecilia quickly became able to identify her pattern of withdrawal; Cecilia noticed that because of the thoughts, she would not initiate contact with peers. These thoughts had generalized to people with whom she used to enjoy spending time (e.g., Mom and friends from middle school). During the second session, she identified a negative spiral when a new girl had invited her to attend a soccer game with her group of friends and Cecilia declined. Cecilia reported as a consequence of this she spent the afternoon feeling down and watching television alone at home. The therapist introduced behavioral activation and how they were going to focus on coming up with a plan to improve her mood. Cecilia's therapist discussed the difference between normal feelings of fatigue and symptoms of depression; her therapist then discussed how these symptoms are common in depression but ultimately serve to maintain negative affect by reducing activity. When discussing things that may help to lift mood, Cecilia identified coming up with a plan to go to a movie with one of her friends. Cecilia also discussed the decrease in family support; she made a plan to do a pleasant activity with her mom at least three times per week starting with going on a walk to a coffee shop that night. Over the course of treatment, Cecilia and her therapist were able to increase her social network starting with making eye contact with others, beginning conversations, asking to sit with other kids at lunch, and eventually planning activities outside of school with others. Cecilia's therapist worked with her on increasing her level of activity more broadly, including walking regularly, doing the hobbies she used to enjoy (e.g., reading and drawing), and planning activities with her mom. Although Cecilia agreed to this plan, she initially had difficulty following through. When coming back for her third session, Cecilia reported that she had completed only one pleasant activity that her mother had initiated. Cecilia's therapist validated how difficult it is to make change but how important the homework is in order for treatment to work. After introducing cognitive restructuring, Cecilia and her therapist discussed how these homework assignments might help her collect evidence to challenge her distorted thoughts. Cecilia discussed the feelings of burdensomeness as a primary barrier to homework completion. Cecilia and her therapist came up with a plan that she would perform her cognitive restructuring homework before completing behavioral activation. Cecilia also decided to talk to her mom about the homework so that her parent could encourage homework completion.

In sessions 4 and 5, Cecilia continued to report limited compliance with homework. Upon further discussion of why Cecilia was having trouble completing the homework, Cecilia became very quiet and reported that she believed the thoughts were true and that others did not want to be around her. Cecilia's therapist asked about her previous relationships with friends as evidence contradicting the distorted thoughts. Cecilia endorsed enjoying being around them and feeling like they enjoyed being around her. Cecilia's therapist further discussed the rationale behind behavioral activation and asked if Cecilia would be willing to try calling one of her friends in session. Cecilia agreed to this activity and, after role-playing how the conversation might go, was able to complete this task. After calling and making plans with her old friend, Cecilia was in much better spirits and was able to come up with alternative thoughts. At the end of session Cecilia and her therapist decided to make a specific plan for performing three pleasant activities over the coming week.

In session 5, Cecilia reported a dramatic change in her mood. Cecilia reported that not only had she followed through on her plan to spend time with her friend but that she had called and made plans with several other friends from her old school. Although scheduling time to spend with her mom had been difficult, they were able to spend time together twice. Cecilia and her therapist discussed whether she might be able to come up with a plan to begin making new friends at school. After the success of the past week, Cecilia was willing to try reaching out to new kids. Cecilia had become considerably withdrawn and had quite a bit of difficulty initiating any social contact. Cecilia decided to start by making eye contact and smiling in the hall to kids at school. By working slowly but persistently, Cecilia was able to work up to talking to new youth and asking to sit with people at lunch. In session 12, Cecilia hit a setback when two girls she had approached to sit with rejected her saying that they wanted to discuss something private. For Cecilia this triggered the thought that "nobody likes me." Cecilia and her therapist were able to challenge the thought using evidence from the past weeks of multiple groups of girls enjoying spending time with her. Cecilia and her therapist were able to identify the more realistic thought that "many people like me, but some people might not want to spend time with me." By session 16, Cecilia had found a group of girls she got along with well. Cecilia noticed that her depressed mood was much less frequent and the thoughts of burdensomeness were less frequent and intense. Cecilia no longer met criteria for MDD or social phobia. Cecilia also had reduced scores on the CDRS-R (=23) and MFQ (=13). At this time, Cecilia and her therapist made the decision to end treatment after reviewing the skills she had learned and how she would continue practicing these skills.

REFERENCES

Asarnow, J. R., Jaycox, L. H., Duan, N., LaBorde, A. P., Rea, M. M., Murray, P., . . . Wells, K. B. (2005). Effectiveness of a quality improvement intervention for adolescent depression in primary care clinics: A randomized controlled trial. *Journal of the American Medical Association, 293,* 311–319.

Birleson, P. (1981). The validity of depressive disorder in childhood and the development of a self-rating scale: A research report. *Journal of Child Psychology and Psychiatry, 22,* 73–88.

Birmaher, B., Brent, D. A., Kolko, D., Baugher, M., Bridge, J., Holder, D., . . . Ulloa, R. E. (2000). Clinical outcome after short-term psychotherapy for adolescents with major depressive disorder. *Archives of General Psychiatry, 57,* 29–36.

Brent, D., Emslie, G., Clarke, G., Wagner, K. D., Asarnow, J. R., Keller, M., . . . Zelazny, J. (2008). Switching to another SSRI or to venlafaxine with or without cognitive behavioral therapy for adolescents with SSRI-resistant depression: The TORDIA randomized controlled trial. *Journal of the American Medical Association, 299,* 901–913.

Brent, D. A., Holder, D., Kolko, D., Birmaher, B., Baugher, M., Roth, C., . . . Johnson, B. A. (1997). A clinical psychotherapy trial for adolescent depression comparing cognitive, family, and supportive therapy. *Archives of General Psychiatry, 54,* 877–885.

Brent, D. A., Kolko, D. J., Birmaher, B., Baugher, M., Bridge, J., Roth, C., Holder, D. (1998). Predictors of treatment efficacy in a clinical trial of three psychosocial treatments for adolescent depression. *Journal of the American Academy of Child & Adolescent Psychiatry, 37,* 906–914.

Caspi, A., Sugden, K., Moffitt, T. E., Taylor, A., Craig, I. W., Harrington, H., . . . Poulton, R. (2003). Influence of life stress on depression: Moderation by a polymorphism in the 5-HTT gene. *Science, 301,* 386–389.

Clarke, G., Debar, L., Lynch, F., Powell, J., Gale, J., O'Connor, E., . . . Hertert, S. (2005). A randomized effectiveness trial of brief cognitive-behavioral therapy for depressed adolescents receiving antidepressant medication. *Journal of the American Academy of Child & Adolescent Psychiatry, 44,* 888–898.

Clarke, G. N., Hornbrook, M., Lynch, F., Polen, M., Gale, J., O'Connor, E., . . . Debar, L. (2002). Group cognitive-behavioral treatment for depressed adolescent offspring of depressed parents in a health maintenance organization. *Journal of the American Academy of Child & Adolescent Psychiatry, 41,* 305–313.

Clarke, G. N., Rohde, P., Lewinsohn, P. M., Hops, H., & Seeley, J. R. (1999). Cognitive-behavioral treatment of adolescent depression: Efficacy of acute group treatment and booster sessions. *Journal of the American Academy of Child & Adolescent Psychiatry, 38,* 272–279.

Costello, E. J., & Angold, A. (1988). Scales to assess child and adolescent depression: Checklists, screens, and nets. *Journal of the American Academy of Child & Adolescent Psychiatry, 27,* 726–737.

David-Ferdon, C., & Kaslow, N. J. (2008). Evidence-based psychosocial treatments for child and adolescent depression. *Journal of Clinical Child & Adolescent Psychology, 37,* 62–104.

Diamond, G. S., Reis, B. F., Diamond, G. M., Siqueland, L., & Isaacs, L. (2002). Attachment based family therapy for depressed adolescents: A treatment development study. *Journal of the American Academy of Child & Adolescent Psychiatry, 41,* 1190–1196.

Diamond, G. S., Wintersteen, M. B., Brown, G. K., Diamond, G. M., Gallop, R., Shelef, K., & Levey, S. (2010). Attachment-based family therapy for adolescents with suicidal ideation: A randomized controlled trial. *Journal of the American Academy of Child & Adolescent Psychiatry, 49,* 122–131.

Friedman, R. J., & Butler, L. F. (1979). *Development and evaluation of a test battery to assess childhood depression.* Final report to Health and Welfare, Canada, for Project #606-1533-44.

Garber, J., Clarke, G. N., Weersing, V. R., Beardslee, W. R., Brent, D. A., Gladstone, T. R. G., . . . Iyengar, S. (2009). Prevention of depression in at-risk children: A randomized controlled trial. *Journal of the American Medical Association, 301,* 2215–2224.

Gazelle, H., & Rudolph, K. D. (2004). Moving toward and away from the world: Social approach and avoidance trajectories in anxious solitary youth. *Child Development, 75,* 829–849.

Goodyer, I., Dubicka, B., Wilkinson, P., Kelvin, R., Roberts, C., Byford, S., . . . Harrington, R. (2007). Selective serotonin reuptake inhibitors (SSRIs) and routine specialist care with and without cognitive behaviour therapy in adolescents with major depression: Randomised controlled trial. *British Medical Journal, 335,* 142–146.

Gould, M. S., King, R., Greenwald, S., Fisher, P., Schwab-Stone, M., Kramer, R., . . . Shaffer, D. (1998). Psychopathology associated with suicidal ideation and attempts in children and adolescents. *Journal of the American Academy of Child & Adolescent Psychiatry, 37*, 915–923.

Hammen, C. (2002). Context of stress in families of children with depressed parents. In S. H. Goodman & I. H. Gotlib (Eds.), *Children of depressed parents: Mechanisms of risk and implications for treatment* (pp. 175–199). Washington, DC: American Psychological Association.

Jayson, D., Wood, A., Kroll, L., Fraser, J., & Harrington, R. (1998). Which depressed patients respond to cognitive-behavioral treatment? *Journal of the American Academy of Child & Adolescent Psychiatry, 37*, 35–39.

Kaufman, J., Birmaher, B., Brent, D., Rao, U., & Ryan, N. (1997). Schedule for Affective Disorders and Schizophrenia for School-Age Children—Present and Lifetime Version (K-SADS-PL): Initial reliability and validity data. *Journal of the American Academy of Child & Adolescent Psychiatry, 36*, 980–988.

Kendler, K. S., Thorton, L. M., & Gardner, C. O. (2001). Genetic risk, number of previous depressive episodes, and stressful life events in predicting onset of major depression. *American Journal of Psychiatry, 158*, 582–586.

Kennard, B. D., Clarke, G. N., Weersing, V. R., Asarnow, J. R., Shamseddeen, W., Porta, G., . . . Brent, D. A. (2009). Effective components of TORDIA cognitive-behavioral therapy for adolescent depression: Preliminary findings. *Journal of Consulting and Clinical Psychology, 77*, 1033–1041.

Kerfoot, M., Harrington, R., Harrington, V., Rogers, J., & Verduyn, C. (2004). A step too far? Randomized trial of cognitive-behaviour therapy delivered by social workers to depressed adolescents. *European Child and Adolescent Psychiatry, 13*, 92–99.

Klerman, G. L., Weissman, M. M., Rounsaville, B. J., & Chevron, E. S. (1984). *Interpersonal psychotherapy of depression*. New York, NY: Basic Books.

Kovacs, M. (1983). *The Children's Depression Inventory: A self report depression scale for school-aged youngsters*. Pittsburgh, PA: University of Pittsburgh School of Medicine.

Kovacs, M., Obrosky, S., Gatsonis, C., & Richards, C. (1997). First-episode major depressive and dysthymic disorder in childhood: Clinical and sociodemographic factors in recovery. *Journal of the American Academy of Child & Adolescent Psychiatry, 36*, 777–784.

Kovacs, M., Sherrill, J., George, C. J., Pollock, M., Tumuluru, R. V., & Ho, V. (2006). Contextual Emotion-Regulation Therapy for childhood depression: Description and pilot testing of a new intervention. *Journal of the American Academy of Child & Adolescent Psychiatry, 45*, 892-903.

Lewinsohn, P. M., Antonuccio, D. O., Steinmetz-Brekenridge, J. L., & Teri, L. (1984). *The Coping with Depression course: A psychoeducational intervention for unipolar depression*. Eugene, OR: Castalia Press.

Lewinsohn, P. M., Clarke, G. N., Hops, H., & Andrews, J. A. (1990). Cognitive-behavioral treatment for depressed adolescents. *Behavior Therapy, 21*, 385–401.

Lewinsohn, P. M., Hops, H., Roberts, R. E., Seeley, J. R., & Andrews, J. A. (1993). Adolescent psychopathology: I. Prevalence and incidence of depression and other DSM-III-R disorders in high school students. *Journal of Abnormal Psychology, 102*, 133–144.

Lewis, G., Rice, F., Harold, G. T., Collishaw, S., & Thapar, A. (2011). Investigating environmental links between parent depression and child depressive/anxiety symptoms: Using an assisted conception design. *Journal of the American Academy of Child & Adolescent Psychiatry, 50*, 451–459.

Mayes, T. L., Bernstein, I. H., Hayley, C. L., Kennard, B. D., & Emslie, G. J. (2010). Psychometric properties of the Children's Depression Rating Scale–Revised in adolescents. *Journal of Child and Adolescent Psychopharmacology, 20*, 513–516.

Mufson, L., Dorta, K. P., Wickramaratne, P., Nomura, Y., Olfson, M., & Weissman, M. M. (2004). A randomized effectiveness trial of interpersonal psychotherapy for depressed adolescents. *Archives of General Psychiatry, 61*, 577–584.

Mufson, L., & Sills, R. (2006). Interpersonal psychotherapy for depressed adolescents (IPT-A): An overview. *Nordic Journal of Psychiatry, 60*, 431–437.

Mufson, L., Weissman, M. M., Moreau, D., & Garfinkel, R. (1999). Efficacy of interpersonal psychotherapy for depressed adolescents. *Archives of General Psychiatry, 56*, 573–579.

Muñoz, R. F., Ying, Y., Bernal, G., Pérez-Stable, E. J., Sorensen, J. L., Hargreaves, W. A., . . . Miller, L. S. (1995). Prevention of depression with primary care patients: A randomized controlled trial. *American Journal of Community Psychology, 23*, 199–222.

Poznanski, E. O., Freeman, L. N., & Mokros, H. B. (1985). Children's Depression Rating Scale–Revised. *Psychopharmacology Bulletin, 21*, 979–989.

Radloff, L. S. (1977). The CES-D scale: A self-report depression scale for research in the general population. *Applied Psychological Measurement, 1*, 385–401.

Rishel, C. W., Greeno, C. G., Marcus, S. C., Sales, E., Shear, M. K., Swartz, H. A., & Anderson, C. (2006). Impact of maternal mental health status on child mental health treatment outcome. *Community Mental Health Journal, 42,* 1–12.

Rohde, P., Clarke, G. N., Mace, D. E., Jorgensen, J. S., & Seeley, J. R. (2004). An efficacy/effectiveness study of cognitive-behavioral treatment for adolescents with comorbid major depression and conduct disorder. *Journal of the American Academy of Child & Adolescent Psychiatry, 43,* 660–668.

Rohde, P., Lewinsohn, P. M., & Seeley, J. R. (1994). Are adolescents changed by an episode of major depression? *Journal of the American Academy of Child & Adolescent Psychiatry, 33,* 1289–1298.

Rosselló, J., & Bernal, G. (1999). The efficacy of cognitive-behavioral and interpersonal treatments for depression in Puerto Rican adolescents. *Journal of Consulting and Clinical Psychology, 67,* 734–745.

Rosselló, J., Bernal, G., Rivera-Medina, C. (2008). Individual and group IPT and CBT for Puerto Rican adolescents with depressive symptoms. *Cultural Diversity and Ethnic Minority Psychology, 14,* 234–245.

Treatment for Adolescents with Depression Study Team. (2004). Fluoxetine, cognitive-behavioral therapy, and their combination for adolescents with depression: Treatment for Adolescents with Depression Study (TADS) randomized controlled trial. *Journal of the American Medical Association, 292,* 807–820.

Treatment for Adolescents with Depression Study Team. (2007). The Treatment for Adolescents with Depression Study (TADS): Long-term effectiveness and safety outcomes. *Archives of General Psychiatry, 64,* 1132–1144.

Vostanis, P., Feehan, C., & Grattan, E. (1998). Two-year outcome of children treated for depression. *European Child and Adolescent Psychiatry, 7,* 12–18.

Vostanis, P., Feehan, C., Grattan, E., & Bickerton, W. (1996a). A randomised controlled out-patient trial of cognitive-behavioural treatment for children and adolescents with depression: 9-month follow-up. *Journal of Affective Disorders, 40,* 105–116.

Vostanis, P., Feehan, C., Grattan, E., & Bickerton, W. (1996b). Treatment for children and adolescents with depression: Lessons from a controlled trial. *Clinical Child Psychology and Psychiatry, 1,* 199–212.

Weersing, V. R., & Brent, D. A. (2003). Cognitive-behavioral therapy for adolescent depression: Comparative efficacy, mediation, moderation, and effectiveness. In A. E. Kazdin & J. R. Weisz (Eds.), *Evidence-based psychotherapies for children and adolescents* (pp. 135–147). New York, NY: Guilford Press.

Weersing, V. R., & Brent, D. A. (2006). Cognitive behavioral therapy for depression in youth. *Child and Adolescent Psychiatric Clinics of North America, 15,* 939–957.

Weersing, V. R., Rozenman, M., & Gonzalez, A. (2008). Core components of therapy in youth: Do we know what to disseminate? *Behavior Modification, 33,* 24–47.

Weersing, V. R., & Weisz, J. R. (2002). Mechanisms of action in youth psychotherapy. *Journal of Child Psychology and Psychiatry, 43,* 3–29.

Weissman, M. M., Wickramaratne, P., Nomura, Y., Warner, V., Pilowsky, D., & Verdeli, H. (2006). Offspring of depressed parents: 20 years later. *American Journal of Psychiatry, 163,* 1001–1008.

Weissman, M. M., Wolk, S., Wickramaratne, P., Goldstein, R. B., Adams, P., Greenwald, S., . . . Steinberg, D. (1999). Children with prepubertal-onset major depressive disorder and anxiety grown up. *Archives of General Psychiatry, 56,* 794–801.

Weisz J. R., Southam-Gerow, M. A., Gordis, E. B., Connor-Smith, J. K., Chu, B. C., Langer, D. A., & Weiss, B. (2009). Cognitive-behavioral therapy versus usual clinical care for youth depression: An initial test of transportability to community clinics and clinicians. *Journal of Consulting and Clinical Psychology, 77,* 383–396.

Wood, A., Harrington, R., & Moore, A. (1996). Controlled trial of a brief cognitive-behavioural intervention in adolescent patients with depressive disorders. *Journal of Child Psychology & Psychiatry & Allied Disciplines, 37,* 737–746.

Wood, A., Kroll, L., Moore, A., & Harrington, R. (1995). Properties of the Mood and Feelings Questionnaire in adolescent psychiatric outpatients: A research note. *Child Psychology & Psychiatry & Allied Disciplines, 36,* 327–334.

World Health Organization. (2012). *Health statistics and health information systems: Regional estimates for 2000–2011.* Retrieved from http://www.who.int/healthinfo/global_burden_disease/estimates_regional/en/index1.html

CHAPTER 11

Bipolar Disorders

AMY E. WEST AND AMY T. PETERS

OVERVIEW OF PEDIATRIC BIPOLAR DISORDER

Bipolar disorder (BD) in children is a complex and severely impairing childhood disorder that has received increasing attention from the psychiatric community in recent years. The accurate phenomenology and characterization of pediatric bipolar disorder (PBD) has been the focus of both empirical investigation and extensive discussion among professionals as the field has endeavored to better understand PBD and its differentiation from other childhood disorders. A bipolar spectrum disorder is diagnosed based on the presence of episodes of either extreme irritability or elevated, expansive mood in combination with other symptoms, including grandiosity, decreased need for sleep, hypersexuality, depressed mood, racing thoughts, and impulsive behavior. Diagnosing PBD requires careful assessment of discrete mood episodes, with sensitivity to the developmental manifestation of symptoms. PBD is distinctive in that, compared to the typical adult presentation of bipolar disorder, children tend to experience longer episodes with rapid-cycling patterns and symptoms of mixed mood states (Leibenluft, Charney, Towbin, Bhangoo, & Pine, 2003). In addition, the diagnosis of PBD is often complicated by significant heterogeneity in symptom presentation and frequent co-occurring disorders, such as attention-deficit/hyperactivity disorder (ADHD), oppositional defiant disorder (ODD), and anxiety disorders.

Recent research has begun to investigate the neurological underpinnings of the various symptoms and functional impairments observed in PBD. Relative to healthy controls and, in some cases, to children with other psychiatric disorders, children with PBD demonstrate impairments in cognitive domains associated with learning, problem solving, and cognitive/emotional modulation, including attention, working memory, executive function, verbal memory, and processing speed (Bearden et al., 2006; Dickstein et al., 2004; Dickstein et al., 2007; Doyle et al., 2005; Henin et al., 2007; McClure et al., 2005; Pavuluri, Schenkel, et al., 2006). These neurocognitive impairments persist over time (Pavuluri, West, Hill, Jindal, & Sweeney, 2009) and occur independent of mood state (Pavuluri, Schenkel, et al., 2006). Passarotti and Pavuluri (2011) proposed an integrated neurobiological model involving altered functioning of the brain circuits responsible for response inhibition, reward, and executive functioning. This model differentiates the pathogenesis of symptoms and impairments in PBD from common co-occurring disorders like ADHD and explains how dysfunction of the brain mechanisms involved in these systems contributes to the affect dysregulation, low frustration tolerance, impulsivity, and maladaptive reward seeking implicated in cognitive, social, and academic impairments (Passarotti & Pavuluri, 2011).

PBD symptoms are associated with chronic and significant impairments in all domains of psychosocial functioning—individual, family, peer, and school/community. Likely due, in part, to the differences in brain functioning and neurocognitive deficits just described, children with PBD demonstrate academic underperformance, including problems with math and reading (Henin et al., 2007;

Pavuluri, O'Connor, Harral, Moss, & Sweeney, 2006), and disruptive school behavior (Geller, Zimerman, et al., 2002). In addition, peer relationships are characterized by limited peer networks, peer victimization, and poor social skills (Geller, Craney, et al., 2002; Wilens et al., 2003). Poor family functioning complicates family support. PBD children often experience strained sibling and parent relationships (Geller et al., 2000; Wilens et al., 2003), characterized by less warmth, affection, and intimacy and more fighting, forceful punishment, and conflict (Schenkel, West, Harral, Patel, & Pavuluri, 2008). These negative experiences accumulate throughout childhood. In adolescence, youth with PBD exhibit low self-esteem, hopelessness, external locus of control, and maladaptive coping strategies (Rucklidge, 2006), poor social functioning (Goldstein, Miklowitz, & Mullen, 2006), high expressed emotion in family relationships and more negative life events and chronic stress in the context of family life (Kim, Miklowitz, Biuckians, & Mullen, 2007), and lower levels of family adaptability and cohesion as a function of aggressive behavior (Keenan-Miller, Peris, Axelson, Kowatch, & Miklowitz, 2012).

The severity of symptoms and accumulation of psychosocial risk throughout development renders PBD a significant public health concern. Children with PBD experience high rates of repeated hospitalization and suicide attempts (Lewinsohn, Olino, & Klein, 2005). In adulthood, PBD patients demonstrate greater mental health care utilization, elevated rates of other chronic disease and health conditions, lower rates of school graduation, and loss of work days and career productivity (Kessler et al., 2006; Kupfer, 2005; Lewinsohn et al., 2005). Thus, PBD places a considerable burden on educational, occupational, and health care systems, not to mention the human cost of loss of individual potential and sense of self, damaged personal relationships, family dysfunction, and suicide. The significant psychosocial deficits and poor long-term prognosis for children with PBD if left untreated (or undertreated) makes high-quality, evidence-based psychosocial treatment an important component of a comprehensive treatment approach. Evidence-based psychosocial methods can be implemented adjunctive to pharmacotherapy to enhance immediate treatment outcomes, improve psychosocial functioning and quality of life, and optimize the global functioning and long-term remission of symptoms for youth with PBD.

EVIDENCE-BASED APPROACHES

Several psychosocial treatment models have been developed and have evidence to support their efficacy. Child- and family-focused cognitive behavioral treatment (CFF-CBT), multifamily psychoeducation groups (MFPGs), and individual family psychoeducation (IFP) have been developed for younger children (7–13), while family-focused treatment (FFT), dialectical behavioral treatment (DBT), and interpersonal and social rhythms therapy (IPSRT) have been developed for adolescents.

Child- and Family-Focused Cognitive Behavioral Treatment

CFF-CBT is a family-focused psychosocial intervention developed for children ages 7 to 13 with bipolar spectrum disorders and their families (West & Weinstein, 2012). CFF-CBT was designed specifically for this age group and incorporates various methods to target the unique symptoms and psychosocial impairments experienced in PBD. Interventions in CFF-CBT integrate cognitive behavioral approaches with psychoeducation, interpersonal psychotherapy, mindfulness, and positive psychology techniques and is employed across multiple domains—individual, family, peer, and school. Practically, CFF-CBT is delivered through 12 weekly sessions; some are child only, some are parent only, but most are family sessions. The key components of CFF-CBT are captured by the acronym RAINBOW, which stands for:

*r*outine
*a*ffect regulation
I can do it (self-efficacy boosting)
*n*o negative thoughts and live in the now
*b*e a good friend and balanced lifestyles for parents
*o*h, how can we solve this problem
*w*ays to get social support

The range of topics covered include establishing a predictable routine, mood monitoring, teaching behavioral management, increasing parent and child self-efficacy, decreasing negative cognitions, improving social functioning, engaging in collaborative problem solving, and increasing social support. Preliminary open trial data support the efficacy of CFF-CBT in individual (Pavuluri et al., 2004), group (West et al., 2009), and maintenance models (West, Henry, & Pavuluri, 2007). A randomized controlled trial of CFF-CBT is currently under way.

Psychoeducation

Fristad and colleagues developed a psychoeducational treatment for children ages 8 to 12 with bipolar and depressive spectrum disorders and their parents (Fristad, Goldberg-Arnold, & Gavazzi, 2002; Fristad, Verducci, Walters, & Young, 2009). This treatment was originally developed to be delivered across eight MFPG sessions. The goals of the intervention include teaching parents and children about the child's illness, treatment approaches, symptom management, problem-solving and communication skills, and coping skills, and providing support for the parents. A randomized clinical trial of MFPG demonstrated efficacy in reducing mood symptoms (Fristad et al., 2009). Fristad and colleagues have also adapted the treatment into an individual family psychoeducational format (IFP) delivered across 24 individual sessions and demonstrated efficacy for this intervention in a small randomized controlled trial (Fristad, 2006).

Family-Focused Treatment for Adolescents

Miklowitz and colleagues (2004) adapted FFT for adults with BD to adolescents (FFT-A). FFT-A aims to reduce symptoms and increase psychosocial functioning through an increased understanding about the disorder and coping skills, decreased family conflict, and improved family communication and problem solving. FFT-A is delivered via 21 individual sessions over the course of 9 months and is organized into three components: psychoeducation (e.g., developing an understanding of the symptoms, etiology, and course of the disorder), communication enhancement training (e.g., active listening skills, role-playing, and offering feedback), and problem solving (e.g., identifying problems and generating effective solutions). A randomized controlled trial of FFT-A indicated that those who participated in the treatment had shorter time to recovery from depression, less time in depressive episodes, and lower depression severity scores for 2 years (Miklowitz et al., 2008).

Dialectical Behavior Therapy for Adolescents

Goldstein, Axelson, Birmaher, and Brent (2007) adapted DBT for adolescents with bipolar disorder. DBT (Linehan et al., 2006) is a psychotherapy originally developed for adults with borderline personality disorder (BPD) that targets emotional instability. DBT for adolescents with BD is delivered over the course of 1 year and is comprised of two modalities: family skills training (delivered to whole family) and individual psychotherapy for the adolescent. The acute treatment phase is 6 months and includes 24 weekly sessions that alternate between individual and family therapy. The continuation treatment is 12 additional sessions tapering in frequency over the rest of the year. A small, preliminary open trial of DBT in 10 adolescents with BD demonstrated decreases in suicidality, nonsuicidal self-injurious behavior, emotional dysregulation, and depression symptoms after the intervention (Goldstein et al., 2007).

Interpersonal and Social Rhythm Therapy for Adolescents

Hlastala and colleagues adapted IPSRT (Frank et al., 2005) for adolescents with BD (Hlastala & Frank, 2006). IPSRT is an evidence-based psychotherapy for adults with BD that targets instability in circadian rhythms and neurotransmitter systems because of their known vulnerability as a precipitant for mood episodes. IPSRT interventions aim to stabilize social and sleep routines and address interpersonal precipitants to dysregulation, such as interpersonal conflict, role transitions, and interpersonal functioning deficits. IPSRT is primarily an individual treatment, but this version does incorporate brief family psychotherapy. A pilot study of IPSRT-A indicated decreased symptoms and improved functioning from pre- to posttreatment (Hlastala, Kotler, McClellan, & McCauley, 2010).

PARENTAL INVOLVEMENT IN TREATMENT

The complex constellation of impairments and negative prognostic indicators associated with PBD places a large burden on the families of affected children to help intervene during this period of significant risk. As caregivers of children with PBD, parents bear a great responsibility to help children seek out treatment resources, attend and adhere to treatment, and reinforce treatment goals outside of sessions. However, families often have difficulty helping to effectively manage their child's illness because of problematic, chaotic, or unsupportive family dynamics. Families of bipolar children report low levels of cohesion, expressiveness, and family activity and high levels of family conflict (Belardinelli et al., 2008; Schenkel et al., 2008). These unstable family dynamics are associated with adverse treatment outcomes. Indeed, a study of pharmacological intervention for children and adolescents with BD found that youth with high levels of family conflict, particularly poor family problem solving, were less likely to benefit from treatment (Townsend, Demeter, Youngstrom, Drotar, & Findling, 2007). In an adjunctive psychosocial FFT study, expressed emotion moderated treatment outcome such that patients of families high in expressed emotion required a more intensive psychosocial intervention to achieve symptomatic improvement than patients of families low in expressed emotion (Miklowitz et al., 2009). In addition, when caregivers of adults with BD experience a high burden, patient adherence and outcome in pharmacological treatment is adversely affected (Perlick et al., 2004). Collectively, these outcomes suggest that assessment of family dynamics provides valuable information for treatment approach and that it is critically important to provide families with the necessary tools to cope with and manage their child's illness.

Recognizing the important role of the family in PBD, several existing psychosocial treatment modalities include the family and utilize strategies to improve family functioning, involvement, and understanding. Psychoeducation is the core of family involvement in treatment. Prior to the introduction of specific skills training, it is important for family members to develop an understanding of PBD and the impact parent and family systems have on its course of illness. More specifically, parents are educated about the nature of mood episodes, risk factors, and comorbidity as well as the role of medications in treatment, how to monitor safety and side effects, and how to navigate the mental health care and educational systems (Fristad et al., 2002). Although IFP and family psychoeducation groups devote the most time to these concepts throughout treatment, psychoeducation is the foundation of other family-based treatment methodologies, such as CFF-CBT and FFT-A, and forms the basis for further skills training (Miklowitz, 2012; West & Weinstein, 2012).

In addition to enhancing parental knowledge and insight regarding PBD, an essential component to treatment gains is boosting parenting efficacy. Boosting parenting efficacy is achieved through the development of affect regulation strategies, both for the parents and children, as well as behavior management and coping strategies. Specific skills in these domains include self-monitoring of mood states, recognizing and labeling feelings, and managing responses to expansive, negative, and irritable moods. Despite their different theoretical underpinnings, psychoeducation interventions, CFF-CBT, and FFT-A each incorporates affect and behavioral regulation strategies into its treatment model (Fristad et al., 2002; Miklowitz, 2012; West & Weinstein, 2012).

It is also especially important to provide parents with support and help them cope with the burden of managing their child's illness. To achieve this goal, several family-based interventions have parent-only sessions, designed to allow parents to process difficult feelings, learn the importance of good self-care, and identify strong social supports. CFF-CBT involves intensive work with the parents parallel to the work with children that addresses the parents' own therapeutic needs and helps them develop an effective parenting style for their child (West & Weinstein, 2012). Similarly, the content covered in parent-only psychoeducation sessions is intended to give parents specific strategies to cope with the variety of challenges associated with their child's illness (Fristad et al., 2002). Although FFT-A is not designed to work with the family individually, the intervention addresses the therapeutic needs of family members by working with the patient and family together throughout treatment to try to decrease family conflict and enhance family communication surrounding the patient's illness (Miklowitz, 2012).

Last, in recognition of the parental burden associated with caring for a child with bipolar disorder, it is as important to teach parents skills to manage their own affect as it is to teach children skills to regulate their emotions. Cognitive behavioral strategies address negative, pessimistic, and hopeless thoughts parents may have as these thoughts relate to their child's illness. Mindfulness skills help parents manage their own difficult emotions and increase the equanimity of their parenting style, especially when faced with managing their child's mood swings or behavioral misconduct. Behavioral interventions are useful for addressing barriers or challenges parents perceive to managing their child's illness as well as maladaptive coping styles parents may have developed. These parent-focused intervention strategies are adapted across treatments. CFF-CBT has a strong foundation in teaching parents cognitive behavioral principles but also reserves sessions to teach mindfulness and behavioral strategies (West & Weinstein, 2012). Psychoeducation-based treatment places a strong emphasis on helping parents to problem-solve and navigate the challenges associated with their child's illness (Fristad et al., 2002). FFT-A helps the family make sense of their child's experiences with mania and depression as well as develop specific plans and coping strategies for when mood swings occur (Miklowitz, 2012).

Existing psychosocial interventions for PBD share the important goal, independent of their particular theoretical orientation, of establishing a family context that facilitates long-term recovery. Children affected by PBD are extremely vulnerable to a variety of negative psychological and psychosocial problems, and their primary caregivers play a critical role in buffering against the onset of these negative outcomes. Development and refinement of psychosocial intervention strategies is warranted, but the positive results of existing family-based models indicate parent and family involvement is an essential ingredient in PBD treatment. In light of the early onset, significant psychosocial risk, and poor long-term prognosis associated with PBD, psychosocial intervention that includes the family is a necessary component to the comprehensive management of the disorder.

ADAPTATIONS AND MODIFICATIONS

There is growing recognition that even the best evidence-based, targeted, and comprehensive manualized interventions cannot be applied to patients in a one-size-fits-all manner. Indeed, a major focus of the National Institute of Mental Health Strategic Plan (2008) is to promote a "personalized" medicine approach in which treatments are adapted and targeted based on individual needs and characteristics. The notion of this approach is that baseline characteristics—whether they are related to symptom experience, parent characteristics, family functioning, or cognitive styles—might contribute to the level of engagement in treatment and the efficacy of particular treatment methods for an individual patient or family. In PBD, given the significant heterogeneity in symptom presentation, high rates of comorbidity, incidence of parent psychopathology, and observed challenges in the family system, it is likely that manual-based interventions for PBD may need to be flexibly implemented or adapted to optimally match patient and family characteristics. Although flexible implementation and adaptation likely happens routinely in clinical practice and in the application of manual-based interventions, this process has not yet been studied systematically.

Of the few manual-based interventions developed for PBD, some adaptations have been made based on clinical and research findings. For example, CFF-CBT was originally developed in an individual family format but later was adapted to a group format based on the observation that parents of youth with PBD were extremely isolated and might benefit significantly from coming together for sharing and support. A preliminary open trial of the group CFF-CBT intervention found decreased parenting stress and increased parent self-efficacy in coping with the disorder posttreatment as well as decreased mania symptoms and increased coping in children (West et al., 2009). In addition, while there was significant improvement in outcomes over the course of the 12-week treatment in early studies of CFF-CBT, study clinicians observed that parents, in particular, expressed desire for ongoing support and intervention, even if in a less intensive way. In most cases, there remained a clinical need for follow-up booster sessions to fine-tune skills, help families further translate skills into their home environment, and focus on areas that were particularly challenging or recurring for patients and families. Therefore, a CFF-CBT maintenance treatment model was developed and studied. Patients who participated in CFF-CBT were followed for 3 years posttreatment and provided a combination of psychopharmacology and psychosocial booster sessions as needed. Results indicated that patients were able to maintain initial positive effects of the treatment with ongoing booster sessions over the course of 3 years (West et al., 2007).

Other manual-based interventions for PBD have been adapted based on identified needs. For example, Fristad (2006) and colleagues adapted their multifamily psychotherapy groups into an individual format to accommodate the fact that not all families are well suited for group treatment and that some have practical barriers that prevent them from attending group sessions. Miklowitz and colleagues (2011) adapted their family-focused treatment for adolescents with BD to be applied to youth at risk for developing BD by virtue of a first-degree relative with the disorder with the goal of preventing or delaying onset by teaching youth important emotion regulation and coping skills. It is hoped that the next wave of research will involve studying how to individually tailor manual-based interventions for PBD to particular patients and families based on baseline character-istics in order to further optimize the impact of these interventions on symptoms and functioning.

MEASURING TREATMENT EFFECTS

It is widely recognized that BD presents differently in children than it does in adults (Leibenluft et al., 2003). Yet, despite recognition of age-dependent distinctions in symptom presentation, there are currently no child-specific *DSM* criteria for PBD. As a consequence, criteria for BDs in adults are used to diagnose and assess the course of PBD. Accordingly, symptom evaluation is often achieved through adapting assessments and ratings designed for adults for use in children. This practice relies on an intersection of knowledge about the existing *DSM-IV-TR* criteria for adults and an understanding of the child-specific distinctions in bipolar symptom presentation and course (e.g., more frequent episodes, mixed states, comorbidity) (Findling et al., 2001; Geller, Craney, et al., 2002). The absence of child-specific diagnostic criteria and lack of child-validated measures has important implications for the reliability and validity of assessing treatment out-come. Specifically, it is possible that changes in pediatric mood symptoms are not adequately captured using adult outcomes.

In an attempt to bridge this gap, development of mania measures for youth has increased in recent years. These measures, however, vary widely in terms of item content, reading level, and validation (Youngstrom, Freeman, & Jenkins, 2009). The two most widely used clinician-rated scales are the Young Mania Rating Scale (YMRS) (Young, Biggs, Ziegler, & Meyer, 1978) and the Children's Depression Rating Scale–Revised (CDRS-R) (Poznanski et al., 1984). Both have shown evidence of good reliability and acceptable validity in pediatric samples (Fristad, Weller, & Weller, 1992, 1995; Youngstrom, Danielson, Findling, Gracious, & Calabrese, 2002), which is particularly encouraging for the YMRS since it was not originally designed for use in children (Young et al., 1978). The best validated and most discriminating informant-report instruments are: the Child Mania Rating Scale (CMRS) (Pavuluri, Henry, Devineni, Carbray, & Birmaher, 2006) and its 10-item form (Henry, Pavuluri, Youngstrom, & Birmaher, 2008); the Parent General Behavior Inventory (Parent GBI) Youngstrom, Findling, Danielson, & Calabrese, 2001) and its 10-item mania form (Youngstrom, Frazier, Demeter, Calabrese, & Findling, 2008); and the Parent Mood Disorder Questionnaire (MDQ) (Pavuluri, 2007; Wagner et al., 2006). These three instruments provide con-sistent and qualitatively similar results in terms of developmentally specific symptom assessment. The advantages of these measures as far as content coverage and developmental appropriateness make them the most reliable candidates for measuring treatment outcome in PBD. Indeed, the CMRS has been shown to be a valid and sensitive measure of symptom change over the course of treatment (West, Celio, Henry, & Pavuluri, 2011). Other instruments have not discriminated pedi-atric mania symptoms as well or have not been validated within an appropriate clinical cohort or context (Youngstrom, Meyers, Youngstrom, Calabrese, & Findling, 2006a).

Additionally, measuring treatment effects in PBD is complicated by cross-informant issues. Information regarding child symptoms and behavior is generally collected from three sources: care-giver, teacher, and child. Findings regarding the validity of caregiver (generally parent) and teacher report consistently demonstrate the greatest validity for parent report, even beyond that of the child (Geller, Warner, Williams, & Zimerman, 1998; Youngstrom, Findling, Calabrese, et al., 2004; Youngstrom et al., 2005). The validity of parent report persists even when the parent has a diagnosed mood disorder (Youngstrom, Meyers, Youngstrom, Calabrese, & Findling, 2006b). Superior validity of parent report relative to self-report contests the generally accepted standard that self-report is the most accurate source of information about mood disorders (Loeber, Green, & Lahey, 1990). In general, children tend to underreport the severity of their mood symptoms (Youngstrom, Findling, & Calabrese, 2004). The lower validity of child self-report is likely attributed to compromised insight and understanding of their own psychopathology (Youngstrom, Findling, & Calabrese, 2004). Thus, in addition to playing a vital role in treatment participation and adherence, parents are an essential source of information for accurately measuring the effectiveness of interventions designed for children.

CLINICAL CASE EXAMPLE

Maggie R (identifying information has been altered to protect confidentiality) was a 9-year-old Caucasian female who lived at home with her biological parents and 13-year-old brother. She was referred to the CFF-CBT/RAINBOW therapy program by her treating psychiatrist in the Pediatric Mood Disorders Program at the University of Illinois at Chicago. At the time of therapy initiation, Maggie was stable on medication and attending regular follow-up appointments with her psychiatrist. Initial assessment via a structured clinical interview and mood symptoms rating scales (parent, child, and clinician report) indicated that Maggie met criteria for bipolar I disorder. Maggie was experiencing frequent irritability, mood lability, and intense periods of anger or "rage attacks." During these episodes Maggie became physically and verbally aggressive and made impulsive decisions (e.g., opening car doors while moving). Maggie also had a history of periods of elated and giddy moods with increased energy, increased activity in several areas, motor hyperactivity, reduced sleep, and racing thoughts. Periods of elated mood were often followed by an increase in irritability and depressed mood, rage, tearfulness, and feelings of worthlessness. Often Maggie would cycle between periods of euphoria and depressed/angry mood within the same day.

Maggie attended treatment sessions with her mother; her father attended parent-only and family sessions when he could. The first phase of treatment was focused on engaging the family in the treatment process and identifying goals. Maggie and her parents were provided psychoeducation about PBD. Her core symptoms were identified and discussed in the context of scientific findings about differences in brain functioning to emphasize that PBD is a brain disorder and to help reduce negative attributions and blaming associated with symptoms. Maggie and her mother also developed a common language for her symptoms (e.g., rage episodes were named "volcanoes" and Maggie's anger was described as "lava"). This process enabled Maggie to distance herself from her symptoms and recognize that they were something that affected her but not defined her. Finally, Mrs. R and Maggie were instructed to monitor Maggie's daily mood states and triggers for any mood fluctuations via a structured mood calendar.

The second phase of treatment focused on Maggie's affect dysregulation and the management of rage episodes. First, the therapist worked with her parents to implement consistent routines to improve two identified areas of difficulty: bedtime and transitions. At bedtime, Mrs. R agreed to incorporate soothing activities prior to bedtime and to issue 30-, 15-, and 5-minute warnings to help Maggie anticipate the approaching transition. To help ease other transitions, Mrs. R committed to provide ample warnings and to post the daily schedule around the house to help Maggie anticipate and prepare for transitions. Parent sessions during this phase also focused on helping manage Maggie's anger outbursts as a family. The analogy of "putting out a fire" was used to facilitate Mr. and Mrs. R's ability to remain neutral and calm while defusing the situation versus engaging in the episode and exacerbating Maggie's distress. Coping plans were developed to help prevent these episodes and to manage them if they did occur. Coping strategies included having Mrs. R use mantras and mindfulness-based techniques to remain focused on the present moment and enhance her ability to stay calm and empathic and to modulate her own responses to Maggie's intense emotion. In addition, the plan included reaching out to Maggie's father for support, implementing soothing activities to help Maggie deescalate her anger, and using appropriate consequences for target negative behaviors (e.g., physical or verbal aggression) only after Maggie and others were feeling calm and emotionally stabilized. Finally, parent sessions during this phase also focused on helping Mrs. and Mr. R to process all of the various feelings they had regarding parenting a child with BD, including anger, helplessness, and guilt. Mr. and Mrs. R were instructed in specific cognitive and mindfulness-based techniques to use during difficult situations (e.g., reframing Maggie's behavior in the context of her neurocircuitry to foster greater empathy and focusing on breathing in the present moment to avoid feeling overwhelmed). Maggie's parents broke down during this session and expressed tremendous relief at being able to disclose such difficult feelings in a safe and nonjudgmental environment.

Child sessions during this phase were primarily focused on helping Maggie to recognize and express her feelings and to better understand the triggers for difficult emotions and negative moods, which were called her "bugs." Games, worksheets, drawings, songs, and role-play were used to help Maggie identify and practice cognitive and behavioral skills for coping with future bugs and difficult emotions. In addition, because Maggie sometimes found it difficult to employ her coping strategies when triggered at home or school, the therapist also helped her normalize the experience of anger and sadness as acceptable emotions.

As Maggie's family became better able to prevent and manage affect dysregulation and rage episodes, the third phase of treatment focused on understanding and managing family and environmental stressors that contributed to stress and poor coping. Child sessions were focused on improving Maggie's social skills and self-esteem. She practiced engaging in appropriate conversations with peers and communicating respectfully with her parents. Additionally, the therapist focused on the recognition of Maggie's positive qualities that comprise the core of her identity and discussed how BD was just one small part of who she was. Parent sessions focused on building Maggie's social competence through supervised play dates with peers and advocating for her social needs in the classroom. In addition, a key component of this phase of treatment was an emphasis on Mrs. R's well-being and balance between self-care and parenting responsibilities to avoid burnout. Last, a family session was held with Maggie, her brother, and her parents. This session was used to provide education on PBD and to improve family interactions through family problem solving. With assistance from the therapist, family members identified their strengths as well as family-wide bugs and developed coping plans for managing their bugs as a team. Maggie's family also agreed on ways to increase positive family interactions (e.g., planned family outings).

The final sessions of the acute treatment phase focused on preparing for the transition from weekly therapy to monthly maintenance sessions. Maggie created a folder of therapy exercises to help her remember and use these therapy tools. The therapist discussed with Mrs. R and Maggie ways to continue to implement therapy strategies at home and how to problem-solve challenges or barriers that arose. Positive changes in the family across treatment were reviewed and celebrated, including Maggie's increased awareness of her moods and triggers and a reduction in her rage episodes from daily outbursts to less frequent and less intense episodes.

Outcomes

Over the course of treatment, Maggie demonstrated greater insight into her symptoms, self-esteem, and ability to cognitively reframe her angry thoughts (e.g., "Nobody loves me"). She was increasingly able to use her coping skills independently and prevent her anger from escalating. Maggie responded well to the presentation of therapy material in a nonthreatening, creative, and engaging manner and also benefited from the therapist's work to help her recognize her many positive qualities. Maggie's parents became increasingly proficient in their ability to recognize warning signs of distress and help soothe Maggie early on to prevent further escalation. As a result of these changes at the individual and family level, Maggie's anger episodes decreased in intensity, frequency, and duration. Mrs. R also reported great improvement in her self-efficacy as a parent and improved family relationships. Objective measures at the conclusion of the treatment indicated significant improvement in Maggie's mania and depression symptoms, family cohesion, and overall global functioning.

REFERENCES

Bearden, C. E., Glahn, D. C., Monkul, E. S., Barrett, J., Najt, P., Kaur, S., . . . Soares, J. C. (2006). Sources of declarative memory impairment in bipolar disorder: Mnemonic processes and clinical features. *Journal of Psychiatric Research, 40*(1), 47–58. doi: 10.1016/j.jpsychires.2005.08.006

Belardinelli, C., Hatch, J. P., Olvera, R. L., Fonseca, M., Caetano, S. C., Nicoletti, M., . . . Soares, J. C. (2008). Family environment patterns in families with bipolar children. *Journal of Affective Disorders, 107*(1–3), 299–305. doi: 10.1016/j.jad.2007.08.011

Dickstein, D. P., Nelson, E. E., McClure, E. B., Grimley, M. E., Knopf, L., Brotman, M. A., . . . Leibenluft, E. (2007). Cognitive flexibility in phenotypes of pediatric bipolar disorder. *Journal of the American Academy of Child & Adolescent Psychiatry, 46*(3), 341–355. doi: 10.1097/chi.0b013e31802d0b3d

Dickstein, D. P., Treland, J. E., Snow, J., McClure, E. B., Mehta, M. S., Towbin, K. E., . . . Leibenluft, E. (2004). Neuropsychological performance in pediatric bipolar disorder. *Biological Psychiatry, 55*(1), 32–39.

Doyle, A. E., Wilens, T. E., Kwon, A., Seidman, L. J., Faraone, S. V., Fried, R., . . . Biederman, J. (2005). Neuropsychological functioning in youth with bipolar disorder. *Biological Psychiatry, 58*(7), 540–548. doi: 10.1016/j.biopsych.2005.07.019

Findling, R. L., Gracious, B. L., McNamara, N. K., Youngstrom, E. A., Demeter, C. A., Branicky, L. A., & Calabrese, J. R. (2001). Rapid, continuous cycling and psychiatric co-morbidity in pediatric bipolar I disorder. *Bipolar Disorders, 3*(4), 202–210.

Frank, E., Kupfer, D. J., Thase, M. E., Mallinger, A. G., Swartz, H. A., Fagiolini, A. M., . . . Monk, T. (2005). Two-year outcomes for interpersonal and social rhythm therapy in individuals with bipolar I disorder. *Archives of General Psychiatry, 62*(9), 996–1004. doi: 10.1001/archpsyc.62.9.996

Fristad, M. A. (2006). Psychoeducational treatment for school-aged children with bipolar disorder. *Developmental Psychopathology, 18*(4), 1289–1306. doi: 10.1017/S0954579406060627

Fristad, M. A., Goldberg-Arnold, J. S., & Gavazzi, S. M. (2002). Multifamily psychoeducation groups (MFPG) for families of children with bipolar disorder. *Bipolar Disorders, 4*(4), 254–262.

Fristad, M. A., Verducci, J. S., Walters, K., & Young, M. E. (2009). Impact of multifamily psychoeducational psychotherapy in treating children aged 8 to 12 years with mood disorders. *Archives of General Psychiatry, 66*(9), 1013–1021. doi: 10.1001/archgenpsychiatry.2009.112

Fristad, M. A., Weller, E. B., & Weller, R. A. (1992). The Mania Rating Scale: Can it be used in children? A preliminary report. *Journal of the American Academy of Child & Adolescent Psychiatry, 31*(2), 252–257. doi: 10.1097/00004583-199203000-00011

Fristad, M. A., Weller, R. A., & Weller, E. B. (1995). The Mania Rating Scale (MRS): Further reliability and validity studies with children. *Annals of Clinical Psychiatry, 7*(3), 127–132.

Geller, B., Bolhofner, K., Craney, J. L., Williams, M., DelBello, M. P., & Gundersen, K. (2000). Psychosocial functioning in a prepubertal and early adolescent bipolar disorder phenotype. *Journal of the American Academy of Child & Adolescent Psychiatry, 39*(12), 1543–1548. doi: 10.1097/00004583-200012000-00018

Geller, B., Craney, J. L., Bolhofner, K., Nickelsburg, M. J., Williams, M., & Zimerman, B. (2002). Two-year prospective follow-up of children with a prepubertal and early adolescent bipolar disorder phenotype. *American Journal of Psychiatry, 159*(6), 927–933.

Geller, B., Warner, K., Williams, M., & Zimerman, B. (1998). Prepubertal and young adolescent bipolarity versus ADHD: Assessment and validity using the WASH-U-KSADS, CBCL and TRF. *Journal of Affective Disorders, 51*(2), 93–100.

Geller, B., Zimerman, B., Williams, M., Delbello, M. P., Frazier, J., & Beringer, L. (2002). Phenomenology of prepubertal and early adolescent bipolar disorder: Examples of elated mood, grandiose behaviors, decreased need for sleep, racing thoughts and hypersexuality. *Journal of Child & Adolescent Psychopharmacology, 12*(1), 3–9. doi: 10.1089/10445460252943524

Goldstein, T. R., Axelson, D. A., Birmaher, B., & Brent, D. A. (2007). Dialectical behavior therapy for adolescents with bipolar disorder: A 1-year open trial. *Journal of the American Academy of Child & Adolescent Psychiatry, 46*(7), 820–830. doi: 10.1097/chi.0b013e31805c1613

Goldstein, T. R., Miklowitz, D. J., & Mullen, K. L. (2006). Social skills knowledge and performance among adolescents with bipolar disorder. *Bipolar Disorders, 8*(4), 350–361. doi: 10.1111/j.1399–5618.2006.00321.x

Henin, A., Mick, E., Biederman, J., Fried, R., Wozniak, J., Faraone, S. V., . . . Doyle, A. E. (2007). Can bipolar disorder-specific neuropsychological impairments in children be identified? *Journal of Consulting and Clinical Psychology, 75*(2), 210–220. doi: 10.1037/0022–006X.75.2.210

Henry, D. B., Pavuluri, M. N., Youngstrom, E., & Birmaher, B. (2008). Accuracy of brief and full forms of the Child Mania Rating Scale. *Journal of Clinical Psychology, 64*(4), 368–381. doi: 10.1002/jclp.20464

Hlastala, S. A., & Frank, E. (2006). Adapting interpersonal and social rhythm therapy to the developmental needs of adolescents with bipolar disorder. *Developmental Psychopathology, 18*(4), 1267–1288. doi: 10.1017/S0954579406060615

Hlastala, S. A., Kotler, J. S., McClellan, J. M., & McCauley, E. A. (2010). Interpersonal and social rhythm therapy for adolescents with bipolar disorder: Treatment development and results from an open trial. *Depression and Anxiety, 27*(5), 457–464. doi: 10.1002/da.20668

Keenan-Miller, D., Peris, T., Axelson, D., Kowatch, R. A., & Miklowitz, D. J. (2012). Family functioning, social impairment, and symptoms among adolescents with bipolar disorder. *Journal of the American Academy of Child & Adolescent Psychiatry, 51*(10), 1085–1094. doi: 10.1016/j.jaac.2012.08.005

Kessler, R. C., Akiskal, H. S., Ames, M., Birnbaum, H., Greenberg, P., Hirschfeld, R. M., . . . Wang, P. S. (2006). Prevalence and effects of mood disorders on work performance in a nationally representative sample of U.S. workers. *American Journal of Psychiatry, 163*(9), 1561–1568. doi: 10.1176/appi.ajp.163.9.1561

Kim, E. Y., Miklowitz, D. J., Biuckians, A., & Mullen, K. (2007). Life stress and the course of early-onset bipolar disorder. *Journal of Affective Disorders, 99*(1–3), 37–44. doi: 10.1016/j.jad.2006.08.022

Kupfer, D. J. (2005). The increasing medical burden in bipolar disorder. *Journal of the American Medical Association, 293*(20), 2528–2530. doi: 10.1001/jama.293.20.2528

Leibenluft, E., Charney, D. S., Towbin, K. E., Bhangoo, R. K., & Pine, D. S. (2003). Defining clinical phenotypes of juvenile mania. *American Journal of Psychiatry, 160*(3), 430–437.

Lewinsohn, P. M., Olino, T. M., & Klein, D. N. (2005). Psychosocial impairment in offspring of depressed parents. *Psychological Medicine, 35*(10), 1493–1503. doi: 10.1017/S0033291705005350

Linehan, M. M., Comtois, K. A., Murray, A. M., Brown, M. Z., Gallop, R. J., Heard, H. L., . . . Lindenboim, N. (2006). Two-year randomized controlled trial and follow-up of dialectical behavior therapy vs therapy by experts for suicidal behaviors and borderline personality disorder. *Archives of General Psychiatry, 63*(7), 757–766.

Loeber, R., Green, S. M., & Lahey, B. B. (1990). Mental health professionals' perception of the utility of children, mothers, and teachers as informants on childhood psychopathology. *Journal of Clinical Child Psychology, 19*, 136–143. doi: 10.1207/s15374424jccp1902_5

McClure, E. B., Treland, J. E., Snow, J., Schmajuk, M., Dickstein, D. P., Towbin, K. E., . . . Leibenluft, E. (2005). Deficits in social cognition and response flexibility in pediatric bipolar disorder. *American Journal of Psychiatry, 162*(9), 1644–1651.

Miklowitz, D. J. (2012). Family-focused treatment for children and adolescents with bipolar disorder. *Israel Journal of Psychiatry and Related Sciences, 49*(2), 95–101.

Miklowitz, D. J., Axelson, D. A., Birmaher, B., George, E. L., Taylor, D. O., Schneck, C. D., . . . Brent, D. A. (2008). Family-focused treatment for adolescents with bipolar disorder: Results of a 2-year randomized trial. *Archives of General Psychiatry, 65*(9), 1053–1061. doi: 10.1001/archpsyc.65.9.1053

Miklowitz, D. J., Axelson, D. A., George, E. L., Taylor, D. O., Schneck, C. D., Sullivan, A. E., . . . Birmaher, B. (2009). Expressed emotion moderates the effects of family-focused treatment for bipolar adolescents. *Journal of the American Academy of Child & Adolescent Psychiatry, 48*(6), 643–651. doi: 10.1097/CHI.0b013e3181a0ab9d

Miklowitz, D. J., Chang, K. D., Taylor, D. O., George, E. L., Singh, M. K., Schneck, C. D., . . . Garber, J. (2011). Early psychosocial intervention for youth at risk for bipolar I or II disorder: A one-year treatment development trial. *Bipolar Disorders, 13*(1), 67–75. doi: 10.1111/j.1399–5618.2011.00890.x

Miklowitz, D. J., George, E. L., Axelson, D. A., Kim, E. Y., Birmaher, B., Schneck, C., . . . Brent, D. A. (2004). Family-focused treatment for adolescents with bipolar disorder. *Journal of Affective Disorders, 82*(Suppl. 1), S113–S128. doi: 10.1016/j.jad.2004.05.020

National Institute of Mental Health Strategic Plan. (2008). NIH Publication No. 08–6368. Retrieved from http://www.nimh.nih.gov/about/strategic-planning-reports/nimh-strategic-plan-2008.pdf

Passarotti, A. M., & Pavuluri, M. N. (2011). Brain functional domains inform therapeutic interventions in attention-deficit/hyperactivity disorder and pediatric bipolar disorder. *Expert Review of Neurotherapeutics, 11*(6), 897–914. doi: 10.1586/ern.11.71

Pavuluri, M. (2007). Comment on: Parental report version of the Mood Disorder Questionnaire for adolescents has good sensitivity and specificity for diagnosing bipolar disorder in psychiatric outpatient clinics. *Evidence-Based Mental Health, 10*(1), 9. doi:10.1136/ebmh.10.1.9

Pavuluri, M. N., Graczyk, P. A., Henry, D. B., Carbray, J. A., Heidenreich, J., & Miklowitz, D. J. (2004). Child- and family-focused cognitive-behavioral therapy for pediatric bipolar disorder: Development and preliminary results. *Journal of the American Academy of Child & Adolescent Psychiatry, 43*(5), 528–537. doi: 10.1097/00004583-200405000–00006

Pavuluri, M. N., Henry, D. B., Devineni, B., Carbray, J. A., & Birmaher, B. (2006). Child Mania Rating scale: Development, reliability, and validity. *Journal of the American Academy of Child & Adolescent Psychiatry, 45*(5), 550–560. doi: 10.1097/01.chi.0000205700.40700.50

Pavuluri, M. N., O'Connor, M. M., Harral, E. M., Moss, M., & Sweeney, J. A. (2006). Impact of neurocognitive function on academic difficulties in pediatric bipolar disorder: A clinical translation. *Biological Psychiatry, 60*(9), 951–956. doi: 10.1016/j.biopsych.2006.03.027

Pavuluri, M. N., Schenkel, L. S., Aryal, S., Harral, E. M., Hill, S. K., Herbener, E. S., & Sweeney, J. A. (2006). Neurocognitive function in unmedicated manic and medicated euthymic pediatric bipolar patients. *American Journal of Psychiatry, 163*(2), 286–293. doi: 10.1176/appi.ajp.163.2.286

Pavuluri, M. N., West, A., Hill, S. K., Jindal, K., & Sweeney, J. A. (2009). Neurocognitive function in pediatric bipolar disorder: 3-year follow-up shows cognitive development lagging behind healthy youths. *Journal of the American Academy of Child & Adolescent Psychiatry, 48*(3), 299–307. doi: 10.1097/CHI.0b013e318196b907

Perlick, D. A., Rosenheck, R. A., Clarkin, J. F., Maciejewski, P. K., Sirey, J., Struening, E., & Link, B. G. (2004). Impact of family burden and affective response on clinical outcome among patients with bipolar disorder. *Psychiatric Services, 55*(9), 1029–1035. doi: 10.1176/appi.ps.55.9.1029

Poznanski, E. O., Grossman, J. A., Buchsbaum, Y., Banegas, M., Freeman, L., & Gibbons, R. (1984). Preliminary studies of the reliability and validity of the children's depression rating scale. *Journal of the American Academy of Child Psychiatry, 23*(2), 191–197.

Rucklidge, J. J. (2006). Psychosocial functioning of adolescents with and without paediatric bipolar disorder. *Journal of Affective Disorders, 91*(2–3), 181–188. doi: 10.1016/j.jad.2006.01.001

Schenkel, L. S., West, A. E., Harral, E. M., Patel, N. B., & Pavuluri, M. N. (2008). Parent-child interactions in pediatric bipolar disorder. *Journal of Clinical Psychology, 64*(4), 422–437. doi: 10.1002/jclp.20470

Townsend, L. D., Demeter, C. A., Youngstrom, E., Drotar, D., & Findling, R. L. (2007). Family conflict moderates response to pharmacological intervention in pediatric bipolar disorder. *Journal of Child and Adolescent Psychopharmacology, 17*(6), 843–852. doi: 10.1089/cap.2007.0046

Wagner, K. D., Hirschfeld, R. M., Emslie, G. J., Findling, R. L., Gracious, B. L., & Reed, M. L. (2006). Validation of the Mood Disorder Questionnaire for bipolar disorders in adolescents. *Journal of Clinical Psychiatry, 67*(5), 827–830.

West, A. E., Celio, C. I., Henry, D. B., & Pavuluri, M. N. (2011). Child Mania Rating Scale–Parent Version: A valid measure of symptom change due to pharmacotherapy. *Journal of Affective Disorders, 128,* 112–119. doi: 10.1016/j.jad.2010.06.013

West, A. E., Henry, D. B., & Pavuluri, M. N. (2007). Maintenance model of integrated psychosocial treatment in pediatric bipolar disorder: A pilot feasibility study. *Journal of the American Academy of Child & Adolescent Psychiatry, 46*(2), 205–212. doi: 10.1097/01.chi.0000246068.85577.d7

West, A. E., Jacobs, R. H., Westerholm, R., Lee, A., Carbray, J., Heidenreich, J., & Pavuluri, M. N. (2009). Child and family-focused cognitive-behavioral therapy for pediatric bipolar disorder: Pilot study of group treatment format. *Journal of the Canadian Academy of Child and Adolescent Psychiatry, 18*(3), 239–246.

West, A. E., & Weinstein, S. M. (2012). A family-based psychosocial treatment model. *Israel Journal of Psychiatry and Related Sciences, 49*(2), 86–93.

Wilens, T. E., Biederman, J., Forkner, P., Ditterline, J., Morris, M., Moore, H., . . . Wozniak, J. (2003). Patterns of comorbidity and dysfunction in clinically referred preschool and school-age children with bipolar disorder. *Journal of Child & Adolescent Psychopharmacology, 13*(4), 495–505. doi: 10.1089/104454603322724887

Young, R. C., Biggs, J. T., Ziegler, V. E., & Meyer, D. A. (1978). A rating scale for mania: Reliability, validity and sensitivity. *British Journal of Psychiatry, 133,* 429–435.

Youngstrom, E., Meyers, O., Demeter, C., Youngstrom, J., Morello, L., Piiparinen, R., . . . Findling, R. L. (2005). Comparing diagnostic checklists for pediatric bipolar disorder in academic and community mental health settings. *Bipolar Disorders, 7*(6), 507–517. doi: 10.1111/j.1399–5618.2005.00269.x

Youngstrom, E., Meyers, O., Youngstrom, J. K., Calabrese, J. R., & Findling, R. L. (2006a). Comparing the effects of sampling designs on the diagnostic accuracy of eight promising screening algorithms for pediatric bipolar disorder. *Biological Psychiatry, 60*(9), 1013–1019. doi: 10.1016/j.biopsych.2006.06.023

Youngstrom, E. [A.], Meyers, O., Youngstrom, J. K., Calabrese, J. R., & Findling, R. L. (2006b). Diagnostic and measurement issues in the assessment of pediatric bipolar disorder: Implications for understanding mood disorder across the life cycle. *Developmental Psychopathology, 18*(4), 989–1021. doi: 10.1017/S0954579406060494

Youngstrom, E. A., Danielson, C. K., Findling, R. L., Gracious, B. L., & Calabrese, J. R. (2002). Factor structure of the Young Mania Rating Scale for use with youths ages 5 to 17 years. *Journal of Clinical Child and Adolescent Psychology, 31*(4), 567–572. doi: 10.1207/S15374424JCCP3104_15

Youngstrom, E. A., Findling, R. L., & Calabrese, J. R. (2004). Effects of adolescent manic symptoms on agreement between youth, parent, and teacher ratings of behavior problems. *Journal of Affective Disorders, 82*(Suppl. 1), S5–S16. doi: 10.1016/j.jad.2004.05.016

Youngstrom, E. A., Findling, R. L., Calabrese, J. R., Gracious, B. L., Demeter, C., Bedoya, D. D., & Price, M. (2004). Comparing the diagnostic accuracy of six potential screening instruments for bipolar disorder in youths aged 5 to 17 years. *Journal of the American Academy of Child & Adolescent Psychiatry, 43*(7), 847–858.

Youngstrom, E. A., Findling, R. L., Danielson, C. K., & Calabrese, J. R. (2001). Discriminative validity of parent report of hypomanic and depressive symptoms on the General Behavior Inventory. *Psychological Assessment, 13*(2), 267–276.

Youngstrom, E. A., Frazier, T. W., Demeter, C., Calabrese, J. R., & Findling, R. L. (2008). Developing a 10-item mania scale from the Parent General Behavior Inventory for children and adolescents. *Journal of Clinical Psychiatry, 69*(5), 831–839.

Youngstrom, E. A., Freeman, A. J., & Jenkins, M. M. (2009). The assessment of children and adolescents with bipolar disorder. *Child and Adolescent Psychiatric Clinics of North America, 18*(2), 353–390, viii–ix. doi: 10.1016/j.chc.2008.12.002

CHAPTER 12

Evidence-Based Treatment of Attention-Deficit/ Hyperactivity Disorder in Children and Adolescents

HEATHER A. JONES AND ANNIE E. RABINOVITCH

OVERVIEW OF THE DISORDER

Attention-deficit/hyperactivity disorder (ADHD) is a neurodevelopmental disorder marked by age-inappropriate levels of inattention and/or hyperactivity and impulsivity. It is one of the most common psychological disorders of childhood (Salmeron, 2009); 8.7% of children ages 8 to 15 in the United States meet diagnostic criteria for ADHD (Froehlich et al., 2007). Although the detection of true sex differences may be limited by an underrepresentation of females in ADHD research (Arnold, 1996), epidemiological data suggest that in nonclinical samples, differences between boys and girls are approximately 3:1 (Szatmari, Offord, & Boyle, 1989). In clinical populations, the ratio climbs to 9:1 (Gershon, 2002). Children and adolescents with ADHD typically present as predominantly inattentive (i.e., solely clinically significant inattentive symptomatology), combined (i.e., clinically significant symptoms of hyperactivity/impulsivity and inattention), or predominantly hyperactive/impulsive (i.e., solely clinically significant symptoms of hyperactivity and impulsivity). Accordingly, symptom profiles for this population are considered to be largely heterogeneous in nature (Musser, Galloway-Long, Frick, & Nigg, 2013). That is to say, two youth with ADHD may look clinically quite distinct from one another.

As a result of their disorder, youth with ADHD experience significant functional impairment most often at home, at school, and with peers. The home lives of youth with ADHD are often marked by high levels of family stress (Deault, 2010) and conflicted parent–child relationships (DuPaul, McGoey, Eckert, & VanBrakle, 2001), as managing the behaviors of children with ADHD can be challenging and stressful (Podolski & Nigg, 2001). With regard to school impairment, symptoms of hyperactivity/impulsivity may make it difficult for children with the disorder to remain seated or still when appropriate. Similarly, symptoms of inattention (e.g., distractibility, difficulty following instructions) may interfere with a child's ability to complete schoolwork successfully. Thus, excessive levels of hyperactivity or intrusiveness may be considered aversive by peers (Whalen & Henker, 1992) and in turn may serve to isolate children with the disorder.

Diagnostic Criteria

Both the fourth text revision and the newly published fifth edition of the *Diagnostic and Statistical Manual of Mental Disorders* (*DSM-IV-TR*, *DSM-5*) (American Psychiatric Association [APA], 2000, 2013) differentiate among three presentations (formerly subtypes) of the disorder: predominantly inattentive, predominantly hyperactive/impulsive, and combined. These presentations are distinguished by specific clusters of symptoms present in the individual. To receive a diagnosis of ADHD, a child or adolescent must demonstrate at least six symptoms of inattention (inattentive presentation), hyperactivity/impulsivity (hyperactive/impulsive presentation), or inattention and hyperactivity/impulsivity respectively (combined). Furthermore, symptomatology must be present for at least 6 months and must coincide with functional impairment in at least two settings (e.g., home, school, with peers).

Four notable changes in the diagnostic criteria for ADHD were made in the *DSM-5*.

1. The threshold of symptoms needed for an adult diagnosis was lowered, given the reduction of symptoms that seem to manifest in adulthood (Kessler et al., 2010).
2. Whereas the *DSM-IV-TR* specified that symptoms must be present before age 7, in the *DSM-5* the age of onset was increased to age 12. Research published since the *DSM-IV-TR* has not found significant differences in functioning, treatment response, or outcomes in comparing youth meeting an earlier relative to a later age of onset threshold (Todd, Huang, & Henderson, 2008).
3. It is no longer necessary for symptoms to be accompanied by *impairment* across multiple settings for an individual to meet diagnostic criteria for ADHD; rather, symptoms must exist across settings.
4. Whereas the *DSM-IV-TR* required "clear evidence of clinically significant impairment in social, academic, or occupational functioning" (APA, 2000 p. 93), language in the *DSM-5* has been modified: "clear evidence that the symptoms interfere with, or reduce the quality of, social, academic, or occupational functioning" (APA, 2013, p. 60).

Thus, recent changes to the diagnostic criteria for ADHD represent advances in the scientific understanding of the disorder and better account for potential diagnostic presentations that may change across the life span.

From a developmental psychopathology perspective, ADHD-associated impairment also changes across development (Seidman, 2006). For instance, toddlers may demonstrate some of the core symptoms typically associated with ADHD (e.g., high energy); however, such symptoms generally are not accompanied by impairment (Campbell & von Stauffenberg, 2009). Longitudinal research suggests that by age 3 or 4, hyperactive/impulsive symptoms can be distinguished from normative disinhibition by virtue of both symptom severity and corresponding impairment (Barkley, 2003).

The demands in middle childhood, such as increased standards for self-control and self-monitoring and expectations of cooperation with family and peers, present many potential ways in which symptoms of ADHD may interfere with functioning. Within the home environment, research suggests that ADHD negatively impacts both the parent–child relationship and overall family functioning (for a review, see Deault, 2010). Parents of children with ADHD report significantly higher levels of parenting stress relative to children without ADHD (Mash & Johnston, 1983). Higher levels of parenting stress among families affected by ADHD may erode parents' ability to engage in effective parenting strategies in order to manage their children's behavior (Podolski & Nigg, 2001). As such, parent–child relationships are often characterized by greater negative emotionality, conflict, and coerciveness (DuPaul et al., 2001) relative to families of children without ADHD. Family functioning is also often affected, with greater family discord (Wells et al., 2000) and higher rates of divorce (Wymbs et al., 2008) observed among families of children with ADHD.

Within the school environment, children in middle childhood with ADHD have significant educational difficulties, including academic underachievement (DeShazo Barry, Lyman, & Klinger, 2002; Fergusson & Horwood, 1995; Fergusson, Horwood, & Lynskey, 1993) relative to control youth. Such children are also more likely to repeat academic grades (Hinshaw, 1992) and receive remedial services (Frick et al., 1991) and are more apt to face school-related disciplinary action (e.g., suspensions) compared to children without the disorder (Loe & Feldman, 2007). They are also more apt to exhibit social impairment. In fact, children with ADHD receive significantly fewer social nominations relative to their nonaffected peers (Hoza, 2007). It may be that the core symptoms of ADHD directly and negatively impact children's ability to establish and maintain peer relationships. Indeed, Whalen and Henker (1992) found that the high levels of impulsivity and hyperactivity often seen in youth with ADHD are found to be aversive and may distance such children from peer social networks. Alternatively, inattentive symptoms may deter children with ADHD from acquiring important social skills (e.g., conversational turn taking) through observational learning (Cunningham, Siegel, & Offord, 1985). The negative impressions made on peers during childhood are resistant to treatment and may continue throughout the school-age years (Price & Dodge, 1989). Thus, the core symptoms of ADHD often result in difficulties in establishing and maintaining healthy peer relationships during childhood.

Moving into adolescence, between 50% and 80% of clinically referred children will continue to experience ADHD-related impairment (Parke et al., 2002). While the symptoms of hyperactivity and impulsivity perhaps distanced middle-age children from their peers, there is evidence to suggest that, in adolescence, these symptoms may translate into greater engagement in risky behaviors, such as dangerous driving habits (Cantwell, 1996). Within the academic realm, adolescents with ADHD fail more classes (Mannuzza, Klein, Bessler, Malloy, & Hynes, 1997), require a greater number of years to graduate high school (Weiss, Hechtman, Milroy, & Perlman,1985), and have lower rates of college attendance and graduation (Barkley, 2006) relative to controls. Research suggests that in adolescence, symptoms of hyperactivity may wane. However, impulsivity and inattention symptoms remain both prominent and impairing. Furthermore, among adolescents with ADHD, a sense of what has been termed "inner restlessness" may begin to pervade the clinical picture for these individuals (Harpin, 2005). Thus, there is evidence to suggest that in adolescence, symptom clusters may become more or less pronounced (i.e., shift from hyperactive to inattentive and impulsive), and types of impairment may also change.

Once conceptualized as a disorder of childhood, there is now evidence that ADHD is a chronic disorder, with symptoms and impairment continuing into adulthood (Pary et al., 2002). Adults affected by ADHD experience greater occupational difficulties (e.g., unemployment) (Mannuzza et al., 1997), have poorer health outcomes (Harpin, 2005), and have fewer intimate relationships (Weiss & Murray, 2003) relative to control adults. Clearly, ADHD has far-reaching developmental implications, as early deficits, particularly if left untreated, may place children with ADHD at risk for significant impairment across multiple domains over a lifetime.

Comorbidity

Complicating the clinical picture for many children with ADHD, comorbidity with other mental disorders is highly prevalent. The most common comorbid disorders are oppositional defiant disorder (ODD) and conduct disorder (CD). Barkley (2003) found that by age 7, 54% to 67% of clinically referred children with ADHD were also diagnosed with ODD. Barkley, Fischer, Smallish, and Fletcher (2004) found that between 20% and 50% of youth with ADHD went on to develop comorbid CD by middle childhood, and by adolescence, 44% to 50% met criteria for a dual diagnosis.

Comorbid internalizing disorders, including anxiety and depression, also are common. Tannock (2000) found that between 10% and 40% of children affected by ADHD within clinical samples are diagnosed with an anxiety disorder. Unlike CD, there is some evidence to suggest that anxiety may mitigate some of the negative consequences of ADHD (Pliszka, 2000). Fewer externalizing behaviors in general and less impulsivity in particular are evidenced among children with comorbid ADHD and anxiety (Jensen et al., 2001; Pliszka, 2000). As such, anxiety may buffer children with

ADHD against some negative sequelae. ADHD is also highly comorbid with depression (Golubchik, Kodesh, & Weizman, 2013), with approximately 20% to 30% of youth meeting diagnostic criteria for both disorders (Barkley et al., 2004). Children with comorbid depression and ADHD may experience greater social and academic impairment relative to those children with ADHD alone (Blackman, Ostrander, & Herman, 2005). It is possible that social isolation and lack of motivation, two hallmark symptoms of depression, exacerbate existing social and academic impairment.

Finally, between 19% and 26% of children with ADHD also have a learning disorder (LD). Eighty percent of children with ADHD have learning difficulties that result in academic performance 2 years behind their nonaffected classmates (Barkley, 2003). A seminal study (Mayes, Calhoun, & Crowell, 2000) compared children with comorbid ADHD and LD to those with ADHD alone and found that both groups experienced significant learning difficulties. However, the difficulties were significantly more severe in the comorbid group, as could be expected. It is possible that LDs and specifically the inattention observed among those with ADHD represent disorders along a common spectrum.

EVIDENCE-BASED APPROACHES TO TREATMENT

From an evolutionary biology perspective, ADHD is conceptualized as a mismatch between a child's interrelated characteristics (e.g., genetic predisposition, temperament, behavior) and his/her environmental demands (Jensen et al., 1997). Accordingly, treatments for the disorder may involve altering a child's behavior, the environment (e.g., home life, school), or a combination of the two, in order to ameliorate consequences of the disorder (Stein, 2007). Currently, most effective interventions utilize multiple treatment components.

The Multimodal Treatment Study of Children with ADHD (MTA Cooperative Group, 1999) was the first large-scale, multisite study designed to evaluate leading treatments for ADHD. The MTA study examined for the first time the safety and relative effectiveness of stimulant medication and behavior therapy alone and in combination. The 14-month clinical trial randomized 579 youth with ADHD to one of four treatment arms: medication management, behavioral treatment, combined treatment (medication management plus behavioral treatment), and community care/referral for assessment. All treatment arms demonstrated a reduction in symptom severity. However, medication management was superior to behavioral treatment and community care. Combined treatment was no better than medication management in reducing symptom severity. In other areas of functioning, however, including child anxiety symptoms, academic performance, and social skills, the combination arm (but not medication or behavioral treatment alone) produced superior outcomes compared to routine community care at the end of treatment. The children in the combination treatment also took lower doses of medication than children in the medication group (MTA Cooperative Group, 1999).

Family and peer-based outcomes from the MTA study also have been investigated. Wells and colleagues (2000) examined parenting and family stress outcomes immediately following treatment, reporting no meaningful group-based differences across the treatment arms. It is possible that child comorbidities, such as ODD, diluted treatment effects on outcome measures. Similar nonsignificant findings were reported by Hoza and colleagues (2005) based on peer-assessed outcomes. Among a subsample of MTA participants, the authors found that despite significant reduction in ADHD symptom severity, peer functioning remained deficient. Thus, family and peer relationships may require more targeted efforts during treatment.

In terms of longer-term outcomes, an 8-year follow-up study of children enrolled in the MTA study (Molina et al., 2009) reported overall maintenance of improvement in functioning relative to pretreatment levels. However, as a whole, children were functioning significantly less well than a comparison non-ADHD classmate sample irrespective of whether children with ADHD did or did not continue to take medication after the 14-month study period. These data point toward a crucial need for treatments (or combination of treatments) that are efficacious over the long term (e.g., into the high school years).

Behavioral Interventions

Just as the symptoms and impairments exhibited by children with ADHD are varied, so too are the behavioral treatment strategies used to reduce these problems. Next we provide an overview of the types of treatment programs that have been examined in empirical research.

Behavioral Parent Training

Behavioral parent training (BPT) is likely the best-studied intervention for children with ADHD. During BPT, the foci of change are the child's unwanted (e.g., noncompliance) and wanted (e.g., compliance) behaviors. Contrary to many other types of therapy, during BPT, the parent is the agent of change. Thus, the therapist's role is to teach the parent to use effective behavior management strategies, monitor change, and troubleshoot difficulties. Using the behavioral principles of reinforcement and punishment, therapists instruct parents to use such skills as rewarding and attending to increase wanted behaviors as well as ignoring and employing time out to decrease unwanted behaviors.

Classroom Behavior Management

The strategies used by parents to increase compliant behaviors and decrease noncompliant behaviors can be implemented in the classroom as well. Teachers can implement reward systems for children with ADHD in the classroom using the same principles of reinforcement and punishment. The Daily Report Card (Chronis, Chacko, Fabiano, Wymbs, & Pelham, 2004; Smith, Waschbusch, Willoughby, & Evans, 2000) is a system that fosters collaboration and communication between parents and teachers. Teachers establish target behaviors, such as in-seat compliance, and send a "report card" home to parents, who then provide rewards.

Intensive Treatment Programs

The range and severity of ADHD symptoms calls for comprehensive and intensive treatment programs. The Summer Treatment Program (STP) is a 2-month, all-day program that combines a behavioral point system, daily report cards, academic skills training, social skills training, problem-solving training, and sports training, all in a summer day camp format. This program has been efficacious in decreasing ADHD symptoms and increasing behavioral functioning (e.g., Pelham et al., 2005).

Peer Interventions

It is becoming increasingly recognized that despite the success of pharmacotherapy and behavioral management to control or change some of the symptoms of ADHD, the interpersonal problems that are part of this disorder remain unchanged. The need to intervene in the area of peer relationships is important for children with ADHD, and accompanying peer problems have significant negative long-term outcomes including criminality, depression, and substance abuse (in boys) (Greene, Biederman, Faraone, Sienna, & Garcia-Jetton, 1997), and school failure, disruptive behaviors, and internalizing symptoms (in girls) (Mikami & Hinshaw, 2006).

Some data suggest that direct attempts to increase peers' social inclusion of children with ADHD may be efficacious (Mikami et al., 2013). One intervention, Making Socially Accepting Inclusive Classrooms (MOSAIC), provides instruction to teachers and peers regarding specific behavioral changes. Teachers are taught to (1) diffuse the frustrations of children with ADHD by providing positive comments, (2) give private reprimands but public praise, (3) promote inclusive behavior by peers by suggesting areas of commonality between children with ADHD and a peer, and (4) publicly attend to the genuine strengths of children with ADHD. In one randomized controlled trial (Mikami et al., 2013), adding MOSAIC to a comprehensive behavioral treatment program resulted in enhanced sociometric ratings, more friendships, and more positive messages by peers for children than among those who received the behavioral treatment program alone.

Neurofeedback Training

Over the past decade, there have been an increasing number of commercial programs that attest to provide improved attention, impulse control, academic functioning, and social functioning as a result of neurofeedback/neurocognitive training. Using computer programs that present puzzles and tasks designed to enhance set shifting, inhibitory control, working memory, or attention, the producers of these products assert efficacious and long-lasting benefits. Unfortunately, these programs have not been subject to rigorous empirical testing, and a recent meta-analysis (Rapport, Orban, Kofler, & Friedman, 2013) suggests that these programs are not efficacious.

PARENTAL INVOLVEMENT IN TREATMENT

Commonly found among interventions for externalizing disorders, parents play an integral role in interventions for children with ADHD. Next, we review how parents contribute to these treatment programs.

Role of Parental Psychopathology

Maternal Depression

In addition to the negative consequences that ADHD can exert on youth outcomes (e.g., social isolation, parent–child conflict, academic underachievement), impairments may be heavily impacted by co-occurring parental psychopathology (e.g., anxiety: Kashdan et al., 2004; depression: Chronis-Tuscano et al., 2011). The bulk of research to date has examined the impact of maternal depression in particular on child outcomes. Despite being more common among children with comorbid ADHD and ODD/CD, mothers of children with ADHD (only) are also more likely to experience depressive symptoms as well as major depression episodes relative to mothers of control children (Chronis et al., 2003). Regardless of diagnostic status, children of depressed mothers are more likely to develop internalizing and externalizing disorders (Weissman et al., 1987), are often less socially competent (Luoma et al., 2001), and experience greater academic underachievement (Beardslee, Bemporand, Keller, & Klerman, 1983) relative to children of nondepressed mothers. Similarly, depressed mothers have been found to be less consistent and more negative in their parenting and to have greater negative expectations of their children (Downey & Coyne, 1990) relative to nondepressed mothers. In considering Patterson's (1982) coercion model, whereby child behavior problems and parental psychopathology interact to perpetuate and maintain one another, maternal depression constitutes a significant risk factor for negative outcomes for children with ADHD (Chronis, Chacko, Fabiano, Wymbs, & Pelham, 2004).

Researchers have started to investigate whether specific treatment components to address parental psychopathology improves child, parent, or family outcomes for BPT. Specifically, Chronis-Tuscano and colleagues (2013) implemented an empirically supported adaptation to CBT targeting maternal stress and depression: the Coping with Depression Course (CWDC) (Lewinsohn, Hoberman, & Clark, 1989). Mothers were randomly assigned to receive traditional BPT or an integrated parenting intervention (IPI-A), which integrates BPT with CWDC. At posttreatment, mothers who were randomized to IPI-A experienced fewer symptoms of maternal depression and small to moderate gains with regard to negative parenting, child deviance, and child impairment. At follow-up, these mothers also saw an improvement in family functioning relative to the BPT group.

Maternal ADHD

Aside from maternal depression, the other form of parental psychopathology most studied among families of children with ADHD is maternal ADHD. Parents of children with ADHD are more likely than nonaffected children to suffer from the disorder (e.g., Alberts-Corush, Firestone, & Goodman, 1986). Some research suggests that maternal ADHD may interfere with the treatment of child ADHD (Weiss, Hechtman, & Weiss, 2000). Symptoms of ADHD (i.e., inattention, difficulty following through on instructions, forgetfulness in daily activities) make it difficult for affected mothers to effectively engage in their child's treatment. Specifically, mothers who are forgetful may not administer ADHD medication on a timely basis or may be absent for treatment sessions. Sonuga-Barke, Daley, and Thompson (2002) specifically found that maternal ADHD hinders child improvement following BPT.

Chronis-Tuscano and colleagues (2011) examined the efficacy of BPT for 70 mothers of children with ADHD who themselves also had ADHD. Mothers with higher levels of ADHD symptomatology reported less improvement in their child's problem behavior relative to mothers with lower levels of symptomatology. Furthermore, the relationship between maternal ADHD symptoms and child behavior outcomes was mediated by negative parenting. Mothers with higher levels of ADHD symptoms demonstrated lower reductions in observed negative parenting. Their children in turn demonstrated less improvement in child behavior problems posttreatment. This study underscores the need for tailored BPT treatment for mothers struggling with their own symptoms of ADHD.

ADAPTATIONS AND MODIFICATIONS TO TREATMENT

Although BPT is considered an effective treatment, its success is notably limited by poor adherence to treatment on the part of families. For instance, Barkley and colleagues (2002) found that despite enrolling in treatment, a significant proportion of families either do not attend or prematurely discontinue such treatment. Among those families that do attend, a large number arrive late to appointments, fail to complete necessary homework assignments, or demonstrate spotty attendance (Cunningham, Davis, Bremner, Dunn, & Rzasa, 1993). As such, significant efforts have been made to identify populations that have notoriously struggled with BPT adherence and to utilize engagement strategies with such populations. Such studies are specifically tailored to address unique populations, including those that are notoriously difficult to engage in treatment, including fathers and families led by single parents.

Adaptations for Specific Populations

Parent management training typically assumes the presence of two caregivers in the household, although fathers are much less likely to attend treatment sessions. Here we present adaptations for different populations.

Fathers

Fathers constitute a subpopulation that has experienced particular difficulty with regard to BPT engagement (Fabiano et al., 2009). As Tiano and McNeil (2005) point out, fathers typically are excluded from research on BPT for children with externalizing difficulties. Fabiano and colleagues (2009) detected a similar pattern within research examining BPT for childhood ADHD. Specifically, research has established that mothers of children with ADHD experience greater levels of stress, marital discord, and conflict in parent–child interactions (Fischer, 1990; Hinshaw, 2002) relative to families unaffected by ADHD. Fathers are significantly and negatively impacted by child ADHD in a number of ways. They report greater impairment in their relationships with both their child and their child's mother (Cunningham, Benness, & Siegel, 1988) relative to fathers of children without ADHD. Further, fathers of children with ADHD report greater daily hassles (i.e., arguments over completing chores, getting to school) relative to mothers (Crnic & Booth, 1991). Thus, it is clear that, in dual-parent households, both parents are negatively impacted by child ADHD.

The rationale for increasing father involvement in BPT among families of children with ADHD is both theoretically and empirically sound. From a developmental standpoint, Parke and colleagues (2002) underscore the important role of fathers in fostering emotion regulation, social competence, and sustained attention in their children. Furthermore, father involvement is linked to a number of positive outcomes in youth across a variety of domains, including fewer behavior problems (Amato & Rivera, 1999) and greater academic achievement (Forehand, Long, Brody, & Fauber, 1986). Thus, identifying ways to involve fathers more heavily in the behavioral treatment of their children holds potential.

The Coaching Our Acting-out Children: Heightening Essential Skills (COACHES) (Fabiano et al., 2012) program combines two evidence-based treatments for child ADHD: the Summer Treatment Program (STP) (Pelham et al., 2005) and group-formatted BPT (Cunningham, Bremner, & Secord, 1998). COACHES is based on a theory that the inclusion of a sports activity within a typical BPT setting would include fathers in an area that is arguably most relevant to their parenting (i.e., settings in which father–child interactions often occur) (Fabiano et al., 2009).

Each intervention session is 2 hours in length. During the first hour, fathers review effective parenting strategies (e.g., praise, time out) in a group setting with other fathers. Children simultaneously practice soccer skill drills with counselors to enhance athleticism. During the second hour, parent and child groups merge, and a soccer game ensues. During the game, fathers utilize these parenting strategies (e.g., effective commands) with their children. Furthermore, clinicians watch the game and provide feedback. Fathers are provided with homework assignments to facilitate practice of such techniques at home with their children. Following participation, fathers demonstrated greater engagement in child treatment (e.g., attended more sessions) as compared to traditional BPT (Fabiano et al., 2012).

The BPT literature including fathers should be considered within the context of several limitations, however. Fabiano and colleagues (2009) note that there are few studies in this area. In addition, the majority of such studies are plagued with methodological limitations, including high attrition rates (e.g., Barkley, Edwards, Laneri, Fletcher, & Metevia, 2001) and lack of improvement for fathers on objective measures of parenting following treatment (e.g., Danforth, Harvey, Ulaszek, & McKee, 2006). Finally, no studies to date have specifically examined the unique effect of paternal involvement on child outcomes.

Single-Parent Households

As mentioned, family adversity (e.g., consistent, high levels of stress) often compromises the benefits of BPT (Chronis et al., 2004). Single mothers are at higher risk for a variety of negative consequences, such as depression and stress (Cairney, Boyle, Offord, & Raccine, 2003), and are also more apt to experience concrete barriers to BPT (e.g., cost of transportation) (Kazdin & Wassell, 2000). Thus, researchers have found that single mothers and their children with ADHD are less likely to enroll in BPT (Cunningham et al., 2000), complete BPT (Kazdin, Mazurick, & Bass, 1993), and improve following receipt of BPT (Webster-Stratton & Hammond, 1990).

To date, two small BPT studies have been conducted with single mothers and their children with ADHD. Pfifner, Jourile, Brown, Etscheidt, and Kelly (1990) conducted a randomized trial of 13 single mothers. Mothers were randomized to BPT or BPT plus a problem-solving component. Mothers who received the latter saw greater improvement in their child's behavior problems relative to the former.

Chacko and colleagues (2008) evaluated the efficacy of the Strategies to Enhance Positive Parenting (STEPP) program, which focused on identifying and tackling barriers to treatment for this population, including concrete barriers to treatment as well as maternal cognitions with regard to child treatment and child problem behaviors. STEPP also incorporated coping and problem-solving enhancement components for mothers. Decreased stress and psychopathology were observed at the end of treatment as well as higher rates of attendance and treatment completion. Significant improvements in child behavior were not found, however.

MEASUREMENT OF TREATMENT OUTCOMES

One primary difficulty with regard to measurement includes teasing apart ADHD as a disorder from its associated impairment (Stein, 2007). The next section focuses on the measurement of treatment outcomes for children with ADHD at the symptom level and at the level of functional impairment.

Measuring ADHD Symptom Outcomes

Studies measuring treatment outcomes often utilize ADHD symptom severity as an index (e.g., Epstein et al., 2010; MTA Cooperative Group, 1999). Such studies typically administer rating scales pretreatment, at subsequent follow-up assessments, and posttreatment. Common instruments include the Swanson, Noland, and Pelham–IV (SNAP-IV) (Swanson, Nolan, & Pelham, in Swanson, 1992), the ADHD Rating Scale (DuPaul, 1991), and the Vanderbilt ADHD Rating Scale (Wolraich et al., 2003). The SNAP-IV includes all 18 *DSM-5* symptoms of ADHD as well as the eight ODD symptoms. Each symptom is assigned a severity rating by the informant on a 4-point Likert scale (0 = not at all to 3 = very much). Separate forms are provided for a child's caregiver and teacher, respectively.

The ADHD Rating Scale includes all *DSM-5* symptoms of ADHD and asks informants to provide an estimate of severity for each symptom on a 4-point Likert scale (0 = never to 3 = very often). Similar to the SNAP-IV, there are separate forms for parents and teachers to complete. While useful in providing a measure of symptom severity improvement, such measures alone do not provide researchers and clinicians with information about treatment gains corresponding to functional impairment (Epstein et al., 2007). The Vanderbilt Rating Scale, however, while assessing the severity of core ADHD symptoms, also requires the informant to rate the degree of functional impairment across eight domains (Wolraich et al., 2003). However, this scale currently does not have published normative data available for clinicians to compare an individual child's scores to the peer group.

The relationship between improvement in core symptoms and corresponding impairment remains unclear (Epstein et al., 2010; Wells et al., 2000). Treatment approaches for youth with ADHD have operated under the assumption that the core symptoms of ADHD (e.g., difficulty with organization, age-inappropriate levels of energy, difficulty sustaining attention in tasks) are directly and caus-ally linked to functional impairment (e.g., Wells et al., 2000). Consequently, decreases in ADHD symptom severity should result in similar reductions in associated impairment. However, empirical data indicate that reduction in ADHD symptoms does not necessarily translate into improvements in functional deficits (Epstein et al., 2010).

Measuring Functional Impairment Outcomes

Other researchers have focused their attention on assessing treatment outcomes as a function of impairment. Measures of changes in functional impairments appear to be far more robust relative to those assessing outcomes at the symptom level. Within the home environment, some research-ers have examined the parent–child relationship as a treatment outcome variable (e.g., Barkley & Cunningham, 1979; Mash & Johnston, 1983). Others have examined parenting sense of competence (e.g., Anastopolous, Shelton, DuPaul, & Guevremont, 1993), given the evidence indicating that par-ents of children with ADHD often perceive themselves to be less competent caregivers (Johnston, 1996) relative to parents of nonaffected youth. Other research has examined the extent to which treatment impacts functional outcomes in academic (e.g., Loe & Feldman, 2007) or peer (e.g., Hoza, 2007) domains.

Home and Family

Specifically within the home environment, where parent–child relationships, family functioning, parenting practices, and parental well-being are particularly salient, outcome measures often take the form of either parent self-report or analog behavioral observation. A common self-report, for instance, used to assess quality of the parent–child relationship among children with ADHD is the Parent-Child Relationship Questionnaire (PCRQ) (Furman & Giberson, 1995). Specifically, this measure assesses five dimensions, including warmth, personal relationship, disciplinary warmth, power assertion, and possessiveness. Caregivers and children endorse the items using a 5-point Likert scale (i.e., "hardly at all" to extremely much"). Administered both pre- and posttreatment, this type of measure has the sensitivity to detect changes in the perceived parent–child relationship (Furman & Giberson, 1995).

Behavioral observation provides another method to assess the parent–child relationship and may serve as an outcome measure for ADHD treatment (e.g., MTA Cooperative Group, 1999). These measures may include video-recorded or live observations of either parent–child interactions or child problem behaviors in multiple settings (e.g., home, school). One commonly used observa-tional measure is the Individualized Target Behavior Evaluation (ITBE) (Pelham et al., 2005). The ITBE operationalizes specific target behaviors germane to the area in which a child is experienc-ing impairment and establishes a criterion for each behavior (e.g., interrupts mother three or fewer times) using a specified time frame (e.g., 2 hours of structured homework). The observer (typically parent or teacher) assesses whether the child has met his/her behavioral goals within the specified time frame and can derive percentages of behavioral successes (e.g., 75% of the time refrained from interrupting during a 2-hour period at home). This type of measure can help define targets for behavioral intervention and monitor treatment progress over time.

Academics

Examination of academic outcomes other than grades may be a challenge. Depending on the outcome measure utilized, available data indicate that results vary greatly. Consistent with MTA findings, an extensive review of academic and educational outcomes among children with ADHD indicates that decreases in symptom severity are linked with greater academic productivity as measured by outcome variables such as note-taking ability and completion of homework assignments (Loe & Feldman, 2007). However, when conceptualizing academic attainment as the outcome measure for treatment, results were insignificant.

Peer Relationships

In the domain of peer relationships, widely used rating scales to measure peer social functioning among children with ADHD include the Social Skills Rating System (SSRS) (Gresham & Elliot, 1989) and the Self-Perception Profile for Children (Harter, 1985). The latter instrument has six subscales of a child's self-perception across multiple domains, including scholastic competence, social competence, athletic competence, physical appearance, behavioral conduct, and global self-worth. Although these two scales are useful, data from these rating scales are confounded by research indicating that children with ADHD often have exaggerated perceptions of their own competence (Ohan & Johnston, 2002) across a variety of domains, including social aptitude (Hoza, 2007). Children's inflated perceptions of their own abilities may in turn limit the accuracy of child-reported data, specifically within the context of peer functioning. Peer social nominations may also provide an accurate assessment of a child's social functioning. However, because peer social nominations tend to be relatively constant throughout the school-age years (Price & Dodge, 1989), this outcome measure may not be sensitive to change in a child's social competence following treatment.

CLINICAL CASE VIGNETTE

Benjamin Randolph (identifying information has been altered to protect confidentiality) is an 8-year-old African American boy, recently diagnosed with ADHD, combined presentation, by his pediatrician. Since age 6, Benjamin's parents have struggled to get their son to follow instructions. At intake, Mrs. Randolph reported that she must repeat herself several times before Benjamin completes a chore, such as putting away toys. If she gives him multistep tasks (e.g., brush his teeth, put on pajamas, and get into bed), Benjamin will brush his teeth and then become distracted by the toys in the corner of his bedroom. Although Mrs. Randolph prides herself on being "patient" and "sensitive", she feels significantly stressed in her role as Benjamin's mother. On two occasions, she has become so frustrated over Benjamin's inability to follow through on instructions that she has turned Benjamin over her knee and given him a light spanking on his bottom. After both of these occasions, Mrs. Randolph was overcome with guilt at having raised a hand to Benjamin and by a growing sense of failure as a mother.

Since Benjamin started the second grade 6 months ago, Mrs. Randolph has received almost weekly phone calls home from his teacher, complaining that he distracts other children during independent work time (e.g., getting out of his seat to talk to classmates) and does not complete classroom assignments. His teacher is concerned that he will not progress sufficiently in his academics for advancement to third grade. Furthermore, Benjamin constantly moves—rocking back and forth in his desk, tapping his feet against the linoleum floor, fidgeting with his hands. He has been struggling to get along with his classmates, particularly during unstructured school periods, such as recess or lunchtime. He bolts to the front of the line, cutting in front of his classmates to be the first to participate in a game on the playground. If other children are engaged in an activity, he has a tendency to intrude on their game, uninvited. Benjamin's teacher noted that she often has found him playing alone during recess, and he complains to his mother that "nobody wants to be his friend."

Evidence-Based Treatment Plan

To address Benjamin's difficulty completing tasks and complying with adult commands within the home environment, Benjamin's parents initiated behavioral parent training, with a local child psychologist. His parents were first provided with psychoeducation about ADHD as well as treatment expectations. She emphasized that Benjamin's parents should provide positive reinforcement for engaging in appropriate behaviors. To teach his parents to provide positive attention for appropriate behaviors, the psychologist taught his parents to verbally broadcast behaviors that they would like to see again (e.g., compliance). For instance, his mother said, "Now you are putting your toys away without my having to tell you twice." The parents were instructed to provide specific verbal praise when Benjamin was behaving appropriately and to reward behaviors that they would like to see again (e.g., putting his clothing in the hamper). For example, Benjamin's father stated, "I really like that you cleared the table after dinner." The parents were taught to ignore minor inappropriate behaviors (e.g., tapping his mother's shoulder while she is on the telephone) until it stopped, with the therapist emphasizing that Benjamin would likely test his limits and that the behavior may escalate before subsiding.

Next, his parents were taught to issue specific, direct, and short commands or instructions, as opposed to vague, indirect, or "chain" commands strung together in one sentence. For instance, instead of "Get ready for bed," his parents might say "Please brush your teeth." His parents were taught logical consequences for managing Benjamin's failure to comply with commands. For instance, his father might say, "If you put your toys away right now, you may have 30 minutes extra on the computer. If you do not put your toys away, you will not have extra computer time this evening." Finally, his parents were taught to use appropriate punishment strategies for moderate to severe misbehavior (e.g., hits his sister), such as time out and removing privileges.

To address Benjamin's difficulties in the classroom, the psychologist implemented a daily report card (DRC). Benjamin's parents set up a meeting with his teacher to discuss the areas in which Benjamin is struggling (i.e., classwork completion, peer relationships). Benjamin's parents and teacher decided on specific target behaviors to track, such as "Morning math assignment is 80% complete." Each day Benjamin's parents received a DRC completed by Benjamin's teacher providing feedback about his target behaviors. The psychologist, Benjamin's parents, and Benjamin decided that a sticker chart would best provide positive reinforcement for achievement of behavioral goals, and his parents worked to consistently provide praise and stickers in response to Benjamin bringing home his DRC daily with goals completed. Furthermore, Benjamin's parents and teacher consistently evaluated the effectiveness of the DRC, with an objective being to maximize Benjamin's successes in achieving goals so as to facilitate self-efficacy.

To further address Benjamin's difficulties with peers, the psychologist encouraged Mr. and Mrs. Randolph to actively network with other parents who have similar-age children to establish a pool of adult friends with whom they might initiate child play dates. Benjamin's parents were further encouraged to increase his peer interactions by setting up play dates with these same-age children and finally to facilitate appropriate social skills during such occasions. For instance, during one such play date, Benjamin's mother said to him, "Please give Jimmy a chance now to play with that toy," and she then praised Benjamin for sharing. Outside of play dates, Benjamin's parents were encouraged to reinforce appropriate social skills through their own interactions with him and through the modeling of such skills.

Following BPT, Mr. and Mrs. Randolph reported drastic improvements in their son's behavior within the home. Specifically, Benjamin was better able to follow instructions within the household, which Benjamin's mother reports has significantly decreased her frustration and has improved her sense of efficacy in managing her son's behavior. Benjamin's parents noted some improvement in his school behavior. Specifically, Benjamin remains seated approximately 65% of independent classwork time. However, Mr. and Mrs. Randolph continue to monitor and adapt his DRC in order to maximize their son's successes. For instance, during a recent parent–teacher conference, it was decided that Benjamin would need to complete 75% of his morning math assignments, as he is having difficulty completing 80% at the present time. Benjamin's parents also continue to encourage positive peer interactions by guiding Benjamin to use appropriate social skills during play dates.

REFERENCES

Alberts-Corush, J., Firestone, P., & Goodman, J. T. (1986). Attention and impulsivity characteristics of biological and adoptive parents of hyperactive and normal children. *American Journal of Orthopsychiatry, 56,* 413–423.

Amato, P. R., & Rivera, F. (1999). Parental involvement and children's behavior problems *Journal of Marriage and Family, 61,* 557–573.

American Psychiatric Association. (2000). *Diagnostic and statistical manual of mental disorders* (4th ed., text rev.). Washington, DC: Author.

American Psychiatric Association. (2013). *Diagnostic and statistical manual of mental disorders* (5th ed.). Arlington, VA: American Psychiatric Publishing.

Anastopoulos, A., Shelton, T., DuPaul, G., & Guevremont, D. (1993). Parent training for attention-deficit hyperactivity disorder: Its impact on parent functioning. *Journal of Abnormal Child Psychology, 21,* 581–596.

Arnold, L. E. (1996). Sex differences in ADHD: Conference summary. *Journal of Abnormal Child Psychology, 2,* 555–569.

Aspland, H., & Gardner, F. (2003). Observational measures of parent-child interaction: An introductory review. *Child and Adolescent Mental Health, 8,* 136–143.

Barkley, R. A. (2003). Issues in the diagnosis of attention-deficit/hyperactivity disorder in children. *Brain and Development, 25,* 77–83.

Barkley, R. A. (2006). *Attention-deficit hyperactivity disorder: A handbook for diagnosis and treatment.* New York, NY: Guilford Press.

Barkley, R. A., & Cunningham, C. E. (1979). The effects of methylphenidate on mother-child interactions of hyperactive children. *Archives of General Psychiatry, 36,* 201–208.

Barkley, R. A., Edwards, G., Laneri, M., Fletcher, K., & Metevia, L. (2001). The efficacy of problem-solving communication training alone, behavior management training alone, and their combination for parent-adolescent conflict in teenagers with ADHD and ODD. *Journal of Consulting and Clinical Psychology, 69,* 926–941.

Barkley, R. A., Fischer, M., Smallish, L., & Fletcher, K. (2004). Young adult follow-up of hyperactive children: Antisocial activities and drug use. *Journal of Child Psychology and Psychiatry, 45,* 195–211.

Barkley, R. A. Shelton, T. L., Crosswait, C., Moorehouse, M., Fletcher, K., Barrett, S., . . . Metevia, L. (2002). Multi-method psychoeducational intervention for preschool children with disruptive behavior: Preliminary results at post-treatment. *Journal of Child Psychology and Psychiatry and Allied Disciplines, 41,* 319–322.

Beardslee, W. R., Bemporand, J., Keller, M. B., & Klerman, G. L. (1983). Children of parents with major affective disorder. *American Journal of Psychiatry, 140,* 825–832.

Blackman, G. L., Ostrander, R., & Herman, K. C. (2005). Children with ADHD and depression: A multisource, multimethod assessment of clinical, social, and academic functioning. *Journal of Attention Disorders, 8,* 195–207.

Cairney, J., Boyle, M., Offord, D., & Racine, Y. (2003). Stress, social support, and depression in single and married mothers. *Social Psychiatry and Psychiatric Epidemiology, 38,* 442–449.

Campbell, S. B., & von Stauffenberg, C. (2009). Delay and inhibition as early predictors of ADHD symptoms in third grade. *Journal of Abnormal Child Psychology, 37,* 1–15.

Cantwell, D. P. (1996). Attention deficit disorder: A review of the past 10 years. *Journal of the Academy of Child and Adolescent Psychiatry, 35,* 978–987.

Chacko, A., Wymbs. B. T., Flammer-River, L., Pelham, W. E., Walker, K. S., & Arnold, F. (2008). A pilot study of the feasibility and efficacy of the Strategies to Enhance Positive Parenting (STEPP) program for single mothers of children with ADHD. *Journal of Attention Disorders, 12,* 270–280.

Chronis, A. M., Chacko, A., Fabiano, G. A., Wymbs, B. T., & Pelham W. E. (2004). Enhancement to the behavioral parent training paradigm for families of children with ADHD: Review and future directions. *Clinical Child and Family Psychology Review, 7,* 1–27.

Chronis, A. M., Lahey, B. B., Pelham, W. E., Kipp, H., Baumann, B., & Lee, S. S. (2003). Psychopathology and substance abuse in parents of young children with attention deficit/hyperactivity disorder. *Journal of the American Academy of Child & Adolescent Psychiatry, 42,* 1425–1423.

Chronis-Tuscano, A., Clarke, T. L., O'Brien, K. A., Raggi, V. L., Diaz, Y., Mintz, A. D., . . . Lewisohn, P. (2013). Development and preliminary evaluation of an integrated treatment targeting parenting and depressive symptoms in mothers of children with attention-deficit/hyperactivity disorder. *Journal of Consulting and Clinical Psychology, 81,* 918–925.

Chronis-Tuscano, A., O'Brien, K. A., Johnston, C., Jones, H. A., Clarke, T. L., Raggi, V. L., Rooney, M. E., . . . Seymour, K. E. (2011). The relation between maternal ADHD symptoms and improvement in child behavior following brief behavioral parent training is mediated by change in negative parenting. *Journal of Abnormal Child Psychology, 39,* 1047–1057.

Crnic, K. A., & Booth, C. L. (1991). Mothers' and fathers' perceptions of daily hassles of parenting across early childhood. *Journal of Marriage and Family, 53,* 1042–1050.

Cunningham, C. E., Benness, B. B., & Siegel, L. S. (1988). Family functioning, time allocation, and parental depression in the families of normal and ADHD children. *Journal of Clinical Child Psychology, 17,* 169–177.

Cunningham, C. E., Boyle, M., Offord, D., Racine, Y., Hundert, J., & Secord, M. (2000). Tri-ministry study: Correlates of school-based parent course utilization. *Journal of Consulting and Clinical Psychology, 68,* 928–933.

Cunningham, C. E., Bremner, R., & Secord, M. (1998). *The Community Parent Education (COPE) program: A school based family systems oriented course for parents of children with disruptive behavior disorders.* Unpublished manual.

Cunningham, C. E., Davis, J. R., Bremner, R., Dunn, K. W., & Rzasa, T. (1993). Coping modeling problem solving versus mastery modeling: Effects on adherence, in-session process, and skill acquisition in a residential parent-training program. *Journal of Consulting and Clinical Psychology, 61,* 871–877.

Cunningham, C. E., Siegel, L. S., & Offord, D. R. (1985). A developmental dose-response analysis of the effects of methylphenidate on the peer interactions of attention deficit disordered boys. *Journal of Clinical Psychology & Psychiatry, 26,* 955–971.

Danforth, J. S., Harvey, E., Ulaszek, W. R., & McKee, T. E. (2006). The outcome of group parent training for families of children with attention-deficit hyperactivity disorder and defiant/aggressive behavior. *Journal of Behavior Therapy and Experimental Psychiatry, 37,* 188–205.

Deault, L. C. (2010). A systematic review of parenting in relation to the development of comorbidities and functional impairments in children with attention-deficit/hyperactivity disorder (ADHD). *Child Psychiatry and Human Development, 2,* 168–182.

DeShazo Barry, T. D., Lyman, R. D., & Klinger, L. G. (2002). Academic underachievement and attention deficit/hyperactivity disorder: The negative impact of symptom severity on school performance. *Journal of School Psychology, 40,* 259–283.

Downey, G., & Coyne, J. C. (1990). Children of depressed parents: An integrative review. *Psychological Bulletin, 108,* 50–76.

DuPaul, G. J. (1991). Parent and teacher ratings of ADHD symptoms: Psychometric properties in a community-based sample. *Journal of Clinical Child Psychology, 20,* 245–253.

DuPaul, G. J., McGoey, K. E., Eckert, T. L., & VanBrakle, J. V. (2001). Preschool children with ADHD: Impairments and behavioral, social and school functioning. *Journal of the American Academy of Child & Adolescent Psychiatry, 40,* 508–515.

Epstein, J. N., Langberg, J. M., Lichtenstein, P., Altaye, M., Brinkman, W. B., House, K., & Stark, L. J. (2010). Attention-deficit/hyperactivity disorder outcomes for children treated in community-based pediatric settings. *Archives of Pediatric Adolescent Medicine, 164,* 160–165.

Epstein, J. N., Rabiner, D., Johnson, D. E., FitzGerald, D. P., Chrisman, A., Erkanli, A., . . . Connors, K. (2007). Improving attention-deficit/hyperactivity disorder treatment outcomes through use of a collaborative consultation treatment service by community-based pediatricians. *Archives of Pediatric Adolescent Medicine, 161,* 835–840.

Fabiano, G. A., Chacko, A., Pelham, W. E., Robb, J. A., Walker, K. S., Wienke, A. L., Arnold, F., . . . Pirvics, L. (2009). A comparison of behavioral parent training programs for fathers of children with attention-deficit/hyperactivity disorder. *Behavior Therapy, 40,* 190–204.

Fabiano, G. A., Pelham, W. E., Cunningham, C. E., Yu, J., Gangloff, B., Buck, M., . . . Gera, S. (2012). A waitlist-controlled trial of behavioral parent training for fathers of children with attention-deficit/hyperactivity disorder. *Journal of Clinical Child and Adolescent Psychology, 41,* 337–345.

Fabiano, G. A., Pelham, W. E., Waschbusch, D. A., Gnagy, E. M., Lahey, B. B., Chronis, A. M., . . . Burrows-MacLean, B. (2006). A practical measure of impairment: Psychometric properties of the Impairment Rating Scale in samples of children with attention deficit hyperactivity disorder and two school-based samples. *Journal of Clinical Child and Adolescent Psychology, 35,* 369–385.

Fergusson, D. M., & Horwood, L. J. (1995). Early disruptive behavior, IQ, and later school achievement and delinquent behavior. *Journal of Abnormal Child Psychology, 23,* 183–199.

Fergusson, D. M., Horwood, L. J., & Lynskey, M. T. (1993). The effects of conduct disorder and attention deficit in middle childhood on offending and scholastic ability at age 13. *Journal of Child Psychology and Psychiatry, 34,* 899–916.

Fischer, M. (1990). Parenting stress and the child with attention-deficit hyperactivity disorder. *Journal of Clinical Child Psychology, 19,* 337–346.

Forehand, R., Long, N., Brody, G. H., & Fauber, R. (1986). Home predictors of young adolescents' school behavior and academic performance. *Child Development, 57,* 1528–1533.

Frick, P. J., Kamphaus, R. W., Lahey, B. B., Loeber, R., Christ, M. A. G., Hart, E. L., & Tannenbaum, L. E. (1991). Academic underachievement and the disruptive behavior disorders. *Journal of Consulting and Clinical Psychology, 59,* 289–294.

Froehlich, T. E., Lanphear, B. P., Epstein, J. N., Barbaresi, W. J., Katusic, S. K., & Kahn, R. S. (2007). Prevalence, recognition, and treatment of attention-deficit/hyperactivity disorder in a national sample of U.S. children. *Archives of Pediatric and Adolescent Medicine, 161,* 857–864.

Furman, W., & Giberson, R. S. (1995). Identifying links between parents and their children's sibling relationships. In S. Shulman (Ed.), *Close relationships in socioemotional development* (pp. 95–108). New York, NY: Ablex.

Gershon, J. (2002). Meta-analytic review of gender differences in ADHD. *Journal of Attention Disorders, 5,* 143–154.

Golubchik, P., Kodesh, A., & Weizman, A. (2013). Attention-deficit/hyperactivity disorder and comorbid subsyndromal depression: What is the impact of methylphenidate on mood? *Clinical Neuropharmacology, 36,* 141–145.

Greene, R. W., Biederman, J., Faraone, S. V., Sienna, M., & Garcia-Jetton, J. (1997). Adolescent outcome of boys with attention deficit/hyperactivity disorder and social disability: Results from a 4-year longitudinal follow-up study. *Journal of Consulting and Clinical Psychology, 65,* 758–767.

Gresham, F. M., & Elliott, S. N. (1989). Social skills assessment technology for LD students. *Learning Disabilities Quarterly, 12,* 141–152.

Harpin, V. A. (2005). The effect of ADHD on the life of an individual, their family, and community from preschool to adult life. *Archives of Disease in Childhood, 90,* 2–7.

Harter, S. (1985). *The Self-Perception Profile for Children: Revision of the Perceived Competence Scale for Children.* Denver, CO: University of Denver.

Hinshaw, S. P. (1992). Externalizing behavior problems and academic underachievement in childhood and adolescence: Causal relationships and underlying mechanisms. *Psychological Bulletin, 111,* 127–155.

Hinshaw, S. P. (2002). Is ADHD an impairing condition in childhood and adolescence? In P. S. Jensen & J. R. Cooper (Eds.), *Attention deficit hyperactivity disorder: State of science, best practices* (pp. 5-1–5-21). Kingston, NJ: Civil Research Institute.

Hoza, B. (2007). Peer functioning in children with ADHD. *Journal of Pediatric Psychology, 32,* 655–663.

Hoza, B., Gerdes, A. C., Mrug, S., Hinshaw, S. P., Bukowski, W. M., Golder, J. A., Arnold, L. E., . . . Wigal, T. (2005). Peer-assessed outcomes in the multimodal treatment study of children with attention deficit hyperactivity disorder. *Journal of Clinical Child and Adolescent Psychology, 34,* 74–86.

Jensen, P. S., Hinshaw, S. P., Kraemer, H. C., Lenora, N., Newcorn, J. H., Abikoff, H. B., . . . Vittiello, B. (2001). ADHD comorbidity findings from the MTA study: Comparing comorbid subgroups. *Journal of the American Academy of Child & Adolescent Psychiatry, 40,* 147–158.

Jensen, P. S., Mrazek, D., Knapp, P. K., Steinberg, L., Pfeffer, C., Schowalter, J., & Shapiro, T. (1997). Evolution and revolution in child psychiatry: ADHD as a disorder of adaption, *Journal of the American Academy of Child and Adolescent Psychiatry, 12,* 1672–1681.

Johnston, C. (1996). Parent characteristics and parent-child interactions in families of nonproblem children and ADHD children with higher and lower levels of oppositional-defiant behavior. *Journal of Abnormal Psychology, 28,* 85–104.

Johnston, C., Weiss, M. D., Murray, C., & Miller, N. V. (2013). The effects of instructions on mothers' ratings of attention-deficit/hyperactivity disorder symptoms on referred children. *Journal of Abnormal Clinical Psychology* [Epub ahead of print].

Kashdan, T. B., Jacob, R. G., Pelham, W. E., Lang, A. R., Hoza, B., Blumenthal, J. D., & Gnagy, E. M. (2004). Depression and anxiety in parents of children with ADHD and varying levels of oppositional defiant behaviors: Modeling relationships with family functioning. *Journal of Clinical Child and Adolescent Psychology, 33,* 169–181.

Kazdin, A. E., Mazurick, J. L., & Bass, D. (1993). Risk for attrition in treatment of antisocial children and families. *Journal of Clinical Child Psychology, 22,* 2–16.

Kazdin, A. E., & Wassell, G. (2000). Predictors of barriers to treatment and therapeutic change in outpatient therapy for antisocial children and their families. *Mental Health Services Research, 2,* 27–40.

Kessler, R., Adler, L., Barkley, R., Biederman, J., Connors, K. C., Demler, O., . . . Zaslavsky, A. M. (2006). The prevalence and correlates of adult ADHD in the United States: Results from the National Comorbidity Survey Replication. *American Journal of Psychiatry, 4,* 716–723.

Lewinsohn, P. M., Hoberman, H. M., & Clark, G. N. (1989). The Coping with Depression course: Review and future directions. *Canadian Journal of Behavioural Science, 21,* 470–493.

Loe, I. M., & Feldman, H. M. (2007). Academic and educational outcomes of children with ADHD. *Ambulatory Pediatrics, 7,* 82–90.

Luoma, I., Tamminen, T., Kaukonen, P., Laippala, P., Purra, K, Salmelin, R., & Almqvist, F. (2001). Longitudinal study of maternal depressive symptoms and child well-being. *Journal of the American Academy of Child & Adolescent Psychiatry, 40,* 1367–1374.

Mannuzza, S., Klein, R. G., Bessler, A., Malloy, P., & Hynes, M. E. (1997). Educational and occupational outcome of hyperactive boys grown up. *Journal of the American Academy of Child & Adolescent Psychiatry, 36,* 1222–1227.

Mash, E. J., & Johnston, C. (1983). Parental perceptions of child behavior problems, parenting self-esteem, and mothers' reported stress in younger and older hyperactive and normal children. *Journal of Consulting and Clinical Psychology, 51*(1), 86–99.

Mayes, S. D., Calhoun, S. L., & Crowell, E. W. (2000). Learning disabilities and ADHD: Overlapping spectrum disorders. *Journal of Learning Disabilities, 33,* 417–424.

Mikami, A. Y., & Hinshaw, S. P. (2006). Resilient adolescent adjustment among girls: Buffers of childhood peer rejection and attention-deficit/hyperactivity disorder. *Journal of Abnormal Child Psychology, 34,* 825–839.

Mikami, A. Y., Swaim Griggs, M., Lerner, M. D., Emeh, C. C., Reuland, M. M., Jack, A., & Anthony, M. R. (2013). A randomized trial of a classroom intervention to increase peers' social inclusion of children with attention-deficit/ hyperactivity disorder. *Journal of Consulting and Clinical Psychology, 81,* 100–112.

Molina, B. S., Hinshaw, S. P., Swanson, J. M., Arnold, L. E., Vitiello, B., Jensen, P. S., . . . MTA Cooperative Group. (2009). The MTA at 8 years: Prospective follow-up of children treated for combined-type ADHD in a multisite study. *Journal of the American Academy of Child & Adolescent Psychiatry, 48,* 484–500.

MTA Cooperative Group. (1999). A 14-month randomized clinical trial of treatment strategies for attention-deficit/hyperactivity disorder. *Archives of General Psychiatry, 56,* 1073–1086.

Musser, E. D., Galloway-Long, H. S., Frick, P. J., & Nigg, J. T. (2013). Emotion regulation and heterogeneity in attention-deficit/hyperactivity disorder. *Journal of the American Academy of Child & Adolescent Psychiatry, 52,* 163–171.

Ohan, J. L., & Johnston, C. (2002). Are the performance overestimates given by boys with ADHD self-protective? *Journal of Clinical Child and Adolescent Psychology, 31,* 230–241.

Parke, R. D., McDowell, D. J., Kim, M., Killian, C., Dennis, J., Flyr, M. R., & Wild, M. N. (2002). Fathers' contribution to children's peer relationships. In C. S. Tamis-Lemonda & N. Carbrera (Eds.), *Handbook of father involvement: Interdisciplinary perspectives* (pp. 141–167). Mahwah, NJ: Erlbaum.

Parker, J. G., & Asher, S. R. (1987). Peer relations and later personal adjustment: Are low-accepted children at risk? *Psychological Bulletin, 102,* 357–389.

Pary, R., Lewis, S., Matuschuka, P. R., Rudzinkiy, P., Safi, M., & Lippmann, S. (2002). Attention deficit disorder in adults. *Annals of Clinical Psychiatry, 14,* 105–111.

Patterson, G. R. (1982). *Coercive family process.* Eugene, OR: Castalia Press.

Pelham, W. E., & Fabiano, G. A. (2008). Evidence-based psychosocial treatments for attention-deficit/hyperactivity disorder. *Journal of Clinical Child and Adolescent Psychology, 37,* 184–214.

Pelham, W. E., Fabiano, G. A., Gnagy, E. M., Greiner, A. R., Hoza, B., & Manos, M. (2005). Comprehensive psychosocial treatment for ADHD. In E. Hibbs & P. Jensen (Eds.), *Psychosocial treatments for child and adolescent disorders: Empirically based strategies for clinical practice* (pp. 377–410). Washington, DC: American Psychological Association Press.

Pfiffner, L. J., Jourile, E. N., Brown, M. M., Etscheidt, M. A., & Kelly, J. A. (1990). Effects of problem solving therapy on outcomes of parent training for single parent families. *Child and Family Behavior Therapy, 12,* 1–11.

Pliszka, S. R. (2000). Patterns of psychiatric comorbidity and attention-deficit/hyperactivity disorder. *Child and Adolescent Clinics of North America, 9,* 525–540.

Podolski, C. L., & Nigg, J. T. (2001). Parent stress and coping in relation to child ADHD severity and associated child disruptive behavior problem. *Journal of Clinical Child Psychology, 4,* 503–513.

Price, J. M., & Dodge, K. A. (1989). Peers' contributions to children's social maladjustment: Description and intervention. In T. J. Berndt & G. W. Ladd (Eds.), *Peer relationships in child development* (pp. 341–370). New York, NY: Wiley.

Rapport, M. D., Orban, S. A., Kofler, M. J., & Friedman, L. M. (2013). Do programs designed to train working memory, other executive functions, and attention benefit children with ADHD? A meta-analytic review of cognitive, academic, and behavioral outcomes. *Clinical Psychology Review, 33,* 1237–1252.

Salmeron, P. A. (2009). Childhood and adolescent attention-deficit hyperactivity disorder: Diagnosis, clinical practice guidelines, and social implications. *Journal of the American Academy of Nurse Practitioners, 21,* 488–497.

Seidman, L. J. (2006). Neuropsychological functioning in people with ADHD across the lifespan. *Clinical Psychology Review, 26,* 446–485.

Smith, B. H., Waschbusch, D. A., Willoughby, M. T., & Evans, S. (2000). The efficacy, safety, and practicality of treatments for adolescents with attention-deficit/hyperactivity disorder (ADHD). *Clinical Child and Family Psychology Review, 3,* 243–267.

Sonuga-Barke, E., Daley, D., & Thompson, M. (2002). Does maternal ADHD reduce the effectiveness of parent training for preschool children's ADHD? *Journal of the American Academy of Child & Adolescent Psychiatry, 41,* 696–702.

Stein, R. K. (2007). Measurement of ADHD outcomes: Implications for the future. *Journal of Pediatric Psychology, 32,* 728–731.

Swanson, J. M. (1992). *School-based assessments and interventions for ADD students.* Irvine, CA: KC Publishing.

Szatmari, P., Offord, D. R., & Boyle, M. H. (1989). Ontario Child Health Study: Prevalence of attention deficit disorder with hyperactivity. *Journal of Child Psychology and Psychiatry, 30,* 219–230.

Tannock, R. (2000). Attention deficit disorders with anxiety disorders. In T. E. Brown (Ed.), *Subtypes of attention deficit disorders in children, adolescents and adults* (pp. 125–170). Washington, DC: American Psychiatric Press.

Tiano, J. D., & McNeil, C. B. (2005). The inclusion of fathers in behavioral parent training: A critical evaluation. *Child and Family Behavior Therapy, 27,* 1–28.

Todd, R. D., Huang, H., & Henderson, C. A. (2008). Poor utility of the age of onset criteria for DSM-IV attention deficit/hyperactivity disorder: Recommendations for DSM-V and ICD-11. *Journal of Child Psychology and Psychiatry, 49,* 942–949.

Webster-Stratton, C. (1994). Advancing videotape parent training: A comparison study. *Journal of Consulting and Clinical Psychology, 62,* 583–593.

Webster-Stratton, C., & Hammond, M. (1990). Predictors of treatment outcome in parent training for families with conduct problem children. *Behavior Therapy, 21,* 319–337.

Weiss, G., Hechtman, L., Milroy, T., & Perlman, T. (1985). Psychiatric status of hyperactives as adults: A controlled prospective 15-year follow-up of 63 hyperactive children. *Journal of the American Academy of Child Psychiatry, 24,* 211–220.

Weiss, M., Hechtman, L., & Weiss, G. (2000). ADHD in parents. *Journal of the American Academy of Child & Adolescent Psychiatry, 39,* 1059–1061.

Weiss, M., & Murray, C. (2003). Assessment and management of attention-deficit hyperactivity disorder in adults. *Canadian Medical Association Journal, 168,* 715–722.

Weissman, M., Gammon, D., John, K., Merikangas, K., Warner, V., Prusoff, B. A., & Sholomskas, D. (1987). Children of depressed parents: Increased psychopathology and early onset of major depression. *Journal of the American Medical Association, 10,* 847–853.

Wells, K. C., Epstein, J. N., Hinshaw, S. P., Conners, C. K., Klaric, J., Abikoff, H. B., . . . Wigal, T. (2000). Parenting and family stress treatment outcomes in attention deficit hyperactivity disorder (ADHD): An empirical analysis in the MTA study. *Journal of Abnormal Child Psychology, 28,* 543–553.

Whalen, C. K., & Henker, B. (1992). The social profile of attention deficit-hyperactivity disorder. *Child and Adolescent Psychiatric Clinics of North America, 1,* 395–410.

Wolraich, M. L., Lambert, E. W., Baumgaertel, A., Garcia-Tornel, S., Feurer, I. D., Bickman, L., & Doffing, M. A. (2003). Teachers' screening for attention-deficit/hyperactivity disorder: Comparing multinational samples on teacher ratings of ADHD. *Journal of Abnormal Child Psychology, 31,* 445–455.

Wymbs, B. T., Pelham, W. E., Molina, B. S., Gnagy, E. M., Wilson, T. K., & Greenhouse, J. B. (2008). Rate and predictors of divorce among parents of youth with ADHD. *Journal of Consulting and Clinical Psychology, 5,* 735–744.

CHAPTER 13

Treatment of Conduct Problems and Disruptive Behavior Disorders

NICOLE P. POWELL, JOHN E. LOCHMAN, CAROLINE L. BOXMEYER, LUIS ALBERTO
JIMENEZ-CAMARGO, MEGAN E. CRISLER, AND SARA L. STROMEYER

BRIEF OVERVIEW OF DISORDERS

Conduct problems and disruptive behaviors are some of the most common reasons that children and adolescents are referred for psychological treatment (Nelson, Finch, & Hart, 2006). In the short term, these behaviors exact a toll, leading, for example, to peer rejection (Coie, Dodge, & Kupersmidt, 1990), academic problems (Risi, Gerhardstein, & Kistner, 2003), and family discord. Long-term effects are perhaps even more concerning, given documented associations between youth conduct problems and poor outcomes in adolescence and adulthood that include substance abuse, delinquency, and incarceration (Brook & Newcomb, 1995). Because of the serious negative implications for disruptive behaviors in children and adolescents, effective intervention is critically important.

Conduct problems tend to be particularly treatment resistant (Kazdin, 2000), underscoring the need for high-quality interventions with documented outcome effects when treating this population. Increasingly, the importance of evidence-based treatments (EBTs) has been recognized in improving the likelihood of successful intervention for childhood disorders. Through a comprehensive literature review employing strict criteria for well-conducted treatment outcome studies, Eyberg, Nelson, and Boggs (2008) have identified 11 EBTs (several of which have multiple versions meeting the EBT criteria) for youth with disruptive behavior. In this chapter, we review each of the identified programs and address topics related to parental involvement, adaptations and modifications of EBTs, and measuring treatment effects. A clinical case example from the Coping Power program is provided to demonstrate treatment processes and procedures.

EVIDENCE-BASED APPROACHES: CHILDREN

EBTs for children can be broadly categorized into cognitive behavioral and behavioral approaches. However, there is substantial overlap between these categories and many behavioral programs have cognitive-behavioral elements (e.g., teaching parents stress management strategies), while most cognitive-behavioral protocols incorporate operant principles.

Research on the Coping Power program described in this chapter has been supported by grants from the National Institute on Drug Abuse (RO1 DA 08453; RO1 DA023156; R41 DA022184–01; R41 DA022184–01S1; RO1 DA 16135), the Centers for Disease Control and Prevention (R49/CCR418569), the Center for Substance Abuse Prevention (RO1 DA 08453), the Office of Juvenile Justice and Delinquency Prevention (2006JLFX0232), and the National Institute of Mental Health (P30 MH086043).

Cognitive Behavioral Approaches

Cognitive behavioral interventions for children with conduct problems generally contain common elements, including emotional awareness, anger management, problem solving, and social skills components. Meta-analytic studies provide support for cognitive behavioral treatment, with effect sizes in the medium to large range (for review see Nock, 2003). When these interventions include both child and parent components, positive effects tend to be broader and more robust over time than protocols with either component alone (e.g., Webster-Stratton & Hammond, 1997).

Anger Control Training

Anger Control Training (Lochman, Barry, & Pardini, 2003) is intended for school-age children and can be delivered in an individual or group-based setting. It is based on social information processing theory (SIP), noting that children assess their environment, interpret their surroundings, and generate goals. As children generate these goals, they are thought to evaluate the consequence of each action and decide on the best response. SIP would indicate that, for children with disruptive behaviors, there are mistakes occurring in this stepwise progression of responses, with actions and goals not being accurately assessed.

During Anger Control Training, children are taught to use problem-solving strategies across hypothetical situations as well as personal, real-life scenarios that they may encounter at school or at home. Behavioral rehearsal of these strategies is relied on earlier in treatment, but in vivo practice is later used to arouse the children's feelings of anger, providing them with the opportunity to practice their new skills within sessions.

Since the inception of Anger Control Training, Anger Coping and Coping Power have been developed as more targeted programs, utilizing and refining the basic tenets of Anger Control Training. Coping Power is the most comprehensive program, including 34 child sessions (Lochman, Wells, & Lenhart, 2008) and a 16-session parent component (Wells, Lochman, & Lenhart, 2008). Several randomized controlled trials of Coping Power have demonstrated its effectiveness in reducing delinquent behaviors and improving teacher reports of behavior, with effects maintained after 1 year (Lochman & Wells, 2003, 2004; Powell et al., 2011).

Problem-Solving Skills Training and Parent-Management Training

Problem-Solving Skills Training and Parent-Management Training (PSST and PMT) are manual-based treatments designed for children between 7 and 12 years of age (Kazdin, 2010). The treatment approaches are based on cognitive behavioral and behavioral concepts. PSST focuses primarily on the child's cognitive experience and how the child is interpreting the environment. In contrast, PMT focuses on parent–child interactions and how parental behavior may modify or alter the child's behavioral patterns (Kazdin, 2010).

Standard administration of PSST involves 12 sessions that focus specifically on problem-solving strategies. An example of this strategy involves four key questions or directives that may be repeated multiple times for a given problem:

1. What am I supposed to do?
2. I need to figure out what to do.
3. What happens when I do this?
4. Make a choice.

Standard administration of PMT also involves 12 sessions. Topics covered during these sessions include positive reinforcement strategies, time-out procedures, and other behavior-shaping strategies (i.e., ignoring, compromising, consequences, etc.) (Kazdin, 2010).

Both PSST and PMT have been assessed as reliable and efficacious across multiple studies either in isolation or together, with the combination of the two improving overall treatment outcomes (Bushman & Peacock, 2010; Eyberg et al., 2008; Kazdin, 2010). Studies examining the effectiveness of PSST have concluded that it produces improvement in both home and school behavior (Kazdin, Bass, Siegel, & Thomas, 1989).

Incredible Years

The Incredible Years (IY) (Webster-Stratton & Reid, 2010) curriculum is primarily designed for children 3 to 10 years of age who present with clinically significant externalizing problems. It is based heavily on cognitive social learning theory and focuses on social/emotional deficits observed in children with conduct-related disorders (Dodge & Price, 1994). The curriculum has modules for parents, teachers, and children that use a variety of methods including video modeling, discussion opportunities, and rehearsal techniques.

Parent modules are based on a 12-week program targeting interactive play, reinforcement strategies, and limit setting, with an optional supplemental program to address specific family problems (i.e., depression, marital discord, etc.). The teacher modules target classroom management skills, including reinforcement strategies and problem-solving strategies. Finally, the child module provides lessons on home and school behaviors, covering topics that include social skills, problem solving, and appropriate classroom behavior.

Published effects for the treatment model are strong, demonstrating reductions in behavioral difficulties at both home and school (Webster-Stratton, Reid, & Hammond, 2004). A randomized trial reported preventive functions of the model across 153 teachers and 1,768 students, indicating that use of the model produced fewer behavior problems across intervention classrooms when compared to control classrooms (Webster-Stratton, Reid, & Stoolmiller, 2008). Similar to other treatments, the combined effect of implementing both parent and child modules remains stronger than treatment effects of either in isolation (Webster-Stratton & Hammond, 1997). Regarding lasting effects of the treatment, a 2011 study reported that at a 10-year follow-up, children receiving IY were less likely to display conduct problems than was predicted by their early-onset conduct problems (Webster-Stratton, Rinaldi, & Jamilia, 2011).

Behavioral Approaches

Behavioral interventions for child conduct problems are characterized by their emphasis on training parents to implement effective behavior modification strategies. Typically, parents learn to reinforce their children's appropriate behaviors and to address problem behaviors with approaches such as ignoring, natural consequences, and time out. In a review of 79 behavioral parent training outcome studies, Maughan, Christiansen, Jenson, Olympia, and Clark (2005) concluded that this type of treatment is effective for reducing behavioral problems in children, and that results tend to be maintained over time.

Helping the Noncompliant Child and Parent–Child Interaction Therapy

Helping the Noncompliant Child (HNC) (Forehand & McMahon, 1981; McMahon & Forehand, 2003) and Parent–Child Interaction Therapy (PCIT) (Brinkmeyer & Eyberg, 2003) are manual-based treatments designed for 2- to 7-year-old children to address issues related specifically to parent–child interactions. Both are based on the Hanf model (Hanf & Kling, 1973) of parent training and may be described as having two phases: (1) the parent learns to apply positive attention skills (i.e., labeling and praise); (2) the parent learns discipline strategies to address unwanted behaviors.

Both models have routinely been cited as being highly effective for use with conduct-related disorders. HNC has been evaluated in over 40 studies that have documented short-term and long-term (up to 14 years posttreatment) effects on child behavior (for a review, see McMahon & Forehand, 2003). Two randomized controlled trials of PCIT have demonstrated positive effects on child disruptive behaviors and parent–child interactions (Bagner & Eyberg, 2007; Schuhmann, Foote, Eyberg, Boggs, & Algina, 1998), and gains have been found to persist up to 6 years posttreatment (Hood & Eyberg, 2003).

Parent-Management Training Oregon Model

Parent-Management Training Oregon Model (PMTO) (Patterson, Reid, Jones, & Conger, 1975) is a treatment approach that teaches parents how to implement specific behavior modification plans that are seated in six key areas:

1. Skill encouragement
2. Positive reinforcement
3. Discipline
4. Monitoring
5. Problem solving
6. Positive involvement

The model is based on social interaction learning, which posits that negative environmental/relationship factors may adversely affect child interaction styles (Reid, Patterson, & Snyder, 2002).

Numerous studies have documented affective change in parents after being taught the model, with these outcomes being directly related to reductions in child behavior problems (e.g., DeGarmo, Patterson, & Forgatch, 2004; Forgatch, Patterson, & DeGarmo, 2005; Kazdin, 1997). Additionally, long-term follow-up studies have indicated that PMTO may be effective at reducing later adolescent delinquency (Forgatch, Patterson, DeGarmo, & Beldavs, 2009).

Positive Parenting Program

The Positive Parenting Program (Triple P) (Sanders, 1999) is a systemically modified treatment plan that allows for five different levels of treatment intensity/focus, ranging from universal prevention to enhanced formats. Standard Individual and Enhanced Triple P are the most extensively studied and, as such, are the levels referenced when Triple P is considered an evidence-based approach. The skills targeted within Triple P include common parenting skills (i.e., positive attention, reinforcement, and limits) as well as problem-solving and coping strategies for parents and children. A detailed meta-analysis documented lasting effects of Triple P on reducing disruptive behaviors over a 12-month period. Results also indicated few moderators, revealing the potential validity of the model across diverse families and children (de Graaf, Speetjens, Smit, de Wolff, & Tavecchio, 2008). A randomized-controlled study showed significant intervention effects on parent–child relationships and disruptive behavior, suggesting that Triple P may have lasting, long-term effects (Wiggins, Sofronoff, & Sanders, 2009).

EVIDENCE-BASED APPROACHES: ADOLESCENTS

In addition to these evidence-based approaches for children, several programs have been developed specifically for adolescents with conduct problems, who are at risk for negative long-term sequelae such as school failure, dropout, substance abuse, arrests, restrictive placements, and chronic delinquent or violent offenses (e.g., Brook & Newcomb, 1995).

School-Based Group Approaches

Schools can be an important setting for intervention, as students with conduct problems often demonstrate behavioral problems in the school setting and may also exhibit academic deficits and attendance problems. School-based interventions for youth conduct problems have been shown to effect positive changes on behavior (e.g., Reese, Prout, Zirkelback, & Anderson, 2010) and academic outcomes (e.g., Lochman, Boxmeyer, et al., 2012). EBTs can allow schools to deliver services in an efficient and effective manner, which may be particularly important given schools' limited resources.

Group Assertiveness Training

In 1976, Winship and Kelley developed a three-part verbal response model of assertiveness, comprising an empathy statement, a conflict statement, and an action statement. Assertiveness training for conduct problems is based on the premise that adolescents exhibiting frequent aggression lack the appropriate skills to deal with interpersonal frustrations. Therefore, assertiveness teaches them more adaptive and socially acceptable ways to express their feelings, from which follows increased self-control.

Huey and Rank (1984) conducted a randomized trial comparing Counselor-Led and Peer-Led Group Assertiveness Training to counselor- and peer-led discussion groups and to a no-treatment control group. Participants were eighth- and ninth-grade African American boys referred for chronic classroom disruption. Compared to the other conditions, boys who received Group Assertiveness Training demonstrated significantly less aggression posttreatment, and analyses revealed that professional and peer counselors were equally effective (Huey & Rank, 1984).

Rational Emotive Mental Health Program

Similar to Group Assertive Training, the Rational Emotive Mental Health Program is based on the idea that adolescents who lack the skills needed to achieve in school can improve their performance by learning self-realization strategies. Block (1978) conducted a randomized trial with minority 10th and 11th graders referred for poor school performance (e.g., low grades, absences, disruptive behavior). Students were assigned to a rational emotive group, a human relations group (i.e., discussion of psychodynamic topics), or a no-treatment control group. The rational emotive sessions included dramatic-emotive exercises, honest expression of feelings, direct confrontation, and risk-taking experiences. Emphasis was placed on cognitive restructuring and self-questioning through these exercises, role-plays, group discussions, and homework assignments. Compared to the other groups, students who received the rational emotive program demonstrated fewer disruptive behaviors and absences and improved grades posttreatment and at a 4-month follow-up (Block, 1978).

Family- and Community-Based Approaches

Given the treatment-resistant nature and pervasive effects of youth conduct problems, interventions that are intensive and comprehensive are often warranted. These interventions, which incorporate a variety of approaches in multiple settings, seek to reduce behavior problems and improve functioning by addressing the contextual processes that contribute to youth conduct problems.

Multisystemic Therapy

Multisystemic Therapy (MST) is a family- and community-based intervention for adolescents with antisocial behavior (Henggeler & Lee, 2003; Henggeler, Schoenwald, Borduin, Rowland, & Cunningham, 1998). MST assumes that adolescents with serious behavioral issues have problems in various settings and that the most effective treatment should intervene within and across these systems. MST combines several evidence-based approaches (i.e., cognitive behavioral, behavioral, parent training, family therapy, school consultation, peer intervention) as needed for each individual. Therapists adapt the approach for each case, and a core focus involves working with the family and addressing the adolescent's role within the system and interrelationships among contexts. Treatment planning is guided by nine core principles (e.g., "Focus on systemic strengths," "Promote responsible behavior and decrease irresponsible behavior among family members," "Interventions should be developmentally appropriate"). Intervention occurs within the adolescent's environment (e.g., home, school); therapists are available whenever needed and are in contact with the family at least weekly.

Extensive research has examined the effects of MST with adolescents demonstrating juvenile offenses, substance abuse, and psychiatric crises (i.e., homicidal, suicidal, psychotic), as well as with maltreating families (Henggeler & Lee, 2003). A randomized trial compared MST to usual community services for adolescents at risk for incarceration and found that, 1-year posttreatment, those who received MST reported fewer conduct problems and were less likely to have been arrested or incarcerated (Henggeler, Melton, & Smith, 1992). Another study randomized seriously delinquent adolescents to MST and alternative community treatments and found that the MST group demonstrated fewer conduct problems, decreased parent psychopathology, and improved parent–youth interaction (Borduin et al., 1995).

Multidimensional Treatment Foster Care

Multidimensional Treatment Foster Care (MTFC) also is a comprehensive and systemic intervention targeting chronic delinquent behavior in adolescents, with the goal of preventing more restrictive placements (e.g., residential treatment) and ultimately returning to the biological family, if possible (Chamberlain & Smith, 2003). For 6 to 9 months, adolescents are placed with foster parents who have been trained to enforce clear, consistent rules and to implement a behavioral point system. Foster parents receive ongoing support, and adolescents meet with therapists for individual issues (e.g., problem-solving training, anger management, social skills building) and with behavioral support specialists who reinforce prosocial behaviors in the community. The biological family or after-care personnel also receive parent training to support the adolescent's transition back into the community following treatment.

Two randomized trials have demonstrated that MTFC is more effective than usual care for adolescents with histories of chronic delinquency. Chamberlain and Reid (1998) compared MTFC to group care placements that involved individual, group, and family therapy. Boys who received MTFC had shorter placements, fewer runaways and arrests, and decreased incarceration and delinquency at 1 year postintervention. At a long-term follow-up, MTFC boys had lower arrest rates than comparison peers (Chamberlain, Fisher, & Moore, 2002). Additionally, Leve, Chamberlain, and Reid (2005) randomized adolescent girls to either MTFC or care as usual (e.g., group homes, hospital, inpatient substance abuse facilities) and found that MTFC girls demonstrated a greater decrease in arrests and fewer hospital days at 1 year postintervention.

PARENT INVOLVEMENT IN TREATMENT

A large body of research has demonstrated that certain parenting practices place children at risk for disruptive behavior. These practices include:

- Nonresponsive parenting at age 1
- Coercive, escalating cycles of harsh parental directives and child noncompliance
- Harsh, inconsistent discipline
- Unclear directions and commands
- Lack of warmth and involvement
- Lack of parental supervision and monitoring as children approach adolescence (e.g., Patterson, Reid, & Dishion, 1992; Shaw, Keenan, & Vondra, 1994)

Parenting programs targeting children's conduct problems often address these variables. A meta-analysis conducted in 2008 investigated the relative importance of various treatment components of parenting programs for children's conduct problems. Promoting positive parent–child interactions and instruction in appropriate limit setting were identified as key factors associated with prevention and remediation of conduct problems (Kaminski, Valle, Filene, & Boyle, 2008). As might be expected, all of the EBTs with parenting components described earlier address these processes. The meta-analysis further identified active practice as an important component for treatment effectiveness. Notably, the majority of the EBTs described here also incorporate in vivo training sessions that include both parents and children.

The importance of including parents in the treatment of children's behavior problems was further demonstrated by the results of a recent meta-analysis that investigated the relative effects of child-only interventions and programs that also included a parenting component. In an examination of 48 studies, Dowell and Ogles (2010) found that the addition of a parenting program resulted in significant benefits in treatment outcomes over child-only interventions. Other research has examined how parent attendance affects treatment outcomes, with results demonstrating greater improvements for children of parents who attend more treatment sessions (e.g., Lavigne et al., 2008; Webster-Stratton & Reid, 2010).

Although current research supports a strong association between effective parenting practices and positive outcomes for children with externalizing behaviors, several barriers impede parental involvement in treatment. With regard to treatment attrition and adherence, lower socioeconomic status is associated with poorer parental engagement (Morrissey-Kane & Prinz, 1999). Likewise, parents who appear uncooperative and negative and who believe that they are ineffective caregivers or that their child's behavior is unchangeable are not as easily engaged in treatment and also tend to be less involved in their children's lives outside of treatment (Frankel & Simmons, 1992; Morrissey-Kane & Prinz, 1999). With regard to externalizing behavior, the literature suggests that parental psychopathology increases negative perceptions, which in turn yield lower parental engagement and less positive involvement (Dowell & Ogles, 2010; Morrissey-Kane & Prinz, 1999). Given these associations, it is not surprising that children of parents who perceive more treatment barriers tend to show less behavioral improvement when receiving treatment (Morrissey-Kane & Prinz, 1999).

Despite these barriers and challenges, some strategies and practices have shown promise in promoting parental involvement in treatment. Some interventions have incorporated child care, transportation services, meals/snacks, make-up sessions, and monetary incentives to help improve parental involvement and engagement (e.g., Dumas, Nissley-Tsiopinis, & Moreland, 2007). Although these approaches have improved involvement in some cases, parent engagement remains a significant challenge in the treatment of child conduct problems. Therefore, continued research on factors that promote parental involvement is critical to the effective delivery of EBTs.

ADAPTATIONS AND MODIFICATIONS

The use of EBTs in clinical settings sometimes elicits concerns about the relevance of the program for specific groups or individual clients. Such concerns may arise out of a perspective that EBTs are inflexible protocols that require rigid adherence (Kendall, Gosch, Furr, & Sood, 2008). When clients differ from the original target group in some important way (e.g., comorbidity, cultural issues), a given EBT may be viewed as inappropriate or potentially ineffective. Fortunately, with creativity and flexibility, EBTs often can be adapted to address clinical concerns not originally encompassed within the program (Kendall et al., 2008). The next examples from Coping Power illustrate how flexible adaptations can increase a program's relevance in different settings and to diverse target groups.

Service Setting Adaptations

Originally designed for implementation in schools, Coping Power has been adapted for use in several different settings. The Utrecht Coping Power Program (UCPP), developed in the Netherlands, involved implementation with youth diagnosed with disruptive behavior disorders at outpatient mental health clinics. Modifications included a reduced number of sessions, addition of active treatment strategies to increase engagement of youth with attention problems, and increased communication with parents about skills taught to youth. Comparison of the UCPP and usual clinic care in a randomized controlled trial indicated that both groups exhibited significantly lower levels of disruptive behavior, but improvements in parent-reported overt aggression and in parenting variables were significantly greater for the UCPP group (van de Wiel, Matthys, Cohen-Kettenis, & van Engeland, 2003; van de Wiel et al., 2007). After 4 years, both treatments had preventive effects on delinquency, but UCPP youth were less likely to have used tobacco or marijuana (Zonnevylle-Bender, Matthys, van de Wiel, & Lochman, 2007).

Clinician-researchers in Canada adapted Coping Power for an intensive after-school program for children with severe behavioral and emotional difficulties. The frequency of the child and parent sessions was increased, but the overall number of sessions was reduced, and Coping Power strategies were incorporated into the overall program, allowing for a unified treatment approach. In a pilot intervention study, parents reported reductions in children's conduct problems, improvements in parenting skills, and reduced functional impairment (Lochman, Powell, et al., 2012).

Coping Power has also been adapted for deaf students with aggressive behavior at a residential school. Materials and teaching strategies were adapted to be more visually focused, and concepts were presented through spatial means. Teaching and residential staff participated in an adapted version of the Coping Power parent component. Posttreatment assessment of Coping Power participants versus students assigned to a wait-list condition indicated that the Coping Power group showed greater teacher-rated behavioral improvements and significant improvements in their social problem-solving skills and communication skills (Lochman et al., 2001).

Adaptations to the Delivery Format

Some researchers and clinicians have expressed concern about the potential for contagion of conduct problems ("deviancy training") within group-based treatments for disruptive youth. Although iatrogenic effects have not been found for group-based Coping Power, whether potentially negative group processes might reduce treatment effects is not known. Our research group has modified the Coping Power child program for individual administration and is currently conducting a randomized controlled trial comparing the group and individual formats. In the individually administered intervention, clinicians take a more active role in role-plays and provide feedback and examples that might otherwise be offered by peers. A prior small-scale randomized controlled trial suggested that intervention formats may have differential effects on different types of outcomes. For example, individual administration of Coping Power appeared to yield greater improvements on adult-rated aggression, while group administration appeared to have stronger effects on social-cognitive and self-regulation outcomes.

Given frequent concerns about client treatment attendance, third-party payer limits on length of treatment, and minimizing educational disruption in school-based interventions, Coping Power has been modified in several different ways with the goal of improving overall program efficiency. For example, Lochman and Wells (2004) assigned at-risk boys to one of three conditions (Coping Power child component only, Coping Power child and parent components, or care as usual) to examine the relative effects of the full versus child-only intervention. Results at 1-year follow-up suggested that while the parent component was critical for preventing delinquent behaviors and substance use, the child component appeared to be responsible for teacher-rated behavioral improvements.

In another study, both Coping Power components were retained but the protocol was reduced to 24 child sessions and 10 parent sessions. Outcome results of a randomized controlled trial revealed significant reductions in teacher-rated externalizing behavior when parent attendance at parent meetings was controlled (Lochman, Boxmeyer, Powell, Roth, & Windle, 2006). After 3 years, sustained and increased reductions were evident in teacher-rated externalizing behavior, proactive and reactive aggression, and psychopathy scores in comparison to control children (Lochman, Boxmeyer, Powell, & Qu, 2011), providing support for the ability of the abbreviated program to effect meaningful changes.

A hybrid version of Coping Power is currently in development that includes substantially fewer face-to-face sessions with clinicians, supplemented with self-administered Internet-based instruction. In addition to improving the overall efficiency of the program, the use of Internet-delivered media is expected to enhance children's and parents' engagement in the program and their retention of information. Another hybrid project incorporates the Family Check Up (FCU) (Dishion & Kavanagh, 2005) with the Coping Power parent component (Herman et al., 2012). The FCU is an assessment that can be used to identify specific Coping Power parenting strategies that address individual family concerns. In this manner, overall treatment length may be reduced, and the consistent delivery of relevant information is likely to enhance parental engagement.

Developmental and Cultural Adaptations

Recent modifications to the Coping Power curriculum have included both upward and downward extensions designed to expand the program's relevance to early adolescent and preschool populations. The early adolescent version of Coping Power includes minor changes to activities (e.g., having students role-play rather than use puppets) as well as newly added content (e.g., cyber-bullying, communication skills, relationship issues) to improve developmental relevance to middle school students. The Coping Power parent component has also been modified for use with parents of preschoolers. Preliminary analyses from a pilot study revealed reductions in preschool teachers' reports of behavior problems and callous-unemotional traits as well as improvements in perceived competence, emotion regulation, and receptive language.

In addition to Dutch, Coping Power has been translated into Spanish and Italian and has been culturally adapted for use with Mexican American children (O'Donnell, Jurecska, & Dyer, 2012). Evaluation of the program adapted for Mexican American students, which included culturally relevant examples and provided a culturally appropriate context for material, revealed no significant outcome differences between Mexican American students who received the adapted program and European American students who received the standard Coping Power program.

Overall, the results of several outcome studies involving modified versions of the Coping Power program indicate that, when thoughtfully planned and implemented with fidelity to the treatment model, adaptations can be applied effectively to broaden the dissemination of EBTs.

MEASURING TREATMENT EFFECTS

The issues in measuring treatment effects are relatively similar for prevention and treatment of conduct problems and for other types of psychopathology in childhood and adolescence, and include a focus on targets of treatment and measurement issues, on issues related to timing of measurement, and on issues related to the timing of termination of treatment. In this section we will discuss measurement issues in intervention research and clinical practice.

Treatment Targets and Measures

Three of the key concerns in measuring treatment effects involve identifying (1) the specific outcomes that will be hypothesized, (2) central active mechanisms that are the critical targets of an intervention, and (3) how many measures and tests of treatment effects will be conducted. Thus, for interventions directed at conduct problems in children, the key behavioral outcomes likely will be measures of aggression and conduct problems. Depending on the nature of the intervention and the age range of the children, other key planned outcomes can involve measures of delinquent acts and arrests, of substance use initiation and substance abuse, and of academic adjustment. For example, in our research on the Coping Power and Fast Track programs, which target at-risk children and which aim to have proximal reductions in aggressive and externalizing behaviors, we have also found intervention effects across time on juvenile arrest rates (Conduct Problems Prevention Research Group [CPPRG], 2010) and self-reported delinquency (Lochman & Wells, 2003, 2004), on substance use according to parent and self-reports (Lochman & Wells, 2003, 2004), and on language arts grades in subsequent years (Lochman, Boxmeyer, et al., 2012). Children's aggressive behaviors are risk predictors for adolescents' later antisocial and academic outcomes, and hence it is sensible to assess a developmental cascade of outcome behaviors that follow anticipated behavioral risk trajectories. This measurement plan would certainly be expected for typical prevention research but also is an important issue in treatment research. For example, as described earlier, the Utrecht Coping Power project included assessment of direct intervention effects on aggression as well as follow-up evaluation documenting the program's preventive effect in reducing later marijuana and tobacco use (Zonnevylle-Bender et al., 2007).

A second measurement issue involves identifying and measuring key active mechanisms and processes leading to and maintaining a type of psychopathology (such as conduct problems in children) and the intervention targets designed to address that type of psychopathology. These active mechanisms typically are clearly apparent in the conceptual model describing the development of the disorder. In the externalizing disorders, such active mechanisms involve aspects of child (hostile attributions; social problem-solving deficits; dysfunctional outcome expectations for aggression and other types of behaviors) and family functioning (harsh, inconsistent parenting; weak parental monitoring and supervision). In clinical settings, identifying the active mechanisms in the child and family that will be addressed over upcoming sessions is an important element of an effective treatment plan. Clinical assessment of child progress in treatment should include measures of these targeted active mechanisms in addition to measures of the behavioral outcomes. In intervention research, this focus on measuring active mechanisms that lead to behavior change essentially addresses a critically important need in the field, and that involves greater attention to processes that mediate intervention effects (La Greca, Silverman, & Lochman, 2009). For example, in our Coping Power research, we have found that intervention effects on delinquency, substance use, and behavioral outcomes at a 1-year follow-up were the result of improvements in key mediators during the intervention period, including children's attributions and outcome expectations and parents' ability to discipline in a consistent manner (Lochman & Wells, 2002).

A third measurement issue involves making decisions about how many measures to collect, and two related topics that involve multimethod-multisource measurement models and transdiagnostic intervention effects should be considered. In both clinical and intervention research, there are clear advantages for having multiple measures of behavioral outcomes. Having behavioral ratings from teachers as well as parents can indicate whether the behavioral problems are cross-situational and can directly affect the focus of intervention (e.g., need for school consultation). From an intervention research perspective, a central tension involves concerns about collecting too many varied measures, which can lead to intervention analyses that seem to be fishing expeditions, versus concerns about limited and potentially biased measures that could confound understanding of intervention effects. Obtaining measures from different sources (parents, teachers, children, observers, school and court records) helps to reduce the likelihood of biased findings (especially if the measures are collected only from individuals directly involved in the treatment). Teacher ratings during follow-up periods and observation measures can be particularly useful nonbiased measures in intervention research because typically they are not influenced by the sources' knowledge of intervention involvement.

Another reason to have multiple outcome measures, for both clinical and research purposes, is to assess for transdiagnostic intervention effects. Transdiagnostic interventions apply the same underlying treatment principles across different disorders (Clark & Taylor, 2009). However, as Clark and Taylor (2009) note, the difference between transdiagnostic and disorder-specific protocols can be a matter of degree. Thus, disorder-specific interventions, such as Coping Power, may have certain key transdiagnostic elements (Lochman, Powell, Boxmeyer, Ford, & Minney, 2013). A focused intervention like Coping Power, which targets certain risk factors, can have an influence on other outcomes (besides aggression) for three reasons: (1) Some other outcomes follow from aggression (e.g., secondary depression in the child, and perhaps even in the parent); (2) some common active mechanisms can influence multiple outcomes (e.g., social problem solving can affect aggression and depression); and (3) aggressive children commonly have co-occurring problems (reactive aggressive children can have co-occurring anxiety). As a result, assessing for anxiety and depression outcome effects even with an intervention targeted for conduct problems can make sense.

Timing of Measurement

Multiple measurement points for children's externalizing behaviors are important for both clinical and research purposes. In clinical settings, frequent (even weekly) and regular assessments of children's aggression or their attainment of positive behavioral goals can indicate whether they are progressively improving, whether their behavioral improvements have stalled, or whether they are not responding in a consistently positive way to the intervention. Each of these observed behavioral patterns can lead to key intervention changes. Multiple assessments, including over longer-term follow-up periods, are also critically important for intervention research and can indicate whether earlier changes are maintained and even amplified during a follow-up period and whether there might be late-blooming effects. For example, the Fast Track project had limited positive outcomes during the middle school years (CPPRG, 2010a), but children who participated in Fast Track had significant relative reductions in their rates of juvenile arrests later during adolescence (CPPRG, 2010b). Follow-up assessments can be scheduled on regular (e.g., yearly) intervals or can be initiated at key developmental transition points, such as the transitions into middle school, into high school, into driving age, and into young adulthood, as new risk and protective factors emerge at these transition times.

When to Terminate Treatment

Although some interventions, such as MST, are purposefully meant to be delivered in a tailored way that is adapted for individuals, most EBTs for children with conduct problems are manualized and have structured treatment time lengths, often fairly lengthy and lasting for 6 months or more. It is incumbent on intervention research, however, to test whether such overall treatment lengths are necessary to produce positive effects and whether all intervention components are necessary. For example, we recently have found that an abbreviated version of Coping Power (one third shorter than the full program) has long-term intervention effects on children's externalizing behavior in school settings (Lochman, Baden, et al., 2013) that are similar to long-term follow-up effects with the full Coping Power program (Lochman, Wells, Qu, & Chen, 2013). It also is essential for intervention research to determine how structured EBTs can be delivered in tailored and adaptive ways, using components such as the FCU to assist with intervention tailoring (Herman et al., 2012). In addition to more flexibly determining the necessary length of intervention for particular children and families, it will be useful to consider whether periodic follow-up booster sessions may be useful. This latter issue should be an important area of focus in its own right, however. Although it seems intuitive that booster interventions should be routinely helpful, research has been limited on this topic, and there are indications that booster interventions, when not structured enough and lacking in parental involvement, have not been useful in some long-term assessments of intervention outcomes (Lochman et al., in press).

CLINICAL CASE EXAMPLE

Wes (identifying information has been altered to protect confidentiality) is a 10-year-old boy in fourth grade. Wes's parents, William and Cynthia, have always found him to be more difficult to handle than their other two children. When he was younger, Wes would throw prolonged temper tantrums when he did not get his way. Now Wes often refuses to follow his parents' directions and becomes angry at the slightest provocation. Wes's parents are tired of dealing with his challenging behavior, which is causing strain in their marriage. Cynthia feels guilty about how often she yells and argues with Wes and wishes that they had a better relationship. She is under quite a bit of stress from working full time and raising three children; William has been out of work for several months.

Wes is also having difficulty at school. His teacher complains that he is disrespectful to her and to his classmates and that he fails to complete his work. Wes was recently suspended from the school bus for fighting. Following the bus incident, Cynthia made an appointment with Dr. Schumann, a local psychologist. Upon assessing Wes's and the family's needs, Dr. Schumann recommended that Wes and his parents participate in the Coping Power program.

The child group was run by Ms. Jackson and Ms. Stanton, both licensed professional counselors. There were four other children in the group. The leaders explained that the purpose of the group was to teach the children skills that would help them meet their personal goals, such as learning to cope with strong feelings and to handle difficult situations. The leaders asked the children to identify a long-term goal that they would like to accomplish. Wes had not given much thought to the future, but his group leaders helped him identify that he would like to join the school drama club. They also helped him think of some short-term goals that he would need to accomplish in order to join the drama club, including improving his grades in social studies, following the teacher's directions more often, and getting along better with classmates. On his first weekly goal sheet, Wes decided that he would set a goal of completing all of his social studies work that week.

During the first parent group, Wes's parents felt relieved to meet other parents who were struggling with similar challenges. Dr. Schumann had some good suggestions about how to develop routines to support academic success. Cynthia and William both agreed that they needed to be more proactive about communicating with Wes's teacher and about making sure he kept track of his assignments and completed his homework each day. Cynthia felt especially relieved when William offered to take responsibility for working with Wes when he got home from school and for requiring Wes to complete his homework before he could play video games.

At home, William made sure to check on Wes's homework each day. Wes became frustrated and yelled at his father one day when he wanted to play video games instead of doing his work. When his dad reminded him of the goal he had set for himself, Wes (grudgingly) finished his homework. Wes was proud when he earned points for meeting his short-term goal at the next Coping Power meeting. The leaders introduced a new unit on identifying emotions and situations that trigger emotional arousal. Wes said that he felt very angry when his father made him do his homework instead of playing video games. Ms. Jackson described to the group that our bodies give us "clues" when we are having a strong feeling and that we can be like "detectives" and notice these clues when they first appear. Wes shared that his face had felt hot and that he felt like yelling when he became angry with his dad. Over the next few sessions, the group leaders taught the children specific strategies for handling emotional arousal, including using distraction to redirect thoughts from the trigger event, using deep breathing to relax, and using coping self-statements to reduce anger-evoking thoughts. The group members practiced these skills with hypothetical and real-life anger triggers during several child group sessions.

During the next few parent sessions, Dr. Schumann led the group in a discussion about the stress of parenting and helped the parents identify ways they could take care of themselves. Cynthia complimented William for becoming more involved in Wes's homework and said that this change had helped her feel less stressed. William agreed to be responsible for getting the children to bed three nights a week so that Cynthia could go for a jog. Dr. Schumann praised them for committing to these changes and pointed out the connection between parents' own mood and the way in which they interact with their children, particularly around challenging child behaviors. Dr. Schumann encouraged the parents to support their children's use of new emotional coping strategies and described the strategies that their children had been learning.

In the next portion of the child group, the leaders worked with group members on learning to take others' perspectives. Wes shared that he frequently became upset with his sister for monopolizing the computer. He felt like she stayed on the computer longer than she was supposed to just to make him angry. With assistance from the group, Wes was able to think of other explanations for his sister's computer use: She had a lot of schoolwork that required the computer, and she also enjoyed communicating with her friends via the computer. Ms. Jackson used this example to illustrate that the way we respond to others often depends on whether we have taken time to see the situation from their perspective. Ms. Jackson also referred back to this example in a later session on problem solving. The group learned to brainstorm a range of solutions when they were having a problem and to think ahead about the consequence of each solution before deciding which one to pick. Wes said that he usually yelled at his sister when she was on the computer too long, which caused him to lose his computer time. He thought that if they posted a schedule for the computer, they might argue less. Another solution might be to try to save money and buy himself a computer, but that could take a long time. The group voted on posting a schedule for the computer as the choice likely to work out best. The group practiced this problem-solving approach for several weeks and then made a video to teach it to others.

In the parent group, Cynthia and William enjoyed watching the problem-solving video that Wes had made with his group. They agreed that it would be helpful to use the same approach at home to solve family problems. They decided to hold weekly family meetings to plan their family's schedule and to address family issues proactively. Over the next few meetings, Dr. Schumann taught the parents a specific approach they could use to encourage positive child behavior, by providing labeled praise (e.g., "I like how you got right to your homework today") and ignoring minor problem behaviors (e.g., whining). He also taught the parents to give clear instructions and to use a specific system for monitoring compliance and addressing noncompliance without becoming engaged in emotionally charged interactions with their child. Cynthia was particularly glad that she and William had learned the same approach so that they could be consistent in how they addressed Wes's challenging behavior at home.

The child group ended with an emphasis on peer issues, including picking friends wisely (i.e., affiliating with nondeviant peers), being the type of person that others want to affiliate with, and resisting peer pressure. The parent group ended with an emphasis on planning for the child's future, including monitoring the friends they spend time with and their activities in the community. By the end of the Coping Power program, Wes had improved his grades and behavior at school well enough to join the drama club. He continued to have angry outbursts; however, they were less frequent, and he seemed to be able to recover from them more quickly. Cynthia and William were working better as a team, and the new parenting strategies they learned helped them keep their cool, even when Wes became angry. This seemed to reduce the level of family conflict substantially. A regular Friday night karaoke night had also helped the family reconnect in a positive way. Dr. Schumann praised Wes and his parents for the improvements they had made and discussed the signs that might indicate they need more services in the future.

REFERENCES

Bagner, D. M., & Eyberg, S. M. (2007). Parent-Child Interaction Therapy for disruptive behavior in children with mental retardation: A randomized controlled trial. *Journal of Child and Adolescent Psychology, 36,* 418–429.

Block, J. (1978). Effects of a rational–emotive mental health program on poorly achieving, disruptive high school students. *Journal of Counseling Psychology, 25*(1), 61–65.

Borduin, C. M., Mann, B. J., Cone, L. T., Henggeler, S. W., Fucci, B. R., Blaske, D. M., & Williams, R. A. (1995). Multisystemic treatment of serious juvenile offenders: Long-term prevention of criminality and violence. *Journal of Consulting and Clinical Psychology, 63,* 569–578.

Brinkmeyer, M. Y., & Eyberg, S. M. (2003). Parent-Child Interaction Therapy for oppositional children. In A. E. Kazdin & J. R. Weisz (Eds.), *Evidence-based psychotherapies for children and adolescents* (pp. 204–223). New York, NY: Guilford Press.

Brook, J. S., & Newcomb, M. D. (1995). Childhood aggression and unconventionality: Impact on later academic achievement, drug use, and workforce involvement. *Journal of Genetic Psychology, 156*(4), 393–410.

Bushman, B., & Peacock, G. G. (2010). Problem-solving skills training: Theory and practice in the school setting. In G. G. Peacock, R. A. Ervin, E. J. Daly III, & K. W. Merrell (Eds.), *Practical handbook of school psychology: Effective practices for the 21st century* (pp. 422–439). New York, NY: Guilford Press.

Chamberlain, P., Fisher, P. A., & Moore, K. (2002). Multidimensional treatment foster care: Application of the OSLC intervention model to high-risk youth and their families. In J. B. Reid, G. R. Patterson, & J. Snyder (Eds.), *Antisocial behavior in children and adolescents: A developmental analysis and model for intervention* (pp. 203–218). Washington, DC: American Psychological Association.

Chamberlain, P., & Reid, J.B. (1998). Comparison of two community alternatives to incarceration for chronic juvenile offenders. *Journal of Consulting and Clinical Psychology, 66,* 624–633.

Chamberlain, P., & Smith, D. K. (2003). Antisocial behavior in children and adolescents: The Oregon multidimensional treatment foster care model. In A. E. Kazdin & J. R. Weisz (Eds.), *Evidence-based psychotherapies for children and adolescents* (pp. 282–300). New York, NY: Guilford Press.

Clark, D. A., & Taylor, S. (2009). The transdiagnostic perspective on cognitive-behavioral therapy for anxiety and depression: New wine for old wineskins? *Journal of Cognitive Psychotherapy: An International Quarterly, 23,* 60–66.

Coie, J. D., Dodge, K. A., & Kupersmidt, J. (1990). Peer group behavior and social status. In S. Asher & J. Coie (Eds.), *Peer rejection in childhood* (pp. 17–59). New York, NY: Cambridge University Press.

Conduct Problems Prevention Research Group. (2010a). The difficulty of maintaining positive intervention effects: A look at disruptive behaviors, deviant peer relations, and social skills during the middle school years. *Journal of Early Adolescence, 30,* 593–624.

Conduct Problems Prevention Research Group. (2010b). Fast Track intervention effects on youth arrests and delinquency. *Journal of Experimental Criminology, 6,* 131–157.

DeGarmo, D. S., Patterson, G. R., & Forgatch, M. S. (2004). How do outcomes in a specified parent training intervention maintain or wane over time? *Prevention Science, 5,* 73–89.

de Graaf, I., Speetjens, P., Smit, F., de Wolff, M., & Tavecchio, L. (2008). Effectiveness of the Triple P Positive Parenting Program on behavioral problems in children: A meta-analysis. *Behavior Modification, 32,* 714–735.

Dishion, T. J., & Kavanagh, K. (2005). *Intervening in adolescent problem behavior: A family-centered approach.* New York, NY: Guilford Press.

Dodge, K. A., & Price, J. M. (1994). Social information processing bases of aggressive behavior in children. *Personality and Social Psychology Bulletin, 16,* 8–22.

Dowell, K. A., & Ogles, B. M. (2010). The effects of parent participation on child psychotherapy outcome: A meta-analytic review. *Journal of Clinical Child and Adolescent Psychology, 39,* 151–162.

Dumas, J. E., Nissley-Tsiopinis, J., & Moreland, A. D. (2007). From intent to enrollment, attendance, and participation in preventive parenting groups. *Journal of Child and Family Studies, 16,* 1–26.

Eyberg, S. M., Nelson, M. N., & Boggs, S. R. (2008). Evidence-based psychosocial treatments for children and adolescents with disruptive behavior. *Journal of Clinical Child and Adolescent Psychology, 37,* 215–237.

Forehand, R., & McMahon, R. J. (1981). *Helping the noncompliant child: A clinician's guide to parent training.* New York, NY: Guilford Press.

Forgatch, M. S., Patterson, G. R., & DeGarmo, D. S. (2005). Evaluating fidelity: Predictive validity for a measure of competent adherence to the Oregon model of parent management training. *Behavior Therapy, 36*(1), 3–13.

Forgatch, M. S., Patterson, G. R., DeGarmo, D. S., & Beldavs, Z. G. (2009). Testing the Oregon delinquency model with 9-year follow-up of the Oregon divorce study. *Development and Psychopathology, 21,* 637–660.

Frankel, F., & Simmons, J. Q. (1992). Parent behavioral training: Why and when some parents drop out. *Journal of Clinical Child Psychology, 21,* 322–330.

Hanf, C., & Kling, J. (1973). *Facilitating parent-child interaction: A two-stage training model.* Unpublished manuscript, University of Oregon Medical School.

Henggeler, S. W., & Lee, T. (2003). Multisystemic treatment of serious clinical problems. In A. E. Kazdin & J. R. Weisz (Eds.), *Evidence-based psychotherapies for children and adolescents* (pp. 301–322). New York, NY: Guilford Press.

Henggeler, S. W., Melton, G. B., & Smith, L.A. (1992). Family preservation using multisystemic therapy: An effective alternative to incarcerating serious juvenile offenders. *Journal of Consulting and Clinical Psychology, 60,* 953–961.

Henggeler, S. W., Schoenwald, S. K., Borduin, C. M., Rowland, M. D., & Cunningham, P. B. (1998). *Multisystemic treatment of antisocial behavior in children and adolescents.* New York, NY: Guilford Press.

Herman, K. C., Reinke, W. M., Bradshaw, C. P., Lochman, J. E., Boxmeyer, C. L., Powell, N. P., . . . Ialongo, N. (2012). Integrating the Family Check-Up and the parent Coping Power program. *Advances in School Mental Health Promotion, 5,* 208–219.

Hood, K. K., & Eyberg, S. M. (2003). Outcomes of Parent-Child Interaction Therapy: Mothers' reports of maintenance three to six years after. *Journal of Clinical Child and Adolescent Psychology, 32,* 419–429.

Huey, W. C., & Rank, R. C. (1984). Effects of counselor and peer-led group assertive training on black adolescent aggression. *Journal of Counseling Psychology, 31*(1), 95–98.

Kaminski, J. W., Valle, L. A., Filene, J. H., & Boyle, C. L. (2008). A meta-analytic review of components associated with parent training program effectiveness. *Journal of Abnormal Child Psychology, 36*(4), 567–589.

Kazdin, A. E. (1997). Parent management training: Evidence, outcomes, and issues. *Journal of the American Academy of Child and Adolescent Psychiatry, 36,* 1349–1356.

Kazdin, A. E. (2000). Treatment for aggressive and antisocial children. *Child and Adolescent Psychiatric Clinics of North America, 9,* 841–858.

Kazdin, A. E. (2010). Problem-solving skills training and parent management training for oppositional defiant disorder and conduct disorder. In A. E. Kazdin & J. R. Weisz (Eds.), *Evidence-based psychotherapies for children and adolescents* (pp. 211–226). New York, NY: Guilford Press.

Kazdin, A. E., Bass, D., Siegel, T., & Thomas C. (1989). Cognitive-behavioral therapy and relationship therapy in the treatment of children referred for antisocial behavior. *Journal of Consulting and Clinical Psychology, 57,* 522–535.

Kendall, P., Gosch, E., Furr, J. M., & Sood, E. (2008). Flexibility within fidelity. *Journal of the American Academy of Child & Adolescent Psychiatry, 47*(9), 987–993.

La Greca, A. M., Silverman, W. K., & Lochman, J. E. (2009). Moving beyond efficacy and effectiveness: Factors influencing the outcome of evidence-based psychological interventions with children and adolescents. *Journal of Consulting and Clinical Psychology, 77,* 373–382.

Lavigne, J. V., LeBailly, S. A., Gouze, K. R., Cicchetti, C., Pochyly, J., Arend, R., . . . Binns, H. J. (2008). Treating oppositional defiant disorder in primary care: A comparison of three models. *Journal of Pediatric Psychology, 33*(5), 449–461.

Leve, L. D., Chamberlain, P., & Reid, J. B. (2005). Intervention outcomes for girls referred from juvenile justice: Effects on delinquency. *Journal of Consulting and Clinical Psychology, 73,* 1181–1185.

Lochman, J. E., Baden, R., Boxmeyer, C. L., Powell, N. P., Qu, L., Salekin, K., & Windle, M. (2013). Does a booster intervention augment the preventive effects of an abbreviated version of the Coping Power program for aggressive children? *Journal of Abnormal Child Psychology.* Advance online publication. doi: 10.1007/s10802-013-9727-y

Lochman, J. E., Barry, T. D., & Pardini, D. A. (2003). Anger control training for aggressive youth. In A. E. Kazdin & J. R. Weisz (Eds.), *Evidence-based psychotherapies for children and adolescents* (pp. 263–281). New York, NY: Guilford Press.

Lochman, J. E., Boxmeyer, C. L., Powell, N., & Qu, L. (2011, November). *Effects of an abbreviated form of the Coping Power intervention on externalizing behaviors in aggressive pre-adolescent children.* Paper presented in a symposium (J. Langberg, Chair) at the 45th annual meeting of the Association for Behavioral and Cognitive Therapies, Toronto, Canada.

Lochman, J. E., Boxmeyer, C. L., Powell, N. P., Qu, L., Wells, K., & Windle, M. (2012). Coping Power dissemination study: Intervention and special education effects on academic outcomes. *Behavioral Disorders, 37,* 192–205.

Lochman, J. E., Boxmeyer, C., Powell, N., Roth, D. L., & Windle, M. (2006). Masked intervention effects: Analytic methods addressing low dosage of intervention. *New Directions for Evaluation, 110,* 19–32.

Lochman, J. E., FitzGerald, D. P., Gage, S. M., Kannaly, M. K., Whidby, J. M., Barry, T. D., . . . McElroy, H. (2001). Effects of social-cognitive intervention for aggressive deaf children: The Coping Power program. *Journal of the American Deafness and Rehabilitation Association, 35,* 39–61.

Lochman, J. E., Powell, N., Boxmeyer, C., Andrade, B., Stromeyer, S. L., & Jimenez-Camargo, L. A. (2012). Adaptations to the Coping Power program's structure, delivery settings, and clinician training. Dissemination study: Intervention and special education effects on academic outcomes. *Psychotherapy, 49,* 135–142.

Lochman, J. E., Powell, N. P., Boxmeyer, C. L., Ford, H. L., & Minney, J. A. (2013). Beyond disruptive behavior diagnoses: Applications of the Coping Power program. In J. Ehrenreich-May & B. Chu (Eds.), *Transdiagnostic treatments for children and adolescents: Principles and practice.* New York, NY: Guilford Press.

Lochman, J. E., & Wells, K. C. (2002). Contextual social-cognitive mediators and child outcome: A test of the theoretical model in the Coping Power Program. *Development and Psychopathology, 14,* 971–993.

Lochman, J. E., & Wells, K. C. (2003). Effectiveness study of Coping Power and classroom intervention with aggressive children: Outcomes at a one-year follow-up. *Behavior Therapy, 34,* 493–515.

Lochman, J. E., & Wells, K. C. (2004). The Coping Power program for preadolescent aggressive boys and their parents: Outcome effects at 1-year follow-up. *Journal of Consulting and Clinical Psychology, 72,* 571–578.

Lochman, J. E., Wells, K. C., & Lenhart, L. (2008). *Coping Power child group program: Facilitator guide.* New York, NY: Oxford University Press.

Lochman, J. E., Wells, K. C., Qu, L., & Chen, L. (2013). Three-year follow-up of Coping Power intervention effects: Evidence of neighborhood moderation? *Prevention Science, 14*(4), 364–376.

Maughan, D. R., Christiansen, E., Jenson, W. R., Olympia, D., & Clark, E. (2005). Behavioral parent training as a treatment for externalizing behaviors and disruptive behavior disorders: A meta-analysis. *School Psychology Review, 34*(3), 267–286.

McMahon, R. J. & Forehand, R. L. (2003). *Helping the noncompliant child: Family-based treatment for oppositional behavior* (2nd ed.). New York, NY: Guilford Press.

Morrissey-Kane, E., & Prinz, R. J. (1999). Engagement in child and adolescent treatment: The role of parental cognitions and attributions. *Clinical Child and Family Psychology Review, 2,* 183–198.

Nelson, W. M., Finch, A. J., & Hart, K. J. (2006). *Conduct disorders: A practitioner's guide to comparative treatments.* New York, NY: Springer.

Nock, M. K. (2003). Progress review of the psychosocial treatment of child conduct problems. *Clinical Psychology: Science and Practice, 10,* 1–28.

O'Donnell, S. L., Jurecska, D. E., & Dyer, R. (2012). Effectiveness of the Coping Power program in a Mexican-American sample: Distinctive cultural considerations. *International Journal of Culture and Mental Health, 5*(1), 30–39.

Patterson, G. R., Reid, J. B., & Dishion, T. J. (1992). *A social learning approach. IV. Antisocial boys.* Eugene, OR: Castalia Press.

Patterson, G. R., Reid, J. B., Jones, R. R., & Conger, R. E. (1975). *A social learning approach to family intervention: Families with aggressive children,* Vol. 1. Eugene, OR: Castalia Press.

Powell, N. P., Boxmeyer, C. L., Baden, R., Stromeyer, S., Minney, J. A., Mushtaq, A., & Lochman, J. E. (2011). Assessing and treating aggression and conduct problems in schools: Implications from the Coping Power program. *Psychology in the Schools, 48,* 233–242.

Reese, R. J., Prout, H. T., Zirkelback, E. A., & Anderson, C. R. (2010). Effectiveness of school-based psychotherapy: A meta-analysis of dissertation research. *Psychology in the Schools, 47*(10), 1035–1045.

Reid, J. B., Patterson, G. R., & Snyder, J. (Eds.). (2002). *Antisocial behavior in children: Developmental theories and models for intervention.* Washington, DC: American Psychological Association.

Risi, S., Gerhardstein, R., & Kistner, J. (2003). Children's classroom peer relationships and subsequent educational outcomes. *Journal of Clinical Child and Adolescent Psychology, 32(3),* 351–361

Sanders, M. R. (1999). Triple P-Positive Parenting Program: Towards an empirically validated multilevel parenting and family support strategy for the prevention of behavior and emotional problems in children. *Clinical Child and Family Psychology Review, 2,* 71–90.

Schuhmann, E. M., Foote, R., Eyberg, S. M., Boggs, S., & Algina, J. (1998). Parent-Child Interaction Therapy: Interim report of a randomized trial with short-term maintenance. *Journal of Clinical Child and Adolescent Psychology, 27,* 34–45.

Shaw, D. S., Keenan, K., & Vondra, J. I. (1994). Developmental precursors of externalizing behavior: Ages 1 to 3. *Developmental Psychology, 30*(3), 355–364.

van de Wiel, N. M. H., Matthys, W., Cohen-Kettenis, P., Maassen, G. H., Lochman, J. E., & van Engeland, H. (2007). The effectiveness of an experimental treatment when compared to care as usual depends on the type of care as usual. *Behavior Modification, 31*(3), 298–312.

van de Wiel, N. M. H., Matthys, W., Cohen-Kettenis, P., & van Engeland, H. (2003). Application of the Utrecht Coping Power program and care as usual to children with disruptive behavior disorders in outpatient clinics: A comparative study of cost and course of treatment. *Behavior Therapy, 34*(4), 421–436.

Webster-Stratton, C., & Hammond, M. (1997). Treating children with early-onset conduct problems: A comparison of child and parent training interventions. *Journal of Consulting and Clinical Psychology, 65,* 93–109.

Webster-Stratton C., & Reid, M. J. (2010). The Incredible Years parents, teachers, and children training series. In J. R. Weisz & A. E. Kazdin (Eds.), *Evidence-based psychotherapies for children and adolescents* (2nd ed., pp. 194–210). New York, NY: Guilford Press.

Webster-Stratton, C., Reid, M. J., & Hammond, M. (2004). Treating children with early onset conduct problems: Intervention outcomes for parent, child, and teacher training. *Journal of Clinical Child and Adolescent Psychology, 33,* 105–124.

Webster-Stratton, C., Reid, M. J., & Stoolmiller, M. (2008). Preventing conduct problems and improving school readiness: Evaluation of the Incredible Years teacher and child training programs in high-risk schools. *Journal of Child Psychology and Psychiatry, 49,* 471–488.

Webster-Stratton, C., Rinaldi, J., & Jamilia, M. R. (2011). Long-term outcomes of Incredible Years parenting program: Predictors of adolescent adjustment. *Child and Adolescent Mental Health, 16,* 38–46.

Wells, K. C., Lochman, J. E., & Lenhart, L. (2008). *Coping Power parent group program: Facilitator guide.* New York, NY: Oxford University Press.

Wiggins, T. L., Sofronoff, K., & Sanders, M. R. (2009). Pathways Triple P-Positive Parenting Program: Effects on parent-child relationships and child behavior problems. *Family Process, 48,* 517–530.

Winship, B. J., & Kelley, J. D. (1976). A verbal response model of assertiveness. *Journal of Counseling Psychology, 23*(3), 215–220.

Zonnevylle-Bender, M. J. S., Matthys, W., van de Wiel, N. M. H., & Lochman, J. E. (2007). Preventive effects of treatment of disruptive behavior disorder in middle childhood on substance use and delinquent behavior. *Journal of the American Academy of Child & Adolescent Psychiatry, 46*(1), 33–39.

CHAPTER 14

Autism Spectrum Disorders

SUSAN W. WHITE, NICOLE L. KREISER, AND MATTHEW D. LERNER

BRIEF OVERVIEW OF AUTISM SPECTRUM DISORDERS

Autism spectrum disorder (ASD) is a neurodevelopmental disability encompassing a group of childhood-onset syndromes that share a severe disability in social interaction. In the fourth edition, text revision of the *Diagnostic and Statistical Manual of Mental Disorders* (*DSM-IV-TR*) (American Psychiatric Association [APA], 2000), ASD comprised distinct diagnostic entities, notably autistic disorder, Asperger's disorder, and pervasive developmental disorder—not otherwise specified. Although considerable debate persists about the scientific merit of grouping versus separating the specific disorders, in the latest revision of the *DSM* (*DSM-5*) (APA, 2013) this subcategorization is replaced with the umbrella diagnostic category.

The spectrum disorders are no longer regarded as rare, nor is identification of ASD restricted to children. Approximately 1 in 88 children meet criteria for an ASD diagnosis (U.S. Centers for Disease Control and Prevention [CDC], 2012). Of this population of approximately 831,507 children with a diagnosis of ASD nationwide (based on a U.S. Census Bureau 2010 report), an estimated 62% are not cognitively impaired (CDC, 2012). Moreover, ASD is a chronic condition; although symptoms often wax and wane over the course of development (Cederlund, Hagberg, Billstedt, Gillberg, & Gillberg, 2008; Howlin, Goode, Hutton, & Rutter, 2004), the diagnosis typically persists through adulthood (Farley et al., 2009). Although children usually are identified by age 5 (CDC, 2012), diagnosis can and often does occur much later (White, Ollendick, & Bray, 2011), especially for individuals who have few or no low-threshold symptoms (i.e., behaviors that are highly atypical and hallmark characteristic of diagnosis, such as stereotyped language) and who are cognitively higher functioning (or at least without co-occurring intellectual disability [ID]. Given the growing population of young people with ASD diagnoses who do not have co-occurring ID and who usually are educated in regular education (i.e., mainstream) classrooms, the focus of this chapter is treatment approaches for those children who are without ID.

Treatment of a client with ASD is usually multifaceted. Unlike many Axis I disorders, the symptom(s) that are diagnostic of ASD often are not the focus of intervention, at least initially (Joshi et al., 2010). For example, a child with ASD may be referred for treatment due to problems with aggression, self-injury, anxiety, or academic difficulties. Moreover, the range of presenting problems is diverse. Although treatment for core symptoms, such as social disability, is often sought, it is typical that other problems are present and uniquely, acutely impairing in the child's life. Effectively reducing co-occurring symptoms (e.g., anxiety) can, in some cases, motivate the child to persist in treatment, contribute directly or indirectly to change in more pervasive or chronic symptoms, and reduce impairment.

The heterogeneity in both symptom profile and treatment needs is also important to bear in mind with respect to discussions of evidence-based treatments (EBTs) for children with ASD.

What is effective for a minimally verbal 4-year-old, for instance, is often inappropriate and ineffective for a highly verbal adolescent, although these two children share the same diagnosis. Given the goal of this volume (i.e., to provide practical, usable information on evidence-based intervention practices), its anticipated consumers (psychologists in practice or training), and the targeted client group (school-age children and adolescents who are without co-occurring ID), we provide information on many of the best-supported treatments based on the extant literature to date. However, there are many treatment options with varying degrees of empirical support and treatments that, although often provided to young people on the spectrum, are not typically delivered by clinical or school psychologists. To balance breadth of coverage with adequate depth and detail, we have opted to cover treatments that are evidence based and promising in terms of efficacy for the most commonly seen clinical referral issues for children and adolescents with ASD. This includes intervention approaches for core (i.e., diagnostic of ASD) and secondary (i.e., problems that frequently co-occur in ASD) symptoms separately.

EVIDENCE-BASED APPROACHES

No specific treatments have been developed for children with ASD that meet the criteria for "empirically validated" treatments, as initially established by the 1995 report from the Society of Clinical Psychology, Task Force on Promotion and Dissemination of Psychological Treatment Procedures. Many, however, likely meet the criteria for "probably efficacious." Notably, Lovaas's Applied Behavior Analysis (ABA) intervention approach, Discrete Trial Training (Lovaas, 1987), was the only treatment determined to be probably efficacious in a review of research on comprehensive treatments for young children with ASD (Rogers & Vismara, 2008). Fortunately, tremendous progress has been made in the field of psychosocial intervention research for ASD in the past 5 years. This body of research is developing rapidly, and the challenges native to this stage of treatment discovery and evaluation (e.g., accruing sufficient size samples to thoroughly assess efficacy, much less moderators and mediators of response, and application of sensitive and valid measures of change) are numerous.

Nonetheless, there are many excellent resources on evidence-based intervention practices for ASD, a full review of which is beyond the scope of this chapter. The National Autism Center (NAC; 2009) has developed empirically informed guidelines for treatment of ASD in the schools, dividing approaches into those that are "emerging" (22 treatments identified as such) and those that are "established" (11 treatments identified as such; e.g., antecedent packages, modeling). The treatment approaches outlined by the NAC are probably best viewed as components of more comprehensive educational and clinical curricula rather than stand-alone interventions. More recently, the National Professional Development Center on ASD (Wong et al., 2014) has identified 27 evidence-based practices, defined as those to be shown effective through high-quality scientific research. There is a lack of consistency in findings across resources, largely owing to use of different systems, or metrics, with which to judge the relative merit of the scientific base. The *Handbook of Autism and Pervasive Developmental Disorders* (Volkmar, Paul, Klin, & Cohen, 2005) and the *Encyclopedia of Autism Spectrum Disorders* (Volkmar, 2013) are also valuable resources (both of which are to have new editions published in the coming year), offering summaries of empirically based interventions and critical analyses of the extant research.

It should also be noted that ABA is the most empirically supported treatment for the core speech and communication deficits of ASD. Intensive ABA programming typically is delivered by board-certified behavior analysts with specialized training in ASD. For children under 4 years of age with ASD, intensive (up to 40 hours per week) is typically the principal recommendation (e.g., Eikeseth, Smith, Jahr, & Eldevik, 2007; Harris & Handleman, 2000; National Research Council, 2001). Without question, treatments based on the principles of ABA (e.g., Lovaas, 2003) continue to be the foundation of most psychosocial interventions for children with ASD. This is particularly true for clients with ID and those who are younger (i.e., under 7 years). Although older children and adolescents can learn from ABA approaches, evidence indicates that the long-term impact is greatest for very young children (Smith, 2010). ABA-based interventions are based in the principles of operant conditioning (Skinner, 1938), such as prompting and reinforcing specific targeted skills. Many of the treatment approaches described in this chapter incorporate aspects of ABA, but we do not describe or explain the Discrete Trial Training approach that is often core to ABA programs for young children with ASD. We instead focus on interventions typically delivered in clinical settings by counselors and psychologists.

Social Disability

The hallmark characteristic of ASD is pervasive social disability (APA, 2000), and social skills instruction often is used to improve general social competence in children with ASD. Although interventions to improve social functioning in youth with ASD generally have demonstrated promising results (Reichow & Volkmar, 2010; Wang & Spillane, 2009), the evidence has not been consistently strong, and common methodological limitations (e.g., primarily parent-report measures and use of wait-list comparison conditions) have hampered comparative evaluation. However, many intervention models target social disability in ASD and have an emerging base of empirical support, including ABA-based behavior modification, peer as interventionist and tutor models, social stories, computer-based training games, and video modeling, many of which we discuss later. Resources also are available on how to design individualized programming to address the social problems of children with ASD (e.g., White, 2011).

Social skills training in a group format is perhaps the most common psychosocial intervention; many commercially available curricula have been developed specifically for young people with ASD (e.g., Baker, 2003; Bellini, 2008; McAfee, 2002). The Program for the Education and Enrichment of Relationship Skills (PEERS) (Laugeson & Frankel, 2010) is perhaps the best-studied specific group treatment package. PEERS is a manualized social skills training intervention developed for adolescents with ASD. Two randomized clinical trials of PEERS have yielded large between-group effects on parent-reported social skills (Laugeson, Frankel, Gantman, Dillon, & Mogil, 2011; Laugeson, Frankel, Mogil, & Dillon, 2009), leading the National Institute for Clinical Excellence to give the PEERS protocol its highest level of recognition as an empirically supported treatment for ASD. Although research on the PEERS program is highly promising, the Skillstreaming approach (Goldstein & McGinnis, 1997; McGinnis & Goldstein, 1997) is arguably the most widely used in this literature and has been successfully adapted for children with ASD (e.g., Lopata et al., 2011).

Shared elements, considered promising components of effective skills training across programs, include consistency in delivery and structure (e.g., a similar sequence of activities and context), direct and immediate feedback to the children, and integration of strategies to promote skill generalization (White, Koenig, & Scahill, 2007). Emerging research supports an additional set of promising components of group social skills training. While PEERS and related models (see Stichter et al., 2010; DeRosier, Swick, Davis, McMillen, & Matthews, 2010) focus on increasing discrete skills through first providing didactic instruction, this alternative set tends to focus on in vivo learning and performance training approaches (Lerner, McMahon, & Britton, 2014; Lerner, Mikami, & Levine,

2011), and there is evidence that such approaches may yield faster improvement in peer functioning relative to didactic approaches (Lerner & Mikami, 2012).

There are many approaches other than traditional group-based or individually delivered social skills training. Peer-mediated interventions involve peers of the child with ASD who are the direct recipients of training to indirectly improve social competence in the identified youth. This training often is conducted with students in mainstream classes, such that effects on socialization are indirect, via social engagement with the trained peer. Recent research indicates that peer-mediated interventions may be superior to interventions that solely target skill development in children with ASD (Kasari, Rotheram-Fuller, Locke, & Gulsrud, 2012), highlighting the importance of training typically developing youth to be supportive and open to peers who have ASD. Video modeling interventions, which provide a visual model of the targeted behavior, also have shown promise in extant research (Charlop-Christy, Le, & Freeman, 2000; Nicopoulos & Keenan, 2004). The model may be the targeted child him- or herself (the client videotaped while using a specific skill) or a peer or sibling. Skills such as conversational speech, perspective taking, and specific social skills to be used in new situations lend themselves easily to this approach. Social Stories, developed by Carol Gray (1998), often are useful in teaching about age-appropriate social behavior and expectations (Rogers & Smith-Myles, 2001). These stories are individualized and used to teach and explain social concepts or situations as well as provide suggestions for what to do in that situation.

Computer-based intervention (CBI) is gaining popularity as an approach to remediate specific processes believed to underlie social disability in ASD, such as deficient emotion recognition and regulation. Several promising CBI programs are available, including *The Transporters* (Golan et al., 2010), an animation series centered around vehicles that demonstrate human emotions; FaceSay (Symbionica), which utilizes realistic avatars to "interact" with users to increase attention toward socially salient features of the face (Hopkins et al., 2011); Let's Face It! (Tanaka et al., 2010), a set of interactive computer games to address face-processing deficits; and the Secret Agent Society (Beaumont, 2009; Beaumont & Sofronoff, 2008), which uses an interactive computer game to teach emotion recognition and regulation skills along with weekly group training sessions. Such approaches have pragmatic benefits, such as transportability (e.g., can be done at home or school), a decreased reliance on therapists, and flexible implementation—all of which may promote a higher treatment "dose" (e.g., the child can be "treated" multiple times weekly or daily). Among children with ASD, moreover, technology is often a particular area of interest. For that reason, these young clients may find CBI more intrinsically interesting and motivating than traditional interpersonal therapies. In a meta-analysis of studies on CBI for individuals with ASD, Ramdoss and colleagues (2012) found considerable range in effect sizes and concluded that further research is needed to determine if CBI can be considered an effective intervention. Regardless, such an approach may be preferred by some children with ASD and may be a useful component of more traditional, face-to-face interventions.

In conclusion, intervention research in this area generally has demonstrated promising, though far from unequivocal, results. In a meta-analysis on the efficacy of school-based social interventions, Bellini, Peters, Benner, and Hopf (2007) reported that the evaluated social skills interventions were minimally effective for most students with ASD. Wang and Spillane (2009), in their meta-analysis, concluded that video modeling was an evidence-based and effective intervention for children with ASD, whereas Social Stories (Gray, 2000) and peer-mediated approaches were found to be less effective. Reichow and Volkmar (2010), in their review, determined that social skills groups could be considered an established, evidence-based intervention, while video modeling is promising. Clearly, there is emerging support for multiple forms of intervention, but the strength of the evidence is quite variable.

Anxiety and Mood Problems

Anxiety is a common co-occurring problem (White, Oswald, Ollendick, & Scahill, 2009), affecting approximately 40% of children and adolescents with ASD (van Steensel, Bogels, & Perrin, 2011). When present, anxiety appears to exacerbate core ASD impairments (Chang, Quan, & Wood, 2012). Several recent clinical trials have indicated that cognitive behavior therapy (CBT) is likely to be effective in reducing symptoms of anxiety (Chalfant et al., 2007; Reaven et al., 2009; Sofronoff, Attwood, & Hinton, 2005; White et al., 2012; Wood et al., 2009). Most such programs have been delivered in a group format, and each program either has been modified from existing programs for youth with ASD or has been developed specifically for children and adolescents with ASD. As several investigators (e.g., Puleo & Kendall, 2011; White, Scarpa, & Attwood, 2013) have observed, however, the clinical need for such adaptations and the merits they afford to eventual treatment outcome have yet to be empirically examined.

Although more treatment research has been afforded to anxiety in young people with ASD, depression is also a common co-occurring problem in this population (Ghaziuddin, Ghaziuddin, & Greden, 2002), affecting approximately 40% of adolescents with diagnosed ASD (Lopata et al., 2010). Yet we know of no studies that have examined the use of CBT for treating depression in youth ASD. Since CBT has promise for the reduction of emotional and behavioral difficulties related to anxiety and anger in ASD, it seems plausible that it also can help with depressive symptomatology.

Aggression and Externalizing Behaviors

Aggression and irritability are common among children with ASD. Because aggression can be severe and can have considerable adverse impacts on family life, functioning in school, and skill development, it is often the primary reason for treatment referral (Johnson et al., 2007). Aggression and severe irritability usually are treated with psychotropic agents, notably atypical antipsychotics (Robb, 2010). Combined pharmacologic and behavioral treatment, however, may be the most effective approach for decreasing severity of aggressive behavior among children with ASD (Frazier et al., 2010). With respect to psychosocial treatment for these behavior problems in children with ASD, the standard treatment approach employs ABA with functional assessment to identify the factors that maintain or exacerbate the behaviors (Matson, 2009). Some such programs have been assembled into treatment manuals. Johnson and colleagues (2007) developed a behavioral parent-training program, based on ABA principles and integrating functional assessment, to treat noncompliance, irritability, and aggression in children with ASD. The treatment was able to be delivered consistently across therapists and clients (therapist integrity across multiple treatment sites), and parents reported being highly satisfied with the intervention (Research Units on Pediatric Psychopharmacology Autism Network, 2007).

Feeding Difficulties

Feeding difficulties, such as sensitivity to food textures, food selectivity, and food refusal, are prevalent among children with ASD, with approximately 60% exhibiting feeding issues (Kerwin, Eicher, & Gelsinger, 2005; Williams, Dalyrmple, & Neal, 2000). If left untreated, such difficulties can result in poor nutrition and other challenging behaviors (e.g., aggression associated with food refusal) (Matson & Fodstad, 2009). Feeding difficulties in children with ASD may stem from a variety of sources, including biological factors and manifestation of ASD symptomology (e.g., cognitive inflexibility, insistence on sameness) (Twachtman-Reilly, Amaral, & Zebrowski, 2008). ABA has been the preferred treatment modality in most types of feeding difficulties (Matson & Fodstad, 2009). Results of single-case studies utilizing behavioral approaches such as behavioral momentum (i.e., requesting desired behavior after trials of high probability compliance tasks) (Patel et al., 2007), differential reinforcement plus response cost (Buckley, Strunck, & Newchok, 2005), positive reinforcement of nonpreferred foods (Luiselli, Ricciardi, & Gilligan, 2005), and pairing nonpreferred foods with preferred foods (Najdowski, Wallace, Doney, & Ghezzi, 2003) have been promising. However, such strategies have not been well examined or compared.

Self-Injury/Suicidality

Self-injurious behavior (SIB) has been conceptualized as a form of repetitive behavior in children with ASD, and some of the most common forms of SIB involve head hitting, hand biting, and skin rubbing (Canitano, 2006; Matson & LoVullo, 2008). However, recent evidence indicates that, among higher-functioning adolescents with ASD, nonsuicidal self-injury is not associated with repetitive or stereotyped behaviors but rather with depression (Maddox & White, 2012). Pharmacological treatment, often with antipsychotic medications such as risperidone, is the most common approach to treating SIB (Canitano, 2006; Matson & LoVullo, 2008). Variants of behavioral modification (e.g., functional assessment, positive reinforcement) also have been employed to target such symptoms, although few efforts have been made to tailor treatment approaches specifically to address SIB and most research in this area has been conducted with individuals who have co-occurring intellectual impairment (Matson & LoVullo, 2008). Although only a handful of reports are available, suicidality has been noted as a problem among some individuals with ASD (Raja, Azzoni, & Frustaci, 2011). In one study, ASD was overrepresented in a sample of adolescents who attempted suicide and were hospitalized (Mikami et al., 2009). It has been hypothesized that factors such as being male, the presence of psychotic symptoms, and pervasive obsessive traits (suggesting a higher degree of planning) are associated with increased suicide completion in people with ASD (Raja et al., 2011). It is also of note that recognizing suicide risk in this population may be quite challenging, given that symptoms typically suggestive of suicide risk may be masked by ASD symptoms (e.g., social withdrawal, inappropriate or bizarre behaviors, negative symptoms). Thus, in working with this population, risk of suicidality should be frequently and explicitly assessed for, even in the absence of typical signs or risk factors related to suicidality (Raja et al., 2011).

Alternative and Untested Treatments

Perhaps just as important as having knowledge of evidence-based and empirically supported interventions for children with ASD is recognizing interventions that are unvalidated and sometimes contraindicated (Lilienfeld, 2007; Smith, 2008). ASD has been described as a "fad magnet" for such treatments (Metz, Mulick, & Butter, 2005), and multiple, widely available treatments simply do not have evidence to support their use clinically (e.g., auditory integration training, bonding therapies, special or restricted diets). This is especially important for clinicians who do not necessarily specialize in treating families affected by ASD. While it is impossible to stay abreast of all new, or even available, treatments for all conditions, especially given the prevalence and proliferation of so many alternative and unvalidated treatments, we recommend that therapists beginning treatment for individuals with ASD avail themselves of current literature to aid families in using caution when considering such treatments.

PARENTAL INVOLVEMENT IN TREATMENT

Parental involvement is important for promoting the child's learning across a range of situations (behavior generalization) and to provide consistent interactions (e.g., response to tantrums), regardless of whether the therapist is present (Matson, Mahan, & Matson, 2009). Parental roles in interventions have included the parent as cotherapist, parent as coach, and less intensive forms of involvement including the provision of psychoeducation and parental support. Despite the noted importance of parental involvement, the specific features of parental involvement that may augment treatment response are largely unexplored.

Caregiver participation in treatment of children with ASD is considered to be imperative, although the intensity of parental involvement varies across interventions (Granger, Rivieres-Pigeon, Sabourin, & Forget, 2012). Interactions between parent and child often are the direct target of treatment, typically via parental training therapies and parent–child interaction therapy (Solomon, Ono, Timmer, & Goodlin-Jones, 2008). Parental involvement in social skills training interventions can vary, with comparably less involvement with school-based programs and more involvement in clinic programs (Karst & Van Hecke, 2012; Sansosti, 2010). For instance, in the PEERS (Laugeson et al., 2009) program, parents participate in concurrent parent groups in which they receive didactic training on how to assist their child in developing friendships and how to effectively assist their teen in weekly homework assignments. In CBT to treat children with ASD and co-occurring anxiety, parents often take a larger role in the treatment, compared to CBT treatment with typically functioning children, owing to the core deficits and other challenges faced by children with ASD (Reaven, 2011). Indeed, evidence suggests that the more severe ASD traits a child exhibits, the more the child benefits from parental involvement in CBT (Puleo & Kendall, 2011). Parents have been involved in various modalities in CBT treatment (i.e., separate parent groups, parent–child dyads, and a combination of both) (Moree & Davis, 2010), and the main components of parental involvement have included parenting training (e.g., psychoeducation), parent coaching, and parental assistance in directing in vivo exposures (Reaven, 2011).

When working with children with ASD, issues such as parental overprotection, child overreliance on parents, and parental variables (e.g., stress, limited self-efficacy) may be important to assess and, when present, to address as they can impact treatment compliance and response. Due to core deficits associated with ASD, affected children and adolescents are often more dependent on their parents than same-age peers are. In some cases, children and teens with ASD may develop a pattern of overreliance on caregivers and feel hesitant to engage in adaptive behaviors, enter social situations, or face anxiety-provoking situations despite possessing the necessary skills to handle such situations. Parents of children with ASD may have realistic, or at least understandable, fears due to the many challenges faced by their children. These fears can lead to patterns of excessive protection and parental attempts to limit exposure to challenging events in which their child may experience failure (Reaven, 2011). From our clinical experience, such patterns may serve to further limit the child's development of independent skills and age-appropriate relationships and may interfere with treatment compliance. Thus, they may need to be addressed in treatment. These patterns may become particularly relevant in treatment during adolescence, when parents may be reluctant to allow their teen to engage in age-appropriate activities, such as driving and unsupervised get-togethers with friends. Psychoeducation related to the role that parental fears may play in adolescents' anxiety and developmental progress, and the distinction between "adaptive" and "excessive" protection, may be helpful (Reaven, 2011). Gains related to adolescents making their own decisions and learning from their success and failure experiences should be emphasized to promote an approach attitude toward greater independence and self-sufficiency.

Also, a number of parental variables, including stress, poor mental health, and low parental self-efficacy, are important to consider and may become a target in treatment. Mothers of children with ASD in particular (who often take on greater parenting responsibility) have significantly higher levels of stress and co-occurring anxiety and depression (Karst & Van Hecke, 2012) and significantly reduced self-efficacy (Sofronoff & Farbotko, 2002) than mothers of typically developing children and children with other developmental disorders or health care needs. High levels of parental stress have consequences for parental physical and emotional well-being, interactions with the child and family (Lerner, Calhoun, Mikami, & De Los Reyes, 2012), and treatment compliance, dropout, and progress (Pisula, 2011; Reaven, 2011), and may exacerbate child behavioral problems (Singh et al., 2006). Reduced parental self-efficacy has been related to poor persistence, higher rates of parental depression, and diminished satisfaction with parenting and increased child behavioral problems (Johnston & Mash, 1989). The impact of having a child with ASD on the family system is also of clinical relevance. Perhaps due to elevated levels of parenting stress, conflict, and child behavior problems, having a child with ASD is associated with reduced marital satisfaction and higher divorce rates as compared to families with typically developing children (Freedman, Kalb, Zaboltsky, & Stuart, 2012; Hartley et al., 2010). Clinicians should be cognizant of parental conflicts during treatment, given that family conflict has been found to be predictive of more severe ASD symptom manifestation (Kelly, Garnett, Attwood, & Peterson, 2008).

Parent support groups, psychoeducation, and various training programs are common components of treatment programs designed for children with ASD, although the specific impact of such components on parental outcomes remains largely unexplored. As reviewed by Karst and Van Hecke (2012), research into parent training programs suggests parental benefits, including improved mental and physical health, reduced levels of stress and depression, greater parenting self-efficacy, and improved responsiveness and emotion regulation, even when training programs are a secondary supplement to programs primarily targeting the child. Programs that teach the use of skills to help deal with the child's challenging behaviors, such as Sofronoff and Farbotko's (2002) adapted parent management training, seem to convey some benefit. Involvement in parent support groups may provide a supportive environment for parents to discuss the unique challenges they face raising a child with ASD and, given the strong relationship between parental stress and lack of social support, may serve to reduce stress (Dyson, 1997; Krauss, 1993), although findings related to the effects of participation in formal support groups on parental stress are mixed (Boyd, 2002). Mobilization of informal support (e.g., family members, relationships with others with children with special needs) appears to have a more powerful influence on reducing parental stress (Boyd, 2002). In summary, parental and family stress and functioning should be considered in treatment in order to gain a better understanding of family strengths and barriers in the child's environment (Karst & Van Hecke, 2012). Group-delivered parent training may be a cost-effective and practical approach while also providing peer support (other parents).

ADAPTATIONS AND MODIFICATIONS

Given the considerable heterogeneity among children with ASD, both in terms of symptomatic impairments (e.g., self-injury, presence of co-occurring psychiatric problems) and in overall functioning (e.g., verbal and cognitive ability), individualization of treatment is a necessity when working with manualized treatment protocols. Some commonly applied adaptations may facilitate the process of treatment and improve outcome. As previously mentioned, however, the merit or incremental benefit of specific modifications has not been well studied. Regardless, while we await such research, many clinicians agree that some modifications to content and delivery are helpful when working with children who have ASD.

Personal insight, or the ability to reflect on one's own thoughts and feelings, is often impaired in children with ASD compared to same-age peers (Hobson, 2010). This impairment affects the youth's pattern of self-report (see Lerner, Calhoun, et al., 2012), which can affect the validity of diagnostic evaluations and the therapeutic process. Difficulties with impulsivity and attention are common (Fein, Dixon, Paul, & Levin, 2005), often necessitating the use of brief therapy sessions, frequent breaks or rewards, and schedules and prompts. Many therapists provide more structure across and within therapy sessions than is typical for clients without ASD, to avoid distress with unanticipated changes or novelty. Impaired social reciprocity, or the ability to sustain a give-and-take social interaction, can influence the dynamic of the therapist–client relationship. In response to questions from the therapist, brief (often one-word) responses to questions are typical, with little spontaneous elaboration for the therapist's benefit or understanding. The therapist often has to explicitly ask for more information or detail and do more directing of the client (e.g., by offering response options in addition to asking open-ended questions) than what may be typical when working with non-ASD children. A larger "dose" of treatment is also typical. For instance, the child may require more sessions than typically would be needed to target the same problem (e.g., separation anxiety) in a child without ASD. Scheduled booster sessions are often helpful, as is parent contact and feedback outside of session.

With respect to the content of treatment, corrective (not just descriptive) feedback is critical for experiential learning to take place. Such feedback should be direct, fairly concrete, and in vivo when possible. Psychoeducation about the nature of ASD, including its chronic course as well as associated strengths and deficits, can be helpful in promoting acceptance and understanding. Unlike many Axis I conditions, remission typically is not sought in treatment. Instead, we focus on decreasing specific symptoms and improving quality of life. As such, integration of strengths-based approaches and helping the young client to develop his or her own interests and skills (e.g., Seligman, Steen, Park, & Peterson, 2005) can be especially useful. Given pervasive problems with emotion recognition, self-regulation of affect, and heightened negative emotionality, a great deal of therapy tends to address the emotional aspects of behavior change (e.g., Attwood, 2004). There are many resources on specific adaptations useful when treating children with ASD (see Attwood & Scarpa, 2013; Lang, Regester, Lauderdale, Ashbaugh, & Haring, 2010; Rotheram-Fuller & MacMullen, 2011).

MEASURING TREATMENT EFFECTS

Evidence-based assessment (e.g., Achenbach, 2005; Mash & Hunsley, 2005) is critical to our ability to determine if treatments work. Unfortunately, there are very few tools validated for the assessment of treatment response in children with ASD (Ollendick & White, 2012). A full review of the most widely used tools for measuring treatment effects is beyond the scope of this chapter (for more information, see: Lord et al., 2005; Mazefsky & White, 2013; Wagner et al., 2007). Regardless of the specific measure or battery of measures that are selected to assess treatment progress, there are six general clinical guidelines to consider.

First, a growing body of research indicates that children and adolescents with ASD, even those who are cognitively higher functioning, tend to underreport psychiatric symptoms (Lerner, Calhoun, et al., 2012; Mazefsky, Kao, Conner, & Oswald, 2011; Russell & Sofronoff, 2005; White, Schry, & Maddox, 2011), a fact that underscores the importance of other reports (e.g., parents) to track treatment progress. We advocate use of multiple raters (e.g., parent, teacher, peers, and child) and evaluation via multiple modalities (e.g., interview, observation, questionnaire) whenever possible.

Second, in light of the heterogeneity of problems and symptoms typically presented by young clients with ASD, it is important to consider change across three domains: (1) in diagnostic status and in specific symptoms continuously, (2) at the global level (i.e., clinical improvement), and (3) in daily functioning or adaptive behavior. As such, a comprehensive battery might include a semi-structured diagnostic interview [domain 1], such as the Autism Comorbidity Interview (Lainhart, Leyfer, & Folstein, 2003) or the Anxiety Disorders Interview Schedule for Children (ADIS-C) (Silverman & Albano, 1996); self- and parent-reports measures of mood and anxiety symptoms [domain 2], such as the Screen for Child Anxiety Related Emotional Disorders (SCARED) (Birmaher et al., 1997) and the Mood and Feeling Questionnaire (MFQ) (Costello & Angold, 1988); and a measure of change in daily functioning [domain 3], such as the Developmental Disability–Global Assessment Scale (DD-CGAS) (Wagner et al., 2007) or the Vineland Adaptive Behavior Scales (Sparrow, Cicchetti, & Balla, 2005). Assessment of complex and multifaceted change, such as improvement in social impairment and symptoms of anxiety within the child, can be challenging (Koenig, De Los Reyes, Cicchetti, Scahill, & Klin, 2009), but evaluating change at multiple levels of analysis is important in developing a full understanding of the influence of the treatment on the whole child (e.g., Kazdin, 2005).

Third, we recommend assessment at multiple time points post-intervention. Although the afore-mentioned interventions are indeed promising, few have demonstrated effects that maintain after treatment cessation (e.g., Lerner et al., 2011). As interventions for ASD, as well as many evidence-based CBT packages, are designed to be time limited, it is crucial that therapists work to ensure they are having an enduring impact.

Fourth, we advocate conducting assessments of fidelity throughout implementation of any EBT (e.g., Koenig et al., 2009). Without such assessment, it is difficult to determine whether associations of treatment with outcome (positive, negative, or null) are truly related to the putative intervention and not other nonspecific factors.

Fifth, we recommend assessing clients' motivation to participate. Given pathognomonic deficits in social motivation in ASD (Chevallier, Kohls, Troiani, Brodkin, & Schultz, 2012), lack of desire to participate may be a particularly powerful impediment to therapeutic change in this population.

Finally, given the aforementioned limitations of informant reports (despite their ecological validity), we recommend complementing them with behavioral and task-based measures of outcomes that maximize internal validity when possible. Some of these measures are computer based (e.g., Tanaka et al., 2010), but others may be psychophysiological. Indeed, recent work suggests that neurobiological markers associated with symptoms of ASD may soon provide both prospective biomarkers of response to treatment and concrete indices of change (Dawson, Bernier, & Ring, 2012; Lerner, White & McPartland, 2012; McPartland & Pelphrey, 2012). For instance, latency of an electrophysiological potential ("spike" in electrical activity) called the N170 has been shown to be slowed in ASD (McPartland et al., 2011), with its speed indexing severity of deficits in processing emotional stimuli (Lerner, McPartland, & Morris, 2013). Thus, this marker could be used prior to treatment to determine whether emotion processing is an appropriate goal for an individual client. Additionally, recent research suggests that this latency may be amenable to intervention (Faja et al., 2012), suggesting that future researchers (and perhaps therapists) may be able to use such neurobiological markers to indicate change in the neural processes subtending social disability in ASD.

CLINICAL CASE EXAMPLE

We present the case of Alisha (identifying information has been altered to protect confidentiality), a 12-year-old African American female referred by her mother for treatment, to exemplify some of the intervention approaches and modifications described in this chapter. Alisha, who was diagnosed with Asperger's disorder by her school psychologist at the age of 11, presented as socially withdrawn and emotionally dysregulated (e.g., frequent, unprompted crying, although she was unable to self-report the cause of her crying). She spoke in a very soft voice, avoided eye contact with the therapist, and often provided one-word responses to questions. Alisha's mother, a single parent, was quite concerned by her daughter's withdrawn behaviors, lack of friendships, and poor performance in school. Alisha's mother reported that she believed that many of Alisha's problems were due to her "laziness, lack of drive, and poor self-esteem."

Although Alisha presented as depressed and her mother described her as experiencing a great deal of anxiety, her scores on self-report measures were consistently (at intake and throughout treatment) not clinically elevated. Behaviorally, however, she frequently pulled her hair out when she became distressed and was very "shy and nervous" (per mother's report) in social interactions. Treatment began slowly with Alisha due to her hesitancy to interact with the therapist. In order to engage Alisha, the therapist incorporated some of her interests into treatment, playing board games with her and drawing cartoons. Due to Alisha's presenting problems related to anxiety and sadness and her difficulty in expressing and regulating her emotions, components of CBT were incorporated into treatment. The therapist assisted Alisha in identifying her emotions and related thoughts using several different visual examples (e.g., emotion thermometers, cartoons). Alisha was able to identify some thoughts and emotions, but her descriptors were vague (e.g., feeling "so-so") and lacked variability. It was most helpful to assist Alisha in identifying the types of situations that she referred to as "hard for her" (e.g., talking to classmates) and assist her in developing helpful thoughts ("This is uncomfortable, but this will help me to make friends") and using relaxation strategies (e.g., deep breathing) in such situations. Imaginal and in vivo exposures to such situations were conducted during treatment sessions (e.g., starting a conversation with a peer), and the use of these strategies was rehearsed.

Individual social skills training was also utilized in Alisha's treatment. Targets for social skills training were developing conversation skills for talking to classmates, asking teachers for help, and phone conversations. The therapist included a didactic portion in some sessions, instructing Alisha on specific social skills (e.g., starting a conversation, using appropriate facial expressions). Role-plays with the therapist and confederates were utilized frequently to practice skills. Alisha was given immediate feedback related to her performance and occasionally was shown videotape of her performance. Each week Alisha was assigned homework to practice the skills learned in session in order to encourage generalization.

The therapist provided Alisha's mother with psychoeducation about ASD and associated concerns (e.g., emotion regulation problems) and worked with her individually and with Alisha in the session, helping her learn how to express her expectations clearly to Alisha. Additionally, Alisha's mother was helped to structure the assistance she provided Alisha with schoolwork (e.g., providing assistance in breaking down homework assignments and organization). The therapist encouraged Alisha's mother to utilize positive reinforcement, using small but meaningful rewards (e.g., a trip to the library), when Alisha made small accomplishments in school and in treatment. By termination of treatment, Alisha had improved her performance in school and had a few friends, with whom she sat during lunch and engaged in conversations within activity groups and in the hallways. Alisha's mother expressed that she noticed her daughter smiling more often and observed her occasionally socializing with classmates she ran into in the community, although no changes were noted throughout treatment on measures of anxiety or depression.

REFERENCES

Achenbach, T. (2005). Advancing assessment of children and adolescents: Commentary on evidence-based assessment of child and adolescent disorders. *Journal of Clinical Child and Adolescent Psychology, 34*(3), 541–547.

American Psychiatric Association. (2000). *Diagnostic and statistical manual of mental disorders* (4th ed., text rev.). Washington, DC: Author.

American Psychiatric Association. (2013). *Diagnostic and statistical manual of mental disorders* (5th ed.). Arlington, VA: American Psychiatric Publishing.

Attwood, T. (2004). Cognitive behavior therapy for children and adults with Asperger's syndrome. *Behaviour Change, 21,* 147–161. doi: 10.1375/bech.21.3.147.55995

Attwood, T., & Scarpa, A. (2013). Modifications of CBT for use with children and adolescents with high functioning ASD and their common difficulties. In A. Scarpa, S. W. White, & T. Attwood (Eds.), *Promising cognitive behavioral interventions for children and adolescents with high-functioning autism spectrum disorders*. New York, NY: Guilford Press.

Baker, J. (2003). *Social skills training for children and adolescents with Asperger syndrome and social-communication problems*. Shawnee Mission, KS: Autism Asperger Publishing.

Beaumont, R. (2009). *Secret Agent Society: Solving the mystery of social encounters* [Computer game]. Queensland, Australia: Social Skills Training Institute, division of Triple P International Pty Ltd.

Beaumont, R., & Sofronoff, K. (2008). A multi-component social skills intervention for children with Asperger syndrome: The Junior Detective Training Program. *Journal of Child Psychology and Psychiatry, 49*(7), 743–753. doi: 10.1111/j.1469–7610.2008.01920.x

Bellini, S. (2008). *Building social relationships: A systematic approach to teaching social interaction skills to children and adolescents with autism spectrum disorders and other social difficulties*. Shawnee Mission, KS: Autism Asperger Publishing.

Bellini, S., Peters, J. K., Benner, L., & Hopf, A. (2007). A meta-analysis of school-based social skills interventions for children with autism spectrum disorders. *Remedial and Special Education, 28,* 153–162. doi: 10.1177/07419325070280030401

Birmaher, B., Khetarpal, S., Brent, D., Cully, M., Balach, L., Kaufman, J., & McKenzie Neer, S. (1997). The Screen for Child Anxiety Related Emotional Disorders (SCARED): Scale construction and psychometric characteristics. *Journal of the American Academy of Child & Adolescent Psychiatry, 36,* 545–553. doi: 10.1097/00004583–199704000–00018

Boyd, B. A. (2002). Examining the relationship between stress and lack of social support in mothers of children with autism. *Focus on Autism & Other Developmental Disabilities, 17*(4), 208–215. doi: 10.1097/00004583–199704000–00018

Buckley, S. D., Strunck, P. G., & Newchok, D. K. (2005). A comparison of two multicomponent procedures to increase food consumption. *Behavioral Interventions, 20,* 139–146. doi: 10.1002/bin.188

Canitano, R. (2006). Self injurious behavior in autism: Clinical aspects and treatment with risperidone. *Journal of Neural Transmission, 113*(3), 425–431. doi:10.1007/s00702–005–0337-x

Cederlund, M., Hagberg, B., Billstedt, E., Gillberg, I. C., & Gillberg, C. (2008). Asperger syndrome and autism: A comparative longitudinal follow-up study more than 5 years after original diagnosis. *Journal of Autism and Developmental Disorders, 38,* 72–85. doi: 10.1007/s10803–007–0364–6

Chalfant, A., Rapee, R., & Carroll, L. (2007). Treating anxiety disorders in children with high-functioning autism spectrum disorders: A controlled trial. *Journal of Autism and Developmental Disorders, 37,* 1842–1857. doi: 10.1007/s10803–006–0318–4

Chang, Y., Quan, J., & Wood, J. J. (2012). Effects of anxiety disorder severity on social functioning in children with autism spectrum disorders. *Journal of Developmental and Physical Disabilities, 24,* 235–245. doi: 10.1007/s10882–012–9268–2

Charlop-Christy, M. H., Le, L., & Freeman, K. A. (2000). A comparison of video modeling with in vivo modeling for teaching children with autism. *Journal of Autism and Developmental Disorders, 30,* 537–552. doi: 10.1023/A:1005635326276

Chevallier, C., Kohls, G., Troiani, V., Brodkin, E. S., & Schultz, R. T. (2012). The social motivation theory of autism. *Trends in Cognitive Sciences, 16*, 231–239. doi: 10.1016/j.tics.2012.02.007

Costello, E. J., & Angold, A. (1988). Scales to assess child and adolescent depression: Checklists, screens, and nets. *Journal of the American Academy of Child & Adolescent Psychiatry, 27*, 726–737. doi: 10.1097/00004583-198811000-00011

Dawson, G., Bernier, R., & Ring, R. H. (2012). Social attention: A possible early indicator of efficacy in autism clinical trials. *Journal of Neurodevelopmental Disorders, 4*, 1–12. doi: 10.1186/1866-1955-4-11

DeRosier, M. E., Swick, D. C., Davis, N. O., McMillen, J. S., & Matthews, R. (2010). The efficacy of a social skills group intervention for improving social behaviors in children with high-functioning autism spectrum disorders. *Journal of Autism and Developmental Disorders, 41*, 1033–1043. doi: 10.1007/s10803-010-1128-2

Dyson, L. I. (1997). Fathers and mothers of school-age children with developmental disabilities: Parental stress, family functioning, and social support. *American Journal of Mental Retardation, 102*, 267–279.

Eikeseth, S., Smith, T., Jahr, E., & Eldevik, S. (2007). Outcome for children with autism who began intensive behavioral treatment between ages 4 and 7: A comparison controlled study. *Behavior Modification, 31*, 264–278. doi: 10.1177/0145445506291396

Faja, S., Webb, S. J., Jones, E., Merkle, K., Kamara, D., Bavaro, J., . . . Dawson, G. (2012). The effects of face expertise training on the behavioral performance and brain activity of adults with high-functioning autism spectrum disorders. *Journal of Autism and Developmental Disorders, 42*, 278–293. doi: 10.1007/s10803-011-1243-8

Farley, M. A., McMahon, W. M., Fombonne, E., Jenson, W. R., Miller, J., Gardner, M., . . . Coon, H. (2009). Twenty-year outcome for individuals with autism and average or near-average cognitive abilities. *Autism Research, 2*, 109–118. doi: 10.1002/aur.69

Fein, D., Dixon, P., Paul, J., & Levin, H. (2005). Pervasive developmental disorder can devolve into ADHD: Case illustrations. *Journal of Autism and Developmental Disorders, 35*, 525–534. doi: 10.1007/s10803-005-5066-3

Frazier, T. W., Youngstrom, E. A., Haycook, T., Sinoff, A., Dimitriou, F., Knapp, J., & Sinclair, L. (2010). Effectiveness of medication combined with intensive behavioral intervention for reducing aggression in youth with autism spectrum disorder. *Journal of Child and Adolescent Psychopharmacology, 20*, 167–177. doi: 10.1089/cap.2009.0048

Freedman, B. H., Kalb, L. G., Zaboltsky, B., & Stuart, E. A. (2012). Relationship status among parents of children with autism spectrum disorders: A population-based study. *Journal of Autism and Developmental Disorders, 42*, 539–548. doi: 10.1007/ s10803-011-1269-y

Ghaziuddin, M., Ghaziuddin, N., & Greden, J. (2002). Depression in persons with autism: Implications for research and clinical care. *Journal of Autism and Developmental Disorders, 32*, 299–306. doi: 10.1023/A:1016330802348

Golan, O., Ashwin, E., Granader, Y., McClintock, S., Day, K., Leggett, V., & Baron-Cohen, S. (2010). Enhancing emotion recognition in children with autism spectrum conditions: An intervention using animated vehicles with real emotional faces. *Journal of Autism and Developmental Disorders, 40*, 269–279. doi: 10.1007/s10803-009-0862-9

Goldstein, A. P., & McGinnis, E. (1997). *Skillstreaming the adolescent: New strategies and perspectives for teaching prosocial skills* (rev. ed.). Champaign, IL: Research Press.

Granger, S., Rivieres-Pigeon, C. D., Sabourin, G., & Forget, J. (2012). Mothers' reports of their involvement in early intensive behavioral intervention. *Topics in Early Childhood Special Education, 32*(2), 68–77. doi: 10.1177/0271121410393285

Gray, C. A. (2000). *The new social story book*. Arlington, TX: Future Horizons.

Harris, S. L., & Handleman, J. S. (2000). Age and IQ at intake as predictors of placement for young children with autism: A four- to six-year follow-up. *Journal of Autism and Developmental Disorders, 30*, 137–142. doi: 10.1023/A:1005459606120

Hartley, S. L., Barker, E. T., Seltzer, M. M., Floyd, F., Greenberg, J., Orsmond, G., & Bolt, D. (2010). The relative risk and timing of divorce in families in children with an autism spectrum disorder. *Journal of Family Psychology, 24*(4), 449–457. doi: 10.1037/ a0019847.

Hobson, R. P. (2010). Explaining autism: Ten reasons to focus on the developing self. *Autism, 14*, 391–407. doi: 10.1177/1362361310364142

Hopkins, I. M., Gower, M. W., Perez, T. A., Smith, D. S., Amthor, F. R., Wimsatt, F. C., & Biasini, F. J. (2011). Avatar assistant: Improving social skills in students with and ASD through a computer-based intervention. *Journal of Autism and Developmental Disorders, 41*, 1543–1555. doi: 10.1007/s10803-011-1179-z

Howlin, P., Goode, J., Hutton, J., & Rutter, M. (2004). Adult outcome for children with autism. *Journal of Child Psychology and Psychiatry, 45*, 212–229. doi: 10.1111/j.1469-7610.2004.00215.x

Johnson, C. R., Handen, B. L., Butter, E., Wagner, A., Mulick, J., Sukhodolsky, D. G., . . . Smith, T. (2007). Development of a parent training program for children with pervasive developmental disorders. *Behavioral Interventions, 22*, 201–221. doi: 10.1002/bin.237

Johnston, C., & Mash, E. J. (1989). A measure of parenting satisfaction and efficacy. *Journal of Clinical Child Psychology, 18*(2), 167–175.

Joshi, G., Petty, C., Wozniak, J., Henin, A., Fried, R., Galdo, M., . . . Biederman, J. (2010). The heavy burden of psychiatric comorbidity in youth with autism spectrum disorders: A large comparative study of a psychiatrically referred population. *Journal of Autism and Developmental Disorders, 40,* 1361–1370. doi: 10.1007/s10803–010–0996–9

Karst, J. S., & Van Hecke, A. V. (2012). Parent and family impact of autism spectrum disorders: A review and proposed model for intervention evaluation. *Clinical Child and Family Psychology Review, 15*(3), 247–277. doi: 10.1007/s10567–012–0119–6

Kasari, C., Rotheram-Fuller, E., Locke, J., & Gulsrud, A. (2012). Making the connection: Randomized controlled trial of social skills at school for children with autism spectrum disorders. *Journal of Child Psychology and Psychiatry, 53,* 431–439. doi: 10.1111/j.1469–7610.2011.02493.x

Kazdin, A. E. (2005). Evidence-based assessment for children and adolescents: Issues in measurement development and clinical application. *Journal of Clinical Child and Adolescent Psychology, 34*(3), 548–558.

Kelly, A. B., Garnett, M. S., Attwood, T., & Peterson, C. (2008). Autism spectrum symptomatology in children: The impact of family and peer relationships. *Journal of Abnormal Child Psychology, 36*(7), 1069–1081. doi: 10.1007/s10802–008–9234–8

Kerwin, M. E., Eicher, P. S., & Gelsinger, J. (2005). Parental report of eating problems and gastrointestinal symptoms in children with pervasive developmental disorders. *Children's Health Care, 34*(3), 217–234. doi: 10.1207/s15326888chc3403_4

Koenig, K., De Los Reyes, A., Cicchetti, D., Scahill, L., & Klin, A. (2009) Group intervention to promote social skills in school-age children with pervasive developmental disorders: Reconsidering efficacy. *Journal of Autism and Developmental Disorders, 39,* 1163–1172. doi: 10.1007/s10803–009–0728–1

Krauss, M. W. (1993). Child-related and parenting stress: Similarities and differences between mothers and fathers of children with disabilities. *American Journal of Mental Retardation, 97,* 393–404.

Lainhart, J. E., Leyfer, O. T., & Folstein, S. E. (2003). *Autism Comorbidity Interview-Present and Lifetime version (ACI-PL).* Salt Lake City: University of Utah Press.

Lang, R., Regester, A., Lauderdale, S., Ashbaugh, K., & Haring, A. (2010). Treatment of anxiety in autism spectrum disorders using cognitive behavior therapy: A systematic review. *Developmental Neurorehabilitation, 13,* 53–63. doi: 10.3109/17518420903236288

Laugeson, E. A., & Frankel, F. (2010). *Social skills for teenagers with developmental and autism spectrum disorders: The PEERS treatment manual.* New York, NY: Routledge.

Laugeson, E. A., Frankel, F., Gantman, A., Dillon, A., & Mogil, C. (2011). Evidence-based social skills training for adolescents with autism spectrum disorders: The UCLA PEERS program. *Journal of Autism and Developmental Disorders, 42,* 1025–1036. doi: 10.1007/s10803–011–1339–1

Laugeson, E. A., Frankel, F., Mogil, C., & Dillon, A. R. (2009). Parent-assisted social skills training to improve friendships in teens with autism spectrum disorders. *Journal of Autism and Developmental Disorders, 39,* 596–606. doi: 10.1007/s10803–008–0664–5

Lerner, M. D., Calhoun, C. D., Mikami, A. Y., & De Los Reyes, A. (2012). Understanding parent-child social informant discrepancy in youth with high functioning autism spectrum disorders. *Journal of Autism and Developmental Disorders, 42,* 2680–2692. doi: 10.1007/s10803–012–1525–9

Lerner, M. D., McMahon, C. M., & Britton, N. (2014). Autism spectrum disorder in adolescents: Promoting social and emotional development. In T. P. Gullotta & M. Bloom (Eds.), *Encyclopedia of primary prevention and health promotion: Adolescence* (Vol. 3, 2nd ed.). New York, NY: Springer.

Lerner, M. D., McPartland, J. C., & Morris, J. P. (2013). Multimodal emotion processing in autism spectrum disorders: An event-related potential study. *Developmental Cognitive Neuroscience, 3,* 11–21. doi: 10.1016/j.dcn.2012.08.005

Lerner, M. D., & Mikami, A. Y. (2012). A preliminary randomized controlled trial of two social skills interventions for youth with high functioning autism spectrum disorders. *Focus on Autism and Other Developmental Disabilities, 27,* 145–155. doi: 10.1177/1088357612450613

Lerner, M. D., Mikami, A. Y., & Levine, K. (2011). Socio-dramatic affective-relational intervention for adolescents with Asperger syndrome & high-functioning autism: Pilot study. *Autism, 15,* 21–42. doi: 10.1177/1362361309353613

Lerner, M. D., White, S. W., & McPartland, J. C. (2012). Mechanisms of change in psychosocial interventions for autism spectrum disorders. *Dialogues in Clinical Neuroscience, 14,* 307–318.

Lilienfeld, S. O. (2007). Psychological treatments that cause harm. *Perspectives on Psychological Science, 2,* 53–70. doi: 10.1111/j.1745–6916.2007.00029.x

Lopata, C., Thomeer, M. L., Volker, M. A., Toomey, J. A., Nida, R. E., Lee, G. K., . . . Rodgers, J. D. (2011). RCT of a manualized social treatment for high-functioning autism spectrum disorders. *Journal of Autism and Developmental Disorders, 40,* 1297–1310. doi: 10.1007/s10803–010–0989–8

Lopata, C., Toomey, J. A., Dox, J. D., Volker, M. A., Chow, S. Y., Thomeer, M. L., . . . Smerbeck, A. M. (2010). Anxiety and depression in children with HFASDs: Symptom levels and source differences. *Journal of Abnormal Child Psychology, 38,* 765–776. doi: 10.1007/s10802–010–9406–1

Lord, C., Wagner, A., Rogers, S., Szatmari, P., Aman, M., Charman, T., . . . Yoder, P. (2005). Challenges in evaluating psychosocial interventions for autistic spectrum disorders. *Journal of Autism and Developmental Disorders, 35,* 695–708. doi: 10.1007/s10803–005–0017–6

Lovaas, O. I. (1987). Behavioral treatment and normal educational and intellectual functioning in young autistic children. *Journal of Consulting and Clinical Psychology, 55,* 3–9. doi: 10.1037/0022–006X.55.1.3

Lovaas, O. I. (2003). *Teaching individuals with developmental delays: Basic intervention techniques.* Austin, TX: Pro-Ed.

Luiselli, J. K., Ricciardi, J. N., & Gilligan, K. (2005). Liquid fading to establish milk consumption by a child with autism. *Behavioral Interventions, 20,* 155–163. doi: 10.1002/bin.187

Maddox, B. B., & White, S. W. *(2012,* May). *Suicidality and non-suicidal self-injury in high-functioning adolescents with autism spectrum disorder.* Poster presented at the 11th annual international meeting for Autism Research, Toronto, ON.

Mash, E., & Hunsley, J. (2005). Special section: Developing guidelines for the evident-based assessment of child and adolescent disorders. *Journal of Clinical Child and Adolescent Psychology, 34*(3), 362–379.

Matson, J. L. (2009). Aggression and tantrums in children with autism: A review of behavioral treatments and maintaining variables. *Journal of Mental Health Research in Intellectual Disabilities, 2,* 169–187. doi: 10.1080/19315860902725875

Matson, J. L., & LoVullo, S. V. (2008). A review of behavioral treatments for self-injurious behaviors of persons with autism spectrum disorders. *Behavior Modification, 32*(1), 61–76. doi: 10.1177/0145445507304581

Matson, M. L., & Fodstad, J. C. (2009). The treatment of food selectivity and other feeding problems in children with autism spectrum disorders. *Research in Autism Spectrum Disorders, 3*(2), 455–461. doi: 10.1016/j.rasd.2008.09.005

Matson, M. L., Mahan, S., & Matson, J. L. (2009). Parent training: A review of methods for children with autism spectrum disorders. *Research in Autism Spectrum Disorders, 3*(4), 868–875. doi: 10.1016/j.rasd.2009.02.003

Mazefsky, C. A., Kao, J., Conner, C., & Oswald, D. P. (2011). Preliminary caution regarding the use of psychiatric self-report measures with adolescents with high-functioning autism spectrum disorders. *Research in Autism Spectrum Disorders, 5,* 164–174. doi: 10.1016/j.rasd.2010.03.006

Mazefsky, C. A., & White, S. W. (in press). Adults with autism. In F. R. Volkmar, R. Paul, S. J. Rogers, & K. A. Pelphrey (Eds.), *Handbook of autism spectrum disorders* (4th ed.). Hoboken, NJ: Wiley.

Mazefsky, C. A., Williams, D. L., & Minshew, N. J. (2008). Variability in adaptive behavior in autism: Evidence for the importance of family history. *Journal of Abnormal Child Psychology, 36,* 591–599. doi: 10.1007/s10802–007–9202–8

McAfee, J. (2002). *Navigating the social world: A curriculum for individuals with Asperger's syndrome, high functioning autism and related disorders.* Arlington, TX: Future Horizons.

McGinnis, E., & Goldstein, A. P. (1997). *Skillstreaming the elementary school child: New strategies and perspectives for teaching prosocial skills* (Rev. ed.). Champaign, IL: Research Press.

McPartland, J. C., & Pelphrey, K. (2012). The implications of social neuroscience for social disability. *Journal of Autism and Developmental Disorders, 1–7.* doi: 10.1007/s10803–012–1514–z

McPartland, J. C., Wu, J., Bailey, C. A., Mayes, L. C., Schultz, R. T., & Klin, A. (2011). Atypical neural specialization for social percepts in autism spectrum disorder. *Social Neuroscience, 6,* 436–451.

Metz, B., Mulick, J. A., & Butter E. M. (2005). Autism: A late 20th century fad magnet. In J. W. Jacobson, R. M. Foxx, & J. A. Mulick (Eds.), *Controversial therapies for developmental disabilities* (pp. 237–264). Mahwah, NJ: Erlbaum.

Mikami, K., Inomata, S., Hayakawa, N., Ohnishi, Y., Enseki, Y., Ohya, A., . . . Matsumoto, H. (2009). Frequency and clinical features of pervasive developmental disorder in adolescent suicide attempts. *General Hospital Psychiatry, 31,* 163–166.

Moree, B. N., & Davis, T. E. (2010). Cognitive-behavioral therapy for anxiety in children diagnosed with autism spectrum disorders: Modification trends. *Research in Autism Spectrum Disorders, 4*(3), 346–354. doi: 10.1016/j.rasd.2009.10.015

Najdowski, A. C., Wallace, M. D., Doney, J. K., & Ghezzi, P. M. (2003). Parental assessment and treatment of food selectivity in natural settings. *Journal of Applied Behavior Analysis, 36,* 383–386. doi: 10.1901/jaba.2003.36–383

National Autism Center. (2009). *A guide to providing appropriate interventions to students with autism spectrum disorders.* Available online at http://www.nationalautismcenter.org/nsp/reports.php

National Research Council. (2001). Educating children with autism. Committee on Educational Interventions for Children with Autism. In C. Lord & J. P. McGee (Eds.), *Division of behavioral and social sciences and education.* Washington, DC: National Academies Press.

Ollendick, T. H., & White, S. W. (2012). Invited commentary: The presentation and classification of anxiety in ASD: Where to from here? *Clinical Psychology: Science and Practice, 19,* 352–355. doi: 10.1111/cpsp.12013

Patel, M., Reed, G. K., Piazza, C. C., Mueller, M., Bachmeyer, M. H., & Layer, S. A. (2007). Use of high-probability instructional sequence to increase compliance to feeding demands in the absence of escape extinction. *Behavioral Interventions, 22*, 305–310. doi: 10.1002/bin.251

Pisula, E. (2011). Parenting stress in mothers and fathers of children with autism spectrum disorders. In M. Mohammadi (Ed.), *A comprehensive book on autism spectrum disorders*. Retrieved from http://www.intechopen.com/books/a-comprehensive-book-on-autism-spectrum-disorders/parenting-stress-in-mothers-and-fathers-of-children-with-autism-spectrum-disorders

Puleo, C. M., & Kendall, P. C. (2011). Anxiety disorders in typically developing youth: Autism spectrum symptoms as a predictor of cognitive-behavioral treatment. *Journal of Autism and Developmental Disorders, 41*, 275–286. doi: 10.1007/s10803–010–1047–2

Raja, M., Azzoni, A., & Frustaci, A. (2011). Autism spectrum disorders and suicidality. *Clinical Practice and Epidemiology in Mental Health, 7*, 97–105. doi: 10.2174/1745017901107010097

Ramdoss, S., Machalicek, W., Rispoli, M., Mulloy, A., Lang, R., & O'Reilly, M. (2012). Computer-based interventions to improve social and emotional skills in individuals with autism spectrum disorders: A systematic review. *Developmental Neurorehabilitation, 15*, 119–135. doi: 10.3109/17518423.2011.651655

Reaven, J. (2011). The treatment of anxiety symptoms in youth with high-functioning autism spectrum disorders: Developmental considerations for parents. *Brain Research, 1380*, 255–263. doi: 10.1016/j.brainres.2010.09.075

Reaven, J. A., Blakeley-Smith, A., Nichols, S., Dasari, M., Flanigan, E., & Hepburn, S. (2009). Cognitive-behavioral group treatment for anxiety symptoms in children with high-functioning autism spectrum disorders: A pilot study. *Focus on Autism and Other Developmental Disabilities, 24*, 27–37. doi: 10.1177/1088357608327666

Reichow, B., & Volkmar, F. R. (2010). Social skills interventions for individuals with autism: Evaluation for evidence-based practices within a best evidence synthesis framework. *Journal of Autism and Developmental Disorders, 40*, 149–166. doi: 10.1007/s10803–009–0842–0

Research Units on Pediatric Psychopharmacology Autism Network. (2007). Parent training for children with pervasive developmental disorders: A multi-site feasibility trial. *Behavioral Interventions, 22*, 179–199. doi: 10.1002/bin.236

Robb, A. S. (2010). Managing irritability and aggression in autism spectrum disorders in children and adolescents. *Developmental Disabilities Research Reviews, 16*, 258–264. doi: 10.1002/ddrr.118

Rogers, M. F., & Smith-Myles, B. (2001). Using social stories and comic strip conversations to interpret social situations for an adolescent with Asperger syndrome. *Intervention in School & Clinic, 36*(5), 310–313.

Rogers, S. J., & Vismara, L. A. (2008). Evidence-based comprehensive treatments for early autism. *Journal of Clinical Child and Adolescent Psychology, 37*, 8–38. doi: 10.1080/15374410701817808

Rotheram-Fuller, E., & MacMullen, L. (2011). Cognitive-behavioral therapy for children with autism spectrum disorders. *Psychology in the Schools, 48*, 263–271. doi: 10.1002/pits.20552

Russell, E., & Sofronoff, K. (2005). Anxiety and social worries in children with Asperger syndrome. *Australian and New Zealand Journal of Psychiatry, 39*, 633–638.

Sansosti, F. J. (2010). Teaching social skills to children with autism spectrum disorders using tiers of support: A guide for school-based professionals. *Psychology in the Schools, 47*(3), 257–281. doi: 10.1002/pits.20469

Seligman, M. E. P., Steen, T. A., Park, N., & Peterson, C. (2005). Positive psychology progress: Empirical validation of interventions. *American Psychology, 60*, 410–421. doi: 10.1037/0003–066X.60.5.410

Silverman, W. K., & Albano, A. M. (1996). *The Anxiety Disorders Interview Schedule for DSM-IV: Child and parent versions*. San Antonio, TX: Graywind.

Singh, N. N., Lancioni, G. E., Winton, A. S., Fisher, B. C., Wahler, R. G., Mcaleavey, K., & McAleavey, K. M. (2006). Mindful parenting decreases aggression, noncompliance, and self-injury in children with autism. *Journal of Emotional and Behavioral Disorders, 14*(3), 169–177. doi: 10.1177/10634266060140030401

Skinner, B. F. (1938). *The behavior of organisms: An experimental analysis*. New York, NY: Appleton-Century.

Smith, T. (2008). Empirically supported and unsupported treatments for autism spectrum disorders. *Scientific Review of Mental Health Practice, 6*, 3–20.

Smith, T. (2010). Early and intensive behavioral intervention in autism. In J. R. Weisz & A. E. Kazdin (Eds.), *Evidence-based psychotherapies for children and adolescents* (2nd ed., pp. 312–326). New York, NY: Guilford Press.

Sofronoff, K., Attwood, T., & Hinton, S. (2005). A randomized controlled trial of a CBT intervention for anxiety in children with Asperger syndrome. *Journal of Child Psychology and Psychiatry, 46*, 1152–1160. doi: 10.1111/j.1469–7610.2005.00411.x

Sofronoff, K., & Farbotko, M. (2002). The effectiveness of parent management training to increase self-efficacy in parents of children with Asperger syndrome. *Autism, 6*(3), 271–286. doi: 10.1177/1362361302006003005

Solomon, M., Ono, M., Timmer, S., & Goodlin-Jones, B. (2008). The effectiveness of parent-child interaction therapy for families of children on the autism spectrum. *Journal of Autism and Developmental Disorders, 38*(9), 1767–1776. doi: 10.1007/s10803–008–0567–5

Sparrow, S. S., Cicchetti, C. V., & Balla, D. A. (2005). *Vineland Adaptive Behavior Scales, second edition (Vineland-II)*. San Antonio, TX: Psychological Corporation.

Stichter, J., Herzog, M. J., Visovsky, K., Schmidt, C., Randolph, J., & Schultz, T. (2010). Social competence intervention for youth with Asperger syndrome and high-functioning autism: An initial investigation. *Journal of Autism and Developmental Disorders, 40,* 1067–1079. doi: 10.1007/s10803–010–0959–1

Tanaka, J., Wolf, J., Klaiman, C., Koenig, K., Cockburn, J., Herlihy, L., . . . Schultz, R. (2010). Using computerized games to teach face recognition skills to children with autism spectrum disorder: The Let's Face It! program. *Journal of Child Psychology and Psychiatry, 51,* 944–952. doi: 10.1111/j.1469–7610.2010.02258.x

Task Force on Promotion and Dissemination of Psychological Treatment Procedures. (1995). Training in and dissemination of empirically validated treatments: Report and recommendations. *Clinical Psychologist, 48,* 3–23.

Twachtman-Reilly, J., Amaral, S. C., & Zebrowski, P. P. (2008). Addressing feeding disorders in children on the autism spectrum in school-based settings: Physiological and behavioral issues. *Language, Speech, and Hearing Services in Schools, 39*(2), 261–272. doi: 10.1044/0161–1461(2008/025)

U.S. Centers for Disease Control and Prevention. (2012). Prevalence of autism spectrum disorders—autism and developmental disabilities monitoring network, United States, 2008. *MMWR Surveillance Summary, 61* (No. SS-3).

van Steensel, F. J. A., Bogels, S. M., & Perrin, S. (2011). Anxiety disorders in children and adolescents with autistic spectrum disorders: A meta-analysis. *Clinical Child and Family Psychology Review, 14,* 302–317. doi: 10.1007/s10567–011–0097–0

Volkmar, F. R. (2013). *The encyclopedia of autism spectrum disorders*. New York, NY: Springer.

Volkmar, F. R., Paul, R., Klin, A., & Cohen, D. (2005). *Handbook of autism and pervasive developmental disorders* (3rd ed.). Hoboken, NJ: Wiley.

Wagner, A., Lecavalier, L., Arnold, L. E., Aman, M. G., Scahill, L., Stigler, K. A., . . . Vitiello, B. (2007). Developmental disabilities modification of the Children's Global Assessment Scale. *Biological Psychiatry, 61,* 504–511. doi: 10.1016/j.biopsych.2007.01.001

Wang, P., & Spillane, A. (2009). Evidence-based social skills interventions for children with autism: A meta-analysis. *Education and Training in Developmental Disabilities, 44,* 318–342.

White, S. W. (2011). *Social skills training for children with Asperger syndrome and high-functioning autism*. New York, NY: Guilford Press.

White, S. W., Koenig, K., & Scahill, L. (2007). Social skills development in children with autism spectrum disorders: A review of the intervention research. *Journal of Autism and Developmental Disorders, 37,* 1858–1868. doi: 10.1007/s10803–006–0320–x

White, S. W., Ollendick, T., Albano, A. M., Oswald, D., Johnson, C., Southam-Gerow, M., . . . Scahill, L. (2013). Randomized controlled trial: Multimodal anxiety and social skill intervention for adolescents with autism spectrum disorder. *Journal of Autism and Developmental Disorder, 43*(2), 382–394. doi: 10.1007/s10803-012-1577-x

White, S. W., Ollendick, T. H., & Bray, B. C. (2011). College students on the autism spectrum: Prevalence and associated problems. *Autism, 15,* 683–670. doi: 10.1177/1362361310393363

White, S. W., Oswald, D., Ollendick, T. H., & Scahill, L. (2009). Anxiety in children and adolescents with autism spectrum disorders. *Clinical Psychology Review, 29,* 216–229. doi: 10.1016/j.cpr.2009.01.003

White, S. W., Scarpa, A., & Attwood, T. (2013). What do we know about psychosocial interventions for youth with high-functioning ASD and where do we go from here? In A. Scarpa, S. W. White, & T. Attwood (Eds.), *Promising cognitive behavioral interventions for children and adolescents with high functioning autism spectrum disorders* (pp. 303–316). New York, NY: Guilford Press.

White, S. W., Schry, A. R., & Maddox, B. B. (2011). Brief report: The assessment of anxiety in high-functioning adolescents with autism spectrum disorder. *Journal of Autism and Developmental Disorders, 42,* 1138–1145. doi: 10.1007/s10803–011–1325–7

Williams, P. G., Dalrymple, N., & Neal, J. (2000). Eating habits of children with autism. *Pediatric Nursing, 26*(3), 259–264.

Wong, C., Odom, S. L., Hume, K. Cox, A. W., Fettig, A., Kucharczyk, S., . . . Schultz, T. R. (2013). *Evidence-based practices for children, youth, and young adults with autism spectrum disorder*. Chapel Hill: The University of North Carolina, Frank Porter Graham Child Development Institute, Autism Evidence-Based Practice Review Group.

Wood, J. J., Drahota, A., Sze, K., Har, K., Chiu, A., & Langer, D. A. (2009). Cognitive behavioral therapy for anxiety in children with autism spectrum disorders: A randomized, controlled trial. *Journal of Child Psychology and Psychiatry, 50,* 224–234. doi: 10.1111/j.1469–7610.2008.01948.x

CHAPTER 15

Evidence-Based Interventions for Eating Disorders

PETER M. DOYLE, CATHERINE BYRNE, ANGELA SMYTH, AND DANIEL LE GRANGE

BRIEF OVERVIEW OF DISORDER/PROBLEM

Eating disorders are serious psychiatric illnesses that can severely impact both the mental and physical health of affected individuals. Diagnostic categories for eating disorders have changed with the publication of the fifth edition of the *Diagnostic and Statistical Manual of Mental Disorders* (*DSM-5*) (American Psychiatric Association, 2013) to include anorexia nervosa (AN), bulimia nervosa (BN), binge eating disorder (BED), and Other Specified Feeding or Eating Disorder. AN is characterized by a failure to achieve or maintain a minimum weight for age and height, fear of gaining weight although underweight, and disturbance in self-perception of body weight or shape or denial of seriousness of low body weight. Patients are given a diagnosis of BN if they are of normal weight but are engaging in regularly occurring episodes of binge eating (i.e., eating large amounts of food with an accompanying sense of loss of control) coupled with compensatory behaviors (e.g., self-induced vomiting, laxative abuse, excessive exercise). Those who are regularly binge eating but do not engage in any kind of compensatory behaviors would meet diagnostic criteria for BED. Outside of these three primary diagnostic categories, patients who engage in some sort of disordered eating are considered to exhibit an Other Specified Feeding or Eating Disorder. Throughout this chapter, we describe these conditions and current evidence-based treatments available when working with eating-disordered children and adolescents.

Rates of eating disorders in the population vary depending on the specific type of eating psychopathology being discussed. By the age of 20, it is estimated that 0.8% of people in the United States will have had AN. Although traditionally thought of as an illness affecting females, approximately 1 to 3 in 10 patients with anorexia are male (Wooldridge, 2012), and that ratio may grow as the stigma of males presenting for treatment of an eating disorder decreases. At this same age cutoff, 2.6% will have had BN, 3.0% will have had BED, and 4.8% to 11.5% will have had an Other Specified Feeding or Eating Disorder (Le Grange, Swanson, Crow, & Merikangas, 2012; Stice, Marti, & Rohde, 2013). The typical age of onset for eating disorders is between 16 and 20 years old. However, increasingly younger cases are being seen in clinics around the country, with some presentations of anorexia nervosa in children as young as 8 years old.

EVIDENCE-BASED APPROACHES

While research in the field of eating disorders is ongoing, there have been some treatments that have been found effective in the improvement and recovery of these disorders.

Anorexia Nervosa

Assessment of patients with AN can be complex, as there are high rates of comorbid psychopathology as well as medical complications that need to be evaluated. Anxiety disorders are the most common comorbidity, with as many as 40% of patients with AN meeting criteria for obsessive-compulsive disorder at some time in their life (Wu, 2008). Of greater concern to the treatment team is the potentially life-threatening consequences of AN. The starvation or semistarvation states in AN can impact every system of the body and lead to disruptions in cardiac, hematological, gastrointestinal, neuroendocrine, skeletal, neurological, and dermatological functioning. Medical complications and the need for close medical monitoring are the norm in patients with AN. The illness has the highest mortality rate of any psychiatric disorder, with 10% of patients ultimately dying from complications (Smink, van Hoeken, & Hoek, 2012). As such, empirically supported treatments for AN include a strong focus on stabilizing the patient's physical health as a means to full recovery. A brief description of these treatments follows.

Family-Based Treatment for Anorexia Nervosa

Originally developed at the Maudsley Hospital in London during the 1980s, family-based treatment for anorexia nervosa (FBT-AN) is commonly referred to as the Maudsley method or Maudsley approach. Theoretically, FBT-AN was influenced by different models of family therapy as well as inpatient eating disorder treatment paradigms. What resulted is a treatment focusing primarily on weight restoration and aiming to empower parents and families to elicit change. The treatment is designed to unfold in three distinct phases. Throughout treatment, the primary therapist serves to coordinate the treatment team, which is comprised of the family, therapist, medical provider, and psychiatrist, if psychotropic medication is necessary. The primary therapist remains in regular contact with all members of the team to ensure consistency of message and focus on eating-disorder symptoms. Except under special circumstances (e.g., suicidal or self-harm behaviors), nothing will take precedence over the task of refeeding and the team's focus on weight restoration.

Phase I   The initial session of FBT-AN is designed to engage the entire family in combating the eating disorder, helping them to conceptualize the eating disorder as separate from the patient, and maximize the family's anxiety in order to motivate them into action. Session 2 is the "family meal," in which the family brings a picnic-style meal to the therapy office. Unlike the standard 60-minute session typical of FBT-AN, this session is 90 minutes long. During this session, parents are given in vivo coaching in how to handle the patient's protestations in a way that is firm but supportive and does not devolve into power plays or arguments. Throughout the family meal, parents are asked to convince their child to eat "one more bite" than he or she is prepared to eat. In order to do so, parents are coached to act together and direct the child to eat in a calm, firm, but supportive manner. Additionally, the therapist will guide the parents on how to persevere until the child eats. The remainder of Phase I is focused on helping parents to problem-solve on a weekly basis in their efforts to help their child gain weight. The primary therapist takes a collaborative stance and works to empower the parents to help them regain trust in their intuition and innate ability to feed their child and make effective decisions in the refeeding process. Instructions regarding food choices or calories are avoided. Instead, parents are encouraged to make these decisions on behalf of their child and to use the weekly weight as data for the effectiveness of their strategies. For example, the therapist will encourage the parents by acknowledging that they have several other children at home who are healthy and have been fed by the parents their whole lives. Additionally, the therapist will support the family in showing them that they had successfully fed their child with anorexia until the anorexia took over. If, for example, the child drops weight in the week before a session, the therapist will encourage the family to identify examples of food that can be added to the child's daily intake in order to increase calories and make up for the weight loss. The therapist also may help the family discover ways in which the patient could have been deficient on calories in the previous week, such as not fully consuming a daily snack at school.

Phase II   Once the patient has reached at least 87% of expected body weight (EBW) and can engage in meals and snacks with minimum resistance, the transition to Phase II can begin. During this phase, control over food decisions is gradually handed back to the child or adolescent. The final disposition of this transition will vary, depending on the age of the patient. A younger patient may not assume full control of all food decisions regardless of progress, whereas an older adolescent might be expected to function more like an adult in terms of food decisions by the end of Phase II of treatment.

Phase III   When the patient's weight is 95% to 100% EBW and he or she can maintain weight without extra parental involvement, treatment can transition into Phase III. The final sessions of FBT-AN are devoted to helping the patient and his or her family navigate a return to a normal trajectory of adolescent development. Often the patient's psychosocial development has been retarded by the presence of AN, and the family must now adjust to what life will look like for a typically functioning preteen or teenager. The therapist reviews the tasks of adolescence and helps the family identify or predict developmental struggles relevant to the patient. These may include peer relationships, sexuality, issues of separation and individuation from parents, and even plans for moving away from home.

FBT is currently the only treatment for adolescent AN that is well established by empirical evidence. The efficacy for FBT-AN has been tested in five randomized control trials (RCTs) (Loeb & Le Grange, 2009). Results from these studies have consistently found that at least 50% of patients experience a full remission of symptoms following 12 months of FBT-AN outpatient treatment. Additionally, the literature has demonstrated that such gains are maintained 4 to 5 years after treatment ends (Eisler et al., 1997; Eisler, Simic, Russell, & Dare, 2007; Lock, Couturier, & Agras, 2006). Accordingly, FBT-AN received the highest rating of any eating disorder treatment from the British National Institute for Health and Clinical Excellence when it published recommended treatment guidelines in 2004 (National Collaborating Centre for Mental Health, 2004). The studies discussed consistently show that adolescents with AN respond well to treatment when their parents are included in the treatment process. However, there is still a substantial population for whom FBT-AN is not successful. Adolescent-focused therapy (AFT, discussed later) seems to be a reasonable alternative to FBT when the latter is not feasible.

Behavioral Family Systems Therapy

Behavioral family systems therapy (BFST) (Robin, Siegal, Koepke, Moye, & Tice, 1994) also utilizes parental involvement and initial control over eating to help patients overcome AN. There are several obvious similarities with FBT-AN, including a three-phase model, the assumption that an underweight patient is unable to make rational decisions about nutrition and healthy eating, and the subsequent control given to parents in Phase I to make decisions on behalf of the patient in terms of food and eating. However, BFST does not focus on empowering the parents to use their own intuition to facilitate changes to meals and food choice. Instead, parents work with a nutritionist, receive concrete directions regarding calories and food choices from the therapist, and record all the meals for therapists' review and feedback.

Phase I   Phase I of BFST consists of an initial assessment followed by parent training relating to the implementation of a behavioral weight gain program. Using straightforward behavioral strategies (e.g., stimulus control and behavioral reward systems), the therapist advises the parents in effectively applying these principles to help their child gain weight. Stimulus control might include removal of "diet" foods from the home. As part of a behavioral reward system, rewards are given for successful performance of some desired behavior, such as meal completion. Depending on the specific family, rewards may take the form of tangible products (e.g., music downloads, clothing, etc.), monetary rewards, or special time spent with family or friends doing a certain activity. These rewards can be negotiated ahead of time with the patient or parents can use their knowledge of the child's preferences to determine rewards.

Phase II   Once the parents are able to consistently achieve weight gain in the patient, Phase II can begin. During this phase, parents continue to maintain control over eating, but the focus of in-session discussions turns to identifying the cognitions that are underlying the patient's eating disorder (e.g., unrealistic fears of unremitting weight gain or all-or-nothing ideas about "good" and "bad" foods). Cognitive behavioral strategies are employed to label the core beliefs and "hot" cognitions that lead to or maintain anorexic behavior. Distorted thoughts are challenged, and patients are encouraged to use rational responses to their distorted automatic thoughts.

Phase III   The final phase of BFST is initiated once patients are able to successfully and consistently challenge their distorted thoughts and manage their own eating and exercise behaviors. Discussions may focus on the parents' activities as a couple and the patient's interests and activities separate from the family. During this final phase of BFST, patients assume responsibility for their own eating and weight maintenance, and the therapist works to help patients individuate and the parents refocus on their marital relationship (something that typically has been deprioritized while their child was acutely ill with AN).

In a design similar to the RCTs for FBT, Robin et al. (1999) compared BFST with ego-oriented individual therapy (EOIT, now known as AFT). Results demonstrated significant improvements for both BFST and EOIT, with 67% of patients reaching target weight and 80% regaining menstruation. At 1-year follow-up, patients had continued to improve, with approximately 75% reaching their target weight and 85% having menses. Results indicated that changes in weight and menses were superior for patients in BFST both at posttreatment and follow-up. Improvements in eating attitudes, mood, and self-reported eating-related family conflict were comparable for the two groups. Therefore, as a close relative to FBT, BFST appears to be a promising treatment option for adolescent AN.

Adolescent-Focused Psychotherapy

Adolescent-focused psychotherapy is a manualized form (Fitzpatrick, Moye, Hoste, Lock, & Le Grange, 2009) of EOIT. AFP is an individual psychotherapy developed from a self-psychology model (Robin et al., 1994, 1999) and based on the tenet that patients with AN are using the disorder to avoid emotional states or developmental tasks of adolescence that they find overwhelming. Consequently, treatment focuses on helping patients to identify, tolerate, and more effectively manage their emotions, thus obviating the need for disordered eating behavior. Similar to other programs, treatment progresses through three phases: (1) building rapport between therapist and patient and developing a mutually understood conceptualization of how AN is being used as a coping strategy; (2) enhancing individuation and independence from parents; (3) developing appropriate coping strategies to deal with the tasks of adolescence and begin engaging in more independent behaviors.

AFP suggests four common themes or coping difficulties as possible paradigms through which to view a patient's anorexic symptoms. *Regressive needs/independence needs* conceptualizes AN as a way of helping the patient to avoid the complex demands of adult life. *Anger/control issues* views the anorexic behavior as a way to communicate feelings of anger or attempt to control others in the patient's life. *Depressive characteristics* focuses on the use of anorexic symptoms as a way to overcome feelings of helplessness through the illusion of control offered by self-denial and starvation. Finally, *deficits in self-esteem* views the function of the eating disorder as a way to bolster the patient's identity and sense of self-worth. Once conceptualization of the illness and its function has been determined, the AFP therapist may employ a host of interventions from a variety of different therapeutic and theoretical backgrounds.

Regardless of what specific AFP paradigm is identified or which strategy is used, all AFP work has a primary emphasis on helping the patient address developmental issues and enhance coping. Issues related to eating and weight gain (or other eating disorder behaviors such as purging, if applicable) are addressed secondarily and incorporated into the primary framework. Weekly 60-minute sessions are held with the adolescent, but collateral sessions can be included in the treatment in order to help parents or other caregivers create a more supportive home environment and enhance familial communication.

Two RCTs have examined the efficacy of AFP for adolescents with a diagnosis of AN. As mentioned previously, the study conducted by Robin and colleagues (1999) comparing BFST with AFP found promising preliminary data for AFP. Findings included large improvements in eating attitudes, depression, and eating-related family conflict in the AFP groups. A second RCT conducted at Stanford University and the University of Chicago evaluated the relative efficacy of FBT-AN and AFT-AN (Lock et al., 2010). These results showed no difference between treatments in achieving full remission at end-of-treatment assessments. However, at both 6- and 12-month follow-up, FBT was significantly superior to AFT in achieving remission from AN (as defined by weight at or above 95% of that expected for age, sex, and height). Given that both treatments led to considerable improvement and similar rates of full remission at end of treatment, AFT appears to be a promising alternative to FBT.

Bulimia Nervosa

Although BN generally presents as ego-dystonic, treatment for this disorder presents its own set of challenges with adolescent patients. Often patients make an effort to stop the binge/purge behavior; however, their lack of success adds to their and the family's fears and doubts about treatment. As with AN, BN also brings with it a host of medical concerns that increase the urgency of treatment. Weight control behaviors and nutritional deficits account for most medical problems in patients with BN; as many as 25% may need to be hospitalized at some point during their illness (Kreipe et al., 1995). Purging can ravage the body as well and cause electrolyte disturbances such as hypokalemia, hyponatremia, and hypochloremia; cardiac arrhythmias; gastroesophageal reflux disease; Mallory-Weiss tears; and periodontal disease due to excessive vomiting (Rome & Ammerman, 2003; Rushing, Jones, & Carney, 2003). Obviously, cessation of purging and the patterns maintaining it is the primary focus of treatment. Following the pattern of treatment development in depression and anxiety, treatments for BN originally were developed for adults and have been adapted for use with child and adolescent populations.

Compared to the adult treatment literature in BN, there is a paucity of research exploring the efficacy of treatments for adolescents. Herein we describe two treatments with empirical support for use in adolescent populations: cognitive behavioral therapy for BN (CBT-BN) and family-based treatment for BN (FBT-BN). Research has established the most support for CBT-BN. A study currently is underway at The University of Chicago and Stanford University comparing CBT-BN and FBT-BN in treating adolescents with BN.

Cognitive Behavioral Therapy for Bulimia Nervosa

Adapted from the adult model of CBT-BN (Fairburn, Marcus, & Wilson, 1993), CBT-BN for adolescents is an individual treatment with three stages. Stage 1 (typically 10 weeks in standard CBT-BN for adults) may be longer to allow for the increased time it may take adolescents to develop a working model of therapy, establish rapport, and increase motivation for treatment. As with adult patients, however, this initial stage of treatment focuses on helping the patient to see the physical and psychological consequences of the eating disorder as well as outlining the CBT model of BN. Self-monitoring is used to help patients make the necessary behavioral changes, including more regular eating that will help reduce intense hunger that can trigger binge episodes and subsequent purging. Stage 2 (7–8 weeks) addresses the distorted cognitions surrounding food, eating, weight, and shape that maintain the bulimic behaviors (e.g., "eating a feared food will instantly make me fat" or "one bite of a feared food means the whole day is ruined and I might as well binge and purge all day"). Patients are helped to understand how their thoughts can influence their behaviors and how to reevaluate and challenge their automatic thoughts to alter behavior. This stage also sees the reintroduction of feared foods into patients' diets via behavioral experiments.

Stage 3 of CBT-BN is adapted for adolescents to consolidate treatment gains and develop a relapse prevention plan. The development of this plan should include a discussion of remaining developmental tasks that may influence relapse of symptoms (e.g., moving away from home).

In the only published case series of CBT-BN adapted for a sample of 34 adolescents, 78% exhibited a reduction in binge/purge frequency, and 56% were binge/purge abstinent at the end of treatment (Lock, 2005). Additionally, 1 randomized control trial compared CBT-guided self-care with a form of family therapy for adolescent BN (Schmidt et al., 2007). At 6 months, binge episodes were significantly reduced in the CBT-guided self-care group compared with the family therapy group; however, this difference was no longer significant at 12-month follow-up. Although no significant group differences were found on measures of purging frequency, body mass index, or concerns about shape and weight, this study demonstrates the efficacy of utilizing CBT strategies in the treatment of adolescent BN.

Family-Based Treatment for Bulimia Nervosa

Using the model of FBT for adolescent AN, FBT-BN relies on family involvement to address eating disorder symptoms (Le Grange & Lock, 2007). (See the description of FBT-AN earlier in this chapter for more details on the FBT model in practice.) Phase I shifts the control of eating over to the parents, who are also charged with the task of monitoring the patient after and between meals to prevent purging episodes. Phase II focuses on shifting control of eating and food-related decisions back to the adolescent in a gradual fashion. Phase III addresses developmental issues and encourages communication between parents and adolescent to navigate future challenges.

Two RCTs have provided empirical evidence for the efficacy of FBT-BN in adolescents. Le Grange and colleagues (2007) reported abstinence rates of 39% at posttreatment (compared to 18% in the individual comparison treatment) and FBT-BN remained superior at 6-month follow-up (29% for FBT-BN versus 10% for comparison treatment) (Le Grange et al., 2007). Schmidt and colleagues (2007) found similar results in that 41% of patients were binge/purge abstinent at 6-month follow-up (Schmidt et al., 2007).

Binge Eating Disorder

No randomized controlled trials have been published examining the efficacy of treatments for adolescents with BED. Research has shown that interpersonal psychotherapy in a group format (Wilfley, Frank, Welch, Spurrell, & Rounsaville, 1998), cognitive behavioral therapy (Grilo, Crosby, Wilson, & Masheb, 2012), and dialectical behavior therapy (Safer, Robinson, & Jo, 2010) are efficacious treatments for BED in adult samples. Interpersonal psychotherapy for the prevention of excess weight gain is a treatment developed to treat binge eating in adolescents (Tanofsky-Kraff, 2012), and preliminary data are promising. Certainly the theoretical arguments for adapting adult BED treatments for use in adolescents are compelling, but currently no evidence exists in the empirical literature.

PARENTAL INVOLVEMENT IN TREATMENT

Parental involvement in a child's recovery from an eating disorder has been examined in treatments for both AN and BN.

Family-Based Treatment for Anorexia Nervosa

As its name suggests, family-based treatment for AN emphasizes parental involvement as critical to helping a child recover from the eating disorder. The role of parents and strategies focusing on their involvement are central to this therapeutic approach, as outlined earlier in this chapter. It is worthwhile to note, however, that unique situations require special consideration.

Parents can get frustrated with their adolescent's refusal to eat and can misinterpret this behavior as willful manipulation or obstinacy. Parents may respond by blaming their child for bringing this stress on the family or may retreat from their role and become overly permissive. Therapists should highlight a separation of the illness from the patient.

Furthermore, in order for parents to be most effective in the process of refeeding, it is important that they are aligned with one another and sending consistent messages regarding decisions about the child's meals and activity level. If there is disagreement between parents or among family members, the therapist should work with them in order to achieve compromise and refocus on the health and safety of the child.

Treatments for Bulimia Nervosa

Because adolescents experience the BN as more ego-dystonic than AN, often they are more motivated during treatment and consequently are less likely to require as much parental involvement. However, parental involvement may vary, depending on the case presentation and family dynamics. At a minimum, parents can provide the instrumental support of having food available in the home and facilitating transportation to and from treatment. Parents may assist with the implementation of the cognitive and behavioral strategies taught during CBT-BN treatment sessions. Younger patients may benefit from reminders to use rational responses to automatic thoughts and may need parents to help shape their environment (e.g., facilitating activities that are incongruent with binge eating or purging). Even in single-parent households, research on the efficacy of FBT-BN has shown that single parents are equally effective as two-parent families in achieving weight restoration (Celio Doyle, McLean, Washington, Hoste, & Le Grange, 2009).

ADAPTATIONS AND MODIFICATIONS

Various adaptations and modifications to eating disorder treatments should be considered, based on unique individual clinical features.

Anorexia Nervosa

The age of the child or adolescent is always a consideration when using family-based treatments for eating disorders. Older adolescents will be expected to take a more active role in their own meals toward the end of Phase II. For example, an 11-year-old child would likely not be expected to prepare all of his or her own meals, regardless of whether this child had an eating disorder. However, a 17-year-old adolescent would be expected to be very independent in his or her own eating by the end of Phase II. Other adaptations of FBT being studied include family-based treatment for pediatric obesity, which targets weight loss, rather than weight gain, as the primary outcome.

Bulimia Nervosa

Adding to concerns about binge eating and purging, it is common for adolescents with BN to have some sort of comorbid psychiatric disorder. Over 60% of patients may meet criteria for another psychiatric disorder (Fischer & Le Grange, 2007). Treatment teams can be expanded to include additional mental health professionals to treat these comorbid disorders. However, unless suicidal ideation, self-harm, or starvation is present, the bulimic symptoms should be the primary focus of treatment.

Binge Eating Disorder

Some authors suggest that perhaps binge eating in children and adolescents has a unique clinical presentation and may require specialized treatment models different from those that have been used with adult populations (Tanofsky-Kraff et al., 2007). Further research is necessary before conclusions can be drawn.

MEASURING TREATMENT EFFECTS

Assessing and monitoring the core behavioral symptoms of eating disorders (weight status, binge eating, and purging) is relatively straightforward. Weight status functions as an objective barometer of progress in treatment and therefore should be measured weekly. Frequency of binge eating and purging behavior is assessed most easily via self-report. To this end, self-monitoring forms often are helpful to track frequently occurring behaviors, such as regular binge eating or purging. Simply attending to these behaviors with self-monitoring can help people with BN to begin curbing them. In CBT, these self-monitoring forms may include space to record cognitions about food, weight, shape, or mood state. Beyond the core symptoms, many aspects of family functioning and quality of life may change as a result of treatment for eating disorders. Attention should be paid to these aspects of the family dynamic and patient experience.

The gold standard of assessment of eating disorder psychopathology is the Eating Disorder Examination (EDE) (Fairburn & Cooper, 1993). The EDE is a semistructured interview conducted by a clinician to assess psychopathology related to eating disorder diagnoses and includes specific binge eating and compensatory behaviors. The EDE measures disordered eating over a 28-day period, with some symptoms also being assessed for up to 2- to 6-month periods. The EDE is rated using four subscales, including (1) Eating Concern, (2) Shape Concern, (3) Weight Concern, and (4) Dietary Restraint, as well as a global score.

A self-report version of this measure has been adapted from the EDE (Fairburn & Beglin, 2008). The Eating Disorder Examination—Questionnaire (EDE-Q) is a 41-item self-report measure and results in the same four subscales used in the EDE.

CLINICAL CASE EXAMPLE

Annalise (identifying information has been altered to protect confidentiality) is a 15-year-old Caucasian female in ninth grade who presented with significant weight loss, secondary amenorrhea, and symptoms of anxiety. Her parents explained that Annalise had begun exercising more often than usual over the summer in attempts to lose weight and become more physically active. Her parents stated that they were initially supportive but became increasingly concerned as Annalise continued to lose weight past her initial goal of 110 lbs (49.90 kg). Previously a social girl with many close friends, Annalise became socially withdrawn. Her mother and father received a phone call from the school social worker reporting that several of Annalise's friends had approached her out of concern for Annalise. This call prompted Mother and Father to bring her in to see a specialist.

Initial Assessment

Assessment began with interviews of Annalise and her parents regarding her eating habits and her feelings about her shape and weight, as well as an interview to assess general psychopathology. Additionally, the assessment included an interview with Annalise's mother and father in order to determine the course of the eating disorder from their perspective. Following the interview, both Annalise and her parents were asked to complete questionnaires regarding her eating behaviors and general family dynamics. Both her parents and Annalise reported that Annalise's weight had started at 115 lbs (52.16 kg). She currently weighed 92 lbs (41.73 kg) and was 64 inches (1.63 m) tall, indicating a body mass index in the 2nd percentile for her gender and age (National Center for Chronic Disease Prevention and Health Promotion, Clinical Growth Charts, Girls BMI-for-age, 2000).While Annalise initially denied most concerns regarding her shape and weight, she did admit to actively restricting her diet on a daily basis, consuming fewer than 1,000 calories per day for most days in the past month. Annalise's parents reported that she frequently complained of distress related to her fears of gaining weight and "becoming fat again"; however, Annalise initially denied experiencing any distress. Following encouragement from the interviewer, Annalise eventually became more open and discussed her negative cognitions concerning her shape and weight as well as her fear of gaining weight.

Assessment of general psychopathology revealed Annalise had a comorbid diagnosis of generalized anxiety disorder. She described her uncontrollable worry about friendships, the future, and school. She reported that these concerns had been going on for about 2 years and existed long before she began losing weight or having eating-disordered cognitions. Specific symptoms of Annalise's anxiety included difficulty concentrating, sleep disturbance, and frequent feelings of restlessness. She reported that these feelings had continued throughout the duration of her weight loss.

Treatment Plan

A treatment plan including the next components was developed.

Family-Based Treatment for Anorexia Nervosa

Annalise and her parents began seeing a therapist weekly in order to assist Annalise and her family with her weight restoration. All three family members were asked to attend every therapy session, and the family was asked to bring Annalise's 12-year-old brother to sessions as often as possible. The treatment included weekly 60-minute sessions focusing on weight restoration and returning to a normal adolescent developmental trajectory. The treatment course included three phases. Phase I consisted of helping Annalise's parents take control of her eating and exercise behaviors in order to help her gain weight. Once Annalise's weight had been restored to about 90% EBW and she was able to make appropriate choices for meals and snacks, control was slowly returned to her. Phase II of treatment focused on helping Annalise regain control of eating and exercise to the point that she no longer required parental monitoring in these domains. Finally, Phase III of treatment came when Annalise was able to maintain her weight on her own at approximately 95% EBW. Phase III was devoted to exploring issues pertinent to normal adolescent development, including physical development and body image, peer relationships, and even future romantic relationships. The role of the therapist throughout treatment was to empower the family to manage Annalise's eating at home effectively and to help Annalise return to a normal pattern of eating. Annalise's weight was taken at the beginning of each session; whether her weight was up or down from the previous week would determine the tone and content of that particular session (i.e., weight gain led to discussions of what was successful, and weight loss led to discussions of what needed to be altered at home the following week).

Medication Management

Annalise and her parents were also asked to begin seeing the team psychiatrist regarding her pre-existing anxiety symptoms. Meeting with the psychiatrist involved initial assessment to evaluate comorbidities and their severity. Following this evaluation, the psychiatrist helped the family determine whether a medication was useful in helping Annalise to manage her symptoms of anxiety. The assessment also served to educate the family about the proper use of medication and the role of psychotropic medications in assisting with psychological symptoms. Follow-up with the psychiatrist included appointments every few weeks to monitor side effects and manage medication dosage.

Medical Monitoring

As eating disorders often come with serious medical consequences, a critical aspect of treatment is monitoring the patient's physical health. In addition to the psychiatrist, Annalise and her parents began seeing the team pediatrician to ensure Annalise's medical stability throughout her treatment. The initial visit included a physical examination and complete blood count. Follow-up appointments continued every few weeks to ensure overall health of the patient.

Outcome Assessment

Treatment progress was tracked weekly by the therapist, who weighed Annalise and assessed her eating disorder and comorbid psychological symptoms. Annalise continued to gain weight weekly with the help of her parents, with the exception of two sessions in which she lost weight from the previous week. After 18 sessions of family-based treatment, Annalise weighed 110 lbs (49.90 kg) and was approximately 97% EBW. End-of-treatment assessment involved the same battery of interviews and questionnaires as those conducted at baseline to assess change in eating disorders behaviors and cognitions. Annalise reported marked improvement in measures of eating restraint, eating concern, weight concern, and shape concern. She reported improvements in anxiety as well. Following the completion of FBT and with her eating disorder symptoms resolved, it was recommended that Annalise begin short-term CBT to help manage her anxiety.

REFERENCES

American Psychiatric Association. (2000). *Diagnostic and statistical manual of mental disorders* (4th ed., text rev.). Washington, DC: Author.

American Psychiatric Association (2013). *Diagnostic and statistical manual of mental disorders* (5th ed.) Arlington, VA: American Psychiatric Publishing.

Celio Doyle, A., McLean, C., Washington, B. N., Hoste, R. R., & Le Grange, D. (2009). Are single-parent families different from two-parent families in the treatment of adolescent bulimia nervosa using family-based treatment? *International Journal of Eating Disorders, 42,* 153–157.

Eisler, I., Dare, C., Russell, G.F.M., Szmukler, G., Le Grange, D., & Dodge, E. (1997). Family and individual therapy in anorexia nervosa. A 5-year follow-up. *Archives of General Psychiatry, 54*(11), 1025–1030.

Eisler, I., Simic, M., Russell, G. F., & Dare, C. (2007). A randomised controlled treatment trial of two forms of family therapy in adolescent anorexia nervosa: A 5-year follow-up. *Journal of Child and Psychology and Psychiatry, and Allied Disciplines, 48*(6), 552–560.

Fairburn, C. G. (1981). A cognitive behavioural approach to the treatment of bulimia. *Psychological Medicine, 11,* 707–711.

Fairburn, C. G., & Beglin, S. (2008). Eating disorder examination questionnaire. In C. G. Fairburn (Ed.), *Cognitive behavior therapy and eating disorders* (pp. 309–313). New York, NY: Guilford Press.

Fairburn, C. G., & Cooper, Z. (1993). The Eating Disorder Examination. In C. G. Fairburn & G. T. Wilson (Eds.), *Binge eating: Nature, assessment, and treatment* (pp. 317–360). New York, NY: Guildford Press.

Fairburn, C. G., Marcus, M. D., & Wilson, G. T. (1993). Cognitive-behavioral therapy for binge eating and bulimia nervosa: A comprehensive treatment manual. In C. G. Fairburn & G. T. Wilson (Eds.), *Binge eating: Nature, assessment, and treatment* (pp. 361–404). New York, NY: Guilford Press.

Fischer, S., & Le Grange, D. (2007). Comorbidity and high-risk behaviors in treatment-seeking adolescents with bulimia nervosa. *International Journal of Eating Disorders, 40,* 751–753.

Fitzpatrick, K., Moye, A., Hoste, R., Lock, J., & Le Grange, D. (2009). Adolescent focused therapy for adolescent anorexia nervosa. *Journal of Contemporary Psychotherapy, 40,* 31–39.

Grilo, C. M., Crosby, R. D., Wilson, G. T., & Masheb, R. M. (2012). 12-month follow-up of fluoxetine and cognitive behavioral therapy for binge eating disorder. *Journal of Consulting and Clinical Psychology, 80,* 1108–1113.

Kreipe, R. E., Golden, N. H., Katzman, D. K., Fisher, M., Rees, J., Tonkin, R. S., . . . Rome, E. S. (1995). Eating disorders in adolescents: Position paper of the Society for Adolescent Medicine. *Journal of Adolescent Health, 16,* 476–479.

Le Grange, D., Crosby, R. D., Rathoiz, P. J., & Leventhal, B. L. (2007). A randomized controlled comparison of family-based treatment and supportive psychotherapy for adolescent bulimia nervosa. *Archives of General Psychiatry, 64,* 1049–1056.

Le Grange, D., & Lock, J. (2007). *Treating bulimia in adolescents: A family-based approach.* New York, NY: Guilford Press.

Le Grange, D., Swanson, S., Crow, S., & Merikangas, K. R. (2012). Eating disorder not otherwise specified presentation in the US population. *International Journal of Eating Disorders, 45,* 711–718.

Lock, J. (2005). Adjusting cognitive behavior therapy for adolescents with bulimia nervosa: Results of a case series. *American Journal of Psychotherapy, 59,* 267–281.

Lock, J., Couturier, J., & Agras, W. S. (2006). Comparison of long-term outcomes in adolescents with anorexia nervosa treated with family therapy. *Journal of the American Academy of Child & Adolescent Psychiatry, 45,* 666–672.

Lock, J., Le Grange, D., Agras, S., Moye, A., Bryson, S.W., & Jo, B. (2010). Randomized clinical trial comparing family-based treatment to adolescent-focused individual therapy for adolescents with anorexia nervosa. *Archives of General Psychiatry, 67,* 1025–1032.

Loeb, K., & Le Grange, D. (2009). Family-based treatment for adolescent eating disorders: Current status, new applications, and future directions. *International Journal of Child and Adolescent Health, 2,* 243–254.

National Center for Chronic Disease Prevention and Health Promotion. (2000). *Clinical Growth Charts, 2 to 20 years: Girls, Body mass index-for-age percentiles*. Retrieved from http://www.cdc.gov/growthcharts

National Collaborating Centre for Mental Health (UK). (2004). *Eating disorders: Core interventions in the treatment and management of anorexia nervosa, bulimia nervosa and related eating disorders*. NICE Clinical Guidelines, No. 9. Leicester, UK: British Psychological Society.

Robin, A., Siegal, P., Koepke, T., Moye, A., & Tice, S. (1994). Family therapy versus individual therapy for adolescent females with anorexia nervosa. *Journal of Developmental and Behavioral Pediatrics, 15,* 111–116.

Robin, A. L., Siegel, P. T., Moye, A. W., Gilroy, M., Dennis, A. B., & Sikand, A. (1999). A controlled comparison of family versus individual therapy for adolescents with anorexia nervosa. *Journal of the American Academy of Child & Adolescent Psychiatry, 38,* 1482–1489.

Rome, E., & Ammerman, S. (2003). Medical complications of eating disorders: An update. *Journal of Adolescent Health, 33,* 418–426.

Rushing, J. M., Jones, L. E., & Carney, C. P. (2003). Bulimia nervosa: A primary care review. *Primary Care Companion to the Journal of Clinical Psychiatry, 5,* 217–224.

Safer, D., Robinson, A. H., & Jo, B. (2010). Outcome from a randomized controlled trial of group therapy for binge eating disorder: Comparing dialectical behavior therapy adapted for binge eating to an active comparison group therapy. *Behavior Therapy, 41,* 106–120.

Schmidt, U., Lee, S., Beecham, J., Perkins, S., Treasure, J., Yim, I., . . . Eisler, I. (2007). A randomized controlled trial of family therapy and cognitive behavior therapy guided self-care for adolescents with bulimia nervosa and related disorders. *American Journal of Psychiatry, 164,* 591–598.

Smink, F. R., van Hoeken, D., & Hoek, H. W. (2012). Epidemiology of eating disorders: Incidence, prevalence, and mortality rates. *Current Psychiatry Reports, 14*(4), 406–414.

Stice, E., Marti, C. N., & Rohde, P. (2013). Prevalence, incidence, impairment, and course of the proposed *DSM-5* eating disorder diagnoses in an 8-year prospective community study of young women. *Journal of Abnormal Psychology, 122,* 445–457.

Tanofsky-Kraff, M. (2012). Psychosocial preventative interventions for obesity and eating disorders in youth. *International Review of Psychiatry, 24,* 262–270.

Tanofsky-Kraff, M., Goossens, L., Eddy, K. T., Ringham, R., Goldschmidt, A., Yanovski, S. Z., . . . Yanovski, J. A. (2007). A multisite investigation of binge eating behaviors in children and adolescents. *Journal of Consulting and Clinical Psychology, 75,* 901–913.

Wilfley, D. E., Frank, M. A., Welch, R. R., Spurrell, E., & Rounsaville, B. J. (1998). Adapting interpersonal psychotherapy to a group format (IPT-G) for binge eating disorder: Toward a model for adapting empirically supported treatments. *Psychotherapy Research, 8,* 379–391.

Wooldridge, T. (2012). An overview of anorexia in males. *Eating Disorders, 20*(5), 368–378.

Wu, K. (2008). Eating disorders and obsessive-compulsive disorder: A dimensional approach to purported relations. *Journal of Anxiety Disorders, 22*(8), 1412–1420.

CHAPTER 16

Elimination Disorders

JACLYN A. SHEPARD, LEE M. RITTERBAND, FRANCES P. THORNDIKE, AND STEPHEN M. BOROWITZ

BRIEF OVERVIEW OF DISORDERS

Elimination disorders are commonly diagnosed in childhood and are characterized by the absence of bladder or bowel control that would be expected based on the child's age or current stage of development. This chapter provides an overview of the two primary elimination disorders identified in the *Diagnostic and Statistical Manual of Mental Disorders* (5th ed.; *DSM-5*) (American Psychiatric Association [APA], 2013): enuresis and encopresis. The chapter reviews the clinical presentation and evidence-based treatment approaches, including parental involvement, modification and adaptations, and measuring treatment efficacy, for each disorder and provides a clinical case example.

Enuresis

Enuresis is characterized by repeated voiding of urine into the bed or clothing in youth at least 5 years of age, chronologically or developmentally (APA, 2013). For children to meet criteria for enuresis, such voiding, whether involuntary or intentional, must occur twice a week for at least 3 months or result in clinically significant distress or functional impairment. Additionally, this behavior cannot be attributed to a medication side effect or a general medical condition (e.g., diabetes, spina bifida, epilepsy). Subtypes are identified as nocturnal only (nighttime bedwetting), diurnal only (wetting during the day), and nocturnal and diurnal. Limitations of the existing criteria have been reviewed in the literature and primarily focus on poorly defined criteria, which are too broad, yield subjective interpretation, or are restrictive to the extent that they result in the exclusion of children who would otherwise need intervention (von Gontard, 2012). It is hypothesized that different underlying etiological pathways exist for diurnal and nocturnal enuresis. Based on the greater medical comorbidities and physiological abnormalities observed in children with diurnal enuresis compared to those who experience nighttime wetting, this chapter focuses primarily on nocturnal enuresis (Järvelin et al., 1991; Rushton, 1995).

Enuresis and subclinical bedwetting are common problems experienced by school-age children. Estimates from a large, longitudinal study indicate that at least 20% of first graders experience occasional bedwetting, while 4% wet the bed at least twice a week (Butler et al., 2008). Approximately 10% of school-age children experience nighttime bedwetting compared to the 2% to 3% who experience daytime wetting (McGrath, Mellon, & Murphy, 2000; von Gontard & Nevéus, 2006). Enuresis is more common in boys than girls, with rates of 9% and 7% in 7- and 9-year-old boys as compared to 6% and 3% in 7- and 9-year-old girls (Byrd, Weitzman, Lanphear, & Auinger, 1996). Early literature suggests that prevalence rates steadily decline as children get older; by adolescence, only approximately 1% to 2% experience enuresis (Feehan, McGee, Stanton, & Silva, 1990; Glazener & Evans, 2004).

Nocturnal enuresis is most commonly conceptualized within a biobehavioral framework, given the strong physiological underpinnings of the problem and the associated behavioral approaches to treatment (Houts, 1991). Specifically, it is characterized by the child's voiding of urine while asleep despite continence during the day (van Gool, Nieuwenhuis, ten Doeschate, Messer, & de Jong, 1999). A minority of these children, approximately 5% to 10%, experience a comorbid dysfunction in daytime urinary abilities (e.g., increased urgency and frequency), and approximately one third of children with nocturnal enuresis experience comorbid constipation (McGrath, Caldwell, & Jones, 2007; Schmitt, 1997). The etiology of enuresis is quite varied, which ultimately reflects the heterogeneous nature of the disorder (McGrath et al., 2000). Many children with nocturnal enuresis exhibit a maturational delay that affects their ability to detect a full bladder overnight (Campbell, Cox, & Borowitz, 2009). Functional bladder capacity may be diminished, production of vasopressin may be decreased, or there may be excessive fluid intake before bedtime, all of which may cause a release of large amounts of urine and exacerbate the child's difficulties with urine retention while asleep (Devitt et al., 1999; Norfolk & Wooton, 2012; Yeung et al., 2002). Evidence of heritability of nocturnal enuresis is strong, as 77% of youth with enuresis have a first-degree relative with a history of the condition (von Gontard, Schaumburg, Hollmann, Eiberg, & Rittig, 2001). Although children with nocturnal enuresis commonly are considered heavy sleepers, this notion likely stems from anecdotal report, as little empirical evidence exists (Nevéus, Stenberg, Läckgren, Tuvemo, & Hetta, 1999).

Psychosocial implications of enuresis have garnered much attention in the literature, but findings are inconsistent. It is estimated that upward of 20% to 30% of children with nocturnal enuresis evidence behavioral difficulties. Although this is 2 to 4 times higher than children without voiding problems, it is comparable to children with other chronic illnesses (Hirasing, van Leerdam, Bolk-Bennink, & Bosch, 1997; Liu, Sun, Uchiyama, & Okawa, 2000). However, inconsistencies across studies as well as the use of small convenience samples have precluded the identification of a definitive relationship between nocturnal enuresis and psychological problems (Wolfe-Christensen, Veenstra, Kovacevic, Elder, & Lakshmanan, 2012). Overall, given the involuntary nature of nocturnal enuresis, bedwetting is not considered a function of psychological disturbance. Rather, emotional and/or behavioral problems may result from the stigma, stress, and embarrassment associated with the child's bedwetting. For example, early literature suggests that the emotional difficulties seen in children with nocturnal enuresis are not the cause of the condition but rather the result of negative parental response to the child's bedwetting (Sharf & Jennings, 1988). Additionally, early studies on self-esteem indicate that bedwetting can have negative emotional effects, as youth's self-esteem improved with treatment, but there is no evidence to support a causal relationship in the opposite direction (Hägglöf, Andrén, Bergström, Marklund, & Wendelius, 1997; Moffatt, Kato, & Pless, 1987; Panides & Ziller, 1981). Although some studies report no increase in psychological problems for children with enuresis, others have demonstrated elevated rates of clinically significant internalizing, externalizing, and attentional problems in this population based on parent report (De Bruyne et al., 2009; Friman, Handwerk, Swearer, McGinnis, & Warzak, 1998; Hirasing et al., 1997; Joinson, Heron, Emond, & Butler, 2007).

Encopresis

Encopresis is a common problem among school-age children, affecting between 1.5% and 7.5% of youth between 6 and 12 years of age and accounting for upward of 25% of visits to a pediatric gastroenterologist and 3% to 6% of psychiatry referrals (Doleys, 1983; Levine, 1975; Olatawura, 1973). The condition is characterized by repeated defecation in inappropriate places (such as in clothing or on the floor), with episodes occurring at least once a month for 3 months (APA, 2013). For children to meet criteria for encopresis, they must be at least 4 years of age, and the behavior must not be exclusively attributed to medications or a general medical condition other than constipation. The diagnosis has two identified subtypes to indicate whether the fecal soiling is a result of constipation: with constipation and overflow incontinence and without constipation and overflow incontinence (APA, 2013).

The majority of children with encopresis have an early history of chronic constipation, typically developing before 3 years of age (Partin, Hamill, Fischel, & Partin, 1992). The underlying pathophysiology of childhood constipation is based on many factors and is somewhat elusive as no specific organic cause can be identified in upward of 90% of young patients (Loening-Baucke, 1993). Characteristics of chronic constipation include infrequent bowel movements (e.g., fewer than three per week), fecal incontinence, active stool withholding, and passage of stools that are large in diameter and hard in consistency. Stool withholding occurs in nearly all (89%–100%) children with chronic constipation and in only 13% of those without (Partin et al., 1992; Taubman, 1997). With such large, hard, and difficult-to-pass stools, children often develop fearful reactions to defecation. As a result, progressive stool retention is common. In fact, children and their parents have identified fear of pain associated with defecation as a very prominent factor in the child's constipation and active withholding (Bernard-Bonnin, Haley, Bélanger, & Nadeau, 1993; Partin et al., 1992). However, with increased stool retention, defecation then becomes even more difficult as stools get progressively larger and more difficult and painful to evacuate (Rasquin et al., 2006).

In addition to pain associated with defecation, active stool retention may also result from a child's fears around toileting, including aversions to public or unfamiliar bathrooms (Benninga, Voskuijl & Taminiau, 2004; Borowitz et al., 2003; Iacono et al., 1998). Stool-specific toileting avoidance, where the child willingly urinates but refuses to defecate in the toilet, occurs in approximately 80% of children with chronic constipation (Taubman, 1997). This behavior also occurs in approximately 20% of children without constipation who are in the toilet training process, often persisting beyond 4 years of age and requiring intervention in 25% of them (Blum, Taubman, & Nemeth, 2004; Taubman, 1997).

Regardless of the etiology, chronic stool retention can result in physical discomfort for the child, including abdominal pain, loss of appetite, early satiety, nausea, and vomiting. In some cases, chronic constipation paired with long-term withholding may lead to acquired megacolon, or the stretching of the rectum walls to accommodate a large amount of retained stool, which ultimately reduces rectal muscle tone, diminishes the child's ability to feel the urge to defecate, and increases the threshold of detection of this urge (Campbell et al., 2009; Voskuijl et al., 2006). The child may then experience overflow fecal incontinence, where fecal matter leaks around a retained mass of stool and into the child's underwear. Such fecal incontinence typically occurs during the day, often multiple times a day, but only rarely occurs overnight, and mostly in cases of severe fecal impaction (Benninga et al., 1996). Overflow incontinence typically improves following a thorough cleanout of the bowel, and if successful cleanout is maintained for several months, defecation sensation and muscle tone often return to normal (Callaghan, 1964; van Dijk, Benninga, Grootenhuis, Nieuwenhuizen, & Last, 2007).

Abnormal defecation dynamics typically develop concurrently with stool retentive behaviors and are present in an estimated 45% to 70% of children with chronic constipation as well as in those with encopresis (Loening-Baucke & Cruikshank, 1986; van der Plas et al., 1996; Weber, Ducrotte, Touchais, Roussignol, & Denis, 1987). Paradoxical contraction of the external anal sphincter (EAS) muscle, or failure to relax the EAS, is commonly associated with chronic constipation. It is hypothesized that paradoxical contraction of the EAS develops in response to painful defecation or out of the child's attempts to control bowel movements during the toilet training process (McGrath et al., 2000). Regardless of whether the pattern was initiated as a response to fear or avoidance of pain associated with defecation or used maladaptively as a regulatory function, it becomes a conditioned response that contributes to the development or further maintenance of the child's chronic constipation.

Psychosocial consequences related to chronic constipation and encopresis remain understudied. Parenting stress associated with the child's fecal incontinence is commonly reported in clinical settings, largely stemming from the child's dishonesty about the occurrence of fecal accidents and the parental burden of frequent laundering of soiled clothing (Cox et al., 2003). In fact, many parents assume that the child's laziness, carelessness, or willfulness is the primary cause of the child's incontinence (Fishman, Rappaport, Schonwald, & Nurko, 2003). However, upon understanding the physiological factors that are involved in encopresis, they often experience feelings of guilt for taking an authoritarian (i.e., blaming or punishing) approach with the child (Campbell et al., 2009). Children with encopresis, particularly those who are older, may be teased and labeled by peers as "dirty" or "stinky." This name-calling can persist even after the fecal incontinence resolves and can result in rejection and social isolation. Ongoing teasing and rejection, whether by peers or by parents, can be devastating for the child and may result in poor self-esteem, hostility, or continued fecal soiling as a result of learned helplessness (Campbell et al., 2009). There is some evidence that perceived quality of life is lower for children with chronic constipation compared to that of healthy children and those with other chronic medical conditions (e.g., inflammatory bowel disease, gastroesophogeal reflux disease) (Youssef, Langseder, Verga, Mones, & Rosh, 2005).

EVIDENCE-BASED APPROACHES

Given the strong physiological underpinnings of enuresis and encopresis, medical management is often the first line of treatment or a prominent component to effective therapies. This section thereby outlines evidence-based approaches for both medical and behavioral/psychological interventions for each disorder.

Enuresis

The spontaneous remission rate for nocturnal enuresis is approximately 15% per year, although for many children, without treatment, remission may take a number of years (Forsythe & Redmond, 1974). Therefore, it is important to initiate treatment as soon as possible to promote rapid resolution of the bedwetting with the goal of minimizing or preventing further psychosocial consequences for the child and his or her family. Prior to mental health treatment, however, children should be referred to their primary care physician or pediatric urologist for a comprehensive assessment to exclude any diseases or structural abnormalities that would cause excessive urination (e.g., urinary tract infection, diabetes, spinal cord abnormalities; Järvelin, Huttunen, Seppanen, Seppanen, & Moilanen, 1990). Additionally, medical practitioners often make recommendations regarding general management strategies, including monitoring fluid intake and routine toileting or treating comorbid constipation prior to referral for more intensive behavioral protocols (Norfolk & Wooton, 2012).

Medical Management

The urine alarm, as discussed in the next section, is typically the first-line treatment for nocturnal enuresis, given its well-established efficacy and superiority over other therapies, including pharmacotherapy. However, desmopressin can be useful in treating enuresis, especially in circumstances where its fast-acting, albeit short-term, effects are desired (e.g., sleepovers) or in situations where the urine alarm or other behavioral methods are deemed inappropriate (e.g., various stressors that preclude consistent implementation of a behavior plan; extreme parental intolerance of bedwetting) (Butler, 2004; Norfolk & Wooton, 2012). Desmopressin is a synthetic analog of the antidiuretic hormone vasopressin, which concentrates urine, decreases urine output, and potentially increases arousability (Norfolk & Wooton, 2012). Efficacy rates vary, likely due to differences in patient populations, dosing, and behavioral therapy recommendations across studies, but, overall, desmopressin successfully reduces bedwetting (Glazener & Evans, 2004). There are few side effects of desmopressin, but children should be instructed to stop fluid intake 2 hours prior to bedtime to prevent hyponatremia with water intoxication (Robson, 2009). Long-term use of desmopressin may result in sustained improvements in bedwetting behavior in some children, but for many children, bedwetting resumes upon discontinuation of the medication (Glazener & Evans, 2004; Norfolk & Wooton, 2012). Use of desmopressin in conjunction with the urine alarm is promising and has demonstrated efficacy in children who are at risk for treatment dropout, including those with severe wetting and comorbid behavioral problems (Bradbury & Meadow, 1995; Houts, 1991).

Imipramine and other tricyclic antidepressants (TCAs) have demonstrated efficacy in reducing bedwetting compared to placebo in children (Deshpande, Caldwell, & Sureshkumar, 2012). Specifically, use of TCAs resulted in reduced frequency of nighttime wetting by 1 night per week, with approximately 20% of children ultimately becoming dry. However, use of these agents in the treatment of enuresis is cautioned due to substantial adverse side effects, which may outweigh the presenting problem (e.g., mood and sleep disturbance, cardiotoxicity, and risk of death with overdose). The International Children's Continence Society, therefore, recommends that TCAs be used only when other therapies have failed and where there is a continued significant impact on the child's functioning (Nevéus et al., 2010).

Behavioral Treatment

The most empirically supported treatment for nocturnal enuresis is the urine alarm (Houts, Berman, & Abramson, 1994). This approach involves the use of an alarm that is activated by moisture sensors that are either worn by the child or placed on the mattress ("bell and pad"). There is ample evidence to support the efficacy of the urine alarm as the primary approach to treatment, and it has been shown to be superior to psychotherapy and medication alone (Wagner, Johnson, Walker, Carter, & Wittner, 1982; Willie, 1986). Results of studies examining the efficacy of the urine alarm in conjunction with other behavioral strategies are promising, with an average cure rate of approximately 79% (Butler, Brewin, & Forsythe, 1988; Fielding, 1985; Geffken, Johnson, & Walker, 1986; Mellon & McGrath, 2000; Wagner et al., 1982; Whelan & Houts, 1990). However, Mellon and McGrath underscore that these combined approaches may represent an additive effect and have not been standardized or empirically tested by other investigators.

Although seemingly straightforward, the urine alarm, whether used independently or in conjunction with other behavioral strategies, requires a considerable investment of time and effort from families. Poor outcome with this approach, including dropout, has been associated with prior failed treatment attempts, family history of enuresis, negative parental attitudes and beliefs about the child's accidents, stressful home environment, and youth's behavioral disturbance (e.g., externalizing problems) (Mellon & Houts, 1995). Therefore, the primary goals of the psychological assessment are to inform families of the demands associated with this approach, including likely disruption of sleep, and to evaluate whether they can realistically and consistently implement the treatment plan (Norfolk & Wooton, 2012; Mellon & McGrath, 2000). Stressful family circumstances, including marital problems, psychiatric or significant behavioral disturbance, and extreme parental intolerance of bedwetting, have served as significant barriers to cooperation and long-term compliance with the urine alarm intervention (Butler, Redfern, & Holland, 1994; Fielding, 1985).

Dry-bed training is another behavioral intervention used to treat nocturnal enuresis. This approach is based on an operant learning model that involves shaping the child's wakefulness by adhering to a waking schedule with predetermined intervals (e.g., waking the child a few hours after he/she has gone to sleep), as well as use of positive practice (i.e., the child practices getting out of bed to toilet and sits despite the lack of urge to urinate) and punishment for bedwetting via cleanliness training (i.e., having the child change soiled bedding and pajamas) (Azrin, Sneed, & Foxx, 1974). Dry-bed training also incorporates the urine alarm, which is likely an important component to this approach, as the use of dry-bed training without it is less effective (Bollard & Nettlebeck, 1981; Keating, Butz, Burke, & Heimburg, 1983). The average cure rate for dry-bed training with urine alarm use is estimated to be 75%, and typically remission is achieved in less than a month (Mellon & McGrath, 2000).

Full Spectrum Home Training is a multicomponent behavioral approach to enuresis treatment that utilizes the urine alarm and several behavioral strategies, such as retention control with monetary rewards, cleanliness training, self-monitoring, and overlearning (i.e., continued use of the urine alarm while drinking increasing quantities of water before bedtime) (Houts & Liebert, 1984). This manualized intervention has demonstrated efficacy in the treatment of nocturnal enuresis, with an average cure rate of 78.5% within 8 to 16 weeks of implementation, but has not been investigated extensively (Houts, Liebert, & Padawer, 1983; Whelan & Houts, 1990). Noted benefits of multicomponent treatment protocols compared to single-method approaches, such as the urine alarm treatment or dry-bed training alone, is the inclusion of relapse prevention components and the reduced burden on the family (Mellon & McGrath, 2000).

Encopresis

Although encopresis is a common pediatric disorder with apparent psychosocial implications for children and their families, no definitive treatment protocol exists (Cunningham & Banez, 2006). Due to the prominent physiological component of constipation and encopresis, medical management is often the first line of treatment. In fact, prior to any behavioral or psychological intervention, children should be referred to their pediatrician or pediatric gastroenterologist to rule out any underlying organic etiology of the constipation and/or fecal incontinence, including Hirschsprung's disease (von Gontard, 2012). Once medical management has been initiated, practitioners typically incorporate straightforward behavioral strategies (e.g., toilet sitting schedule) or make a referral to a mental health specialist for an enhanced behavioral treatment protocol. Again, no criteria exist to inform a treatment timeline, but in general, if constipation and fecal soiling persist beyond 6 months despite consistent medical intervention, etiology of the symptoms remains unclear, and psychosocial functioning of the child or family is clearly affected, further psychobehavioral intervention likely is warranted (Cunningham & Banez, 2006).

Medical Management

According to guidelines set by the North American Society for Pediatric Gastroenterology and Nutrition, essential medical treatment strategies for chronic constipation include education, fecal disimpaction, and maintenance laxative therapy (Baker et al., 1999). It is important to begin the treatment process by educating families about the physiological aspects of the condition and address any misconceptions parents may have about the deliberate nature of the child's fecal incontinence. Given the high incidence of chronic constipation in children with encopresis, medical management generally begins with disimpaction of the colon, either via high-dose laxatives or enemas, and continues with a prolonged laxative regimen to promote daily, soft bowel movements to prevent the reaccumulation of stool (Borowitz et al., 2003; van Dijk et al., 2007). Efficacy of laxative therapy alone has not been established, as the majority of examined treatment strategies combine the use of laxatives with behavioral interventions. Information about efficacy related to specific maintenance laxative dosing and duration is also unclear, although there is some evidence that polyethylene glycol has a higher success rate than lactulose and milk of magnesia in the treatment of functional constipation (Loening-Baucke, 2002; Voskuijl et al., 2004).

Behavioral and Psychological Interventions

Once an organic etiology has been ruled out and medical intervention has begun, it is common for practitioners to incorporate behavioral strategies in the child's treatment plan (Sutphen, Borowitz, Hutchison, & Cox, 1995). Behavioral strategies, such as positive reinforcement, exposure, and skills building (e.g., scheduled toilet sits, dietary education, instruction/modeling of defecation dynamics), have been utilized over the past few decades and are the most common protocols used in conjunction with medical interventions (Campbell et al., 2009; Levine & Bakow, 1976). These added behavioral protocols aim to decrease fecal incontinence, establish regular bowel habits, and resolve fears around toileting (Borowitz et al., 2003). However, efficacy data on these approaches are varied, likely due to the lack of consistent definition of "improvement" across studies and, therefore, no single, well-established intervention has been clearly identified (Brooks et al., 2000). In general, combination medical-behavioral interventions, with and without dietary recommendations, appear to be the most promising interventions to date (see review by McGrath et al., 2000; Borowitz et al., 2003; Brazzelli & Griffiths, 2006; Stark et al., 1997; Stark, Owens-Stively, Spirito, Lewis, & Guevremont, 1990).

Similarly, enhanced toilet training (ETT), which pairs behavioral strategies with medical management, has demonstrated efficacy in the treatment of encopresis. In addition to skills building and positive reinforcement of self-initiated toileting and lack of fecal accidents, ETT adds instruction to parents and their children about the physiology of overflow incontinence, training and modeling of appropriate defecation dynamics, and exercises promoting the child's ability to control the EAS muscle (Ritterband et al., 2003). When compared to intense medical management, ETT demonstrated a significantly greater reduction in symptoms, and youth who received ETT required significantly fewer treatment sessions and lower daily doses of maintenance laxatives (Cox, Sutphen, Borowitz, Kovatchev, & Ling, 1999). These gains were maintained at both 6-month and 12-month follow-up (Borowitz et al., 2003).

Medical interventions that incorporate biofeedback also have been used in the treatment of constipation and abnormal defecation dynamics, although their independent effects remain unclear (Brazzeli & Griffiths, 2007; McGrath et al., 2000). Biofeedback, through the use of electromyographic monitoring, targets the paradoxical contraction of the EAS and teaches the child to relax the EAS during straining (Borowitz et al., 2003). Early studies examining the efficacy of biofeedback in the treatment of encopresis have demonstrated some benefits in decreasing paradoxical contraction of the EAS, but methods were notably focused on the use of this technique in conjunction with medical-behavioral management (Cox et al., 1994; Cox, Sutphen, Ling, Quillian, & Borowitz, 1996; Loening-Baucke, 1996). Overall, its use has not added a significant benefit in the majority of randomized studies.

PARENTAL INVOLVEMENT IN TREATMENT

Parental involvement is central in the treatment of elimination disorders. Both enuresis and encopresis have underlying pathophysiology that should be clearly explained to the parents to promote a better understanding of their children's condition and to dispel any myths related to psychopathology causing or maintaining the condition (Cunningham & Banez, 2006). Additionally, the behavioral strategies involved in the treatment of both enuresis and encopresis can be demanding and require consistent follow-through on the parents' part. It is therefore crucial not only to conduct a comprehensive assessment of the potential barriers related to parental cooperation and compliance (e.g., marital stressors, existing psychiatric conditions) and the support mechanisms that are in place, but also to have a thorough discussion with the family about the demands and foreseeable challenges that may affect treatment success.

Parental stress and anxiety may be an important facet of the treatment model for elimination disorders. An association between maternal anxiety about children's health and use of pediatric health services has been established for several chronic conditions (Brown, Connelly, Rittle, & Clouse, 2006; Janicke, Finney, & Riley, 2001; Spurrier et al., 2000). For encopresis, there is support for an association between higher baseline parental anxiety and greater use of an online intervention (Magee, Ritterband, Thorndike, Cox, & Borowitz, 2009). Additionally, parents of children with enuresis endorse higher overall stress than do parents of controls, and stress in parents of children with enuresis is significantly related to increased report of children's behavior problems (De Bruyne et al., 2009). Although it can be argued that parental stress leads to increased problem behaviors in children with enuresis, it also may be the case that parental stress and frustration may lead to overestimation of the severity of problem behaviors in their children (Butler & McKenna, 2002; Joinson et al., 2008; van Hoecke, Hoebeke, Braet, & Walle, 2004). Further investigation into the role of parental stress in the maintenance or exacerbation of elimination problems in the child is clearly warranted, as it may have implications for treatment beyond the initial educational component of an intervention.

ADAPTATIONS AND MODIFICATIONS

As discussed, treatment approaches for elimination disorders are understudied. From the available evidence, it appears as if a combination of medical and behavioral management is most effective. However, limitations associated with these approaches preclude their routine use in clinical settings. The combination of behavioral intervention with medical management requires expertise in both arenas (e.g., medical knowledge about defecation dynamics and laxative therapy, psychological knowledge relevant to intensive behavioral management, child development, and family systems), which few practitioners possess (Ritterband et al., 2003). Additionally, time and cost associated with medical appointments, as well as potential psychosocial implications such as embarrassment, serve as salient barriers to more widespread implementation of these interventions (Ritterband et al., 2003).

To address these challenges, a fully automated Internet-based version of ETT, entitled UCanPoopToo, was created to promote increased access for parents seeking treatment for their children with encopresis. The initial version of the 3-week program was designed for parents and children to complete together and consisted of educational content delivered via three core modules focusing on the anatomy and pathophysiology involved in defecation, bowel cleanout and laxative therapy, and behavioral treatment of encopresis. The program was designed to be engaging and interactive and, thus, incorporated numerous illustrations, animated tutorials, and reinforcing quizzes (Ritterband et al., 2003). Initial findings suggest this Internet intervention is a promising method for the delivery of enhanced behavioral treatment of encopresis (Ritterband et al., 2003). Specifically, children who participated in the Internet-based intervention demonstrated reduced frequency of fecal soiling (i.e., from an average of 6 fecal accidents per week to an average of 0.5 accidents per week after the intervention), increased defecation in the toilet, and increased self-initiated trips to the bathroom as compared to controls receiving routine care from their primary care physician. The cure rate was 70% for children who received the Internet intervention compared to 45% for controls.

More recently, UCanPoopToo underwent a revision to incorporate additional educational content, online diaries, and arcade-style video games used as a reward for completing the educational components of the program (Ritterband et al., 2013). A 1-week follow-up was also added to the intervention, lengthening it to a total of 4 weeks. Consistent with previous findings, results from a larger randomized controlled trial indicate that children who received the intervention in conjunction with routine care not only had significantly fewer fecal accidents at postintervention compared to those who had received only routine care, but they had fewer accidents at 1-year follow-up as well (Ritterband et al., 2013). Specifically, children who used the UCanPoopToo intervention demonstrated a 50% reduction in fecal accidents at 4 to 6 weeks as compared to controls. They also experienced a gain in encopresis-specific knowledge. The majority of children and their parents liked the program and perceived it to be useful, convenient, easy to use, and understandable. Clinically, the rapid gains attained through the program are notable given the chronicity of the condition for these youth, and they underscore the potential of the intervention as an adjunctive component to treatment, particularly for families with limited resources and for providers with limited expertise in the behavioral treatment of encopresis. A third national trial is under way and is in the final phase of data collection.

MEASURING TREATMENT EFFECTS

Despite the involvement of pediatric psychologists in the treatment of these functional disorders over the past few decades, barriers still exist that limit empirical examination of treatment approaches and outcome. At present, diagnostic limitations associated with these conditions make it difficult to study interventions and their effects systematically (von Gontard, 2012). These limitations include criteria that are not well defined or, in some cases, too restrictive (e.g., for enuresis, the frequency of urinary accidents two times per week for at least 3 months), thereby resulting in possible exclusion of children who may otherwise benefit from treatment and, overall, limiting sample size (von Gontard, 2012). Similarly, in the case of encopresis, there are general guidelines for the treatment of constipation and fecal incontinence, but much less information is available for treatment of fecal incontinence without constipation (Stark, 2000). The treatment literature often does not specify these subtypes, which is highly relevant to the determination of efficacy and clinical implications (McGrath et al., 2000). Consistent with these limitations, the lack of well-defined and systematically implemented treatment strategies remains problematic and makes it difficult to draw conclusions about treatment efficacy. Medical intervention, for example, may require bowel disimpaction and maintenance laxative therapy, but the approaches taken vary across practitioners, making outcomes related to this approach difficult to study systematically. Another prominent barrier in treatment outcome research is the use of convenience samples, specifically those who have failed medical intervention and are referred subsequently for more intensive behavioral treatment

(Stark, 2000). Collectively, these barriers underscore the need for improved diagnostic criteria, more systematic methods for documenting/coding treatment strategies and adherence, and more controlled, between-groups studies with larger samples.

CLINICAL CASE EXAMPLE

Jack (identifying information has been altered to protect confidentiality), a nearly 7-year-old, Caucasian boy, was toilet trained for urination by 3 years of age but was never fully toilet trained for defecation. He developed chronic constipation around 3½ years of age, which resulted in the passage of large, painful bowel movements and associated fecal incontinence. Aside from encopresis, medical history was unremarkable. His primary care physician began treatment for constipation and fecal incontinence via stool softeners when Jack turned 4 years of age. When his symptoms persisted after several months, his primary care physician referred him to a pediatric gastroenterologist, who recommended disimpaction with enemas followed by daily administration of stool softeners, paired with a toilet sitting schedule of four to five times per day. This approach continued for more than 2 years with minimal success. At the time of referral for intensive behavioral treatment, Jack was having several fecal accidents every day, and he was passing two large, very soft bowel movements in the toilet every day. He always required prompting by his parents to attend the toilet. His medical regimen, which he had been on for approximately 2 years, consisted of 17 mg polyethylene glycol daily supplemented by fiber three times per week. Jack frequently engaged in retentive behaviors, including crossing his legs and hiding behind furniture. Emotionally, he began experiencing anger and poor self-esteem secondary to encopresis, and over the past several years, he had been seen by several therapists to address these concerns. Jack's father expressed frustration and anger secondary to beliefs that the soiling was intentional, and his mother was concerned that his retentive behaviors were so ingrained that they were now "subconscious." However, Jack reported that he often did not feel the urge to defecate.

Treatment began by educating the family about encopresis and the associated pathophysiology. Goals of treatment were outlined, including helping Jack become more responsible for his toileting behavior and fecal accidents as well as ensuring that he had the requisite skills, such as proper defecation dynamics and effective toilet sitting, to pass at least one formed, easy-to-pass bowel movement in the toilet every day. In consultation with a pediatric gastroenterologist, Jack underwent a clean-out the following weekend using high-dose polyethylene glycol, and his medication regimen was changed to incorporate a laxative to promote a more robust urge to defecate. The timing of the laxative dose was shifted to the afternoon to allow more time for Jack to have a bowel movement in the evening and to prevent fecal accidents during the school day. Toilet sits were reduced to two per day, approximately 20 minutes after meals (i.e., breakfast and dinner), during which time he was encouraged to practice the appropriate defecation dynamics that were described in detail and modeled during the evaluation. To address retentive behaviors and fecal accidents, a behavioral incentive plan was initiated that included a monetary reward for self-initiating toileting when he felt the urge to defecate and a disincentive when his parents noticed retentive behaviors and had to remind him to go to the toilet. The importance of immediate and consistent rewards, as well as having both parents on board with this approach to promote consistency, was underscored to the parents. Last, the family was provided access to the Internet intervention UCanPoopToo to provide adjunctive psychoeducational information about the physiology of defecation, clean-out and laxative therapy, and the behavioral treatment of encopresis.

Jack made several gains in the first 2 weeks of treatment, most notably with remittance of fecal accidents and passing spontaneous, formed bowel movements in the toilet before school each morning. He demonstrated improved self-confidence and was motivated and empowered by the reward system that was in place. Specifically, Jack was enthusiastic to receive the monetary reward at each self-initiated trip to the toilet associated with an urge to defecate, and he reported looking forward to buying a toy of his choosing at the end of the week with "his own" money. Additionally, his mother reported feeling less frustrated, although she was cautiously optimistic given the chronicity of Jack's condition.

Jack maintained these improvements for several months, during which time he was weaned off laxatives. He experienced a relapse in fecal accidents twice over the course of 2 years following this intervention. On both occasions, it coincided with changes to the family's daily schedule (i.e., travel and during the holidays). Jack consequently experienced reimpaction but underwent a clean-out followed by a period of maintenance laxatives each time. Jack has remained asymptomatic since that time, although his parents were encouraged to continue to monitor his bowel habits to prevent reimpaction.

REFERENCES

American Psychiatric Association. (2013). *Diagnostic and statistical manual of mental disorders* (5th ed.). Arlington, VA: American Psychiatric Publishing.

Azrin, N. H., Sneed, T. J., & Foxx, R. M. (1974). Dry-bed training: Rapid elimination of childhood enuresis. *Behaviour Research and Therapy, 12,* 147–156.

Baker, S. S., Liptak, G. S., Colletti, R. B., Croffie, J. M., Di Lorenzo, C., Ector, W., & Nurko, S. (1999). Constipation in infants and children: Evaluation and treatment. A medical position statement of the North American Society for Pediatric Gastroenterology and Nutrition. *Journal of Pediatric Gastroenterology and Nutrition, 29,* 612–626.

Benninga, M. A., Büller, H. A., Tytgat, G. N., Akkermans, L. M., Bossuyt, P. M., & Taminiau, J. A. (1996). Colonic transit time in constipated children: Does pediatric slow-transit constipation exist? *Journal of Pediatric Gastroenterology and Nutrition, 23,* 241–251.

Benninga, M. A., Voskuijl, W. P., & Taminiau, J. A. (2004). Childhood constipation: Is there new light in the tunnel? *Journal of Pediatric Gastroenterology Nutrition, 39,* 448–464.

Bernard-Bonnin, A. C., Haley, N., Bélanger, S., & Nadeau, D. (1993). Parental and patient perceptions about encopresis and its treatment. *Journal of Developmental and Behavioral Pediatrics, 14,* 397–400.

Blum, N. J., Taubman, B., & Nemeth, N. (2004). Why is toilet training occurring at older ages? A study of factors associated with later training. *Journal of Pediatrics, 145,* 107–111.

Bollard, J., & Nettlebeck, T. (1981). A comparison of dry bed training and standard urine alarm conditioning treatment of childhood bedwetting. *Behaviour Research and Therapy, 19,* 215–226.

Borowitz, S., Ritterband, L. M., Cox, D. J., Walker, L. S., Kovatchev, B., McKnight, . . . Sutphen, J. (2003). An Internet intervention as adjunctive therapy for pediatric encopresis. *Journal of Consulting and Clinical Psychology, 71,* 910–917.

Bradbury, M., & Meadow, S. (1995). Combined treatment with enuresis alarm and desmopressin for nocturnal enuresis. *Acta Paediatrica Scandinavia, 84,* 1014–1018.

Brazzelli, M., & Griffiths, P. (2006). Behavioural and cognitive interventions with or without other treatments for the management of faecal incontinence in children (review). *Cochrane Database of Systematic Reviews, 2006*(4), CD002240. doi: 10.1002/14651858.CD002240.pub3

Brooks, R. C., Copen, R. M., Cox, D. J., Morris, J., Borowitz, S., & Sutphen, J. (2000). Review of the treatment literature for encopresis, functional constipation, and stool-toileting refusal. *Annals of Behavioral Medicine, 22,* 260–267.

Brown, R. T., Connelly, M., Rittle, C., & Clouse, B. (2006). A longitudinal examination predicting emergency room use in children with sickle cell disease and their caregivers. *Journal of Pediatric Psychology, 31,* 163–173.

Butler, R. J. (2004). Childhood nocturnal enuresis: Developing a conceptual framework. *Clinical Psychology Review, 24,* 909–931.

Butler, R. J., Brewin, C. R., & Forsythe, W. I. (1988). Relapse in children treated for nocturnal enuresis: Prediction of response using pre-treatment variables. *Behavioural Psychotherapy, 18,* 65–72.

Butler, R. J., & McKenna, S. (2002). Overcoming parental intolerance in childhood nocturnal enuresis: A survey of professional opinion. *British Journal of Urology International, 89,* 295–297.

Butler, R. J., Redfern, E. J., & Holland, P. (1994). Children's notions about enuresis and the implications for treatment. *Scandinavian Journal of Nephrology, 163*(Suppl.), 39–47.

Butler, U., Joinson, C., Heron, J., von Gontard, A., Golding, J., & Emond, A. (2008). Early childhood risk factors associated with daytime wetting and soiling in school-age children. *Journal of Pediatric Psychology, 33,* 739–750.

Byrd, R. S., Weitzman, M., Lanphear, N. E., & Auinger, P. (1996). Bed-wetting in US children: Epidemiology and related behavior problems. *Pediatrics, 98,* 414–419.

Callaghan, R. P. (1964). Megarectum: Physiologic observations. *Archives of Diseases in Childhood, 39,* 153–157.

Campbell, L. K., Cox, D. J., & Borowitz, S. M. (2009). Elimination disorders: Enuresis and encopresis. In M. C. Roberts & R. G. Steele (Eds.), *Handbook of pediatric psychology* (4th ed., pp. 481–490). New York, NY: Guilford Press.

Cox, D. J., Ritterband, L. M., Quillian, W., Kovatchev, B., Morris, J., Sutphen, J., & Borowitz, S. (2003). Assessment of behavioral mechanisms maintaining encopresis: Virginia Encopresis-Constipation Apperception Test. *Journal of Pediatric Psychology, 28,* 375–382.

Cox, D. J., Sutphen, J., Borowitz, S., Dickens, M. N., Singles, J., & Whitehead, W. E. (1994). Simple electromyographic biofeedback treatment for chronic pediatric constipation/encopresis: Preliminary report. *Biofeedback and Self-Regulation, 19,* 41–50.

Cox, D. J., Sutphen, J., Borowitz, S., Kovatchev, B., & Ling, W. (1999). Contribution of behavior therapy and biofeedback to laxative therapy in the treatment of pediatric encopresis. *Annals of Behavioral Medicine, 20,* 70–76.

Cox, D. J., Sutphen, J., Ling, W., Quillian, W., & Borowitz, S. (1996). Additive benefits of laxative, toilet training, and biofeedback therapies in the treatment of pediatric encopresis. *Journal of Pediatric Psychology, 21,* 659–670.

Cunningham, C. L., & Banez, G. A. (2006). *Pediatric gastrointestinal disorders: Biopsychosocial assessment and treatment.* New York, NY: Springer.

De Bruyne, E., Van Hoecke, E., Van Gompel, K., Verbeken, S., Baeyens, D., Hoebeke, P. & Vande Walle, J. (2009). Problem behavior, parental stress, and enuresis. *Journal of Urology, 182,* 2015–2021.

Deshpande, A. V., Caldwell, P.H.Y., & Sureshkumar, P. (2012). Drugs for nocturnal enuresis in children (other than desmopressin and tricyclics). *Cochrane Database of Systematic Reviews, 2012*(1), CD002238. doi: 10.1002/14651858 .CD002238.pub2

Devitt, H., Holland, P., Butler, R., Redfern, E., Hiley, E., & Roberts, G. (1999). Plasma vasopressin and response to treatment in primary nocturnal enuresis. *Archives of Disease of Childhood, 80,* 448–451.

Doleys, D. M. (1983). Enuresis and encopresis. In T. Ollendick & M. Hersen (Eds.), *Handbook of child psychopathology* (pp. 201–226). New York, NY: Plenum Press.

Feehan, M., McGee, R., Stanton, W., & Silva, P. (1990). A 6-year follow-up of childhood enuresis: Prevalence in adolescence and consequences for mental health. *Journal of Paediatrics and Child Health, 26,* 75–79.

Fielding, D. (1985). Factors associated with drop out, relapse and failure in the conditioning treatment of nocturnal enuresis. *Behavioral Psychotherapy, 13,* 174–185.

Fishman, L., Rappaport, L., Schonwald, A., & Nurko, S. (2003). Trends in referral to a single encopresis clinic over 20 years. *Pediatrics, 111,* e604–e607.

Forsythe, W. I., & Redmond, A. (1974). Enuresis and spontaneous cure rate. Study of 1129 enuretics. *Archives of Disease in Childhood, 49,* 259–263.

Friman, P. C., Handwerk, M. L., Swearer, S. M., McGinnis, C., & Warzak, W. J. (1998). Do children with primary nocturnal enuresis have clinically significant behavior problems? *Archives of Pediatric and Adolescent Medicine, 152,* 537–539.

Geffken, G. R., Johnson, S. B., & Walker, D. (1986). Behavioral interventions for childhood nocturnal enuresis: The differential effect of bladder capacity on treatment progress and outcome. *Health Psychology, 5,* 261–272.

Glazener, C. M. A., & Evans, J.H.C. (2004). Simple behavioural and physical interventions for nocturnal enuresis in children. *Cochrane Database of Systematic Reviews, 2004*(2), CD003637. doi: 10.1002/14651858.CD003637

Hägglöf, B., Andrén, O., Bergström, E., Marklund, L., & Wendelius, M. (1997). Self-esteem before and after treatment in children with nocturnal enuresis and urinary incontinence. *Scandinavian Journal of Urology and Nephrology, 31,* 79–82.

Hirasing, R. A., van Leerdam, F. J., Bolk-Bennink, L. B., & Bosch, J. D. (1997). Bedwetting and behavioural and/or emotional problems. *Acta Paediatrica, 86,* 31–34.

Houts, A. C. (1991). Nocturnal enuresis as a biobehavioral problem. *Behavior Therapy, 22,* 133–151.

Houts, A. C., Berman, J. S., & Abramson, H. A. (1994). The effectiveness of psychological and pharmacological treatments for nocturnal enuresis. *Journal of Consulting and Clinical Psychology, 62,* 737–745.

Houts, A. C., & Liebert, R. M. (1984). *Bedwetting: A guide for parents and children.* Springfield, IL: Charles C Thomas.

Houts, A. C., Liebert, R. M., & Padawer, W. (1983). A delivery system for the treatment of primary enuresis. *Journal of Abnormal Child Psychology, 11,* 513–519.

Iacono, G., Cavataio, F., Montalto, G., Florena, A., Tumminello, M., Soresi, M., . . . Carroccio, A. (1998). Intolerance of cow's milk and chronic constipation in children. *New England Journal of Medicine, 339,* 1100–1104.

Janicke, D. M., Finney, J. W., & Riley, A. W. (2001). Children's health care use: A prospective investigation of factors related to care-seeking. *Medical Care, 39,* 990–1001.

Järvelin, M. R., Huttunen, N., Seppanen, J., Seppanen, U., & Moilanen, I. (1990). Screening for urinary tract abnormalities among day and night wetting children. *Scandinavian Journal of Urology and Nephrology, 24,* 181–189.

Järvelin, M. R., Moilanen, I., Kangas, P., Moring, K., Vikeväinen-Tervonen, L., Huttunen, N. P., & Seppänen, J. (1991). Aetiological and precipitating factors for childhood enuresis. *Acta Paediatrica Scandinavica, 80,* 361–369.

Joinson, C., Heron, J., Emond, A., & Butler, R. (2007). Psychological problems in children with bedwetting and combing (day and night) wetting: A UK population-based study. *Journal of Pediatric Psychology, 32,* 605–616.

Joinson, C., Heron, J., von Gontard, A., Butler, U., Golding, J., & Emond, A. (2008). Early childhood risk factors associated with daytime wetting and soiling in school-age children. *Journal of Pediatric Psychology, 33,* 739–750.

Keating, J., Butz, R., Burke, E., & Heimburg, R. (1983). Dry-bed training without a urine alarm: Lack of effect setting and therapist contact with child. *Journal of Behaviour Therapy and Experimental Psychiatry, 14,* 109–115.

Levine, M. D. (1975). Children with encopresis: A descriptive analysis. *Pediatrics, 56,* 412–416.

Levine, M. D., & Bakow, H. (1976). Children with encopresis: A study of treatment outcome. *Pediatrics, 58,* 845–852.

Liu, X., Sun, Z., Uchiyama, M., & Okawa, M. (2000). Attaining nocturnal urinary control, nocturnal enuresis, and behavioral problems in Chinese children aged 6 through 16 years. *Journal of the American Academy of Child and Adolescent Psychiatry, 39,* 1557–1564.

Loening-Baucke, V. (1993). Constipation in early childhood: Patient characteristics, treatment, and long-term follow up. *Gut, 34,* 400–404.

Loening-Baucke, V. (1996). Balloon defecation as a predictor of outcome in children with functional constipation and encopresis. *Journal of Pediatrics, 128,* 336–340.

Loening-Baucke, V. (2002). Polyethylene glycol without electrolytes for children with constipation and encopresis. *Journal of Pediatric Gastroenterology and Nutrition, 34,* 372–377.

Loening-Baucke, V. A., & Cruikshank, B. M. (1986). Abnormal defecation dynamics in chronically constipated children with encopresis. *Journal of Pediatrics, 108,* 562–566.

Magee, J. C., Ritterband, L. M., Thorndike, F. P., Cox, D. J., & Borowitz, S. M. (2009). Exploring the relationship between parental worry about their children's health and usage of an Internet intervention for pediatric encopresis. *Journal of Pediatric Psychology, 34,* 530–538.

McGrath, K. H., Caldwell, P. H. Y., & Jones, M. P. (2007). The frequency of constipation in children with nocturnal enuresis: A comparison with parental reporting. *Journal of Pediatrics and Child Health, 44,* 19–27.

McGrath, M. L., Mellon, M. W., & Murphy, L. (2000). Empirically supported treatments in pediatric psychology: Constipation and encopresis. *Journal of Pediatric Psychology, 25,* 225–254.

Mellon, M. W., & Houts, A. C. (1995). Elimination disorders. In R. T. Ammerman & M. Hersen (Eds.), *Handbook of child behavior therapy in the psychiatric setting* (pp. 341–366). New York, NY: Wiley.

Mellon, M. W., & McGrath, M. L. (2000). Empirically supported treatments in pediatric psychology: Nocturnal enuresis. *Journal of Pediatric Psychology, 25,* 193–214.

Moffatt, M. E., Kato, C., & Pless, N. B. (1987). Improvements in self-concept after treatment of nocturnal enuresis: Randomized controlled trial. *Journal of Paediatrics, 110,* 647–652.

Nevéus, T. (2001). Oxybutynin, desmopressin, and enuresis. *Journal of Urology, 166,* 2459–2462.

Nevéus, T., Eggert, P., Evans, J., Macedo, A., Rittig, S., Tegül, S., . . . Robson, L. (2010). Evaluation and treatment of monosymptomatic enuresis: A standardization document from the International Children's Continence Society. *Journal of Urology, 183,* 441–447.

Nevéus, T., Stenberg, A., Läckgren, G., Tuvemo, T., & Hetta, J. (1999). Sleep of children with enuresis: A polysomnographic study. *Pediatrics, 103,* 1193–1197.

Norfolk, S., & Wooton, J. (2012). Nocturnal enuresis in children. *Nursing Standard, 27,* 49–56.

Olatawura, M. O. (1973). Encopresis: A review of thirty-two cases. *Acta Paediatrica Scandinavica, 62,* 358–364.

Panides, W. C., & Ziller, R. C. (1981). The model of nocturnal enuresis management of children in Leeds. *Health Visitor, 70,* 10.

Partin, J. C., Hamill, S. K., Fischel, J. E., & Partin, J. S. (1992). Painful defecation and fecal soiling in children. *Pediatrics, 89,* 1007–1009.

Rasquin, A., Di Lorenzo, C., Forbes, D., Guiraldes, E., Hyams, J. S., Staiano, A., & Walker, L. S. (2006). Childhood functional gastrointestinal disorders: Child/adolescent. *Gastroenterology, 130,* 1527–1537.

Ritterband, L. M., Cox, D. J., Walker, L. S., Kovatchev, B., McKnight, L., Patel, K., . . . Sutphen, J. (2003). An Internet intervention as adjunctive therapy for pediatric encopresis. *Journal of Consulting and Clinical Psychology, 71,* 910–917.

Ritterband, L. M., Thorndike, F. P., Lord, H. R., Borowitz, S., Walker, L. S., Ingersoll, K. S., . . . Cox, D. J. (2013). An RCT of an Internet intervention for pediatric encopresis with one-year follow-up. *Clinical Practice in Pediatric Psychology, 1,* 68–80.

Robson, W. L. M. (2009). Evaluation and management of enuresis. *New England Journal of Medicine, 360,* 1429–1436.

Rushton, H. G. (1995). Wetting and functional voiding disorders. *Urologic Clinics of North America, 22,* 75–93.

Schmitt, B. D. (1997). Nocturnal enuresis. *Pediatrics in Review, 18,* 183–190.

Sharf, M. B., & Jennings, S. W. (1988). Childhood enuresis: Relationship to sleep, etiology, evaluation, and treatment. *Annals of Behavioral Medicine, 10,* 113–120.

Spurrier, N. J., Sawyer, M. G., Staugas, R., Martin, A. J., Kennedy, D., & Steiner, D. L. (2000). Association between parental perceptions of children's vulnerability to illness and management of children's asthma. *Pediatric Pulmonology, 29,* 88–93.

Stark, L. (2000). Treatment of encopresis: Where do we go from here? *Journal of Pediatric Psychology, 25,* 255–256.

Stark, L. J., Opipari, L. C., Donaldson, D. L., Danovsky, M. B., Rasile, D. A., & DelSanto, A. F. (1997). Evaluation of a standard protocol for retentive encopresis: a replication. *Journal of Pediatric Psychology, 22,* 619–633.

Stark, L. J., Owens-Stively, J., Spirito, A., Lewis, A., & Guevremont, D. (1990). Group behavioral treatment of retentive encopresis. *Journal of Pediatric Psychology, 15,* 659–671.

Sutphen, J. L., Borowitz, S. M., Hutchison, R. L., & Cox, D. J. (1995). Long-term follow-up of medically treated childhood constipation. *Clinical Pediatrics, 34,* 576–580.

Taubman, B. (1997). Toilet training and toileting refusal for stool only: A prospective study. *Pediatrics, 99,* 54–58.

van der Plas, R. N., Benninga, M. A., Büller, H. A., Bossuyt, P. M., Akkermans, L. M., Redekop, W. K., & Taminiau, J. A. (1996). Biofeedback training in treatment of childhood constipation: A randomised controlled study. *Lancet, 348,* 776–780.

van Dijk, M., Benninga, M. A., Grootenhuis, M. A., Nieuwenhuizen, A. M., & Last, B. F. (2007). Chronic childhood constipation: A review of the literature and the introduction of a protocolized behavioral intervention program. *Patient Education and Counseling, 67,* 63–77.

van Gool, J. D., Nieuwenhuis, E., ten Doeschate, I. O., Messer, T. P., & de Jong, T. P. (1999). Subtypes in monosymptomatic nocturnal enuresis. II. *Scandinavian Journal of Urology and Nephrology* (Suppl.), *202,* 8–11.

Van Hoecke, E., Hoebeke, P., Braet, C., & Walle, J. V. (2004). An assessment of internalizing problems in children with enuresis. *Journal of Urology, 171,* 2580–2583.

von Gontard, A. (2012). The impact of *DSM-5* and guidelines for assessment and treatment of elimination disorders. *European Child and Adolescent Psychiatry, 22*(Suppl. 1), 61–67.

von Gontard, A., & Nevéus, T. (2006). *Management of disorders of bladder and bowel control in childhood.* London, England: MacKeith Press.

von Gontard, A., Schaumburg, H., Hollmann, E., Eiberg, H., & Rittig, S. (2001). The genetics of enuresis: A review. *Journal of Urology, 166,* 2438–2443.

Voskuijl, W. P., van der Zaag-Loonen, H. J., Ketel, I. J., Grootenhuis, M. A., Derkx, B. H., & Benninga, M. A. (2004). Health related quality of life in disorders of defecation: The Defecation Disorder List. *Archives of Disease in Childhood, 89,* 1124–1127.

Voskuijl, W. P., van Ginkel, R., Benninga, M. A., Hart, G. A., Taminiau, J. A., & Boeckxstaens, G. E. (2006). New insight into rectal function in pediatric defecation disorders: Disturbed rectal compliance is an essential mechanism in pediatric constipation. *Journal of Pediatrics, 148,* 62–67.

Wagner, W., Johnson, S., Walker, D., Carter, R., & Wittner, J. (1982). A controlled comparison of two treatments for nocturnal enuresis. *Journal of Pediatrics, 101,* 302–307.

Weber, J., Ducrotte, P., Touchais, T. Y., Roussignol, C., & Denis, P. (1987). Biofeedback training for constipation in adults and children. *Diseases of the Colon and Rectum, 30,* 844–846.

Whelan, J. P., & Houts, A. C. (1990). Effects of a waking schedule on primary enuretic children with full-spectrum home training. *Health Psychology, 9,* 164–176.

Willie, S. (1986). Comparison of desmopressin and enuresis alarm for nocturnal enuresis. *Archives of Disease in Childhood, 61,* 30–33.

Wolfe-Christensen, C., Veenstra, A. L., Kovacevic, L., Elder, J. S., & Lakshmanan, Y. (2012). Psychosocial difficulties in children referred by pediatric urology: A closer look. *Urology, 80,* 907–913.

Yeung, C. K., Sit, F. K., To, L. K., Chiu, H. N., Sihoe, J. D., Lee, E., & Wong, C. (2002). Reduction in nocturnal functional bladder capacity is a common factor in the pathogenesis of refractory nocturnal enuresis. *BJU International, 90,* 302–307.

Youssef, N. N., Langseder, A. L., Verga, B. J., Mones, R. L., & Rosh, J. R. (2005). Chronic childhood constipation is associated with impaired quality of life: A case-controlled study. *Journal of Pediatric Gastroenterology and Nutrition, 41,* 56–60.

SECTION III

Other Interventions for Children

CHAPTER 17

Treatment of Insomnia and Nighttime Fears

MICHELLE A. CLEMENTI, JESSICA BALDERAS, JENNIFER COWIE, AND CANDICE A. ALFANO

BRIEF OVERVIEW OF DISORDER/PROBLEM

Intermittent problems sleeping and nighttime fears are typical features of child development, affecting up to 25% of all children (Meltzer & Mindell, 2006). Conversely, when these problems persist over periods of time, are markedly severe, and/or impair daytime functioning, a sleep disorder diagnosis may be appropriate. Insomnia is one of the most common sleep disorders in children (Owens, 2005) and typically is characterized by difficulty initiating sleep, although problems with sleep maintenance also may be present. As compared to the fourth edition of the *Diagnostic and Statistical Manual of Mental Disorders*, text revision (*DSM-IV-TR*) (American Psychiatric Association, 2000), the second edition of the *International Classification of Sleep Disorders* (*ICSD-2*) (American Academy of Sleep Medicine, 2005) provides diagnostic criteria for insomnia that occurs specifically during the childhood years (see Table 17.1). Consensus nonetheless exists that identification of insomnia in children is more challenging than in adults (Owens & Mindell, 2011). First, children with insomnia may not complain of sleepiness or necessarily view their sleep patterns as problematic. Caregivers more commonly serve as reporters of these problems. Meanwhile, parental understanding and awareness of children's sleep varies based on a range of factors, including a child's age, a family's culture, socioeconomic status, and personal habits and experience (Owens, 2005). Thus, insomnia in children must be viewed against a backdrop of developmental, cultural, and familial considerations.

The *ICSD-2* definition of behavioral insomnia of childhood (BIC) specifies two developmental subtypes of the disorder: *sleep-onset association subtype* and *limit-setting subtype*. The former, which predominantly presents in infancy, is characterized by difficulty falling asleep in the absence of certain conditions (e.g., singing, rocking, nursing) both at bedtime and after nighttime awakenings. The latter, more commonly diagnosed in preschool and school-age children and the focus of this chapter, refers to difficulty initiating sleep and resisting/refusing bed due to inadequate structure, limit setting, and/or behavior management by a caregiver. Thus, inconsistently set limits surrounding sleep serve to intermittently reinforce poor sleep and negative bedtime behaviors.

The presence of BIC may be influenced by a range of biological, temperamental, and behavioral factors (Owens, 2005). From a clinical standpoint, however, one of the most frequent causes of BIC is sleep-related or nighttime fears. Such fears include a broad array of content, including fear of the dark/shadows, separation from caregivers, bad dreams/nightmares, strange noises, and intruders/burglars. Although common in childhood (Gordon, King, Gullone, Muris, & Ollendick, 2007), fearful nighttime behaviors that are chronic and/or severe often require direct intervention and may signify a co-occurring or nascent anxiety disorder, such as separation or generalized anxiety disorder (Alfano & Lewin, 2008). Accordingly, comprehensive assessment in such cases should include a specific focus on anxiety and fear. In light of the common overlap of insomnia and nighttime fears

TABLE 17.1   *ICSD-2*: Diagnostic Criteria for Behavioral Insomnia of Childhood

A. A child's symptoms meet the criteria for insomnia based upon reports of parents or other adult caregivers. (Note: ICSD-II general criteria for insomnia includes a complaint of difficulty initiating sleep, difficulty maintaining sleep, or waking up too early or sleep that is chronically nonrestorative or poor in quality.)

B. The child shows a pattern consistent with either the sleep-onset association or limit-setting type of insomnia described below.

   i. Sleep-onset association type includes each of the following:

      1. Falling asleep is an extended process that requires special conditions.

      2. Sleep-onset associations are highly problematic or demanding.

      3. In the absence of the associated conditions, sleep onset is significantly delayed or sleep is otherwise disrupted.

   ii. Limit-setting type includes each of the following:

      1. The individual has difficulty initiating or maintain sleep.

      2. The individual stalls or refuses to go to bed at an appropriate time or refuses to return to bed following a nighttime awakening.

      3. The caregiver demonstrates insufficient or inappropriate limit setting to establish appropriate sleeping behavior in the child.

C. The sleep disturbance is not better explained by another sleep disorder, medical or neurological disorder, mental disorder, or medication use.

Note: Adapted from American Academy of Sleep Medicine. (2005). *International Classification of Sleep Disorders: Diagnostic and coding manual (2nd ed.)*. Westchester, IL: Author.

in children, this chapter provides a review of evidence-based approaches for the treatment of both problems in children and adolescents.

EVIDENCE-BASED APPROACHES

Evidence-based approaches for treatment of BIC and nighttime fears are separately outlined next.

Behavioral Insomnia of Childhood

The efficacy of various behavioral approaches and techniques for BIC has been established in controlled studies (Mindell, Kuhn, Lewin, Meltzer, & Sadeh, 2006; Sadeh, 2005). Specific approaches/techniques are outlined in Table 17.2. Although prescriptive interventions corresponding with parental attitudes, abilities, and goals should be used, extinction-based procedures represent the cornerstone of most treatments for BIC. Both standard and graduated extinction interventions are used with the goal of reducing inappropriate child behaviors during bedtime by altering parental responses. *Standard extinction* involves completely ignoring all inappropriate behaviors (e.g., crying, yelling, tantrums, or unreasonable demands) after bedtime once the child has been put to bed and until wake time (except those posing a danger to the child). Several studies have demonstrated the efficacy of this approach in reducing bedtime resistance and sleep onset (Reid, Walter, & O'Leary, 1999; Rickert & Johnson, 1988; Seymour, Brock, During, & Poole, 1989). Although relatively straightforward, this approach may be particularly challenging for parents to implement consistently. Postextinction bursts, which include a sudden, temporary reemergence of the behavior, also are common (Owens, France, & Wiggs, 1999).

Graduated extinction consists of ignoring inappropriate behaviors and systematically increasing the amount of time before responding. Because the reward of parental attention is withdrawn gradually, graduated extinction often is easier than standard extinction for both parents and children. Using a graduated extinction approach, a parent might put a child to bed and then check on the child after progressively longer periods of time (e.g., 5, 7, 10 minutes) with the goals of having

TABLE 17.2   Description of Evidence-Based Approaches for Behavioral Insomnia of Childhood and
Child Nighttime Fears

Approach/Technique	Description
Behavioral Insomnia of Childhood	
Standard extinction	Withdrawing all attention in response to problem behavior from bedtime until morning
Graduated extinction	Ignoring inappropriate behavior and gradually increasing the intervals between parental attention
Bedtime fading	Delaying bedtime until sleep initiation is highly probable and incrementally moving toward an earlier bedtime
Positive routines	Incorporating pleasant and relaxing activities into the bedtime routine
Response cost	Removing a child from bed after a sleep-onset latency greater than approximately 20 minutes
Stimulus control	Pairing sleep-appropriate cues and activities with the sleeping environment
Cognitive techniques	Directly identifying and challenging maladaptive sleep cognitions
Progressive muscle relaxation	Systematically tensing and relaxing muscle groups throughout the body
Nighttime Fears	
Self-control training	Teaching skills that empower children to develop their own sense of agency in response to their fear(s)
Relaxation training	Guided exercises that promote relaxation
Positive imagery	Guiding a child to remember and focus on a pleasant and relaxing memory
Positive self-statements	Repeating statements that promote courage and increase self-esteem
Differential reinforcement	A process of shaping behavior through the principles of operant conditioning
Desensitization	Diminishing negative responsiveness to aversive stimuli through repeated exposure

the child fall asleep independently. In between checks, the parent follows an extinction procedure and continues to ignore any inappropriate behaviors until the next check. Checks should include only brief periods of parental presence and praise; excessive dialogue, prolonged physical contact, or placating the child's demands is avoided (Taylor & Roane, 2010). Theoretically, checks are aimed at modifying schedules of reinforcement so that the time interval rather than the child's (inappropriate) behavior determines parental attention. Using this approach, checks may be faded out in one night or over successive nights, with the fading schedule determined by parental/child preference, the child's age and temperament, and overall chronicity/intensity of the problem. The efficacy of graduated extinction in reducing noncompliant bedtime behavior is well established (see Mindell et al., 2006).

Extinction procedures also are frequently combined with other procedures to increase bedtime compliance and facilitate easier transitions to sleep (Kuhn & Elliot, 2003; Tikotzky & Sadeh, 2010). *Bedtime fading* involves delaying bedtime until the child appears naturally sleepy and then systematically moving to an earlier bedtime based on mastery of sleep initiation. This procedure reduces the amount of time spent in bed awake (i.e., stimulus control) while strengthening a child's intrinsic sleep drive. Sadeh, Gruber, and Raviv (2003) have demonstrated that a delayed bedtime alone results in decreased sleep-onset latency in school-age children.

Positive routines incorporate pleasant and structured presleep activities into the bedtime routine as environmental sleep cues. For example, a school-age child might brush his or her teeth, put on pajamas and read a story independently, and then spend time reviewing the day with a parent leading up to bedtime. Throughout the routine, parents provide praise for compliant behaviors and avoid responding to negative behaviors. Based on review by Mindell and colleagues (2006), positive routines are at least equally as effective as extinction-based approaches and may provide a preferred alternative to extinction in reducing the likelihood of extinction bursts.

Response cost involves removing a child from bed if he or she is unable to initiate sleep within about 20 minutes. However, it is critical that children be allowed to engage only in calming, quiet activities during such periods in order to avoid increased levels of nighttime arousal. Bedtime may be delayed accordingly on subsequent nights based on the timing of successful sleep initiation on the previous night (Taylor & Roane, 2010). Research has shown that bedtime fading with and without response cost is an effective intervention in reducing bedtime resistance (Ashbaugh & Peck, 1998; Piazza & Fisher, 1991a, 1991b).

Although few controlled studies have focused on the treatment of insomnia in adolescents specifically, many of the cognitive behavioral treatment (CBT) components shown to be effective in adults (Taylor & Roane, 2010) can be used among teenagers. *Stimulus control* aims to strengthen the association between the bed and sleep by encouraging the individual to go to bed when feeling sleepy, removing clocks from the bedroom (e.g., since they can trigger frustration and arousal at night), and using the bed for sleep only. *Cognitive techniques* target maladaptive beliefs or attitudes about sleep (e.g., "I am a bad sleeper"; "I won't be able to function tomorrow"), which may serve to fuel sleep problems, by directly challenging such thoughts (e.g., "Everyone experiences sleep problems sometimes"; "Poor sleep does not feel good but will not hurt you"). Cognitive techniques sometimes are used with *relaxation training*, which focuses on slow and deep breathing, progressive muscle relaxation, and/or visualizing a peaceful scene. *Progressive muscle relaxation* involves tensing (for 4–7 seconds) and then relaxing (for 30–40 seconds) different muscle groups throughout the body, including forehead, face, neck, shoulders, arms, wrists, hands, abdomen, buttocks, thighs, ankles, and feet. Preliminary research using such CBT techniques in substance-abusing adolescents is promising (Bootzin & Stevens, 2005).

Nighttime Fears

A variety of cognitive behavioral techniques have been examined in the treatment of children's nighttime fears, including self-control training, relaxation training, positive imagery, positive self-statements, and differential reinforcement (Sadeh, 2005; Tikotzky & Sadeh, 2010). These approaches/techniques are outlined in Table 17.2. Because a combination of multiple techniques has been examined in most studies, the contribution of individual components is largely unclear at this time; however, the overall effectiveness of such interventions is high. For example, in a study of 33 school-age children with severe nighttime fears, self-control training, relaxation, positive imagery, and "brave" self-statements were used (Graziano & Mooney, 1980). During weekly group meetings, a trained therapist instructed the children to lie on the floor for 1 minute and practice maintaining a quiet and relaxed position while the therapist spoke in a soothing voice (relaxation training). Then the children imagined a pleasant scene (incorporated a comforting memory) that they described in detail to the therapist who recorded it in the child's journal (positive imagery). Brave self-statements involved having children repeat positive statements, such as "I am brave" or "I can take care of myself in the dark" at the end of the exercise. Children were encouraged to practice these self-control skills for 5 minutes at night with the parents and alone when feeling afraid. As part of an additional contingency management component, parents gave tokens for "brave" behaviors (differential reinforcement were awarded for remaining in bed throughout the night and independently following the self-control training skills). In comparison to a wait-list control group, children receiving CBT evidenced significant reduction in frequency, intensity, and duration of nighttime fears as well as overall disruptive nighttime behavior, which was maintained at 1-year follow-up.

Several studies that have utilized various combinations of slightly modified self-control strategies with small sample sizes have achieved similar results (see King, Ollendick & Tonge, 1997). McMenamy and Katz (1989) conducted an intervention with five children that included relaxation training, positive self-statements, and storytelling. Following the reading of a story, the children were encouraged to model the characters acting bravely in fearful situations. Nighttime fear ratings and problem behaviors as indicated by ratings on the Child Behavior Checklist (CBCL) (Achenbach & Edelbrock, 1981) were significantly improved after 6 weeks. Giebenhain and O'Dell (1984) used similar techniques (relaxation training and positive self-statements) and added a *desensitization* component. Six school-age children gradually dimmed a night-light each night and earned a reward each morning for their compliance. Rewards included verbal and physical praise and tangible items. Children experienced a significant reduction in fear up to 12 months posttreatment. More recently, Ollendick, Hagopian, and Huntzinger (1991) demonstrated the importance of adding differential reinforcement to self-control training in order to significantly improve treatment efficacy.

PARENT INVOLVEMENT IN TREATMENT

The parent–child interaction is the primary context for behavior change in the treatment of BIC (Sadeh, 2005). Difficulty setting firm nighttime limits is strongly associated with increased sleep disturbances in school-age children (Owens-Stively et al., 1997). Thus, parental understanding of and compliance with prescribed interventions are critical for successful outcomes, particularly among young children. Specific strategies for increasing limit setting in relation to sleep were discussed in the previous section, but a range of parent-related factors may interfere with the correct implementation of these approaches. For example, increased levels of family discord/stress, parental psychopathology, and single-parent status have each been associated with higher rates of child sleep disturbance (Byars, Yeomans-Maldonado, & Noll, 2011; Gregory et al., 2005; Sadeh, Raviv, & Gruber, 2000). Although precise mechanisms underlying these relationships remain unknown, such problems/issues may directly (or indirectly) hinder a parent's ability to successfully establish and/or enforce adaptive bedtime routines and sleep practices in the home. Clinicians therefore need to consider whether additional intervention recommendations, such as referring a parent for individual/couples-based mental health services or identifying additional sources of social support for parents, will maximize the possibility of treatment success.

Parental beliefs and attitudes also can have a significant impact on the development and maintenance of sleep disturbances in children (Johnson & McMahon, 2008; Owens, Jones, & Nash, 2011; Tikotsky & Shaashua, 2012) and therefore may be considered an important target of cognitive behavioral interventions. Faulty beliefs (e.g., "My child needs me in order to feel safe and fall asleep") can maintain maladaptive parenting behaviors at night and ultimately serve to reinforce bedtime resistance and insomnia. Negative parental attitudes about treatment (e.g., "Ignoring my child's crying is harmful or cruel") similarly can impede successful implementation of behavioral strategies. If parents experience emotions such as fear, guilt, or shame when attempting to use extinction techniques, for example, they will most likely use such intervention inappropriately, and thus it will fail. Identification and correction of faulty beliefs/attitudes at the outset of treatment through the use of psychoeducation about sleep and cognitive techniques can circumvent such problems.

Sleep intervention research in infants has found that parental expectations regarding the effects and course of treatment on child sleep problems can impact treatment adherence and outcome significantly (Sadeh, Flint-Ofir, Tirosh, & Tikotzky, 2007; Tse & Hall, 2007). To ensure that behavioral

techniques are implemented consistently and correctly, clinicians should prepare parents for potential increases in problem behaviors both during and after the course of treatment. *Extinction bursts*
(i.e., a temporary increase in a behavior following the removal of a reinforcer) and *spontaneous*
recovery (i.e., the reemergence of a previously extinguished conditioned response after a delay) are
commonly observed phenomena during treatment for BIC or nighttime fears and can represent pivot
points in treatment, particularly if parents are not properly prepared for such events. Setting realistic
goals and ensuring that parents understand the basic principles of operant and classic conditioning
underlying prescribed behavioral techniques often increases the likelihood of parents responding
appropriately to such events.

ADAPTATIONS AND MODIFICATIONS

There are several circumstances under which behavioral sleep interventions require some form of
modification in order to ensure their appropriateness. Notably, since sleep patterns and practices are
shaped by a range of demographic, racial/ethnic, and cultural factors, clinicians need to consider a
child's sleep behaviors within these contexts. Research indicates that children of racial/ethnic minorities are more likely to cosleep, obtain less sleep at night, and give up daytime naps at later ages than
nonminority children (Crabtree et al., 2005; Crosby, LeBourgeois, & Harsh, 2005). Children from
lower socioeconomic status (SES) groups experience a greater number of sleep-related problems
and daytime sleepiness compared to their peers (Crabtree et al., 2005). Although it is tempting to
speculate that the latter finding may be explained simply by a greater number of persons living in
the home, longer parent work schedules, increased family stress, and the like, other data show that
racial/ethnic and SES variables interact with regard to children's sleep in complex ways. In a study
examining cosleeping and sleep problems in children from White lower-SES, White higher-SES,
Black lower-SES, and Black higher-SES families, cosleeping was associated with increased night
waking and bedtime resistance in White lower-SES and Black higher-SES children only (Lozoff,
Askew, & Wolf, 1996). Interestingly, White parents were more likely than Black parents to consider
their child's sleep behavior to be a problem. Such findings underscore the fact that, although a
child's sleep needs to be considered within the context of these variables, successful approaches to
treatment ultimately need to align with parent practices, beliefs, and expectations.

   Children with developmental disorders as well as other syndromes associated with cognitive and
behavioral deficits (Down syndrome, Prader-Willi syndrome) often experience frequent, severe,
and chronic sleep problems requiring intervention (Wiggs, 2001). The transition from wake to
sleep requires learning a bedtime routine and developing self-regulatory skills, and children with
autism spectrum disorders (ASDs) can have difficulty learning these behavioral sequences as well
as reading and/or responding to social cues that signal sleep. Stereotypic behaviors also can render
bedtime routines problematic. In addition to problems at the beginning of the night, children with
developmental disorders commonly awaken in the middle of the night and experience difficulty
transitioning back to sleep (Johnson, 1996). The content of treatment approaches for such problems does not differ significantly from those used among typically developing children, although
the duration and pace of treatment may. In general, more gradual treatment approaches are favored
(Vriend, Corkum, Moon, & Smith, 2011). For example, greater repetition in the demonstration
and reinforcement of specific bedtime routines may be needed before consistent changes in sleep
patterns are observed. Because many children with ASD respond more favorably to visual rather
than verbal instruction, the same series of pictures can be used nightly to remind the child of
nighttime routines.

A host of biological, psychosocial, and developmental factors can make working with adolescent patients particularly challenging. Lifestyle demands, such as early school start times, after-school sports and jobs, homework, and social activities can significantly interfere with adequate sleep during the teenage years (Carskadon, Wolfson, Acebo, Tzischinsky, & Seifer, 1998). Additionally, increased nightly use of electronic media (e.g., cell phones, texting, video games, television, the Internet), a favorite activity among this age group, is associated with shortened sleep duration and daytime sleepiness (Calamaro, Watson, & Ratclifffe, 2009). These lifestyle changes are in sync with well-established circadian changes that occur with the onset of puberty and cause adolescents to want to go to bed later at night and sleep later in the morning (Carskadon et al., 1998). It is important to consider this convergence of factors when beginning treatment with adolescent patients since they may well require considerable support in making lasting changes in their sleep. Also, educating families about predictable, developmentally based sleep changes can help alleviate conflict between adolescents and their parents (i.e., "These problems are not all his/her fault!") and bolster therapeutic alliance. Effective intervention strategies often incorporate elements from both child and adult-based treatments (depending on the adolescent's age, specific sleep problem, motivation level, etc.). For example, maintaining a consistent sleep schedule on weekdays and weekends, avoiding daytime napping and caffeine, and creating a sleep-friendly environment (e.g., dark room, cool temperature) are staples of insomnia interventions among adults and should be used with adolescents as well. However, parental involvement in the form of ensuring appropriate bedtimes, taking away cell phones at a certain time of night, and/or rewarding compliant nighttime behaviors (differential reinforcement) may be equally essential for success.

ASSESSMENT/MEASURING TREATMENT EFFECTS

Based in part on the continual development changes in sleep patterns and need that occur across early development, valid and reliable assessment is critical for both accurate diagnosis and treatment planning. Although objective measures such as polysomnography and actigraphy are considered the gold standard for measuring sleep, evaluation among children with suspected BIC does not necessitate the use of such measures. However, to the extent that other sleep disorders also are suspected and must be ruled out (e.g., to rule out sleep-disordered breathing in children who snore/gasp during sleep), an overnight sleep study may be indicated.

Clinical Interviews

Diagnostic evaluation for behavioral sleep problems such as insomnia or nighttime fears typically includes a structured interview with parents and children. Information regarding a child's current and historical sleep patterns/behaviors, duration and chronicity of the sleep problem, and description of the child's sleep routine and environment should be collected in detail. Further, parental responses to child nighttime behaviors (e.g., bedtime resistance, requests to cosleep) are particularly important to evaluate since certain behaviors may serve as primary reinforcers of sleep problems. Other potential contributing factors include late-day caffeine consumption, overly committed academic/social schedules, and nighttime interaction with peers via electronic media (texting, online chatting, etc.).

Certain medical problems and conditions, such as eczema, gastroesophageal reflux, and pain syndromes, may contribute to a child's behavioral sleep difficulties. Clinicians should therefore query the presence of such symptoms and complaints during the interview. A thorough developmental history can assist in understanding the presence of other problems/disorders (e.g., mental retardation, ASD) that may influence the choice of the most appropriate sleep intervention strategies.

Finally, sleep problems in children overlap to a large extent with psychiatric disorders including anxiety, attention-deficit/hyperactivity disorder, and depression (Alfano & Gamble, 2009). Whether a psychiatric disorder may underlie a child's sleep problem or, alternatively, whether ongoing sleep disruption contributes to problems with daytime behavioral/emotional regulation can be difficult to determine since this relationship has been shown to be reciprocal (e.g., Cousins et al., 2011). However, when behavioral indicators of insufficient sleep are present, such as an inability to awaken in the morning, increased sleep on weekends, and sleepiness in inappropriate settings (e.g., school), sleep-based intervention should be considered. Such information should be collected at the beginning and at the end of treatment in order to determine the intervention's effectiveness in reducing daytime sleepiness.

Sleep Logs/Diaries

Although numerous formats are available, sleep logs/diaries usually consist of a one-page, 24-hour grid used to record specific sleep–wake patterns and behaviors on a prospective basis (commonly 7 days). Information captured includes daily bedtimes and wake times, time required to fall asleep after getting in bed, number and length of awakenings during the night, and daytime naps. These data can be used to calculate key sleep variables, including average sleep-onset latency, variability in nightly bedtimes, and sleep efficiency (ratio of time spent asleep to time spent in bed). Other information, which may be central to effective intervention, might include the use of medications and other sleep aids (e.g., melatonin), frequency of nightmares, or cosleeping behaviors and serve as reference points for progress during treatment. Sleep logs/diaries are inexpensive, easy to use, and provide detailed, visual depiction of a child's sleep. They can be completed throughout or at specific points during treatment.

Validated Sleep Questionnaires

In recent years, there has been an exponential increase in the number of parent and child questionnaires designed to assess sleep–wake patterns and problems in youth. Of available measures, however, very few have been developed based on fundamental operational principles of instrument development (see Spruyt & Gozal, 2011). Based on a comprehensive review of the research, Spruyt and Gozal (2011) found that the Sleep Disturbance Scale for Children (SDSC) (Bruni et al., 1996) is one of the only measures to have been validated and standardized using appropriate psychometric criteria. The SDSC, which is available at no cost, assesses a range of sleep disorders, including disorders of initiating/maintaining sleep, sleep-related breathing disorders, disorders of arousal, sleep–wake transition disorders, disorders of excessive somnolence, and sleep hyperhidrosis in children ages 6.5 to 15 years. The 27-item scale asks parents to rate child sleep behavior and disturbances during the past 6 months using a 5-point Likert scale.

The Children's Sleep Habits Questionnaire (CHSQ) (Owens, Spirito & McGuinn, 2000) is a widely used albeit somewhat less well-validated measure that yields a total sleep problems score and eight subscales among children 4 to 10 years of age. Among the subscales, scores on the bedtime resistance and sleep anxiety scales may be particularly helpful in determining the specific nature of sleep initiation/maintenance problems. The CSHQ also assesses average total sleep time and nightly bedtime and is available in an abbreviated 33-item format. In contrast to the SDSC, parents use a 3-point Likert scale to rate the frequency of sleep behaviors/problems during the past week.

The CSHQ also is available free of charge from the authors. Parent-report measures such as the SDSC and CSHQ can be completed in approximately 10 to 15 minutes, making them an efficient option for assessment at the start and throughout treatment.

CLINICAL CASE EXAMPLE

Xavier (identifying information has been altered to protect confidentiality) is a 7-year-old Hispanic boy in the first grade who presented with difficulty falling asleep, fear of the dark, and defiant nighttime behaviors. His mother explained that while he had never been a "great sleeper," his sleep-related problems increased significantly when he started kindergarten (full time) during the previous school year. Although Xavier likes school, his mother reported that he frequently worried about his performance, following the rules, things his teacher says to him, and/or whether the other kids like him. Both Xavier and his parents also complain of excessive tiredness during the daytime.

Initial Assessment

Assessment included an interview with Xavier and his parents as well as completion of parent and child questionnaires regarding sleep and daytime behavior. A sleep diary was mailed to the family ahead of time to be completed during the 1-week period leading up the evaluation appointment. The sleep diary completed by Xavier's parents indicated the presence of several sleep-related problems, including inconsistent bed and wake times, prolonged sleep-onset latency (i.e., >20 minutes) on a nightly basis, and periodic nighttime awakenings. Overall, Xavier was receiving an inadequate amount of sleep for his age: an average of 8.25 hours per night (compared to a recommended 10 hours for his age group) (Mindell & Owens, 2005). During the interview, the family agreed that Xavier had been experiencing problems falling asleep by himself since kindergarten. On a nightly basis he insists that one of his parents stay with him in his room until he falls asleep. If his parents refuse his request, Xavier becomes angry, cries, and refuses to stay in his room. Even though he insists that he can fall asleep only when a parent is with him, Xavier still requires 30 to 45 minutes to initiate sleep with a parent at his bedside. If Xavier wakes up during the night (two to three times per week), he calls out to his parents to come stay with him so he can fall back to sleep. He is also afraid of the dark and insists on having several night-lights on and the door to his room kept wide open at all times. Xavier's parents have found it easier to just comply with his nighttime requests since his crying and tantrums can persist for hours. These problems also have caused daytime fatigue and conflict between Xavier's parents.

Treatment Plan

A behavioral treatment plan including five components was developed.

Psychoeducation

The entire family was first educated about the role of sleep in relation to numerous aspects of functioning, including feeling anxious/nervous. The following explanation was given:

> Falling asleep at night is not something we are born knowing how to do. As we grow up, our task is to learn to fall asleep based on the presence of certain appropriate internal (e.g., feelingy sleepy, body temperature) and external (e.g., lying down in our own bed, darkness) signals or cues. However, if we get in the habit of using the wrong signals/cues for sleep, the correct signals no longer work and might even make us feel

more awake. This is when sleep can become a problem. When this happens, we have to do some things to "reset" our own sleep clock. It is easiest to do this when everyone in the family works together.

It was further explained how, in Xavier's case, his parents had become the cues for sleeping. Xavier agreed that in order to do be able to do things like sleepovers and camp, he needed to use/learn different signals for sleep.

Sleep Hygiene

The concept of sleep hygiene was reviewed with the family as well:

Just like dental hygiene means keeping your teeth and gums healthy, sleep hygiene refers to keeping your sleep healthy so that we feel rested and strong during the daytime.

Five new sleep rules were implemented:

1. Keeping a regular sleep schedule 7 days a week by going to bed and waking up at the same time every day
2. Avoiding daytime napping (which might interfere with Xavier's ability to fall asleep at the same time every night)
3. Creating a sleep environment that is quiet, cool, and dimly lit
4. Avoiding caffeine after lunch (e.g., from soda or chocolate)
5. Developing a calm and relaxing bedtime routine

Positive Bedtime Routine

It was decided that approximately 45 minutes before bedtime, Xavier would take a warm shower. In addition to the fact that Xavier found this activity relaxing, it was explained that the warm water would work with his own body temperature to create a good (internal) signal for sleep. After his shower, Xavier was responsible for brushing his teeth and putting on his pajamas independently, after which he would have 15 minutes of reading time with one parent. Reading time was to take place on the living room sofa under dim light (i.e., not in Xavier's room). Xavier's parents understood that if he protested or complained at any time during the bedtime routine, they were to ignore these behaviors.

Graduated Extinction

Following reading time, Xavier was to go to his bedroom alone and get in bed. He was allowed to keep his bedroom door open and turn on one of his night-lights when getting into bed. As long as Xavier remained in his bed and quiet, one parent would come to his room to check on him every few minutes. Nighttime check-ins consisted only of a parent standing in the doorway to his bedroom (for no more than 30 seconds) and providing verbal praise for his brave behavior. Check-ins were allowed to continue (over increasingly longer intervals) for up to 20 minutes. Xavier was also told that at any time during this 20-minute period, he had the option to tell his parent that he did not need any more check-ins that night. In the event that this occurred, he could have whatever breakfast he wanted the next morning (e.g., Xavier chose ice cream one morning). Alternatively, if Xavier whined or protested at any time during check-ins, his behavior was ignored. If he got out of bed, his parents were instructed to leave the room immediately and not return until he got back into bed. When/if Xavier woke up in the middle of the night and called out to his parents, they were allowed only to go to his doorway in the same manner as at the beginning of the night.

Sticker Chart

Xavier could earn one sticker each night for practicing good sleep hygiene, following the bedtime routine, and being compliant with check-ins (e.g., up to three stickers per night). He was allowed to design his own chart and pick out the stickers he liked best. At the end of the week, Xavier earned a small reward for getting a certain number of stickers. This amount was increased over time as Xavier showed greater levels of success (contingency management).

Outcome Assessment

Treatment progress was tracked with both sticker charts and completion of weekly sleep diaries, which showed that Xavier was able to stay and sleep in his room by himself every night within 3 weeks of beginning treatment. After an initial increase in Xavier's average sleep-onset latency (during weeks 1 and 2), he was able to initiate sleep (independently) within 20 minutes of getting into bed by week 4 of treatment. Behaviors such as crying, whining, and calling out to his parents at night also ceased after approximately 4 weeks. His sleep diaries simultaneously indicated an increase in average total sleep time (from 8.25 to 9 hours) and number of nighttime awakenings. Based on parent report 6 weeks after the start of treatment, Xavier was also less sleepy during the day.

REFERENCES

Achenbach, T. M., & Edelbrock, C. (1981). Behavioral problems and competencies reported by parents of normal and disturbed children aged 4–16. *Monographs of the Society for Research in Child Development, 46,* 88.

Alfano, C. A., & Gamble, A. (2009). The role of sleep in childhood psychiatric disorders. *Child Youth Care Forum, 38,* 327–340.

Alfano, C. A., & Lewin, D. S. (2008). Sleep in children with anxiety disorders. In A. Ivanenko (Ed.), *Sleep and psychiatric disorders in children and adolescents* (pp. 315–328). New York, NY: Informa Healthcare.

American Academy of Sleep Medicine. (2005). *International classification of sleep disorders. Diagnostic and coding manual* (2nd ed.). Westchester, IL: Author.

American Psychiatric Association. (2000). *Diagnostic and statistical manual of mental disorders* (4th ed., text rev.). Washington, DC: Author.

Ashbaugh, R., & Peck, S. M. (1998). Treatment of sleep problems in a toddler: A replication of the faded bedtime with response cost protocol. *Journal of Applied Behavior Analysis, 31,* 127–129.

Bootzin, R. R., & Stevens, S. J. (2005). Adolescents, substance abuse, and the treatment of insomnia and daytime sleepiness. *Clinical Psychology Review, 25,* 629–644.

Bruni, O., Ottaviano, S., Guidetti, V., Romoli, M., Innocenzi, M., & Cortesi, F. (1996). The Sleep Disturbance Scale for Children (SDSC): Construction and validation of an instrument to evaluate sleep disturbances in childhood and adolescence. *Journal of Sleep Research, 5*(4), 251–261.

Byars, K. C., Yeomans-Maldonado, G., & Noll, J. G. (2011). Parental functioning and pediatric sleep disturbance: An examination of factors associated with parenting stress in children clinically referred for evaluation of insomnia. *Sleep Medicine, 12,* 898–905.

Calamaro, C. J., Mason, T. B. A., & Ratcliffe, S. J. (2009). Adolescents living the 24/7 lifestyle: Effects of caffeine and technology on sleep duration and daytime functioning. *Pediatrics, 123*(6), e1005–e1010.

Carskadon, M. A., Wolfson A. R., Acebo, C., Tzischinsky, O., & Seifer, R. (1998). Adolescent sleep patterns, circadian timing, and sleepiness at a transition to early school days. *Sleep, 21*(8), 871–881.

Cousins, J. C., Whalen, D. J., Dahl, R. E., Forbes, E. E., Olino, T. M., Ryan, N. D., & Silk, J. S. (2011). The bidirectional association between daytime affect and nighttime sleep in youth with anxiety and depression. *Journal of Pediatric Psychology, 36*(9), 969–979. doi: 10.1093/jpepsy/jsr036

Crabtree, V. M., Korhonen, J. B., Montgomery-Downs, H. E., Jones, V. F., O'Brien, L. M., & Gozal, D. (2005). Cultural influences on the bedtime behaviors of young children. *Sleep Medicine, 6,* 319–324.

Crosby, B., LeBourgeois, M., & Harsh, J. (2005). Ethnic differences in reported napping and nighttime sleep in 2–8-year-old children. *Pediatrics, 115,* 225–232.

Giebenhain, J. E., & O'Dell, S. L. (1984). Evaluation of a parent-training manual for reducing children's fear of the dark. *Journal of Applied Behavior Analysis, 17*(1), 121–125.

Gordon, J., King, N., Gullone, E., Muris, P., & Ollendick, T. H. (2007). Nighttime fears of children and adolescents: Frequency, content, severity, harm expectations, disclosure, and coping behaviours. *Behaviour Research and Therapy, 45,* 2464–2472.

Graziano, A. M., & Mooney, K. C. (1980). Family self-control instruction for children's nighttime fear reduction. *Journal of Consulting and Clinical Psychology, 48*(2), 206–213.

Gregory, A. M., Avshalom, C., Eley, T. C., Moffitt, T. E., O'Connor, T. G., & Poulton, R. (2005). Prospective longitudinal associations between persistent sleep problems in childhood and anxiety and depression disorders in adulthood. *Journal of Abnormal Child Psychology, 33*(2), 157–163.

Johnson, C. (1996). Sleep problems in children with mental retardation and autism. *Child and Adolescent Psychiatric Clinics of North America: Sleep Disorder, 5,* 673–683.

Johnson, N., & McMahon, C. (2008). Preschoolers' sleep behaviour: Associations with parental hardiness, sleep-related cognitions and bedtime interactions. *Journal of Child Psychology and Psychiatry, 49*(7), 765–773.

King, N., Ollendick, T. H., & Tonge, B. J. (1997). Children's nighttime fears. *Clinical Psychology Review, 17*(4), 431–443.

Kuhn, B. R., & Elliot, A. J. (2003). Treatment efficacy in behavioral pediatric sleep medicine. *Journal of Psychosomatic Research, 54,* 587–597.

Lozoff, B., Askew, G., & Wolf, A. W. (1996). Cosleeping and early childhood sleep problems: Effects of ethnicity and socio-economic status. *Journal of Developmental and Behavioral Pediatrics, 17,* 9–15.

McMenamy, C., & Katz, R. C. (1989). Brief parent-assisted treatment for children's nighttime fears. *Developmental and Behavioral Pediatrics, 10*(3), 145–148.

Meltzer, L. J., & Mindell, J. A. (2006). Sleep and sleep disorders in children and adolescents. *Psychiatric Clinics of North America, 29*(4), 1059–1076.

Mindell, J. A., Kuhn, B., Lewin, D. S., Meltzer, L. J., & Sadeh, A. (2006). Behavioral treatment of bedtime problems and night wakings in infants and young children. *Sleep, 29*(10), 1263–1276.

Mindell, J. A., & Owens, J. A. (2005). *A clinical guide to pediatric sleep.* Philadelphia, PA: Lippincott Williams & Wilkins.

Ollendick, T. H., Hagopian, L. P., & Huntzinger, R. M. (1991). Cognitive-behavior therapy with nighttime fearful children. *Journal of Behavior Therapy and Experimental Psychiatry, 22*(2), 113–121.

Owens, J. A. (2005). *Epidemiology of sleep disorders during childhood.* Philadelphia, PA: Elsevier Saunders.

Owens, J. A., Jones, C., & Nash, R. (2011). Caregivers' knowledge, behavior, and attitudes regarding healthy sleep in young children. *Journal of Clinical Sleep Medicine, 7*(4), 345–350.

Owens, J. A., & Mindell, J. A. (2011). Pediatric insomnia. *Pediatric Clinics of North America, 58,* 555–569.

Owens, J. A., Spirito, A., & McGuinn, M., (2000). The Children's Sleep Habits Questionnaire (CSHQ): Psychometric properties of a survey instrument for school-aged children. *Sleep, 23,* 1043–1051.

Owens, L. J., France, K. G., & Wiggs, L. (1999). Behavioural and cognitive-behavioural interventions for sleep disorders in infants and children: A review. *Sleep Medicine Reviews, 3*(4), 281–302.

Owens-Stively, J., Frank, N., Smith, A., Hagino, O., Spirito, A., Arrigan, M., & Alario, A. (1997). Child temperament, parenting discipline style, and daytime behavior in childhood sleep disorders. *Journal of Developmental and Behavioral Pediatrics, 18,* 314–321

Piazza, C., & Fisher, W. (1991a). Bedtime fading in the treatment of pediatric insomnia. *Journal of Behavior Therapy and Experimental Psychiatry, 22*(1), 53–56.

Piazza, C., & Fisher, W. (1991b). A faded bedtime with response cost protocol for treatment of multiple sleep problems in children. *Journal of Applied Behavioral Analysis, 24,* 129–140.

Reid, M. J., Walter, A. L., & O'Leary, S. G. (1999). Treatment of young children's bedtime refusal and nighttime wakings: A comparison of "standard" and graduated ignoring procedures. *Journal of Abnormal Child Psychology, 27,* 5–16.

Rickert, V. I., & Johnson, C. M. (1988). Reducing nocturnal awakening and crying episodes in infants and young children: A comparison between scheduled awakenings and systematic ignoring. *Pediatrics, 81*(2), 203–212.

Sadeh, A. (2005). Cognitive-behavioral treatment for childhood sleep disorders. *Clinical Psychology Review, 25,* 612–628.

Sadeh, A., Flint-Ofir, E., Tirosh, T., & Tikotzky, L. (2007). Infant sleep and parental sleep-related cognitions. *Journal of Family Psychology, 21*(1), 74–87.

Sadeh, A., Gruber, R., & Raviv, A. (2003). The effects of sleep restriction and extension on school-age children: What a difference an hour makes. *Child Development, 74*(2), 444–455.

Sadeh, A., Raviv, A., & Gruber, R. (2000). Sleep patterns and sleep disruptions in school-age children. *Developmental Psychology 36*(3), 291–301.

Seymour, F. W., Brock, P., During, M., & Poole, G. (1989). Reducing sleep disruptions in young children: Evaluation of a therapist-guided and written information approaches: A brief report. *Journal of Child Psychology and Psychiatry, 30*(6), 913–918.

Spruyt, K., & Gozal, D. (2011). Pediatric sleep questionnaires as diagnostic or epidemiological tools: A review of currently available instruments. *Sleep Medicine Reviews, 15*(1), 19–32. doi:10.1016/j.smrv.2010.07.005

Taylor, D. J., & Roane, B. M. (2010). Treatment of insomnia in adults and children: A practice-friendly review of research. *Journal of Clinical Psychology: In Session, 66*(11), 1137–1147.

Tikotzky, L., & Sadeh, A. (2010). The role of cognitive-behavior therapy in behavioral childhood insomnia. *Sleep Medicine, 11,* 686–691.

Tikotzky, L., & Shaashua, L. (2012). Infant sleep and early parental sleep-related cognitions predict sleep in pre-school children. *Sleep Medicine, 13,* 185–192.

Tse, L., & Hall, W. (2007). A qualitative study of parents' perceptions of behavioural sleep intervention. *Child: Care, Health, and Development, 34*(2), 162–172.

Vriend, J. L., Corkum, P. V., Moon, E. C., & Smith. I. M. (2011). Behavioral interventions for sleep problems in children with autism spectrum disorders: Current findings and future directions. *Journal of Pediatric Psychology, 36*(9), 1017–1029.

Wiggs, L. (2001). Sleep problems in children with developmental disorders. *Journal of the Royal Society of Medicine, 94*(4), 177–179.

CHAPTER 18

Problematic School Absenteeism

CHRISTOPHER A. KEARNEY AND EMMA ROSS

BRIEF OVERVIEW OF PROBLEMATIC SCHOOL ABSENTEEISM

Problematic school absenteeism is a complex and serious problem for many youth referred for treatment. Youth with problematic school absenteeism (1) have missed at least 25% of total school time for at least 2 weeks, (2) experience severe difficulty attending classes for at least 2 weeks, with significant interference in a youth's or family's daily routine, and/or (3) are absent for at least 10 days of school during any 15-week period while school is in session, with an absence defined as 25% or more of school time missed (Kearney, 2008a). Problematic absenteeism thus includes complete absences from school, skipped classes, tardiness, morning misbehaviors in an attempt to miss school, and/or substantial distress at school that precipitates pleas for future nonattendance (Kearney, 2003).

Problematic school absenteeism in its various forms may occur at some time in as many as 28% to 35% of youth (Piña, Zerr, Gonzales, & Ortiz, 2009). A large community survey of youth with truancy and anxiety-based school refusal that required actual time missed from school revealed a more narrow prevalence of 8.2% (Egger, Costello, & Angold, 2003). Still, high school graduation rates are exceedingly poor in many American cities, such as Los Angeles (45.3%), New York (45.2%), Baltimore (34.6%), and Detroit (24.9%) (EPE Research Center, 2008). In addition, a recent national study revealed that the rate of chronic absenteeism (i.e., missing 10+% of the school year) among American youth may be 10% to 15%. Chronic absenteeism is higher among low-income students, and school dropout rates are highest among Hispanics (Balfanz & Byrnes, 2012).

Some youth are referred to treatment because of absentee problems, but such problems also can be part of broader anxiety, mood, or disruptive behavior disorders (McShane, Walter, & Rey, 2001). Key concomitants of problematic school absenteeism include substance abuse, violence, suicide attempt, risky sexual behavior, pregnancy, delinquency-related behaviors, injury, illness, and school dropout. Longitudinal studies reveal severe consequences of school absenteeism into adulthood, including economic deprivation and psychiatric, social, marital, and occupational problems (Kearney, 2008b).

EVIDENCE-BASED APPROACHES

Evidence-based approaches for problematic school absenteeism include preventive, early, and later interventions. These interventions can be conceptualized along a tier system and are described next.

Introduction

A key challenge for those who address problematic school absenteeism is that researchers from many different disciplines study this population. Researchers in education, psychology, criminal justice, law, social work, nursing, medicine, and sociology have devised various definitions as well as different classification, assessment, and treatment strategies for this population. Mental health professionals often concentrate on anxiety-based school refusal, for example, whereas educators and criminal justice experts often concentrate on delinquent-related truancy. Thus, little standardization across research articles has emerged.

Several scholars in recent years have called for more integrated and comprehensive approaches to address problematic school absenteeism (Kearney, 2008a; Lyon & Cotler, 2009; Reid, 2011). Such approaches would: encompass all youth with difficulties attending school; incorporate prevention as well as intervention strategies; resonate with health, mental health, and educational professionals; and be tailored to the developmental and academic needs of a given student.

One approach that may fit these criteria is a response to intervention (RtI) model, or a systematic decision-making process to assign evidence-based strategies based on student need (Fox, Carta, Strain, Dunlap, & Hemmeter, 2010). RtI involves a proactive focus on early identification of learning and behavior problems and immediate, effective intervention. RtI includes a three-tiered approach of universal, targeted, and intensive interventions. Tier 1, or universal, interventions are directed toward all students and involve a core set of strategies and regular screening to identify students who are not benefiting from these core strategies. Tier 2, or targeted, interventions are directed toward at-risk students who require additional support beyond Tier 1 strategies. Tier 3, or intensive, interventions are directed toward students with severe problems who require a more concentrated approach and constant progress monitoring.

An RtI model may be compatible for problematic school absenteeism. RtI and problematic absenteeism scholars focus on the need for early intervention with progress monitoring, functional behavioral assessment, empirically supported treatments to reduce obstacles to academic achievement (including absenteeism), multitier organization, and a team-based approach for implementation. Early intervention is crucial, given that even moderate rates of absenteeism are linked to substantial academic and behavioral problems (Henry, 2007). The next sections outline Tier 1, 2, and 3 interventions for problematic school absenteeism that have received considerable empirical support.

Tier 1 Interventions

Tier 1 interventions are directed toward all students and are largely preventive. Tier 1 interventions are "whole school" in nature and focus on risk factors that contribute to absenteeism on a wide scale. Such risk factors include poor school climate, school violence and bullying, unhealthy learning environments, and student mental health concerns. Tier 1 interventions thus include strategies to improve school climate and safety as well as student health and social-emotional development.

Whole-school interventions to improve school climate include the Positive Behavioral Intervention and Supports (PBIS) program, which emphasizes prosocial behaviors, frequent monitoring of disciplinary issues, and evidence-based practices for academic and behavior problems. PBIS is implemented by school officials and does improve academic gains and student perceptions of school safety; the program also reduces office disciplinary referrals and school suspensions (Lassen, Steele, & Sailor, 2006). PBIS may be adapted for attendance issues to include examination of patterns in attendance data and increased student involvement in attendance policies. The role of the homeroom teacher also can be restructured to identify students at risk for absenteeism and to inform school officials and parents about an absence (Graeff-Martins et al., 2007).

Climate approaches also include developing school cultures that recognize academic accomplishments. Award ceremonies for good attendance, frequent monitoring of absences, and quicker notification of parents following an absence thus are advisable (Epstein & Sheldon, 2002). Others have advocated that school climate approaches to boost attendance must involve flexible responses to absenteeism (as opposed to legal referral), customizing curriculum and instruction to individual academic needs, and alternative educational methods to allow for more gradual accumulation of academic credit (Archambault, Janosz, Fallu, & Pagani, 2009; Martin, 2011).

Whole-school interventions that reduce problematic school absenteeism also include bullying and violence prevention and conflict resolution. Bullying prevention focuses on clear and well-enforced school rules regarding social violence, classroom interventions, parental engagement, community participation, curriculum changes, increased supervision, social skills and support groups, behavioral contracts, counseling for victims and perpetrators, and mentoring (Olweus & Limber, 2010; Vreeman & Carroll, 2007). Beane, Miller, and Spurling (2008) found that their Bully Free Program enhanced school attendance between baseline (90.8%) and after 175 days of program implementation (97.8%). Other school-wide practices to reduce violence include security enforcement, crisis plans for violent acts, anger management classes, parent training and family therapy, and peer mediation. Truancy and dropout prevention programs often involve enhancing safe learning environments (Smink & Reimer, 2005).

Whole-school interventions to reduce problematic absenteeism also include health-based programs. These interventions focus on hand washing, flu immunization, asthma and lice management, specialized educational services for those with chronic medical conditions, and routine medical care for pregnant youth. These programs boost overall attendance levels. Other school-based health services that may reduce absenteeism include health and nutrition education as well as HIV and STD prevention (Freudenberg & Ruglis, 2007).

Whole-school interventions to reduce problematic school absenteeism also include programs to address students' mental health needs. Substance abuse prevention, coping skills, and treatments for emotional, learning, and disruptive behavior disorders are good examples (Weist, Stiegler, Stephan, Cox, & Vaughan, 2010). Other programs focus on conflict resolution, anger management, coping with divorce or family conflict, and sex education (Brown & Bolen, 2008). Mental health programs in schools are sometimes combined with academic remediation strategies and have led sometimes to improvements in tardiness, absenteeism, and dropout rates (Hoagwood et al., 2007).

Tier 1 approaches for problematic absenteeism also include social and emotional learning programs, such as character education. The latter emphasizes core values and life skills to promote social competence and learning. Snyder and colleagues (2010) implemented a social-emotional and character development program that involved six areas:

1. Self-concept
2. Physical and intellectual actions (e.g., nutrition, decision-making skills)
3. Social and emotional actions (self-control, time management)
4. Interpersonal skills (e.g., empathy, conflict resolution)
5. Integrity and self-appraisal
6. Self-improvement (e.g., problem solving, persistence)

Schools with the intervention had significantly lower absenteeism than control schools.

Tier 2 Interventions

Tier 2 interventions are directed toward at-risk students who require additional support beyond Tier 1. Students at Tier 2 include those who are beginning to refuse school, which may involve obvious behaviors, such as scattered absences, or subtle behaviors, such as escalating distress about attending school. Some students also have difficulty transitioning from one school to another and begin missing school. Key goals for treatment include stabilizing school attendance, reintegrating a youth to school, reducing emerging distress and obstacles to attendance, and addressing school-based threats. Tier 2 interventions include those for (1) anxiety- and non–anxiety-based cases of school refusal behavior and (2) student engagement.

Interventions for anxiety-based school refusal help students manage physical and cognitive anxiety symptoms, ease reentry to classes, and resolve obstacles to attendance. These interventions often consist of relaxation training and breathing retraining, cognitive therapy, gradual reintegration into classes, participation in extracurricular activities, social skills training, and conflict resolution. Detailed guidelines for these procedures are available (Eisen & Engler, 2006; Heyne & Rollings, 2002; Kearney & Albano, 2007).

King and colleagues (1998) found that cognitive behavioral therapy (CBT) for six sessions was superior to wait-list control for attendance, fear, anxiety, and depression. Treatment was especially effective if a youth returned swiftly to school and if parents and youth were involved in the intervention. Last, Hansen, and Franco (1998) found that both CBT and education support (control), which consisted of allowing youth to express concerns about school, produced substantial improvements in school attendance, fear, anxiety, and depression over 12 weeks. Bernstein and colleagues (2000) found that CBT with imipramine was superior to placebo for improving attendance and depression over 8 weeks. Better response to treatment was predicted by higher baseline attendance and less separation anxiety and avoidant disorder (Layne, Bernstein, Egan, & Kushner, 2003). Heyne and colleagues (2002, 2011) also have found that youth-/parent-based CBT produced improvements in attendance and distress.

Tier 2 cases also involve non–anxiety-based problems that contribute to nonattendance. Kearney (2007) identified several functions of school refusal behavior: avoidance of school-based stimuli that provoke negative affectivity, escape from aversive school-based social and/or evaluative situations, pursuit of attention from significant others, and pursuit of tangible rewards outside of school. The functional model of school refusal behavior thus covers anxiety- and non–anxiety-based cases. The School Refusal Assessment Scale–Revised is used to identify the key maintaining variables of a child's absenteeism (Haight, Kearney, Hendron, & Schafer, 2011).

Kearney and colleagues designed a prescriptive treatment approach to tailor interventions to a child's primary function for missing school. Youth who refuse school to avoid school-based stimuli that provoke negative affectivity receive child-based somatic control exercises and gradual reintegration to school. Youth who refuse school to escape aversive school-based social and/or evaluative situations receive child-based somatic control exercises, cognitive therapy, and gradual reintegration to school. Youth who refuse school to pursue attention from significant others receive parent-based contingency management to establish set morning routines and provide attention-based consequences. Youth who refuse school to pursue tangible rewards outside of school receive family-based contingency contracting to boost incentives for attendance and disincentives for nonattendance (Kearney & Albano, 2007). A functionally based, prescriptive treatment approach has empirical support (see Kearney, 2008b). Intervention administered on the basis of a youth's primary function of school refusal behavior has been found superior to intervention administered on the basis of a youth's least influential function of school refusal behavior (Kearney & Silverman, 1999).

Piña and colleagues (2009) conducted a meta-analysis of psychosocial (and largely cognitive behavioral) interventions for school refusal behavior. Across group design studies, school attendance improved from 30% at pretest to 75% at posttest (range at posttest: 47% to 100%). Effect sizes were also calculated for continuous variables associated with school refusal behavior, such as anxiety, fear, and depression. These effect sizes were quite variable (range, –0.40 to 4.64), leading the authors to conclude that CBT may be effective for some domains (e.g., anxiety) more so than others (e.g., depression). These authors and others have contended that greater research is needed to pinpoint mediators of behavior change and which interventions are best for individual cases. Psychosocial interventions also require refinement to maximize effectiveness for a wider swath of youth who refuse school (Tolin et al., 2009).

Another, more systemic Tier 2 approach for problematic school absenteeism involves boosting student engagement with school. The Check and Connect model, for example, includes building relationships between school officials and family members, routine monitoring of absentee and other misbehaviors, and cognitive behavioral problem solving to enhance social and coping skills and to remove obstacles to attendance (Sinclair, Christenson, Lehr, & Anderson, 2003). School-based monitors meet individually with students and family members and check attendance and behavior referrals. The Check and Connect program reduces tardiness and absenteeism (Anderson, Christenson, Sinclair, & Lehr, 2004).

A related strategy involves peer mentors who contact absentee youth, encourage them to return to school, and help remove obstacles to attendance. Peers can also escort at-risk students to school, offer companionship to students with social anxiety problems, and ease the transition process to a new school (Reid, 2007). Peer mentors can supplement teacher mentors who offer tutoring, advocacy, and support (DeSocio et al., 2007). Teacher and community mentoring programs are effective for reducing truancy rates (DuBois, Portillo, Rhodes, Silverthorn, & Valentine, 2011).

Tier 3 Interventions

Tier 3 interventions are directed toward students with complex or severe problems who require concentrated approaches and frequent progress monitoring. Youth in Tier 3 have likely surpassed a legal limit for truancy. Such chronic absenteeism may be defined operationally as 20% of missed class time in 6 weeks (McCluskey, Bynum, & Patchin, 2004). Students in Tier 3 may have a lengthy history of attendance problems that have escalated over time. Tier 3 interventions for problematic school absenteeism include alternative educational programs and legal strategies.

Tier 3 interventions include alternative and self-contained educational programs that focus on part-time and/or highly supervised attendance and academic work (Lever et al., 2004). Alternative educational programs, such as career academies, emphasize small class size, project-based and cooperative learning, interdisciplinary instruction such as technical skills training, apprenticeships, and diverse instructional methods. Students receive extended instruction and specialized training and earn college course credit (Detgen & Alfeld, 2011). Alternative schools may utilize home study and laboratory work, extended class time, work release, or summer or evening classes. Such schools emphasize academic remediation and credit accrual at a modified pace, individualized curricula and psychosocial services, and links to the business community.

Alternative educational programs are best for reducing dropout and enhancing attendance, academic achievement, and graduation rates compared to other methods (Klima, Miller, & Nunlist, 2009). Successful programs tailor intervention to the specific academic, health, skills, social, and resource needs of students and their families (Christenson & Thurlow, 2004). Career academy graduates are more likely to plan for college and have greater earning potential than controls (Fleischman & Heppen, 2009).

Legal strategies to address severe absenteeism are also part of a Tier 3 approach. Such strategies include referring youth with chronic attendance problems to truancy court or juvenile detention as well as police "sweeps" to return truant youths to school. These strategies are more effective if utilized consistently and if linked to tracking attendance, educating support staff about attendance policies, and providing citations to parents for educational neglect (Jonson-Reid et al., 2007). Numerous laws also have been passed to deter truancy but are not highly effective (Markussen & Sandberg, 2011).

A hybrid model of legal intervention has evolved in recent years as a contrast to traditional truancy courts. Fantuzzo, Grim, and Hazan (2005) found that placing court proceedings within school buildings and linking families with case workers from service organizations improved attendance compared to a control group at 1-year follow-up. Richtman (2007) referred absentee students and their parents to school-based meetings with a county attorney, school social worker or counselor, and probation officer to create a school attendance plan. The meetings also included referrals to social services agencies, substance use and mental health evaluations, and student or family counseling to address nonattendance. Truancy petitions were reduced 57.8% over a 10-year period for youth under age 16 years. Shoenfelt and Huddleston (2006) instituted school personnel home visits to investigate factors related to absenteeism, meetings with a judge, and interventions such as parenting classes, academic tutoring, anger management, mentoring, and support groups. The truancy diversion group evidenced significant reductions in unexcused absences and improved grades compared to a control group.

Sutphen, Ford, and Flaherty (2010) found that the most effective truancy interventions involved student- and family-based approaches that relied on contingency management, student support programs, and increased monitoring of attendance. Effective broader interventions for truancy included school-based structural changes, such as smaller and more independent academic units, as well as alternative educational programs.

PARENTAL INVOLVEMENT IN TREATMENT

Parental involvement is a key element at each tier of intervention for problematic school absenteeism. Parental involvement is targeted at Tiers 1 and 3 to prevent attendance problems and thus has been pursued at a systemic level. Sheldon (2007) examined a school partnership program to help families establish supportive home environments, increase parent–school official communication, recruit parents to help at school and serve on school committees, provide information to families about how to help students with homework, and integrate community-based resources to strengthen school programs. Attendance was significantly higher in schools that implemented the partnership program than control schools.

Other Tier 1 and 3 strategies to boost parental involvement include bridging language and cultural differences between school faculty and parents. These strategies include interpreters, home visits, culturally responsive curricula, integration of cultures within a school, school-based child care during parent–teacher conferences, recruiting parents into school-based governing positions and parent–teacher associations, matching the ethnicity of school personnel to the surrounding community, and special school-based events that are conducted in various languages (Broussard, 2003; Garcia-Gracia, 2008; Reid, 2007). A key element of these parental involvement tactics is to help parents better understand their child's homework, progress notes, and report cards.

Tier 2 interventions for problematic school absenteeism tend to be more effective with parental involvement (e.g., King et al., 1998). Many Tier 2 interventions also include procedures designed specifically for parents, especially contingency management. Contingency management procedures for problematic school absenteeism include restructuring parent commands, establishing fixed routines, and implementing rewards and disincentives. Contingency management procedures tend to be most useful for children who refuse school to gain attention from parents. Parent commands in these situations often are given in the form of questions, lectures, or criticism, or they are linked to negotiated rewards to end noncompliance and return to school (usually without success). Parent commands thus are restructured toward greater brevity, clarity, and frequency.

Parent commands are linked to establishing fixed routines during the day and especially in the morning prior to school. A morning routine would involve consistent times for rising from bed, eating breakfast, getting dressed, brushing teeth and washing, and preparing materials for school. Midday routines are necessary if a child is home on a school day and should involve academic work. Evening routines focus on set times for homework, dinner, chores, free time, and bedtime.

Parent commands and fixed routines are linked to rewards for compliance and disincentives for noncompliance. Youth who are the target of a contingency management approach typically refuse school for attention, so rewards and disincentives are attention based (e.g., extra time with parents, early bedtime). Parents reward compliance to morning and other routines, appropriate school entry behavior, and full-time attendance. Increased supervision of a child, particularly one who has demonstrated a penchant for leaving school before the end of the day, is often necessary as well.

ADAPTATIONS AND MODIFICATIONS

Protocols for addressing youth with problematic school absenteeism will require adaptations for comorbid problems and academic issues as well as modifications based on constraints provided by school officials. The pace of treatment, for example, will have to be slower for youth with developmental disorders, long-standing absenteeism, severe family dysfunction (including detachment from the educational process), and friction with school officials. In other cases, however, the pace of treatment will necessarily be urgent, given pressing academic demands and the risk of declining grades.

Modifications to treatment protocols will be necessary following consultation with key school officials, such as guidance counselors, deans or principals, and school psychologists. A key aspect of initial treatment for school refusal behavior, for example, is establishing a part-time attendance schedule with gradual increases in attendance time. This may consist of having a child attend school for part of the morning or afternoon and then scheduling additional time each week. This process is effective but will fail if school officials are unaware of the plan or inadvertently sabotage it by insisting on full-time attendance once a child is in school. Treatment plans for school refusal behavior thus must be developed in concert with relevant school officials.

MEASURING TREATMENT EFFECTS

Assessment is a critical aspect of a multitiered approach to problematic school absenteeism. Assessment at Tier 1 is designed to identify youth with emerging attendance problems who may require Tier 2 interventions. Assessment at Tier 1 is thus conducted by school officials who should routinely review attendance at least twice per month (Mac Iver & Mac Iver, 2010). In addition, school officials should look closely at partial absences and difficulties getting to school, including tardiness. Clinicians who are treating youth with behavior problems should monitor school attendance closely as well. Other relevant Tier 1 data include office disciplinary referrals; suspensions; behavioral observations of noncompliance or distress regarding school; and reports from parents, teachers, and other school personnel, such as guidance counselors and school nurses.

Teachers in particular can reveal early-warning signs of absenteeism by noting subtle behaviors, such as repeated visits to the nurse's office or frequent requests to leave the classroom or to use the restroom. Another early-warning sign is persistent distress in the form of crying or clinging when separating from family members. Resistance to entering class, reluctance to participate in the classroom, persistent illness, and pleas to parents for future nonattendance are also common warning signs for later absenteeism.

Assessment at Tier 2 as school attendance problems emerge is also crucial and should include a detailed and daily log of hours spent in school (Thambirajah, Grandison, & De-Hayes, 2008). Such data are available online in many school districts and can be easily accessed by parents. In addition, many youth at Tier 2 display various forms of absenteeism, including surreptitious and subtle absenteeism, so home-based misbehaviors in the morning (e.g., noncompliance, dawdling) that set the stage for potential absence or tardiness should be monitored as well.

Other assessment methods for youth with problematic absenteeism have been utilized in several treatment outcome studies. Primary examples include structured diagnostic interviews, questionnaires of internalizing and externalizing behavior problems, behavioral observations, and review of attendance and academic records (Kearney, Gauger, Schafer, & Day, 2011). The purpose of these assessment methods is to better understand the forms, contextual variables, and function of a child's school refusal behavior to help determine treatment direction (e.g., anxiety management, parent-focused contingency management, family therapy).

Assessment at Tier 3 typically is much more extensive due to the wide array of psychopathology and parent, family, and peer factors that complicate nonattendance at this stage (Uppal, Paul, & Sreenivas, 2010). These cases may involve comorbid conditions such as agoraphobia, depression, and disruptive behavior disorder. Assessment at Tier 3 thus could involve psychoeducational testing and psychological evaluation to help inform appropriate educational placement, treatment for learning and other disorders, and community-based supports (Dube & Orpinas, 2009). Assessment at Tier 3 also must involve comprehensive medical evaluations because chronic health problems, such as recurrent abdominal pain, are not uncommon at this stage.

CLINICAL CASE EXAMPLES

Two clinical case examples are presented here, one for Tier 2 and one for Tier 3. In both, identifying information has been altered to protect confidentiality.

Consider this vignette for Tier 2: Amelia is a 12-year-old girl who entered middle school and was daunted by the new array of classes, teachers, peers, and academic demands. Amelia experienced escalating distress that led to several absences due to somatic complaints. Amelia's school attendance was intermittent during September and was marked by missed classes, tardy arrivals to school, avoidance, and requests to leave the classroom to visit the nurse's office. Amelia's grades thus suffered, and she was referred twice to the dean's office for a required parent conference.

Many youth have difficulty transitioning from elementary to middle school and experience general and social anxiety in the new setting. Amelia's assessment revealed that she was having difficulty attending school because of negative affectivity while there as well as intense social anxiety around older students. She avoided the cafeteria and other common areas where younger and older students mingled. Amelia also had considerable difficulty speaking before others in class.

Treatment for cases like Amelia's initially focus on stabilizing school attendance, developing a strategy for gradual reintegration to school, reducing distress and obstacles to attendance, and addressing school-based threats. Secondary goals include establishing regular parent–school contact, resolving emerging academic deficiencies from nonattendance, and supplying academic work if a child remains home from school. More formal treatment to address the child's anxiety can involve somatic control exercises, cognitive therapy, and exposure-based practice, which was utilized for Amelia. Amelia initially attended school for four periods and was allowed to spend remaining time in the counselor's office. She engaged in anxiety management practices and some social skills training to address her concerns about interacting with older students and teachers. Amelia returned to full-time school attendance within 4 weeks.

Consider the next vignette for Tier 3: Emilio is a 16-year-old boy in 11th grade who has missed the last several weeks of school. Emilio has a history of poor attendance that escalated from middle to high school and that was marked by low grades. He attended school briefly at the beginning of the year but later spent more time with friends outside of school. Emilio received several truancy citations and surpassed the legal limit for absenteeism in October. He was referred to a truancy court and treatment.

Cases such as Emilio are more likely to be seen in legal, educational, or social service settings. Intervention typically involves an initial discussion as to whether full reintegration into a regular classroom setting is feasible. If so, clinical procedures may be used. If not, which is often the case, alternative educational placements, such as those discussed earlier for Tier 3, may be more appropriate. Emilio and his parents were presented with various educational options that included a vocational program, part-time attendance at his high school for partial credit, and an alternative school placement with smaller class size. Emilio and his parents opted for the vocational learning center administered by the school district. Such learning centers often are linked to local businesses that help provide training and internships for the students. Emilio opted for the electrician training program and was able to maintain attendance at a modified pace.

FINAL COMMENTS

Problematic school absenteeism is a serious public health issue that demands a sophisticated and nuanced approach. Researchers traditionally have examined subsets of youth with absenteeism and have provided valuable data regarding assessment and treatment methods, but a model is needed that is sensitive to the demanding and complex nature of many of these cases. This is especially true given the abysmal high school graduation rates in many geographical areas. A multitiered approach to various levels of school absenteeism that includes a focus on prevention can accommodate youth with varying levels of absenteeism severity, contextual factors, and intervention targets.

REFERENCES

Anderson, A. R., Christenson, S. L., Sinclair, M. F., & Lehr, C. A. (2004). Check & connect: The importance of relationships for promoting engagement with school. *Journal of School Psychology, 42,* 95–113.

Archambault, I., Janosz, M., Fallu, J.-S., & Pagani, L. S. (2009). Student engagement and its relationship with early high school dropout. *Journal of Adolescence, 32,* 651–670.

Balfanz, R., & Byrnes, V. (2012). *Chronic absenteeism: Summarizing what we know from nationally available data.* Baltimore, MD: Johns Hopkins University Press.

Beane, A., Miller, T. W., & Spurling, R. (2008). The Bully Free program: A profile for prevention in the school setting. In T. W. Miller (Ed.), *School violence and primary prevention* (pp. 391–405). New York, NY: Springer.

Bernstein, G. A., Borchardt, C. M., Perwein, A. R., Crosby, R. D., Kushner, M. G., Thuras, P. D., & Last, C. G. (2000). Imipramine plus cognitive-behavioral therapy in the treatment of school refusal. *Journal of the American Academy of Child & Adolescent Psychiatry, 39,* 276–283.

Broussard, C. A. (2003). Facilitating home-school partnerships for multiethnic families: School social workers collaborating for success. *Children and Schools, 25,* 211–222.

Brown, M. B., & Bolen, L. M. (2008). The school-based health center as a resource for prevention and health promotion. *Psychology in the Schools, 45,* 28–38.

Christenson, S. L., & Thurlow, M. L. (2004). School dropouts: Prevention considerations, interventions, and challenges. *Current Directions in Psychological Science, 13,* 36–39.

DeSocio, J., VanCura, M., Nelson, L. A., Hewitt, G., Kitzman, H., & Cole, R. (2007). Engaging truant adolescents: Results from a multifaceted intervention pilot. *Preventing School Failure, 51,* 3–11.

Detgen, A., & Alfeld, C. (2011). *Replication of a career academy model: The Georgia Central Educational Center and four replication sites.* Washington, DC: U.S. Department of Education, Institute of Education Sciences, National Center for Education Evaluation and Regional Assistance, Regional Educational Laboratory Southeast.

Dube, S. R., & Orpinas, P. (2009). Understanding excessive school absenteeism as school refusal behavior. *Children and Schools, 31,* 87–95.

DuBois, D. L., Portillo, N., Rhodes, J. E., Silverthorn, N., & Valentine, J. C. (2011). How effective are mentoring programs for youth? A systematic assessment of the evidence. *Psychological Science in the Public Interest, 12,* 57–91.

Egger, H. L., Costello, E. J., & Angold, A. (2003). School refusal and psychiatric disorders: A community study. *Journal of the American Academy of Child & Adolescent Psychiatry, 42,* 797–807.

Eisen, A. R., & Engler, L. B. (2006). *Helping your child overcome separation anxiety or school refusal: A step-by-step guide for parents.* Oakland, CA: New Harbinger.

EPE Research Center. (2008). *Closing the graduation gap: Educational and economic conditions in America's largest cities.* Bethesda, MD: Editorial Projects in Education.

Epstein, J. L., & Sheldon, S. B. (2002). Present and accounted for: Improving student attendance through family and community involvement. *Journal of Educational Research, 95,* 308–318.

Fantuzzo, J., Grim, S., & Hazan, H. (2005). Project START: An evaluation of a community-wide school-based intervention to reduce truancy. *Psychology in the Schools, 42,* 657–667.

Fleischman, S., & Heppen, J. (2009). Improving low-performing high schools: Searching for evidence of promise. *The Future of Children, 19,* 105–133.

Fox, L., Carta, J., Strain, P. S., Dunlap, G., & Hemmeter, M. L. (2010). Response to Intervention and the pyramid model. *Infants and Young Children, 23,* 3–13.

Freudenberg, N., & Ruglis, J. (2007). Reframing school dropout as a public health issue. *Preventing Chronic Disease, 4,* 1–11.

Garcia-Gracia, M. (2008). Role of secondary schools in the face of student absenteeism: A study of schools in socially underprivileged areas. *International Journal of Inclusive Education, 12,* 263–280.

Graeff-Martins, A. S., Dmitrieva, T., El Din, A. S., Caffo, E., Flament, M. F., Nurcombe, B., . . . Rohde, L. A. (2007). School dropout: A systematic worldwide review concerning risk factors and preventive interventions. In H. Remschmidt, B. Nurcombe, M. L. Belfer, N. Sartorius, & A. Okasha (Eds.), *The mental health of children and adolescents: An area of global neglect* (pp. 165–178). Hoboken, NJ: Wiley.

Haight, C., Kearney, C. A., Hendron, M., & Schafer, R. (2011). Confirmatory analyses of the School Refusal Assessment Scale–Revised: Replication and extension to a truancy sample. *Journal of Psychopathology and Behavioral Assessment, 33,* 196–204.

Henry, K. L. (2007). Who's skipping school: Characteristics of truants in 8th and 10th grade. *Journal of School Health, 77,* 29–35.

Heyne, D., King, N. J., Tonge, B. J., Rollings, S., Young, D., Pritchard, M., & Ollendick, T. H. (2002). Evaluation of child therapy and caregiver training in the treatment of school refusal. *Journal of the American Academy of Child & Adolescent Psychiatry, 41,* 687–695.

Heyne, D., & Rollings, S. (2002). *School refusal.* Malden, MA: Blackwell.

Heyne, D., Sauter, F. M., Van Widenfelt, B. M., Vermeiren, R., & Westenberg, P. M. (2011). School refusal and anxiety in adolescence: Non-randomized trial of a developmentally sensitive cognitive behavioral therapy. *Journal of Anxiety Disorders, 25,* 870–878.

Hoagwood, K. E., Olin, S. S., Kerker, B. D., Kratochwill, T. R., Crowe, M., & Saka, N. (2007). Empirically based school interventions targeted at academic and mental health functioning. *Journal of Emotional and Behavioral Disorders, 15,* 66–92.

Jonson-Reid, M., Kim, J., Barolak, M., Citerman, B., Laudel, C., Essma, A., . . . Thomas, C. (2007). Maltreated children in schools: The interface of school social work and child welfare. *Children and Schools, 29,* 182–191.

Kearney, C. A. (2003). Bridging the gap among professionals who address youth with school absenteeism: Overview and suggestions for consensus. *Professional Psychology: Research and Practice, 34,* 57–65.

Kearney, C. A. (2007). Forms and functions of school refusal behavior in youth: An empirical analysis of absenteeism severity. *Journal of Child Psychology and Psychiatry, 48,* 53–61.

Kearney, C. A. (2008a). An interdisciplinary model of school absenteeism in youth to inform professional practice and public policy. *Educational Psychology Review, 20,* 257–282.

Kearney, C. A. (2008b). School absenteeism and school refusal behavior in youth: A contemporary review. *Clinical Psychology Review, 28,* 451–471.

Kearney, C. A., & Albano, A. M. (2007). *When children refuse school: A cognitive-behavioral therapy approach/Therapist guide.* New York, NY: Oxford University Press.

Kearney, C. A., Gauger, M., Schafer, R., & Day, T. (2011). Social and performance anxiety and oppositional and school refusal behavior in adolescents. In C. A. Alfano & D. C. Beidel (Eds.), *Social anxiety disorder in adolescents and young adults: Translating developmental science into practice* (pp. 125–141). Washington, DC: American Psychological Association.

Kearney, C. A., & Silverman, W. K. (1999). Functionally-based prescriptive and nonprescriptive treatment for children and adolescents with school refusal behavior. *Behavior Therapy, 30,* 673–695.

King, N. J., Tonge, B. J., Heyne, D., Pritchard, M., Rollings, S., Young, D., . . . Ollendick, T. H. (1998). Cognitive-behavioral treatment of school-refusing children: A controlled evaluation. *Journal of the American Academy of Child & Adolescent Psychiatry, 37,* 395–403.

Klima, T., Miller, M., & Nunlist, C. (2009). *What works? Targeted truancy and dropout programs in middle and high school.* Olympia: Washington State Institute for Public Policy.

Lassen, S. R., Steele, M. M., & Sailor, W. (2006). The relationship of school-wide positive behavior support to academic achievement in an urban middle school. *Psychology in the Schools, 43,* 701–712.

Last, C. G., Hansen, C., & Franco, N. (1998). Cognitive-behavioral treatment of school phobia. *Journal of the American Academy of Child & Adolescent Psychiatry, 37,* 404–411.

Layne, A. E., Bernstein, G. A., Egan, E. A., & Kushner, M. G. (2003). Predictors of treatment response in anxious-depressed adolescents with school refusal. *Journal of the American Academy of Child & Adolescent Psychiatry, 42,* 319–326.

Lever, N., Sander, M. A., Lombardo, S., Randall, C., Axelrod, J., Rubenstein, M., & Weist, M. D. (2004). A drop-out prevention program for high-risk inner-city youth. *Behavior Modification, 28,* 513–527.

Lyon, A. R., & Cotler, S. (2009). Multi-systemic intervention for school refusal behavior: Integrating approaches across disciplines. *Advances in School Mental Health Promotion, 2,* 20–34.

Mac Iver, M. A., & Mac Iver, D. J. (2010). How do we ensure that everyone graduates? An integrated prevention and tiered intervention model for schools and districts. *New Directions for Youth Development, 127,* 25–35.

Markussen, E., & Sandberg, N. (2011). Policies to reduce school dropout and increase completion. In S. Lamb, E. Markussen, R. Teese, N. Sandberg, & J. Polesel (Eds.), *School dropout and completion: International comparative studies in theory and policy* (pp. 391–406). New York, NY: Springer.

Martin, A. J. (2011). Holding back and holding behind: Grade retention and students' non-academic and academic outcomes. *British Educational Research Journal, 37,* 739–763.

McCluskey, C. P., Bynum, T. S., & Patchin, J. W. (2004). Reducing chronic absenteeism: An assessment of an early truancy initiative. *Crime and Delinquency, 50,* 214–234.

McShane, G., Walter, G., & Rey, J. M. (2001). Characteristics of adolescents with school refusal. *Australian and New Zealand Journal of Psychiatry, 35,* 822–826.

Olweus, D., & Limber, S. P. (2010). Bullying in school: Evaluation and dissemination of the Olweus Bullying Prevention Program. *American Journal of Orthopsychiatry, 80,* 124–134.

Piña, A. A., Zerr, A. A., Gonzales, N. A., & Ortiz, C. D. (2009). Psychosocial interventions for school refusal behavior in children and adolescents. *Child Development Perspectives, 3,* 11–20.

Reid, K. (2007). The views of learning mentors on the management of school attendance. *Mentoring and Tutoring, 15,* 39–55.

Reid, K. (2011). The strategic management of truancy and school absenteeism: Finding solutions from a national perspective. *Educational Review, 64,* 1–12.

Richtman, K. S. (2007). The truancy intervention program of the Ramsey County Attorney's Office: A collaborative approach to school success. *Family Court Review, 45,* 421–437.

Sheldon, S. B. (2007). Improving school attendance with school, family, and community partnerships. *Journal of Educational Research, 100,* 267–275.

Shoenfelt, E. L., & Huddleston, M. R. (2006). The Truancy Court Diversion Program of the Family Court, Warren Circuit Court Division III, Bowling Green, Kentucky: An evaluation of impact on attendance and academic performance. *Family Court Review, 44,* 683–695.

Sinclair, M. F., Christenson, S. L., Lehr, C. A., & Anderson, A. R. (2003). Facilitating student engagement: Lessons learned from Check & Connect longitudinal studies. *California School Psychologist, 8,* 29–41.

Smink, J., & Reimer, M. S. (2005). *Fifteen effective strategies for improving student attendance and truancy prevention.* Clemson, SC: National Dropout Prevention Center.

Snyder, F. J., Flay, B. R., Vuchinich, S., Acock, A., Washburn, I. J., Beets, M. W., & Li, K.-K. (2010). Impact of a social-emotional and character development program on school-level indicators of academic achievement, absenteeism, and disciplinary outcomes: A matched-pair, cluster randomized, controlled trial. *Journal of Research on Educational Effectiveness, 3,* 26–55.

Sutphen, R. D., Ford, J. P., & Flaherty, C. (2010). Truancy interventions: A review of the research literature. *Research on Social Work Practice, 20,* 161–171.

Thambirajah, M. S., Grandison, K. J., & De-Hayes, L. (2008). *Understanding school refusal: A handbook for professionals in education, health and social care.* Philadelphia, PA: Kingsley.

Tolin, D. F., Whiting, S., Maltby, N., Diefenbach, G. J., Lothstein, M. A., Hardcastle, S., . . . Gray, K. (2009). Intensive (daily) behavior therapy for school refusal: A multiple baseline case series. *Cognitive and Behavioral Practice, 16,* 332–344.

Uppal, P., Paul, P., & Sreenivas, V. (2010). School absenteeism among children and its correlates: A predictive model for identifying absentees. *Indian Pediatrics, 47,* 925–929.

Vreeman, R. C., & Carroll, A. E. (2007). A systematic review of school-based interventions to prevent bullying. *Archives of Pediatric and Adolescent Medicine, 161,* 78–88.

Weist, M. D., Stiegler, K., Stephan, S., Cox, J., & Vaughan, C. (2010). School mental health and prevention science in the Baltimore city schools. *Psychology in the Schools, 47,* 89–100.

CHAPTER 19

Trauma-Related Problems and Disorders

BRIAN FISAK

BRIEF OVERVIEW OF DISORDER/PROBLEM

Potentially traumatic events (PTEs) include a range of experiences, such as physical or sexual abuse, exposure to domestic or school violence, traumatic death of a loved one, injuries and accidents, exposure to community violence, and severe illnesses (American Academy of Child and Adolescent Psychiatry [AACAP], 2010). Unfortunately, exposure to PTEs in childhood and adolescence is common. In particular, based on conservative estimates, approximately 25% of children and adolescents experience a PTE (Costello, Erkanli, Fairbank, & Angold, 2002), with some epidemiological studies reporting rates exceeding 60% (Turner, Finkelhor, & Ormrod, 2010). Further, specific groups may be at elevated risk. Briggs-Gowan, Ford, Fraleigh, McCarthy, and Carter (2010) found that poverty, single parenting, and parent depression symptoms were associated with increased likelihood of exposure to PTEs. Exposure to PTEs also appears to be common in clinical outpatient settings, with estimates ranging from 60% to 90% of children and adolescents (Ford et al., 1999).

Although many children and adolescents who are exposed to PTEs recover naturally and without the need for intervention, long-term disruption in multiple areas of functioning is not uncommon. In particular, children and adolescents are at risk for developing posttraumatic stress disorder (PTSD), along with a number of other behavioral and emotional problems, including depression symptoms, emotional dysregulation, and oppositional behaviors and aggression (Cohen, Mannarino, & Deblinger, 2006). Further, sexualized behaviors and shame are common in youth who have been sexually abused. Rate of PTSD among children and adolescents exposed to a PTE varies considerably and is influenced by a number of factors, including the nature of the trauma, pretrauma psychopathology, and duration of time following the occurrence of the traumatic event (Cox, Kenardy, & Hendrikz, 2008; Smith, Perrin, Yule, & Clark, 2010).

Overall, it is likely that practitioners will encounter children and adolescent clients who have been exposed to trauma and who experience trauma-related disruptions in functioning. This chapter provides an overview of evidence-based approaches and standards of practice for clinicians working with traumatized children and adolescents.

EVIDENCE-BASED APPROACHES

A number of comprehensive reviews have been conducted to identify the best evidence-based interventions for children and adolescents who have experienced trauma. One comprehensive review was prepared by the National Crime Victims Research and Treatment Center and the Center for Sexual Assault and Traumatic Stress (Saunders, Berliner, & Hanson, 2004). This review identified and categorized the common psychosocial treatments for trauma in youth, and treatments were rated on several dimensions, including level of empirical support, acceptance/use in clinical practice, potential for harm, and theoretical basis. Each treatment was rated on a Likert scale ranging from 1 (well-supported efficacious treatment) to 6 (concerning treatment). Trauma-Focused Cognitive-Behavioral Therapy (TF-CBT) was the only treatment to receive a top rating. An additional 12 treatments received a rating of 3, meaning that they were considered to be generally supported and acceptable.

Another reviewed conducted by the Kauffman Best Practices Project (Chadwick Center on Children and Families, 2004) identified three specific interventions as "best practices" for children and adolescents who experience trauma-related symptoms following abuse. Again, TF-CBT was listed as a best practice. In addition, Abuse Focused Cognitive Behavioral Therapy (AF-CBT) and Parent–Child Interaction Therapy (PCIT) were also listed as best practices. Of these three treatments, TF-CBT was the only treatment specifically designed to address trauma symptoms in youth and their nonoffending parents.

A number of other factors strengthen the argument for TF-CBT as a standard of practice for traumatized children and adolescents. In particular, the efficacy of TF-CBT has been supported by several controlled clinical trials (see Cary & McMillen, 2012). Further, TF-CBT was found to be effective in a multisite, randomized clinical trial, with significant reductions in PTSD symptoms, depression symptoms, behavior problems, shame, and negative abuse-related attributions in children and adolescents who had been sexually abused (Cohen, Deblinger, Mannarino, & Steer, 2004). Treatment gains were maintained at 12-month follow-up (Deblinger, Mannarino, Cohen, & Steer, 2006).

Another reason that TF-CBT has become a standard of practice is due to the widespread and successful dissemination of this model (Cohen & Mannarino, 2008). In particular, readily accessible resources have been provided for dissemination, including a published treatment manual (Cohen et al., 2006) and web-based training, referred to as TF-CBTWeb, which is accessible at www.musc.edu/tfcbt (Allen & Johnson, 2012; Cohen & Mannarino, 2008). Although other models show promise for the treatment of traumatized children and adolescents, TF-CBT appears to have reached the strongest evidence-based standards for the treatment of traumatized children and adolescents and their parents. Consequently, the remainder of this section focuses on TF-CBT.

Trauma-Focused Cognitive-Behavioral Therapy

Overview of TF-CBT

TF-CBT is a manualized treatment designed to help children and adolescents who are experiencing PTSD and other trauma-related symptoms, including depression, anxiety, externalizing behavior problems, sexualized behaviors, and trauma-related shame (e.g., Cohen et al., 2004, 2006; TF-CBTWeb, www.musc.edu/tfcbt). The program also has benefits for parents, including reduction in emotional distress related to the child's trauma, improved ability to support the child, improved general parenting practices, and reductions in depression and PTSD symptoms. It is noteworthy that most of the research on TF-CBT focuses on children with a history of sexual abuse; however, the model can be applied to other forms of trauma, including children with a history of physical abuse and children who have witnessed violence.

TF-CBT Treatment Components

TF-CBT includes nine modules, which are based on common cognitive behavioral interventions for children who experience dysfunction in response to trauma (Cohen et al., 2006). The duration of treatment is typically 12 to 16 sessions but can be extended if necessary. Further, the treatment was designed to include individual sessions with the child and parent, along with conjoint parent–child sessions. The nine basic modules (skill sets) can be remembered with the acronym PRACTICE:

1. Psychoeducation
2. Parenting
3. Relaxation
4. Affective expression
5. Cognitive coping
6. Trauma narrative development and processing
7. In vivo exposure
8. Conjoint parent–child sessions
9. Enhancing safety and future development

The modules are designed to be implemented in a flexible manner. A summary of each of the modules, based on the treatment manual published by Cohen at al. (2006) and the TF-CBT*Web* program (www.musc.edu/tfcbt), is provided next.

Psychoeducation   Psychoeducation usually is implemented near the beginning of treatment but often continues throughout the course of treatment. Psychoeducation typically consists of normalization of the child and parent experiences in response to the trauma, including discussion of common responses to trauma. Information about the nature of the particular trauma often is provided, including the frequency and causes of trauma. Clinicians also address common myths and misconceptions about abuse. Psychoeducational handouts are available for distribution (see Cohen et al., 2006; TF-CBT*Web*, www.musc.edu/tfcbt).

In relation to sexual abuse, psychoeducation typically includes three basic components:

1. *Information about the traumatic event.* This typically includes defining sexual abuse, discussions about the reasons that perpetrators commit sexual abuse, typical responses to abuse, and the reasons that children do not immediately tell others about the abuse.
2. *Sex education.* Children and adolescents are provided with factual information, and misinformation about sexual abuse is clarified. Further, body awareness and the child or adolescent's feelings about sexuality are discussed, and health-related issues, such as sexually transmitted diseases, often are discussed.
3. *Risk reduction.* Children and adolescents learn how to identify high-risk situations and how to develop a safety plan if they were to end up in a high-risk situation in the future. The difference between appropriate touch and inappropriate touch also is discussed, and a child's right to say no is reinforced. Further, role-plays can be used to practice effective limit setting.

Parenting Skills   The clinician discusses the use of basic parenting skills, such as praise, selective attention, time-out, and contingency reinforcement. These skills may serve to improve the parent–child relationship and reduce disruptive behaviors. Further, a discussion of parenting skills may be particularly helpful for parents who experience less effective parenting in response to the trauma or who exhibited ineffective parenting skills before the occurrence of the trauma. Although a discussion of basic parenting skills may be particularly beneficial for the parents of children and adolescents who exhibit externalizing symptoms, these skills also are likely to be beneficial for parents of children who are not exhibiting behavioral difficulties. More specifically, these skills may enhance the effectiveness of other components of TF-CBT. For example, parent praise is an important skill for parents to use when children and adolescents begin to engage in exposure later in treatment (see the sections titled "Trauma Narrative Development and Processing" and "In Vivo Exposure").

Relaxation/Stress Management   Relaxation strategies can be particularly beneficial to manage physiological arousal due to trauma-related memories and triggers. In this module, children and adolescents typically learn a variety of skills. One skill that is introduced is controlled breathing (diaphragmatic breathing), and for older children and adolescents, meditation also can be taught. Muscle relaxation (progressive muscle relaxation) typically is included as well. In addition, thought stopping often is introduced as a strategy to manage intrusive thoughts that occur at inopportune times.

In general, all these skills should be introduced and practiced in session. Clinicians also should make an effort to adjust technique descriptions to the developmental level of the child or adolescent. Further, parents typically are taught the relaxation strategies in session, often by the child or adolescent. As a result, parents develop strategies to manage their own stress and can assist the child and adolescent with between-session practice. Especially detailed descriptions of these relaxation strategies, including scripts, are provided in the TF-CBT*Web* training program (www.musc.edu/tfcbt).

Affective Expression and Modulation Training   The purpose of this module is to help children and adolescents develop the ability to identify and label emotions so that they can appropriately express and manage emotions. First, the clinician works with the child or adolescent to identify and rate the intensity of emotions. Next, strategies to address appropriate management of emotions are discussed. For example, children or adolescents are taught effective communication skills, including the use of I statements, active listening, and the benefit of sharing feelings in the appropriate context. Further, children and adolescents are encouraged to use the previously discussed relaxation skills as a strategy when negative emotions are experienced. Finally, role-plays often are conducted in session.

Cognitive Coping   In this module, children and adolescents discuss how to identify and challenge inaccurate and unhelpful thoughts. In particular, clinicians often begin with the connection among thoughts, feelings, and behaviors, which usually is presented in the form of a cognitive triangle. The clinician typically discusses how some thoughts can be inaccurate and/or unhelpful and how these thoughts may lead to negative emotions and behaviors, including avoidance. Further, the clinician and the child or adolescent work together to identify and challenge unhelpful thoughts and to generate helpful/accurate thoughts. Finally, generalization of this skill is discussed. It is noteworthy that skills from this module can be helpful in the cognitive processing of the trauma narrative (see next module).

Trauma Narrative Development and Processing   The goal of trauma narrative development and processing is to break the connection between thoughts and memories of the traumatic event and both negative emotions and physiological arousal. Through gradual exposure and repetition, habituation occurs, and the end result is that trauma-related thoughts no longer lead to excessive distress.

The trauma narrative is developed in a gradual, progressive manner. In particular, the child or adolescent is asked to provide an account of the trauma over time, with increased detail. One option is for the child or adolescent to develop the narrative in sections, starting with sections of the narrative that create the lowest level of distress and eventually progressing to the most distressful components of the narrative. During the development of the narrative, the clinician also asks the child or adolescent to describe feelings and cognitions about the trauma, which can assist in the integration and processing of the traumatic event. Older children and adolescents typically are asked to provide a written narrative; however, therapists often dictate the narrative for younger children. The narrative also can be made into a book, and younger children can include drawings.

Cognitive and emotional processing typically occurs following the completion of the narrative. The purpose of this processing is to elicit and modify distorted thoughts about the trauma, and this process allows thoughts and feelings to be consolidated into an understandable experience. Through this experience, the child or adolescent can recognize that the trauma is *part of* his or her self-concept rather than *central to* his or her self-concept.

As part of the trauma narrative process, the child or adolescent typically is asked to read the narrative out loud to the therapist, and, typically, the narrative eventually is shared with the parent. The parent is often exposed to the narrative in a stepwise manner. First the therapist may read the narrative to the parent, and eventually the child is asked to read the narrative in the presence of the parent. This task provides the parent an opportunity to model positive coping behavior and also serves to improve support and communication between the parent and child in relation to the trauma.

In Vivo Exposure   The trauma narrative likely will decrease reactivity to thoughts and images that remind the child or adolescent of traumatic event; however, children and adolescents still may experience continued fear and avoidance of external cues that serve as reminders of the traumatic event. For example, a child may continue to experience a fear of the dark, even when safe in his or her own bedroom. As a result, in vivo exposure can be used to overcome the fear and avoidance of these external cues. As with the narrative, in vivo exposure should be gradual. It is noteworthy that in vivo exposure is not recommended for situations that may signify an actual threat to the child or adolescent's safety.

Conjoint Parent–Child Sessions   Parent involvement is considered an important component of TF-CBT, and sessions with both the parent and child typically occur throughout treatment. Conjoint sessions may be particularly important when discussing components of the psychoeducational module. Further, as discussed earlier, conjoint sessions are an important component of review of the trauma narrative. In particular, once the child and parent are adequately prepared, the child typically is asked to read the narrative to the parent and therapist. The parent and child are then provided an opportunity to ask each other questions about the trauma. In addition to desensitization, these conjoint sessions provide parents and children an opportunity to learn how to communicate about the trauma in a more open manner.

Enhancing Safety and Future Development   This module typically is conducted near the end of treatment—after the trauma narrative is complete. An exception to this guideline is that if ongoing safety is an issue, steps to enhance safety often occur at the beginning of treatment and continue throughout the course of treatment. This model includes an assessment of the child's or adolescent's knowledge regarding particular trauma-related dangers and relative risk. The therapist then focuses on psychoeducation and the development of skills to enhance safety, including assertiveness training, problem-solving skills, and body safety.

TF-CBT Contraindications/Precautions

Circumstances exist in which other clinical issues should be addressed before implementation of TF-CBT or in which TF-CBT may be contraindicated (Child Sexual Abuse Task Force, 2004). In particular, conduct problems and significant premorbid behavioral problems may need to be addressed before TF-CBT is implemented. Further, gradual exposure, including the trauma narrative and in vivo exposure, may not be appropriate for youth who are acutely suicidal, exhibit substance abuse symptoms, engage in self-harm and parasuicidal behavior, or are experiencing severe depression. These symptoms should be addressed before exposure techniques are implemented. In addition, the listed symptoms may be signs of complex trauma, and as a result, guidelines for complex trauma may also be relevant (see the section titled "Complex Trauma" later in the chapter). In addition, TF-CBT should be conducted only with nonoffending parents (e.g., Stauffer & Deblinger, 1996), and TF-CBT was not designed to be implemented within the first month of the occurrence of a trauma.

PARENTAL INVOLVEMENT IN TREATMENT

Parent involvement is an important component of TF-CBT. As mentioned, parents are involved throughout treatment through individual sessions and joint parent–child sessions. One benefit to parent involvement is that parents can be a source of support, encouragement, and positive modeling throughout treatment. This may be particularly helpful during the narrative and in vivo exposure. Further, parent management of behavioral difficulties is considered a core component of TF-CBT. Finally, psychoeducation often is beneficial for parents.

The added benefit of including parents in treatment has received consistent empirical support (see Cohen et al., 2006). For example, Deblinger, Lippmann, and Steer (1996) compared the effectiveness of TF-CBT administered under three conditions: parent only, child only, and combined parent and child. Parent involvement led to a greater reduction in child externalizing symptoms and depression symptoms. Further, based on other studies, parent participation has been found to help parents manage their own dysfunctional beliefs about trauma and their own trauma-related symptoms (see Cohen et al., 2006; Dalgleish, Meiser-Stedman, & Smith, 2005). In addition, parent variables, including higher levels of support and lower levels of emotional distress, have been found to be associated with improved treatment outcome (e.g., Cohen & Mannarino 1998, 2000; Lang, Ford, & Fitzgerald, 2010).

Although parent involvement is considered an important component of TF-CBT, circumstances exist in which treatment can be implemented without parent involvement. In particular, the Cognitive-Behavioral Intervention for Trauma in Schools (CBITS) model is a group-based program conducted in school settings, and this model has yielded promising findings without direct parental involvement (Stein et al., 2003). Further, children and adolescents currently in foster care may benefit from TF-CBT, even if parent involvement is not feasible (Dorsey & Deblinger, 2012). In addition, clinicians need to use discretion regarding level of parent involvement, and under particular circumstances, it may be necessary to limit involvement. For example, it may be detrimental to the child or adolescent to share trauma narratives with parents who are unlikely to respond supportively or appropriately (Cohen et al., 2006).

ADAPTATIONS AND MODIFICATIONS

Particular circumstances exist in which significant modifications of the TF-CBT model may be necessary or in which alternative treatment approaches may be indicated. These circumstances are discussed next.

Traumatic Grief

When addressing grief, the distinction between uncomplicated grief and traumatic grief is noteworthy. In particular, uncomplicated grief is considered a normative response related to the loss of an important relationship (Cohen et al., 2006). Cohen et al. (2006) indicate that this form of grief typically is not associated with increased risk for ongoing disruption in functioning, assuming that the child or adolescent receives adequate social support and parenting. As a result, intensive intervention often is not indicated. In contrast, traumatic grief occurs when a child is exposed to a death of a love one, and the death was violent, gory, and/or unexpected (Cohen et al., 2006). Traumatic grief typically includes a grief response along with PTSD symptoms. In cases of traumatic grief, intensive intervention may be indicated.

The Childhood Traumatic Grief (CTG) model is used in conjunction with TF-CBT. The model is described in detail in Cohen et al. (2006), and an online training is available at musc.edu/ctg. It is recommended that the treatment be conducted in two phases. Trauma-related issues typically are addressed before specific grief-related issues. Specific components of grief therapy include (1) grief psychoeducation, (2) grieving the loss and resolving ambivalent feelings, (3) preserving positive memories, and (4) redefining the relationship and committing to present relationships. A brief overview of each component is provided here.

The primary goal of the first stage, grief psychoeducation, is to introduce and expose the child or adolescent to the topic of death. In a developmentally appropriate and culturally sensitive manner, the clinician aims to clarify misconceptions about death. Psychoeducation for parents typically includes normalizing grief responses. As part of this psychoeducation, therapists discuss with the parent that there is no "normal" or standard grieving process. For example, it is not uncommon for some children and adolescents to exhibit limited emotional response following a death. The therapist also can help the parent understand the child's concept of death, as young children may not fully understand the finality of death. Further, the therapist and the parent can discuss developmentally appropriate explanations of death.

The second stage involves grieving the loss and resolving ambivalent feelings. This component includes discussion of the loss of the relationship and the loss of what may have occurred in the future. The child or adolescent typically is asked to remember, identify, and name the things that he or she did with the deceased loved one. The special aspects of the relationship that have been lost also are discussed. It may be helpful for the therapist to help the child or adolescent prepare for future losses. Further, unresolved conflicts often are addressed, including what was or was not said to the deceased loved one. Finally, the therapist can discuss inaccurate or unhelpful thoughts about the death.

The next stage emphasizes preserving positive memories about the deceased loved one. This can include a variety of strategies, such as collecting and organizing photographs or videos. Parents should be encouraged to assist the child. For example, the parent can contribute fond memories about the loved one. Other family members and friends also can be asked to include pictures, videos, and shared memories.

The final stage involves redefining the relationship and helping the child or adolescent commit to present relationships. The child or adolescent is often asked to list loved ones and friends who are still in his or her life, and how he/she will commit to these relationships.

Cultural Adaptations

Cultural sensitivity is a core value of the TF-CBT model, and cultural considerations are addressed within each of the modules (TF-CBT*Web*). In addition, detailed recommendations for adaptation of TF-CBT models to meet the needs of specific cultural groups, including Latino and Native American families are provided (e.g., BigFoot & Schmidt, 2012; de Arellano, Danielson, & Felton, 2012). These adaptations are briefly summarized here.

De Arellano et al. (2012) provide specific suggestions for modification of each of the PRACTICE components of TF-CBT for Latino families. For example, the authors suggest specific modifications of the stated rationale of the program to fit with experiences and beliefs common in Latino culture. In particular, a strong rationale for the trauma narrative may be particularly important, as discussion of abuse may be discouraged in Latino culture. Further, it may be beneficial to include discussion of the family's religious beliefs during the cognitive processing stage of the trauma narrative, such as the importance of the concept of virginity.

BigFoot and Schmidt (2010, 2012) developed a modified version of the TF-CBT model for use with American Indian/Alaska Native children; the model has been named the Honoring Children-Mending the Circle (HC-MC) program. The program merges TF-CBT with the indigenous practices and beliefs of the American Indian culture. Underlying themes emphasized in the model include spirituality, interconnectedness, and the role of extended family. Each of the treatment components were modified to fit with the concept of a symbolic circle, which is often referred to as the medicine wheel. Other specific modifications are suggested, including the use of cultural analogies and the incorporation of spiritual practices into relaxation training.

Finally, the model also has been adapted to a number of international settings, including nations in Western Europe, Africa, and Asia (Murray & Skavenski, 2012). Murray and Skavenski (2012) indicate that the model has been effective in a number of international settings that are considered "low-resource" settings.

Complex Trauma (Complex PTSD)

The term "complex trauma" is used to describe instances in which a child or adolescent has been exposed to multiple and often chronic trauma experiences, resulting in substantial impairment in a number of areas of functioning (Cohen et al., 2006; Cohen, Mannarino, Kliethermes, & Murray, 2012). Common difficulties for individuals with complex trauma include problems with emotional regulation, self-injurious behaviors, substance abuse, and intense interpersonal distrust (see Cohen et al., 2006; Cohen et al., 2012; Cook et al., 2005).

As discussed in Cohen et al. (2012), significant modifications to the traditional TF-CBT model may be necessary for individuals with complex trauma. In particular, treatment often is extended to approximately 25 sessions, and it is recommended that clinicians begin with an initial stabilization phase. This phase emphasizes initial relationship building with the therapist and the development of basic coping skills. This phase typically is the longest in duration (i.e., approximately 50% of the treatment sessions). In addition to coping skills discussed in traditional TF-CBT, other coping strategies often are included, such as distraction, mindfulness, perceptional bias modification, and self-awareness skills. Further, establishing safety, which usually is reserved for the final phase of treatment, is addressed in the first phase of treatment. Guidelines for modifying Phase 2, trauma narration and processing, and Phase 3, consolidation and closure, also can be found in Cohen et al. (2012).

Ongoing Trauma

Modifications to the TF-CBT model may be necessary for children and adolescents who are at substantial risk for ongoing trauma (Cohen, Mannario, & Murray, 2011). First, because the child or adolescent is at risk for ongoing trauma, maximizing safety may need to be a primary focus of treatment. This includes safety planning, such as identification of safe places for the child or adolescent to go if in danger. The level of risk related to the perpetrator being in the home or in the child's life and risk related to disclosure of information about the perpetrator's behavior also should be evaluated and addressed. The second consideration relates the potential need to increase parental engagement in treatment. In particular, in the case of situations in which the nonoffending parent has remained with an abusive partner, the parent may experience ambivalence about remaining in the relationship. Consequently, it can be helpful for therapists to acknowledge factors that have led the parent to remain in the relationship. Third, clinicians should be aware that the development and processing of the narrative may have a number of unique benefits for children and adolescents at risk for ongoing trauma. For example, the parent may not have known that the child witnessed episodes of domestic violence and may not be aware of the impact of these episodes. The parent may develop a better understanding of the impact of trauma experiences on the child or adolescent.

Treatment With an Offending Parent

Involvement of offending parents in TF-CBT is contraindicated. However, two interventions may be indicated for parents who have been physically abusive but still have custody (Chadwick Center on Children and Families, 2004). In particular, Abuse-Focused Cognitive Behavioral Therapy for Child Physical Abuse (AF-CBT) (see Kolko, Iselin, & Gully, 2011) and Parent-Child Interaction Therapy (PCIT) (McNeil et al., 2010) have been found to be effective for parents who have a history of physical abuse.

Intervention for Trauma Other Than Sexual Abuse

TF-CBT was developed primarily as a treatment for children and adolescents who have experienced sexual abuse, and the clinical trials providing support for TF-CBT focus almost exclusively on this population. Surprisingly few systematic studies have examined the effectiveness of interventions for children and adolescents who have been exposed to other forms of trauma, including interpersonal violence and accidents. However, the TF-CBT model does include modifications for children who have been physically abused and children who have witnessed violence (Cohen et al., 2006; TF-CBT*Web*, www.musc.edu/tfcbt). Further, Smith et al. (2007) developed a model to treat PTSD related to traumas other than sexual abuse, including accidents and involvement with and/or witnessing interpersonal violence. Based on a randomized trial, the intervention was found to be effective, with a 92% recovery rate in the intervention condition. The model developed by Smith and colleagues is available for clinician use (see Smith et al., 2010).

Early Intervention

Although TF-CBT trials include a percentage of children referred immediately following disclosure of a trauma, research focused exclusively on the effectiveness of intervention within the first month of a trauma is relatively sparse, and a number of concerns have been raised regarding the implantation of early intervention programs (Cohen, 2003). In particular, it is possible that early intervention may call undue attention to the trauma, which may increase the child's or adolescent's negative perceptions about the trauma. Further, interventions, such as psychological debriefing, often occur in a group format, and listening to others' trauma-related experiences potentially may worsen symptoms.

Based on initial research, psychological debriefing and related intervention models were found to be ineffective in the prevention of PTSD symptoms, and in some cases, these interventions may have been detrimental (Cohen, 2003). However, more recent trials, in which children and adolescents receive brief intervention within the first month of a PTE, have yielded more mixed results. For example, two recent studies found that a brief intervention for children who had recently experienced a traffic accident had no added benefit when compared to the control group (Stallard et al., 2006; Zehnder, Meuli, & Landolt, 2010). In contrast, Kenardy and colleagues found brief interventions, implemented within 1 month of an accidental injury, to be effective in the reduction of anxiety symptoms (Cox, Kenardy, & Hendrikz, 2010; Kenardy, Thompson, Le Brocque, & Olsson, 2008). Further, Berkowitz, Stover, and Marans (2011) found a four-session program implemented within 1 month of exposure to a PTE to be effective. In addition, emerging research from the adult trauma literature has provided support for the effectiveness of intervention within the first month. In particular, based on systematic reviews, TF-CBT for adults with acute stress disorder has been found to be effective in the prevention of PTSD symptoms (see Kornør et al., 2008; Roberts, Kitchiner, Kenardy, & Bisson, 2009).

Overall, the effectiveness of cognitive behavioral interventions within the first month of a trauma appears to be inconclusive at this time, and more research is needed. Moreover, based on initial findings by Cohen (2003), group-based intervention seems to be contraindicated. One exception is group intervention for children and adolescents who have been exposed to war, as they may benefit from the reestablishment of social contacts. Further, exposure is not likely to be indicated within the first month of exposure to a trauma. Overall, until more research is conducted in this area, it may be best to provide supportive intervention, including social support, enhancing basic caregiver coping, and making sure that the basic needs of the family are met.

MEASURING TREATMENT EFFECTS

In cases of suspected trauma, it is recommended that multiple domains of functioning are assessed. In particular, Cohen et al. (2006) use the acronym CRAFTS in reference to the relevant domains of functioning, which include cognitive problems, relationship problems, affective problems, family problems, traumatic behavior problems, and somatic problems. Further, American Academy of Child and Adolescent Psychiatry recommendations indicate that screening for PTSD should be a standard part of the assessment process, and if PTSD is present, symptom severity and level of functional impairment should be assessed (AACAP, 2010).

In addition to information obtained from a basic clinical interview, a number of assessment tools are available to assist in the assessment of PTSD and other trauma-related symptoms (see AACAP, 2010; Cohen et al., 2006; Smith et al., 2010). In particular, clinician-administered measures, such as the Clinician-Administered PTSD Scale for Children and Adolescents, are available (Nader et al., 1996). Further, self-report measures often are utilized, including the Child PTSD Symptom Scale (Foa, Johnson, Feeny, & Treadwell, 2001) and the Children's Revised Impact of Events Scale (Perrin, Meiser-Stedman, & Smith, 2005). In addition to the assessment for the presence of PTSD, it is recommended that clinicians assess for the presence of other psychiatric disorders and symptoms often associated with trauma, including depression, suicidality, substance abuse, other anxiety symptoms, externalizing problems, and parenting behaviors and beliefs in relation to the trauma. See Cohen et al. (2006) and Smith et al. (2010) for suggested measures to assess these relevant constructs.

CLINICAL CASE EXAMPLE

Brittany (identifying information has been altered to protect confidentiality) is a 10-year-old Caucasian female. She is an only child who lives with her mother, who is single. Brittany and her mother presented at the clinic because Brittany had been experiencing ongoing symptoms following sexual abuse that occurred 6 months prior to the intake. In particular, Brittany was sexually abused by a biological uncle on three occasions over a span of approximately 1 month. Brittany told her mother about the abuse approximately 2 weeks after the third incident, and her uncle recently pled guilty to charges resulting from the abuse.

Following the abuse, Brittany exhibited a number of symptoms. In particular, she reported embarrassment and shame because she did not immediately tell her mother about the abuse. Further, she experienced nightmares approximately three times a week and fear and avoidance of stimuli that reminded her of the event, including fear of the dark. Due to her fear of the dark, Brittany had slept in her mother's bed every night following the occurrence of the abuse. She was also reluctant to go into other safe, dark places, including movie theaters, even with her mother. In addition, Brittany was reluctant to separate from her mother, and she was reluctant to leave the home during the weekends. Brittany's mother was able to get her to go to school, despite resistance from Brittany. However, when Brittany was at school, she had difficulty concentrating and sometimes would experience intrusive thoughts about the abuse. It was also apparent that Brittany's mother had had some unhelpful beliefs about the trauma. In particular, she was concerned that Brittany would likely experience permanent psychological harm as a result of the abuse and that Brittany would not be able to develop healthy relationships with males. She was reluctant to discuss the trauma with her daughter because she was afraid of making her daughter worse and was concerned about her own reactions. It is noteworthy that Brittany had no prior psychiatric history and no premorbid psychological disorders. Based on the assessment, it was apparent that Brittany met criteria for PTSD and separation anxiety disorder.

Consistent with the TF-CBT model, the initial step of treatment was psychoeducation, which seemed to be beneficial to Brittany. Prior to intervention, Brittany was not provided with opportunities to discuss the abuse with an adult. The only exception was initial disclosure to her mother and police interviews. As a result, psychoeducation provided Brittany with an opportunity to clarify misconceptions about sexual abuse. Due to her level of shame, she also benefited from a discussion of the reasons that children do not immediately tell others when abused. Her mother also appeared to benefit from psychoeducation. In particular, she benefited from the knowledge that Brittany's responses are normal and that she will likely recover from the trauma. Relaxation training was also helpful for Brittany. She found controlled breathing to be particularly beneficial and practiced at home with her mother. Further, she was able to generalize the technique to situations in which she experienced anxiety at inopportune times and when she faced cues that reminded her of the trauma.

The trauma narrative and in vivo exposure were important components of treatment. Brittany developed her trauma narrative over a number of sessions, and beliefs and emotions in relation to the trauma were reviewed and processed. After significant preparation, Brittany was able to read the narrative to her mother, and her mother was able to listen and discuss the trauma while modeling positive coping skills. Further, through the use of in vivo exposure, Brittany was able to overcome a number of her other fears, including her fear of the dark, and sleep in her own room.

Overall, Brittany and her mother were responsive to treatment. Although she continued to experience distressful thoughts about the trauma on occasion, Brittany no longer met criteria for PTSD and separation anxiety disorder at the completion of treatment.

REFERENCES

Allen, B., & Johnson, J. C. (2012). Utilization and implementation of trauma-focused cognitive-behavioral therapy for the treatment of maltreated children. *Child Maltreatment, 17,* 80–85.

American Academy of Child and Adolescent Psychiatry. (2010). Practice parameter for the assessment and treatment of children and adolescents with posttraumatic stress disorder. *Journal of the American Academy of Child & Adolescent Psychiatry, 49,* 414–430.

Berkowitz, S. J., Stover, C., & Marans, S. R. (2011). The child and family traumatic stress intervention: Secondary prevention for youth at risk of developing PTSD. *Journal of Child Psychology and Psychiatry, 52*(6), 676–685. doi: 10.1111/j.1469–7610.2010.02321.x

BigFoot, D., & Schmidt, S. R. (2010). Honoring children, mending the circle: Cultural adaptation of trauma-focused cognitive-behavioral therapy for American Indian and Alaska Native children. *Journal of Clinical Psychology, 66,* 847–856. doi: 10.1002/jclp.20707

BigFoot, D., & Schmidt, S. R. (2012). American Indian and Alaska Native children: Honoring children—Mending the circle. In J. A. Cohen, A. P. Mannarino, & E. Deblinger (Eds.), *Trauma-focused CBT for children and adolescents: Treatment applications* (pp. 280–300). New York, NY: Guilford Press.

Briggs-Gowan, M. J., Ford, J. D., Fraleigh, L., McCarthy, K., & Carter, A. S. (2010). Prevalence of exposure to potentially traumatic events in a healthy birth cohort of very young children in the northeastern United States. *Journal of Traumatic Stress, 23,* 725–733. doi: 10.1002/jts.20593

Cary, C. E., & McMillen, J. (2012). The data behind the dissemination: A systematic review of trauma-focused cognitive behavioral therapy for use with children and youth. *Children and Youth Services Review, 34,* 748–757. doi: 10.1016/j.childyouth.2012.01.003

Chadwick Center on Children and Families. (2004). *Closing the quality chasm in child abuse treatment: Identifying and disseminating best practices.* Available at http://www.chadwickcenter.org/Kauffman/kauffman.htm

Child Sexual Abuse Task Force. (2004). *How to implement trauma-focused cognitive behavioral therapy (TF-CBT)* (Version 2). National Child Traumatic Stress Network. Available online at www.NCTSN.org

Cohen, J., & Mannarino, A. P. (2008). Disseminating and implementing trauma-focused CBT in community settings. *Trauma, Violence, & Abuse, 9*(4), 214–226. doi: 10.1177/1524838008324336

Cohen, J. A. (2003). Treating acute posttraumatic reactions in children and adolescents. *Biological Psychiatry, 53,* 827–833. doi: 10.1016/S0006–3223(02)01868–1

Cohen, J. A., Deblinger, E., Mannarino, A. P., & Steer, R. A. (2004). A multisite, randomized controlled trial for children with sexual abuse-related PTSD symptoms. *Journal of the American Academy of Child & Adolescent Psychiatry, 43*(4), 393–402. doi: 10.1097/00004583–200404000–00005

Cohen, J. A., & Mannarino, A. P. (1998). Factors that mediate treatment outcome of sexually abused preschool children: Six- and 12-month follow-up. *Journal of the American Academy of Child & Adolescent Psychiatry, 37,* 44–51.

Cohen, J. A., & Mannarino, A. P. (2000). Predictors of treatment outcome in sexually abused children. *Child Abuse & Neglect, 24,* 983–994. doi: 10.1016/S0145–2134(00)00153–8

Cohen, J. A., Mannarino, A. P., & Deblinger, E. (2006). *Treating trauma and traumatic grief in children and adolescents.* New York, NY: Guilford Press.

Cohen, J. A., Mannarino, A. P., Kliethermes, M., & Murray, L. A. (2012). Trauma-focused CBT for youth with complex trauma. *Child Abuse & Neglect, 36,* 528–541. doi: 10.1016/j.chiabu.2012.03.007

Cohen, J. A., Mannarino, A. P., & Murray, L. K. (2011). Trauma-focused CBT for youth who experience ongoing traumas. *Child Abuse & Neglect, 35,* 637–646. doi: 10.1016/j.chiabu.2011.05.002

Cook, A., Spinazzola, J., Ford, J., Lanktree, C., Blaustein, M., Cloitre, M., . . . van der Kolk, B.(2005). Complex trauma in children and adolescents. *Psychiatric Annals, 35,* 390–398.

Costello, E., Erkanli, A., Fairbank, J. A., & Angold, A. (2002). The prevalence of potentially traumatic events in childhood and adolescence. *Journal of Traumatic Stress, 15,* 99–112. doi: 10.1023/A:1014851823163

Cox, C. M., Kenardy, J. A., & Hendrikz, J. K. (2008). A meta-analysis of risk factors that predict psychopathology following accidental trauma. *Journal for Specialists in Pediatric Nursing, 13*(2), 98–110. doi: 10.1111/j.1744–6155.2008.00141.x

Cox, C. M., Kenardy, J. A., & Hendrikz, J. K. (2010). A randomized controlled trial of a web-based early intervention for children and their parents following unintentional injury. *Journal of Pediatric Psychology, 35,* 581–592. doi: 10.1093/jpepsy/jsp095

Dalgleish, T., Meiser-Stedman, R., & Smith, P. (2005). Cognitive aspects of posttraumatic stress reactions and their treatment in children and adolescents: An empirical review and some recommendations. *Behavioural and Cognitive Psychotherapy, 33,* 459–486. doi: 10.1017S1352465805002389

de Arellano, M., Danielson, C., & Felton, J. W. (2012). Children of Latino descent: Culturally modified TF-CBT. In J. A. Cohen, A. P. Mannarino, & E. Deblinger (Eds.), *Trauma-focused CBT for children and adolescents: Treatment applications* (pp. 253–279). New York, NY: Guilford Press.

Deblinger, E., Lippmann, J., & Steer, R. (1996). Sexually abused children suffering posttraumatic stress symptoms: Initial treatment outcome findings. *Child Maltreatment, 1,* 310–321.

Deblinger, E., Mannarino, A. P., Cohen, J. A., & Steer, R. A. (2006). A follow-up study of a multisite, randomized, controlled trial for children with sexual abuse-related PTSD symptoms. *Journal of the American Academy of Child & Adolescent Psychiatry, 45,* 474–1484. doi: 10.1097/01.chi.0000240839.56114.bb

Dorsey, S., & Deblinger, E. (2012). Children in foster care. In J. A. Cohen, A. P. Mannarino, & E. Deblinger (Eds.), *Trauma-focused CBT for children and adolescents: Treatment applications* (pp. 49–72). New York, NY: Guilford Press.

Foa, E. B., Johnson, K. M., Feeny, N. C., & Treadwell, K. H. (2001). The Child PTSD Symptom Scale: A preliminary examination of its psychometric properties. *Journal of Clinical Child Psychology, 30,* 376–384. doi: 10.1207/S15374424JCCP3003_9

Ford, J. D., Racusin, R., Daviss, W. B., Ellis, C. G., Thomas, J., Rogers, K., . . . Sengupta, A. (1999). Trauma exposure among children with oppositional defiant disorder and attention deficit–hyperactivity disorder. *Journal of Consulting and Clinical Psychology, 67,* 786–789. doi: 10.1037/0022–006X.67.5.786

Kenardy, J., Thompson, K., Le Brocque, R., & Olsson, K. (2008). Information-provision intervention for children and their parents following pediatric accidental injury. *European Child & Adolescent Psychiatry, 17,* 316–325. doi: 10.1007/s00787–007–0673–5

Kolko, D. J., Iselin, A. R., & Gully, K. J. (2011). Evaluation of the sustainability and clinical outcome of Alternatives for Families: A cognitive-behavioral therapy (AF-CBT) in a child protection center. *Child Abuse & Neglect, 35,* 105–116. doi: 10.1016/j.chiabu.2010.09.004

Kornør, H., Winje, D., Ekeberg, Ø., Weisæth, L., Kirkehei, I., Johansen, K., & Steiro, A. (2008). Early trauma-focused cognitive-behavioural therapy to prevent chronic post-traumatic stress disorder and related symptoms: A systematic review and meta-analysis. *BMC Psychiatry, 8.*

Lang, J.M., Ford, J.D., & Fitzgerald, M.M. (2010). An algorithm for determining the use of trauma-focused cognitive behavioral therapy. *Psychotherapy: Theory, Practice, Research, Training, 47,* 554–569. doi: 10.1037/a0021184

McNeil, C., Hembree-Kigin, T. L., Anhalt, K., Bjørseth, Å., Borrego, J., Chen, Y., . . . Wormdal, A. (2010). *Parent–child interaction therapy* (2nd ed.). New York, NY: Springer Science Business Media.

Murray, L. K., & Skavenski, S. A. (2012). International settings. In J. A. Cohen, A. P. Mannarino, & E. Deblinger (Eds.), *Trauma-focused CBT for children and adolescents: Treatment applications* (pp. 225–252). New York, NY: Guilford Press.

Nader, K., Kriegler, J. A., Blake, D. D., Pynoos, R. S., Newman, E., & Weathers, F. W. (1996). *Clinician Administered PTSD Scale, Child and Adolescent Version.* White River Junction, VT: National Center for PTSD.

Perrin, S., Meiser-Stedman, R., & Smith, P. (2005). The Children's Revised Impact of Event Scale (CRIES): Validity as a screening instrument for PTSD. *Behavioural and Cognitive Psychotherapy, 33,* 487–498. doi: 10.1017/S1352465805002419

Roberts, N. P., Kitchiner, N. J., Kenardy, J., & Bisson, J. I. (2009). Systematic review and meta-analysis of multiple-session early interventions following traumatic events. *American Journal of Psychiatry, 166,* 293–301. doi: 10.1176/appi.ajp.2008.08040590

Saunders, B. E., Berliner, L., & Hanson, R. F. (Eds.). (2004). *Child physical and sexual abuse: Guidelines for treatment* (Revised Report: April 26, 2004). Charleston, SC: National Crime Victims Research and Treatment Center.

Smith, P., Perrin, S., Yule, W., & Clark, D. M. (2010). *Post traumatic stress disorder: Cognitive therapy with children and young people.* New York, NY: Routledge/Taylor & Francis.

Smith, P., Yule, W., Perrin, S., Tranah, T., Dalgleish, T., & Clark, D. M. (2007). Cognitive-behavioral therapy for PTSD in children and adolescents: A preliminary randomized controlled trial. *Journal of the American Academy of Child & Adolescent Psychiatry, 46,* 1051–1061. doi: 10.1097/CHI.0b013e318067e288

Stallard, P., Velleman, R., Salter, E., Howse, I., Yule, W., & Taylor, G. (2006). A randomized controlled trial to determine the effectiveness of an early psychological intervention with children involved in road traffic accidents. *Journal of Child Psychology and Psychiatry, 47,* 127–134. doi: 10.1111/j.1469–7610.2005.01459.x

Stauffer, L. B., & Deblinger, E. (1996). Cognitive behavioral groups for nonoffending mothers and their young sexually abused children: A preliminary treatment outcome study. *Child Maltreatment, 1,* 65–76. doi: 10.1177/1077559596001001007

Stein, B. D., Jaycox, L. H., Kataoka, S. H., Wong, M., Tu, W., Elliott, M. N., & Fink, A. (2003). A mental health intervention for schoolchildren exposed to violence: A randomized controlled trial. *Journal of the American Medical Association, 290,* 603–611. doi: 10.1001/jama.290.5.603

Turner, H. A., Finkelhor, D., & Ormrod, R. (2010). Child mental health problems as risk factors for victimization. *Child Maltreatment, 15,* 132–143. doi: 10.1177/1077559509349450

Zehnder, D., Meuli, M., & Landolt, M. A. (2010). Effectiveness of a single-session early psychological intervention for children after road traffic accidents: A randomised controlled trial. *Child and Adolescent Psychiatry and Mental Health, 4.* doi: 10.1186/1753-2000-4-7

CHAPTER 20

Bullied Children

JUVENTINO HERNANDEZ RODRIGUEZ, SAMANTHA J. GREGUS, JAMES T.
CRAIG, FREDDIE A. PASTRANA, AND TIMOTHY A. CAVELL

BRIEF OVERVIEW OF THE PROBLEM

The term "bullying" often is defined as behavior toward another that is: (1) aggressive or intentionally harmful; (2) done repeatedly over time; and (3) in the context of an interpersonal relationship marked by an actual or perceived imbalance of power (Olweus, 1993; Olweus & Limber, 2010). The term focuses on the perpetrator's behavior. The term *peer victimization*, often used interchangeably with bullying, shifts the focus to the plight of the victim. Peer victimization occurs in the context of relationships or roles that children develop among peers (Gazelle & Ladd, 2002). It is a group process (Salmivalli, Lagerspetz, Björkqvist, Osterman, & Kaukiainen, 1996) often reinforced by peers either passively (e.g., not intervening) or actively (e.g., laughing at bullying behavior). Peer support for bullying and the failure of peers to intervene on behalf of victims usually is compounded by ineffective strategies on the part of victims to escape from or cope with bullying and its aversive consequences (Kochenderfer & Ladd, 1997; Salmivalli, 2010). The combination of peer- and child-related factors conspires to perpetuate a cycle of victimization, leading some children to become chronically bullied and at risk for negative sequelae (Rudolph, Troop-Gordon, Hessel, & Schmidt, 2011).

The prevalence of children who report being bullied ranges from 20% to 30% (Nansel et al., 2001). Generally, younger children report more peer victimization experiences than adolescents (Whitney & Smith, 1993). However, rates for self-reported bullying remain the same or increase from elementary school through high school, suggesting that as children get older, some are being singled out and bullied more often (Boulton & Underwood, 1992). It is estimated that about 75% to 80% of children are relatively uninvolved in bullying, 10% to 15% are occasionally involved, and 5% to 10% are frequently, chronically bullied (Craig & Pepler, 2003; Craig, Pepler, Murphy, & McCuaig-Edge, 2010). There is also some overlap between bullies and victims, with some children occupying both positions (Solberg, Olweus, & Endresen, 2007). These children typically evince a provocative, impulsive, and emotionally reactive interpersonal style that is thought to compromise their capacity to manage peer conflict situations and lead to being labeled as both a bully and a victim (Schwartz, 2000). Outcomes for the bully–victim subtype typically are worse compared to children who are bullies or victims only (Kaltiala-Heino, Rimpela, Marttunen, Rimpela, & Rantanen, 1999), but the prevalence of this subtype is relatively low, estimated to be around 2% for youth in grades 4 to 10 (Solberg et al., 2007).

Bullying can occur in multiple ways: verbally, physically, and relationally (Olweus, 1993). Verbal and physical bullying types are observed more readily as direct forms of aggression. Relational aggression, the act of hurting others' relationships or hurting others via manipulating relationships, is less easily observed due to the fact it is indirect and more subtle (Crick & Grotpeter,

1995). It is thought that boys are more likely to act physically aggressive when bullying and that for girls, bullying is through relational means, such as excluding others or gossiping (Carbone-Lopez, Esbensen, & Brick, 2010). Recently, cyberbullying (i.e., aggressive acts perpetrated by cell phone or the Internet) has emerged as another type of victimization, with consequences similar to that of in-school bullying (Mitchell, Ybarra, & Finkelhor, 2007).

The experience of repeated peer victimization can have harmful effects (see Card, Isaacs, & Hodges, 2007, for a review). Chronic victimization can lead to serious psychosocial maladjustment in childhood and can carry forward into adulthood (Rigby & Slee, 1999; Roth, Coles, & Heimberg, 2002). The probability of having a psychiatric disorder is higher for chronically bullied children and for bully–victims than for children rarely involved in bullying (Kumpulainen, Rasanen, & Puura, 2001). A meta-analysis of cross-sectional studies revealed that chronic victimization is associated significantly with depression, loneliness, social and generalized anxiety, and low self-esteem (Hawker & Boulton, 2000). Chronic bully–victims in particular are at risk for depression, anxiety, psychosomatic complaints, eating disorders, and substance abuse (Due et al., 2005; Kaltiala-Heino, Rimpelä, Rantanen, & Laippala, 2000). Additionally, compared to children rarely involved in bullying, chronic bully–victims are more likely to have a psychiatric disorder of attention-deficit/hyperactivity disorder, oppositional defiant disorder/conduct disorder, or depression (Kumpulainen et al., 2001). A prospective study by Kim, Leventhal, Koh, and Boyce (2009) indicated that chronically bullied children and bully–victims are at an increased risk of persistent suicidal ideation and behaviors, especially for girls.

In this chapter, we discuss evidence-based interventions for children who are victims of school bullying. We outline effective programs and highlight key features and then describe adaptations to more established evidence-based interventions, including recently developed approaches that are being evaluated. We also cover involvement by parents and teachers in interventions for bullied children followed by strategies for measuring intervention effects. Our chapter concludes with two case examples.

EVIDENCE-BASED APPROACHES

There have been many attempts to reduce occurrences of peer victimization and prevent the problems associated with school bullying. Because there are several mechanisms by which school bullying is caused and maintained, a range of intervention strategies have been suggested. Most focus on the whole school, but some focus on specific groups or individual bullies and victims. Whole-school interventions generally are used as universal prevention programs designed to reduce the students' involvement in school bullying, whether as bullies or victims. This is a public health approach designed to reducing overall levels of school bullying, but whole-school interventions also are used to address systemic factors that contribute to peer victimization or to promote a more positive school climate as a way to counter school bullying. Thus, it often is recommended that anti-bullying interventions be broad based, multifaceted, and capable of making positive changes to the existing school culture (e.g., Smith, Schneider, Smith, & Ananiadou, 2004). Beginning with the early work of Olweus (1978), the vast majority of outcome studies have involved whole-school programs. We describe three of the more established such programs and then consider recent efforts (e.g., meta-analyses) to review the current status of existing outcome research.

Olweus Bullying Prevention Program

The Olweus Bullying Prevention Program (OBPP) (1993) was the first large-scale, comprehensive intervention program to be implemented fully and evaluated systematically. The main goals of the

OBPP are to reduce the prevalence of school victimization and to prevent new incidences of bullying (Olweus, 1993; Olweus, Limber, & Mihalic, 1999). These goals are met by changing schoolwide norms and structures (e.g., teacher supervision, consequences) so as to decrease opportunities and rewards for school bullying (Olweus, 1993). The OBPP also includes components that address bullying at the level of the classroom and the individual student, when needed. Intervention effects were evaluated first in the 1980s during the 2.5-year-long New Bergen Project, which followed 2,500 elementary children in an open trial of OBPP. Results were impressive in that reductions in self-reported victimization were at 62% and 64% following 8 and 20 months of intervention, respectively (Olweus, 1991; Olweus & Limber, 2010). A subsequent project examined the OBPP in a comprehensive, nationwide implementation and evaluation project in Norwegian schools over several years. Results from the first three cohorts indicated a roughly 33% reduction in the number of bullied students in grades 4 to 7 (Olweus & Limber, 2010).

Because of initial promising results, several efforts to replicate the OBPP's effectiveness soon followed. These efforts have produced mixed results. Two studies yielded reductions in the prevalence of bullied students that were similar to those found in the original OBPP studies (O'Moore & Minton, 2005; Ortega & Lera, 2000). Other studies failed to replicate those findings. In the first evaluation of the OBPP in the United States, there were no significant decreases in children's reports of being bullied (Limber, Nation, Tracy, Melton, & Flerx, 2004). A second study (also in the United States) found no significant differences in peer victimization between intervention and control groups (Bauer, Lozano, & Rivara, 2007). When faithfully implemented and sustained, the OBPP is an intervention that can produce substantial reductions in the number of children who are bullied at school (Farrington & Ttofi, 2010; Merrell, Gueldner, Ross, & Isava, 2008; Olweus, 1993; Smith, Ananiadou, & Cowie, 2003; Stassen Berger, 2007). The reasons why implementation of the OBPP might lead to null effects or negative outcomes are unclear. It is also unclear why it appears difficult to replicate the impressive findings reported from studies conducted in northern Europe in the United States (Swearer, Espelage, Vaillancourt, & Hymel, 2010).

Steps to Respect

Another universal, school-wide intervention that has shown positive results in reducing bullying is the Steps to Respect Program (Committee for Children, 2001). It uses a multilevel approach that attempts to increase adults' awareness and monitoring of school bullying, support a culture of prosocial behavior, and teach social-emotional skills specific to peer relationships and school bullying (Frey et al., 2005). The Steps to Respect classroom curriculum targets children in grades 3 to 6, is teacher-led, and lasts 12 to 14 weeks. Specific skills focus on identifying various forms of bullying, assertiveness, and conflict resolution (Hirschstein & Frey, 2006). The program also involves more focused skills coaching for individual students identified as bullied.

Intervention effects, for the most part, have been favorable. In an early randomized control trial conducted at six schools, researchers found significant program effects on observed bullying and argumentative behavior as well as agreeable interactions after 6 months of the program. Also found were nonsignificant trends for reduced negative bystander behavior and self-reported peer victimization (Frey et al., 2005). Frey and colleagues posited that it might take several years before schools can fully adopt and implement anti-bullying policies (Frey, Hirschstein, Edstrom, & Snell, 2009). Thus, in an extension of their 2005 study, they reexamined outcomes after 18 months of the intervention. Results showed that observed playground bullying and victimization consistently declined from pre-intervention to the 18-month posttest for children in the intervention group but increased or remained stable for the control group (Frey et al., 2009). Unexpected were significant increases in self-reported aggression and declines in self-reported peer victimization for children in both groups. The authors suggested that observations were conducted on the playground whereas behaviors assessed via self-report were not limited to the playground.

KiVa

KiVa is a Finnish acronym for "against bullying," and the KiVA Anti-Bullying Program is a school-based program used in schools across Finland (see Salmivalli, Kärnä, & Poskiparta 2009a, 2009b). Like Steps to Respect, it is a comprehensive program that targets school-, classroom-, and individual-level factors over the course of an entire school year. KiVa emphasizes universal prevention but also includes indicated prevention components. An important aspect of this program is its focus on peer group factors that maintain school bullying. Teachers implement monthly lessons designed to educate students about the role of the peer group, promote empathy toward victims, increase bystander intervention, and enhance children's coping with peer victimization. A novel feature of the KiVA program is a virtual learning environment wherein students use computer games or Internet forums linked to lesson topics as a way to enhance the acquisition and application of knowledge gained. Indicated components are geared toward victims and bullies as well as selected bystanders. A small team of school personnel is trained to meet with bullies and victims, while classroom teachers hold separate meetings with peers who might support victims.

Published outcomes for KiVa are promising. A large randomized control trial (39 intervention schools, 39 control schools) targeting children in grades 4 to 6 revealed significant reductions after 9 months of program implementation for self- and peer-reported levels of victimization and for self-reported bullying (Kärnä et al., 2011). Schools receiving the KiVa intervention reported on average 46% reduction in victimization and 61% reduction in bullying. Another study investigated the effectiveness of KiVa for grades 1 to 3 versus grades 7 to 9. Similar reductions in bullying and victimization were found, although effects were more mixed in the upper grades (Kärnä et al., 2013).

PARENT (AND TEACHER) INVOLVEMENT IN TREATMENT

Given that the school environment is where most bullying occurs, teachers are often the first adults to witness peer victimization and thus are ideally situated to influence bullying behavior (Troop-Gordon & Quenette, 2010). As noted earlier, empirically supported anti-bullying programs rely heavily on teacher-implemented lessons and strategies, and the success of those programs is closely tied to level of teacher implementation (Kallestad & Olweus, 2003). Less is known about the level and nature of teacher involvement in the absence of formal bullying prevention programs. Besag (1989) suggested that teachers can help manage the problem of bullying in school by becoming more knowledgeable and cognizant of bullying behaviors. However, many teachers are often unsure of how and when to intervene (Newman-Carlson & Horne, 2004).

Commonly recommended teacher strategies include enlisting other adults (e.g., principals, parents), supporting the victim, advocating that victims avoid bullies, disciplining bullies, and seeking ways to promote greater empathy for victims among bullies (Bauman, Rigby, & Hoppa, 2008; Kochenderfer-Ladd & Pelletier, 2008). Yoon and Kerber (2003) found that teachers are more likely to get involved in physical and verbal bullying compared to relational bullying. Only one cross-sectional study examined specific strategies teachers use in response to victimization (Kochenderfer-Ladd & Pelletier, 2008). These authors found that teachers' beliefs about bullying (e.g., bullying is normative) predicted which strategies they were likely to use. Teachers' endorsement of separating students was predictive of lower levels of peer victimization, whereas ignoring the situation or telling children to avoid bullies was predictive of higher levels of victimization.

Some bully prevention programs directly target teachers' attitudes and behaviors in an effort to reduce levels of peer victimization (Newman, Horne, & Bartolumucci, 2000). Class-wide, teacher-implemented programs can be used separate from or alongside school-wide approaches. Bully Busters (Newman et al., 2000) is a psychoeducational prevention strategy directed specifically at teachers. This program trains teachers to be aware of bullying, to recognize the bully and the victim, to intervene in instances of bullying, and to assist victims. A secondary goal is to increase teacher self-efficacy in dealing with bullying situations. This is important, as research has shown that teachers who report higher self-efficacy report a greater likelihood of intervening (Yoon, 2004). Published outcomes suggest that Bully Busters is an effective means of increasing teacher knowledge and recognition of bullying behaviors, use of intervention skills, and teacher self-efficacy (Newman-Carlson & Horne, 2004). There is also some evidence that Bully Busters can have an impact on bullying behavior as measured by disciplinary referrals (Newman-Carlson & Horne, 2004). A recent study of an abbreviated version of Bully Busters yielded mixed results in terms of changes in students' bullying behavior but a positive impact on teacher reports of self-efficacy in managing bullying behavior (Bell, Raczynski, & Horne, 2010).

Compared to the critical role that teachers play in established anti-bullying interventions, parent-based interventions are notably lacking in the literature, despite evidence that bullied children are more likely to report concerns to parents than to teachers (e.g., Fekkes, Pipjers, & Verloove-Vanhorick, 2005). Social ecological systems theory would suggest that parents can influence children's involvement in school bullying and their efforts to cope with peer victimization and other forms of peer conflict (Espelage & Swearer, 2003; Swearer & Doll, 2001). For example, there is evidence that bullies are more likely to experience harsh parenting at homes marked by violence and chaos (see Card et al., 2007, for a review). Less clear is the research examining parents' contribution to children's level of peer victimization (Veenstra et al., 2005). Card et al. (2007) noted some support for the notion that the relation between parenting and peer victimization is gender specific (e.g., overprotection for boys, coercive parenting behavior for girls). It also appears that family conflict and low parental involvement are risk factors for peer victimization (Jeynes, 2008; Mohr, 2006). Although the number of documented familial correlates of peer victimization is small, there is reason to believe that parenting factors can be protective. For example, supportive (Abecassis, Hartup, Haselager, Scholte, & van Lieshout, 2002; Haynie et al., 2001), involved (Haynie et al., 2001; Nansel et al., 2001), and responsive (Ladd & Ladd, 1998) parenting behaviors have been found to be negatively correlated with peer victimization.

Waasdorp, Bradshaw, and Duong (2011) examined parents' use of various strategies in response to their child's victimization. Included were contacting school personnel, talking to their child, talking to the bully, talking to the bully's parents, or doing nothing. The most commonly endorsed response was talking with their child after they disclosed victimization (Waasdorp et al., 2011). Related research would suggest this strategy can be helpful when parents are able to teach children more adaptive ways to cope with peer conflicts and negative emotions (Conners-Burrow, Johnson, Whiteside-Mansell, McKelvey, & Gargus, 2009). Other research points to parent strategies that are potentially counterproductive: These might include calling the bully's parents or encouraging children to use inappropriate retaliatory behavior (Mishna, Pepler, & Wiener, 2006; Rigby, 2008). Waasdorp and colleagues (2011) found that parents' choice of strategies was associated with school climate. Specifically, parents who perceived the school climate to be responsive to and supportive of bullied students were less likely to talk to their child about being bullied and were less likely to contact teachers or administrators than parents who viewed the school climate as less supportive.

We could find no published studies that specifically evaluated parent-based interventions for bullied children, although a version of the Triple P program designed to help families with concerns about bullying currently is being evaluated (M. R. Sanders, personal communication, January 22, 2013). Many bullying prevention programs include materials or informational meetings that give parents opportunities to learn about school bullying. And some programs include more focused talks or conferences with the parents of bullies and victims. As noted previously, Ttofi and Farrington (2010) found that efforts to involve parents were related significantly to decreases in both bullying and victimization.

ADAPTATIONS AND MODIFICATIONS

Some adaptations or modifications to evidence-based anti-bullying programs include selective or indicated components embedded within school-wide universal prevention programs (e.g., Frey et al., 2005; Olweus, 1993). Unfortunately, details concerning these components often are lacking, as are studies evaluating their outcomes (cf. Garandeau, Little, Kärnä, Poskiparta, & Salmivalli, 2011). Other adaptations are stand-alone programs geared specifically for individual bullies or victims and designed to operate with or without the added infrastructure of school-wide interventions (e.g., Elledge, Cavell, Ogle, & Newgent, 2010).

Nonpunitive Interventions

In most bullying prevention programs, school staff members directly address the behavior of bullies and issue firm consequences for such actions. This confronting approach has been challenged by proponents of nonpunitive programs, such as the Shared Concern method (Pikas, 1989). This program attempts to guide students—victims and perpetrators—to solve the problems caused by bullying behavior (Rigby, 2005). The program involves a series of interviews with bullies, then victims, and finally group discussions with all involved in the bullying episode. It is thought to be most appropriate with secondary school students. A handful of anti-bullying programs have included the method of Shared Concern, with programs that used the approach reporting that it helped some children (Smith, Pepler, & Rigby, 2004) and most cases reporting successful outcomes (Duncan, 1996). In Pikas's (1989) study, the method was reportedly successful in 34 of 38 cases, of which most involved children between 8 and 12 years of age. Rigby and Griffiths (2011) evaluated this approach in a study of 17 schools involving students across all 12 grades. The intervention focused on 49 bullies (5 to 16 years of age) as well as a number of students considered victims of bullying. Participating children in 12 of the 17 schools reported that bullying had ceased and that their situation had improved (15 out of 17 schools). Practitioners reported that bullying had stopped (15 of 17 schools), and all indicated a desire to use the method in the future. In contrast to these supportive findings, Wurf (2012) found that the Shared Concern method was less effective than a whole-school approach when examined in a randomized controlled trial.

In the No-Blame or Support Group approach (Maines & Robinson, 1994, 1998), bullying behavior is addressed through attempts to promote empathy, unselfishness, and concern for others. In contrast to the Shared Concern method, it focuses primarily on the victim in an effort to draw attention away from blaming the bully. Teachers or counselors follow several steps, including interviewing victims, meeting with bullies and bystanders and giving voice to victims' concerns, promoting shared responsibility within the group, asking the group for solutions, and passing responsibility for a solution to the group. Based on teacher reports, this approach was described as being successful in 80% of cases (Young & Holdorf, 2003).

Recently, KiVa researchers compared the nonpunitive approach to working with individual cases of school bullying to the more traditional strategy of confronting bullies (Garandeau et al., 2011). Findings indicated that the *confronting* method was less effective for cases involving long-term victimization and more effective when addressing instances of group bullying. The nonpunitive method was more effective in primary schools, and direct confrontation appeared to work better with adolescents. For both strategies, overall effectiveness was greater when victims had been bullied for only a short time and when bullying did not involve relational victimization.

Child-Focused Skills Training Interventions

Social skills training interventions are conceptualized as a way to teach bullied children new and more adaptive responses to their victimization experiences (Fox & Boulton, 2003). The underlying rationale is that chronically bullied children use ineffective interpersonal strategies to deal with instances of school bullying because they lack important social skills (Hanish & Guerra, 2000). There is clear support for this notion, but there are also reports indicating that chronically bullied children's use of ineffective strategies could be a consequence of repeated victimization (e.g., Elledge et al., 2010).

Fox and Boulton's (2003) Social Skills Training (SST) Programme is designed to reduce victims' use of behaviors (e.g., looking scared) that could lead to targeting by other children and behaviors that might be reinforcing to bullies (e.g., crying). SST groups (5–10 children) usually are led by two trainers and involve eight 1-hour training sessions for children ages 9 to 11. Session topics included friendship skills, body language, assertiveness, and dealing with bullies. Additional exercises focused on increasing self-esteem, problem solving, relaxation, and challenging negative thoughts. Fox and Boulton conducted a small pilot study without random assignment that involved 15 children in the SST condition and 13 children in a wait-list condition. Participating children were nominated by peers as bullied, scored greater than the mean on a measure of social skill deficits, and did not qualify as bully–victims. Children in the SST condition had significantly higher global self-worth scores; there were nonsignificant trends in other areas, including number of friends, level of peer acceptance, and reduced depression and anxiety. However, SST was not associated with significant changes in victim status or social skill deficits. Fox and Boulton speculated that children in the SST program failed to generalize their new skills to the natural environment and therefore recommended using SST in the context of a whole-school anti-bullying program.

The Social Skills Group Intervention (S.S. Grin) (DeRosier & Marcus, 2005) aims to build cognitive and behavioral skills, reinforce prosocial attitudes and behaviors, and promote adaptive coping strategies for peer pressure and victimization. S.S. Grin is a manualized program that includes both scripted didactic sessions and practice-oriented activities, such as role playing and modeling. An interesting aspect of this intervention is that it is broadly focused on children who have a range of social difficulties, including children who are socially anxious or peer rejected. DeRosier and Marcus (2005) used a randomized controlled trial to investigate the benefits of their program in a large sample of third-graders (187, experimental; 194, control). Results indicated gains for children participating in S.S. Grin on self-report measures of school adjustment, self-esteem, social efficacy, and social anxiety. Program effects also were found at 1-year follow-up on peer-report measures of social acceptance, fighting, and symptoms of anxiety and depression. Unfortunately, program effects on self- and peer-reported victimization were not significant, although there was some evidence that S.S. Grin led to reduced victimization for girls.

Mentor-Based Interventions

For any intervention designed to help individual children who are bullied, the challenge is to overcome peer-mediated contingencies and reputational biases that tacitly support school bullying while not causing harm to children who are identified and treated (Card et al., 2007; Pepler, 2006; Rodkin & Hodges, 2003; Salmivalli & Voeten, 2004). One indirect strategy involves the use of school-based mentors, an intervention that has been shown to improve the peer relationships of children in the elementary grades (Herrera, 2004). Despite the intuitive appeal of school-based mentoring, few studies have examined the benefits for bullied children. Some anecdotal reports describe mentoring as part of a larger intervention program, but most of the programs involved peer mentoring (e.g., Mahdavi & Smith, 2002), an approach called into question by the findings of Farrington and Ttofi (2010). Other reports identify mentoring as a potentially useful strategy for bullied children based on qualitative interviews with children (e.g., Espelage & Asidao, 2001).

There are several mechanisms through which school-based mentoring could benefit chronically bullied children. Given prior research indicating that adult monitoring of contexts that occasion bullying is critical to intervention success (Olweus, 1993; Smith et al., 2004), the mere presence of an adult mentor could reduce school bullying, at least when the mentor is present. It is also possible that mentors embedded in the school context could use praise or reprimands to alter the contingencies that maintain peer bullying; other mentors might model conversational skills or conflict-resolution strategies that are adopted by bullied children and peers (Cavell & Henrie, 2010). The desire to interact with visiting mentors could also mean that nearby peers begin to view bullied children in a less negative light (Hymel, 1986).

A recent study examined changes in bullied children following their participation in an open trial of the Lunch Buddy (LB) mentoring program (Elledge, Cavell, Ogle, & Newgent, 2010). LB mentors were college students who met with their mentee (identified as bullied based on self- and teacher reports) twice a week in the school cafeteria. Mentors were given two goals: enhance both the mentee's social reputation and interactions with lunchtime peers (Cavell & Henrie, 2010). Outcomes for children in the LB program ($n = 12$) were compared with those of 24 matched-control children: 12 from the same school ("Same" controls) and 12 from a different school ("Different" controls). Compared to Different controls, LB children experienced significantly greater reductions in peer reports of peer victimization from fall to spring semesters. Teachers and parents were very satisfied with the LB mentoring program, and children viewed the mentoring as positive and nonharmful. An extension of this study (Craig, Gregus, Faith, Gomez, & Cavell, 2012) found significant decreases in child- and teacher-reported victimization after three semesters of mentoring.

MEASURING TREATMENT EFFECTS

Assessment procedures for interventions designed to address school bullying should be tailored to the goals of the intervention and to the specified unit of analysis (e.g., school, class, individual children). A number of psychometrically sound measures are available for obtaining self-, peer, and teacher reports of school bullying and peer victimization. These measures can be used to detect program-related changes in bullying and victimization but also have been used to assess population levels of student involvement in school bullying or to test hypothesized relations between peer victimization and related constructs, such as school performance or psychological adjustment (Buhs & Ladd, 2001; Juvonen, Nishina, & Graham, 2006; Rudolph et al., 2011). When used in the context of universal prevention, these measures are given to all students in a school or a grade and usually are completed anonymously. These same measures can be used to identify children who are bullied and would benefit from selective interventions or to assess the impact of bullying prevention programs on those children who are chronically bullied (e.g., DeRosier, 2004; Elledge et al., 2010). In general, however, the development of practical, applied measures that can be used with individual cases of school bullying have received far less attention from researchers (Card & Hodges, 2008).

Assessing Changes in Prevalence or Children's Level of Victimization

Efforts to estimate changes in the prevalence of school bullying or changes in children's degree of exposure to peer victimization have included a variety of procedures, including direct observation, self-report measures, peer ratings or nominations, and ratings from teachers (Card & Hodges, 2008). Efforts to observe instances of school bullying directly have provided valuable insights into this troubling phenomenon and the social processes that maintain it (Craig, Pepler, & Atlas, 2000; Parault, Davis, & Pellegrini, 2007). As an assessment strategy, however, direct observations are quite costly to use, and often they are too impractical to be used routinely. A more feasible and common approach to estimating changes in the prevalence of bullying or victimization or children's level of victimization is the use of self-report measures. These measures typically are brief and can be administered to large groups of students simultaneously. Currently, several self-report measures are available that have been shown to be reliable, valid, and practical. The most widely used instrument is the Olweus Bully-Victim Questionnaire (OBVQ). The OBVQ offers a definition of bullying and then asks students to indicate how often they have experienced various forms of bullying in the past 2 months (Solberg & Olweus, 2003). Solberg and Olweus presented findings that supported a recommended cutoff on the OBVQ (i.e., a frequency of at least two or three times a month) and also made the case for using a single, broad item when assessing prevalence ("How often have you been bullied at school in the past couple of months?"). It is useful to distinguish between the OBVQ and self-report measures that assess the experience of being victimized by peers without regard to whether children apply the label of "bullying" (Vaillancourt, McDougall, Hymel, & Sunderani, 2010). This difference aside, most self-report scales yield a total score reflecting overall level of victimization as well subscales that measure the extent to which children experience different forms of bullying (see Crick & Grotpeter, 1996; Hunt, Peters, & Rapee, 2012; Kochenderfer-Ladd, 2004, for examples of other self-report scales).

Some researchers see value in using teacher- or peer-report instruments, in part as a way to circumvent children's reluctance to disclose their own level of involvement in school bullying (Card & Hodges, 2008). Peer-report procedures typically ask students to identify classmates who fit certain roles—for instance, "Someone who gets teased, called names, or made fun of by other children" (Ladd & Kochenderfer-Ladd, 2002, p. 77). Nominations then are tallied and standardized by the number of class participants (Ladd & Kochenderfer-Ladd, 2002; Salmivali & Nieminen, 2002). Teacher-report measures typically ask teachers to rate students using items that parallel those used on child-report measures of peer victimization (Cullerton-Sen & Crick, 2005; Elledge et al., 2010).

Identifying Bullied Children

As noted previously, one limitation of research evaluating universal bullying prevention programs is the use of anonymous surveys, which severely hampers the opportunity to assess outcomes for chronically bullied children (Kumpulainen et al., 2001; Reijntjes, Kamphuis, Prinzie, & Telch, 2010; Rigby & Slee, 1999; Roth et al., 2002). There has been little research examining practical strategies for identifying bullied children (Card & Hodges, 2008), which is a serious obstacle for practitioners trying to discern when efforts to identify and intervene on behalf of bullied children are justified, given the level of risk involved (Newgent, Seay, Malcolm, Keller, & Cavell, 2010). One way to identify bullied children is to gather information from multiple sources over time (Crick & Bigbee, 1998; Goldbaum, Craig, Pepler, & Connolly, 2003; Graham & Juvonen, 1998; Ladd & Kochenderfer-Ladd, 2002), but procedures that maximize accuracy often are not feasible in applied settings (Card & Hodges, 2008; Newgent et al., 2010).

A trend common in studies that identify victims of school bullying for research purposes is to use sample-specific statistics (Kochenderfer-Ladd, 2003; Ladd & Kochenderfer-Ladd, 2002; Salmivali & Nieminen, 2002). Identifying as victims all children who score at or above 1 standard deviation above the mean on a measure will mean that roughly 16% of children are categorized as victims. This figure is in line with published estimates of the frequency with which children experience bullying on at least an occasional basis (Craig & Pepler, 2003; Craig et al., 2010; Nansel et al., 2001). Another strategy for identifying victims is to rely on preestablished cutoff scores that are thought to indicate a significant level of risk. For example, Solberg and Olweus (2003) found evidence for recommending a cutoff score of two or three times a month on the Olweus Bully-Victim Questionnaire. Studies using this cutoff find that 10% to 20% of children are identified as victims (Hunt et al., 2012; Salmivali, 2010; Solberg & Olweus, 2003).

CLINICAL CASE EXAMPLES

The next two cases involved bullied children participating in a pilot investigation of the Lunch Buddy mentoring program. The children were enrolled in a public elementary school and had been identified based on a combination of scores from measures completed by children and teachers (Kochenderfer-Ladd, 2004). In both cases, identifying information has been altered to protect confidentiality.

Case Study 1: "Anna"

Anna was a Hispanic fourth-grade girl who lived with her mother, father, and three sisters. According to self- and teacher report, Anna was the most bullied girl in her class. The school counselor noted that Anna had a history of bullying problems prior to mentoring. In particular, she had an ongoing conflict with a group of girls in her same grade.

From pre- to postmentoring, Anna's own report as well as her teacher's report of peer victimization decreased from 1.67 to 1.00 and from 1.33 to 0.67 (on a 0–3 scale), respectively. Additionally, sociometric data indicated that Anna's level of peer acceptance increased after the semester of mentoring: Her standardized social preference scores increased from –.50 to .39, indicating that by the end of mentoring, she had moved from below the class mean to above the mean. Both her parents and her teacher reported high satisfaction and perceived little harm associated with her participation in the mentoring program. Anna and her mentor met a total of 15 times over the course of mentoring.

Anna disclosed that she liked the mentoring program and that it helped "fix problems." Her mother said Anna "loved" her mentor, and her mother had noticed greater confidence in her daughter. Her mother reported that LB mentoring "helped a lot," especially in regard to improving her daughter's peer relationships. Anna's mother did not see any harm caused by the program. Anna's teacher reported that having a mentor helped Anna "feel special," that it seemed to be an experience she enjoyed, and that it appeared to be "a big deal" to invite friends to sit by her mentor. Anna's teacher also reported that she thought other teachers would like the program because it did not interfere with class times. Anna's teacher added that LB mentoring helped increase Anna's confidence and concluded by saying, "There was nothing but good to come out of it." The mentor questioned whether Anna needed mentoring at the outset, did not see much change, but said it caused no harm. The counselor stated that with mentoring, Anna was less likely to come to his office seeking help with her peer problems as she had previously. He also indicated that the program "probably" helped boost Anna's self-esteem.

Case Study 2: "Darcy"

Darcy was a Caucasian fifth-grade girl who lived with her father, mother, one brother, and one sister. According to self- and teacher report, Darcy was the most bullied girl in her class. Her teacher reported Darcy had severe difficulties getting along with peers and notable behavioral problems, including lying, stealing, and not completing academic work.

Darcy's self-report of victimization (on a scale of 0–3) decreased from 1.89 to 0.44 following mentoring. Ratings by Darcy's teacher indicated less of a decline in victimization, with only a .11 point decrease in scores from pre- to postmentoring. Darcy's standardized social preference score increased from –0.92 to –0.53, indicating that she experienced sizable gains but was still below average on peer acceptance after mentoring. And as was the case with Anna, teachers and parents reported low levels of harm and high levels of satisfaction with the program. Darcy and her mentor met a total of 16 times.

Darcy reported that she liked the LB mentoring program and that her mentor helped her "stop arguments" with other students and helped her "talk to other kids more." Postmentoring, her teacher reported that Darcy had been struggling with "many problems at home" and was not sure "a regular school setting was appropriate" for her. The teacher also reported that Darcy's problems appear to worsen over time, but this had "nothing to do with the program." Darcy's teacher reported she was "glad the girl had someone" and that "it made her feel special." The mentor believed that mentoring boosted Darcy's self-esteem and improved her interactions with other children. The mentor did not believe that the program was harmful and also noted that Darcy recounted having significant problems outside of school. The school counselor noted these same difficulties and was concerned that these difficulties led to an increase in Darcy's behavioral problems over the course of the school year. He also noted that she was still not well liked by peers and that her self-esteem had "plummeted." However, he noted that LB mentoring gave her a "positive experience in relating to other kids" and did not believe it was harmful or was responsible for Darcy's increased problems at school.

REFERENCES

Abecassis, M., Hartop, W. W, Haselager, G. J. T., Scholte, R., & van Lieshout, C. F. M. (2002). Mutual antipathies and their significance in middle childhood and early adolescence. *Child Development, 73,* 1543–1556.

Bauer, N. S., Lozano, P., & Rivara, F. P. (2007). The effectiveness of the Olweus Bullying Prevention Program in public middle schools: A controlled trial. *Journal of Adolescent Health, 40,* 266–274. doi: 10.1016/j.jadohealth.2006.10.005

Bauman, S., Rigby, K., & Hoppa, K. (2008). US teachers' and school counsellors' strategies for handling school bullying incidents. *Educational Psychology, 28,* 837–856. doi: 10.1080/01443410802379085

Bell, C. D., Raczynski, K. A., & Horne, A. M. (2010). Bully Busters abbreviated: Evaluation of a group-based bully intervention and prevention program. *Group Dynamics: Theory, Research, and Practice, 14,* 257. doi: 10.1037/a0020596

Besag, V. (1989). *Bullies and victims in schools.* Bristol, PA: Open University Press.

Boulton, M. J., & Underwood, K. (1992). Bully/victim problems among middle school children. *British Journal of Educational Psychology, 62,* 73–87. doi: 10.1111/j.2044–8279.1992.tb01000.x

Buhs, E. S., & Ladd, G. W. (2001). Peer rejection as antecedent of young children's school adjustment: An examination of mediating processes. *Developmental Psychology, 37,* 550–560. doi: 10.1037/0012-1649.37.4.550

Carbone-Lopez, K., Esbensen, F. A., & Brick, B. T. (2010). Correlates and consequences of peer victimization: Gender differences in direct and indirect forms of bullying. *Youth Violence and Juvenile Justice, 8,* 332–350. doi: 10.1177/1541204010362954

Card, N. A., & Hodges, E. V. E. (2008). Peer victimization among school children: Correlations, causes, consequences, and considerations in assessment and intervention. *School Psychology Quarterly, 23,* 451–461. doi: 10.1037/a0012769

Card, N. A., Isaacs, J., & Hodges, E. V. E. (2007). Correlates of school victimization: Implications for prevention and intervention. In J. E. Zins, M. J. Elias, & C. A. Maher (Eds.), *Bullying, victimization, and peer harassment: A handbook of prevention and intervention* (pp. 339–368). New York, NY: Haworth Press.

Cavell, T. A., & Henrie, J. L. (2010). Deconstructing serendipity: Focus, purpose, and authorship in lunch buddy mentoring. *New Directions for Youth Development, 2010*(126), 107–121. doi: 10.1002/yd.352

Committee for Children. (2005). *Review of research. Steps to Respect program guide.* Retrieved from http://www.cfchildren. org/Portals/0/STR/STR_DOC/Research_Review_STR.pdf

Conners-Burrow, N. A., Johnson, D. L., Whiteside-Mansell, L., McKelvey, L., & Gargus, R. A. (2009). Adults matter: Protecting children from the negative impacts of bullying. *Psychology in the Schools, 46,* 593–604. doi: 10.1002/pits.20300

Craig, J. T., Gregus, S. J., Faith, M. A., Gomez, D., & Cavell, T. (2012). *School-based mentoring for bullied children: Replication and extension.* Poster presented at the biannual meeting of the Society for Prevention Research, Washington, DC.

Craig, W. M., & Pepler, D. (2003). Identifying and targeting risk for involvement in bullying and victimization. *Canadian Journal of Psychiatry, 48,* 577–582.

Craig, W. M., Pepler, D., & Atlas, R. (2000). Observations of bullying in the playground and in the classroom. *School Psychology International, 21,* 22–36. doi: 10.1177/0143034300211002

Craig, W. M., Pepler, D. J., Murphy, A., & McCuaig-Edge, H. (2010). Intervening in bullying: A review of what works. In E. Vernberg & B. Biggs (Eds.), *Preventing and treating bullying and victimization.* London, England: Oxford University Press.

Crick, N. R., & Bigbee, M. A. (1998). Relational and over forms of peer victimization: A multiinformant approach. *Journal of Consulting and Clinical Psychology, 66,* 337–347.

Crick, N. R., & Grotpeter, J. K. (1995). Relational aggression, gender, and social-psychological adjustment. *Child Development, 66,* 710–722. doi: 10.2307/1131945

Crick, N. R., & Grotpeter, J. K. (1996). Children's treatment by peers: Victims of relational and overt aggression. *Development and Psychopathology, 8,* 367–380. doi: 10.1017/S0954579400007148

Cullerton-Sen, C., & Crick, N. R. (2005). Understanding the effects of physical and relational victimization: The utility of multiple perspectives in predicting social-emotional adjustment. *School Psychology Review, 34,* 147–160.

DeRosier, M. E. (2004). Building relationships and combating bullying: Effectiveness of a school-based social skills group intervention. *Journal of Clinical Child and Adolescent Psychology, 33,* 196–201. doi: 10.1207/S15374424JCCP3301_18

DeRosier, M. E., & Marcus, S. R. (2005). Building friendships and combating bullying: Effectiveness of SS GRIN at one-year follow-up. *Journal of Clinical Child and Adolescent Psychology, 34,* 140–150. doi: 10.1207/s15374424jccp3401_13

Due, P., Holstein, B. E., Lynch, J., Diderichsen, F., Gabhain, S., Scheidt, P., & Currie, C. (2005). Bullying and symptoms among school-aged children: International comparative cross sectional study in 28 countries. *European Journal of Public Health, 15,* 128–132. doi:10.1093/eurpub/cki105

Duncan, A. (1996). The shared concern method of resolving group bullying in schools. *Educational Psychology in Practice, 12,* 94–98. doi: 10.1080/0266736960120206

Elledge, L. C., Cavell, T. A., Ogle, N., & Newgent, R. A. (2010). Lunch buddy mentoring as selective prevention for bullied children. *Journal of Primary Prevention, 31,* 171–187.

Elledge, L. C., Cavell, T. A., Ogle, N., Newgent, R. A., Malcolm, K. T., & Faith, M. A. (2010). History of peer victimization and children's response to instances of school bullying. *School Psychology Quarterly,* 129–141.

Espelage, D., & Swearer, S. (2003). Research on school bullying and victimization: What have we learned and where do we go from here? *School Psychology Review, 32,* 365–383.

Espelage, D. L., & Asidao, C. S. (2001). Conversations with middle school students about bullying and victimization. *Journal of Emotional Abuse, 2,* 49–62. doi: 10.1300/J135v02n02_04

Farrington, D. P., & Ttofi, M. M. (2010). School-based programs to reduce bullying and victimization. *Campbell Systematic Reviews, 2009, 6,* 1–148. doi:10.4073/csr.2009.6

Fekkes, M., Pipjers, F. I., M., & Verloove-Vanhorick, S. P. (2005). Bullying: Who does what, when and where? Involvement of children, teachers, and parents in bullying behavior. *Health Education Research: Theory & Practice, 20,* 81–91.

Fox, C., & Boulton, M. (2003). Evaluating the effectiveness of a social skills training (SST) programme for victims of bullying. *Educational Research, 45,* 231–247. doi: 10.1080/0013188032000137238

Frey, K. S., Hirschstein, M. K., Edstrom, L. V., & Snell, J. L. (2009). Observed reductions in school bullying, nonbullying aggression, and destructive bystander behavior: A longitudinal evaluation. *Journal of Educational Psychology, 101,* 466–481. doi: 10.1037/a0013839

Frey, K. S., Hirschstein, M. K., Snell, J. L., Edstrom, L., MacKenzie, E. P., & Broderick, C. J. (2005). Reducing playground bullying and supporting beliefs: An experimental trial of the Steps to Respect Program. *Developmental Psychology, 41,* 479–491. doi: 10.1037/0012-1649.41.3.479

Garandeau, C. F., Little, T., Kärnä, A., Poskiparta, E., & Salmivalli, C. (2011). Dealing with bullies at school: Which approach for which situations. In M. Sainio & C. F. Garandeau (Chairs), *KiVa antibullying program: Practical viewpoints on implementation and effectiveness, and an innovative perspective from social network analysis.* Symposium presented at the Biennial Meeting of the European Society for Developmental Psychology, Bergen, Norway.

Gazelle, H., & Ladd, G. W. (2002). Interventions for children victimized by peers. In P. A. Schewe (Eds.), *Preventing violence in relationships: Interventions across the life span* (pp. 55–78). Washington, DC: American Psychological Association.

Goldbaum, S., Craig, W. M., Pepler, D., & Connolly, J. (2003). Developmental trajectories of victimization: Identifying risk and protective factors. *Journal of Applied School Psychology, 19,* 139–156. doi: 10.1300/J008v19n02_09

Graham, S., & Juvonen, J. (1998). Self-blame and peer victimization in middle school: An attributional analysis. *Developmental Psychology, 34,* 587. doi: 10.1037/0012-1649.34.3.587

Hanish, L., & Guerra, N. (2000). Children who get victimized at school: What is known? What can be done? *Professional School Counseling, 4,* 113–119.

Hawker, D., & Boulton, M. (2000). Twenty years' research on peer victimization and psychosocial maladjustment: A meta-analytic review of cross-sectional studies. *Journal of Child Psychology and Psychiatry, 41,* 441–455. doi: 10.1111/1469-7610.00629

Haynie, D. L., Nansel, T., Eitel, P., Crump, A. D., Saylor, K., Yu, K., & Simons-Morton, B. (2001). Bullies, victims, and bully/victims: Distinct groups of at-risk youth. *Journal of Early Adolescence, 21,* 29–49.

Herrera, C. (2004). *School-based mentoring: A closer look.* Philadelphia, PA: Public/Private Ventures.

Hirschstein, M. K., & Frey, K. S. (2006). Promoting behavior and beliefs that reduce bullying: The Steps to Respect Program. In S. R. Jimerson, and M. J. Furlong (Eds.), *The handbook of school violence and school safety: From research to practice.* Mahwah, NJ: Erlbaum.

Hunt, C., Peters, L., & Rapee, R. M. (2012). Development of a measure of the experience of being bullied in youth. *Psychological Assessment, 24,* 156–165. doi: 10.1037/a0025178

Hymel, S. (1986). Interpretations of peer behavior: Affective bias in childhood and adolescence. *Child Development, 57,* 431–445.

Jeynes, W. H. (2008). Effects of parental involvement on experiences of discrimination and bullying. *Marriage & Family Review, 43,* 255–268. doi: 10.1080/01494920802072470

Juvonen, J., Nishina, A., & Graham, S. (2006). Ethnic diversity and perceptions of safety in urban middle schools. *Psychological Science, 17,* 393–400. doi: 10.1111/j.1467-9280.2006.01718.x

Kallestad, J. H., & Olweus, D. (2003). Predicting teachers' and schools' implementation of the Olweus Bullying Prevention Program: A multilevel study. *Prevention and Treatment, 6,* 1–27. doi: 10.1037/1522-3736.6.1.621a

Kaltiala-Heino, R., Rimpelä, M., Marttunen, M., Rimpelä, A., & Rantanen, P. (1999). Bullying, depression, and suicidal ideation in Finnish adolescents: School survey. *British Medical Journal, 319,* 348–351. doi: 10.1136/bmj.319.7206.348

Kaltiala-Heino, R., Rimpelä, M., Rantanen, P., & Laippala, P. (2000). Adolescent depression: The role of discontinuities in life course and social support. *Journal of Affective Disorders, 64,* 155–166. doi: 10.1016/S0165-0327(00)00233-0

Kärnä, A., Voeten, M., Little, T. D., Alanen, E., Poskiparta, E., & Salmivalli, C. (2013). Effectiveness of the KiVa Antibullying Program: Grades 1–3 and 7–9. *Journal of Educational Psychology, 105,* 535–551.

Kärnä, A., Voeten, M., Little, T. D., Poskiparta, E., Kaljonen, A., & Salmivalli, C. (2011). A large scale evaluation of the KiVa Antibullying Program: Grades 4–6. *Child Development, 82,* 311–330. doi: 10.1111/j.1467-8624.2010.01557.x

Kim, Y., Leventhal, B., Koh, Y., & Boyce, W. (2009). Bullying increased suicide risk: Prospective study of Korean adolescents. *Archives of Suicide Research, 13,* 15–30. doi: 10.1080/13811110802572098

Kochenderfer, B. J., & Ladd, G. W. (1997). Victimized children's responses to peers' aggression: Behaviors associated with reduced versus continued victimization. *Development and Psychopathology, 9,* 59–73. doi: 10.1017/S0954579497001065

Kochenderfer-Ladd, B. (2003). Identification of aggressive and asocial victims and the stability of their peer victimization. *Merrill-Palmer Quarterly, 49,* 401–425. doi: 10.1353/mpq.2003.0022

Kochenderfer-Ladd, B. (2004). Peer victimization: The role of emotions in adaptive and maladaptive coping. *Social Development, 13,* 329–349. doi: 10.1111/j.1467-9507.2004.00271.x

Kochenderfer-Ladd, B., & Pelletier, M. (2008). Teachers' views and beliefs about bullying: Influences on classroom management strategies and students coping with peer victimization. *Journal of School Psychology, 46,* 431–453. doi: 10.1016/j.jsp.2007.07.005

Kumpulainen, K., Rasanen, E., & Puura, K. (2001). Psychiatric disorders and the use of mental health services among children involved in bullying. *Aggressive Behavior, 27,* 102–110. doi: 10.1002/ab.3

Ladd, B., & Kochenderfer-Ladd, G. W. (2002). Identifying victims of peer aggression from early to middle childhood: Analysis of cross-informant data for concordance, estimation of relational adjustment, prevalence of victimization, and characteristics of identified victims. *Psychological Assessment, 14,* 74–96. doi: 10.1037/1040–3590.14.1.74

Ladd, G. W., & Ladd, B. K. (1998). Parenting behaviors and parent-child relationships: Correlates of peer victimization in kindergarten? *Developmental Psychology, 34,* 1450–1458.

Limber, S. P., Nation, M., Tracy, A. J., Melton, G. B., & Flerx, V. (2004). Implementation of the Olweus Bullying Prevention Program in the southeastern United States. In P. K. Smith, D. Pepler, & K. Rigby (Eds.), *Bullying in schools: How successful can interventions be?* (pp. 55–79). Cambridge, UK: Cambridge University Press.

Mahdavi, J., & Smith, P. K. (2002). The operation of a bully court and perceptions of its success a case study. *School Psychology International, 23,* 327–341. doi: 10.1177/0143034302023003235

Maines, B., & Robinson, G. (1994, September). *The no blame approach to bullying.* Paper presented at the Meeting of the British Association for the Advancement of Science, Briston, England.

Maines, B., & Robinson, G. (1998). The no blame approach to bullying. In D. Shorrocks-Taylor (Ed.), *Directions in educational psychology* (pp. 281–295). Philadelphia, PA: Whurr.

Merrell, K. W., Gueldner, B. A., Ross, S. W., & Isava, D. M. (2008). How effective are school bullying intervention programs? A meta-analysis of intervention research. *School Psychology Quarterly, 23,* 26–42. doi: 10.1037/1045–3830.23.1.26

Mishna, F., Pepler, D., & Wiener, J. (2006). Factors associated with perceptions and responses to bullying situations by children, parents, teachers, and principals. *Victims & Offenders, 1,* 255–288. doi: 10.1080/15564880600626163

Mitchell, K. J., Ybarra, M., & Finkelhor, D. (2007). The relative importance of online victimization in understanding depression, delinquency, and substance use. *Child Maltreatment, 12*(4), 314–324. doi: 10.1177/1077559507305996

Mohr, A. (2006). Family variables associated with peer victimization: Does family violence enhance the probability of being victimized by peers? *Swiss Journal of Psychology, 65,* 107–116.

Nansel, T. R., Overpeck, M., Pilla, R. S., Ruan, W. J., Simons-Morton, B., & Scheidt, P. (2001). Bullying behaviors among US youth: Prevalence and association with psychosocial adjustment. *Journal of the American Medical Association, 285,* 2094–2100. doi: 10.1001/jama.285.16.2094

Newgent, R. A., Seay, A. D., Malcolm, K. T., Keller, E. A., & Cavell, T. A. (2010). Identifying children potentially at-risk for serious maladjustment due to peer victimization: A new model using receiver operating characteristics (ROC) analysis. In J. M. Lampinen & K. Sexton-Radek (Eds.), *Protecting children from violence: Evidence based intervention* (pp. 79–104). London, England: Psychology Press.

Newman, D., Horne, A., & Bartolomucci, C. (2000). *Bullybusting: A psychoeducational program for helping bullies and their victims.* Champaign, IL: Research Press.

Newman-Carlson, D., & Horne, A. (2004). Bully Busters: A psychoeducational intervention for reducing bullying behavior in middle school students. *Journal of Counseling and Development, 82,* 259–267. doi: 10.1002/j.1556–6678.2004.tb00309.x

Olweus, D. (1978). *Aggression in the schools: Bullies and whipping boys.* Washington, DC: Hemisphere (Wiley).

Olweus, D. (1991). Bully/victim problems among school children: Basic facets and effects of a school based intervention program. In D. J. Pepler & K. H. Rubin (Eds.), *The development and treatment of childhood aggression.* Hillsdale, NJ: Erlbaum.

Olweus, D. (1993). *Bullying at school: What we know and what we can do.* Cambridge, MA: Blackwell.

Olweus, D., & Limber, S. P. (2010). Bullying in school: Evaluation and dissemination of the Olweus Bullying Prevention Program. *American Journal of Orthopsychiatry, 80*(1), 124–134.

Olweus, D., Limber, S. P., & Mihalic, S. F. (1999). *Blueprints for violence prevention, book nine: Bullying prevention program.* Boulder, CO: Center for the Study and Prevention of Violence.

O'Moore, A. M., & Minton, S. J. (2005). Evaluation of the effectiveness of an anti-bullying programme in primary schools. *Aggressive Behavior, 31,* 609–622. doi: 10.1002/ab.20098

Ortega, R., & Lera, M. J. (2000). The Seville anti-bullying in school project. *Aggressive Behavior, 26,* 113–123. doi: 10.1002/(SICI)1098–2337(2000)26:1<113::AID-AB9>3.0.CO;2-E

Parault, S. J., Davis, H. A., & Pellegrini, A. D. (2007). The social contexts of bullying and victimization. *Journal of Early Adolescence, 27,* 145–174. doi: 10.1177/0272431606294831

Pepler, D. (2006). Bullying interventions: A binocular perspective. *Journal of the Canadian Academy of Child and Adolescent Psychiatry, 15,* 16–20.

Pikas, A. (1989). A pure concept of mobbing gives the best results for treatment. *School Psychology International, 10,* 95–104. doi: 10.1177/0143034389102003

Reijntjes, A. H. A., Kamphuis, J. H., Prinzie, P., & Telch, M. J. (2010). Peer victimization and internalizing problems in children: A meta-analysis of longitudinal studies. *Child Abuse & Neglect, 34,* 244–252. doi: 10.1016/j.chiabu.2009.07.009

Rigby, K. (2005). The method of Shared Concern as an intervention technique to address bullying in schools: An overview and appraisal. *Australian Journal of Guidance & Counseling, 15,* 27–34. doi: 10.1375/ajgc.15.1.27

Rigby, K. (2008). *Children and bullying: How parents and educators can reduce bullying at school.* Malden, MA: Blackwell.

Rigby, K., & Griffiths, C. (2011). Addressing cases of bullying through the Method of Shared Concern. *School Psychology International, 32,* 345–357. doi: 10.1177/0143034311402148

Rigby, K., & Slee, P. (1999). Suicidal ideation among adolescent school children involvement in bully-victim problems, and perceived social support. *Suicide and Life-Threatening Behavior, 29,* 119–130. doi: 10.1111/j.1943–278X.1999.tb01050.x

Rodkin, P. C., & Hodges, E. V. (2003). Bullies and victims in the peer ecology: Four questions for psychologists and school professionals. *School Psychology Review, 32,* 384–400.

Roth, D. A., Coles, M. E., & Heimberg, R. G. (2002). The relationship between memories for childhood teasing and anxiety and depression in adulthood. *Journal of Anxiety Disorders, 16,* 149–164. doi: 10.1016/S0887–6185(01)00096–2

Rudolph, K. D., Troop-Gordon, W., Hessel, E. T., & Schmidt, J. D. (2011). A latent growth curve analysis of early and increasing peer victimization as predictors of mental health across elementary school. *Journal of Clinical Child & Adolescent Psychology, 40,* 111–122. doi: 10.1080/15374416.2011.533413

Salmivalli, C. (1999). Participant role approach to school bullying: Implications for intervention. *Journal of Adolescence, 22,* 453–459. doi: 10.1006/jado.1999.0239

Salmivalli, C. (2010). Bullying and the peer group: A review. *Aggression and Violent Behavior, 15,* 112–120. doi: 10.1016/j.avb.2009.08.007

Salmivalli, C., Kärnä, A., & Poskiparta, E. (2009a). Development, evaluation, and diffusion of a national anti-bullying program (KiVa). In B. Doll, W. Pfohl, & J. Yoon (Eds.), *Handbook of youth prevention science* (pp. 238–252). New York, NY: Routledge.

Salmivalli, C., Kärnä, A., & Poskiparta, E. (2009b). From peer putdowns to peer support: A theoretical model and how it translated into a national anti-bullying program. In S. Shimerson, S. Swearer, & D. Espelage (Eds.), *The handbook of bullying in schools: An international perspective* (pp. 441–454). New York, NY: Routledge.

Salmivalli, C., Lagerspetz, K., Björkqvist, K., Österman, K., & Kaukiainen, A. (1996). Bullying as a group process: Participant roles and their relations to social status within the group. *Aggressive Behavior, 22,* 1–15. doi: 10.1002/(SICI)1098–2337(1996)22:1<1::AID-AB1>3.0.CO;2-T

Salmivalli, C., & Nieminen, E. (2002). Proactive and reactive aggression among school bullies, victims, and bully-victims. *Aggressive Behavior, 28,* 30–44. doi: 10.1002/ab.90004

Salmivalli, C., & Voeten, M. (2004). Connections between attitudes, group norms, and behaviour in bullying situations. *International Journal of Behavioral Development, 28,* 246–258. doi: 10.1080/01650250344000488

Schwartz, D. (2000). Subtypes of victims and aggressors in children's peer groups. *Journal of Abnormal Child Psychology, 28,* 181–192.

Smith, J. D., Ananiadou, K., & Cowie, H. (2003). Interventions to reduce school bullying. *Canadian Journal of Psychiatry, 48,* 591–599.

Smith, J. D., Schneider, B. H., Smith, P. K., & Ananiadou, K. (2004). The effectiveness of whole-school antibullying programs: A synthesis of evaluation research. *School Psychology Review, 33,* 547–560.

Smith, P. K., Pepler, D., & Rigby, K. (Eds.). (2004). *Bullying in schools: How successful can interventions be?* Cambridge, UK: Cambridge University Press.

Solberg, M. E., & Olweus, D. (2003). Prevalence estimation of school bullying with the Olweus Bully/Victim Questionnaire. *Aggressive Behavior, 29,* 239–268. doi: 10.1002/ab.10047

Solberg, M. E., Olweus, D., & Endresen, I. M. (2007). Bullies and victims at school: Are they the same pupils? *British Journal of Educational Psychology, 77*(2), 441–464.

Stassen Berger, K. (2007). Update on bullying at school: Science forgotten. *Developmental Review, 27,* 90–126. doi: 10.1016/j.dr.2006.08.002

Swearer, S. M., & Doll, B. (2001). Bullying in schools: An ecological framework. *Journal of Emotional Abuse, 2,* 7–23. doi: 10.1300/J135v02n02_02

Swearer, S. M., Espelage, D. L., Vaillancourt, T., & Hymel, S. (2010). What can be done about school bullying? Linking research to educational practice. *Educational Researcher, 39,* 38–47. doi: 10.3102/0013189x09357622

Troop-Gordon, W., & Quenette, A. (2010). Children's perceptions of their teacher's responses to students' peer harassment: Moderators of victimization-adjustment linkages. *Merrill-Palmer Quarterly, 56,* 333–360. doi: 10.1353/mpq.0.0056

Ttofi, M. M., & Farrington, D. P. (2011). Effectiveness of school-based programs to reduce bullying: A systematic and meta-analytic review. *Journal of Experimental Criminology, 7,* 27–56. doi: 10.1007/s11292–010–9109–1

Ttofi, M. M., Farrington, D. P., & Baldry, A. C. (2008). *Effectiveness of programmes to reduce school bullying.* Stockholm, Sweden: Swedish National Counsil for Crime Prevention.

Vaillancourt, T., McDougall, P., Hymel, S., & Sunderani, S. (2010). Respect or fear? The relationship between power and bullying behavior. In S. R. Jimerson, S. M. Swearer, & D. L. Espelage (Eds.), *Handbook of bullying in schools: An international perspective* (pp. 211–222). New York, NY: Routledge.

Veenstra, R., Lindenberg, S., Oldehinkel, A. J., De Winter, A. F., Verhulst, F. C., & Ormel, J. (2005). Bullying and victimization in elementary schools: A comparison of bullies, victims, bully/victims, and uninvolved preadolescents. *Developmental Psychology, 41*(4), 672–682.

Waasdorp, T., Bradshaw, C. P., & Duong, J. (2011). The link between parents' perceptions of the school and their responses to school bullying: Variation by child characteristics and the forms of victimization. *Journal of Educational Psychology, 103,* 324–335. doi: 10.1037/a0022748

Whitney, I., & Smith, P. K. (1993). A survey of the nature and extent of bullying in junior/middle and secondary schools. *Educational Research, 35,* 3–25. doi: 10.1080/0013188930350101

Wurf, G. (2012). High school anti-bullying interventions: An evaluation of curriculum approaches and the method of shared concern in four Hong Kong international schools. *Australian Journal of Guidance and Counselling, 22,* 139–149. doi: 10.1017/jgc.2012.2

Yoon, J. (2004). Predicting teacher interventions in bullying situations. *Education and Treatment of Children, 27,* 37–45.

Yoon, J., & Kerber, K. (2003). Bullying: Elementary teachers' attitudes and intervention strategies. *Research in Education, 69,* 27–35.

Young, S., & Holdorf, G. (2003). Using solution focused brief therapy in individual referrals for bullying. *Educational Psychology in Practice, 19,* 271–282. doi: 10.1080/0266736032000138526

CHAPTER 21

Adherence to Medical Regimens

ALAN M. DELAMATER, ASHLEY N. MARCHANTE, AND AMBER L. DAIGRE

BRIEF OVERVIEW OF PROBLEM

Regimen adherence is critical to chronic illness management. It has been generally acknowledged for years that nonadherence rates for chronic illness regimens and for lifestyle changes in adults are around 50% (Haynes, Taylor, & Sackett, 1979). Poor regimen adherence is also a major health concern among youth with chronic illnesses, with the same approximate rate of 50% average adherence (Drotar, 2000; La Greca & Mackey, 2009; Rapoff, 2010).

For example, in the case of type 1 diabetes, the regimen is complex and consists of multiple components, including blood glucose monitoring, insulin administration, and monitoring and modification of dietary intake and physical activity. The aim of the regimen is to balance all of the components in order to achieve close-to-normal blood glucose levels while at the same time avoiding hypo- and hyperglycemia. Achieving optimal glycemic control requires the integration of considerable amounts of information concerning factors affecting blood glucose levels on an ongoing basis and then applying problem-solving techniques to manage blood glucose. This is particularly challenging for children and adolescents, where parental involvement is one of the key elements to successful diabetes management (Anderson, Ho, Brackett, Finkelstein, & Laffel, 1997).

Not surprisingly, research has shown that optimal regimen adherence and glycemic control is difficult to achieve for many youth with diabetes (Delamater, 2012). For example, studies have shown that blood glucose monitoring typically was not performed as often as prescribed, and blood glucose data were not routinely used to make appropriate changes in the regimen (Delamater et al., 1989; Weissberg-Benchell et al., 1995; Wysocki et al., 2008). Insulin often is omitted, particularly for adolescent girls concerned with body weight issues, underdosing is common, and youth frequently do not take insulin boluses when they eat (Bryden et al., 1999; Burdick et al., 2004; Neumark-Sztainer et al., 2002; Weissberg-Benchell et al., 1995). It is important to note that early adolescence represents a high-risk time for diabetes management, with worsening of regimen adherence and glycemic control typically observed over time (Helgeson et al., 2010; Jacobson et al., 1990; Johnson et al., 1992).

In understanding regimen adherence in children and adolescents with chronic health conditions, it is helpful to use an ecological model in which the child's adherence is determined by multiple levels of influence, including child characteristics (e.g., age, temperament, psychological functioning); parent, family, and social factors (e.g., parental psychological functioning, family structure and socioeconomic status, parental monitoring and support of regimen, family conflict, peer relationships); medical system factors (e.g., relationships with doctors, frequency of contact with health care team); as well as cultural factors (e.g., culture-specific health beliefs) (Delamater, 2012).

It is also helpful to consider the constructs of regimen compliance and adherence. Most health care providers use the term "compliance" instead of "adherence," although these concepts are conceptually very different. Compliance has been defined as "the extent to which a person's behavior coincides with medical advice" (Haynes et al., 1979). With this definition, noncompliance essentially means that patients disobey the advice of their doctors. Patient noncompliance is attributed to personal qualities of patients, such as lack of will power or discipline, forgetfulness, or low level of education. The concept of noncompliance assumes a negative attitude toward patients and also places them in a passive, unequal role in relationship to their health care providers.

Adherence has been defined as the "active, voluntary collaborative involvement of the patient in a mutually acceptable course of behavior to produce a therapeutic result" (Meichenbaum & Turk, 1987, p. 20). The concept of adherence implies choice and mutuality in goal setting, treatment planning, and implementation of the regimen. Patients internalize treatment recommendations and then either adhere to these internal guidelines or do not adhere (i.e., volitional nonadherence).

However, the concept of adherence itself has been criticized because of its focus on patients and because of the nature of medical regimens, which often are dynamic rather than static (Glasgow & Anderson, 1999). It is useful to think of adherence as a multidimensional rather than unitary construct, because patients may adhere well to one aspect of the regimen but not to others. Another way to conceptualize patient behavior related to disease management is to use terms such as "self-care behaviors" or "self-management," which simply describe the types of and frequencies of specific behaviors patients engage in to manage their health condition.

In this chapter, we review research related to regimen adherence in pediatric patients with chronic health conditions. Because considerable research has been conducted in the areas of pediatric diabetes and asthma, we focus on illustrative research in these areas of chronic illness (with an emphasis on diabetes). We first review research on evidence-based interventions to promote adherence and then consider the issues of parental involvement, adaptations to interventions, and assessment of regimen adherence. After describing an illustrative case example, we conclude the chapter with a summary of the main points.

EVIDENCE-BASED APPROACHES TO DEALING WITH NONADHERENCE

Given that about one half of chronically ill children struggle with nonadherence, researchers have paid significant attention to the development and implementation of evidence-based interventions (Drotar, 2000; Graves, Roberts, Rapoff, & Boyer, 2010; Kahana, Drotar, & Frazier, 2008; La Greca et al., 2009; Lemanek, Kamps, & Chung, 2001; Stark, 2013). Interventions that promote increased adherence among children and adolescents span a wide range of medical illnesses; however, the areas of asthma and diabetes have been especially well studied (Kahana et al., 2008).

Interventions to improve regimen adherence include three main approaches: educational, behavioral, and psychologically based interventions. Knowledge- and education-based interventions seek to increase disease education and skills; behavioral interventions seek to alter specific behaviors involved in disease management (e.g., blood glucose monitoring); and psychologically based interventions target the emotional and social effects of the disorder as they may impact on regimen adherence (Hood, Rohan, Peterson, & Drotar, 2010).

Our review highlights results from adherence intervention studies for young patients with type 1 diabetes to illustrate the approaches used. In pediatric diabetes, increased adherence has been associated with improved glycemic control (Delamater, 2012; Johnson et al., 1992; Silverstein et al., 2005). A number of controlled studies document the efficacy of various interventions to improve regimen adherence in youth with type 1 diabetes (Delamater, 2009). With regard to asthma, higher levels of regimen adherence have been associated with improved lung functioning as well as decreased school absenteeism and reduction in nights disturbed by asthma attacks (Wolf, Guevara, Grum, Clark, & Cates, 2008).

Educational Interventions

Educational interventions for adherence provide verbal or written information about the nature of childhood illness and the various treatment options and strategies for disease management (Dean, Walters, & Hall, 2010). The assumption of this approach is that patients and their parents lack important disease-specific knowledge and skills, and therefore teaching them about disease management will improve regimen adherence. Didactic educational approaches, however, typically do not include exploration of individual barriers that are specific to each patient; rather, they offer a straightforward instructional format that is applicable across patients with the same diagnosis. Educational interventions may be provided in a single session or across several sessions and may be conducted with individuals or with groups (Farber & Oliveria, 2004; Hughes, McLeod, Garner, & Goldbloom, 1991).

Research in adult asthma populations has shown that purely informational education has little impact on health outcomes (Gibson et al., 2002); however, results with pediatric populations are somewhat more promising. In a review of educational interventions for children and adolescents with asthma, Guevara, Wolf, Grum, and Clark (2003) examined 32 studies and found that significant improvements in lung function were associated with self-management education programs. Additionally, for randomized educational intervention studies in which one group received usual care, significant effects were seen between the intervention and control groups. Specifically, children receiving the educational interventions demonstrated reduced days of school absence, reduced restriction of activity, and decreased emergency department utilization (Guevera et al., 2003).

Educational interventions to increase disease-related knowledge and skills clearly are necessary and important but may not be sufficient to lead to behavior change. While the evidence from this review suggests the utility of educational interventions within pediatric populations, it is important to note that educational interventions focusing on self-management may include behavioral components, such as goal setting and self-monitoring, which may have stronger effects on regimen adherence. In the pediatric obesity intervention literature, nutrition education (without behavioral components) has been utilized as a control group for family-based intervention studies and has consistently been shown to not be effective at behavior change leading to weight control (Epstein, Valoski, Wing, & McCurly, 1994).

Behavioral Interventions

Behavioral interventions are problem focused and address specific behaviors and barriers that preclude patients from optimal regimen adherence. Systematic reviews indicate that controlled studies have shown the efficacy of behavioral interventions for children and adolescents with diabetes (Delamater, 2009, 2012; Hood et al., 2010), although this literature does have some methodological limitations (Northam, Todd, & Cameron, 2005). Most of these interventions have included parents as an integral part of treatment.

Results indicate that family-based, behavioral strategies, such as self-monitoring of regimen behaviors, goal setting, positive reinforcement, behavioral contracts, supportive parental communications, and appropriately shared responsibility for diabetes management, have improved regimen adherence as well as glycemic control of youth with diabetes (Anderson et al., 1997; Satin, La Greca, Zigo, & Skyler, 1989). Besides improving regimen adherence, family-based behavioral interventions also have improved the parent–adolescent relationship, reduced family conflict, and improved long-term glycemic control (Wysocki et al., 2006, 2007).

Given the crisis that diagnosis presents for children and families, the period just after diagnosis presents opportunities for behavioral and psychological interventions. Psychoeducational family-based behavioral interventions with children and their families that promote problem-solving skills and increase parental support through training in positive reinforcement early in the disease course have improved long-term glycemic control of children (Delamater et al., 1990).

Research findings indicate that when parents allow older children and adolescents to have self-care autonomy without sufficient cognitive and social maturity, they are more likely to have regimen adherence problems and poor glycemic control (Wysocki et al., 1996). Thus, a critical aspect of behavioral family management of diabetes is finding ways for parents and family members to remain involved and supportive, but not intrusive, in their youngsters' daily care. An intervention to promote family teamwork increased family involvement without causing family conflict or adversely affecting youth quality of life and also prevented worsening of glycemic control (Laffel et al., 2003). This type of psychoeducational intervention to change family behavior was delivered during regular outpatient visits and shown to improve the frequency of outpatient visits and reduce acute adverse outcomes, such as hypoglycemia and emergency department visits (Svoren, Butler, Levine, Anderson, & Laffel, 2003).

A recent multisite controlled trial evaluated the effects of a family teamwork intervention implemented during routine clinic visits over a 2-year period with 9- to 14-year-old children with diabetes (Nansel, Iannotti, & Liu, 2012). Those assigned to the family teamwork group received a behavioral, problem-focused intervention focused on identifying strengths, barriers, and benefits of behavior change. After identifying these components, therapists and families worked together to resolve maladaptive communication patterns, solidify concrete action plans, and define roles and responsibilities. Results revealed a significant improvement in glycemic control from the baseline to 2-year assessment for the older adolescent participants (12–14 years). When compared to the usual-care group, the effect of intervention began after 12 months (approximately three to four sessions) and consistently increased in magnitude until the final 24-month assessment. Interestingly, there were no effects noted on the measure of regimen adherence, and regimen adherence was only weakly associated with the measure of glycemic control (glycosylated hemoglobin A1c). A recent randomized trial of a similar parent–youth teamwork intervention was shown to improve regimen adherence and health outcomes in youth with asthma (Duncan et al., 2012).

Another behavioral intervention approach utilized intensive home-based multisystemic therapy with inner-city adolescents in chronically poor metabolic control, a patient population that is at high risk for poor health outcomes and has not received much attention in the intervention literature. The results of a controlled trial indicated this approach improved frequency of blood glucose monitoring and glycemic control and reduced inpatient admissions and medical costs (Ellis, Frey, et al., 2005; Ellis, Naar-King, et al., 2005).

Motivational interviewing appears to be a promising intervention approach for adolescents with diabetes. The results of a multicenter randomized trial demonstrated that motivational interviewing with adolescents improved long-term glycemic control and quality of life (Channon et al., 2007). Another study targeting motivation with an individualized personal trainer showed improved glycemic outcomes in older but not younger adolescents (Nansel et al., 2007). A recent uncontrolled pilot study examined the effects of a multicomponent motivational intervention for adolescents with poor glycemic control (Stanger et al., 2013). Included in the intervention approach was family-based contingency management. Results indicated increased blood glucose monitoring and improved glycemic control over time, suggesting that this approach may be clinically effective. Similarly, the use of motivational interviewing has been useful with youth who have asthma. A recent study provides pre-liminary support for the use of motivation interviewing intervention to increase regimen adherence in inner-city, African American youth with asthma (Riekert, Borrelli, Bilderback, & Rand, 2011).

Psychological/Psychosocial Interventions

Psychological interventions for disease management provide a comprehensive approach to address-ing adherence. These interventions often target self-management skills as well as emotional com-ponents, such as patient and family adjustment to the diagnosis. Some studies in the diabetes area target psychological conditions that may influence regimen adherence, but more research is needed addressing psychological functioning. For example, depression in youth has been shown to be asso-ciated with decreased regimen adherence over time (McGrady & Hood, 2010), but intervention studies to reduce depression and evaluate the effects on regimen adherence have not been reported yet. Similarly, given the high rate of eating disorders among youth with diabetes and the relation-ship of eating disorders to poor disease management (Neumark-Sztainer et al., 2002; Rydall, Rodin, Olmsted, Devenyi, & Daneman, 1997), it would be important to examine the effects on regimen adherence of interventions addressing disordered eating in youth.

The stress of diagnosis of a disease like diabetes is significant for children and their parents. Trials involving psychosocial intervention for children and parents after the diagnosis of type 1 diabetes showed improved family functioning but no effects on glycemic control (Sullivan-Bolyai, 2004; Sundelin, Forsander, & Matttson, 1996).

Several reports of interventions for youth with diabetes target stress management and coping skills; typically the interventions are conducted in small groups of youth rather than with indi-vidual patients. This is important because research has shown that anxious youth have lower levels of regimen adherence (Herzer & Hood, 2010), and higher levels of stress and poor coping have been associated with lower regimen adherence and poor glycemic control (Delamater, Patino-Fernandez, Smith, & Bubb, 2013; Graue, Wentzel-Larsen, Bru, Hanestad, & Sovir, 2004; Hanson et al., 1989). Stress management and coping skills training including problem solving has reduced diabetes-related stress (Boardway, Delamater, Tomakowsky, & Gutai, 1993; Hains, Davies, Parton, Totka, & Amoroso-Camarata, 2000), improved social interaction (Mendez & Belendez, 1997), and increased glucose monitoring and improved glycemic control (Cook, Herold, Edidin, & Briars, 2002). Controlled studies of coping skills training have demonstrated improved glycemic control and quality of life for adolescents on intensive insulin regimens (Grey, Boland, Davidson, Li, & Tamborlane, 2000).

Brazil, McLean, Abbey, and Musselman (1997) compared inpatient versus outpatient psychoso-cial interventions for children and families dealing with childhood asthma. The outpatient interven-tion was a summer day camp that targeted management of physical and emotional components of the disease. Children were taught relaxation techniques, and social workers addressed the social and emotional issues associated with asthma. The inpatient intervention contained similar components but was implemented in a 3-month inpatient asthma rehabilitation program. Findings indicated sig-nificant differences between the groups, with the inpatient group demonstrating greater improve-ments, including fewer asthma attacks and more positive emotions about having asthma.

Intervention Meta-Analyses

Several meta-analyses have evaluated regimen adherence interventions across all evidence-based treatment approaches, providing the opportunity to examine the relative efficacy of various approaches (Dean et al., 2010; Graves et al., 2010; Kahana et al., 2008). In general, results indicate that improved health outcomes were significantly better for studies using a combination of behavioral and educational interventions (Dean et al., 2010; Graves et al., 2010). Similarly, the analysis by Kahana et al. (2008) revealed that purely educational interventions were related to negligible changes in adherence while psychological and behavioral approaches yielded greater improvements in adherence behaviors with medium effect sizes (mean $d = .44$ and .54, respectively).

Summary of Intervention Research

The results of controlled intervention research in the area of pediatric diabetes have shown that family-based interventions utilizing positive reinforcement and behavioral contracts, communication skills training, negotiation of diabetes management goals, and collaborative problem-solving skills training have led to improved regimen behaviors, glycemic control, and family relationships. Group interventions for young people with diabetes targeting stress management and coping skills also have shown positive effects on regimen adherence, glycemic control, and quality of life. Individual interventions with adolescents have shown motivational interviewing to improve long-term glycemic control and psychosocial outcomes. More research is needed to address psychological conditions such as depression and eating disorders in youth and to evaluate the effects on regimen adherence and health outcomes.

PARENTAL INVOLVEMENT

The regimens associated with childhood chronic illness are often rigorous and may contain several components. In the case of childhood diabetes, a single day may include several blood glucose checks (at mealtimes, prior to engaging in physical activity, and before bedtime), close monitoring of carbohydrate intake, correct measurement and administration of insulin, and ensuring easy access to necessary medical supplies (American Diabetes Association, 2011; Hansen, Weissbrod, Schwartz, & Taylor, 2012; Silverstein et al., 2005). Given the numerous responsibilities of managing chronic illness, it is essential that parents play an integral role in the management of their child's illness (Laffel et al., 2003; Wysocki, Buckloh, & Greco, 2009).

   Research has documented the significant impact of family functioning on diabetes management, suggesting that parenting behaviors may be important in promoting healthy adaptation to the disease (Grey et al., 2000; Hamilton & Daneman, 2002; Wysocki, 1993). Studies have shown that parental involvement may be essential for successful diabetes management (Ellis et al., 2007; Skinner, Murphy, & Huws-Thomas, 2005). Parents provide an example of goal setting and planning for their chronically ill children, both of which are important components of regimen adherence (Robinson et al., 2011). Parenting style also can influence self-management behaviors, with parental warmth being associated with better regimen adherence and parental restrictiveness associated with poorer glycemic control in young children with type 1 diabetes (Davis et al., 2001; Shorer et al., 2011). Family organization also plays an important role. Children who are a part of families with more organization and routine demonstrate better regimen adherence (Herge et al., 2012).

   Research with adult chronic illness populations underscores the impact of family function on self-management behaviors (Rosland, Heisler, & Piette, 2012). Across several diagnoses, including diabetes, arthritis, cardiovascular disease, and end-stage renal disease, family behaviors that focus on control, criticism, and overprotection are associated with negative health outcomes. This is certainly a finding that can be applied to parenting of young children with chronic illness.

Although a positive influence in many respects, parental involvement in caring for a child with chronic illness may represent a significant stressor for parents. The impact of this stressor has been well documented in pediatric literature, outlining the increased rates of parental stress and risk for parental mental health problems (Jaser, Whittemore, Ambrosino, Lindemann, & Grey, 2008; Quittner, DiGirolamo, Michel, & Eigen, 1992; Streisand, Braniecki, Tercyak, & Kazak, 2001; Thompson et al., 1994). These findings are most applicable to mothers who more frequently take on the caregiving tasks related to disease management. The impact on fathers also has been examined in research where results revealed similar psychological distress in fathers (Hansen et al., 2012). These included clinically significant sleep problems, anxiety, and depressive symptoms.

ADAPTATIONS AND MODIFICATIONS

There are several important factors to consider when assessing regimen adherence and intervening to improve it in youth with chronic illnesses. These factors may include developmental effects, demographic variables such as culture and socioeconomic status, illness comorbidity, and health beliefs. It is important to consider each of these variables in the context of regimen adherence to guide adherence-promoting interventions.

Developmental Issues

Throughout development, youth experience many biological, cognitive, emotional, and social changes. These age-related changes often play an interactive role in affecting illness management. For example, a review of diabetes-related barriers highlighted the metabolic changes that occur during puberty, paired with transitions in family and social roles, that make it more difficult to achieve optimal glycemic control (Anderson & McKay, 2011). During adolescence, youth tend to gain more independence and increased responsibility for illness management, which may affect their regimen adherence (Anderson et al., 2009). Studies have shown that regimen adherence is higher during childhood and declines during adolescence (McQuaid et al., 2012). Recent research has shown that youth with higher levels of executive functioning have better regimen adherence (Miller et al., 2013). Additionally, as adolescents transition into young adulthood, they face challenges associated with moving from pediatric health care into adult health care, with typically lower rates of adherence (Pai & Ostendorf, 2011).

Family Demographic Variables and Functioning

Research suggests that low socioeconomic status and minority ethnic/racial group status is associated with increased risk for poor adherence and health outcomes (Anderson & McKay, 2011; Hood et al., 2010). According to a review on the influences of adherence in pediatric asthma patients, race, single-parent homes, parental education, and income were consistently associated with nonadherence (Drotar & Bonner, 2009). McQuaid et al. (2012) found that when comparing medication adherence in Latino and non-Latino White children with asthma, the non-Latino White families reported higher levels of adherence than Latino families. These results remained even for Latino youth who had higher rates of health care coverage (McQuaid et al., 2012). However, medication adherence was associated with family organization across both cultures, suggesting that family-based interventions should focus on strategies to improve family organization. Parental beliefs about medication necessity also were associated with adherence across cultural groups.

Therefore, it is important to discuss cultural beliefs about medication with families of distinct cultural backgrounds.

Family factors play a critical role in pediatric illness management. Studies across illness groups have indicated that family support is positively associated with adherence and health outcomes (Mackey et al., 2011; Rhee, Belyea, & Brasch, 2010), while family conflict is consistently associated with poorer health outcomes in youth with chronic illness. For example, in the diabetes literature, family conflict consistently has been associated with poor regimen adherence and glycemic control (Hilliard, Guilfoyle, Dolan, & Hood, 2011; Ingerski, Anderson, Dolan, & Hood, 2010; Wysocki, 1993).

Parent and Child Psychological Factors

Studies indicate that rates of mental health symptoms are higher among youth with chronic illness. For example, adolescents with type 1 diabetes are at increased risk for anxiety, depression, and disordered eating (Delamater, 2009; Grey, Whittemore, & Tamborlane, 2002; Herzer et al., 2010; Neumark-Sztainer et al., 2002). Research in adults supports the effectiveness of cognitive behavioral therapy to improve regimen adherence in patients with diabetes who are depressed (Gonzalez & McCarl, 2010). Similar disease management interventions should be tailored for youth with chronic illness, as the mental health symptoms they experience may be highly associated with their physical symptoms and regimen adherence.

Additionally, illness perceptions may affect illness management. For example, reviews of treatment barriers to pediatric asthma have found that parental health beliefs about their child's illness and treatment are associated with adherence: for example, parents who perceived the treatment as more effective were more likely to adhere to the regimen (Drotar et al., 2009; Kaptein, Klok, Moss-Morris, & Brand, 2010). Drotar et al. (2009) also highlighted that child perceptions about the illness, such as self-efficacy and hope, were positively associated with adherence. This is consistent with reports for other chronic illness groups, such as diabetes (Grossman, Brink, & Hauser, 1987) and cystic fibrosis (Ricker, Delamater, & Hsu, 1998).

Adaptations for Adherence-Promoting Interventions

There are several factors to consider when tailoring interventions to promote regimen adherence for youth with pediatric chronic illness. As mentioned, developmental stages, demographic and family factors, and the health care system all affect illness management in different ways. For years, researchers have emphasized the importance of targeting issues related to many of these factors to promote better adherence and improve health outcomes for youth.

For example, researchers in one study with low-income Puerto Rican families tailored a culturally relevant asthma intervention to improve health outcomes (Canino et al., 2008). As part of the education program, research staff discussed common myths that Puerto Rican families believe about asthma and common triggers of asthma on their island, and how to increase their empowerment in dealing with the Puerto Rican health system (Canino et al., 2008). Families in the culturally adapted intervention group reported better asthma control and fewer hospitalizations than the control group.

Considering the numerous factors that affect regimen adherence and health outcomes in youth across chronic illnesses, it is evident that individually tailored, "multicomponent" adherence interventions seem to be most effective (Kahana et al., 2008). Future behavioral and educational adherence-promoting intervention programs should assess their effectiveness across different developmental, ethnic, and socioeconomic groups.

MEASURING TREATMENT EFFECTS

Several direct and indirect, objective and subjective measures have been developed to assess regimen adherence behaviors (Drotar, 2000; Graves et al., 2010; Quittner, Modi, Lemanek, Levers-Landis, & Rapoff, 2008). Typically, serum assays are used as a direct objective measure of adherence; pill counts and electronic monitors may be used as objective or indirect measures of adherence; and self-report, 24-hour recall, and diaries are used as subjective measures of adherence (Graves et al., 2010). Each measure has its own strengths and weaknesses. Selection of adherence measures depends on the nature and complexity of the illness.

Direct Measures

Drug assays, such as blood, urine, or saliva samples, may provide an objective measure of regimen adherence. Drug assays can be used to identify the amount of a prescribed medication present in the body; however, results from drug assays can be affected by individual differences in the body's rate of drug absorption, metabolism, and food interactions (Drotar, 2000; Epstein & Cluss, 1982). With the half-life of certain medications being relatively brief, assays would reflect adherence over only a short time period. In diabetes, glycosylated hemoglobin A1c provides an average of blood glucose levels over a 2- to 3-month period; A1c may be used to reflect or infer levels of regimen adherence but does not actually measure regimen adherence. Overall, assays may be expensive and therefore often are not feasible to use as a measure of adherence over long periods of time (La Greca et al., 2009).

Indirect Measures

Pill counts often have been used to assess adherence by comparing the dose of a prescription that is taken from the pill bottle to the dosage prescribed. Although using pill counts as a measure of adherence is simple and inexpensive, it poses a few problems. When using the pill count method, researchers cannot be certain that patients actually took the pill that they removed from the pill bottle. Patients also may take more than the prescribed amount of medication out at once (Drotar, 2000).

New technologies have allowed for the development of electronic monitors to more objectively and accurately assess regimen adherence. Electronic monitors now are considered one of the most objective ways to measure adherence after serum assays (Ingerski, Hente, Modi, & Hommel, 2011). These monitors can be used to assess glucose testing, insulin bolusing, oral medication use, inhaled medication use, and nebulized medication use across various pediatric chronic illness groups. For example, data from blood glucose monitors in patients with diabetes can be downloaded to assess the time and results of blood glucose tests; data from insulin pumps can be downloaded to measure timing and amount of insulin boluses. Although electronic monitors make up for some of the shortcomings of using the pill count method by monitoring the time and frequency that the pill bottle is opened, there are also some disadvantages.

The most commonly used measure of oral medication use is the Medication Event Monitoring System (MEMS), which records "date, time, and frequency of pill bottle openings" (Ingerski et al., 2011, p. 2). MEMS provides a measure of adherence issues, such as underdosing, overdosing, delayed dosing, drug holidays, or "white-coat" adherence (taking medication more often right before their scheduled appointment) in real time over a long period of time (Ingerski et al., 2011; Quittner et al., 2008).

Although research studies suggest that there are many strengths to using MEMS to measure adherence with strong correlations between serum assay and pharmacy refill data (Farley, Hines, Musk, Ferrus, & Tepper, 2003), there are some disadvantages to consider. For one, MEMS can record only the number of pill bottle openings rather than the actual number of pills taken out of the bottle or ingested. For example, a patient may take more than one dose of pills at once or not take the pills removed from the bottle. Additionally, studies have reported that electronic monitors or software for downloading data often malfunction (Helgeson, Honcharuk, Becker, Escobar, & Siminerio, 2011). Other widely used electronic monitors include inhaled medication monitors, such as DOSER, and nebulized medication monitors for asthma. Similar issues in using these methods of assessment include high cost and high rates of malfunction (Ingerski et al., 2011). Further technological advances may improve the quality of electronic monitoring devices and decrease costs.

Subjective Measures

Self-Report Questionnaires and Structured Interviews

Child, parent, and physician report questionnaires or structured interviews are the most commonly used measures of adherence in research and clinical practice across many pediatric chronic illnesses, including diabetes, asthma, HIV-AIDS, and cystic fibrosis (Quittner et al., 2008; Wu et al., 2013). In a review of evidence-based adherence assessment tools, Quittner and colleagues (2008) highlighted the most widely used measures of adherence. Among the well-established measures were the Self-Care Inventory for parents and adolescents (Lewin et al., 2009), Diabetes Regimen Adherence Questionnaire (DRAQ) (Brownlee-Duffeck et al., 1987), and Disease Management Interview-CF (Quittner et al., 2000).

A reliable, validated structured interview method is available for the assessment of diabetes self-management behaviors: the Diabetes Self-Management Profile (DSMP) (Harris et al., 2000). This measure provides information on all aspects of diabetes self-care, including glucose monitoring, insulin use, dietary intake and exercise, and how these behaviors are modified depending on glucose levels. In addition, the measure assesses how hypoglycemia is treated. The interview is conducted separately with youth and parents and provides information about usual self-care behaviors over the preceding 3 months. A self-report measure of type 1 diabetes self-management based on the DSMP was published recently (Wysocki, Buckloh, Antal, Lochrie, & Taylor, 2012). The self-report version of the DSMP consists of 24 items with five subscales (blood glucose monitoring, insulin use, eating, physical exercise, and hypoglycemia management) with excellent reliability and validity reported. The measure is available as a youth self-report and also as a parent report about their child.

There are several relative strengths and weaknesses to using self-report measures to assess adherence. Self-report measures are inexpensive, easy to obtain, and easily scored, and they can be modified to capture multiple perspectives (e.g., parent, child, and physician). However, individuals tend to overestimate adherence and have problems with accurate recall; self-report measures also tend to assess "global perceptions" of adherence rather than specific behaviors (Quittner et al., 2008). Thus, it may be more productive to request information about specific regimen adherence behaviors rather than general adherence over a period of time (Rapoff, 2010).

Diaries

Daily diaries can include handwritten logs, computerized devices, or cellular phones. Through the diary method of adherence assessment, youth record their daily adherence behaviors. Although research has shown that youth have difficulty complying with written diary methods of assessment, more recent diary methods have been more effective (Mulvaney et al., 2012; Quittner et al., 2008). For example, ecological momentary assessment (EMA) is used as a way to collect data in real time.

Recent research has focused on the use of EMA through cell phones (Kuntsche & Labhart, 2013; Mulvaney et al., 2012).

In a recent study, adolescents with type 1 diabetes used a cell phone–based EMA for blood glucose monitoring and insulin administration (Mulvaney et al., 2012). Youth were called twice a day for 10 days and asked specific questions about their most recent glucose monitoring patterns and insulin administrations. Through this real-time method, youth are better able to recall their routine self-care behaviors. Results also showed that adherence was lower in the mornings and higher in the evenings. Through these mobile monitoring devices, researchers and clinicians may be better able to tailor cell phone–based interventions to address particular barriers (e.g., send prompts through the cell phone at particular times of day). As with other technologies, cell phone–based EMA's pose some challenges. For one, they require a certain knowledge of cell phone use that may be difficult for different groups (e.g., young children). Using cell phone methods for measurement of regimen adherence also can be costly and pose a challenge for low-income families.

24-Hour Recall

The 24-hour recall method often is employed as a self-report measure to record the events of the previous day. This 24-hour recall (or "cued recall") method helps to obtain more specific information about most recent adherence behaviors. The Diabetes Management Interview, for example, obtains information such as frequency of injections, eating, and exercise (Johnson, Silverstein, Rosenbloom, Carter, & Cunningham, 1986). However, the 24-hour recall, done over a 2-week period, requires greater time from interviewer and patient as well as more complex data management and analysis.

Considerations for Clinicians and Researchers

A number of evidence-based approaches are available for measurement of regimen adherence in children and adolescents with various types of diseases. Due to the challenges in assessing adherence behaviors accurately, it is recommended that researchers and clinicians use more than one kind of measure to assess adherence. According to a recent survey administered to pediatric psychologists, psychologists tend to use multiple methods to measure adherence but also report time limitations as the most common barrier to adherence assessment (Wu et al., 2013). Future research should focus on tailoring methods of assessment to be shorter while maintaining their effectiveness. Additionally, it is important for pediatric psychologists to continue working with multidisciplinary teams to promote strategies for improving adherence in youth.

CLINICAL CASE EXAMPLE

The patient was a 13-year-old boy with type 1 diabetes living with both parents. (Identifying information has been altered to protect confidentiality.) He was diagnosed when he was 4 years old. He was doing well socially and academically. For the past 2 years he was on an insulin pump regimen. However, his glycemic control, determined by measurement of glycosylated hemoglobin A1c at the time of the initial evaluation, was 9.2%, indicating poor glycemic control. He and his parents agreed to participate in a research study to evaluate the effects of a family-based intervention to improve diabetes self-management.

Besides measurement of hemoglobin A1c, the baseline evaluation consisted of interviews with the patient and his mother to determine current levels of regimen adherence using the DSMP

(Harris et al., 2000). In addition, several standardized questionnaires were used to assess diabetes-related family conflict, support, responsibilities, and quality of life. These measures were repeated 6 and 12 months later for study purposes.

The intervention was standardized but flexible, consistent with the approach used in motivational interviewing. At each session, there was a menu of regimen-related issues that could be addressed, and it was the decision of the patient to make a choice about which issues he wanted to deal with during each session. One parent (either the mother or father, and sometimes both) participated in each session along with the child. There were six possible topics in the program, including: learning more about diabetes ("Diabetes 101"), using glucose monitoring to understand blood glucose changes, insulin use, food, physical activity, and family communication.

Following motivational interviewing principles, with each issue there was a discussion of its importance, information sharing as appropriate, and goal setting for specific regimen-related behaviors. A discussion of confidence with respect to meeting the goal also occurred, and a corresponding goal was set for the parent to support the youth-selected goal. If confidence was low due to some barriers, problem solving was applied to make a better plan. A goal sheet was signed at the conclusion of each session. At the subsequent session, progress was reviewed, and then a new issue was chosen for that session, although the choice could be made to continue working on the same issue. Sessions were held approximately every 2 weeks for a 4-month period, with a booster session held 6 months after beginning the program.

In this case, the patient first chose to discuss family communication. The parents were very concerned that they were nagging their son too much and that they argued about his blood glucose readings. They reported that he hoarded candy and would eat it surreptitiously at night in his room; the father searched the room and found many candy wrappers. Because they did not want to be nagging too much, they often avoided discussions about diabetes management and allowed their son to have considerable autonomy with regard to self-care tasks. "Nagging" was reframed as "caring" about the health of their son, and the patient agreed that he did not mind being "nagged" in this way—in fact, he told his parents that he appreciated them nagging him.

Over the next few sessions, the patient wanted to learn more about diabetes and discuss use of blood glucose monitoring, diet, and insulin administration to improve diabetes control, as he was aware of the fact that his A1c was too high and placed him at risk for poor health. Goals were set regarding eating food as he wished, contingent on monitoring blood glucose and taking insulin boluses as needed; he also set goals to begin reading food labels and counting carbohydrates so that he could adjust his insulin more effectively. The therapist asked the mother if she ever looked at the patient's insulin pump and meter to review glucose levels and insulin boluses. She indicated she did not. A goal was set to have her use the computer program to download the meter and pump data so that they could review this together at the next session.

At the subsequent session, the patient and mother, along with the therapist, reviewed the data documenting blood glucose checks and insulin boluses. Although the patient was measuring his blood glucose regularly about six times each day, he only bolused on average three times (with breakfast, lunch, and dinner); he did not bolus at other times when he snacked. Through a discussion about these issues, the patient realized this was contributing to his poor glycemic control, and a goal was set to increase bolusing so that every time he snacked, he would also bolus. In addition, he set a goal to bolus whenever he checked his blood glucose and found he was out of range. Goals also were set for the parents to praise this behavior, and the issue of sneaking food was overcome as the patient and parents agreed that snacking was acceptable as long as appropriate bolusing occurred. Sessions addressing diet focused on being more accurate about carbohydrate counting so that he could be more effective with bolusing the correct amount of insulin.

During one of the sessions where only the father attended, it became clear that he had only limited diabetes management knowledge and skills, as he deferred responsibility for monitoring his son's diabetes care to his wife. Through participation in the program, however, he increased his skills and confidence with diabetes management. The patient and parents responded very well to this approach, and the patient began bolusing more consistently when he snacked. The family attended seven sessions over about 4 months and then was seen for a booster session 2 months later to review progress and discuss the changes made by the patient and parents.

The patient's hemoglobin A1c at 6 months after beginning treatment showed a clinically significant improvement, from 9.2% to 8.3%. The DSMP total score from the mother's interview improved from 34 to 47, while the patient's DMSP total score decreased slightly from 51 at baseline to 47 at 6 months. The DSMP subscales showing the greatest increases from the mother's report were eating and blood glucose monitoring. Reports from both patient and mother revealed no changes in quality of life or responsibilities for diabetes management tasks. While the patient reported a decrease in family conflict (from 30 to 27), the mother reported an increase (from 32 to 58), probably reflecting her greater involvement in daily diabetes management.

The family was not seen again outside of regular outpatient clinic appointments for 6 months, at which time they completed the assessment protocol to determine if gains were maintained without further behavioral intervention. Results indicated that the A1c was 8.5%; patient DSMP total score increased from the 6-month score of 47 to 53, while the mother's DSMP total score declined from 47 to 40; the child ratings of diabetes family conflict remained the same, but the mother's ratings showed a decrease from 58 to 48; diabetes responsibilities were unchanged from 6 to 12 months in both patient and parent ratings; and quality-of-life scores increased from 51 at 6 months to 64 at 12 months for the patient, while the mother's report of child quality-of-life scores similarly showed improvements from 61 at 6 months to 68 at 12 months.

This case study illustrates a number of important issues in addressing regimen adherence in diabetes. First, it was clear that the patient's glycemic control was poor and could be attributed in part to lack of insulin bolusing when eating snacks. Although the patient was recording blood glucose values frequently and regularly, he was not using that information for making appropriate changes in dietary intake and insulin use. Through the use of motivational interviewing, the patient selected issues for discussion and set specific individual behavioral goals to work on, and the parents made their own goals to specifically support their child's goals. With this approach, the parents became more involved in their son's daily diabetes management and praised him more frequently for his self-care efforts. The family began reviewing records of both blood glucose results and insulin boluses, and the child began bolusing more frequently; additionally, the patient became more skilled at carbohydrate counting, and eating snacks, including candy, was not restricted, as long as appropriate bolusing followed. The results of this family-based behavioral intervention indicated improvements in regimen adherence, glycemic control, and quality of life.

REFERENCES

American Diabetes Association. (2011). Executive summary: Standards of medical care in diabetes—2011. *Diabetes Care, 34*(Suppl.), S4–S10.

Anderson, B. J., Ho, J., Brackett, J., Finkelstein, D., & Laffel, L. (1997). Parental involvement in diabetes management tasks: Relationships to blood glucose monitoring adherence and metabolic control in young adolescents with insulin-dependent diabetes mellitus. *Journal of Pediatrics, 130,* 257–265.

Anderson, B. J., Holmbeck, G., Iannotti, R. J., McKay, S. V., Lochrie, A., Volkening, L. K., & Laffel, L. (2009). Dyadic measures of the parent–child relationship during the transition to adolescence and glycemic control in children with type 1 diabetes. *Families, Systems, & Health, 27*(2), 141–152.

Anderson, B. J., & McKay, S. V. (2011). Barriers to glycemic control in youth with type 1 diabetes and type 2 diabetes. *Pediatric Diabetes, 12,* 197–205.

Boardway, R. H., Delamater, A. M., Tomakowsky, J., & Gutai, J. P. (1993). Stress management training for adolescents with diabetes. *Journal of Pediatric Psychology, 18,* 29–45.

Brazil, K., McLean, L., Abbey, D., & Musselman, C. (1997). The influence of health education on family management of childhood asthma. *Patient Education and Counseling, 30*(2), 107–118.

Brownlee-Duffeck, M., Peterson, L., Simonds, J. F., Goldstein, D., Kilo, C., & Hoette, S. (1987). The role of health beliefs in the regimen adherence and metabolic control of adolescents and adults with diabetes mellitus. *Journal of Consulting and Clinical Psychology, 55*(2), 139–144.

Bryden, K. S., Neil, A., Mayou, R. A., Peveler, R. C., Fairburn, C. G., & Dunger, D. B. (1999). Eating habits, body weight, and insulin misuse. A longitudinal study of teenagers and young adults with type 1 diabetes. *Diabetes Care, 22*(12), 1956–1960.

Burdick, J., Chase, H. P., Slover, R. H., Knievel, K., Scrimgeour, L., Maniatis, A. K., & Klingensmith, G. J. (2004). Missed insulin meal boluses and elevated hemoglobin A1c levels in children receiving insulin pump therapy. *Pediatrics, 113*(3), 221–224.

Canino, G., Vila, D., Normand, S. T., Acosta-Pérez, E., Ramírez, R., García, P., & Rand, C. (2008). Reducing asthma health disparities in poor Puerto Rican children: The effectiveness of a culturally tailored family intervention. *Journal of Allergy and Clinical Immunology, 121*(3), 665–670.

Channon, S. J., Huws-Thomas, M. V., Rollnick, S., Hood, K., Cannings-John, R. L., Rogers, C., & Gregory, J. W. (2007). A multicenter randomized controlled trial of motivational interviewing in teenagers with diabetes. *Diabetes Care, 30*(6), 1390–1395.

Cook, S., Herold, K., Edidin, D.V., & Briars, R. (2002). Increasing problem solving in adolescents with type 1 diabetes: The Choices Diabetes program. *Diabetes Educator, 28,* 115–124.

Davis, C. L., Delamater, A. M., Shaw, K. H., La Greca, A. M., Eidson, M. S., Perez-Rodriguez, J. E., & Nemery, R. (2001). Parenting styles, regimen adherence, and glycemic control in 4- to 10-year-old children with diabetes. *Journal of Pediatric Psychology, 26*(2), 123–129.

Dean, A. J., Walters, J., & Hall, A. (2010). A systematic review of interventions to enhance medication adherence in children and adolescents with chronic illness. *Archives of Disease in Childhood, 95*(9), 717–723.

Delamater, A. M. (2009). Psychological care of children and adolescents with diabetes. *Pediatric Diabetes, 10,* 175–184.

Delamater, A. M. (2012). Successful team management of type 1 diabetes in children and young people: Key psychosocial issues. *Diabetes Care in Children & Young People, 1,* 10–116.

Delamater, A. M., Bubb, J., Davis, S., Smith, J., Schmidt, L., White, N., & Santiago, J. V. (1990). Randomized, prospective study of self-management training with newly diagnosed diabetic children. *Diabetes Care, 13*(5), 492–498.

Delamater, A. M., Davis, S. G., Bubb, J., Santiago, J. V., Smith, J. A., & White, N. H. (1989). Self-monitoring of blood glucose by adolescents with diabetes: technical skills and utilization of data. *Diabetes Educator, 15*(1), 56–61.

Delamater, A. M., Patino-Fernandez, A. M., Smith, K. E., & Bubb, J. (2013). Measurement of diabetes stress in older children and adolescents with type 1 diabetes. *Pediatric Diabetes, 14,* 50–56.

Drotar, D. (Ed.). (2000). *Promoting adherence to medical treatment in chronic childhood illness: Concepts, methods, and interventions.* Mahwah, NJ: Erlbaum.

Drotar, D., & Bonner, M. S. (2009). Influences on adherence to pediatric asthma treatment: A review of correlates and predictors. *Journal of Developmental & Behavioral Pediatrics, 30*(6), 574–582.

Duncan, C. L., Hogan, M. B., Tien, K. J., Graves, M. M., Chorney, J. M., Zettler, M. D., & Portnoy, J. (2012). Efficacy of a parent–youth teamwork intervention to promote adherence in pediatric asthma. *Journal of Pediatric Psychology, 38*(6), 617–628.

Ellis, D., Frey, M., Naar-King, S., Templin, T., Cunningham, P., & Cakan, N. (2005). Use of multisystemic therapy to improve regimen adherence among adolescents with type 1 diabetes in chronic poor metabolic control. *Diabetes Care, 28*(7), 1604–1610.

Ellis, D., Naar-King, S., Frey, M., Templin, T., Rowland, M., & Cakan, N. (2005). Multisystemic treatment of poorly controlled type 1 diabetes: Effects on medical resource utilization. *Journal of Pediatric Psychology, 30,* 656–666.

Ellis, D. A., Podolski, C., Frey, M., Naar-King, S., Wang, B., & Moltz, K. (2007). The role of parental monitoring in adolescent health outcomes: Impact on regimen adherence in youth with type 1 diabetes. *Journal of Pediatric Psychology, 32*(8), 907–917.

Epstein, L. H., & Cluss, P. A. (1982). A behavioral medicine perspective on adherence to long-term medical regimens. *Journal of Consulting and Clinical Psychology, 50*(6), 950–971.

Epstein, L. H., Valoski, A., Wing, R. R., & McCurley, J. (1994). Ten-year outcomes of behavioral family-based treatment for childhood obesity. *Health Psychology, 13*(5), 373–383.

Farber, H. J., & Oliveria, L. (2004). Trial of an asthma education program in an inner-city pediatric emergency department. *Pediatric Asthma, Allergy & Immunology, 17*(2), 107–115.

Farley, J., Hines, S., Musk, A., Ferrus, S., & Tepper, V. (2003). Assessment of adherence to antiviral therapy in HIV-infected children using the Medication Event Monitoring System, pharmacy refill, provider assessment, caregiver self-report, and appointment keeping. *Journal of Acquired Immune Deficiency Syndromes, 33*(2), 212–218.

Gibson, P. G., Powell, H., Wilson, A., Abramson, M. J., Haywood, P., Bauman, A., . . . Roberts, J. L. (2002). Self-management education and regular practitioner review for adults with asthma. *Cochrane Database of Systematic Reviews, 2002*(3), 1–59.

Glasgow, R. E., & Anderson, R. M. (1999). In diabetes care, moving from compliance to adherence is not enough. *Diabetes Care, 22*(12), 2090–2092.

Gonzalez, J. S., & McCarl, L. A. (2010). Cognitive-behavioral therapy for adherence and depression (CBT-AD) in type 2 diabetes. *Journal of Cognitive Psychotherapy, 24*(4), 329–343.

Graue, M., Wentzel-Larsen, T., Bru, E., Hanestad, B., & Sovir, O. (2004). The coping styles of adolescents with type 1 diabetes are associated with degree of metabolic control. *Diabetes Care, 27*(6), 1313–1317.

Graves, M. M., Roberts, M. C., Rapoff, M., & Boyer, A. (2010). The efficacy of adherence interventions for chronically ill children: A meta-analytic review. *Journal of Pediatric Psychology, 35*(4), 368–382.

Grey, M., Boland, E. A., Davidson, M., Li, J., & Tamborlane, W. V. (2000). Coping skills training for youth with diabetes mellitus has long-lasting effects on metabolic control and quality of life. *Journal of Pediatrics, 137*(1), 107–113.

Grey, M., Whittemore, R., & Tamborlane, W. (2002). Depression in type 1 diabetes in children: Natural history and correlates. *Journal of Psychosomatic Research, 53*(4), 907–911.

Grossman, H. Y., Brink, S., & Hauser, S. T. (1987). Self-efficacy in adolescent girls and boys with insulin-dependent diabetes mellitus. *Diabetes Care, 10*(3), 324–329.

Guevara, J. P., Wolf, F. M., Grum, C. M., & Clark, N. M. (2003). Effects of educational interventions for self management of asthma in children and adolescents: Systematic review and meta-analysis. *British Medical Journal, 326,* 1308–1314.

Hains, A. A., Davies, W. H., Parton, E., Totka, J., & Amoroso-Camarata, J. (2000). A stress management intervention for adolescents with type 1 diabetes. *Diabetes Educator, 26,* 417–424.

Hamilton, J., & Daneman, D. (2002). Deteriorating diabetes control during adolescence: Physiological or psychosocial? *Journal of Pediatric Endocrinology and Metabolism, 15*(2), 115–126.

Hansen, J. A., Weissbrod, C., Schwartz, D. D., & Taylor, W. P. (2012). Paternal involvement in pediatric type 1 diabetes: Fathers' and mothers' psychological functioning and disease management. *Families, Systems, & Health, 30*(1), 47–59.

Hanson, C. L., Cigrant, J. A., Harris, M., Carle, D. L., Relyea, G., & Burghen, G. A. (1989). Coping styles in youths with insulin-dependent diabetes mellitus. *Journal of Consulting and Clinical Psychology, 57,* 644–651.

Harris, M. A., Wysocki, T., Sadler, M., Wilkinson, K., Harvey, L. M., Buckloh, L. M., . . . White, N. H. (2000). Validation of a structured interview for the assessment of diabetes self-management. *Diabetes Care, 23*(9), 1301–1304.

Haynes, R. B., Taylor, D. W., & Sackett, D. L. (1979). *Compliance in health care.* Baltimore, MD: Johns Hopkins University Press.

Helgeson, V. S., Honcharuk, E., Becker, D., Escobar, O., & Siminerio, L. (2011). A focus on blood glucose monitoring: Relation to glycemic control and determinants of frequency. *Pediatric Diabetes, 12*(1), 25–30.

Helgeson, V. S., Snyder, P. R., Seltman, H., Escobar, O., Becker, D., & Siminerio, L. (2010). Brief report: Trajectories of glycemic control over early to middle adolescence. *Journal of Pediatric Psychology, 35*(10), 1161–1167.

Herge, W. M., Streisand, R., Chen, R., Holmes, C., Kumar, A., & Mackey, E. R. (2012). Family and youth factors associated with health beliefs and health outcomes in youth with type 1 diabetes. *Journal of Pediatric Psychology, 37*(9), 980–989.

Herzer, M., & Hood, K. K. (2010). Anxiety symptoms in adolescents with type 1 diabetes: Association with blood glucose monitoring and glycemic control. *Journal of Pediatric Psychology, 35*(4), 415–425.

Hilliard, M. E., Guilfoyle, S. M., Dolan, L. M., & Hood, K. K. (2011). Prediction of adolescents' glycemic control 1 year after diabetes-specific family conflict: The mediating role of blood glucose monitoring adherence. *Archives of Pediatrics & Adolescent Medicine, 165*(7), 624–629.

Hood, K. K., Rohan, J. M., Peterson, C. M., & Drotar, D. (2010). Interventions with adherence-promoting components in pediatric type 1 diabetes meta-analysis of their impact on glycemic control. *Diabetes Care, 33*(7), 1658–1664.

Hughes, D. M., McLeod, M., Garner, B., & Goldbloom, R. B. (1991). Controlled trial of a home and ambulatory program for asthmatic children. *Pediatrics, 87*(1), 54–61.

Ingerski, L. M., Anderson, B. J., Dolan, L. M., & Hood, K. K. (2010). Blood glucose monitoring and glycemic control in adolescence: Contribution of diabetes-specific responsibility and family conflict. *Journal of Adolescent Health, 47*(2), 191–197.

Ingerski, L. M., Hente, E. A., Modi, A. C., & Hommel, K. A. (2011). Electronic measurement of medication adherence in pediatric chronic illness: A review of measures. *Journal of Pediatrics, 159*(4), 528–534.

Jacobson, A. M., Hauser, S. T., Lavori, P., Wolfsdorf, J., Herskowitz, R., Milley, J., . . . Stein, J. (1990). Adherence among children and adolescents with insulin-dependent diabetes mellitus over a four-year longitudinal follow-up: I. The influence of patient coping and adjustment. *Journal of Pediatric Psychology, 15*, 511–526.

Jaser, S. S., Whittemore, R., Ambrosino, J. M., Lindemann, E., & Grey, M. (2008). Mediators of depressive symptoms in children with type 1 diabetes and their mothers. *Journal of Pediatric Psychology, 33*(5), 509–519.

Johnson, S. B., Kelly, M., Henretta, J. C., Cunningham, W. R., Tomer, A., & Silverstein, J. H. (1992). A longitudinal analysis of adherence and health status in childhood diabetes. *Journal of Pediatric Psychology, 17*(5), 537–553.

Johnson, S. B., Silverstein, J., Rosenbloom, A., Carter, R., & Cunningham, W. (1986). Assessing daily management in childhood diabetes. *Health Psychology, 5*(6), 545–564.

Kahana, S., Drotar, D., & Frazier, T. (2008). Meta-analysis of psychological interventions to promote adherence to treatment in pediatric chronic health conditions. *Journal of Pediatric Psychology, 33*(6), 590–611.

Kaptein, A. A., Klok, T., Moss-Morris, R., & Brand, P. L. (2010). Illness perceptions: Impact on self-management and control in asthma. *Current Opinion in Allergy and Clinical Immunology, 10*(3), 194–199.

Kuntsche, E., & Labhart, F. (2013). Using personal cell phones for ecological momentary assessment: An overview of current developments. *European Psychologist, 18*(1), 3.

La Greca, A. M., & Mackey, E. R. (2009). Adherence to pediatric treatment regimens. In M. C. Roberts & R. G. Steele (Eds.), *Handbook of pediatric psychology* (4th ed., pp. 130–152). New York, NY: Guilford Press.

Laffel, L., Vangsness, L., Connell, A., Goebel-Fabbri, A., Butler, D., & Anderson, B. J. (2003). Impact of ambulatory, family-focused teamwork intervention on glycemic control in youth with type 1 diabetes. *Journal of Pediatrics, 142*(4), 409–416.

Lemanek, K. L., Kamps, J., & Chung, N. B. (2001). Empirically supported treatments in pediatric psychology: Regimen adherence. *Journal of Pediatric Psychology, 26*(5), 253–275.

Lewin, A. B., LaGreca, A. M., Geffken, G. R., Williams, L. B., Duke, D. C., Storch, E. A., & Silverstein, J. H. (2009). Validity and reliability of an adolescent and parent rating scale of type 1 diabetes adherence behaviors: The self-care inventory (SCI). *Journal of Pediatric Psychology, 34*(9), 999–1007.

Mackey, E. R., Hilliard, M. E., Berger, S. S., Streisand, R., Chen, R., & Holmes, C. (2011). Individual and family strengths: An examination of the relation to disease management and metabolic control in youth with type 1 diabetes. *Families, Systems & Health, 29*(4), 314–326.

McGrady, M. E., & Hood, K. K. (2010). Depressive symptoms in adolescents with type 1 diabetes: Associations with longitudinal outcomes. *Diabetes Research and Clinical Practice, 88*, 35–37.

McQuaid, E. L., Everhart, R. S., Seifer, R., Kopel, S. J., Mitchell, D. K., Klein, R. B., . . . Canino, G. (2012). Medication adherence among Latino and non-Latino white children with asthma. *Pediatrics, 129*(6), e1404–e1410.

Meichenbaum, D., & Turk, D. C. (1987). *Facilitating treatment adherence: A practitioner's guidebook.* New York, NY: Plenum Press.

Mendez, F., & Belendez, M. (1997). Effects of a behavioral intervention on treatment adherence and stress management in adolescents with IDDM. *Diabetes Care, 20*(9), 1370–1375.

Miller, M., Rohan, J., Delamater, A., Shroff-Pendley, J., Dolan, L., Reeves, G., & Drotar, D. (2013). Changes in executive functioning and self-management in adolescents with type 1 diabetes: A growth curve analysis. *Journal of Pediatric Psychology, 38*, 18–29.

Mulvaney, S. A., Rothman, R. L., Dietrich, M. S., Wallston, K. A., Grove, E., Elasy, T. A., & Johnson, K. B. (2012). Using mobile phones to measure adolescent diabetes adherence. *Health Psychology, 31*(1), 43.

Nansel, T. R., Iannotti, R. J., & Liu, A. (2012). Clinic-integrated behavioral intervention for families of youth with type 1 diabetes: Randomized clinical trial. *Pediatrics, 129*(4), e866–e873.

Nansel, T. R., Iannotti, R. J., Simons-Morton, B. G., Cox, C., Plotnick, L. P., Clark, L. M., & Zeitzoff, L. (2007). Diabetes personal trainer outcomes: Short-term and 1-year outcomes of a diabetes personal trainer intervention among youth with type 1 diabetes. *Diabetes Care, 30*(10), 2471–2477.

Neumark-Sztainer, D., Patterson, J., Mellin, A., Ackard, D. M., Utter, J., Story, M., & Sockalosky, J. (2002). Weight control practices and disordered eating behaviors among adolescent females and males with type 1 diabetes: Associations with sociodemographics, weight concerns, familial factors, and metabolic outcomes. *Diabetes Care, 25*(8), 1289–1296.

Northam, E. A., Todd, S., & Cameron, F. J. (2005). Interventions to promote optimal health outcomes in children with type 1 diabetes—are they effective? *Diabetic Medicine, 23*, 113–121.

Pai, A. L., & Ostendorf, H. M. (2011). Treatment adherence in adolescents and young adults affected by chronic illness during the health care transition from pediatric to adult health care: A literature review. *Children's Health Care, 40*(1), 16–33.

Quittner, A. L., DiGirolamo, A. M., Michel, M., & Eigen, H. (1992). Parental response to cystic fibrosis: A contextual analysis of the diagnosis phase. *Journal of Pediatric Psychology, 17*(6), 683–704.

Quittner, A. L., Drotar, D., Levers-Landis, C., Slocum, N., Seidner, D., & Jacobsen, J. (2000). Adherence to medical treatments in adolescents with cystic fibrosis: The development and evaluation of family-based interventions. In D. Drotar (Ed.), *Promoting adherence to medical treatment in chronic childhood illness: Concepts, methods, and interventions* (pp. 383–407). Mahwah, NJ: Erlbaum.

Quittner, A. L., Modi, A. C., Lemanek, K. L., Levers-Landis, C. E., & Rapoff, M. A. (2008). Evidence-based assessment of adherence to medical treatments in pediatric psychology. *Journal of Pediatric Psychology, 33*(9), 916–936.

Rapoff, M. A. (2010). *Adherence to pediatric medical regimens* (2nd ed.). New York, NY: Springer.

Rhee, H., Belyea, M. J., & Brasch, J. (2010). Family support and asthma outcomes in adolescents: Barriers to adherence as a mediator. *Journal of Adolescent Health, 47*(5), 472–478.

Ricker, J. H., Delamater, A. M., & Hsu, J. (1998). Correlates of regimen adherence in cystic fibrosis. *Journal of Clinical Psychology in Medical Settings, 5*(2), 159–172.

Riekert, K. A., Borrelli, B., Bilderback, A., & Rand, C. S. (2011). The development of a motivational interviewing intervention to promote medication adherence among inner-city, African-American adolescents with asthma. *Patient Education and Counseling, 82*(1), 117–122.

Robinson, E. M., Iannotti, R. J., Schneider, S., Nansel, T. R., Haynie, D. L., & Sobel, D. O. (2011). Parenting goals: Predictors of parent involvement in disease management of children with type 1 diabetes. *Journal of Child Health Care, 15*(3), 199–209.

Rosland, A., Heisler, M., & Piette, J. D. (2012). The impact of family behaviors and communication patterns on chronic illness outcomes: A systematic review. *Journal of Behavioral Medicine, 35*(2), 221–239.

Rydall, A. C., Rodin, G. M., Olmsted, M. P., Devenyi, R. G., & Daneman, D. (1997). Disordered eating behavior and microvascular complications in young women with insulin-dependent diabetes mellitus. *New England Journal of Medicine, 336*, 1849–1854.

Satin, W., La Greca, A. M., Zigo, M. A., & Skyler, J. S. (1989). Diabetes in adolescence: Effects of multifamily group intervention and parent simulation of diabetes. *Journal of Pediatric Psychology, 14*(2), 259–275.

Shorer, M., David, R., Schoenberg-Taz, M., Levavi-Lavi, I., Phillip, M., & Meyerovitch, J. (2011). Role of parenting style in achieving metabolic control in adolescents with type 1 diabetes. *Diabetes Care, 34*(8), 1735–1737.

Silverstein, J., Klingensmith, G., Copeland, K., Plotnick, L., Kaufman, F., Laffel, L., . . . Holzmeister, L. A. (2005). Care of children and adolescents with type 1 diabetes: A statement of the American Diabetes Association. *Diabetes Care, 28*(1), 186–212.

Skinner, T. C., Murphy, H., & Huws-Thomas, M. (2005). Diabetes in adolescents. In F. J. Snoek & T. C. Skinner (Eds.), *Psychology in Diabetes Care* (2nd ed., pp. 27–52). West Sussex, UK: Wiley.

Stanger, C., Ryan, S. R., Delhey, L. M., Thrailkill, K., Li, Z., Li, Z., & Budney, A. J. (2013). A multicomponent motivational intervention to improve adherence among adolescents with poorly controlled type 1 diabetes: A pilot study. *Journal of Pediatric Psychology, 38*(6), 629–637.

Stark, L. J. (2013). Introduction to the special issue on adherence in pediatric medical conditions. *Journal of Pediatric Psychology, 38*(6), 589–594.

Streisand, R., Braniecki, S., Tercyak, K. P., & Kazak, A. E. (2001). Childhood illness-related parenting stress: The pediatric inventory for parents. *Journal of Pediatric Psychology, 26*(3), 155–162.

Sullivan-Bolyai, S. (2004). Helping other mothers effectively work at raising young children with type 1 diabetes. *Diabetes Educator, 30*(3), 458–461.

Sundelin, J., Forsander, G. A., & Mattson, S. E. (1996). Family-oriented support at the onset of diabetes mellitus: A comparison of two group conditions during 2 years following diagnosis. *Acta Paediatrica, 85*, 49–55.

Svoren, B. M., Butler, D., Levine, B. S., Anderson, B. J., & Laffel, L. M. (2003). Reducing acute adverse outcomes in youths with type 1 diabetes: A randomized, controlled trial. *Pediatrics, 112*(4), 914–922.

Thompson, R. J., Gil, K. M., Gustafson, K. E., George, L. K., Keith, B. R., Spock, A., & Kinney, T. R. (1994). Stability and change in the psychological adjustment of mothers of children and adolescents with cystic fibrosis and sickle cell disease. *Journal of Pediatric Psychology, 19*(2), 171–188.

Weissberg-Benchell, J., Glasgow, A. M., Tynan, W. D., Wirtz, P., Turek, J., & Ward, J. (1995). Adolescent diabetes management and mismanagement. *Diabetes Care, 18*(1), 77–82.

Wolf, F., Guevara, J. P., Grum, C. M., Clark, N. M., & Cates, C. J. (2008). Educational interventions for asthma in children (Review). *Cochrane Library, 2008*(4), 2–62.

Wu, Y. P., Rohan, J. M., Martin, S., Hommel, K., Greenley, R. N., Loiselle, K., . . . Fredericks, E. M. (2013). Pediatric psychologist use of adherence assessments and interventions. *Journal of Pediatric Psychology, 38*(6), 595–604.

Wysocki, T. (1993). Associations among teen-parent relationships, metabolic control, and adjustment to diabetes in adolescents. *Journal of Pediatric Psychology, 18*(4), 441–452.

Wysocki, T., Buckloh, L., Antal, H., Lochrie, A., & Taylor, A. (2012). Evaluation of a self-report version of the Diabetes Self-Management Profile. *Pediatric Diabetes, 13,* 438–443.

Wysocki, T., Buckloh, L. M., & Greco, P. (2009). The psychological context of diabetes mellitus in youth. In M. C. Roberts & R. G. Steele (Eds.), *Handbook of pediatric psychology* (4th ed., pp. 287–302). New York, NY: Guilford Press.

Wysocki, T., Harris, M., Buckloh, L., Mertlich, D., Lochrie, A., Mauras, N., & White, N. (2007). Randomized trial of behavioral family systems therapy for diabetes: Maintenance of effects on diabetes outcomes in adolescents. *Diabetes Care, 30*(3), 555–560.

Wysocki, T., Harris, M., Buckloh, L., Mertlich, D., Lochrie, A., Taylor, A., . . . White, N. (2006). Effects of behavioral family systems therapy for diabetes on adolescents' family relationships, treatment adherence, and metabolic control. *Journal of Pediatric Psychology, 31,* 928–938.

Wysocki, T., Iannotti, R., Weissberg-Benchell, J., Laffel, L., Hood, K., Anderson, B., & Chen, R. (2008). Diabetes problem solving by youths with type 1 diabetes and their caregivers: Measurement, validation, and longitudinal associations with glycemic control. *Journal of Pediatric Psychology, 33*(8), 875–884.

Wysocki, T., Taylor, A., Hough, B., Linscheid, T., Yeates, K., & Naglieri, J. (1996). Deviation from developmentally appropriate self-care autonomy: Association with diabetes outcomes. *Diabetes Care, 19*(2), 119–125.

CHAPTER 22

Overweight and Obesity

ANNA VANNUCCI AND MARIAN TANOFSKY-KRAFF

OVERVIEW OF THE PROBLEM

Obesity among children and adolescents is a pressing public health concern. Rates of pediatric obesity saw staggering increases over the past several decades. Although the overall prevalence of obesity appears to have stabilized in recent years, it remains high. Estimates from 2009 to 2010 indicate that more than one third of children and adolescents in the United States are overweight (body mass index [BMI] ≥ 85th percentile for age and sex) or obese (BMI ≥ 95th percentile) (Ogden, Carroll, Kit, & Flegal, 2012). Of serious concern, rates of extreme obesity (BMI ≥ 99th percentile) are increasing disproportionately faster than the rates of moderate levels of obesity (BMI between the 95th and 98th percentiles) (Koebnick et al., 2010).

Obesity in youth has been linked to numerous medical conditions. Pediatric obesity is not only associated with cardiovascular disease risk factors such as hypertension, dyslipidemia, carotid artery atherosclerosis, insulin resistance, and type 2 diabetes (Freedman, Dietz, Srinivasan, & Berenson, 2009; Rosenbloom, Joe, Young, & Winter, 1999; Weiss et al., 2004), but it is also predictive of coronary artery disease and early death during adulthood (Baker, Olsen, & Sorensen, 2007; Franks et al., 2010). Orthopedic problems, asthma, and allergies are more common in obese youths as compared to their nonobese peers (Halfon, Larson, & Slusser, 2013). Pediatric obesity also is associated with a poor health-related quality of life (Fallon et al., 2005; Schwimmer, Burwinkle, & Varni, 2003; Tsiros et al., 2009).

In addition to adverse medical sequelae, pediatric obesity has detrimental effects on psychosocial functioning. Overweight and obese children and adolescents are more likely than nonoverweight children to report symptoms of depression, anxiety, disordered eating, and attention-deficit/hyperactivity disorder (Kalarchian & Marcus, 2012). Obese youth frequently have a negative body image and low self-esteem (Puder & Munsch, 2010). These emotional issues may be linked to the social problems reported by this vulnerable population, including stigmatization, social discrimination and exclusion, and teasing and bullying (Gundersen, Mahatmya, Garasky, & Lohman, 2011).

This chapter puts forth the rationale for the early identification of and intervention regarding eating- and weight-related problems in youth and reviews the current evidence-based guidelines for the screening and treatment of pediatric overweight and obesity. This review summarizes the key components of family-based behavioral interventions, a treatment modality that has the greatest evidence base, as well as the role of parental involvement. In addition, we describe common adaptations of family-based behavioral interventions. Novel targeted interventions that address aberrant eating patterns associated with childhood overweight and are currently under development are discussed. Common measures of treatment outcome are reviewed. Finally, clinical cases are reviewed that highlight the heterogeneity of youth presenting with weight problems and the distinct intervention recommendations.

Importance of Early Intervention

Despite the sobering statistics linking pediatric obesity to numerous medical and psychological problems, prospective data indicate that the pediatric obesity-related consequences can be prevented or potentially reversed. One study following individuals for 23 years found that obese children who developed into nonobese adults had a similar cardiovascular profile to adults who were never obese (Juonala et al., 2011). Weight reduction has also been associated with improvements in socio-emotional outcomes among youth (Lloyd-Richardson et al., 2012). However, the reality is that pediatric obesity does not spontaneously resolve with age, as childhood overweight is a robust predictor of obesity during adolescence and young adulthood (Nader et al., 2006). The tendency for obesity to track across the life span starts as early as 6 months of age (Taveras et al., 2009), which underscores the need for early identification and intervention of pediatric weight problems.

Childhood is an ideal point of behavioral intervention for four reasons.

1. Children's eating and activity behaviors may be more amenable to change because these habits are not yet fully ingrained (Wilfley, Vannucci, & White, 2010).
2. Natural increases in height during childhood create a circumstance where even small weight loss reductions, weight maintenance, or excess weight gain prevention over time are sufficient for overweight and obese children to satisfy criteria for normal weight (Goldschmidt, Wilfley, Paluch, Roemmich, & Epstein, 2013).
3. Traditional low-intensity universal prevention programs, psychoeducation, and usual care do not yield significant weight reductions (Haynos & O'Donohue, 2012).
4. Early behavioral intervention has the potential to reduce the high health care costs resulting from obesity-related illness, which are estimated to be over $190 billion annually (O'Grady & Capretta, 2012). Targeted interventions that reduce modifiable risk factors for pediatric obesity may be especially cost effective (Ma & Frick, 2011), as there is substantial heterogeneity in the causes of obesity in youth.

EVIDENCE-BASED APPROACHES

This section reviews the current evidence-based guidelines for the screening and treatment of pediatric overweight and obesity and the key components of family-based behavioral interventions, which have the greatest evidence base for improvements in weight outcomes.

Expert Treatment Guidelines

The U.S. Preventive Services Task Force (Barton, 2010) and the American Academy of Pediatrics (Barlow, 2007) have published expert guidelines for the screening, prevention, and treatment of pediatric obesity. The importance of identifying at-risk youth as early as possible is stressed so that targeted interventions may be explored before more costly, intensive treatments are needed (Barlow, 2007). It is recommended that primary care and child health providers track BMI percentiles (Barton, 2010) and assess children's medical and behavioral risk factors for obesity (Barlow, 2007). The American Academy of Pediatrics guidelines encourage providers to deliver obesity prevention messages to all youth (i.e., guidelines for fruit and vegetable intake and daily activity) and to provide specific behavior change targets for families with overweight children (Barlow, 2007). Finally, providers should establish procedures for making referrals to community resources that can provide the treatment appropriate for children's level of adiposity and risk factors (Barlow, 2007; Barton, 2010).

The U.S. Preventive Services Task Force recommends that overweight and obese children receive specialty treatment of moderate to high intensity that incorporates behavioral counseling targeting diet and physical activity (Barton, 2010). Many pediatric obesity interventions use a "life-style change" approach, which refers to the notion that weight-related behaviors should be modified in a manner that is compatible with daily living so that healthful changes may be more sustainable over time (Wilfley, Vannucci, et al., 2010). According to Task Force recommendations (Barton, 2010), parents are expected to play a pivotal role in treatment. Family-based behavioral weight loss treatment is one example of a lifestyle intervention, and it is currently considered the first line of treatment for pediatric overweight and obesity (Wilfley, Vannucci, et al., 2010). There is also evidence that preventive interventions targeting modifiable risk factors, such as disordered eating patterns, may be effective (Tanofsky-Kraff, 2012).

The use of pharmacotherapy or surgical options is recommended for older children and adolescents with extreme obesity and severe medical comorbidities (Barlow, 2007). Although orlistat, roux-en-Y gastric bypass, and laparoscopic adjustable gastric banding have demonstrated efficacy for the reduction of BMI in severely obese adolescents (de la Cruz-Muñoz et al., 2010; Viner, Hsia, Tomsic, & Wong, 2010; Widhalm et al., 2011), there are high rates of side effects and complications and cogent concerns about strict adherence to dietary regimens and the continued cost of medical management. It must be emphasized that pharmacologic and surgical options should be considered only if good adherence to an intensive lifestyle intervention for 3 to 6 months was ineffective at reducing weight or improving medical comorbidities (Barlow, 2007). The implementation of intensive behavioral lifestyle interventions and targeted interventions for obesity risk factors is still indicated alongside the use of pharmacotherapy and surgical options.

Family-Based Behavioral Intervention

Family-based behavioral interventions are often considered the first line of treatment for pediatric overweight and obesity due to their demonstrated efficacy in reducing adiposity (Wilfley, Vannucci, et al., 2010). The most efficacious family-based interventions incorporate these components: dietary modification, changes in energy expenditure, behavior change techniques, and parental involvement across all levels of change. Treatment is time-limited in scope; weekly sessions are comprised of separate parent and child groups as well as brief individual family meetings, which occur for 4 to 6 months with trained leaders.

Dietary Modification

The general aim of dietary modification strategies is to induce an overall negative energy balance, as obese children consume greater overall calories and have a higher fat intake than nonobese youth (Davis et al., 2007). The most widely studied dietary modification approach to achieve such a caloric deficit is the Traffic Light Diet (Epstein & Squires, 1988), which classifies foods into three categories: red (low in nutrients, high in calories), yellow (high in nutrients and calories), and green (high in nutrients, low in calories). Families are taught that "red" foods signal "stop"; any foods containing 5 grams or more of fat per serving, sugary cereals, and fast food items should be eaten sparingly and limited to no more than 10 to 15 servings per week (Epstein, Paluch, Beecher, & Roemmich, 2008). Decreases in specific "red" foods known to be associated with excess weight gain—sugar-sweetened beverages and unhealthy snacks, such as fried potato chips—are also recommended (Davis et al., 2007). Families learn that "green" foods signal "go," and increased consumption of fruits and vegetables is often targeted (five servings daily are recommended) (Epstein, Paluch, et al., 2008). "Yellow" foods are items that are highly nutritious, contain "good" fats, or have high fiber but are also high in calories, such as fish or raisins. Families are not discouraged from consuming "yellow" foods but learn to eat them in moderation. In addition to modifying the types of foods consumed, limiting portion sizes to age-appropriate standards is also crucial (Orlet Fisher, Rolls, & Birch, 2003). These strategies—when tested independently and in combination—have been shown to reduce energy intake and adiposity in children and adolescents (Wilfley, Vannucci, et al., 2010).

Energy Expenditure Modification

Changes in activity patterns are critical to induce an overall caloric deficit needed for sustained weight management success. Children are encouraged to work toward engaging in approximately 60 minutes of moderate to vigorous physical activity every day, and engagement in muscle- and bone-strengthening exercises, which includes activities involving jumping or climbing, is recommended to prevent a loss of muscle mass during weight loss efforts (U.S. Department of Health and Human Services, 2008). Parents are encouraged to find activities that their children enjoy, are age appropriate, and offer variety. Inactive children should gradually increase their level of exercise and be monitored closely to prevent injuries. Evidence suggests that increasing lifestyle activity (e.g., taking the stairs instead of the elevator) is effective for sustaining weight loss (Davis et al., 2007). Decreasing the time that children and adolescents spend engaging in sedentary behaviors—those that burn a minimal number of calories, such as television watching and computer time—to no more than 2 hours per day also has a potent impact on weight loss efforts (Epstein, Paluch, Gordy, & Dom, 2000; Epstein, Roemmich, et al., 2008). Notably, reductions in sedentary behaviors have been associated with less overall energy intake (Coon, Goldberg, & Rogers, 2001), since many children snack while watching television.

Behavior Change Techniques

Interventions that incorporate behavior change strategies are more effective at achieving weight loss and the prevention of excess weight gain in youth than approaches that offer primarily psychoeducation (Wilfley, Tibbs, et al., 2007). Working with families to set feasible, specific goals is central to being successful in making behavior changes (Wilfley, Kass, & Kolko, 2011). Goals should be determined collaboratively between families and providers, and they should change gradually throughout treatment to accommodate for progress in children's eating and activity behaviors. Parents and children are also taught to engage in regular self-monitoring, a practice that is a strong predictor of long-term weight loss maintenance (Theim et al., 2012). Families learn to pay close attention to their daily dietary and activity behaviors and to record their patterns in a log. Through weekly weight monitoring, children learn the association between their energy balance behaviors and changes in their weight (Wilfley, Vannucci, et al., 2010). It is also helpful to set up a family-based reward system to reinforce behavior changes; families develop a list of acceptable rewards or privileges, and parents provide contingent rewards to their children for achieving behavioral goals (Epstein, Paluch, Kilanowski, & Raynor, 2004). It is strongly recommended that food not be used as a reward, as it can promote overeating in a subset of vulnerable youth. Stimulus control—defined as restructuring the environment to increase desired behaviors—within the home setting also supports healthful behavior change (Epstein et al., 2004).

PARENT INVOLVEMENT IN TREATMENT

The inclusion of parents in lifestyle interventions is critical for successful child weight outcomes. Greater degree of parental involvement in behavioral weight loss treatment leads to greater child

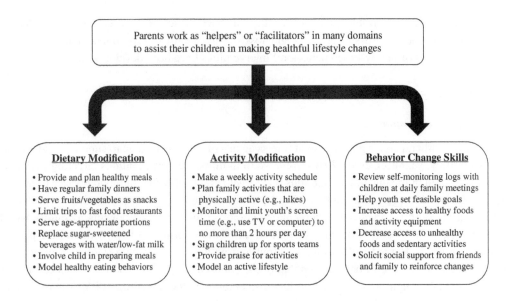

Figure 22.1   Examples of Parent Involvement in Family-Based Behavioral Interventions

weight loss and maintenance outcomes (Heinberg et al., 2010; Wadden, Butryn, & Byrne, 2004). Parents are actively involved at all stages of family-based behavioral lifestyle interventions (see Figure 22.1). Parents play a crucial role as key agents of change in a child's daily life (Wilfley, Vannucci, et al., 2010). Therefore, parents most often are conceptualized in a "facilitator" role. They are taught to encourage their children in making healthy choices and to create "healthy eating and activity zones" by modifying the shared home environment. Parents play a particularly important role in controlling the availability of healthful foods, access to unhealthy foods, and the amount of physical activity and screen time. Teaching parenting skills is also required to enforce healthful changes (Young, Northern, Lister, Drummond, & O'Brien, 2007).

Targeting healthful behavior changes and weight loss in parents is an important component of family-based behavioral interventions. Findings indicate that targeting both the parent and the child directly is associated with more robust child weight loss outcomes than targeting the child alone (Epstein, Wing, Koeske, Andrasik, & Ossip, 1981; Golan & Crow, 2004). Moreover, the degree of parental weight loss is positively correlated with child weight loss (Wrotniak, Epstein, Roemmich, Paluch, & Pak, 2005). During family-based behavioral interventions, parents participate in group sessions focused on teaching them how to use the Traffic Light Diet, increase their activity levels, and implement behavior change techniques for themselves. The same material is covered in separate parent and child groups each week, and the individual family meeting allows for the discussion of how parents and children will implement what they have learned into their daily routines.

ADAPTATIONS AND MODIFICATIONS

Family-based behavioral interventions have demonstrated their efficacy in achieving long-term improvements in weight outcomes. However, the intensive nature of involving the entire family may not be feasible in many real-world settings. Additionally, despite the success of family-based interventions, there is a sizable subset of youth who have difficulty making sustained behavior changes and do not achieve sufficient weight loss during treatment. To address these concerns, several adaptations of family-based behavioral interventions have been developed and tested.

Adaptations of Family-Based Lifestyle Interventions

Parent-Only Interventions

As discussed earlier, parents play a critical role as agents of lifestyle change to support child weight control (Wilfley, Vannucci, et al., 2010). Relative to family-based interventions targeting both parents and children in treatment, interventions that target parents only in childhood obesity treatment have the potential to provide more flexibility for families and be more cost effective for providers (Janicke et al., 2009). Parent-only interventions comprise the same components as family-based interventions, with the only difference being that all of the information is provided to the parent, who applies newly learned skills to the children and within the household (Golan, Kaufman, & Shahar, 2006). Some studies have shown that obese children assigned to parent-only interventions exhibited greater weight loss than family-based interventions (Golan et al., 2006), whereas other studies demonstrated no differences in child weight outcomes when comparing parent-only and family-based interventions (Boutelle, Cafri, & Crow, 2011; Janicke et al., 2008). Parent-only interventions may be most appropriate for use in very young children who developmentally assume only very limited responsibility for their behavior management.

Family-Based Behavioral Social Facilitation Treatment

To overcome the challenge of weight loss and its maintenance presented by genetic vulnerability and the obesogenic environment, family-based interventions have expanded the focus of sustained behavior change beyond the individual and home (Wilfley, Van Buren, et al., 2010). This family-based behavioral social facilitation treatment builds on the lifestyle change skills learned in family-based behavioral interventions by extending treatment duration and practicing new skills across contexts (Wilfley, Van Buren, et al., 2010). Individual barriers to sustained self-regulation (e.g., impulsivity) are identified and addressed with tailored evidence-based strategies (for review, see Vannucci & Wilfley, 2012). Empowering families to build social support systems that promote healthy lifestyle choices is also a critical focus, as is increasing families' awareness of environmental cues for making sustainable lifestyle changes (Wilfley, Van Buren, et al., 2010). These strategies have been shown to be effective in sustaining weight loss maintenance following participation in a traditional family-based behavioral intervention (Wilfley, Stein, et al., 2007; Wilfley, Van Buren, et al., 2010).

Novel Targeted Interventions

Despite the success of family-based behavioral interventions, approximately 50% of youth either do not lose weight during treatment or regain weight soon after treatment cessation (Wilfley, Vannucci, et al., 2010). This is unsurprising, as the causes of obesity are heterogeneous in nature. Numerous risk factors that may predict excessive weight gain are not addressed in family-based interventions. Therefore, there has been a call for targeted interventions for youth who either exhibit a poor treatment response or report modifiable obesity risk factors (Ma & Frick, 2011). Targeting reductions in such aberrant eating patterns linked to obesity—including loss-of-control eating, eating in the absence of hunger, and emotional eating—may be important for achieving weight maintenance and obesity prevention (Shomaker, Tanofsky-Kraff, & Yanovski, 2010). Indeed, obese children and

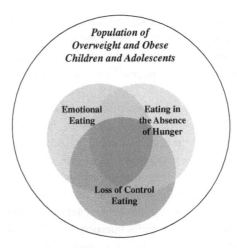

Figure 22.2   Proportion of Overweight and Obese Youth Reporting Aberrant Eating Patterns

adolescents who are engaging in aberrant eating behaviors prior to the start of behavioral weight loss treatment may exhibit poorer weight outcomes in the short term (Wildes et al., 2010). Moreover, a sizable proportion (~30%–45%) of obese youths report these aberrant eating patterns (see Figure 22.2; Shomaker, Tanofsky-Kraff, & Yanovski, 2010). Although many novel targeted interventions are under development, three programs focused on reducing aberrant eating patterns during adolescence, middle childhood, and early childhood are reviewed briefly here.

Interpersonal Psychotherapy for the Prevention of Excess Weight Gain

The phrase "loss-of-control eating" refers to a child's personal sensation of being unable to control what or how much one is eating, regardless of the amount of food actually consumed (Tanofsky-Kraff, Yanovski, & Yanovski, 2011). Pediatric loss-of-control eating predicts excessive body weight and fat gain (Tanofsky-Kraff et al., 2006, 2009), the onset of obesity (Sonneville et al., 2012), components of the metabolic syndrome (Tanofsky-Kraff et al., 2012), and partial or full-syndrome binge eating disorder (Tanofsky-Kraff, Shomaker, et al., 2011). In adult studies evaluating psychological treatments for binge eating disorder, individuals who cease to binge eat tend to maintain their body weight or exhibit modest weight loss during and after treatment (Tanofsky-Kraff et al., 2007). There is also evidence that reducing binge episodes may impact body weight in adolescents (Jones et al., 2008; Tanofsky-Kraff et al., 2010).

The *interpersonal model of loss-of-control eating* posits that social problems, such as being involved in high-conflict relationships or rejected by peers, leads to the experience of negative affect, which precipitates loss-of-control eating episodes (Tanofsky-Kraff et al., 2007). There is cross-sectional support for the interpersonal model in children and adolescents (Elliott et al., 2010). In a pilot study, adolescents at risk for obesity who participated in an interpersonal psychotherapy group had greater reductions in loss-of-control eating and were less likely to experience excess weight gain compared to those randomly assigned to a health education group (Tanofsky-Kraff et al., 2010). These data are comparable to adult findings, which indicate that interpersonal psychotherapy is effective in reducing loss-of-control eating and achieving weight maintenance or modest weight loss (Hilbert et al., 2012; Wilson, Wilfley, Agras, & Bryson, 2010). Interpersonal psychotherapy may be particularly appealing for use in adolescents at high risk for obesity, as overweight teens often report poor social functioning (Strauss & Pollack, 2003) and adolescents frequently use their relationships as vital markers for self-evaluation (Mufson, Dorta, Moreau, & Weissman, 2004). However, other therapies effective for reducing binge eating in adults, such as cognitive behavior therapy (Fairburn, 1995) or dialectic behavior therapy (Telch, Stewart, & Linehan, 2001), are also worth investigating as potential targeted interventions for children and adolescents with loss-of-control eating.

Interpersonal psychotherapy for the prevention of excess weight gain is a time-limited program that targets reductions in loss-of-control eating by improving interpersonal functioning, which reduces negative affect and, in turn, emotional and loss-of-control eating (Tanofsky-Kraff et al., 2007). The intended result is decreased weight gain attributable to loss-of-control eating. Interpersonal psychotherapy for the prevention of excess weight gain was adapted from interpersonal psychotherapy for binge eating disorder in adults (Wilfley, Frank, Welch, Spurrell, & Rounsaville, 1998) and for depression in adolescents (Mufson, Gallagher, Dorta, & Young, 2004). At a pre-group individual meeting, each girl's interpersonal relationships and eating patterns are reviewed. The manifestation of the adolescent's symptoms is then conceptualized into one of four problem areas, and specific, feasible goals are collaboratively developed. Then the program consists of three phases in a group setting that occurs over approximately 12 weeks:

1. Initial (providing the rationale for the approach and developing rapport among group members)
2. Middle (the work phase during which members share personal relationship experiences and role-play new ways of communication)
3. Termination (preparing to say good-bye and for future work on goals)

The seven specific communication skills taught during the initial phase create the foundation for working on adolescents' interpersonal goals during the middle phase. Throughout the intervention, adolescents are continually encouraged to link social interactions and their mood to loss-of-control eating patterns.

Regulation of Cues Intervention

The phrase "eating in the absence of hunger" refers to eating in response to the presence of palatable foods despite an absence of physiological hunger, which is thought to be reflective of poor responsivity to internal satiety cues (Birch & Fisher, 1998). For example, children who eat in the absence of hunger will eat lunch until they say they are completely full but then continue to eat snacks available to them soon afterward. In studies across a wide range of age groups (i.e., from toddlers to adolescents), a cross-sectional relationship between eating in the absence of hunger and BMI or overweight status has been demonstrated consistently in controlled laboratory paradigms (Fisher & Birch, 2002; Shomaker, Tanofsky-Kraff, Zocca, et al., 2010), in ecologically valid naturalistic settings (Hill et al., 2008), and when assessed via child or parent reports (Shomaker et al., 2013; Tanofsky-Kraff et al., 2008).

The *externality theory of obesity* proposes that individuals who eat in the absence of hunger are more responsive to environmental, external cues, such as the smell, taste, and sight of food, and have a poor responsiveness to internal physiological cues signaling hunger and fullness (Schachter, 1971). This heightened external responsivity is thought to result in an "obese eating style" that promotes excess weight gain (Schachter, 1971). *Classical conditioning models* are useful for understanding the development of sensitivity to external food cues (Jansen, 1998), which posit that environmental cues that signal food intake—when paired with actual eating in the absence of hunger—can come to elicit physiological responses experienced as cravings for food over time. In support of these models, a pilot study comparing two treatments targeting either increases in awareness of internal hunger and satiety cues or decreases in cravings and responsivity to external food cues found that both programs demonstrated loss-of-control eating and that only the cue-responsivity program reduced eating in the absence of hunger among overweight children (Boutelle, Cafri, et al., 2011).

The *regulation of cues intervention* is a time-limited program that targets eating in the absence of hunger in overweight children and their parents by teaching families to be more sensitive to internal hunger and fullness cues and to learn to resist eating in the absence of hunger when exposed to external food cues (Boutelle & Tanofsky-Kraff, 2011). This program was adapted directly from the appetite awareness and cue-responsivity programs that were compared in the pilot study just described (Boutelle, Zucker, et al., 2011). Information is covered in separate parent and child groups, and experiential learning occurs in parent/child dyads. During the first five sessions, youth are taught to recognize internal, physiological signals that their bodies are hungry and how to use these signals when deciding what and how much to eat. In the last seven sessions, psychoeducation about overeating, craving, and external food cues is provided and skills for managing "tricky hungers" are taught. Behavioral parenting skills are taught so that intervention messages are reinforced in the home.

Group Parent Training for the Prevention of Obesity

The term *emotional eating* refers to consuming food in an attempt to cope with transient or enduring negative emotions (Heatherton & Baumeister, 1991). A positive relationship between emotional eating and overweight status has been found in youth (Braet & van Strien, 1997; Viana, Sinde, & Saxton, 2008). Pediatric emotional eating has been linked to excess overall energy intake and consumption of high-fat foods (Braet & van Strien, 1997; Vannucci et al., 2012, 2013), which may contribute to excess weight gain.

Affective theories propose that emotional eating results can be conceptualized as an ineffective attempt to regulate (i.e., alleviate, escape) negative emotions (Heatherton & Baumeister, 1991). *Theories of parenting style* suggest that a warm and responsive, yet directive, approach to parenting leads children to develop adaptive means of regulating emotions and behavior, while parenting practices marked by excessive control or harshness are related to a reduced ability of children to self-regulate during stressful times (Baumrind, 1966). In particular, *parental feeding practices* may impact very young children's aberrant eating patterns, as pressuring children to eat (Carper, Fisher, & Birch, 2000) and feeding toddlers in response to negative emotion (Blissett, Haycraft, & Farrow, 2010) are associated with emotional eating. *Social cognitive theory* emphasizes the role of vicarious learning and child modeling of parental behaviors as youth learn self-regulation strategies (Bandura, 1986). Indeed, toddler emotional eating is related to the parent's own reported use of food for emotion regulation (Blissett et al., 2010). Parental stress may serve as a particularly important treatment target for reducing emotional eating in very young children, as perceived stress has a negative impact on parenting strategies and modeling of appropriate emotion and behavioral regulation (Jones & Prinz, 2005).

Group parent training for the prevention of obesity is an eight-session program that is administered solely to parents or guardians of overweight preschool-age children in three stages (Elliott, Zucker, & Tanofsky-Kraff, 2012). This program was adapted from a similar group parent training program (Zucker, 2006) and a mother–child program design to enhance healthful behaviors in overweight preschool-age children (Østbye et al., 2012). The first stage provides parents with parenting tools to decrease parental stress, including a general approach to parenting and strategies for parent and child emotion regulation, behavior modification strategies, and mindfulness. The second stage focuses on improving household structure through modification of mealtimes and bedtimes. Stage 3 emphasizes the importance of parental role modeling of healthy lifestyle behaviors and provides skills to help parents teach their children effective ways to identify and respond appropriately to hunger versus emotional cues. At each session, parents identify a specific goal for the upcoming week and use problem-solving strategies to minimize potential barriers to implementation. Preliminary findings are promising (Elliott et al., 2012; Zucker, 2006).

MEASURING TREATMENT EFFECTS

Changes in weight outcomes are used to measure the effects of pediatric obesity interventions. Several metrics have been used to measure weight outcomes, including BMI, BMI z-score, and percentage overweight. Research shows that even modest weight loss in obese children and adolescents is associated with reductions in cardiovascular disease risk factors, which are important secondary health outcomes that can be assessed.

BMI is calculated from a person's weight (kg) and height (m) using a standard formula (kg/m^2). Examining changes in solely BMI over time has disadvantages in pediatric samples because BMI does not take into account youth's normative changes in BMI over time, which differs by age and sex. Estimates are available that indicate the amount of weight-for-height change required for overweight and obese boys and girls to achieve nonoverweight status over a 1- or 2-year span (Goldschmidt, et al., 2013). One method used to overcome the limitations of using BMI as an outcome is to compare children's *actual versus expected BMI change* (Tanofsky-Kraff et al., 2010), which can be calculated based on the Centers for Disease Control (CDC) pediatric BMI growth chart data (Kuczmarski et al., 2002).

BMI z-scores are adjusted for age and sex and determined from a person's height and weight using the CDC pediatric BMI growth charts (Kuczmarski et al., 2002). BMI z-scores are most useful for classifying children at a single point in time rather than for describing changes over time, as within-subject changes in BMI z-scores vary depending on youth's degree of adiposity (Berkey & Colditz, 2007; Cole, Faith, Pietrobelli, & Heo, 2005). Among obese youth participating in lifestyle interventions, research has shown that a BMI z-score reduction of 0.5 or greater was associated with improvements in all components of metabolic syndrome, including waist circumference, triglycerides, high-density lipoprotein cholesterol, blood pressure, and fasting glucose (Reinehr & Andler, 2004; Reinehr, de Sousa, & Wabitsch, 2006; Reinehr, Kleber, & Toschke, 2009).

Percentage overweight is most often calculated as the percentage over a child's ideal BMI for sex and age, as indicated by the CDC BMI growth charts (Kuczmarski et al., 2002). Percentage overweight has also been calculated as children's percentage over a sample's median BMI in randomized controlled trials (Epstein, Valoski, Wing, & McCurley, 1990, 1994; Quattrin et al., 2012). Change in percentage overweight often has been used to report children's relative body weight change throughout the course of a pediatric obesity intervention (McGovern et al., 2008; Wilfley, Tibbs, et al., 2007). Estimates from a meta-analysis suggest that lifestyle interventions resulted in an average decrease in percentage overweight of 8.9%, as compared to education-only controls, which resulted in an average increase in percentage overweight of 2.7% at follow-up (Wilfley, Tibbs, et al., 2007).

CLINICAL CASES

Here we review several clinical cases meant to illustrate differences in the conceptualization of and treatment goals for targeting eating- and weight-issues in youth spanning a broad age range and with different factors contributing their weight issues. Please note that identifying information has been altered to protect confidentiality.

"Uncomplicated" Obesity

Sean is a 12-year-old obese boy. Both of his parents are obese, as are his two brothers. His family often eats very large, rich meals, and family time is often spent around the dinner table. After school, Sean does his homework and then plays video games with friends and watches television while indulging in his favorite snacks, such as potato chips. He rarely needs to move from the living room couch until dinnertime. He continues to eat and enjoy large, heavy meals and, despite a desire to lose weight, often goes back for second helpings. Sean's percentage overweight has slowly increased since he was a toddler. Sean and his family are most appropriate for enrollment in a family-based behavioral intervention. Following their initial meeting, it was determined that Sean's initial goals should include logging his eating and activity behaviors daily, reducing afternoon snacking behaviors, and replacing some of his time spent playing video games with an outdoor activity with friends.

Loss-of-Control Eating Promoting Excess Weight Gain

Becky is a 16-year-old overweight girl with recurrent loss-of-control eating and concerns about her weight. Becky lives at home with her 14-year-old brother and parents. Becky experienced her first loss-of-control eating episode at 11 years old and started gaining a lot of weight. Notably, Becky's loss-of-control eating began shortly after her mother changed jobs, leading Becky to take on more caregiving responsibilities for her brother, who was difficult to manage. Becky's mom often blamed Becky when her brother's chores or homework were not completed after she returned home from work. Becky's stress of anticipating her mother's return from work was a common precipitant for her loss-of-control eating episodes. Shortly after Becky began interpersonal psychotherapy for the prevention of excess weight gain, the group leaders conceptualized Becky as having a "role dispute" since it appeared that Becky and her mother had difficulty negotiating their relationship and had different expectations about the roles they should play in the relationship. The leaders and Becky agreed on these goals: (1) learn strategies to express her feelings about her stress about caring for her brother more directly to her mother; and (2) begin sharing feelings more to reduce her feelings of being overwhelmed and turning to food for comfort.

Eating in the Absence of Hunger Leading to Overconsumption

Dillon was an overweight 8-year-old boy who frequently ate in the absence of hunger. Dillon and his father found it very difficult to resist eating snack foods that were around the house. Dillon would often come home from school and immediately ask about having a snack and then about dinner, saying he was "always" hungry. Further, Dillon often asks for "just one more" bite or serving while eating meals and snacks. Outside the home, Dillon and his father reported craving "comfort foods" after passing fast food restaurants while driving through town, which they would often indulge in. Even though Dillon wants to lose weight, he becomes frustrated because he has so much difficulty resisting his cravings. As such, Dillon and his father decide to enroll in the regulation of cues intervention, where they both set goals of improving their awareness of and response to internal hunger and fullness cues and resisting cravings in response to external cues. In addition, Dillon's father also sought to improve his parenting skills to create a home environment with fewer food cues.

Emotional Eating and Parenting Stress Exacerbating Obesity Risk

Katrina is a 4-year-old girl who is at high risk for obesity by virtue of being at the 87th BMI percentile. Katrina lives with her mother and three siblings (ages 1, 3, and 6 years), each of whom is at risk for overweight. Katrina's mother feels overwhelmed as she attempts to work full time and care for her children as a single parent. When she gets home from work, she has little patience for misbehavior and so she yells at her children when they get "out of line." Recently, Katrina has been bursting into severe temper tantrums nearly every day at preschool and at home. Katrina's mother has learned that the only thing that seems to calm Katrina down is giving her cookies. Katrina's mother also finds herself frequently emotionally eating in an attempt to reduce her anxiety and stress momentarily. Upon joining the group parent training program targeting parental stress, Katrina's mother had the initial goals of improving the way that she deals with stress in her life, using consistent yet warm parenting approaches, and decreasing emotional eating in herself and her children.

CONCLUSIONS AND FUTURE DIRECTIONS

The reduction of pediatric obesity is paramount to improving health outcomes in the United States. Early intervention and targeted prevention of pediatric obesity have the potential to be the most cost-efficient approaches (Ma & Frick, 2011), which is important for the feasible implementation of and insurance coverage for such programs. Effective treatments for pediatric obesity, such as family-based behavioral interventions, have been identified, but more work is needed to develop programs that focus on reducing obesity risk factors since the causes of obesity are heterogeneous. Several promising novel targeted interventions focusing on reductions in aberrant eating patterns that promote overeating and excess weight gain are currently under development. Programs targeting obesity risk factors other than aberrant eating patterns also require evaluation. Improving access to evidence-based care is a crucial next step, and this may be accomplished by sharing knowledge and the responsibility for the health of children across sectors.

To further accelerate obesity prevention and support ongoing intervention efforts taking place on the individual level, the Institute of Medicine (2012) called for systematic changes to physical activity environments, food and beverage availability, media messages about lifestyle behaviors and marketing toward children, health care and work environments, and schools. If implemented, these changes likely would enhance intervention outcomes and reduce the likelihood of weight regain following treatment cessation. Schools may be especially compelling contexts to create healthy eating and activity zones, since school is where children spend most of their time and consume a significant proportion of their daily calories. Moving forward, establishing communication and cooperative networks among families, health care professionals, schools, community organizations, and policy makers likely would facilitate the dissemination of cohesive health messages and the sustained implementation of best evidence-based practices.

REFERENCES

Baker, J. L., Olsen, L. W., & Sorensen, T. I. A. (2007). Childhood body-mass index and the risk of coronary heart disease in adulthood. *New England Journal of Medicine, 257,* 2329–2337.

Bandura, A. (1986). *Social foundations of thought and action: A social cognitive theory.* Englewood Cliffs, NJ: Prentice-Hall.

Barlow, S. E. (2007). Expert committee recommendations regarding the prevention, assessment, and treatment of child and adolescent overweight and obesity: Summary report. *Pediatrics, 120*(Suppl. 4), S164–S192.

Barton, M. (2010). Screening for obesity in children and adolescents: US Preventive Services Task Force recommendation statement. *Pediatrics, 125*(2), 361–367.

Baumrind, D. (1966). Effects of authoritative parental control on child behavior. *Child Development, 37*(4), 887–907.

Berkey, C. S., & Colditz, G. A. (2007). Adiposity in adolescents: Change in actual BMI works better than change in BMI z score for longitudinal studies. *Annals of Epidemiology, 17*(1), 44–50.

Birch, L. L., & Fisher, J. O. (1998). Development of eating behaviors among children and adolescents. *Pediatrics, 101,* 539–549.

Blissett, J., Haycraft, E., & Farrow, C. (2010). Inducing preschool children's emotional eating: Relations with parental feeding practices. *American Journal of Clinical Nutrition, 92*(2), 359–365.

Boutelle, K. N., Cafri, G., & Crow, S. (2011). Parent-only treatment for childhood obesity: A randomized controlled trial. *Obesity, 19*(3), 574–580.

Boutelle, K. N., & Tanofsky-Kraff, M. (2011). Treatments targeting aberrant eating patterns in overweight youth. In D. Le Grange & J. Lock (Eds.), *Eating disorders in children and adolescents: A clinical handbook* (pp. 381–401). New York, NY: Guilford Press.

Boutelle, K. N., Zucker, N. L., Peterson, C. B., Rydell, S. A., Cafri, G., & Harnack, L. (2011). Two novel treatments to reduce overeating in overweight children: A randomized controlled trial. *Journal of Consulting and Clinical Psychology, 79*(6), 759–771.

Braet, C., & van Strien, T. (1997). Assessment of emotional, externally induced and restrained eating behaviour in nine- to twelve-year-old obese and non-obese children. *Behavior Research and Therapy, 35*(9), 863–873.

Carper, J. L., Fisher, J. O., & Birch, L. L. (2000). Young girls' emerging dietary restraint. *Appetite, 35*(2), 121–129.

Cole, T. J., Faith, M., Pietrobelli, A., & Heo, M. (2005). What is the best measure of adiposity change in growing children: BMI, BMI %, BMI z-score or BMI percentile? *European Journal of Clinical Nutrition, 59*(3), 419–425.

Coon, K. A., Goldberg, J. P., & Rogers, B. L. (2001). Relationships between use of television during meals and children's food consumption patterns. *Pediatrics, 140*(3), 334–339.

Davis, M. M., Gance-Cleveland, B., Hassink, S., Johnson, R., Paradis, G., & Resnicow, K. (2007). Recommendations for prevention of childhood obesity. *Pediatrics, 120*(Suppl. 4), S229–S252.

de la Cruz-Muñoz, N., Messiah, S. E., Cabrera, J. C., Torres, C., Cuesta, M., Lopez-Mitnik, G., & Arheart, K. L. (2010). Four-year weight outcomes of laparoscopic gastric bypass surgery and adjustable gastric banding among multiethnic adolescents. *Surgery for Obesity and Related Diseases, 6*(5), 542–547.

Elliott, C., Zucker, N., & Tanofsky-Kraff, M. (2012). *Group parenting training for the prevention of obesity.* [Therapy manual.] Bethesda, MD: Uniformed Services University of the Health Sciences.

Elliott, C. A., Tanofsky-Kraff, M., Shomaker, L. B., Columbo, K. M., Wolkoff, L. E., Ranzenhofer, L. M., & Yanovski, J. A. (2010). An examination of the interpersonal model of loss-of-control eating in children and adolescents. *Behavior Research and Therapy, 48*(5), 424–428.

Epstein, L. H., Paluch, R. A., Beecher, M. D., & Roemmich, J. N. (2008). Increasing healthy eating vs. reducing high energy-dense foods to treat pediatric obesity. *Obesity, 16*(2), 318–326.

Epstein, L. H., Paluch, R. A., Gordy, C. C., & Dom, J. (2000). Decreasing sedentary behaviors in treating pediatric obesity. *Archives of Pediatric and Adolescent Medicine, 154,* 220–226.

Epstein, L. H., Paluch, R. A., Kilanowski, C. K., & Raynor, H. A. (2004). The effect of reinforcement or stimulus control to reduce sedentary behaviors in the treatment of pediatric obesity. *Health Psychology, 23,* 371–380.

Epstein, L. H., Roemmich, J. N., Robinson, J. L., Paluch, R. A., Winiewicz, D. D., Fuerch, J. H., & Robinson, T. N. (2008). A randomized trial of the effects of reducing television viewing and computer use on body mass index in young children. *Archives of Pediatric and Adolescent Medicine, 162*(3), 239–245.

Epstein, L. H., & Squires, S. (1988). *The stoplight diet for children.* Boston, MA: Little, Brown.

Epstein, L. H., Valoski, A., Wing, R. R., & McCurley, J. (1990). Ten-year follow-up of behavioral, family-based treatment for obese children. *Journal of the American Medical Association, 264*(19), 2519–2523.

Epstein, L. H., Valoski, A., Wing, R. R., & McCurley, J. (1994). Ten-year outcomes of behavioral family-based treatment for childhood obesity. *Health Psychology, 13*(5), 373–383.

Epstein, L. H., Wing, R. R., Koeske, R., Andrasik, F., & Ossip, D. J. (1981). Child and parent weight loss in family-based behavior modificatin programs. *Journal of Consulting and Clinical Psychology, 49,* 672–685.

Fairburn, C. G. (1995). *Overcoming binge eating.* New York, NY: Guilford Press.

Fallon, E. M., Tanofsky-Kraff, M., Norman, A. C., McDuffie, J. R., Taylor, E. D., Cohen, M. L., . . . Yanovski, J. A. (2005). Health-related quality of life in overweight and nonoverweight black and white adolescents. *Journal of Pediatrics, 147*(4), 443–450.

Fisher, J. O., & Birch, L. L. (2002). Eating in the absence of hunger and overweight in girls from 5 to 7 years of age. *American Journal of Clinical Nutrition, 76,* 226–231.

Franks, P. W., Hanson, R. L., Knowler, W. C., Sievers, M. L., Bennett, P. H., & Looker, H. C. (2010). Childhood obesity, other cardiovascular risk factors, and premature death. *New England Journal of Medicine, 362*(6), 485–493.

Freedman, D. S., Dietz, W. H., Srinivasan, S. R., & Berenson, G. S. (2009). Risk factors and adult body mass index among overweight children: The Bogalusa Heart Study. *Pediatrics, 123*(3), 750–757.

Golan, M., & Crow, S. (2004). Targeting parents exclusively in the treatment of childhood obesity: Long-term results. *Obesity Reviews, 12*(2), 357–361.

Golan, M., Kaufman, V., & Shahar, D. R. (2006). Childhood obesity treatment: Targeting parents exclusively v. parents and children. *British Journal of Nutrition, 95*(5), 1008–1015.

Goldschmidt, A. B., Wilfley, D. E., Paluch, R. A., Roemmich, J. N., & Epstein, L. H. (2013). Indicated prevention of adult obesity: How much weight change is necessary for normalization of weight status in children? *Journal of the American Medical Association for Pediatrics, 167*(1), 21–26.

Gundersen, C., Mahatmya, D., Garasky, S., & Lohman, B. (2011). Linking psychosocial stressors and childhood obesity. *Obesity Research, 12*(5), e54–e63.

Halfon, N., Larson, K., & Slusser, W. (2013). Associations between obesity and comorbid mental health, developmental, and physical health conditions in a nationally representative sample of US children aged 10 to 17. *Academy of Pediatrics, 13*(1), 6–13.

Haynos, A. F., & O'Donohue, W. T. (2012). Universal childhood and adolescent obesity prevention programs: Review and critical analysis. *Clinical Psychology Review, 32*(5), 383–399.

Heatherton, T. F., & Baumeister, R. F. (1991). Binge eating as escape from self-awareness. *Psychological Bulletin, 110,* 86–108.

Heinberg, L. J., Kutchman, E. M., Berger, N. A., Lawhun, S. A., Cuttler, L., Seabrook, R. C., & Horwitz, S. M. (2010). Parent involvement is associated with early success in obesity treatment. *Clinical Pediatrics, 49*(5), 457–465.

Hilbert, A., Bishop, M. E., Stein, R. I., Tanofsky-Kraff, M., Swenson, A. K., Welch, R. R., & Wilfley, D. E. (2012). Long-term efficacy of psychological treatments for binge eating disorder. *British Journal of Psychiatry, 2000*(3), 232–237.

Hill, C., Llewellyn, C. H., Saxton, J., Webber, L., Semmler, C., Carnell, S., . . . Wardle, J. (2008). Adiposity and "eating in the absence of hunger" in children. *International Journal of Obesity, 32*(10), 1499–1505.

Institute of Medicine. (2012). *Accelerating progress in obesity prevention: Solving the weight of the nation.* Washington, DC: Institute of Medicine of the National Academies.

Janicke, D. M., Sallinen, B. J., Perri, M. G., Lutes, L. D., Huerta, M., Silverstein, J. H., & Brumback, B. (2008). Comparison of parent-only vs. family-based interventions for overweight children in underserved rural settings: Outcomes from project STORY. *Archives of Pediatric and Adolescent Medicine, 162*(12), 1119–1925.

Janicke, D. M., Sallinen, B. J., Perri, M. G., Lutes, L. D., Silverstein, J. H., & Brumback, B. (2009). Comparison of program costs for parent-only and family-based interventions for pediatric obesity in medically underserved rural settings. *Journal of Rural Health, 25*(3), 326–330.

Jansen, A. (1998). A learning model of binge eating: Cue reactivity and cue exposure. *Behavior Research and Therapy, 36*(3), 257–272.

Jones, M., Luce, K. H., Osborne, M. I., Taylor, K., Cunning, D., Celio Doyle, A., . . . Taylor, C. B. (2008). Randomized controlled trial of an Internet-facilitated intervention for reducing binge eating and overweight in adolescents. *Pediatrics, 123*(3), 453–462.

Jones, T. L., & Prinz, R. J. (2005). Potential roles of parental self-efficacy in parent and child adjustment: A review. *Clinical Psychology Review, 25*(3), 341–363.

Juonala, M., Magnussen, C. G., Berenson, G. S., Venn, A., Burns, T. L., Sabin, M. A., . . . Raitakari, O. T. (2011). Childhood adiposity, adult adiposity, and cardiovascular risk factors. *New England Journal of Medicine, 365*(20), 1876–1885.

Kalarchian, M. A., & Marcus, M. D. (2012). Psychiatric comorbidity of childhood obesity. *International Review of Psychiatry, 24*(3), 241–246.

Koebnick, C., Smith, N., Coleman, K. J., Getahun, D., Reynolds, K., Quinn, V. P., . . . Jacobsen, S. J. (2010). Prevalence of extreme obesity in a multiethnic cohort of children and adolescents. *Journal of Pediatrics, 157*(1), 1–6.

Kuczmarski, R. J., Ogden, C. L., Guo, S. S., Grummer-Strawn, L. M., Flegal, K. M., Mei, Z., . . . Johnson, C. L. (2002). 2000 CDC Growth Charts for the United States: Methods and development. *Vital Health Statistics, 11*(246), 1–190.

Lloyd-Richardson, E. E., Jelalian, E., Sato, A. F., Hart, C. N., Mehlenbeck, R., & Wing, R. R. (2012). Two-year follow-up of an adolescent behavioral weight control intervention. *Pediatrics, 130*(2), e281–288.

Ma, S., & Frick, K. D. (2011). A simulation of affordability and effectiveness of childhood obesity interventions. *Academy of Pediatrics, 11*(4), 342–350.

McGovern, L., Johnson, J. N., Paulo, R., Hettinger, A., Singhal, V., Kamath, C., . . . Montori, V. M. (2008). Clinical review: Treatment of pediatric obesity: A systematic review and meta-analysis of randomized trials. *Journal of Clinical Endocrinology and Metabolism, 93*(12), 4600–4605.

Mufson, L., Dorta, K. P., Moreau, D., & Weissman, M. M. (2004). *Interpersonal Psychotherapy for depressed adolescents* (2nd ed.). New York, NY: Guilford Press.

Mufson, L., Gallagher, T., Dorta, K. P., & Young, J. F. (2004). A group adaptation of interpersonal psychotherapy for depressed adolescents. *American Journal of Psychotherapies, 58*(2), 220–237.

Nader, P. R., O'Brien, M., Houts, R., Bradley, R., Belsky, J., Crosnoe, R., . . . Susman, E. J. (2006). Identifying risk for obesity in early childhood. *Pediatrics, 118*(3), 594–601.

Ogden, C. L., Carroll, M. D., Kit, B. K., & Flegal, K. M. (2012). Prevalence of obesity and trends in body mass index among US children and adolescents, 1999–2010. *Journal of the American Medical Association, 307*(5), 483–490.

O'Grady, M. J., & Capretta, J. C. (2012, March). *Assessing the economics of obesity and obesity interventions.* Washington, DC: Campaign to End Obesity.

Orlet Fisher, J., Rolls, B. J., & Birch, L. L. (2003). Children's bite size and intake of an entree are greater with larger portions than with age-appropriate or self-selected portions. *American Journal of Clinical Nutrition, 77,* 1164–1170.

Østbye, T., Krause, K. M., Stroo, M., Lovelady, C. A., Evenson, K. R., Peterson, B. L., . . . Zucker, N. L. (2012). Parent-focused change to prevent obesity in preschoolers: Results from the KAN-DO study. *Preventive Medicine, 55*(3), 188–195.

Puder, J. J., & Munsch, S. (2010). Psychological correlates of childhood obesity. *International Journal of Obesity, 34*(Suppl. 2), S37–S43.

Quattrin, T., Roemmich, J. N., Paluch, R. A., Yu, J., Epstein, L. H., & Ecker, M. A. (2012). Efficacy of family-based weight control program for preschool children in primary care. *Pediatrics, 130*(4), 660–666.

Reinehr, T., & Andler, W. (2004). Changes in the atherogenic risk factor profile according to degree of weight loss. *Archives of Diseases in Childhood, 89*(5), 419–422.

Reinehr, T., de Sousa, G., & Wabitsch, M. (2006). Changes of cardiovascular risk factors in obese children effects of inpatient and outpatient interventions. *Journal of Pediatric Gastroenterology and Nutrition, 43*(4), 506–511.

Reinehr, T., Kleber, M., & Toschke, A. M. (2009). Lifestyle intervention in obese children is associated with a decrease of the metabolic syndrome prevalence. *Atherosclerosis, 207*(1), 174–180.

Rosenbloom, A. L., Joe, J. R., Young, R. S., & Winter, N. E. (1999). Emerging epidemic of type 2 diabetes in youth. *Diabetes Care, 22,* 345–354.

Schachter, S. (1971). Some extraordinary facts about obese humans and rats. *American Psychologist, 26*(2), 129–144.

Schwimmer, J. B., Burwinkle, T. M., & Varni, J. W. (2003). Health-related quality of life of severely obese children and adolescents. *Journal of the American Medical Association, 289*(14), 813–819.

Shomaker, L. B., Tanofsky-Kraff, M., Mooreville, M., Reina, S. A., Courville, A. C., Field, A. E., . . . Yanovski, J. A. (2013). Relationships of adolescent- and parent-reported eating in the absence of hunger with observed eating in the absence of hunger in the laboratory. *International Journal of Obesity, 2*(16), 1243–1250.

Shomaker, L. B., Tanofsky-Kraff, M., & Yanovski, J. A. (2010). Disinhibited eating and body weight in youth. In V. R. Preedy, R. R. Watson, & C. R. Martin (Eds.), *International handbook of behavior, diet, and nutrition* (pp. 2183–2200). New York: Springer.

Shomaker, L. B., Tanofsky-Kraff, M., Zocca, J. M., Courville, A., Kozlosky, M., Columbo, K. M., . . . Yanovski, J. A. (2010). Eating in the absence of hunger in adolescents: Intake after a large-array meal compared with that after a standardized meal. *American Journal of Clinical Nutrition, 92*(4), 697–703.

Sonneville, K. R., Horton, N. J., Micali, N., Crosby, R. D., Swanson, S. A., Solmi, F., & Field, A. E. (2012). Longitudinal associations between binge eating and overeating and adverse outcomes among adolescents and young adults: Does loss of control matter? *Archives of Pediatric and Adolescent Medicine, 10,* 1–7.

Strauss, R. S., & Pollack, H. A. (2003). Social marginalization of overweight children. *Archives of Pediatric and Adolescent Medicine, 157*(8), 746–752.

Tanofsky-Kraff, M. (2012). Psychosocial preventive interventions for obesity and eating disorders in youths. *International Review of Psychiatry, 24*(3), 262–270.

Tanofsky-Kraff, M., Cohen, M. L., Yanovski, S. Z., Cox, C., Theim, K. R., Keil, M., . . . Yanovski, J. A. (2006). A prospective study of psychological predictors of body fat gain among children at high risk for adult obesity. *Pediatrics, 117,* 1203–1209.

Tanofsky-Kraff, M., Ranzenhofer, L. M., Yanovski, S. Z., Schvey, N. A., Faith, M., Gustafson, J., & Yanovski, J. A. (2008). Psychometric properties of a new questionnaire to assess eating in the absence of hunger in children and adolescents. *Appetite, 51*(1), 148–155.

Tanofsky-Kraff, M., Shomaker, L. B., Olsen, C., Roza, C. A., Wolkoff, L. E., Columbo, K. M., . . . Yanovski, J. A. (2011). A prospective study of pediatric loss-of-control eating and psychological outcomes. *Journal of Abnormal Psychology, 120*(1), 108–118. doi: 10.1037/a0021406

Tanofsky-Kraff, M., Shomaker, L. B., Stern, E. A., Miller, R., Sebring, N. G., Dellavalle, D., . . . Yanovski, J. A. (2012). Children's binge eating and development of metabolic syndrome. *International Journal of Obesity, 36*(7), 956–962.

Tanofsky-Kraff, M., Wilfley, D. E., Young, J. F., Mufson, L., Yanovski, S. Z., Glasofer, D. R., & Salaita, C. (2007). Preventing excessive weight gain in adolescents: Interpersonal psychotherapy for binge eating. *Obesity, 15*(6), 1345–1355.

Tanofsky-Kraff, M., Wilfley, D. E., Young, J. F., Mufson, L., Yanovski, S. Z., Glasofer, D. R., . . . Schvey, N. A. (2010). A pilot study of interpersonal psychotherapy for preventing excess weight gain in adolescent girls at-risk for obesity. *International Journal of Eating Disorders, 43*(8), 701–706.

Tanofsky-Kraff, M., Yanovski, S. Z., Schvey, N. A., Olsen, C. H., Gustafson, J., & Yanovski, J. A. (2009). A prospective study of loss-of-control eating for body weight gain in children at high risk for adult obesity. *International Journal of Eating Disorders, 42*(1), 26–30.

Tanofsky-Kraff, M., Yanovski, S. Z., & Yanovski, J. A. (2011). Loss of control over eating in children and adolescents. In R. H. Striegel-Moore, S. A. Wonderlich, B. T. Walsh, & J. E. Mitchell (Eds.), *Developing an evidence-based classification of eating disorders: Scientific findings for DSM-5* (pp. 221–236). Washington, DC: American Psychiatric Association Press.

Taveras, E. M., Rifas-Shiman, S. L., Belfort, M. B., Kleinman, K. P., Oken, E., & Gillman, M. W. (2009). Weight status in the first 6 months of life and obesity at 3 years of age. *Pediatrics, 123*(4), 1177–1183.

Telch, C. F., Stewart, W. S., & Linehan, M. M. (2001). Dialectical behavior therapy for binge eating disorder. *Journal of Consulting and Clinical Psychology, 69*(6), 1061–1065.

Theim, K. R., Sinton, M. M., Goldschmidt, A. B., Van Buren, D. J., Doyle, A. C., Saelens, B. E., . . . Wilfley, D. E. (2012). Adherence to behavioral targets and treatment attendance during a pediatric weight control trial. *Obesity, 2*(12), 294–297.

Tsiros, M. D., Olds, T., Buckley, J. D., Grimshaw, P., Brennan, L., Walkley, J., . . . Coates, A. M. (2009). Health-related quality of life in obese children and adolescents. *International Journal of Obesity, 33*(4), 387–400.

U.S. Department of Health and Human Services. (2008). *Physical activity guidelines Advisory Committee Report.* Washington, DC: Author.

Vannucci, A., Tanofsky-Kraff, M., Crosby, R. D., Ranzenhofer, L. M., Shomaker, L. B., Field, S. E., . . . Yanovski, J. A. (2013). Latent profile analysis to determine the typology of disinhibited eating behaviors in children and adolescents. *Journal of Consulting and Clinical Psychology, 8*(13), 494–507.

Vannucci, A., Tanofsky-Kraff, M., Shomaker, L. B., Ranzenhofer, L. M., Matheson, B. E., Cassidy, O. L., . . . Yanovski, J. A. (2012). Construct validity of the Emotional Eating Scale adapted for children and adolescents. *International Journal of Obesity, 36*(7), 938–943.

Vannucci, A., & Wilfley, D. E. (2012). Behavioral interventions and cardiovascular risk in obese youth: Current findings and future directions. *Current Cardiovascular Risk Reports, 6*(6), 567–578.

Viana, V., Sinde, S., & Saxton, J. C. (2008). Children's Eating Behaviour Questionnaire: Associations with BMI in Portuguese children. *British Journal of Nutrition, 100*(2), 445–450.

Viner, R. M., Hsia, Y., Tomsic, T., & Wong, I. C. (2010). Efficacy and safety of anti-obesity drugs in children and adolescents: Systematic review and meta-analysis. *Obesity Reviews, 11*(8), 593–602.

Wadden, T. A., Butryn, M., & Byrne, K. (2004). Efficacy of lifestyle modifcation for long-term weight control. *Obesity Research, 12,* 151–162S.

Weiss, R., Dziura, J., Burgert, T. S., Tamborlane, W. V., Taksali, S. E., Yeckel, C. W., . . . Caprio, S. (2004). Obesity and the metabolic syndrome in children and adolescents. *New England Journal of Medicine, 350,* 2362–2374.

Widhalm, K., Fritsch, M., Widhalm, H., Silberhumer, G., Dietrich, S., Helk, O., & Prager, G. (2011). Bariatric surgery in morbidly obese adolescents: Long-term follow-up. *International Journal of Pediatric Obesity, 6*(Suppl. 1), S65–S69.

Wildes, J. E., Marcus, M. D., Kalarchian, M. A., Levine, M. D., Houck, P. R., & Cheng, Y. (2010). Self-reported binge eating in severe pediatric obesity: Impact on weight change in a randomized controlled trial of family-based treatment. *International Journal of Obesity, 34*(7), 1143–1148.

Wilfley, D. E., Frank, M. A., Welch, R. R., Spurrell, E., & Rounsaville, B. J. (1998). Adapting interpersonal psychotherapy to a group format (IPT-G) for binge eating disorder: Toward a model for adapting empirically supported treatments. *Psychotherapy Research, 8,* 379–391.

Wilfley, D. E., Kass, A. E., & Kolko, R. P. (2011). Counseling and behavior change in pediatric obesity. *Pediatric Clinics of North America, 58,* 1403–1424.

Wilfley, D. E., Stein, R. I., Saelens, B. E., Mockus, D. S., Matt, G. E., Hayden-Wade, H. A., . . . Epstein, L. H. (2007). Efficacy of maintenance treatment approaches for childhood overweight: A randomized controlled trial. *Journal of the American Medical Association, 298*(14), 1661–1673.

Wilfley, D. E., Tibbs, T. L., Van Buren, D. J., Reach, K. P., Walker, M. S., & Epstein, L. H. (2007). Lifestyle interventions in the treatment of childhood overweight: A meta-analytic review of randomized controlled trials. *Health Psychology, 26*(5), 521–532.

Wilfley, D. E., Van Buren, D. J., Theim, K. R., Stein, R. I., Saelens, B. E., Ezzet, F., . . . Epstein, L. H. (2010). The use of biosimulation in the design of a novel multilevel weight loss maintenance program for overweight children. *Obesity, 18*(Suppl. 1), S91–S98.

Wilfley, D. E., Vannucci, A., & White, E. K. (2010). Family-based behavioral interventions. In M. Freemark (Ed.), *Pediatric obesity: Etiology, pathogenesis, and treatment* (pp. 281–302). New York, NY: Humana Press.

Wilson, G. T., Wilfley, D. E., Agras, W. S., & Bryson, S. W. (2010). Psychological treatments of binge eating disorder. *Archives of General Psychiatry, 67*(1), 94–101.

Wrotniak, B. H., Epstein, L. H., Roemmich, J. N., Paluch, R. A., & Pak, Y. (2005). The relationship between parent weight change and child weight change from 6 months to 10 years in family-based behavioral weight control treatment. *Obesity Research, 13*(6), 1089–1096.

Young, K. M., Northern, J. J., Lister, K. M., Drummond, J. A., & O'Brien, M. (2007). A meta-analysis of family-behavioral weight loss treatments for children. *Clinical Psychology Review, 27,* 240–249.

Zucker, N. (2006). *The H.O.U.S.E. program (a humorous, open-minded, understanding, strong, and explicit approach to parenting).* [Therapy manual.] Durham, NC: Duke University.

CHAPTER 23

Obsessive-Compulsive Disorder and Trichotillomania

JENNIFER COWIE, MICHELLE A. CLEMENTI, DEBORAH C. BEIDEL, AND CANDICE A. ALFANO

BRIEF OVERVIEW OF DISORDERS/PROBLEMS

Previously categorized as an anxiety disorder, obsessive-compulsive disorder (OCD) is now listed under a separate obsessive-compulsive and related disorders category in the fifth edition of the *Diagnostic and Statistical Manual of Mental Disorders* (*DSM-5*) (American Psychiatric Association, 2013). Trichotillomania (TTM) is included in this category as well. Many suggest that OCD and TTM are related disorders due to the presence of (commonly secretive) repetitive behaviors, their response to similar pharmacological treatments, higher than expected rates of TTM among the relatives of OCD patients, and vice versa (Bienvenu et al., 2000; Swedo & Rapoport, 1991). There are also, however, some clear differences between the disorders (King, Ollendick, & Montgomery, 1995), and the relationship between TTM and OCD is not entirely clear.

Obsessive-Compulsive Disorder

Epidemiological studies indicate lifetime prevalence rates of OCD from 2% to 3% by late adolescence (Zohar, 1999). The average age of onset among children is approximately 10 years, but OCD has been reported to occur in children from 5 to 18 years (Flament et al., 1988; Geller et al., 1998; Leonard et al., 1993; Masi et al., 2005). As indicated in *DSM-5*, obsessions and compulsions are core features of OCD. Obsessions are characterized by intrusive, unwanted thoughts or feelings that create significant distress, while compulsions are ritualistic behaviors performed in an effort to relieve distress. More specifically, patients with OCD feel compelled to engage in rituals that counteract their obsessions and thus temporarily alleviate their anxiety. According to *DSM-5* diagnostic criteria, individuals with OCD may have either obsessions or compulsions. When only one component is present, children, in comparison to adolescents, are much more likely to present with compulsions rather than obsessions (Geller et al., 1998; Last & Strauss, 1989). When obsessions are present, most children with OCD report one predominant type of obsession (Masi et al., 2005).

   With respect to content, the most common obsessions include contamination fears and concerns about illness and disease. Also common but somewhat less frequently reported by children with OCD are thoughts of aggression (e.g., inflicting harm on oneself or others), symmetry/exactness, religion, sex, and somatization. The most prevalent compulsions include checking, handwashing, and cleaning. Other common rituals include repeating, ordering/arranging, touching, counting, and hoarding/saving (Barrett & Healy-Farrell, 2003; Flament et al., 1988; Hanna, 1995; Last & Strauss, 1989; Riddle et al., 1990; Swedo, Rapoport, Leonard, Lenane, & Cheslow, 1989).

Trichotillomania

As discussed in *DSM-5*, recurrent pulling out of one's hair is the core feature of TTM. Although data focused on children with TTM are more limited, a lifetime prevalence rate of approximately 0.6% has been found in two separate studies primarily including adults (Christenson, Pyle, & Mitchell, 1991; Duke, Bodzin, Tavares, Geffken, & Storch, 2009). The hair-pulling often occurs in conjunction with: (1) negative emotions such as stress, irritation, or doubt; (2) when the individual is sitting alone, perhaps doing homework, watching television, or reading; and/or (3) after significant life events (e.g., starting school, moving to a new city, automobile accident) (Chang, Lee, Chiang, & Lü, 1991; Christenson, Ristvedt, & Mackenzie, 1993; Hanna, 1995; Reeve, Bernstein, & Christenson, 1992). Two primary subtypes of hair pulling have been identified: (1) a "focused" subtype in which pulling occurs under conscious awareness, and (2) an "autonomic" subtype in which pulling occurs outside of awareness, usually during sedentary or mindless activities like watching television (Flessner, Berman, Garcia, Freeman, & Leonard, 2009). Hair may be pulled from the head, eyebrows, eyelashes, or pubic area. A survey study among 133 youth with TTM ages 10 to 17 years found the most common sites of hair-pulling are the scalp (86%), eyelashes (52%), eyebrows (38%), pubic region (27%), legs (18%), and arms (9%) (Franklin et al., 2008). Hair selected to be pulled is described as feeling different in some way (too kinky or straight, too short or long, or just odd). In some instances, hairs are pulled only from areas where it is easy to cover bald spots; in other cases, the baldness may be so extensive that concealment is not possible. Some children eat the hair, and in certain instances hair-pulling co-occurs with thumb-sucking (Walsh & McDougle, 2001).

Mean age of onset in some TTM samples is reported during early to mid-adolescence (Duke et al., 2009; King et al., 1995; Swedo & Leonard, 1992). However, in other samples, approximately one third of children had an onset prior to age 10, and 14% had an onset prior to age 7 (Muller, 1987; Walsh & McDougle, 2001). According to Flessner et al. (2009), TTM often co-occurs with OCD, and children presenting with both disorders report more obsessions and compulsions than those with OCD alone. Further, children with comorbid OCD and TTM more commonly report contamination, aggressive, sexual, somatic, and religious obsessions and washing/cleaning, checking, repeating, and counting compulsions. Parents of children with both disorders more commonly report the presence of tactile/sensory sensitivities than do parents of children with OCD alone (Flessner et al., 2009).

EVIDENCE-BASED APPROACHES

Although included in the same diagnostic category, the two disorders differ considerably in the types of treatment strategies employed and the breadth and depth of the existing efficacy studies. Therefore, the next section outlines the empirical research separately for each disorder.

Psychosocial Treatment for Obsessive-Compulsive Disorder

Cognitive behavioral therapy (CBT) consisting of *exposure and response prevention* (ERP) is the treatment of choice for children and adolescents with OCD, according to Expert Consensus Guidelines (March, Frances, Carpenter, & Kahn, 1997) and the American Academy of Child and Adolescent Psychiatry practice parameters (Geller & March, 2012). The goal of ERP is to weaken associations between obsessions and anxiety and between compulsions and experiencing anxiety relief. The child or adolescent confronts the stimuli that evoke obsessional anxiety (e.g., touching a "dirty" bathroom doorknob) while simultaneously refraining from compulsive behaviors (e.g., washing hands). An *exposure hierarchy* is developed so that exposure tasks begin with less anxiety-provoking stimuli and gradually move toward tasks of increased difficulty. Exposures that elicit moderate levels of anxiety are thought to be optimal for promoting within-session habituation and to decrease the likelihood of treatment dropout (Norton, Hayes-Skelton, & Klenck, 2011).

During exposure sessions, therapists provide support and encourage the child to confront the feared stimuli via modeling, instruction (e.g., "Try a little bit at a time"), and verbal praise (e.g., "You're doing great!"). Subjective units of distress (SUD) ratings (i.e., a Likert-type scale) are recorded at brief intervals throughout the exposure to help the therapist gauge the child's level of habituation. Ideally, exposures should not be discontinued until the child's SUD ratings have decreased by at least 50% from the peak anxiety rating. SUD ratings can be tracked visually on a graph during exposures to promote learning that anxiety eventually will decrease on its own in the absence of compulsions and/or avoidance. Tracking progress in treatment both within and across sessions may also build motivation for more difficult exposures. Also, since most treatment gains are made outside of treatment sessions (Piacentini & Bergman, 2000), homework assignments in which children practice ERP between sessions is critically important.

ERP can be delivered in either an in vivo or an imaginal format, depending on the nature of the child's obsessions and/or compulsions as well as the age of the child. Compared to adolescents, children may experience difficulty holding the feared stimulus in their mind for long periods of time, making in vivo exposures more ideal for younger patients. During *in vivo exposures*, the child actually confronts the feared stimulus (i.e., touching an item believed to be contaminated). In order to facilitate generalization, exposures may also be conducted outside of sessions in other anxiety-provoking settings, such as at school, at home, or in a hospital. *Imaginal exposures* may be necessary when obsessions include inappropriate content or are not easily reproduced in the treatment setting. As an example, a child who fears s/he will physically harm a loved one might be encouraged to imagine carrying out this act. Generally, exposures that are more vivid and realistic are more effective (Piacentini, Gitow, Jaffer, Graae, & Whitaker, 1994). In vivo and imaginal exposures can also be used in combination. In an evaluation of the efficacy of a CBT treatment package in which ERP was conducted utilizing both in vivo and imaginal exposures, Piacentini, Bergman, Jacobs, McCracken, and Kretchman (2002) found a response rate of 79%.

Research examining the efficacy of ERP alone (Bolton & Perrin, 2008) or as part of a treatment package (see Barrett, Farrell, Piña, Peris, & Piacentini, 2008; Freeman et al., 2013) suggests that exposure is the most critical component in the treatment of pediatric OCD. An initial open trial of ERP-focused CBT conducted by Franklin and colleagues (1998) revealed that 12 out of 14 youth experienced a 50% reduction in scores on a measure of symptom severity (i.e., Children's Yale-Brown Obsessive Compulsive Scale [CY-BOCS]). In comparing ERP alone to a wait-list control condition, Bolton and Perrin (2008) found statistically significant improvement in OCD symptoms (46%) from pre- to posttreatment in 20 youth (8–17 years). Several other randomized control trials have demonstrated the efficacy of CBT protocols utilizing ERP (see Watson & Rees, 2008), and a meta-analysis by Abramowitz, Whiteside, and Deacon (2006) found that CBT incorporating ERP produces larger effect sizes than selective serotonin reuptake inhibitors (SSRIs) alone.

Cognitive restructuring techniques are also helpful in the treatment of pediatric OCD (Bolton et al., 2011; Williams et al., 2010). Based on the principles outlined by Salkovskis (1998), *cognitive restructuring* consists of identifying and relabeling obsessive thoughts in order to achieve some "distancing" from OCD symptoms (e.g., "I'm not really going to make my mom die if I don't say good-bye to her. It's just my OCD talking"). Cognitions that are commonly identified for relabeling include exaggerated responsibility appraisals (e.g., "It's my responsibility to tap three times to

356 Obsessive-Compulsive Disorder and Trichotillomania

keep my mother healthy") or thought-action fusions (i.e., the belief that thinking about something is as bad as doing it). Strategies aimed at normalizing these intrusive thoughts, such as surveying friends and family or conducting Internet-based research, can help the child reappraise the situation in a less threatening way. Behavioral experiments may also be used to directly test the veracity of thoughts (i.e., testing the power of a thought to make something happen). Unlike ERP, these experiments are designed to challenge maladaptive cognitions instead of promoting habituation to anxiety-provoking stimuli. Cognitive restructuring may also help some children cope with extreme anxiety during difficult exposures (Piacentini et al., 1994). In a sample of 21 youth ages 9 to 18 years, Williams and colleagues (2010) compared cognitive-focused CBT with a wait-list control group and found a large treatment effect (Cohen's $d = 1.07$) and a significant reduction in CY-BOCS scores. Another study by Bolton and colleagues (2011) revealed that both brief (an average of five sessions) and longer (an average of 12 sessions) treatment with CBT emphasizing cognitive restructuring significantly improved OCD symptoms (i.e., CY-BOCS scores) among 96 youth ages 10 to 18 years as compared with a wait-list condition.

CBT protocols for OCD may sometimes incorporate other components as well, including psychoeducation (Bjorgvinsson et al., 2008; March & Mulle, 1995), anxiety management techniques (March et al., 2004), contingency management (Piacentini et al., 1994), and relapse prevention (Barrett, Healy-Farrell, & March, 2004). During *psychoeducation*, OCD is described as a neurobiological disorder using a medical model. Consequently, symptoms are viewed as external from the child, and the child and family work together against OCD. The principles of behavioral theory and the process of ERP are also explained. *Anxiety management training* may include diaphragmatic breathing, progressive muscle relaxation (PMR), constructive self-talk (i.e., "If I can just wait a little while longer, my anxiety will go down"), and humorous visualizations (i.e., picturing OCD as a funny cartoon character). *Contingency management* consists of rewarding a child for attempting or completing in-session exposures or homework. The nature of rewards depends on the developmental level and preferences of the child. During *relapse prevention*, any unrealistic expectations (e.g., the belief that symptoms will disappear completely) are addressed. The child is asked to identify stressors or situations that may increase risk for a relapse or exacerbate symptoms and to establish a plan for ongoing support.

Combining Psychosocial With Pharmacological Treatments for OCD

SSRIs, including fluoxetine, fluvoxamine, paroxetine, sertraline, and a tricyclic antidepressant, clomipramine, are also commonly used to treat pediatric OCD (Geller et al., 2003). Until recently, these medications were presumed to have a good safety profile, as few changes in blood pressure, pulse, weight, or electrocardiogram were reported (e.g., Liebowitz et al., 2002; Riddle et al., 1990). However, many of the SSRIs now carry a "black box warning" due to an association with increased suicidal ideation. Meta-analytic results (Abramowitz et al., 2006) also indicate that while children treated with SSRIs report reduced symptoms, obsessions and compulsions often remain severe enough to meet entrance criteria for most clinical trials (March et al., 2004). Overall, about 33% of pediatric patients fail to benefit from pharmacotherapy alone, and medication is less likely to be associated with long-term improvements than CBT (O'Leary, Barrett, & Fjermestad, 2009; Shalev et al., 2009).

In a randomized, placebo-controlled comparison trial (Pediatric OCD Treatment Study [POTS]) (March et al., 2004), CBT, sertraline, their combination, and pill placebo were compared among 112 youth with OCD ages 7 to 17 years. At posttreatment, scores on a measure of symptom severity (i.e., CY-BOCS) indicated significant improvement in all three active treatment conditions, but children in the combination condition showed significantly greater symptom reductions on the CY-BOCS compared to those treated with sertraline or CBT. However, when clinical remission rates were examined (defined as posttreatment CY-BOCS score ≤10), 53.6% of the combination group, 39% of the CBT group, 21% of the sertraline group, and 3% taking placebo reached remission status. Statistically, combination treatment was superior to sertraline alone based on remission rates, and sertraline did not differ from placebo. Effect sizes for combined treatment, CBT alone, and sertraline were 1.4, 0.97, and 0.67, respectively. Other more recent studies have provided further support for the increased efficacy of combination therapy as opposed to pharmacological monotherapies (Franklin, Edson, Ledley, & Cahill, 2011; Storch et al., 2010). Psychosocial interventions are therefore considered the first line of treatment for pediatric OCD, with pharmacological interventions recommended in combination with CBT for more severe cases of the illness (Geller & March, 2012).

Treatment for Trichotillomania

The efficacy of behavior therapy (BT) with habit reversal training (HRT) (Azrin & Nunn, 1973) for treating adults with TTM is well established (Stemberger, McCombs-Thomas, MacGlashan, & Mansueto, 2000; Wetterneck, Woods, Norberg, & Begotka, 2006). Studies evaluating the efficacy of behavioral treatment in children and adolescents with TTM are limited, however. When pulling behavior occurs in conjunction with thumb-sucking, elimination of thumb-sucking may eliminate TTM (Watson & Allen, 1993). In a review of available case studies, Bruce, Barwick, and Wright (2005) concluded that behavioral treatments have the greatest support in young patients. For example, Blum, Barone, and Friman (1993) and Vitulano, King, Scahill, and Cohen (1992) reported some success with a range of traditional behavioral interventions, such as overcorrection, annoyance review, and differential reinforcement of other behaviors. *Overcorrection* usually has aversive connotations (Foxx & Bechtel, 1982), but in the case of children with TTM, it has been used in the form of positive practice by having the children comb or brush their hair (Vitulano et al., 1992). *Annoyance review* simply refers to having the children acknowledge the problematic nature of hair-pulling and their reasons for wanting to stop. This approach is probably most effective for preadolescents and adolescents rather than younger children. *Differential reinforcement of other behavior* means giving the child attention only when pulling behavior is absent. Positive touches (in young children) and compliments (in older children and adolescents) are also commonly used (Blum et al., 1993).

Only one randomized controlled trial to date has demonstrated the efficacy of BT in the treatment of children and adolescents with TTM (Franklin et al., 2011). In this study, 24 youth ages 7 to 17 years were treated with the primary components of HRT: awareness training, stimulus control, and competing response training. Given that children often report "automatic" as opposed to "focused" hair-pulling (Flessner et al., 2009), *awareness training* is implemented to increase awareness of pulling behavior and urges by identifying situations (i.e., sleep onset or television watching) and/or triggers (i.e., bathroom mirror) that increase risk for pulling. *Self-monitoring* strategies, such as using a mirror or keeping a diary (in older children), may be helpful. *Stimulus control* strategies involve creating barriers to pulling during high-risk situations (i.e., wearing gloves or covering nails with bandages while falling asleep) or placing visual reminders near triggers (i.e., a sign placed by the bathroom mirror or television).

During *competing response training*, the child or adolescent is taught to engage in an alternative, opposite movement when becoming aware of an urge to pull. The competing response should be physically incompatible with pulling, such as playing with clay or holding a tight fist. Given the theoretical association between stress and pulling behavior, *progressive muscle relaxation* was also implemented to (indirectly) reduce pulling. Finally, *cognitive restructuring* was used to challenge negative autonomic thoughts associated with pulling. Compared with a minimal attention control condition, this combined treatment package resulted in a significant reduction in scores on the National Institute of Mental Health Trichotillomania Severity Scale (NIMH-TSS) at posttreatment and at an 8-week follow-up assessment (Franklin et al., 2011). These results are promising overall, but more controlled treatment research is needed to more definitively establish the efficacy of HRT and its individual components in treating youth with TTM.

PARENT INVOLVEMENT IN TREATMENT

An important issue for clinicians is the role of the family in the perpetuation of symptoms of OCD and TTM. Family interaction patterns may have a significant impact on treatment, and specific strategies for guiding parental involvement during treatment for each disorder separately are outlined in the next section.

Obsessive-Compulsive Disorder

The distress experienced by children with OCD is a major source of stress and disruption for the family (Barrett et al., 2004). In attempting to manage distress and avoid conflict, parents and siblings often accommodate a child's ritualistic behavior by avoiding obsessional triggers, becoming involved in or assisting with compulsions (e.g., helping with washing rituals, such as always disinfecting silverware before meals), and/or providing excessive reassurance. These behaviors serve to reinforce the child's irrational beliefs and may undermine the success of ERP by limiting the child's experience of habituation outside of the treatment session. Family accommodation may also reduce the aversive consequences of symptoms, which ultimately may decrease a child's motivation for change. Parental involvement in symptoms has been found to be related to greater symptom severity (Bipeta, Yerramilli, Pingali, Karredla, & Ali, 2013; Peris et al., 2012) and OCD-related functional impairment (Bipeta et al., 2013). Families of youth with OCD are also less likely to use positive problem-solving strategies and reward independence (Barrett, Shortt, & Healy, 2002), and overall family dysfunction is associated with poorer treatment outcomes (Barrett, Farrell, Dadds, & Boulter, 2005).

Therefore, family members may play an important role in treatment (Waters & Barrett, 2000). For example, parents who participate in their child's rituals should be instructed to cease any assistance and to provide encouragement for compliance with the treatment program. Parents who are hostile toward their children require education regarding the nature of OCD, what the child should be expected to be able to do and not do at various treatment phases, and how the parents can be active, positive participants in the treatment process. The need to formally address these issues has led some investigators to develop behavioral treatments that include a family intervention component. However, given the diversity of family responses to a child's OCD, it is unclear that any one intervention would work for all families.

In an initial open trial (Waters, Barrett, & March, 2001), a parent skills training component was added to psychoeducation, anxiety management and cognitive training, and graduated ERP. The parent skills training consisted of educating parents about OCD and its treatment, reducing parental involvement in the child's symptoms, encouraging family support of home-based exposure and response prevention, and increasing family problem-solving skills. Children reported significant improvement in OCD symptoms, and there was significant decrease in family accommodation behaviors. However, contrary to expectations, there was no change in parental functioning as a result of the intervention.

Additional studies establishing the efficacy of family-based CBT in treating pediatric OCD have recently emerged (see Freeman et al., 2013). A follow-up controlled trial compared individual cognitive behavioral family treatment (CBFT), group CBFT, and a 6-week wait-list control (Barrett et al., 2004). Again, significant improvement in OCD symptoms was evident for both active treatment conditions. Sibling level of accommodation and depression also decreased across both treated groups. However, similar to pilot data, there was no significant change in parental functioning or parental distress, and families scored in the unhealthy range of functioning at both pre- and post-treatment. Additionally, the family component did not affect family dysfunction. As such, inclusion of parents and family members as a necessary treatment component remains unclear. There may nonetheless be important benefits in terms of preventing relapse. Treatment gains were maintained at 6-month (Barrett et al., 2004), 1-year (Barrett et al., 2005), and 7-year follow-up assessments (O'Leary et al., 2009), providing some initial evidence for the potential importance of the family in relapse prevention.

In another study, Piacentini and colleagues (2011) found that family-focused CBT resulted in faster improvement in CY-BOCS scores and OCD-related impairment than psychoeducation/relaxation training; however, the groups did not differ significantly on these measures at posttreatment. Results also revealed that reduction in family accommodation preceded symptom change, shedding light on the temporal relationships of outcomes. Collectively, although available research focused on family-based interventions has led both expert consensus and professional groups to recommend some degree of family involvement in treatment (Geller & March, 2012; March et al., 1997), there remains a lack of head-to-head comparison trials examining more traditional individual child CBT with family-focused CBT for pediatric OCD.

Trichotillomania

Parents appear to be critical to the treatment success of youth with TTM for three reasons. First, during the awareness training component of HRT, parents may play an essential role in assisting with the identification of pulling behavior, especially in children who engage in autonomic versus focused hair-pulling. Second, parents of children with TTM may unintentionally reinforce pulling behavior by providing negative attention (i.e., "Stop that!") or access to tangible items (i.e., giving a child a toy to discourage pulling) in response to pulling (Park, Rahman, Murphy, & Storch, 2012). As mentioned previously, it is important to assist the parent in utilizing consistent reinforcement of positive rather than negative behaviors. Third, family conflict and parental frustration can confound treatment outcome (Vitulano et al., 1992). Parents may feel reduced competency and express uncertainty as to how to avoid exacerbating pulling behavior (Bruce et al., 2005) and/or how to track the child's progress in treatment if pulling is performed in secret. Educating parents about treatment and helping them distance themselves from the treatment program and from the child's behavior may therefore be critical in reducing family conflict and enhancing treatment compliance and outcome.

ADAPTATIONS AND MODIFICATIONS

Current evidence-based treatments for both OCD and TTM require adapting treatment procedures for the specific child and the context in which the symptoms are present. For OCD, several specific adaptations of current treatments have been examined in the literature, and here we briefly review efforts addressing developmental challenges, comorbidities, and alternate delivery methods. Special considerations for evidence-based approaches in the treatment of TTM are also described.

Obsessive-Compulsive Disorder

Adaptations and/or modifications may be warranted in order to ensure appropriateness of treatment across a range of situations and patient characteristics. Psychosocial interventions can be modified for younger children with OCD so that those even as young as age 5 can be treated with evidence-based approaches (March et al., 2004). Freeman and colleagues (2012) are currently conducting a controlled trial evaluating the efficacy of an adapted version of family-based CBT (Choate-Summers et al., 2008) for a younger sample of children with OCD (ages 5–8). Several developmentally driven modifications have been made, although the primary components and goals of CBT remained unchanged. For example, since many young children have difficulty fully understanding the rationale of exposure tasks, psychoeducation was conducted separately with the parent to ensure parental understanding of treatment. During psychoeducation sessions with the child, ERP was explained utilizing large drawings and more developmentally appropriate metaphors (i.e., the "worry monster") in order to facilitate the child's engagement and understanding. During the course of treatment, parents also participated in additional parent training and played more of an active role in promoting behavioral change. Finally, because young children struggle to accurately identify and express increases in anxiety during ERP, exposures began with particularly low anxiety-provoking stimuli and incorporated more play and humor throughout treatment.

The presence of comorbidities may also impact on treatment. In a reanalysis of the data from the POTS study (2004), March and colleagues (2007) found that comorbid tic disorder attenuated the response rate for medication but not CBT or combination therapy. In a naturalistic treatment study by Masi and colleagues (2005) including 94 youth with OCD (ages 7–18), children and adolescents with primary contamination fears and rituals tended to respond best to SSRI monotherapy. Among a sample of 96 youth with OCD (range 7–19 years), Storch and colleagues (2008) found that comorbid disruptive behavior disorders including attention-deficit/hyperactivity disorder (ADHD) and major depressive disorder (MDD) were related to lower CBT response rates.

A few treatment studies have emerged to address the challenges that specific comorbidities present for treatment. Among six youth (age range 9–14 years) with OCD and co-occuring disruptive behavior disorders, Sukhodolsky, Gorman, Scahill, Findley, and McGuire (2013) demonstrated that treatment outcome can be enhanced by implementing parent management training (PMT) prior to implementing ERP. Meyer and colleagues (2013) found that CBT treatment for OCD improved both obsessive-compulsive and depressive symptoms in a sample of youth ages 7 to 17 diagnosed with both conditions. The authors concluded that clinicians should first target OCD in youth presenting with OCD and co-occurring depression.

To examine whether intensive treatment might produce better outcomes than standard weekly sessions for pediatric OCD patients 7 to 17 years, Storch and colleagues (2007) compared the efficacy of fourteen 90-minute CBT sessions delivered daily over a 3-week period to 90-minute weekly sessions held over 14 weeks. At posttreatment, 75% of the intensive treatment group and 50% of the weekly treatment group reached remission status (based on CY-BOC scores of ≤10). Further, 90% of youth in the intensive group and 65% in the weekly group were deemed treatment responders based on global improvement scores at posttreatment. Although neither group difference was statistically significant, effect sizes for intensive and weekly treatment were 2.62 and 1.73, respectively.

Also, a significant difference was detected for level of family accommodation at posttreatment, with the intensive group showing a greater reduction in the degree to which family members accommodated the child's OCD symptoms. At the 3-month follow-up assessment, outcomes for both groups were largely similar, due primarily to a slight decrease in treatment effectiveness among the intensive group. Overall, both treatments appear to be highly efficacious, and youth treated with either protocol may require some level of additional care during the initial follow-up period. A more recent open trial by Whiteside and Jacobsen (2010) found that ten 50-minute CBT sessions delivered over 5 days significantly reduced CY-BOCS scores at posttreatment and follow-up. However, symptom improvements were less than those found in 3-week intensive program by Storch and colleagues (2007).

For youth with treatment-resistant OCD, more intensive treatments may offer better outcomes. Bjorgvinsson and colleagues (2008) conducted an open trial with a sample of 23 adolescents who had failed to respond to outpatient treatment (65% with comorbid diagnoses). Participants stayed at an inpatient unit for an average of 9.5 weeks, and treatment consisted of medication management and 90-minute ERP sessions each morning followed by 60 minutes of self-directed exposure sessions at least 3 evenings per week. Participants were also encouraged to practice ERP in practice groups or during scheduled community outings. Results revealed significant reductions in obsessions, compulsions, state and trait anxiety, and a host of other symptom measures. Additionally, 70% of participants exhibited clinically significant reductions in CY-BOCS scores (Jacobson & Traux, 1991).

Research has also begun to explore the efficacy of group-based CBT for pediatric OCD, although many studies are limited by the lack of a control group and small sample sizes. For instance, a group adaptation of March and Mulle's (1998) CBT program implemented among 18 adolescent patients (Thienemann, Martin, Cregger, Thompson, & Dyer-Friedman, 2001) produced statistically significant changes on the CY-BOCS and on a global rating of OCD severity. However, the degree of improvement was substantially less than that reported for individual CBT trials, as only 50% of group patients achieved a 25% or greater improvement in symptoms. It may be that group treatment dilutes the amount of time required for efficacious ERP tasks, thereby attenuating outcomes. Olino and colleagues (2011) conducted an open trial treating 41 youth ages 6 to 17 in an intensive outpatient group treatment (4 times per week) for 12 weeks. Participants experienced a significant decrease in both OCD and depressive symptoms pre- to posttreatment; however, no comparison control group was examined.

Studies examining technology-based dissemination of CBT are emerging as well and yielding promising results. Turner, Heyman, Futh, and Lovell (2009) explored the efficacy of CBT delivered weekly via telephone to 10 teenagers. The treatment resulted in a reduction in CY-BOCS scores below clinical levels for 70% of participants, and families reported good feasibility and acceptability of the treatment. Storch and colleagues (2011) compared family-focused CBT delivered via webcam with a wait-list control group among 31 youth ages 7 to 16. At posttreatment, 56.1% of the treatment group demonstrated a significant reduction in CY-BOCS scores compared to 12.9% of those on the wait list. Additionally, 81% of participants in the treatment group were identified as treatment responders compared to only 13% in the wait-list condition. Although CY-BOCS scores increased for the treatment group at 3-month follow-up, scores remained significantly below baseline. Most recently, Comer and colleagues (2014) conducted a preliminary case-series study delivering real-time, empirically based CBT via Internet videoconferencing to four children with OCD. All children showed symptom improvement and reduction in global impairment, and 60% no longer met diagnostic criteria posttreatment. This novel approach to dissemination represents an exciting area for future research.

Trichotillomania

Given the lack of evidence from controlled treatment trials among children with TTM coupled with the typical secrecy associated with the disorder, there are considerable challenges for clinicians treating children with TTM. Similar to OCD treatment, the selection of the specific intervention components will be dependent on the child's age. For example, cognitive strategies may be more appropriate for older children and adolescents, given that urges rather than cognitions are associated with hair-pulling in younger children and preteens (Malhotra, Grover, Baweja, & Bhateja, 2008). Likewise, younger children may be more motivated by sticker charts and small rewards. Vitulano and colleagues (1992) have identified low compliance and motivation for change as a challenge to successfully treating children and adolescents with TTM. Children sometimes find it difficult to adhere to self-monitoring procedures and can be embarrassed to collect their hairs and bring them to the therapist. Among children and adolescents who are reluctant to participate in treatment, two factors seem to increase the likelihood of compliance: (1) keeping the self-monitoring as simple as possible (no more than one page per day) and (2) small rewards for completion of self-monitoring and/or behavioral assignments.

MEASURING TREATMENT EFFECTS

Valid and reliable assessment of OCD and TTM symptoms are critical for treatment planning and evaluation of treatment effects. Although far fewer assessment options are available for TTM relative to OCD, the commonly used approaches for each disorder are reviewed in the next section.

Obsessive-Compulsive Disorder

Various strategies may be used for assessment and measurement of treatment effects in children and adolescents with OCD, including diagnostic interviews and clinician ratings, child- and parent-report, self-monitoring, and behavioral assessment. Younger patients may be unable to articulate the content of obsessions or aim of their compulsions, making assessment particularly challenging for clinicians. Thus, thorough assessment strategies should be applied in a clinically sensitive and developmentally appropriate manner. For instance, depending on the child's age, diagnostic and clinical interviews might be conducted privately with adolescents but in the presence of parents for younger children. Self-monitoring strategies also should be tailored to age and developmental status.

OCD treatment effects are often measured with semistructured diagnostic interviews and clinician rating scales, such as the Anxiety Disorders Interview Schedule for Children/Parent (ADIS-C/P; Silverman & Albano, 1996) and the Children's Yale-Brown Obsessive-Compulsive Scale (CY-BOCS) (Scahill et al., 1997). The CY-BOCS, a clinician-administered interview, assesses a broad range of obsessions and compulsions as well as severity, interference, and ability to control/resist obsessions and compulsions. Scores range from 0 to 40; scores of 20 or higher indicate at least moderate severity, whereas scores of 10 or below indicate subclinical OCD. Few empirical data on the reliability and validity of the CY-BOCS are available, but clinically, it is very useful for case conceptualization and treatment planning and has become a mainstay of pharmacological research trials. Another commonly used clinician scale, the NIMH Global Scale, is a 15-point, 1-item scale that rates OCD severity and impairment. Scores of 7 or greater are indicative of clinically significant OCD (Insel et al., 1983). The scale often is used in pharmacological studies of OCD treatment.

Relatively few self-report measures have been developed to directly assess OCD in children and adolescents. The Leyton Obsessional Inventory–Child Version (LOI-CV), originally a card-sorting task, is now commonly used as a 20-item self-report measure rating the presence of obsessions and compulsions on a 4-point Likert scale (Berg, Rapoport, & Flament, 1986; Berg, Whitaker, Davies, Flament, & Rapoport, 1988). The scale has good psychometric properties and items load onto four factors: general-obsessive, dirt-contamination, numbers-luck, and school (Berg et al., 1988; Roussos et al., 2003). A shorter 11-item screening version with three subscales (compulsions, obsessions/completeness, and cleanliness) has also been developed and appears to have good reliability and the ability to discriminate children with OCD from normal controls and depressed children (Bamber, Tamplin, Park, Kyte, & Goodyer, 2002).

The Child Obsessive Compulsive Impact Scale–Revised (COIS-R) (Piacentini, Peris, Bergman, Chang, & Jaffer, 2007) was developed to assess functional impairments associated with pediatric OCD. Parallel parent and child report versions are available. The parent version yields four distinct areas of impairment (daily living skills, family, social, and school) while the youth version yields three areas (school, social, and activities). Both measures appear to have good internal consistency, concurrent validity, and test–retest reliability. The measure also has been shown to be sensitive to the effects of both medication (Geller et al., 2001; Liebowitz et al., 2002) and CBT (Martin & Thienemann, 2005; Valderhaug, Larsson, Götestam, & Piacentini, 2007) in alleviating impairment associated with OCD.

Behavioral avoidance tests (BATs) may also be used to provide an objective assessment of OCD symptoms. BATs have moderate convergent validity with self-report measures of OCD and are sensitive to the effects of treatment (Barrett, Healy, & March, 2003). Most BATs ask the child to approach and, it is hoped, touch the "feared object" (e.g., contaminated object), measuring the actual distance that a child is able to cover. In addition, rituals performed during the BAT are assessed (see Barrett et al., 2003, for a detailed description of how to conduct a BAT for OCD). BATs provide a much more objective assessment of psychopathology than self-report or clinician ratings. Even so, demand characteristics play a role, as children may feel pressure to do more than they normally would because of the assessment environment. An additional limitation is that BATs are most appropriate for obsessions and rituals involving contamination (washing) and, in some cases, future events (checking). It is more difficult to construct BATs for covert compulsions, such as cognitive rituals.

Self-monitoring can provide information on the daily frequency of obsessions and compulsions as well as daily information on emotional distress prior to implementing an intervention. A key challenge, particularly with children, is ensuring compliance with the monitoring task. Given that familial relationships are already under some strain as a result of the child's disorder, it is important that parents do not attempt to force compliance. Clinicians can increase compliance by constructing self-monitoring forms that are simple to use and require no more than 5 minutes a day to complete. Daily rating of distress as well as estimates of the time spent carrying out obsessions and compulsions can provide needed information by which to gauge treatment success while at the same time not being overly burdensome to the child. Small, developmentally appropriate reinforcers can also increase compliance with self-monitoring procedures (Beidel, Neal, & Lederer, 1991).

Trichotillomania

Currently, there is no gold standard for assessing TTM and very few assessments exist to evaluate TTM specifically in children and adolescents. Most tools were designed for adult populations, including the commonly used clinician rating scales: the NIMH Trichotillomania Impairment Scale (NIMH-TIS) and the NIMH Trichotillomania Symptom Severity Scale (NIMH-TSS) (Swedo et al.,

1989). The NIMH-TIS is a one-item measure that provides an impairment score based on degree of hair loss, time spent pulling or concealing hair loss, and control over behavior (Swedo et al., 1989). The NIMH-TSS includes five items that assess time spent pulling in the past week and in the previous day, resistance to pulling, distress, and interference; this scale shows adequate internal consistency and excellent interrater agreement (Diefenbach, Tolin, Crocetto, Maltby, & Hannan, 2005). However, it is important to note that these assessment measures have not been validated in child and adolescent populations.

Diagnostic interviews exist specifically for assessing TTM in pediatric populations, including the NIMH Diagnostic Interview Schedule for Children (DISC-IV) (Shaffer, Fisher, Lucas, Dulcan, & Schwab-Stone, 2000). Only one validated self-report measure, the Massachusetts General Hospital Hairpulling Scale (O'Sullivan et al., 1995), exists for adolescent patients, but none exists for younger children. However, self-monitoring procedures similar to those noted in the OCD assessment section should be implemented to gauge treatment success related to changes in hair pulling urges and frequency.

CLINICAL CASE EXAMPLES

The following section provides a case example in order to illustrate the characteristics, assessment, treatment plan, and outcomes for clinical practice associated with each disorder separately.

Obsessive-Compulsive Disorder

Mark (identifying information has been altered to protect confidentiality) is a 12-year-old boy referred for evaluation of compulsive behaviors that include excessive hand-washing, the need to touch objects that he feels compelled to carry with him at all times, and the need to complete rituals in symmetry (e.g., carry out his hand-washing ritual until he is sure both sides of his body are equally clean). At the time of the evaluation, he has intrusive thoughts that harm might come to him or his family. Most of the time, the thoughts are uncontrollable, and repetitive behaviors designed to relieve them bring only temporary relief. The behaviors cause disruption in his schoolwork, family interactions, and peer socialization. He often refuses to go to school due to concerns he will not be able to carry out his compulsions to a satisfactory level, and his grades at school have decreased.

Initial Assessment

The initial diagnostic interview confirmed the presence of OCD but did not indicate the presence of any other disorder. Further information on Mark's specific pattern of obsessions and compulsions was collected with the CY-BOCS. Intrusive thoughts occurred 1 to 3 hours per day, were disturbing, resulted in moderate interference with social and school activities, and only sometimes were able to be controlled. Rituals also occupied 1 to 3 hours per day, and although they could be delayed, they could not be prevented. As with the obsessions, the rituals impacted Mark's academic and family functioning. Consistent with the diagnostic interview, scores on Mark's self-report inventories indicated the lack of psychopathology other than OCD. His baseline self-monitoring data depict the presence of moderate distress and a significant number of intrusive thoughts per day.

Treatment Plan

Mark's treatment plan included imaginal and in vivo exposure with response prevention. Imaginal sessions conducted in the office included scripts outlining a scenario in which his parents were harmed in an accident. The in vivo exposure and response prevention program occurred outside of the clinic sessions. Mark was given a detailed response prevention program related to hand-washing compulsions to ensure that the instructions were implemented correctly. Mark was instructed that he could wash his hands for 30 seconds with nonantiseptic hand soap only after using the bathroom or 30 minutes before he eats. He was not allowed to wash his hands immediately before eating. Specifically, his plan included having a snack before bedtime that he must eat with his fingers without washing his hands first. Mark was told that if he felt an urge to wash his hands, he should get someone to distract him until the urge went away.

Outcome Assessment

Treatment consisted of 14 clinic sessions and the accompanying homework assignments. At the end of the treatment, rituals were decreased to less than 5 minutes per day and obsessions to less than 10 minutes per day. Mark's score on the CY-BOCS dropped to subclinical levels (below 10). Further, his posttreatment self-monitoring data indicated the presence of mild distress and a minimal number of intrusive thoughts per day.

Trichotillomania

Melanie (identifying information has been altered to protect confidentiality) is a 6-year-old girl referred for treatment for chronic hair-pulling. At the time of the initial evaluation, Melanie had pulled out most of the hair on her head. This behavior began about 12 months ago and was continuous since that time. Melanie also tended to suck her thumb at night while pulling her hair. Melanie's parents and teachers often talked to Melanie about why she should stop pulling her hair. Thus, she received substantial attention for her behavior, which likely played a role in the maintenance of her hair-pulling. Further, Melanie's parents had recently separated and her father moved out of the house. The recent arguments and changes in the family unit no doubt contributed to Melanie's emotional distress. Finally, Melanie's older sister had recently been diagnosed with OCD, which caused further stress on the family.

Treatment Plan

The initial treatment program consisted of psychoeducation about TTM and eliminating attention for hair-pulling. Parents were instructed to ignore Melanie when she pulled her hair and provide positive attention when she was not pulling her hair. Furthermore, an hourly sticker program was implemented. Specifically, at the top of every hour, if Melanie's hands were not near her face or head, she earned a sticker. After 5 weeks, there was a slight, but not substantial, decrease in nightly hair-pulling. Further evaluation indicated that Melanie's parents were inconsistent in implementing the sticker program when she switched between her parents' homes. Therefore, at week 6, a small alarm was used in both settings to help her parents to remember to provide stickers as appropriate throughout the day. Additionally, both parents and Melanie were taught relaxation exercises and were instructed to do them at home together. To deal with nighttime hair-pulling, a contract was implemented in which Melanie was instructed to wear mittens at night. If she wore her mittens all night (i.e., they were still on when she woke up in the morning), she could choose any special food she wanted for breakfast. Implementation of the contract was necessary only for a 5-week period. After that, Melanie's newly growing hair and her pride in her new appearance negated the need for rewards.

Outcome Assessment

Treatment outcome was measured by counting the number of hairs pulled daily. Given Melanie's age and the fact that parental attention appeared to be a maintaining factor for the behavior, a decision was made to use the number of hairs specifically pulled at night as an indication of treatment outcome. Each morning, Melanie's mother collected the hair on the pillow and each week, her mother brought the hairs to the clinic where they were counted and the total number graphed. Thus, self-monitoring data were useful in determining the efficacy of the program and making alterations when the data indicated that ongoing strategies had reached maximal effectiveness.

REFERENCES

Abramowitz, J. S., Whiteside, S. P., & Deacon, B. J. (2006). The effectiveness of treatment for pediatric obsessive-compulsive disorder: A meta-analysis. *Behavior Therapy, 36*(1), 55–63.

American Psychiatric Association. (2013). *Diagnostic and statistical manual of mental disorders* (5th ed.). Arlington, VA: American Psychiatric Publishing.

Azrin, N., & Nunn, R. (1973). Habit-reversal: A method of eliminating nervous habits and tics. *Behaviour Research and Therapy, 11*(4), 619–628.

Bamber, D., Tamplin, A., Park, R., Kyte, Z., & Goodyer, I. (2002). Development of a short Leyton Obsessional Inventory for Children and Adolescents. *Journal of the American Academy of Child & Adolescent Psychiatry, 41*(10), 1246–1252. doi: 10.1097/00004583–200210000–00015

Barrett, P., Farrell, L., Dadds, M., & Boulter, N. (2005). Cognitive-behavioral family treatment of childhood obsessive-compulsive disorder: Long-term follow-up and predictors of outcome. *Journal of the American Academy of Child & Adolescent Psychiatry, 44*(10), 1005–1014.

Barrett, P., Farrell, L., Piña, A., Peris, T., & Piacentini, J. (2008). Evidence-based psychosocial treatments for child and adolescent obsessive-compulsive disorder. *Journal of Clinical Child & Adolescent Psychology, 37*(1), 131–155.

Barrett, P., Healy, L., & March, J. (2003). Behavioral avoidance test for childhood obsessive-compulsive disorder: A home-based observation. *American Journal of Psychotherapy, 57*(1), 80–100.

Barrett, P., & Healy-Farrell, L. (2003). Perceived responsibility in juvenile obsessive-compulsive disorder: An experimental manipulation. *Journal of Clinical Child & Adolescent Psychology, 32*(3), 430–441. doi: 10.1207/S15374424JCCP3203_11

Barrett, P., Healy-Farrell, L., & March, J. (2004). Cognitive-behavioral family treatment of childhood obsessive-compulsive disorder: A controlled trial. *Journal of the American Academy of Child & Adolescent Psychiatry, 43*(1), 46–62.

Barrett, P., Shortt, A., & Healy, L. (2002). Do parent and child behaviours differentiate families whose children have obsessive-compulsive disorder from other clinic and non-clinic families? *Journal of Child Psychology and Psychiatry, 43*(5), 597–607.

Beidel, D., Neal, A., & Lederer, A. (1991). The feasibility and validity of a daily diary for the assessment of anxiety in children. *Behavior Therapy, 22*(4), 505–517. doi: 10.1016/S0005–7894(05)80342–9

Berg, C., Rapoport, J., & Flament, M. (1986). The Leyton Obsessional Inventory–Child Version. *Journal of the American Academy of Child Psychiatry, 25*(1), 84–91. doi: 10.1016/S0002–7138(09)60602–6

Berg, C., Whitaker, A., Davies, M., Flament, M., & Rapoport, J. (1988). The survey form of the Leyton Obsessional Inventory–Child Version: Norms from an epidemiological study. *Journal of the American Academy of Child & Adolescent Psychiatry, 27*(6), 759–763. doi: 10.1097/00004583–198811000–00017

Bienvenu, O., Samuels, J., Riddle, M., Hoehn-Saric, R., Liang, K., Cullen, B., . . . Nestadt, G. (2000). The relationship of obsessive-compulsive disorder to possible spectrum disorders: Results from a family study. *Biological Psychiatry, 48*(4), 287–293. doi: 10.1016/S0006–3223(00)00831–3

Bipeta, R., Yerramilli, S. S., Pingali, S., Karredla, A. R., & Ali, M. O. (2013). A cross-sectional study of insight and family accommodation in pediatric obsessive-compulsive disorder. *Child and Adolescent Psychiatry and Mental Health, 7*(1), 20. doi: 10.1186/1753–2000–7–20

Bjorgvinsson, T., Wetterneck, C., Powell, D., Chasson, G., Webb, S., Hart, J., . . . Davidson, J. (2008). Treatment outcome for adolescent obsessive-compulsive disorder in a specialized hospital setting. *Journal of Psychiatric Practice, 14*(3), 137–145.

Blum, N. J., Barone, V. J., & Friman, P. C. (1993). A simplified behavioral treatment for trichotillomania: Report of two cases. *Pediatrics, 91*(5), 993–995.

Bolton, D., & Perrin, S. (2008). Evaluation of exposure with response-prevention for obsessive compulsive disorder in childhood and adolescence. *Journal of Behavior Therapy and Experimental Psychiatry, 39*(1), 11–22.

Bolton, D., Williams, T., Perrin, S., Atkinson, L., Gallop, C., Waite, P., & Salkovskis, P. (2011). Randomized controlled trial of full and brief cognitive-behaviour therapy and wait-list for paediatric obsessive-compulsive disorder. *Journal of Child Psychology and Psychiatry, 52*(12), 1269–1278.

Bruce, T. O., Barwick, L. W., & Wright, H. H. (2005). Diagnosis and management of trichotillomania in children and adolescents. *Pediatric Drugs, 7*(6), 365–376.

Chang, C., Lee, M., Chiang, Y., & Lü, Y. (1991). Trichotillomania: A clinical study of 36 patients. *Journal of the Formosan Medical Association, 90*(2), 176–180.

Choate-Summers, M., Freeman, J., Garcia, A., Coyne, L., Przeworski, A., & Leonard, H. (2008). Clinical considerations when tailoring cognitive behavioral treatment for young children with obsessive compulsive disorder. *Education and Treatment of Children, 31*(3), 395–416.

Christenson, G., Pyle, R., & Mitchell, J. (1991). Estimated lifetime prevalence of trichotillomania in college students. *Journal of Clinical Psychiatry, 52*(10), 415–417.

Christenson, G., Ristvedt, S., & Mackenzie, T. (1993). Identification of trichotillomania cue profiles. *Behaviour Research and Therapy, 31*(3), 315–320. doi: 10.1016/0005-7967(93)90030-X

Comer, J. S., Furr, J. M., Cooper-Vince, C. E., Kerns, C. E., Chan, P. T., Edson, A. L., . . . Freeman, J. B. (2014). Internet-delivered, family-based treatment for early-onset OCD: A preliminary case series. *Journal of Clinical Child & Adolescent Psychology, 43*(1), 74–87.

Diefenbach, G., Tolin, D., Crocetto, J., Maltby, N., & Hannan, S. (2005). Assessment of trichotillomania: A psychometric evaluation of hair-pulling scales. *Journal of Psychopathology and Behavioral Assessment, 27*(3), 169–178. doi: 10.1007/s10862-005-0633-7

Duke, D., Bodzin, D., Tavares, P., Geffken, G., & Storch, E. (2009). The phenomenology of hairpulling in a community sample. *Journal of Anxiety Disorders, 23*(8), 1118–1125. doi: 10.1016/j.janxdis.2009.07.015

Flament, M., Whitaker, A., Rapoport, J., Davies, M., Berg, C., Kalikow, K., . . . Shaffer, D. (1988). Obsessive compulsive disorder in adolescence: An epidemiological study. *Journal of the American Academy of Child & Adolescent Psychiatry, 27*(6), 764–771. doi: 10.1097/00004583-198811000-00018

Flessner, C., Berman, N., Garcia, A., Freeman, J., & Leonard, H. (2009). Symptom profiles in pediatric obsessive-compulsive disorder (OCD): The effects of comorbid grooming conditions. *Journal of Anxiety Disorders, 23*(6), 753–759. doi: 10.1016/j.janxdis.2009.02.018

Foxx, R., & Bechtel, D. (1982). *Overcorrection*. In M. Hersen, R. Eisler, & P. Miller (Eds.), *Progress in behavior modification,* Vol. 13 (pp. 227–288). Newbury Park, CA: Sage.

Franklin, M., Edson, A., Ledley, D., & Cahill, S. (2011). Behavior therapy for pediatric trichotillomania: A randomized controlled trial. *Journal of the American Academy of Child & Adolescent Psychiatry, 50*(8), 763–771.

Franklin, M., Flessner, C., Woods, D., Keuthen, N., Piacentini, J., Moore, P., . . . Trichotillomania Learning Center–Scientific Advisory Board. (2008). The child and adolescent trichotillomania impact project: Descriptive psychopathology, comorbidity, functional impairment, and treatment utilization. *Journal of Developmental and Behavioral Pediatrics, 29*(6), 493–500. doi: 10.1097/DBP.0b013e31818d4328

Franklin, M. E., Kozak, M. J., Cashman, L. A., Coles, M. E., Rheingold, A. A., & Foa, E. B. (1998). Cognitive-behavioral treatment of pediatric obsessive-compulsive disorder: An open clinical trial. *Journal of the American Academy of Child & Adolescent Psychiatry, 37*(4), 412–419.

Freeman, J., Garcia, A., Benito, K., Conelea, C., Sapyta, J., Khanna, M., . . . Franklin, M. (2012). The pediatric obsessive compulsive disorder treatment study for young children (POTS Jr): Developmental considerations in the rationale, design, and methods. *Journal of Obsessive-Compulsive and Related Disorders, 1*(4), 294–300. doi: 10.1016/j.jocrd.2012.07.010

Freeman, J., Garcia, A., Frank, H., Benito, K., Conelea, C., Walther, M., & Edmunds, J. (2013). Evidence base update for psychosocial treatments for pediatric obsessive-compulsive disorder. *Journal of Clinical Child & Adolescent Psychology, 43*(1): 7–26. doi: 10.1080/15374416.2013.804386

Geller, D., Biederman, J., Jones, J., Park, K., Schwartz, S., Shapiro, S., & Coffey, B. (1998). Is juvenile obsessive-compulsive disorder a developmental subtype of the disorder? A review of the pediatric literature. *Journal of the American Academy of Child & Adolescent Psychiatry, 37*(4), 420–427. doi: 10.1097/00004583-199804000-00020

Geller, D., Biederman, J., Stewart, S., Mullin, B., Martin, A., Spencer, T., & Faraone, S. (2003). Which SSRI? A meta-analysis of pharmacotherapy trials in pediatric obsessive-compulsive disorder. *American Journal of Psychiatry, 160*(11), 1919–1928.

Geller, D., Hoog, S., Heiligenstein, J., Ricardi, R., Tamura, R., Kluszynski, S., & Jacobson, J. (2001). Fluoxetine treatment for obsessive-compulsive disorder in children and adolescents: A placebo-controlled clinical trial. *Journal of the American Academy of Child & Adolescent Psychiatry, 40*(7), 773–779. doi: 10.1097/00004583-200107000-00011

Geller, D., & March, J. (2012). Practice parameter for the assessment and treatment of children and adolescents with obsessive-compulsive disorder. *Journal of the American Academy of Child & Adolescent Psychiatry, 51*(1), 98–113.

Hanna, G. (1995). Demographic and clinical features of obsessive-compulsive disorder in children and adolescents. *Journal of the American Academy of Child & Adolescent Psychiatry, 34*(1), 19–27. doi: 10.1097/00004583-199501000-00009

Insel, T., Murphy, D., Cohen, R., Alterman, I., Kilts, C., & Linnoila, M. (1983). Obsessive-compulsive disorder in five U.S. communities. *Archives of General Psychiatry, 40,* 605–612.

Jacobson, N. S., & Truax, P. (1991). Clinical significance: A statistical approach to defining meaningful change in psychotherapy research. *Journal of Consulting and Clinical Psychology, 59*(1), 12–19.

King, M., Ollendick, T., & Montgomery, I. (1995). Obsessive-compulsive disorder in children and adolescents. *Behaviour Change, 12,* 51–58.

Last, C., & Strauss, C. (1989). Obsessive-compulsive disorder in childhood. *Journal of Anxiety Disorders, 3*(4), 295–302. doi: 10.1016/0887–6185(89)90020–0

Leonard, H., Swedo, S., Lenane, M., Rettew, D., Hamburger, S., Bartko, J., & Rapoport, J. (1993). A 2- to 7-year follow-up study of 54 obsessive-compulsive children and adolescents. *Archives of General Psychiatry, 50*(6), 429–439.

Liebowitz, M., Turner, S., Piacentini, J., Beidel, D., Clarvit, S., Davies, S., . . . Sallee, F. (2002). Fluoxetine in children and adolescents with OCD: A placebo-controlled trial. *Journal of the American Academy of Child & Adolescent Psychiatry, 41*(12), 1431–1438.

Malhotra, S., Grover, S., Baweja, R., & Bhateja, G. (2008). Trichotillomania in children. *Indian Pediatrics, 45*(5), 403.

March, J., Foa, E., Gammon, P., Chrisman, A., Curry, J., Fitzgerald, D., . . . Team, P. (2004). Cognitive-behavior therapy, sertraline, and their combination for children and adolescents with obsessive-compulsive disorder:—The Pediatric OCD Treatment Study (POTS) randomized controlled trial. *Journal of the American Medical Association, 292*(16), 1969–1976.

March, J., Frances, A., Carpenter, L., & Kahn, D. (1997). Expert consensus treatment guidelines for obsessive-compulsive disorder: A guide for patients and families. *Journal of Clinical Psychiatry, 58*(Suppl. 4), 65–72.

March, J., & Mulle, K. (1995). Manualized cognitive-behavioral psychotherapy for obsessive-compulsive disorder in childhood: A preliminary single case study. *Journal of Anxiety Disorders, 9*(2), 175–184.

March, J., & Mulle, K. (1998). *OCD in children and adolescents: A cognitive-behavioral treatment manual.* New York, NY: Guilford Press.

March, J. S., Franklin, M. E., Leonard, H., Garcia, A., Moore, P., Freeman, J., & Foa, E. (2007). Tics moderate treatment outcome with sertraline but not cognitive-behavior therapy in pediatric obsessive-compulsive disorder. *Biological Psychiatry, 61*(3), 344–347. doi: 10.1016/j.biopsych.2006.09.035

Martin, J., & Thienemann, M. (2005). Group cognitive-behavior therapy with family involvement for middle-school-age children with obsessive-compulsive disorder: A pilot study. *Child Psychiatry and Human Development, 36*(1), 113–127. doi: 10.1007/s10578–005–3496-y

Masi, G., Millepiedi, S., Mucci, M., Bertini, N., Milantoni, L., & Arcangeli, F. (2005). A naturalistic study of referred children and adolescents with obsessive-compulsive disorder. *Journal of the American Academy of Child & Adolescent Psychiatry, 44*(7), 673–681. doi: 10.1097/01.chi.0000161648.82775.ee

Meyer, J. M., McNamara, J. P., Reid, A. M., Storch, E. A., Geffken, G. R., Mason, D. M., . . . Bussing, R. (2013). Prospective relationship between obsessive-compulsive and depressive symptoms during multimodal treatment in pediatric obsessive-compulsive disorder. *Child Psychiatry and Human Development* [Epub ahead of print], 1–10. doi: 10.1007/s10578–013–0388–4

Muller, S. (1987). Trichotillomania. *Dermatologic Clinics, 5*(3), 595–601.

Norton, P., Hayes-Skelton, S., & Klenck, S. (2011). What happens in session does not stay in session: Changes within exposures predict subsequent improvement and dropout. *Journal of Anxiety Disorders, 25*(5), 654–660.

O'Leary, E., Barrett, P., & Fjermestad, K. (2009). Cognitive-behavioral family treatment for childhood obsessive-compulsive disorder: A 7-year follow-up study. *Journal of Anxiety Disorders, 23*(7), 973–978.

Olino, T. M., Gillo, S., Rowe, D., Palermo, S., Nuhfer, E. C., Birmaher, B., & Gilbert, A. R. (2011). Evidence for successful implementation of exposure and response prevention in a naturalistic group format for pediatric OCD. *Depression and Anxiety, 28*(4), 342–348.

O'Sullivan, R., Keuthen, N., Hayday, C., Ricciardi, J., Buttolph, M., Jenike, M., & Baer, L. (1995). The Massachusetts General Hospital (MGH) Hairpulling Scale: 2. Reliability and validity. *Psychotherapy and Psychosomatics, 64*(3–4), 146–148. doi: 10.1159/000289004

Park, J. M., Rahman, O., Murphy, T. K., & Storch, E. A. (2012). Early childhood trichotillomania: Initial considerations on phenomenology, treatment, and future directions. *Infant Mental Health Journal, 33*(2), 163–172.

Peris, T. S., Sugar, C. A., Bergman, R. L., Chang, S., Langley, A., & Piacentini, J. (2012). Family factors predict treatment outcome for pediatric obsessive-compulsive disorder. *Journal of Consulting and Clinical Psychology, 80*(2), 255.

Piacentini, J., & Bergman, R. (2000). Obsessive-compulsive disorder in children. *Psychiatric Clinics of North America, 23*(3), 519–533.

Piacentini, J., Bergman, R., Jacobs, C., McCracken, J., & Kretchman, J. (2002). Open trial of cognitive behavior therapy for childhood obsessive-compulsive disorder. *Journal of Anxiety Disorders, 16*(2), 207–219.

Piacentini, J., Bergman, R. L., Chang, S., Langley, A., Peris, T., Wood, J. J., & McCracken, J. (2011). Controlled comparison of family cognitive behavioral therapy and psychoeducation/relaxation training for child obsessive-compulsive disorder. *Journal of the American Academy of Child & Adolescent Psychiatry, 50*(11), 1149–1161.

Piacentini, J., Gitow, A., Jaffer, M., Graae, F., & Whitaker, A. (1994). Outpatient behavioral treatment of child and adolescent obsessive compulsive disorder. *Journal of Anxiety Disorders, 8*(3), 277–289.

Piacentini, J., Peris, T., Bergman, R., Chang, S., & Jaffer, M. (2007). Brief report: Functional impairment in childhood OCD: Development and psychometrics properties of the Child Obsessive-compulsive Impact Scale–Revised (COIS-R). *Journal of Clinical Child & Adolescent Psychology, 36*(4), 645–653. doi: 10.1080/15374410701662790

Reeve, E., Bernstein, G., & Christenson, G. (1992). Clinical characteristics and psychiatric comorbidity in children with trichotillomania. *Journal of the American Academy of Child & Adolescent Psychiatry, 31*(1), 132–138. doi: 10.1097/00004583-199201000-00020

Riddle, M., Scahill, L., King, R., Hardin, M., Towbin, K., Ort, S., . . . Cohen, D. (1990). Obsessive compulsive disorder in children and adolescents: Phenomenology and family history. *Journal of the American Academy of Child & Adolescent Psychiatry, 29*(5), 766–772. doi: 10.1097/00004583-199009000-00015

Roussos, A., Francis, K., Koumoula, A., Richardson, C., Kabakos, C., Kiriakidou, T., . . . Karamolegou, K. (2003). The Leyton Obsessional Inventory–Child Version in Greek adolescents. *European Child & Adolescent Psychiatry, 12*(2), 58–66. doi: 10.1007/s00787-003-0308-4

Salkovskis, P. M. (1998). *Psychological approaches to the understanding of obsessional problems*. New York, NY: Guilford Press.

Scahill, L., Riddle, M., McSwiggin-Hardin, M., Ort, S., King, R., Goodman, W., . . . Leckman, J. (1997). Children's Yale-Brown Obsessive Compulsive Scale: Reliability and validity. *Journal of the American Academy of Child & Adolescent Psychiatry, 36*(6), 844–852. doi: 10.1097/00004583-199706000-00023

Shaffer, D., Fisher, P., Lucas, C., Dulcan, M., & Schwab-Stone, M. (2000). NIMH Diagnostic Interview Schedule for Children Version IV (NIMH DISC-IV): Description, differences from previous versions, and reliability of some common diagnoses. *Journal of the American Academy of Child & Adolescent Psychiatry, 39*(1), 28–38. doi: 10.1097/00004583-200001000-00014

Shalev, I., Sulkowski, M., Geffken, G., Rickets, E., Murphy, T., & Storch, E. (2009). Long-term durability of cognitive behavioral therapy gains for pediatric obsessive-compulsive disorder. *Journal of the American Academy of Child & Adolescent Psychiatry, 48*(7), 766–767.

Silverman, W., & Albano, A. (1996). *The Anxiety Disorders Interview Schedule for Children DSM–IV: (Child and Parent Versions)*. San Antonio, TX: Psychological Corporation.

Stemberger, R. M., McCombs-Thomas, A., MacGlashan, S., & Mansueto, C. (2000). Cognitive behavioral treatment of trichotillomania. In M. Hersen & M. Biaggio (Eds.), *Effective brief therapies: A clinician's guide* (pp. 319–334). San Diego, CA: Academic Press.

Storch, E., Geffken, G., Merlo, L., Mann, G., Duke, D., Munson, M., . . . Goodman, W. (2007). Family-based cognitive-behavioral therapy for pediatric obsessive-compulsive disorder: Comparison of intensive and weekly approaches. *Journal of the American Academy of Child & Adolescent Psychiatry, 46*(4), 469–478.

Storch, E., Merlo, L., Larson, M., Geffken, G., Lehmkuhl, H., Jacob, M., . . . Goodman, W. (2008). Impact of comorbidity on cognitive-behavioral therapy response in pediatric obsessive-compulsive disorder. *Journal of the American Academy of Child & Adolescent Psychiatry, 47*(5), 583–592.

Storch, E., Murphy, T., Goodman, W., Geffken, G., Lewin, A., Henin, A., . . . Bengtson, M. (2010). A preliminary study of D-cycloserine augmentation of cognitive-behavioral therapy in pediatric obsessive-compulsive disorder. *Biological Psychiatry, 68*(11), 1073–1076.

Storch, E. A., Caporino, N. E., Morgan, J. R., Lewin, A. B., Rojas, A., Brauer, L., . . . Murphy, T. K. (2011). Preliminary investigation of web-camera delivered cognitive-behavioral therapy for youth with obsessive-compulsive disorder. *Psychiatry Research, 189*(3), 407–412.

Sukhodolsky, D. G., Gorman, B. S., Scahill, L., Findley, D., & McGuire, J. (2013). Exposure and response prevention with or without parent management training for children with obsessive-compulsive disorder complicated by disruptive behavior: A multiple-baseline across-responses design study. *Journal of Anxiety Disorders, 27*(3), 298–305. doi: 10.1016/j.janxdis.2013.01.005

Swedo, S., & Leonard, H. (1992). Trichotillomania: An obsessive compulsive spectrum disorder? *Psychiatric Clinics of North America, 15*(4), 777–790.

Swedo, S., & Rapoport, J. (1991). Trichotillomania. *Journal of Child Psychology and Psychiatry, 32*, 401–409.

Swedo, S., Rapoport, J., Leonard, H., Lenane, M., & Cheslow, D. (1989). Obsessive-compulsive disorder in children and adolescents: Clinical phenomenology of 70 consecutive cases. *Archives of General Psychiatry, 46*(4), 335. doi: 10.1001/archpsyc.1989.01810040041007

Thienemann, M., Martin, J., Cregger, B., Thompson, H. B., & Dyer-Friedman, J. (2001). Manual-driven group cognitive-behavioral therapy for adolescents with obsessive-compulsive disorder: A pilot study. *Journal of the American Academy of Child & Adolescent Psychiatry, 40*(11), 1254–1260.

Turner, C., Heyman, I., Futh, A., & Lovell, K. (2009). A pilot study of telephone cognitive-behavioural therapy for obsessive-compulsive disorder in young people. *Behavioural and Cognitive Psychotherapy, 37*(4), 469.

Valderhaug, R., Larsson, B., Götestam, K., & Piacentini, J. (2007). An open clinical trial of cognitive-behaviour therapy in children and adolescents with obsessive-compulsive disorder administered in regular outpatient clinics. *Behaviour Research and Therapy, 45*(3), 577–589. doi: 10.1016/j.brat.2006.04.011

Vitulano, L.A., King, R.A., Scahill, L., & Cohen, D. J. (1992). Behavioral treatment of children and adolescents with trichotillomania. *Journal of the American Academy of Child & Adolescent Psychiatry, 31*(1), 139–146.

Walsh, K., & McDougle, C. (2001). Trichotillomania. *American Journal of Clinical Dermatology, 2*(5), 327–333. doi: 10.2165/00128071-200102050-00007

Waters, T. L., & Barrett, P. M. (2000). The role of the family in childhood obsessive-compulsive disorder. *Clinical Child and Family Psychology Review, 3*(3), 173–184.

Waters, T. L., Barrett, P. M., & March, J. S. (2001). Cognitive-behavioral family treatment of childhood obsessive-compulsive disorder: Preliminary findings. *American Journal of Psychotherapy, 55*(3), 372–387.

Watson, H. J., & Rees, C. S. (2008). Meta-analysis of randomized, controlled treatment trials for pediatric obsessive-compulsive disorder. *Journal of Child Psychology and Psychiatry, 49*(5), 489–498.

Watson, T. S., & Allen, K. D. (1993). Elimination of thumb-sucking as a treatment for severe trichotillomania. *Journal of the American Academy of Child & Adolescent Psychiatry, 32*(4), 830–834.

Wetterneck, C. T., Woods, D. W., Norberg, M. M., & Begotka, A. M. (2006). The social and economic impact of trichotillomania: Results from two nonreferred samples. *Behavioral Interventions, 21*(2), 97–109.

Whiteside, S. P., & Jacobsen, A. B. (2010). An uncontrolled examination of a 5-day intensive treatment for pediatric OCD. *Behavior Therapy, 41*(3), 414–422.

Williams, T., Salkovskis, P., Forrester, L., Turner, S., White, H., & Allsopp, M. (2010). A randomised controlled trial of cognitive behavioural treatment for obsessive compulsive disorder in children and adolescents. *European Child & Adolescent Psychiatry, 19*(5), 449–456.

Zohar, A. (1999). The epidemiology of obsessive-compulsive disorder in children and adolescents. *Child and Adolescent Psychiatric Clinics of North America, 8*(3), 445–460.

Author Index

Clouse, B., 250
Cluss, P. A., 325
Cobham, V. E., 8, 101, 116
Cohen, D., 214
Cohen, D. J., 3, 357
Cohen, J., 288
Cohen, J. A., 287, 288, 289, 292, 293, 294, 295, 296
Cohen, J. S., 112
Cohen-Kettenis, P., 202
Coie, J. D., 195
Colditz, G. A., 81, 344
Cole, T. J., 344
Coles, E. K., 59
Coles, M. E., 302
Collica, T. J., 120
Collins, N., 23
Collishaw, S., 153
Comer, J. S., xv, 4, 55, 56, 58, 59, 64, 65, 66, 361
Compton, S. N., 114
Condie, L. O., 23
Conger, R. E., 198
Connelly, M., 250
Conner, C., 222
Conners-Burrow, N. A., 305
Connolly, J., 310
Conover, N. C., 4
Conradt, J., 102, 111
Contreras, R., 85
Cook, A., 294
Cook, S., 321
Cooley, M. R., 50
Cooley-Strickland, M., 50
Coon, K. A., 338
Cooper, Z., 57, 238
Cooper-Vince, C., 64, 66
Cooper-Vince, C. E., 59, 64, 65, 66
Corda, B., 115
Corkum, P. V., 266
Cornwall, E., 98
Costa, N., 102
Costa, N. M., 3
Costello, 104
Costello, A. J., 4
Costello, E., 287
Costello, E. J., 94, 129, 140, 156, 222, 275
Costello, J., 111
Cotler, S., 276
Cousins, J. C., 268
Couturier, J., 233
Cowan, P. A., 7
Cowart, M., 103
Cowie, H., 303
Cowie, J., xv, 261, 353
Cox, A., 61

Cox, C. M., 287, 296
Cox, D. J., 63, 244, 246, 249, 250
Cox, J., 277
Coyne, J. C., 182
Crabtree, V. M., 266
Craig, G., 35
Craig, J. T., xv, 301, 308
Craig, T., 35
Craig, W. M., 301, 309, 310
Craighead, W. E., 3
Craney, J. L., 164, 169
Craske, M. G., 57
Crawley, S. A., 115
Cregger, B., 361
Crick, N. R., 301–302, 309, 310
Crisler, M. E., xv, 195
Crnic, K. A., 184
Crocetto, J., 364
Crosby, B., 266
Crosby, R. D., 237
Crosthwaite, J., 23
Crow, S., 231, 339, 340
Crowell, E. W., 180
Cruikshank, B. M., 245
Crump, A. D., 51
Crystal, S., 56
Cuellar, J., 62
Cullerton-Sen, C., 309
Cummings, C., 61
Cunningham, C. E., 179, 183, 184, 185, 186
Cunningham, C. L., 248, 250
Cunningham, M. J., 61, 118
Cunningham, P. B., 83, 200
Cunningham, W., 327

Dadds, M., 358
Dadds, M. R., 4, 8, 96, 97, 98, 99, 101, 103, 116
Daigre, A. L., xvi, 317
Dailor, A. N., 23, 25
Daleiden, E. L., 73, 82
Daley, D., 183
Dalgleish, T., 113, 292
Dalrymple, N., 217
Damschroder, L. J., 74, 79
Dancu, C. V., 119
Daneman, D., 321, 322
Danforth, J. S., 184
Danielson, C., 294
Danielson, C. K., 169
Dare, C., 233
Darney, D., 50
David-Ferdon, C., 130, 153
Davidov, B. J., 17
Davidson, K. W., 16
Davidson, M., 321
Davidson, P. W., 18

Davies, E., 63
Davies, M., 363
Davies, W. H., 321
Davis, A. C., 75
Davis, C. L., 322
Davis, H., 4
Davis, H. A., 309
Davis, J. R., 183
Davis, M. M., 337, 338
Davis, N. O., 215
Davis, T. E., 16, 98, 101, 219
Davis, T. L., 7
Dawson, G., 222
Day, T., 282
Deacon, B. J., 355
Dean, A. J., 319, 322
de Arellano, M., 294
Deas, D., 5
Deault, L. C., 177, 178
Deblinger, E., 287, 288, 292
De Bruyne, E., 244, 250
DeGarmo, D. S., 198
de Graaf, I., 198
Degroot, J., 4
De-Hayes, L., 282
de Jong, T. P., 244
DeKraai, M. B., 19
de la Cruz-Muñoz, N., 337
Delamater, A. M., xvi, 317, 320, 321, 324
De Los Reyes, A., 118, 220, 222
DeMartino, R. A., 17
Demeter, C., 169
Demeter, C. A., 166
Demler, O., 111
Dempsey, P., 55
Denis, P., 245
Dent, H. C., 119
Depp, C. A., 21
DeRosier, M. E., 215, 307, 309
DeShazo Barry, T. D., 178
Deshpande, A. V., 247
DeSocio, J., 279
de Sousa, G., 344
Detgen, A., 279
Devenyi, R. G., 321
Devineni, B., 169
Devitt, H., 244
DeWit, D. J., 5
de Wolff, M., 198
Diamond, G. M., 153
Diamond, G. S., 153
Dickstein, D. P., 163
DiClemente, R. J., 5, 24, 51
Diefenbach, G., 364
Diehle, J., 93
Dietz, W. H., 335
DiGirolamo, A. M., 323

Subject Index

Aarons et al.'s multilevel, multiphase implementation model, 80
Abstract reasoning, 6–7
Abuse. *See* Child abuse; Substance abuse
Abuse-focused cognitive behavioral therapy (AF-CBT), 288, 295
Academics. *See* School and education
ACTION Treatment Program for Girls, 138–139
Adaptations and modifications:
  for anxiety disorders interventions, 101–102, 117–118
  for attention-deficit/ hyperactivity disorder interventions, 183–185
  for autism spectrum disorders interventions, 220–221
  for bipolar disorder interventions, 168–169
  for bullying/bullied children interventions, 306–308
  for conduct and disruptive behavior disorders interventions, 202–204
  cultural adaptation as, 44, 49, 50–51, 139, 155, 204, 293–294
  for depression/depressive disorders interventions, 137–139, 153–155
  dissemination and implementation improvement through, 81–82
  for eating disorders, 238
  for elimination disorders interventions, 250–251
  to medical regimen adherence interventions, 323–324
  for obsessive-compulsive disorder interventions, 359–361
  for overweight and obesity interventions, 339–344

  for school absenteeism/refusal interventions, 281
  for sleep disorders interventions, 266–267
  for trauma-related problems/ disorders interventions, 292–296
  for trichotillomania interventions, 362
ADHD. *See* Attention-deficit/ hyperactivity disorder
ADHD Rating Scale, 185
Adolescent-focused psychotherapy (AFP), 234–235
Adolescents. *See* Children and adolescents
African American youth. *See also* Ethnic minority youth
  anxiety disorders in, 45, 46, 49, 50, 103
  attention-deficit/hyperactivity disorder in, 45, 48, 49, 187–189
  conduct and disruptive behavior disorders in, 45, 46–47, 49
  cultural factors influencing, 45, 49–50
  depression/depressive disorders in, 45, 50, 139
  interventions and treatments for, 43, 45–48, 49–50, 52, 103, 139, 187–189, 266, 321
  medical regimen adherence of, 321
  population of, 43
  sexual behavior among, 5
  sleep disorders in, 266
  socioeconomic status of, 49, 50
Aggression. *See* Bullying/bullied children; Conduct and disruptive behavior disorders
Agoraphobia, 111, 115, 282
Alcohol abuse. *See* Substance abuse
American Academy of Child and Adolescent Psychiatry, 354
American Academy of Pediatrics, 336

American Psychiatric Association, *Diagnostic and Statistical Manual. See Diagnostic and Statistical Manual of Mental Disorders*
American Psychological Association, Code of Ethics, 15, 25, 39
Anger control training, 196
Anxiety disorders:
  adaptations and modifications to interventions for, 101–102, 117–118
  in adolescents, specifically, 3, 4, 111–122, 157–159, 232, 239–241
  agoraphobia as, 111, 115, 282
  anxiety management training for, 356
  aromatherapy as treatment for, 32
  assessments and diagnosis of, 3, 4, 93–94, 102–105, 114, 118–120, 121, 122, 157
  bibliotherapy for, 102
  breathing skills training for, 36, 112, 115, 278
  bullying relationship to, 302
  case example of, 105–106, 120–122, 157–159
  in children, specifically, 3, 4, 93–106
  cognitive behavioral therapy for, 8, 46, 48–49, 50, 57, 60, 61, 82, 95–106, 112–122, 157–159, 217, 241, 278, 279, 282–283, 356
  cognitive restructuring for, 57, 96, 113, 115–116, 158
  communication skill training for, 99, 100, 117
  community intervention and prevention efforts for, 102
  comorbidity with, 94, 103, 105, 111–112, 121, 129, 157–159, 163, 179–180, 206, 217, 223, 232, 239–241, 261, 268, 275, 278, 279, 282–283, 297, 302, 324, 335

as translational research, 74
treatment adaptation for improved, 81–82
Distance and Internet-based therapies:
computerized treatments with minimal therapist involvement as, 60–61, 102, 117–118, 216, 250–251, 252
confidentiality issues with, 20, 61, 66
Coping Power program as, 203
costs associated with, 63, 327
ethical and legal considerations with, 20
smartphone technology leveraged in, 61–63, 327
technology-based treatment delivery formats for, 60–66, 102, 117–118, 121–122, 134, 203, 216, 250–251, 252, 327, 361
text messaging as tool in, 63
videoconferencing as tool in, 20, 64–66, 134, 361
virtual environments in, 121–122
Drug abuse. *See* Substance abuse
Drug Abuse Resistance Education (D.A.R.E.), 34–35
Drug treatments. *See* Pharmacological treatments
Dry-bed training, 248
Dysthymic disorder, 129. *See also* Depression/depressive disorders

Eating Disorder Examination (EDE), 238–239
Eating Disorder Examination-Questionnaire (EDE-Q), 239
Eating disorders. *See also* Food and feeding difficulties
adaptations and modifications to interventions for, 238
adolescent-focused psychotherapy for, 234–235
anorexia nervosa as, 231, 232–235, 237, 238, 240
assessments and diagnosis of, 156, 231, 238–239, 240–241
behavioral family systems therapy for, 233–234
binge eating disorder as, 231, 237, 238, 341–342
bulimia nervosa as, 231, 235–236, 237, 238
bullying relationship to, 302

case example of, 239–241
cognitive behavioral therapy for, 234–237, 341
comorbidity with, 232, 238, 239–241, 302, 321, 324, 335, 341–342
developmental considerations in, 233, 238
dialectical behavior therapy for, 237, 341
family-based therapy for, 232–234, 236, 237, 240–241
interpersonal psychotherapy for, 237, 341–342
interventions and treatments for, 8, 62, 231–241, 341–342
measuring treatment effects for, 238–239
other specified feeding or eating disorder as, 231
overview of, 231
overweight and obesity relationship to, 335, 341–342
parental involvement in treatment for, 232–234, 236, 237, 240–241
service delivery methods for, 62, 238
technology-based treatment formats for, 62
therapy format used for, 8
Ecological momentary assessment (EMA), 326–327
Education. *See* School and education; Training and education
Educational interventions, 319, 322, 328. *See also* Psychoeducation
Electronically mediated therapies. *See* Distance and Internet-based therapies
Elimination disorders:
adaptations and modifications to interventions for, 250–251
assessments and diagnosis of, 243, 251–252
behavioral treatment for, 247–248, 249–250, 252–253
biofeedback for, 249
case example of, 252–253
constipation and, 244, 245–246, 248–249, 251, 252
dry-bed training for, 248
encopresis as, 244–246, 248–253
enhanced toilet training for, 249, 250–251

enuresis as, 243–244, 246–248, 250, 251
Full Spectrum Home Training for, 248
Internet-based interventions for, 250–251, 252
interventions and treatments for, 246–253
measuring treatment effects for, 251–252
medical management for, 246–247, 248–249, 251, 252–253
overview of, 243–246
parental involvement in treatment for, 250
physical health relationship to, 243, 245–246, 248
psychoeducation for, 248–249
relapse prevention for, 248
urine alarms for, 246, 247–248
Emancipated minors, 18
Emotional Freedom Technique (EFT), 35–36
Emotionally Attuned Parenting, 136
Emotion Detectives, 59–60, 207
Emotions:
anxiety disorders impacting (*see* Anxiety disorders)
Contextual Emotion-Regulation Therapy, 134, 153
emotional eating, 343–344, 346
Emotional Freedom Technique, 35–36
Emotionally Attuned Parenting, 136
emotionally descriptive language, 8
emotional understanding, 7–8
emotion awareness therapy/education, 57, 95, 112, 150, 290
Emotion Detectives, 59–60, 207
emotion-focused skills training, 60, 167
mood disorders impacting (*see* Bipolar disorder; Depression/depressive disorders)
Parent-Child Interaction Therapy Emotion Development, 136
play to act out, 9, 47
Encopresis, 244–246, 248–253. *See also* Elimination disorders